OFF-HOLLYWOOD MOVIES

OFF-HOLLYWOOD MOVIES

A Film Lover's Guide

Richard Skorman

With Contributors
Gail Bradney
Tony Etz

Harmony Books/New York

To Albert and Gladys

Grateful acknowledgment is given to the following for permission to include photographs: New Yorker Films, photographs copyright © 1986, 1985, 1981, 1980, 1978, 1976, 1974, 1973, 1953 by New Yorker Films. All rights reserved. Almi Pictures, Inc., photographs copyright © 1985, 1983, 1981, 1978, 1977, 1976, 1973, 1966 by Almi Pictures Inc. All rights reserved. Cinecom Pictures, photographs copyright © 1987, 1986, 1985, 1984 by Cinecom Pictures. All rights reserved. Kino International, photographs copyright © 1986, 1985, 1982 by Kino International. All rights reserved. Institute for Regional Education, photograph copyright © 1983 by Institute for Regional Education. All rights reserved. Skouras Pictures, photograph copyright © 1987 by Skouras Pictures. All rights reserved. Jim Jarmusch, photograph copyright © 1986 by Black Snake, Inc. All rights reserved. Promovision International Films Ltd., photograph copyright © 1981 by Promovision International Films Ltd. All rights reserved.

Published by Harmony Books, a division of Crown Publishers, Inc., 225 Park Avenue South, New York, New York 10003

HARMONY and colophon are trademarks of Crown Publishers, Inc.

Manufactured in the United States of America

Library of Congress Cataloging-in-Publication Data

Skorman, Richard.
  Off-Hollywood Movies : a film lover's guide / Richard Skorman.
    p.   cm.
  1. Motion pictures—Reviews.   2. Video recordings—Reviews
I. Title.
PN1995.S528 1988
791.43'75—dc19   88–2093
ISBN 0-517-56863-2   CIP

10 9 8 7 6 5 4 3 2 1
First Edition

Contents

Acknowledgments

I received a great deal of help in writing this book, but I would especially like to thank Gail Bradney and Tony Etz, who both worked long and hard to assist me in watching movies, writing reviews, and gathering information, who both lent their editing skills to every single word appearing in this book at the same time they gave me an enormous amount of moral support and encouragement from this project's inception.

I would also like to extend special thanks to J. LeRoy Sole, the publicist at New Yorker Films, for helping compile the directors' bio index, opening up the New Yorker Films library to me, and offering invaluable suggestions on my reviews. I would like to express my gratitude to Suzy Oboler for dropping everything else in her life to give me much-needed editing help during the final panic moments close to the deadline. And a special thanks to Janet Alexander for her encouragement and artistic contributions, and Carol Andreas for her help with the revisions.

I also greatly appreciate the advice, generosity, and fun movie facts from Linda Duchin and Wayne Salazar at Cinecom, Dennis Doros at Kino International Films, Lee Krugman at Almi Pictures, Matthew Curtis at Corinth Films, Nancy Gerstman at First Run Features, Judy Levitow at the Samuel Goldwyn Company, Steve Benz at Swank Motion Pictures, Jeff Capp and Amy Hiller at New Yorker Films, Ralph Sevush at New Line Cinema, Steve Buck at AMC Theaters, and Ruth Robbins at Castle Hill Films.

I would like to express my gratitude to Lala Brooks at New Yorker Films for cheerfully loaning me prints at a moment's notice, to Milos Stehlik at Facets Video in Chicago for opening up his video library to me, and Ken Petchenik at Cinebooks for his help in getting me important reference information at the last minute.

I also owe a great deal to my family and friends, particularly my brother, Stuart, for our initial brainstorming session while we were soaking in a Colorado hot springs together, and my apartment mates, Michael Gibbs and Ann Bradney, for their constant generosity and support, as well as Jeff Livesay, Jeff Dworkin, Salvatore Bizzarro, Steven Brunner, Jeff Eichengreen, Jody Alyn, Tom O'Donnald, Tom Mawn, Anthony Russo, Suwat Charnond, Anthony Garrett, Kim Bayles, Bill and Mikey Drummond, Ed Zasadny, Jerry Best, Tim Remington, Sarah McCoy, Marv Skorman and Pam Gallagher for their understanding ears and contributions.

Finally, a special thanks to Patricia Seator for her loving support and patience; to my agent, Kate Hartson, for having so much faith in me from the onset; to Harmony Editorial Director Esther Mitgang for giving me a chance; and Harmony editor Liz Sonneborn for her reassurance, understanding and honesty.

Introduction

I had an eye-opening experience during a visit to my hometown, Akron, Ohio. I accompanied my friend Tim to his favorite video store because he was complaining that he had seen "everything good there was to rent." When I suggested what I thought were well-known, independently produced films such as *Choose Me, Streetwise, The Brother from Another Planet* and *Paris, Texas,* I was surprised to discover that Tim had never heard of any of these films.

But I shouldn't have been surprised. After all, they hadn't played at an Akron-area movie theater, so the *Akron Beacon Journal*'s film critic never reviewed them. Likewise, video-store clerks seemed to know little about them, the local FM stations hadn't promoted them, and none of these films' stars had appeared on Johnny Carson's show. And most important, not one of the guidebooks to which Tim had access gave these films more than a two- or three-line capsule, if they were mentioned at all.

In operating a revival house movie theater in Colorado Springs for the last six years, I have run into a similar information gap about the same kinds of movies. Often there are only the catalogue blurbs or capsule guidebooks to use when I am trying to order films. I have been unpleasantly surprised more than a few times because I have had only my distributor's opinion, incomplete filmbooks and my pocketbook to guide me in my selection process. I hope that *Off-Hollywood Movies* will help fill that gap for people like Tim, and me, in places such as Akron and Colorado Springs.

The term *off-Hollywood* was first coined by Annette Insdorf in a May 12, 1987, *New York Times* article, and is starting to be used in the movie industry to describe films that had previously been labeled with the more pretentious-sounding expression, *art film*. These are the kinds of movies that traditionally play at first-run art houses, repertoire and revival theaters, film societies and film festivals. Some are products of Hollywood's major studios, but most are independent American and foreign films.

At the risk of oversimplifying, Off-Hollywood movies can be distinguished from commercial releases in many of the same ways literature is distinguished from pop fiction. Whereas a Hollywood film might move quickly from one scene to the next, off-Hollywood movies often develop plot, characters and atmosphere more deliberately. Many are both entertaining and challenging, and deal with psychologically complex themes or thought-provoking social and political issues. Some are simply personal artistic statements by filmmakers not especially interested in wooing a mass audience. But by their very nature, off-Hollywood movies have much smaller production budgets, so character development, cinematography and mood have to take precedence over elaborate action sequences, special effects and sets.

In the past, most of these movies were produced and/or released through the classics divisions of major Hollywood studios. Today, while these studios are preoccupied with huge-budget blockbusters, a whole new group of successful, cost-effective independent American production and distribution companies (such as Island, Skouras, Circle, Cinecom, Samuel Goldwyn, and New Yorker) have come into their own. Many filmmakers, such as Robert Altman, Alan Rudolph and Jonathan Demme, prefer the special attention they get from the smaller companies.

Independent productions now account for nearly 70 percent of the films on the market, although many are exploitation and specialty releases.

Another important new trend in the movie business is the advent of "art" screens in multiplex chain theaters. Many national theater corporations, including AMC, Cineplex-Odeon, General Cinema, Commonwealth and U.S.A. Cinema, have designated one screen at selected multiplexes for first-run independent and foreign films with positive results. Market studies show an increased interest in independent and foreign movies, in part because college-educated baby boomers aren't satisfied with youth-oriented Hollywood releases. While overall box-office receipts were down 11 percent in 1985 from 1984, receipts at first-run art houses actually rose in 1985.

Off-Hollywood movies are becoming an important part of the cable market because the movie channels are desperate for new product. But off-Hollywood movies not only provide variety for cable companies who have played out their Hollywood hits, they give the image-conscious cable companies prestige. Why prestige? Because even though many off-Hollywood movies have not had widespread exposure at the movie theater, they are often critically acclaimed and international award winners.

Another factor in cable television's future is subscription or pay-for-what-you-watch movies. Industry analysts are predicting that in the next two to five years you will be able to select from huge cable movie libraries the film you want, when you want it. Here again, off-Hollywood movies will become more accessible in a market where variety is the only solution to oversaturation by Hollywood's formula movies and movie burnout (a term now coined by the video and cable industry).

As for video outlets, convenience stores and supermarkets are getting more involved in cassette rentals, taking over a large share of the best-seller/mass-market video business and forcing the mom-and-pop stores to close. Consequently, larger video stores are thriving. Proliferating nationwide are "superstores" that carry 3,000 to 6,000 titles, including hundreds of off-Hollywood movies. Within the next five years, every large metropolitan area and most medium-size ones will have at least one "superstore" with plenty of off-Hollywood titles on its shelves.

Unfortunately the widespread availability of these movies on video and cable has dealt a fatal blow to many repertoire and revival theaters and university film societies. Combined with the high cost of running a theater and rising rents, this has caused hundreds of single-screen revival theaters across the country to close. Speaking as an art-theater owner myself, I urge you to support your local repertoire theater and film society because they are a dying breed. If we continue to choose video and cable over the theater for second-run films, the option to view them on a larger screen won't exist much longer.

Watching off-Hollywood movies on video or cable is a problem because the visuals are often so integrally connected to these films' emotional content that much of their impact can be lost on a TV screen. Cinematography that creates a dark, brooding atmosphere, for example, might be powerful on a big screen but seem pretentious on TV. Unlike some major studio releases, most off-Hollywood movies weren't made with a video audience in mind.

In response to the new demand for foreign films, many producers and their video distributors are making a concerted effort to give viewers quality subtitles. Now they often outline the letters in a dark color to avoid the white-letters-on-white-background problem, making both home and theater viewing much easier. Some video companies are even going back and resubtitling classics that they have already released. First-run foreign films and older foreign titles released on video in the last two years are virtually guaranteed to have very readable subtitles. Unfortunately, the readability of many older classics varies (I indicate this in my reviews whenever possible, especially for public domain prints and unauthorized reproductions of films for which the video rights have yet to be negotiated).

Another problem to be aware of with off-Hollywood movies on video is that some of them were originally shot in Cinemascope. Because of the long, horizontal image of Cinemascope, these films would naturally appear on the television screen as a smaller image with a black strip on the top and bottom. Instead of releasing them in their original form, many video producers are employing a technique called "pan and scan," in which they enlarge the image so it fills the entire screen, leaving a portion of the shot out. Needless to say, this technique can seriously affect the visuals of a film. Kurosawa's *Ran* is perhaps the most notable example of this. The filmmaker's carefully composed battle scenes, which are supposed to be viewed taking in entire vistas from one horizon to the other, are practically ruined on video. (Again, I try to flag in my reviews which video releases use this technique.)

With a few exceptions (most notably the films of Ingmar Berman, who took great care to reshoot scenes dubbed), dubbing seriously undermines the quality of foreign movies. Some films are available both subtitled and dubbed, and in these cases I almost always recommend the subtitled version. You can do your bit by urging your video store to carry only subtitled films. Maybe video and film producers will eventually get the hint and stop butchering their films with dubbing.

After viewing over 1,000 films before selecting the 445 movies reviewed in *Off-Hollywood Movies,* I based my choices on the following criteria. All of these movies can be seen currently at first-run art houses, repertoire theaters, and film societies and festivals. With a couple dozen exceptions, all are readily available on video or will be soon. I have focussed on lesser-known independent American films and foreign classics of the recent past, but in some cases I included a movie merely because it is considered so important in the history of its genre. Of course, many of these selections are my personal favorites. I am particularly fond of filmmakers who see their art as a means of political expression. Thus you'll find in the book a good number of movies dealing with subjects such as sex roles, Third World cultures and class differences.

Some of the films I chose to exclude from the book were ones I simply felt were unworthy of mention. But by no means does an omission reflect the value of a particular film. Several films were virtually impossible for me to track down before my deadline. Other excellent films, such as *Bread and Chocolate, The Chant of Jimmy Blacksmith* and *Tell Me a Riddle,* have disappeared from distribution or were never released on video. I also veered away from films that are well known, such as Woody Allen's movies and some of Peter Weir's most recent releases (*Witness* and *The Year of Living Dangerously*), since I assume most moviegoers are already familiar with them.

In order to help you select movies that will be of greatest interest to you, the films in *Off-Hollywood Movies* are indexed in the front of the book by director, actor, cinematographer and country.

In the reviews themselves, I have tried to give you more than a capsule's worth of information, while keeping each shorter than the average newspaper review. I hope you can use this guide as a quick but detailed resource without getting bogged down, and without learning so much about a movie that it is spoiled for you. The plot synopsis in every review appears first, the critique second, so you can disregard one or the other, if that's your preference.

I have rated each film on a 1-to-5 scale, explained below:

★ .... POOR

★ ★ .... FAIR

★ ★ ½ .... DECENT

★ ★ ★ .... GOOD

★ ★ ★ ★ .... VERY GOOD

★ ★ ★ ★ ★ .... EXCELLENT

Again, these ratings are purely subjective, and I recommend that you read the review to find out more about the movie yourself.

You may also notice some inconsistencies in the credits given with each review. Sometimes a piece of information simply wasn't available for a certain film, as in the case of many Eastern European films that were produced by the state and don't have individual producers. For every movie, I've tried to list the director, screenwriter, producer, cinematographer, distributor and the principal members of the cast. When the music, costumes, makeup, set design and art direction are important in a production, I include these in the credits as well.

At the end of the book you'll find a list of companies you can contact to rent prints of these films to show in classrooms and at film societies (nontheatrical). There is information on how to buy and rent them on video through the mail. I've also included an appendix list of fifty-four of the most prominent directors represented in *Off-Hollywood,* with a brief personal history, description of why they are important and a filmography of their best work.

Happy movie selecting!

OFF-HOLLYWOOD MOVIES

Off-Hollywood Movies

Absolute Beginners
The Adventures of Buckaroo Bonzai Across
   the 8th Dimension
After Hours
After the Rehearsal
Aguirre, the Wrath of God
Ali: Fear Eats the Soul
All Screwed up (All in Place, Nothing in
   Order)
Allegro non Troppo
Alphaville
Alsino and the Condor
Altered States
Always
Amarcord
The American Friend
And the Ship Sails On
Angelo, My Love
Angry Harvest
Another Country
Aparajito . . . The Unvanquished
The Assault
Atlantic City
The Atomic Cafe
Au Revoir les Enfants (Goodbye, Children)
Autumn Sonata
L'Avventura
Babette's Feast
Badlands
Le Bal
La Balance
The Ballad of Gregorio Cortez
Ballad of Narayama
Barfly
The Basileus Quartet
Le Beau Mariage
Beau Père
Beauty and the Beast
Being There
Belizaire the Cajun
Bellissima

Berlin Alexanderplatz
Betrayal
Betty Blue
Between the Lines
Beyond the Walls
The Bicycle Thief
Birdy
Blade Runner
Bliss
Blood Simple
Blood Wedding
Blue Collar
Blue Velvet
Boat People
Bob le Flambeur
Das Boot (The Boat)
The Bostonians
A Boy and His Dog
Brazil
Breaker Morant
Breathless
Brimstone and Treacle
Britannia Hospital
The Brother from Another Planet
Brother Sun, Sister Moon
The Buddy Holly Story
Burden of Dreams
Burroughs
Bye Bye Brazil
La Cage aux Folles—The Mad Cage: Birds
   of a Feather
Cal
Camila
Can She Bake Cherry Pie?
Caravaggio
Careful, He Might Hear You
Carmen
Chan Is Missing
Chicken Ranch
Chilly Scenes of Winter
Choose Me

1

The Clockmaker
A Clockwork Orange
Closely Watched Trains
The Clowns
The Coca-Cola Kid
Colonel Redl
Come Back to the Five and Dime, Jimmy
   Dean, Jimmy Dean
Comfort and Joy
The Company of Wolves
Les Compères
Confidentially Yours
The Conformist
Coup de Grace
Coup de Torchon (Clean Slate)
Cousin, Cousine
Cries and Whispers
Cross Creek
Crossover Dreams
Cutter's Way
Dance with a Stranger
Dancing in the Dark
Dangerous Moves
Danton
Day for Night
Days of Heaven
The Dead
Death in Venice
Deathwatch
The Decline of the American Empire
Decline of Western Civilization
Dersu Uzala
Desert Bloom
Desert Hearts
Despair
Desperately Seeking Susan
Les Diaboliques
Diary of a Country Priest
Dim Sum: A Little Bit of Heart
Diner
El Diputado (The Deputy)
The Discreet Charm of the Bourgeoisie
Diva
Dodes'ka-den
La Dolce Vita (The Sweet Life)
Dona Flor and Her Two Husbands
Don's Party
Don't Look Now
Down by Law
Dreamchild
The Dresser
Eating Raoul
8½
84 Charing Cross Road

Eleni
The Elephant Man
Enormous Changes at the Last Minute
Entre Nous
Equus
Eraserhead
Erendira
Eureka
The Europeans
Evil Dead II: Dead by Dawn
Experience Preferred . . . But Not Essential
Exposed
The Exterminating Angel
The Eyes, The Mouth
Fanny and Alexander
Female Trouble
The Festival of Claymation
Fitzcarraldo
A Flash of Green
Fool for Love
The 400 Blows
The 4th Man
Fox and His Friends
The Fringe Dwellers
From Mao to Mozart: Isaac Stern in China
Full Moon in Paris
Gal Young 'Un
Gallipoli
The Garden of the Finzi-Continis
Gates of Heaven
General Della Rovere
George Stevens: A Filmmaker's Journey
Get Out Your Handkerchiefs
The Getting of Wisdom
Ginger and Fred
The Girl in the Picture
The Gods Must Be Crazy
Going Places
The Good Father
The Gospel According to St. Matthew
Gospel According to Vic
Greaser's Palace
The Green Room
Gregory's Girl
The Grey Fox
Hail Mary/The Book of Mary
Hammett
Hanna K.
The Harder They Come
Harlan County, U.S.A.
Harold and Maude
Heart Like a Wheel
Heart of the Stag
Heartbreakers

Heartland
Heat and Dust
Heaven
Hester Street
The Hidden Fortress
Hiroshima Mon Amour
The Hit
Hollywood Shuffle
The Home and the World
The Honeymoon Killers
Hour of the Star
I Married a Shadow
If . . .
Ikiru (To Live)
Improper Conduct
The Inheritors
Insignificance
Jean de Florette
A Joke of Destiny, Lying in Wait Around
    the Corner Like a Bandit
Jules and Jim
Kagemusha—the Shadow Warrior
Kamikaze '89
Kangaroo
Kerouac
The King of Comedy
King of Hearts
Kipperbang
Kiss of the Spider Woman
Knife in the Water
Koyaanisqatsi
The Lacemaker
The Last Métro
Last Night at the Alamo
Last Tango in Paris
The Last Waltz
The Last Wave
Last Year at Marienbad
Latino
Law of Desire
Letter to Brezhnev
Lianna
Liquid Sky
Local Hero
Lola
Lonely Hearts
The Long Good Friday
The Lost Honor of Katharina Blum
Love and Anarchy
A Love in Germany
Love Streams
Loves of a Blonde
Loyalties
McCabe and Mrs. Miller

Mad Max
Malcolm
A Man and a Woman
Man Facing Southeast
Man of Flowers
Man of Marble
The Man Who Fell to Earth
The Man Who Loved Women
Marlene
The Marriage of Maria Braun
Masculin-Féminin
Matewan
A Matter of Heart
Maurice
Mean Streets
Men
Mephisto
Merry Christmas, Mr. Lawrence
Mikey and Nicky
Mishima: A Life in Four Chapters
Missing
Mr. Love
Mixed Blood
Modern Romance
The Moderns
Mon Oncle D'Amerique
Mona Lisa
Montenegro (Pigs and Pearls)
Monty Python and the Holy Grail
Moonlighting
Morgan (A Suitable Case for Treatment)
Moscow Does Not Believe in Tears
My Beautiful Laundrette
My Brilliant Career
My Dinner with Andre
My First Wife
My Life as a Dog
My New Partner
My Sweet Little Village
The Mystery of Kaspar Hauser—Every
    Man for Himself and God Against All
The Mystery of Picasso
Native Son
Night of the Shooting Stars
90 Days
El Norte
A Nos Amours
La Nuit de Varennes
O Lucky Man!
The Official Story
Los Olvidados (The Young and the
    Damned)
One Sings, The Other Doesn't
Outrageous

Padre Padrone
Paris, Texas
Parting Glances
The Passenger
Passione d'Amore (Passion of Love)
Pather Panchali (Song of the Road)
Pauline at the Beach
Persona
Personal Services
Picnic at Hanging Rock
Pixote
Playtime
The Ploughman's Lunch
The Plumber
Poetry in Motion
Prick Up Your Ears
A Private Function
Private Practices: The Story of a Sex
  Surrogate
Privates on Parade
Providence
Pumping Iron II: The Women
Quadrophenia
Querelle
A Question of Silence
The Quiet Earth
Raising Arizona
Ramparts of Clay
Ran
Rashomon
Real Life
Remember My Name
Repo Man
The Return of Martin Guerre
The Return of the Secaucus Seven
Reuben, Reuben
The Revolt of Job
River's Edge
The Road Warrior
Rockers
A Room With a View
Round Midnight
The Ruling Class
The Sacrifice
Saint Jack
Salvador
Sammy and Rosie Get Laid
Sanjuro
Say Amen, Somebody
Scene of the Crime
Scenes From a Marriage
Secret Honor
The Seduction of Mimi
The Serpent's Egg

Seven Beauties
Seven Samurai
The Seventh Seal
Sherman's March: An Improbable Quest
  for Love
She's Gotta Have It
Shoah
Shoot the Piano Player
The Shooting Party
The Shop on Main Street
Short Eyes
Sid and Nancy
Silver City
Simon of the Desert
Sisters, or The Balance of Happiness
Sitting Ducks
A Slave of Love
Small Change
Smash Palace
Smiles of a Summer Night
Smithereens
Smooth Talk
Soldier of Orange
Something Wild
Sotto Sotto (Softly Softly)
A Special Day
Starstruck
State of Siege
Steaming
Stevie
Stolen Kisses
Stop Making Sense
The Story of Adele H.
La Strada
Stranger Than Paradise
Strangers Kiss
Streamers
Streetwise
Stroszek
Suburbia (The Wild Side)
Subway
Sugar Cane Alley
Sugarbaby
Summer
Sunday in the Country
Swann in Love
Swept Away
Swimming to Cambodia
The Tall Blonde Man with One Black Shoe
Tampopo
Taxi Driver
Taxi Zum Klo
Tchao Pantin
Testament

That Obscure Object of Desire
That Sinking Feeling
Thérèse
This Is Spinal Tap
Three Men and a Cradle
Ticket to Heaven
Time Stands Still
The Times of Harvey Milk
The Tin Drum
Tokyo Story
Trash
The Tree of Wooden Clogs
The Trip to Bountiful
Trouble in Mind
True Stories
La Truite (The Trout)
Turtle Diary
28/Up
Under the Volcano
Utu
Vagabond
Vengeance Is Mine
Veronika Voss
Viridiana

Waiting for the Moon
Walkabout
Water
We All Loved Each Other So Much
We of the Never Never
The Weavers: Wasn't That a Time!
Welcome to L.A.
Wetherby
What Happened to Kerouac?
When Father Was Away on Business
Where the Buffalo Roam
Who Am I This Time?
Wild Style
Wings of Desire
Winter Kills
Wise Blood
Woman in the Dunes
The Woman Next Door
Working Girls
WR: Mysteries of the Organism
A Year of the Quiet Sun
Yojimbo
Yol
Z

Directors

PERCY ADLON
Sugarbaby

CHARLIE AHEARN
Wild Style

NESTOR ALMENDROS
Improper Conduct

PEDRO ALMODOVAR
Law of Desire

ROBERT ALTMAN
Come Back to the Five and Dime, Jimmy Dean, Jimmy Dean; Fool for Love; McCabe and Mrs. Miller; Secret Honor; Streamers

SUZANA AMARAL
Hour of the Star

LINDSAY ANDERSON
Brittania Hospital; If . . . ; O Lucky Man!

JOHN ANTONELLI
Kerouac

MICHELANGELO ANTONIONI
L'Avventura; The Passenger

MICHAEL APTED
Kipperbang; 28/Up

DENYS ARCAND
The Decline of the American Empire

GILLIAN ARMSTRONG
My Brilliant Career; Starstruck

HAL ASHBY
Being There; Harold and Maude

IGOR AUZINS
We of the Never Never

GABRIEL AXEL
Babette's Feast

HECTOR BABENCO
Kiss of the Spider Woman; Pixote

THEODOROS BAFALOUKOS
Rockers

MIRRA BANK
Enormous Changes at the Last Minute (co-directors: Muffie Meyer, Ellen Hovdie)

WALTER BANNERT
The Inheritors

URI BARBASH
Beyond the Walls

BRUNO BARRETO
Dona Flor and Her Two Husbands

PAUL BARTEL
Eating Raoul

ROY BATTERSBY
Mr. Love

JEAN-JACQUES BEINEIX
Betty Blue; Diva

MARTIN BELL
Streetwise (co-directors: Mary Ellen Mark, Cheryl McCall)

MARCO BELLOCCHIO
The Eyes, the Mouth

MARIA LUISA BEMBERG
Camila

RICHARD BENNER
Outrageous

BRUCE BERESFORD
Breaker Morant; Don's Party; The Fringe Dwellers; The Getting of Wisdom

INGMAR BERGMAN
After the Rehearsal; Autumn Sonata; Cries and Whispers; Fanny and Alexander; Persona; Scenes from a Marriage; The Serpent's Egg; The Seventh Seal; Smiles of a Summer Night

CHRIS BERNARD
Letter to Brezhnev

CLAUDE BERRI
Jean de Florette; Tchao Pantin

BERNARDO BERTOLUCCI
The Conformist; Last Tango in Paris

JEAN-LOUIS BERTUCELLI
Ramparts of Clay

MICHAEL BLAKEMORE
Privates on Parade

LES BLANK
Burden of Dreams

BERTRAND BLIER
Beau Père; Get Out Your Handkerchiefs; Going Places

PETER BOGDANOVICH
Saint Jack

LIZZIE BORDEN
Working Girls

PHILIP BORSOS
The Grey Fox

BRUNO BOZZETTO
Allegro non Troppo

LUC BRESSON
Subway

ROBERT BRESSON
Diary of a Country Priest

ALAN BRIDGES
The Shooting Party

HOWARD BROOKNER
Burroughs

ALBERT BROOKS
Modern Romance; Real Life

NICK BROOMFIELD
Chicken Ranch (co-director: Sandi Sissel)

JIM BROWN
The Weavers: Wasn't That a Time!

LUIS BUÑUEL
The Discreet Charm of the Bourgeoisie; The Exterminating Angel; Los Olvidados; Simon of the Desert; That Obscure Object of Desire; Viridiana

TIM BURSTALL
Kangaroo

GEORGE BUTLER
Pumping Iron II: The Women

DAVID BYRNE
True Stories

FABIO CARPI
Basileus Quartet

JOHN CASSAVETES
Love Streams

ALAIN CAVALIER
Thérèse

MATTHEW CHAPMAN
Strangers Kiss

JOYCE CHOPRA
Smooth Talk

DICK CLEMENT
Water

HENRI-GEORGES CLOUZOT
Les Diaboliques; The Mystery of Picasso

JEAN COCTEAU
Beauty and the Beast

JOEL COEN
Blood Simple; Raising Arizona

EUGENE CORR
Desert Bloom

CONSTANTINE COSTA-GAVRAS
Hanna K; Missing; State of Siege; Z

ALEX COX
Repo Man; Sid and Nancy

PAUL COX
Lonely Hearts; Man of Flowers; My First Wife

ROBIN DAVIS
I Married a Shadow

PHILIPPE DE BROCA
King of Hearts

ELOY DE LA IGLESIA
El Diputado

VITTORIO DE SICA
The Bicycle Thief; The Garden of the Finzi-Continis

DONNA DEITCH
Desert Hearts

RICHARD DEMBO
Dangerous Moves

JONATHAN DEMME
Something Wild; Stop Making Sense; Swimming to Cambodia; Who Am I This Time?

KIRBY DICK
Private Practices: The Story of a Sex Surrogate

CARLOS DIEGUES
Bye Bye Brazil

ROGER DONALDSON
Smash Palace

DORIS DORRIE
Men

ROBERT DOWNEY
Greaser's Palace

PETER DUFFELL
Experience Preferred . . . But Not Essential

ROBERT DUVALL
Angelo, My Love

ROBERT ENDERS
Stevie

ROBERT EPSTEIN
The Times of Harvey Milk

RICHARD EYRE
The Ploughman's Lunch

RAINER WERNER FASSBINDER
Ali: Fear Eats the Soul; Berlin Alexanderplatz; Despair; Fox and His Friends: Right of Freedom; Lola; The Marriage of Maria Braun; Querelle; Veronika Voss

FEDERICO FELLINI
Amarcord; And the Ship Sails On; The Clowns; La Dolce Vita; 8½; Ginger and Fred; La Strada

MICHAEL FIRTH
Heart of the Stag

MILOS FOREMAN
Loves of a Blonde

BILL FORSYTH
Comfort and Joy; Gregory's Girl; Local Hero; That Sinking Feeling

STEPHEN FREARS
The Hit; My Beautiful Laundrette; Prick Up Your Ears; Sammy and Rosie Get Laid

JERROLD FREEDMAN
Native Son

TERRY GILLIAM
Brazil; Monty Python and the Holy Grail (co-director: Terry Jones)

JEAN-LUC GODARD
Alphaville; Breathless; Hail Mary/The Book of Mary (co-director: Anne-Marie Mievelle); Masculin-Féminin

JILL GODMILOW
Waiting for the Moon

SERIF GOREN
Yol (co-director: Yilmaz Gurney)

CLAUDE GORETTA
The Lacemaker

CHARLES GORMLEY
Gospel According to Vic

MARLEEN GORRIS
A Question of Silence

PETER GOTHAR
Time Stands Still

WOLF GREMM
Kamikaze '89

RUY GUERRA
Erendira

YILMAZ GURNEY
Yol (co-director: Serif Goren)

IMRE GYONGYOSSY
The Revolt of Job (co-director: Barna Kabay)

LASSE HALLSTROM
My Life as a Dog

DAVID HARE
Wetherby

PERRY HENZELL
The Harder They Come

WERNER HERZOG
Aguirre, the Wrath of God; Fitzcarraldo; The Mystery of Kaspar Hauser; Stroszek

AGNIESZKA HOLLAND
Angry Harvest

ELLEN HOVDIE
Enormous Changes at the Last Minute (co-directors: Muffie Meyer, Mirra Bank)

ANN HUI
Boat People

TIM HUNTER
River's Edge

JOHN HUSTON
The Dead; Under the Volcano; Wise Blood

LEON ICHASO
Crossover Dreams

SHOHEI IMAMURA
The Ballad of Narayama; Vengeance Is Mine

JOHN IRVIN
Turtle Diary

JUZO ITAMI
Tampopo

JAMES IVORY
The Bostonians; The Europeans; Heat and Dust; Maurice; A Room with a View

HENRY JAGLOM
Always; Can She Bake Cherry Pie?; Sitting Ducks

DEREK JARMAN
Caravaggio

JIM JARMUSCH
Down by Law; Stranger Than Paradise

DAVID JONES
Betrayal; 84 Charing Cross Road

L. Q. JONES
A Boy and His Dog

TERRY JONES
Monty Python and the Holy Grail (co-director: Terry Gilliam); Personal Services

NEIL JORDAN
The Company of Wolves; Mona Lisa

BARNA KABAY
The Revolt of Job (co-director: Imre Gyongyossy)

JAN KADAR
The Shop on Main Street (co-director: Elmar Klos)

MAREK KANIEVSKA
Another Country

JONATHAN KAPLAN
Heart Like a Wheel

LEONARD KASTLE
The Honeymoon Killers (co-director: Oliver Wood)

DIANE KEATON
Heaven

ELMAR KLOS
The Shop on Main Street (co-director: Jan Kadar)

BARBARA KOPPLE
Harlan County, U.S.A.

STANLEY KUBRICK
A Clockwork Orange

AKIRA KUROSAWA
Dersu, Uzala; Dodes'ka-den; The Hidden Fortress; Ikiru; Kagemusha (The Shadow Warrior); Ran; Rashomon; Sanjuro; Seven Samurai; Yojimbo

DIANE KURYS
Entre Nous

EMIR KUSTURICA
When Father Was Away on Business

CLAUDE LANZMANN
Shoah

RAY LAWRENCE
Bliss

SPIKE LEE
She's Gotta Have It

CLAUDE LELOUCH
A Man and a Woman

MURRAY LERNER
From Mao to Mozart: Isaac Stern in China

RICHARD LERNER
What Happened to Kerouac? (co-director: Lewis MacAdams)

BARRY LEVINSON
Diner

ART LINSON
Where the Buffalo Roam

MIGUEL LITTIN
Alsino and the Condor

LYNNE LITTMAN
Testament

JAYNE LOADER
The Atomic Cafe (co-directors: Kevin Rafferty, Pierce Rafferty)

RICHARD LONCRAINE
Brimstone and Treacle

JOSEPH LOSEY
Steaming; La Truite

SIDNEY LUMET
Equus

DAVID LYNCH
Blue Velvet; The Elephant Man; Eraserhead

LEWIS MACADAMS
What Happened to Kerouac? (co-director: Richard Lerner)

JOHN MACKENZIE
The Long Good Friday

DUSAN MAKAVEJEV
The Coca-Cola Kid; Montenegro (Pigs and Pearls); WR: Mysteries of the Organism

TERRENCE MALICK
Badlands; Days of Heaven

LOUIS MALLE
Atlantic City; Au Revoir les Enfants (Goodbye, Children); My Dinner with Andre

RON MANN
Poetry in Motion

MARY ELLEN MARK
Streetwise (co-directors: Martin Bell, Cheryl McCall)

LEON MARR
Dancing in the Dark

PETER MASTERSON
The Trip to Bountiful

ELAINE MAY
Mikey and Nicky

CHERYL MCCALL
Streetwise (co-directors: Martin Bell, Mary Ellen Mark)

ROSS MCELWEE
Sherman's March: An Improbable Quest
for Love

PETER MEDAK
The Ruling Class

JEAN-PIERRE MELVILLE
Bob le Flambeur

VLADIMIR MENSHOV
Moscow Does Not Believe in Tears

JIRI MENZEL
Closely Watched Trains; My Sweet Little
Village

MUFFIE MEYER
Enormous Changes at the Last Minute
(co-directors: Ellen Hovdie, Mirra Bank)

ANNE-MARIE MIEVELLE
Hail Mary/The Book of Mary (co-
director: Jean-Luc Godard)

NIKITA MIKHALKOV
A Slave of Love

GAVIN MILLAR
Dreamchild

GEORGE MILLER
Mad Max; The Road Warrior

ROBERT ELLIS MILLER
Reuben, Reuben

EDOUARD MOLINARO
La Cage aux Folles

ERROL MORRIS
Gates of Heaven

PAUL MORRISSEY
Mixed Flood; Trash

MALCOLM MOWBRAY
A Private Function

GEOFF MURPHY
The Quiet Earth; Utu

GREGORY NAVA
El Norte

GEORGE T. NEIRENBERG
Say Amen, Somebody

MICHAEL NEWELL
Dance with a Stranger; The Good Father

VICTOR NUNEZ
A Flash of Green; Gal Young 'Un

PAT O'CONNOR
Cal

ERMANNO OLMI
The Tree of Wooden Clogs

NAGISA OSHIMA
Merry Christmas, Mr. Lawrence

YASUJIRO OZU
Tokyo Story

EUZHAN PALCY
Sugar Cane Alley

ALAN PARKER
Birdy

CARY PARKER
The Girl in the Picture

PIER PAOLO PASOLINI
The Gospel According to St. Matthew

IVAN PASSER
Cutter's Way

RICHARD PEARCE
Heartland

EAGLE PENNELL
Last Night at the Alamo

WOLFGANG PETERSON
Das Boot

MAURICE PIALAT
A Nos Amours

GLEN PITRE
Belizaire the Cajun

ROMAN POLANSKI
Knife in the Water

LUIS PUENZO
The Official Story

FONS RADEMAKERS
The Assault

KEVIN RAFFERTY
The Atomic Cafe (co-directors: Pierce Rafferty, Jayne Loader)

PIERCE RAFFERTY
The Atomic Cafe (co-directors: Kevin Rafferty, Jayne Loader)

SAM RAIMI
Evil Dead II: Dead by Dawn

STEVE RASH
The Buddy Holly Story

SATYAJIT RAY
Aparajito . . . The Unvanquished; The Home and the World; Pather Panchali (Song of the Road)

GODFREY REGGIO
Koyaanisqatsi

ROB REINER
This Is Spinal Tap

KAREL REISZ
Morgan (A Suitable Case for Treatment)

ALAIN RESNAIS
Hiroshima Mon Amour; Last Year at Marienbad; Mon Oncle d' Amerique; Providence

WILLIAM RICHERT
Winter Kills

W. D. RICHTER
The Adventures of Buckaroo Bonzai Across the 8th Dimension

FRANK RIPPLOH
Taxi Zum Klo

MARTIN RITT
Cross Creek

YVES ROBERT
The Tall Blond Man with One Black Shoe

FRANC RODDAM
Quadrophenia

NICOLAS ROEG
Don't Look Now; Eureka; Insignificance; The Man Who Fell to Earth; Walkabout

ERIC ROHMER
Le Beau Mariage; Full Moon in Paris; Pauline at the Beach; Summer

ROBERTO ROSSELLINI
General della Rovere

BOBBY ROTH
Heartbreakers

ALAN RUDOLPH
Choose Me; Remember My Name; The Moderns; Trouble in Mind; Welcome to L.A.

KEN RUSSELL
Altered States

CARLOS SAURA
Blood Wedding; Carmen

JOHN SAYLES
The Brother from Another Planet; Lianna; Matewan; The Return of the Secaucus Seven

MAXIMILIAN SCHELL
Marlene

VOLKER SCHLONDORFF
Coup de Grace; The Lost Honor of Katharina Blum (co-director: Margarethe von Trotta); Swann In Love; The Tin Drum

PAUL SCHRADER
Blue Collar; Mishima: A Life in Four Chapters

BARBET SCHROEDER
Barfly

CARL SCHULTZ
Careful, He Might Hear You

ETTORE SCOLA
Le Bal; La Nuit de Varennes; Passione d'Amore; A Special Day; We All Loved Each Other So Much

MARTIN SCORSESE
After Hours; The King of Comedy; The Last Waltz; Mean Streets; Taxi Driver

RIDLEY SCOTT
Blade Runner

SUSAN SEIDELMAN
Desperately Seeking Susan; Smithereens

COLINE SERREAU
Three Men and a Cradle

BILL SHERWOOD
Parting Glances

JOAN MICKLIN SILVER
Between the Lines; Chilly Scenes of Winter; Hester Street

SANDI SISSEL
Chicken Ranch (co-director: Nick Broomfield)

JERZY SKOLIMOWSKI
Moonlighting

PENELOPE SPHEERIS
The Decline of Western Civilization; Suburbia (The Wild Side)

GEORGE STEVENS, JR.
George Stevens: A Filmmaker's Journey

OLIVER STONE
Salvador

ELISEO SUBIELA
Man Facing·Southeast

BOB SWAIM
La Balance

ISTVAN SZABO
Colonel Redl; Mephisto

JEAN-CHARLES TACCHELLA
Cousin, Cousine

ANDREI TARKOVSKY
The Sacrifice

NADIA TASS
Malcolm

JACQUES TATI
Playtime

BERTRAND TAVERNIER
The Clockmaker; Coup de Torchon (Clean Slate); Deathwatch; Round Midnight; Sunday in the Country

PAULO TAVIANI
The Night of the Shooting Stars (co-director: Vittorio Taviani); Padre Padrone (co-director: Vittorio Taviani)

VITTORIO TAVIANI
The Night of the Shooting Stars (co-director: Paulo Taviani); Padre Padrone (co-director: Paulo Taviani)

ANDRE TECHINE
Scene of the Crime

JULIEN TEMPLE
Absolute Beginners

HIROSHI TESHIGAHARA
Woman in the Dunes

RALPH THOMAS
Ticket to Heaven

JAMES TOBACK
Exposed

ROBERT TOWNSEND
Hollywood Shuffle

FRANCOIS TRUFFAUT
Confidentially Yours; Day for Night; The 400 Blows; The Green Room; Jules and Jim; The Last Metro; The Man Who Loved Women; Shoot the Piano Player; Small Change; Stolen Kisses; The Story of Adele H.; The Woman Next Door

SLAVA TSUCKERMAN
Liquid Sky

SOPHIA TURKIEWICZ
Silver City

JAMIE UYS
The Gods Must Be Crazy

AGNES VARDA
One Sings, The Other Doesn't; Vagabond

FRANCIS VEBER
Les Compères

PAUL VERHOEVEN
The 4th Man; Soldier of Orange

DANIEL VIGNE
The Return of Martin Guerre

WILL VINTON
The Festival of Claymation

LUCHINO VISCONTI
Bellissima; Death in Venice

MARGARETHE VON TROTTA
The Lost Honor of Katharina Blum (co-director: Volker Schlondorff); Sisters, or The Balance of Happiness

ANDRZEJ WAJDA
Danton; A Love in Germany; Man of Marble

GILES WALKER
90 Days

WAYNE WANG
Chan Is Missing; Dim Sum: A Little Bit of Heart

JOHN WATERS
Female Trouble

PETER WEIR
Gallipoli; The Last Wave; Picnic at Hanging Rock; The Plumber

WIM WENDERS
The American Friend; Hammett; Paris, Texas; Wings of Desire

LINA WERTMULLER
All Screwed Up (All in Place, Nothing in Order); A Joke of Destiny; Love and Anarchy; The Seduction of Mimi; Seven Beauties; Sotto, Sotto; Swept Away

HASKELL WEXLER
Latino

ANNE WHEELER
Loyalties

MARK WHITNEY
A Matter of Heart

OLIVER WOOD
The Honeymoon Killers (co-director: Leonard Kastle)

PETER YATES
The Dresser; Eleni

ROBERT YOUNG
The Ballad of Gregorio Cortez; Short Eyes

KRZYSZTOF ZANUSSI
A Year of the Quiet Sun

FRANCO ZEFFIRELLI
Brother Sun, Sister Moon

CLAUDE ZIDI
My New Partner

Actors

DIAHNNE ABBOTT
King of Comedy; Love Streams; Taxi Driver

BROOKE ADAMS
Days of Heaven

ISABELLE ADJANI
The Story of Adele H.; Subway

JENNY AGUTTER
Equus; Walkabout

ANOUK AIMEE
8½; La Dolce Vita; A Man and a Woman

NORMA ALEANDRO
The Official Story

STEVE ALLEN
Kerouac; What Happened to Kerouac?

HECTOR ALTERIO
The Basileus Quartet; Camila; The Official Story

BIBI ANDERSSON
Exposed; Persona; Scenes from a Marriage; The Seventh Seal; Smiles of Summer Night

LAURA ANTONELLI
Passione d'Amore

FANNY ARDANT
Confidentially Yours; Swann in Love; The Woman Next Door

ROSANNA ARQUETTE
After Hours; Desperately Seeking Susan

KEVIN BACON
Enormous Changes at the Last Minute; Diner

ANNE BANCROFT
84 Charing Cross Road; The Elephant Man

BRIGITTE BARDOT
Masculin-Féminin

ELLEN BARKIN
The Adventures of Buckaroo Bonzai; Enormous Changes at the Last Minute; Desert Bloom; Diner; Down by Law

PAUL BARTEL
Eating Raoul; Heart Like a Wheel

RICHARD BASEHART
Being There; La Strada

ALAN BATES
King of Hearts

NATHALIE BAYE
The Green Room; I Married a Shadow; La Balance; The Man Who Loved Women; The Return of Martin Guerre

NED BEATTY
Mikey and Nicky; Wise Blood

WARREN BEATTY
George Stevens: A Filmmaker's Journey; McCabe and Mrs. Miller

BONNIE BEDELIA
Heart Like a Wheel

JEAN-PAUL BELMONDO
Breathless

JIM BELUSHI
Salvador

ROBERT BELTRAN
Eating Raoul; Latino

INGRID BERGMAN
Autumn Sonata

SANDRA BERNHARD
King of Comedy

TED BERRIGAN
Poetry in Motion

JACQUELINE BISSET
Day for Night; Under the Volcano

GUNNAR BJORNSTRAND
Autumn Sonata; The Seventh Seal; Smiles of a Summer Night

KAREN BLACK
Can She Bake Cherry Pie?; Come Back to the Five and Dime, Jimmy Dean, Jimmy Dean

DIRK BOGARDE
Death in Venice; Despair; Providence

PETER BOGDONAVICH
Saint Jack

SANDRINE BONNAIRE
A Nos Amours; Vagabond

SUDIE BOND
Enormous Changes at the Last Minute; Come Back to the Five and Dime, Jimmy Dean, Jimmy Dean

DAVID BOWIE
Absolute Beginners; The Man Who Fell to Earth

JUDY BOWKER
Brother Sun, Sister Moon; The Shooting Party

PETER BOYLE
Hammett; Taxi Driver; Where the Buffalo Roam

SONIA BRAGA
Dona Flor and Her Two Husbands; Kiss of the Spider Woman

KLAUS MARIA BRANDAUER
Colonel Redl; Mephisto

MARLON BRANDO
Last Tango in Paris

JEFF BRIDGES
Cutter's Way; Winter Kills

ALBERT BROOKS
Modern Romance; Real Life; Taxi Driver

BLAIR BROWN
Altered States; A Flash of Green

WILLIAM F. BUCKLEY
Kerouac; What Happened to Kerouac?

GENEVIEVE BUJOLD
Choose Me; King of Hearts; The Moderns; Trouble in Mind

CHARLES BUKOWSKI
Barfly; Poetry in Motion

WILLIAM F. BURROUGHS
Burroughs; Kerouac; Poetry in Motion; What Happened to Kerouac?

ELLEN BURSTYN
Providence

RICHARD BURTON
Equus

GARY BUSEY
The Buddy Holly Story; Insignificance

DAVID BYRNE
Stop Making Sense; True Stories

NICOLAS CAGE
Birdy; Raising Arizona

MICHAEL CAINE
Mona Lisa; Water

SIMON CALLOW
The Good Father; Maurice

CLAUDIA CARDINALE
Burden of Dreams; 8½; Fitzcarraldo

ANNE CARLISLE
Desperately Seeking Susan; Liquid Sky

FABIO CARPI
The Basileus Quartet

KEITH CARRADINE
Choose Me; McCabe and Mrs. Miller; The Moderns; The Serpent's Egg; Trouble in Mind; Welcome to L.A.

JOHN CASSAVETES
Love Streams; Mikey and Nicky

FIDEL CASTRO
Improper Conduct

RICHARD CHAMBERLAIN
The Last Wave

GERALDINE CHAPLIN
Remember My Name; The Moderns; Welcome to L.A.

CHER
Come Back to the Five and Dime, Jimmy Dean, Jimmy Dean

THOMAS CHONG
After Hours

JULIE CHRISTIE
Don't Look Back; Heat and Dust; McCabe and Mrs. Miller

ERIC CLAPTON
The Last Waltz; Water

JILL CLAYBURGH
Hanna K.

JOHN CLEESE
Monty Python and the Holy Grail; Privates on Parade

JIMMY CLIFF
The Harder They Come

TOM CONTI
Gospel According to Vic; Merry Christmas, Mr. Lawrence; Reuben, Reuben

GREGORY CORSO
Burroughs; Poetry in Motion; What Happened to Kerouac?

BUD CORT
Harold and Maude

TOM COURTENAY
The Dresser

PETER COYOTE
Cross Creek; Heartbreakers; Strangers Kiss

TONY CURTIS
Insignificance

JOE DALLESANDRO
Trash

JEFF DANIELS
Something Wild

RAY DAVIES
Absolute Beginners

BRAD DAVIS
Querelle

JUDY DAVIS
Kangaroo; My Brilliant Career

REBECCA DE MORNAY
Testament; The Trip to Bountiful

ROBERT DE NIRO
Brazil; The King of Comedy; Mean Streets; Taxi Driver

LAURA DEL SOL
Carmen; The Hit

VITTORIO DE SICA
General Della Rovere; We All Loved Each Other So Much

JUDY DENCH
84 Charing Cross Road; Wetherby

CATHERINE DENEUVE
The Last Métro; Scene of the Crime

CHARLES DENNER
The Man Who Loved Women; Z

SANDY DENNIS
Come Back to the Five and Dime, Jimmy Dean, Jimmy Dean

GÉRARD DEPARDIEU
Danton; Get Out Your Handkerchiefs; Going Places; Jean de Florette; The Last Métro; Mon Oncle d'Amerique; The Return of Martin Guerre; The Woman Next Door

LAURA DERN
Blue Velvet; Smooth Talk

PATRICK DEWAERE
Beau Père; Get Out Your Handkerchiefs; Going Places

MARLENE DIETRICH
Marlene

MATT DILLON
Native Son

DIVINE
Female Trouble; Trouble in Mind

DIANA DORS
Come Back to the Five and Dime, Jimmy Dean, Jimmy Dean; Steaming

BRAD DOURIF
Blue Velvet; Wise Blood

FAYE DUNAWAY
Barfly

GRIFFIN DUNNE
After Hours; Chilly Scenes of Winter

SHELLY DUVALL
McCabe and Mrs. Miller

BOB DYLAN
The Last Waltz

ANITA ECKBERG
La Dolce Vita

LISA EICHORN
Cutter's Way; The Europeans

DENHOLM ELLIOT
Brimstone and Treacle; Maurice; A Private Function; A Room with a View; Saint Jack

MICHAEL EMIL
Always; Can She Bake Cherry Pie?; Insignificance; Sitting Ducks

EMILIO ESTEVEZ
Repo Man

RUPERT EVERETT
Another Country; Dance with a Stranger

PETER FALK
Mikey and Nicky; Wings of Desire

RAINER WERNER FASSBINDER
Ali: Fear Eats the Soul; Fox and His Friends; Kamikaze '89; The Marriage of Maria Braun; Querelle

FREDERICO FELLINI
The Clowns; We All Loved Each Other So Much

LAWRENCE FERLINGHETTI
Kerouac; Poetry in Motion

ALBERT FINNEY
The Dresser; Under the Volcano

LINDA FIORENTINO
After Hours; The Moderns

PETER FIRTH
Equus; Letter to Brezhnev

EDWARD FOX
The Dresser; The Shooting Party; Soldier of Orange

COLIN FRIELS
Kangaroo; Malcolm

ANTONIO GADES
Blood Wedding; Carmen

BRUNO GANZ
The American Friend; Wings of Desire

BEN GAZZARA
Saint Jack

RICHARD GERE
Days of Heaven

GIANCARLO GIANNINI
Love and Anarchy; The Seduction of Mimi; Seven Beauties; Swept Away

MEL GIBSON
Gallipoli; Mad Max; The Road Warriors

JOHN GIELGUD
The Elephant Man; Providence; The Shooting Party

TERRY GILLIAM
Monty Python and the Holy Grail

ALLEN GINSBERG
Burroughs; Kerouac; Poetry in Motion; What Happened to Kerouac?

JEFF GOLDBLUM
The Adventures of Buckaroo Bonzai; Between the Lines; Remember My Name

JOHN GOODMAN
Raising Arizona; True Stories

DEXTER GORDON
Round Midnight

RUTH GORDON
Harold and Maude

ROBERT GOULET
Atlantic City

SPALDING GRAY
Swimming to Cambodia, True Stories

ANDRE GREGORY
Always; My Dinner with Andre

MELANIE GRIFFITHS
Something Wild

ALEC GUINNESS
Brother Sun, Sister Moon

STEVE GUTTENBERG
Diner

DAVID GUMPILIL
The Last Wave; Walkabout

GENE HACKMAN
Eureka

HERBIE HANCOCK
Round Midnight

DARYL HANNAH
Blade Runner

JOHN HARGREAVES
Don's Party; Careful He Might Hear You; Malcolm; My First Wife

ED HARRIS
A Flash of Green

GEORGE HARRISON
Water

KATHRYN HARROLD
Heartbreakers; Modern Romance

RUTGER HAUER
Blade Runner; Eureka; Soldier of Orange

JOHN HEARD
After Hours; Between Lines; Cutter's Way; The Chilly Scenes of Winter; The Trip to Bountiful

RICHARD HELL
Smithereens

MARILU HENNER
Between the Lines; Hammett

BUCK HENRY
Eating Raoul; The Man Who Fell to Earth

WERNER HERZOG
Burden of Dreams; Man of Flowers

WILLIAM HICKEY
Mikey and Nicky

IAN HOLM
Brazil; Dance with a Stranger; Dreamchild; Wetherby

ANTHONY HOPKINS
84 Charing Cross Road; The Elephant Man; The Good Father

DENNIS HOPPER
The American Friend; Blue Velvet; River's Edge

BOB HOSKINS
Brazil; The Long Good Friday; Mona Lisa

WENDY HUGHES
Careful He Might Hear You; Lonely Hearts; My Brilliant Career; My First Wife

LINDA HUNT
The Bostonians; Eleni; Waiting for the Moon

HOLLY HUNTER
Raising Arizona

ISABELLE HUPPERT
Entre Nous; Coup de Torchon; Going Places; The Lacemaker; La Truite

JOHN HURT
The Elephant Man; The Hit

WILLIAM HURT
Altered States; Kiss of the Spider Woman

ANJELICA HUSTON
The Dead

JOHN HUSTON
George Stevens: A Filmmaker's Journey; Winter Kills; Wise Blood

JEREMY IRONS
Betrayal; Moonlighting; Swann in Love

GREGORY ISSACS
Rockers

GLENDA JACKSON
Stevie; Turtle Diary

MICK JAGGER
Burden of Dreams

HENRY JAGLOM
Always; Sitting Ducks

ANNA JEMISON
My First Wife; Silver City; Smash Palace

JAMES EARL JONES
Matewan

ERLAND JOSEPHSON
After the Rehearsal; Autumn Sonata; Cries and Whispers; Fanny and Alexander; Montenegro; The Sacrifice; Scenes from a Marriage

RAOUL JULIA
Kiss of the Spider Woman

CARL JUNG
A Matter of Heart

CAROL KANE
Hester Street

IVAR KANTS
The Plumber; Silver City

NORMAN KAYE
Lonely Hearts; Man of Flowers

HARVEY KEITEL
Blue Collar; Deathwatch; Exposed; La Nuit de Varennes; Mean Streets; Taxi Driver; Welcome to L.A.

SALLY KELLERMAN
Welcome to L.A.

JACK KEROUAC
Kerouac; What Happened to Kerouac?

BEN KINGSLEY
Betrayal; Maurice; Turtle Diary

KLAUS KINSKI
Aguirre, the Wrath of God; Fitzcarraldo

NASTASSJA KINSKI
Aguirre, the Wrath of God; Exposed; Paris, Texas

BRUNO KIRBY
Between the Lines; Birdy; Modern Romance; This Is Spinal Tap; Where the Buffalo Roam

JEROEN KRABBE
The 4th Man; Soldier of Orange

KRIS KRISTOFFERSON
Trouble in Mind

SWOOZIE KURTZ
True Stories

BURT LANCASTER
Atlantic City; Local Hero

CAROL LAURE
Get Out Your Handkerchiefs; Heartbreakers

BRUNO LAWRENCE
Heart of the Stag; The Quiet Earth; Smash Palace; Utu

JEAN-PIERRE LEAUD
Day for Night; The 400 Blows; Last Tango in Paris; Masculin-Féminin; Stolen Kisses

SPIKE LEE
She's Gotta Have It

DARLING LEGITIMUS
Last Tango in Paris; Sugar Cane Alley

DANIEL DAY LEWIS
My Beautiful Laundrette; A Room with a View

JOHN LITHGOW
The Adventures of Buckaroo Bonzai

SOPHIA LOREN
A Special Day

JOHN LURIE
Down by Law; Stranger Than Paradise

MADONNA
Desperately Seeking Susan

ANNA MAGNANI
Bellissima

JOHN MALKOVICH
Eleni

GUY MARCHAND
Coup de Torchon; Cousin, Cousine; Entre Nous

CHEECH MARIN
After Hours

GIULIETTA MASINA
Ginger and Fred; La Strada

JAMES MASON
The Shooting Party

EDITH MASSEY
Female Trouble

MARCELLO MASTROIANNI
8½; Ginger and Fred; La Dolce Vita; La Nuit de Varennes; A Special Day; We All Loved Each Other So Much

ALEC MCCOWEN
Personal Services; Stevie

MALCOLM MCDOWELL
Britannia Hospital; A Clockwork Orange; Cross Creek; If . . .; O Lucky Man!

MARIANGELA MELATO
Love and Anarchy; The Seduction of Mimi; Swept Away

TOSHIRO MIFUNE
The Hidden Fortress; Rashomon; Sanjuro; Seven Samurai; Winter Kills; Yojimbo

SARAH MILES
Steaming

HARVEY MILK
The Times of Harvey Milk

SANDRA MILO
8½; General Della Rovere

MIOU-MIOU
Entre Nous; Going Places

BRIGITTE MIRA
Ali: Fear Eats Soul; Berlin Alexanderplatz; Kamikaze '89; The Mystery of Kaspar Hauser

HELEN MIRREN
Cal; Gospel According to Vic; The Long Good Friday; O Lucky Man!

JONI MITCHELL
The Last Waltz

MATTHEW MODINE
Birdy; Streamers

ANGELA MOLINA
The Eyes, the Mouth; That Obscure Object of Desire

YVES MONTAND
Jean de Florette; State of Siege; Z

JEANNE MOREAU
Going Places; Jules and Jim; La Truite; Querelle

JOE MORTON
The Brother from Another Planet; Trouble in Mind

ARMIN MUELLER-STAHL
Angry Harvest; Colonel Redl; Lola; A Love in Germany

BILL MURRAY
Where the Buffalo Roam

TATSUYA NAKADAI
Kagemusha; Ran; Sanjuro

JOHN NANCE
Eraserhead

KATE NELLIGAN
Eleni

JACK NICHOLSON
The Passenger

PHILIPPE NOIRET
The Clockmaker; Coup de Torchon; My New Partner; Round Midnight

WARREN OATES
Badlands

KEN OGATA
Ballad of Narayama; Mishima: A Life in Four Chapters; Vengeance Is Mine

GARY OLDMAN
Prick Up Your Ears; Sid and Nancy

EDWARD JAMES OLMOS
The Ballad of Gregorio Cortez; Blade Runner

PETER O'TOOLE
The Ruling Class

GERALDINE PAGE
Native Son; The Trip to Bountiful

IRENE PAPAS
Erendira; Z

MICHAEL PALIN
Brazil; Monty Python and the Holy Grail; A Private Function

ANTHONY PERKINS
Remember My Name; Winter Kills

PABLO PICASSO
The Mystery of Picasso

MICHAEL PICCOLI
Atlantic City; Dangerous Moves; The Discreet Charm of the Bourgeoisie; The Eyes, the Mouth; La Nuit de Varennes

HAROLD PINTER
Turtle Diary

MARY KAY PLACE
Smooth Talk

JOAN PLOWRIGHT
Brimstone and Treacle; Britannia Hospital; Equus

MICHAEL J. POLLARD
Between the Lines

JONATHAN PRYCE
Brazil; The Ploughman's Lunch

RICHARD PRYOR
Blue Collar

RANDY QUAID
Fool for Love

ANTHONY QUINN
La Strada

BEATRICE RAYMOND
Summer; Le Beau Mariage

ROCKETS REDGLARE
Down by Law

VANESSA REDGRAVE
The Bostonians; Morgan; Prick Up Your Ears; Steaming; Wetherby

WILHEIM REICH
WR: The Mysteries of the Organism

ROB REINER
This Is Spinal Tap

ALBERT REMY
The 400 Blows; Shoot the Piano Player

FERNANDO REY
The Discreet Charm of the Bourgeoisie; The Hit; Padre Nuestro; Seven Beauties; That Obscure Object of Desire; Viridiana

PETER RIEGERT
Local Hero

FRANK RIPPLOH
Kamikaze '89; Taxi Zum Klo

JASON ROBARDS, JR.
A Boy and His Dog; Burden of Dreams

ROBBIE ROBERTSON
The Last Waltz

MICKEY ROURKE
Barfly; Diner

GINA ROWLANDS
Love Streams

CRAIG RUSSELL
Outrageous

THERESA RUSSELL
Eureka; Insignificance

BRUNO S.
The Mystery of Kaspar Hauser; Stroszek

MARIANNE SAGEBRECHT
Sugarbaby

WILL SAMPSON
Insignificance

DOMINIQUE SANDA
The Conformist; The Garden of the Finzi Continis

SUSAN SARANDON
Atlantic City; Who Am I This Time?

JOHN SAYLES
The Brother from Another Planet; Lianna; The Return of the Secaucus Seven

GRETTA SCACCHI
The Coca-Cola Kid; Heat and Dust

MAXIMILIAN SCHELL
Marlene

MARIA SCHNEIDER
Last Tango in Paris; The Passenger

ROMY SCHNEIDER
Deathwatch

HANNA SCHYGULLA
Berlin Alexanderplatz; La Nuit de Varennes; A Love in Germany; The Marriage of Maria Braun

MARTIN SCORSESE
King of Comedy; The Last Waltz; Round Midnight; Taxi Driver

JEAN SEBERG
Breathless

PETE SEEGER
The Weavers: Wasn't That a Time!

PETER SELLERS
Being There

MICHAEL SERRAULT
Get Out Your Handkerchiefs; La Cage aux Folles; Les Diaboliques

DELPHINE SEYRIG
The Discreet Charm of the Bourgeoisie; Last Year at Marienbad; Stolen Kisses

HELEN SHAVER
Desert Hearts; Outrageous

WALLACE SHAWN
Atlantic City; The Bostonians; The Moderns; My Dinner With Andre

SAM SHEPARD
Days of Heaven; Fool for Love

TAKASHI SHIMURA
Ikiru; Rashomon; Sanjuro; Seven Samurai; Yojimbo

SIMONE SIGNORET
Les Diaboliques

GORDON JOHN SINCLAIR
Gregory's Girl; That Sinking Feeling; The Girl in the Picture

LILA SKALA
Heartland; Testament

IONE SKYE
The River's Edge

CHARLES MARTIN SMITH
The Buddy Holly Story

MAGGIE SMITH
A Private Function; A Room with a View

SUSAN SONTAG
Improper Conduct

SISSY SPACEK
Badlands; Missing; Welcome to L.A.

TERENCE STAMP
The Hit

HARRY DEAN STANTON
Deathwatch; Fool for Love; Paris, Texas; Repo Man; Wise Blood

RINGO STARR
The Last Waltz; Water

MARY STEENBURGEN
Cross Creek

DANIEL STERN
Diner

STING
Brimstone and Treacle; Quadrophenia

DEAN STOCKWELL
Alsino and the Condor; Blue Velvet; Paris, Texas

MINK STOLE
Female Trouble

SHIRLEY STOLER
The Honeymoon Killers; Seven Beauties

BARBARA SUKOWA
Berlin Alexanderplatz; Lola

DONALD SUTHERLAND
Don't Look Now

ELIZABETH TAYLOR
Winter Kills

JACQUES TATI
Playtime

MARGARET THATCHER
The Ploughman's Lunch

UGO TOGNAZZI
A Joke of Destiny; La Cage aux Folles

RIP TORN
Cross Creek; Heartland

ROBERT TOWNSHEND
Hollywood Shuffle

JEAN-LOUIS TRINTIGNANT
Confidentially Yours; The Conformist; La Nuit de Varennes; A Man and a Woman; Passion D'Amore; Z

FRANÇOIS TRUFFAUT
Breathless; Day for Night; The Green Room

LIV ULLMANN
Autumn Sonata; Cries and Whispers; Dangerous Moves; Persona; Scenes from a Marriage; The Serpent's Egg

JON VOIGHT
Desert Bloom

MAX VON SYDOW
Deathwatch; The Seventh Seal

MARGARETHE VON TROTTA
Coup de Grace

TOM WAITS
Down by Law; Poetry in Motion

CHRISTOPHER WALKEN
Who Am I This Time?

E. EMMETT WALSH
Blade Runner; Blood Simple; Mikey and Nicky

JULIE WALTERS
Personal Services; Prick Up Your Ears

DAVID WARNER
The Company of Wolves; Morgan; Providence

LESLIE ANN WARREN
Choose Me

MONA WASHBOURNE
Stevie

JOHN WATERS
Something Wild

MUDDY WATERS
The Last Waltz

PETER WELLER
The Adventures of Buckaroo Bonzai

JAMES WHITEMORE
The Serpent's Egg

TREAT WILLIAMS
Smooth Talk

OPRAH WINFREY
Native Son

ALFRE WOODARD
Cross Creek; Remember My Name

HOLLY WOODLAWN
Trash

JAMES WOODS
Salvador

VICTOR WONG
Chan Is Missing; Dim Sum: A Little Bit of Heart

Cinematographers

HENRI ALEKAN
Beauty and the Beast; Wings of Desire

NESTOR ALMENDROS
Confidentially Yours; Days of Heaven; The Green Room; The Last Métro; The Man Who Loved Women; Pauline at the Beach; The Story of Adele H.

RICARDO ARONOVICH
Le Bal; Hanna K.; Missing; Providence

JOHN BAILY
Mishima: A Life in Four Chapters; Swimming to Cambodia

MICHAEL BALLHAUS
After Hours; Despair; Heartbreakers; Fox and His Friends; The Marriage of Maria Braun

RUSSELL BOYD
Gallipoli; The Last Wave; Picnic at Hanging Rock; Starstruck

RAOUL COUTARD
Alphaville; Breathless; Dangerous Moves; Jules and Jim; Shoot the Piano Player; Z

JORDAN CRONENWETH
Altered States; Blade Runner; Cutter's Way; Stop Making Sense

HENRI DECAE
Bob le Flambeur; Exposed; The 400 Blows

FREDERICK ELMES
Blue Velvet; Eraserhead; Heaven; River's Edge

GABRIEL FIGUEROA
The Exterminating Angel; Los Olvidados; Under the Volcano

TAK FUJIMOTO
Heart Like a Wheel; Remember My Name; Something Wild; Where the Buffalo Roam

PIERRE-WILLIAM GLENN
The Clockmaker; Coup de Torchon; Day for Night; Deathwatch; Small Change; State of Siege

PETER HANNAN
Brimstone and Treacle; Dance with a Stranger; Insignificance; Turtle Diary

IGOR LUTHER
Coup de Grace; Danton; A Love in Germany; The Tin Drum

THOMAS MAUCH
Aguirre, the Wrath of God; Fitzcarraldo

DON MCALPINE
Breaker Morant; Don's Party; The Fringe Dwellers; The Getting of Wisdom; My Brilliant Career

CHRIS MENGES
Comfort and Joy; Local Hero

PIERRE MIGNOT

Come Back to the Five and Dime, Jimmy Dean, Jimmy Dean; Fool for Love; Secret Honor; Streamers

ROBBY MULLER

The American Friend; Barfly; Down by Law; Paris, Texas; Repo Man; Saint Jack

FRED MURPHY

The Dead; Heartland; The Trip to Bountiful; Trouble in Mind

ASAISHI NAKAI

Dersu Uzala; Ikiru; Kagemusha; Ran; Seven Samurai

VICTOR NUNEZ

A Flash of Green; Gal Young 'Un

SVEN NYKVIST

After the Rehearsal; Autumn Sonata; Cries and Whispers; Fanny and Alexander; Persona; The Sacrifice; Scenes from a Marriage; The Serpent's Egg; Swann in Love

TONY PIERCE-ROBERTS

Kipperbang; Moonlighting; A Private Function; A Room with a View

GIUSEPPE ROTUNNO

All Screwed Up; Amarcord; And the Ship Sails On; Love and Anarchy; The Seduction of Mimi

PHILIPPE ROUSSELOT

Diva; Thérèse

XAVER SCHWARZENBERGER

Berlin Alexanderplatz; Kamikaze '89; Lola; Querelle; Veronika Voss

PETER SOVA

Diner; Rockers; Short Eyes

OLIVER STAPLETON

Absolute Beginners; My Beautiful Laundrette; Prick Up Your Ears; Sammy and Rosie Get Laid

JOST VACANO

Das Boot; The Lost Honor of Katherina Blum; Soldier of Orange

SACHA VIERMY

Beau Père, Hiroshima Mon Amour; Last Year at Marienbad; Mon Oncle d'Amerique

HASKELL WEXLER

Days of Heaven; Matewan

VILMOS ZSIGMOND

McCabe and Mrs. Miller; Winter Kills

Countries

ALGERIA

Ramparts of Clay (co-production:
  Tunisia)
Z (co-production: France)

ARGENTINA

Camila
Man Facing Southeast
The Official Story

AUSTRALIA

Bliss
Breaker Morant
Careful, He Might Hear You
The Coca-Cola Kid
Don's Party
The Fringe Dwellers
Gallipoli
The Getting of Wisdom
Kangaroo
The Last Wave
Lonely Hearts
Mad Max
Malcolm
Man of Flowers
My Brilliant Career
My First Wife
Picnic at Hanging Rock
The Plumber
The Road Warrior
Silver City
Starstruck
Walkabout
We of the Never Never

AUSTRIA

Colonel Redl (co-production: Hungary,
  West Germany)
The Inheritors

BELGIUM

Get Out Your Handkerchiefs (co-production: France)

BRAZIL

Bye Bye Brazil
Dona Flor and Her Two Husbands
Hour of the Star
Kiss of the Spider Woman (co-produc-
  tion: U.S.A.)
Pixote

CANADA

Atlantic City (co-production: U.S.A.)
Dancing in the Dark
The Decline of the American Empire
The Grey Fox
Loyalties
90 Days
Outrageous
A Special Day (co-production: Italy)
Ticket to Heaven

CZECHOSLOVAKIA

Closely Watched Trains
Loves of a Blonde
My Sweet Little Village
The Shop on Main Street

DENMARK

Babette's Feast

ENGLAND

Absolute Beginners
Another Country
Betrayal
Brazil (co-production: U.S.A.)
Brimstone and Treacle
Brittania Hospital
Caravaggio

A Clockwork Orange
The Company of Wolves
Dance with a Stranger
Don't Look Now
Dreamchild
The Dresser
84 Charing Cross Road
The Elephant Man
Eraserhead
The Europeans (co-production: U.S.A.)
Experience Preferred . . . But Not Essential
The Good Father
Heat and Dust
The Hit
If . . .
Insignificance
Kipperbang
Letter to Brezhnev
The Long Good Friday
The Man Who Fell to Earth
Maurice
Merry Christmas, Mr. Lawrence (co-production: Japan)
Mr. Love
Mona Lisa
Montenegro (Pigs and Pearls) (co-production: Sweden)
Monty Python and the Holy Grail
Moonlighting
Morgan (A Suitable Case for Treatment)
My Beautiful Laundrette
O Lucky Man!
Personal Services
The Ploughman's Lunch
Prick Up Your Ears
A Private Function
Privates on Parade
Providence
Quadrophenia
A Room with a View
The Ruling Class
Sammy and Rosie Get Laid
The Shooting Party
Sid and Nancy (co-production: U.S.A.)
Steaming
Stevie
Turtle Diary
28/Up
Water
Wetherby

FRANCE

Alphaville
Always
Au Revoir les Enfants (Goodbye, Children)
Le Bal (co-production: Italy)
La Balance
Basileus Quartet (co-production: Italy)
Le Beau Mariage
Beau Père
Beauty and the Beast
Betty Blue
Bob le Flambeur
Breathless
La Cage aux Folles (co-production: Italy)
The Clockmaker
The Clowns (co-production: Italy)
Confidentially Yours
Les Compères
Coup de Grace (co-production: West Germany)
Coup de Torchon (Clean Slate)
Cousin, Cousine
Danton
Day for Night
Death in Venice (co-production: Italy)
Deathwatch (co-production: West Germany)
Les Diaboliques
Diary of a Country Priest
The Discreet Charm of the Bourgeoisie
Diva
Entre Nous
The Eyes, the Mouth (co-production: Italy)
The 400 Blows
Full Moon in Paris
General della Rovere
Get Out Your Handkerchiefs (co-production: Belgium)
Going Places
The Gospel According to St. Matthew (co-production: Italy)
The Green Room
Hail Mary/The Book of Mary
Hanna K. (co-production: U.S.A.)
Hiroshima Mon Amour
I Married a Shadow
Improper Conduct
Jean de Florette
Jules and Jim

King of Hearts
The Last Métro
Last Tango in Paris (co-production:
    Italy)
Last Year at Marienbad (co-production:
    Italy)
A Man and a Woman
The Man Who Loved Women
Masculin-Féminin
Mon Oncle d'Amerique
My New Partner
The Mystery of Picasso
A Nos Amours
La Nuit de Varennes (co-production:
    Italy)
One Sings, The Other Doesn't
Passione d' Amore (co-production: Italy)
Pauline at the Beach
Playtime
The Return of Martin Guerre
Round Midnight (co-production: U.S.A.)
The Sacrifice (co-production: Sweden)
Scene of the Crime
Shoah
Shoot the Piano Player
Small Change
State of Siege (co-production: U.S.A.,
    Italy)
Stolen Kisses
The Story of Adele H.
Subway
Summer
Sunday in the Country
Swann in Love (co-production: West
    Germany)
*The Tall Blond Man with One Black
    Shoe*
Tchao Pantin
That Obscure Object of Desire (co-pro-
    duction: Spain)
Thérèse
Three Men and a Cradle
The Tin Drum (co-production: West
    Germany, Poland, Yugoslavia)
La Truite
Vagabond
The Woman Next Door
Z (co-production: Algeria)

HOLLAND
The Assault
The 4th Man
A Question of Silence
Soldier of Orange

HONG KONG
Boat People

HUNGARY
Colonel Redl (co-production: Austria,
    West Germany)
Mephisto (co-production: West Ger-
    many)
The Revolt of Job (co-production: West
    Germany)
Time Stands Still

INDIA
Aparajito . . . The Unvanquished
The Home and the World
Pather Panchali (Song of the Road)

IRELAND
Cal

ISRAEL
Beyond the Walls

ITALY
*All Screwed Up (All in Place, Nothing in
    Order)*
Allegro non Troppo
Amarcord
And the Ship Sails On
L'Avventura
Le Bal (co-production: France)
Basileus Quartet (co-production: France)
Bellissima
The Bicycle Thief
La Cage aux Folles (co-production:
    France)
The Clowns (co-production: France)
The Conformist
Death in Venice (co-production: France)
La Dolce Vita
8½
The Eyes, the Mouth (co-production:
    France)
The Garden of the Finzi-Continis
General della Rovere

Ginger and Fred
The Gospel According to St. Matthew
  (co-production: France)
A Joke of Destiny, Lying in Wait Around
  the Corner Like a Bandit
Last Tango in Paris (co-production:
  France)
Last Year at Marienbad (co-production:
  France)
Love and Anarchy
The Night of the Shooting Stars
La Nuit de Varennes (co-production:
  France)
Padre Padrone
The Passenger
Passione d'Amore (co-production: France)
The Seduction of Mimi
Seven Beauties
Sotto, Sotto
A Special Day (co-production: Canada)
State of Siege (co-production: France,
  U.S.A.)
La Strada
Swept Away
The Tree of Wooden Clogs
We All Loved Each Other So Much

JAMAICA

The Harder They Come
Rockers

JAPAN

The Ballad of Narayama
Dersu Uzala (co-production: U.S.S.R.)
Dodes'ka-den
The Hidden Fortress
Ikiru
Kagemusha (The Shadow Warrior)
Merry Christmas, Mr. Lawrence (co-
  production: England)
Mishima: A Life in Four Chapters (co-
  production: U.S.A.)
Ran
Rashomon
Sanjuro
Seven Samurai
Tampopo
Tokyo Story
Vengeance Is Mine
Woman in the Dunes
Yojimbo

MARTINIQUE

Sugar Cane Alley

MEXICO

Erendira
The Exterminating Angel
Los Olvidados
Simon of the Desert

NEW ZEALAND

Heart of the Stag
The Quiet Earth
Smash Palace
Utu

NICARAGUA

Alsino and the Condor

POLAND

Knife in the Water
Man of Marble
The Tin Drum (co-production: West
  Germany, France)
A Year of the Quiet Sun (co-production:
  West Germany, U.S.A.)

SCOTLAND

Comfort and Joy
The Girl in the Picture
Gospel According to Vic
Gregory's Girl
Local Hero
That Sinking Feeling

SOUTH AFRICA

The Gods Must Be Crazy

SPAIN

Blood Wedding
Carmen
El Diputado
Law of Desire
That Obscure Object of Desire (co-pro-
  duction: France)
Viridiana

SWEDEN

After the Rehearsal
Autumn Sonata
Cries and Whispers
Fanny and Alexander
Montenegro (Pigs and Pearls) (co-pro-
  duction: England)
My Life as a Dog

Persona
The Sacrifice (co-production: France)
Scenes from a Marriage
The Seventh Seal
Smiles of a Summer Night

SWITZERLAND
Dangerous Moves
The Lacemaker

TUNISIA
Ramparts of Clay (co-production: Algeria)

TURKEY
Yol

UNITED STATES
The Adventures of Buckaroo Bonzai Across the 8th Dimension
After Hours
Altered States
Always
Angelo, My Love
Atlantic City (co-production: Canada)
The Atomic Café
Badlands
The Ballad of Gregorio Cortez
Barfly
Being There
Belizaire the Cajun
Between the Lines
Birdy
Blade Runner
Blood Simple
Blue Collar
Blue Velvet
The Bostonians
A Boy and His Dog
Brazil (co-production: England)
The Brother from Another Planet
Brother Sun, Sister Moon
The Buddy Holly Story
Burden of Dreams
Burroughs
Can She Bake Cherry Pie?
Chan Is Missing
Chicken Ranch
Chilly Scenes of Winter
Choose Me
Come Back to the Five and Dime, Jimmy Dean, Jimmy Dean

Cross Creek
Crossover Dreams
Cutter's Way
Days Of Heaven
The Dead
Decline of Western Civilization
Desert Bloom
Desert Hearts
Desperately Seeking Susan
Dim Sum: A Little Bit of Heart
Diner
Down by Law
Eating Raoul
Eleni
Enormous Changes at the Last Minute
Equus
Eureka
The Europeans (co-production: England)
Evil Dead II: Dead by Dawn
Exposed
Female Trouble
The Festival of Claymation
A Flash of Green
Fool for Love
From Mao to Mozart: Isaac Stern in China
Gal Young 'Un
Gates of Heaven
George Stevens: A Filmmaker's Journey
Greaser's Palace
Hammett
Hanna K.
Harlan County, U.S.A.
Harold and Maude
Heart Like a Wheel
Heartbreakers
Heartland
Heaven
Hester Street
Hollywood Shuffle
The Honeymoon Killers
Kerouac
The King of Comedy
Kiss of the Spider Woman (co-production: Brazil)
Koyaanisquatsi
Last Night at the Alamo
The Last Waltz
Latino
Lianna

Liquid Sky
Love Streams
Matewan
A Matter of Heart
McCabe and Mrs. Miller
Mean Streets
Mikey and Nicky
Mishima: A Life in Four Chapters (co-production: Japan)
Missing
Mixed Blood
Modern Romance
The Moderns
My Dinner with Andre
Native Son
El Norte
Paris, Texas
Parting Glances
Poetry in Motion
Private Practices: The Story of a Sex Surrogate
Pumping Iron II: The Women
Raising Arizona
Real Life
Remember My Name
Repo Man
The Return of the Secaucus Seven
Reuben, Reuben
River's Edge
Round Midnight (co-production: France)
Saint Jack
Salvador
Say Amen, Somebody
Secret Honor
The Serpent's Egg (co-production: West Germany)
Sherman's March: An Improbable Quest for Love
She's Gotta Have It
Short Eyes
Sid and Nancy (co-production: England)
Sitting Ducks
Smithereens
Smooth Talk
Something Wild
State of Siege (co-production: France, Italy)
Stop Making Sense
Stranger Than Paradise
Strangers Kiss
Streamers

Streetwise
Suburbia (The Wild Side)
Swimming to Cambodia
Taxi Driver
Testament
This Is Spinal Tap
Ticket to Heaven
The Times of Harvey Milk
Trash
The Trip to Bountiful
Trouble in Mind
True Stories
Under the Volcano
Waiting for the Moon
The Weavers: Wasn't That a Time!
Welcome to L.A.
What Happened to Kerouac?
Where the Buffalo Roam
Who Am I This Time?
Wild Style
Winter Kills
Wise Blood
Working Girls
A Year of the Quiet Sun (co-production: West Germany, Poland)

U.S.S.R.

Dersu Uzala (co-production: Japan)
Moscow Does Not Believe in Tears
A Slave of Love

WEST GERMANY

Aguirre, the Wrath of God
Ali: Fear Eats the Soul
The American Friend
Angry Harvest
Berlin Alexanderplatz
Das Boot
Colonel Redl (co-production: Hungary, Austria)
Coup de Grace (co-production: France)
Deathwatch (co-production: France)
Despair
Fitzcarraldo
Fox and His Friends
Kamikaze '89
Lola
The Lost Honor of Katharina Blum
A Love in Germany
Marlene
The Marriage of Maria Braun

Men
Mephisto (co-production: Hungary)
The Mystery of Kaspar Hauser
Querelle
The Revolt of Job (co-production: Hungary)
The Serpent's Egg (co-production: U.S.A.)
Sisters, or The Balance of Happiness
Stroszek
Sugarbaby
Swann in Love (co-production: France)
Taxi Zum Klo
The Tin Drum (co-production: France, Poland, Yugoslavia)

Veronika Voss
Wings of Desire
WR: Mysteries of the Organism (co-production: Yugoslavia)
A Year of the Quiet Sun (co-production: Poland, U.S.A.)

YUGOSLAVIA

The Tin Drum (co-production: France, West Germany, Poland)
WR: Mysteries of the Organism (co-production: West Germany)
When Father Was Away on Business

Reviews

ABSOLUTE BEGINNERS
(Video)

Rock Musical

England

1986   107 Min.   Color

CREDITS: *Directed by Julien Temple.
Written by Richard Burridge, Christopher
Wicking and Don MacPherson, based on
the novel by Colin MacInnes. Produced by
Stephen Wooley and Chris Brown. Music
by Gil Evans. Cinematography by Oliver
Stapleton. Set design by John Beard. Re-
leased by Palace-Virgin/Goldencrest. Dis-
tributed nontheatrically by Films Inc. Star-
ring Eddie O'Connell, Patsy Kensit, David
Bowie, James Fox, Ray Davies, Eve Ferret,
Anita Morris, Steven Berkoff, Mandy Rice-
Davies, Bruce Payne and Tenpole Tudor.*

With *Absolute Beginners,* director Julien
Temple *(The Secret Policeman's Other
Ball)* creates a dark but effervescent musical
about love and social justice, against the
unlikely backdrop of London's Kensington
Race Riots of 1958.

The hero of the story is Colin (Eddie
O'Connell), an idealistic young Mod
photographer who lives for capturing the
excitement of the teen movement on film,
and for his beautiful girlfriend, Suzette (Patsy Kensit). When Suzette leaves him for
Henley (James Fox), a dress designer who
can further her career, the brokenhearted
Colin sells out to the highest bidder, an ad
executive (David Bowie) who exploits the
Mod movement for profit. As Colin abandons his friends to become the spokesman
for this entrepreneur's plastic image of the
new generation, he becomes oblivious to
the tensions building in his neighborhood—
the racially mixed, lower-income Kensington. Henley and his cronies are using white,
racist teddy boys to push the blacks out of
their homes in order to build a high-rise.
When Colin finally snaps out of his moral
lethargy to see the threat to himself and his
friends, it's too late to prevent the race riot
that explodes one hot summer night.

Despite Temple's inexperience in feature
films (he mostly directed music videos before this release), he does an extraordinary
job creating *Absolute Beginners's* exuberant and jazzy atmosphere. Several set pieces
are outstanding, including the opening
scene of Colin darting through the streets of
Soho snapping pictures to upbeat music,
and Bowie's seduction of Colin—a big band
introduction to the world of advertising
that takes place on monstrous typewriters
and globes. Although the film's characters
are caricatures, there are some entertaining
performances: Ray Davies of the Kinks in a
cameo as Colin's father, Bowie as the
lizard-voiced oily adman, and O'Connell
and Kensit as the appealing but troubled
teens. But Temple doesn't balance the various moods in this movie as well as he styles
the music and the visuals. Colin's disillusionment with his slum existence clashes
with the energy of his idealism and love for
Suzette. The film also slips a bit at the end.
The final riot comes off stiff and stagey and
doesn't carry the emotional weight that the
events leading up to that cathartic moment
warrant.

RATING: *PG-13 for sexual situations and
mild profanity.*
WARNING: *Because the sets, cinematography and music are so important in
Absolute Beginners, the quality of the
film is decreased on video.*
FILMNOTE: *During production, Absolute
Beginners was surrounded by more hype
than any British film in recent years. But
in spite of all the buildup, the film actually was received far better in the United
States.*

THE ADVENTURES OF BUCKAROO BONZAI ACROSS THE 8TH DIMENSION
(Video)

Science Fiction Satire

U.S.A.

1984   103 Min.   Color

CREDITS: *Directed by W. D. Richter. Written by W. D. Richter and Earl Mac. Produced by Neil Canton. Cinematography by Koenekamp. Released by 20th Century Fox. Distributed nontheatrically by Films Inc. Starring Peter Weller, Jeff Goldblum, John Lithgow, Christopher Lloyd, Ellen Barkin, Lewis Smith and Rosalind Cash.*

Buckaroo Bonzai is a science fiction spoof full of absurd characters and imaginative sets, but it's so frenetically paced that it fails to convey its humor or story line.

Buckaroo (Peter Weller), a brain surgeon from New Jersey, and his rock band, The Hong Kong Cavaliers, get mixed up in a war between good and bad aliens from the mysterious Planet 10. The bad guys are imprisoned in the 8th dimension until Buckaroo accidentally breaks into that netherworld with his souped-up Ford and inadvertently unleashes them to commit dastardly deeds. He spends the rest of the movie trying to fight the aliens and the evil Dr. Lizardo (John Lithgow) for the Oscillator Overthruster, a machine that allows humans and aliens alike to penetrate solid matter. Whoever controls the Overthruster will control the world.

Confused? Sitting through Buckaroo Bonzai won't help. So many disconnected subplots and characters are thrown together here that the whole film becomes a blur. The talents of fine performers such as John Lithgow, Jeff Goldblum and Ellen Barkin have never been so gloriously wasted—their characters are elaborately costumed but vacuous. Even the good-looking hero, Peter Weller, conveys little screen presence beyond his sex appeal. For all of its pumped-up atmosphere and hipness, there is little about Buckaroo Bonzai that is entertaining or clever.

RATING: PG, *with nothing objectionable.*

AFTER HOURS
(Video)

Urban Satire

U.S.A.

1985   118 Min.   Color

CREDITS: *Directed by Martin Scorsese. Written by Joseph Minion. Produced by Amy Robinson, Griffin Dunne and Robert Colesberry. Cinematography by Michael Ballhaus. Released by Warner Brothers. Distributed nontheatrically by Swank Motion Pictures. Starring Griffin Dunne, Rosanna Arquette, John Heard, Teri Garr, Cheech Marin, Thomas Chong, Linda Fiorentino, Verna Bloom, Catherine O'Hara, Dick Miller, Will Patton, Robert Plunkett and Bronson Pinchot.*

If you've ever had one of those days when everything goes wrong, you should be able to empathize with the protagonist in Martin Scorsese's After Hours.

Paul Hackett (Griffin Dunne), a lonely computer operator, meets a woman named Marcy (Rosanna Arquette) in a diner and makes a late-night date with her. When he gets into a cab to go over to her place, his disastrous adventure in New York's SoHo district begins. In the course of the evening, he loses all of his money, is mistaken for a neighborhood prowler, and is attacked by punks who try to give him a mohawk. Marcy, who turns out to be seriously depressed, is just one of the weird characters he meets. He also encounters a confused homosexual looking for his first gay experience, an artist who tries to turn him into a human statue, and a Mister Softee ice cream vendor who sics a vigilante mob on him. The whole time, he is just trying to end his terrible night and make it home, but each attempt to flee one bizarre situation leads him right into another.

Although the plot is unfathomable (Why doesn't he just walk home?), each scene in *After Hours* is shot so that Paul's thoughts are transparent and his dilemma is frighteningly real. Scorsese's direction and Michael Ballhaus's camera work are brilliant, so that what is happening in the corners of the screen is just as important as the focus of the shot. All the players give fine performances and there are some hilarious jabs at artists, yuppies, guppies (gay yuppies), cabbies, cops, punks and bikers. But mostly, it's about lonely and frightened people in the big city. Through this crazy gang of neurotic urbanites, Scorsese is really making fun of us all, and sometimes his jokes can hit too close for comfort.

RATING: R for brief nudity, adult situations and marijuana smoking.
AWARDS: Best Director award (Martin Scorsese) at the 1986 Cannes Film Festival.
WARNING: The cinematography is so important that much is lost on the video.
FILMNOTE: Joseph Minion wrote the screenplay for After Hours *while he was still a student at Columbia University.*

AFTER THE REHEARSAL
(Video, subtitled)

Pschological Drama

Sweden	Swedish
1984 72 Min.	Color

CREDITS: *Directed and written by Ingmar Bergman. Produced by Jorn Donner. Cinematography by Sven Nykvist. Released by Columbia Pictures/Triumph Films. Distributed nontheatrically by Swank Motion Pictures. Starring Erland Josephson, Ingrid Thulin, Lena Olin, Nadja Palmstjerna-Weiss and Bertil Guve.*

Ingmar Bergman's last movie, *After the Rehearsal,* is a low-budget, made-for-TV drama that was probably only released in theaters because of the tremendous success of his alleged final film, *Fanny and Alexander.*

Erland Josephson stars as Henrik, an aging director who is aloof and godlike in his arrogance but increasingly obsessed by his own mortality. One day, after rehearsing a play by Strindberg, he is visited backstage by the play's main actress, Anna (Lena Olin)—a sexy and talented twenty-three-year-old who idolizes Henrik and fantasizes about having an affair with him. Anna is the daughter of Rakel, a now-deceased actress whom Henrik daydreams about while talking to Anna. Through his flashbacks, we see Rakel (Ingrid Thulin) as an alcoholic, has-been actress who begs Henrik to cast her in a starring role and sleep with her again. It's here we also discover the film's crusher: unbeknownst to Anna, the man she is trying to seduce is really her father.

After the Rehearsal is another bout with some of Bergman's favorite depressing themes—power, incest, death, loneliness and alienation. The performances by all three actors are excellent, typically Bergmanesque in their austerity. Their intense faces fill the screen in close-ups, and their dialogue is underscored with meaningful glances. Cinematographer Sven Nykvist has done so many similar movies for Bergman that he has the camera angles and pans down perfectly. But none of these Bergman trademarks give life to *After the Rehearsal,* which is hampered by its claustrophobic setting, cryptic dialogue and slow pacing. This last film by Bergman is ultimately a disappointment, especially when compared to *Fanny and Alexander,* a wonderful tribute to a brilliant and prolific career.

RATING: No MPAA rating, with nothing objectionable.

AGUIRRE, THE WRATH OF GOD

(Video, subtitled)

Wilderness Adventure

West Germany   German

1972   90 Min.   Color

CREDITS: Directed, written and produced by Werner Herzog. Cinematography by Thomas Mauch. Music by Popol Vuh. Released and distributed nontheatrically by New Yorker Films. Starring Klaus Kinski, Ruy Guerra, Del Negro, Helena Rojo, Cecilia Rivera, Peter Berling, Danny Ades and Nastassja Kinski.

Werner Herzog's *Aguirre* is an epic story of the sixteenth-century Spanish conquistadors' search for El Dorado (the legendary city of gold). It begins when Pizarro assigns a group of forty men, including Aguirre, to travel down the Amazon to explore this uncharted jungle. The charismatic Aguirre quickly takes control of the group, and then proceeds to lead his men into disaster. They not only lose their raft and supplies, but one by one, Aguirre's men lose their lives to the dangerous river, cannibals, dart-throwing Indians and disease. Despite these horrors, Aguirre pushes on, determined to reach El Dorado, ruthless in his quest for power and fortune.

One of the most expensive independent films ever made, *Aguirre* is thought by many to be Herzog's major accomplishment to date. Although there is little action or dialogue, the film abounds with metaphors—Aguirre's armor-laden men intent on conquering nature come to symbolize the arrogance of civilized man. In a greater sense, Aguirre's drive to reach El Dorado and even Herzog's obsession with making movies under physically inhospitable conditions can be traced to the "superman complex" that is prevalent in all of his films.

Filmed in the jungles of Peru, Thomas Mauch's cinematography resists static, tranquil shots of nature's wonderment. Instead it portrays the power of nature as something to be feared and respected. Herzog is a master at capturing the terror of the Amazon's deadly whirlpools and the strange silences that befall the jungle when a killer is stalking its prey. Most astonishing, though, is Kinski's powerful performance as Aguirre. "If I ask birds to fall from the trees, they will," he exclaims to his beleaguered men. As a power-monger who defies God in his lust for power, he is unforgettable.

RATING: No MPAA rating, with nothing objectionable.
FILMNOTE: Rumor has it that during the filming of Aguirre, Kinski threatened to quit the film because Herzog was driving him too hard. He was persuaded to stay only when Herzog pulled a gun on him. Herzog carried the gun with him for the rest of the production.

ALI: FEAR EATS THE SOUL

Psychological Romance

West Germany   German

1974   94 Min.   Color

CREDITS: Directed, written and produced by Rainer Werner Fassbinder. Cinematography by Jurgen Jurges. Released and distributed nontheatrically by New Yorker Films. Starring Brigitte Mira, El Hedi Ben Salem, Barbara Valentin, Rainer Werner Fassbinder, Irm Hermann, Peter Gauhe, Karl Scheydt, Marquard Bohm and Walter Sedlmayer.

In his prolific but short career, Rainer Werner Fassbinder was called the most important and disciplined filmmaker of his time by many critics. One of the main reasons for this is his remarkable ability to take a simple story and turn it into a profound exploration of sexuality, alienation and despair. *Ali: Fear Eats the Soul* is a perfect example.

The film begins when an overweight sixty-year-old widow named Emmi (Brigitte Mira) ducks into an Arab bar in Berlin to get out of the rain. While uncomfortably nursing her Coke waiting for the rain to stop, Emmi is interrupted by Ali (El Hedi Ben Salem), a young black Moroccan, who asks her to dance. They dance and talk for a while, although it's not easy because Ali barely speaks German. Then, as unlikely as it seems, Ali pronounces his love for her. Emmi comes back the next day, orders a Coke and sits at the same table, and sure enough, Ali asks her to dance again.

Soon they get married and are very happy together until Emmi introduces Ali to her children. One son (Fassbinder) throws his fist through the TV set, and another exclaims he'll never speak to her again. Emmi's friends, neighbors and co-workers are just as astounded at her marital choice as her children. Naturally, all of this prejudice begins to take a toll on their relationship, and though Emmi isn't conscious of it, she wishes that Ali was more Western. Emmi's cultural racism, on top of his feeling of displacement, finally destroys Ali.

Although at first glance, Salem's Ali doesn't seem to express himself well enough for us to know what's really going on inside him, Ali's love for Emmi and his tragic fate make perfect sense. Both Salem and Mira are curiously appealing misfits, and they make a wonderful couple. Their affection for each other is genuine and tender, and the racism they experience is also realistically presented, even if Fassbinder drives the point home a few too many times when, after they are married, nearly every person they meet scorns them. Still, *Ali: Fear Eats the Soul* pronounces loud and clear that no matter how different a person's culture, looks, age or race, there is an enormous potential for love between two people.

RATING: No MPAA rating, with brief nudity.
AWARDS: International Critics Award at the 1974 Cannes Film Festival. Silver Hugo at the 1974 Chicago Film Festival.

ALL SCREWED UP (ALL IN PLACE, NOTHING IN ORDER)
(Video, dubbed)

Political Satire

Italy		Italian
1976	105 Min.	Color

CREDITS: *Directed and written by Lina Wertmuller. Produced by Romano Cardarelli. Cinematography by Giuseppe Rotunno. Music by Piero Piccioni. Released and distributed nontheatrically by New Line Cinema. Starring Luigi Diberti, Nino Bignamini, Lina Polito, Sara Rapisarda, Guiliana Calandra, Isa Danieli and Eros Pagni.*

All Screwed Up is the final film in Lina Wertmuller's trilogy (including *Love and Anarchy* and *The Seduction of Mimi*) on class and sex roles in industrial Italy, and it's definitely the weakest.

Set in Milan in the late sixties, the film centers around Carletto (Luigi Diberti) and Gigi (Nino Bignamini), two carefree young rural men who come to the city looking for love and work. They end up sharing a rundown tenement with a bunch of women who turn their lives into disaster. A pushy prostitute organizes the household so that Carletto and Gigi have to pay for everything, including watching TV and drinking a cup of coffee. Gigi falls for a pretty young virgin who teases him to the point of insanity. Carletto gets involved with Mariaccia, an extremely fertile woman who gives birth to twins, then nine months later, to quintuplets.

Carletto and Gigi have to hold a variety of degrading jobs just to make ends meet. Once again, Wertmuller expertly dismantles the working-class dream of finding happiness in the big city, as every job Carletto and Gigi take is more mindless and oppressive than the last. *All Screwed Up*'s sharpest satire is in Carletto's and Gigi's battles with vicious bosses and nasty coworkers.

Unfortunately, the film isn't nearly as successful as a sex farce. We are supposed to laugh at the two heroes for being fools, and the women for being coy, servile or bitchy. Because of the film's hurried pacing, neither gender is well enough developed for the jokes to stick or for Wertmuller to get us to love her devilish men despite their less than appealing attitudes toward women. The women in *All Screwed Up* are all degrading stereotypes who aren't in the least funny.

RATING: *No MPAA rating, with sexual content and mild language.*
WARNING: *The dubbing on the video is only fair.*

ALLEGRO NON TROPPO
(Video, dubbed)

Animated Musical

Italy		Italian
1977	75 Min.	B&W/Color

CREDITS: *Directed by Bruno Bozzetto. Written by Bruno Bozzetto, Guido Manuli, Maurizio Nichetti. Animation by Bruno Bozzetto, Giuseppe Lagana, Walter Cavazzuti and Guido Manudi. Music by Debussey, Ravel, Dvorak, Sibelius, Vivaldi and Stravinsky. Editing and sound by Giancarlo Rossini. Released and distributed nontheatrically by New Line Cinema. Live sequences starring Maurisio Nichetti, Nestor Garay, Maurizio Mitchel and Maria Luisa Giovanninni.*

Like Walt Disney's *Fantasia*, *Allegro non Troppo* links six pieces of classical music to short, often humorous animated vignettes. In one of the best, a sagging old professor gets a facelift from Mother Nature to aid him in his pursuit of a beautiful young woman. In another, set to Ravel's "Bolero," a primordial slug evolves from the fizz in the bottom of a Coke bottle until it becomes a huge, gap-toothed monster. And in a third, sad segment, a scraggly cat wanders through the post-war rubble of his old home, remembering happier times. Interspersed among the animated sequences

are live-action slapstick scenes of the frazzled director's attempts to bring a fat conductor, an animator recently released from a dungeon, and an orchestra composed of elderly ladies in step with his artistic vision.

In terms of production and narrative quality, *Allegro non Troppo* is schizophrenic. Most of the animation is excellent, particularly the colorization and originality in the drawings of the main characters (although the detail work in the background isn't very sharp). The classical music works very well with the animation, capturing just the right emotional shades to enhance the action of the story. But the plots of three of the six animated sequences are trite, and the live segments don't work at all. These scenes are full of the most obvious kind of Italian slapstick, complete with pies in the face, a gorilla run amok and cheap laughs at the expense of fat and old people. There's nothing clever about this kind of comedy, and its presence simply detracts from the film's marvelous animation.

RATING: *No MPAA rating, with mild violence.*

ALPHAVILLE
(Video, subtitled)

Political Science Fiction

France		French
1965	100 Min.	B&W

CREDITS: *Directed and written by Jean-Luc Godard. Produced by Andre Michelin. Released and distributed nontheatrically by New Yorker Films and Kit Parker Films. Cinematography by Raoul Coutard. Music by Paul Misraki. Starring Eddie Constantine, Anna Karina, Akim Tamiroff, Howard Vernon, Laszlo Szabo, Michel Delahaye, Jean-Andre Fieschi and Jean-Louis Comolli.*

Jean-Luc Godard's *Alphaville* is about a futuristic, Big Brother society ruled by an evil despot named Professor Von Braun.

Von Braun controls his subjects with drugs and terror, and his most important decree is that expressing emotions or displaying illogical behavior is a crime punishable by death. Execution Alphaville-style means that the victim is shot from behind while standing on a diving board, and beautiful women retrieve the body as onlookers watch without emotion. When Alphaville's lobotomized women aren't fishing out corpses, they walk around in trances and provide sex for any man who desires them.

Into this insanity comes Lemmy Caution (Eddie Constantine), a secret agent from the "normal" world who pretends to be a reporter doing a story on Von Braun. His real purpose is to blow up Alphaville's central computer system and free its inhabitants from Von Braun's tyranny. This isn't an easy task because he falls for Von Braun's beautiful daughter Natasha (Anna Karina), and love is strictly forbidden in Alphaville.

In our age of big-budget science fiction adventures, *Alphaville's* special effects appear unsophisticated. The plot is scattered, and some of the acting is uninspired, particularly Constantine's Lemmy Caution. But in order to appreciate this film, you have to look past its surface to the themes that drive it. Not only is *Alphaville* filled with Big Brother/police-state metaphors, but it lashes out at the impersonalization of modern France. Instead of building science fiction sets in the studio, Godard filmed *Alphaville* in his native Paris, using the city's neomodern architecture for his futuristic sets. He also is fascinated with the Pop-Art aspect of comic strips in this film, so *Alphaville's* story, pacing and characters are straight from American comics. But visually, with Raoul Coutard's swirling and jumpy camera work and strange, powerful images piling up in nearly every scene, *Alphaville* is pure Godard.

RATING: *No MPAA rating, with mild violence.*

AWARDS: *Golden Bear for Best Film at the 1965 Berlin Film Festival.*

ALSINO AND THE CONDOR
(Video, subtitled)

Political Drama

Nicaragua		Spanish and English
1982	89 Min.	Color

CREDITS: *Directed by Miguel Littin. Written by Miguel Littin, Tomas Perez Turrent and Isidore Aguirre. Produced by Herman Littin. Cinematography by Jorge Herrera. Music by Leo Brower. Released and distributed nontheatrically by Almi Pictures. Starring Alan Esquivel, Dean Stockwell, Carmen Bunster, Alejandro Parodi, Delia Casanova, Mart Lorena Perez and Reinaldo Miravalle.*

Alsino and the Condor was the first fictional feature made in Nicaragua after the overthrow of Somoza. It's about a peasant boy named Alsino (Alan Esquivel) whose dreams of one day flying come true when a patronizing U.S. military adviser to the Somoza junta (Dean Stockwell) takes him up for a ride in his helicopter. Though exciting for Alsino, the flight only increases his desire to soar like a real bird. Soon after, Alsino climbs to the top of a very large tree, jumps off, and plummets to the ground, severely injuring himself and becoming a hunchback. When he is well enough to walk again, Alsino witnesses the atrocities of the junta. Eventually he does what he can to help the Sandinistas fight against the Somoza soldiers and their American helpers, including the pilot who gave him a ride in his helicopter.

Alsino is more than a boy living inside his fantasies and trying to deal with the harsh realities of his country's civil war. He's also a metaphor for the emerging national consciousness that was taking place in both Nicaragua and El Salvador when *Alsino and the Condor* was made. Jorge Herrera's cinematography is of very high quality, especially in the allegorical dream sequences of Alsino flying, while the first half of *Alsino and the Condor* isn't nearly as didactic as it could be. Stockwell's character, for instance, is allowed to be caring and human, and the hypocrisy of his mission is made even more evident by his concern for Alsino. But as the young boy gets caught up in the revolutionary fervor, *Alsino and the Condor* eventually evolves into a full-fledged Sandinista propaganda film.

The atrocities of the Somoza National Guard and Americans are portrayed in all their graphic detail, while the Sandinistas appear as angelic liberators who kill because they have to (the camera doesn't linger long on their victims). Upbeat folk music even plays when they are on the screen. You can't fault Chilean filmmaker Miguel Littin for his intentions, but the film's important issues concerning Alsino's struggle of growing up in poverty and political repression, established early on, are finally lost in all the orchestration.

RATING: R for profanity and a lot of violence.
AWARDS: 1982 Academy Award nomination for Best Foreign Film.

ALTERED STATES
(Video)

Science Fiction

U.S.A.

1980   102 Min.   Color

CREDITS: *Directed by Ken Russell. Written by Sidney Aaron, based on the book by Paddy Chayevsky. Produced by Howard Gottfried. Cinematography by Jordan Cronenweth. Music by John Corigliano. Special effects by Bran Ferren. Makeup by Dick Smith. Released by Warner Brothers. Distributed nontheatrically by Swank Motion Pictures. Starring William Hurt, Blair Brown, Bob Balaban, Charles Haid, Thaao Penghlis, Miguel Godreau and Dori Brenner.*

Altered States is a Dr. Jeckyl and Mr. Hyde story with a New Age twist. Its hero is Eddie Jessup (William Hurt), a scientist who, instead of ingesting a frothing concoction out of a test tube, eats mind-altering mushrooms and floats in a sensory-deprivation tank. Eddie is conducting rebirthing experiments at his Harvard laboratory and is all too successful: he not only goes back to the time of his own birth but also travels all the way back to the beginning of mankind. For some unexplained reason, Eddie gets stuck in the ape phase of his evolutionary passage, and like a recurring bad acid trip, he not only switches back and forth between man and ape during his experiments, but outside the lab he suddenly turns into a Neanderthal, running wild through the streets. His journeys are accompanied by a tremendous force of energy—a virtual psychedelic light show coming out of his body. He convulses uncontrollably, sometimes even being hurled across the room.

Based on John Lilly's research on isolation tanks, *Altered States* starts out with a well-developed scientific framework. Hurt gives a strong performance as Eddie and is particularly adept at capturing his character's anguish during the rebirthing process. But about halfway through it becomes evident that Eddie's experiments are little more than glorified acid trips. *Altered States* fizzles because too many important scientific and metaphysical questions are left unexplained. Still, all of these shenanigans are ideal for the special effects talents of director Ken Russell (*The Devils* and *The Music Lovers*). When Eddie whirls back to mankind's dawning, his body, the tank and the lab explode with energy, color and light.

RATING: R for nudity, sex, profanity and violence.
AWARDS: 1980 Academy Award nominations for Best Sound (Arthur Piantadosi, Les Fresholtz, Michael Minklen and Willie D. Burton) and Best Original Score (John Corigliano).
WARNING: Because the visuals are so important, much is lost on video.

ALWAYS
(Video)

★ ★ ½

Romantic Comedy

U.S.A.

1985   105 Min.   Color

CREDITS: *Directed and written by Henry Jaglom. Produced by Henry Jaglom and Judith Wolinski. Cinematography by Hanania Baer. Music by Ike Megal. Released and distributed nontheatrically by The Samuel Goldwyn Company. Starring Henry Jaglom, Patrice Townsend, Joanna Frank, Allan Rachins, Melissa Leo, Jonathan Kaufer, Bob Rafelson and Michael Emil.*

Sitting through Henry Jaglom's *Always* is like eavesdropping on a stranger's psychotherapy session. Too many of the personal details of Jaglom's breakup with his wife are revealed in this movie, and after a while this confessional becomes uncomfortable. Filmed with cinema verité techniques, the self-effacing orgy begins with Dave Townsend (Jaglom) explaining that his wife Judy (played by Jaglom's ex-wife Patrice Townsend) left him two years before. He announces to the audience that he is finally over the heartbreak and that she is coming to dinner that night to sign the divorce papers in the presence of a notary.

Despite his brave monologue, Dave's façade crumbles when Judy walks through the door. They don't sign the papers, and when Judy agrees to stay the weekend at his house, Dave spends the next two days desperately trying to win her back. The two aren't alone in their misery. Judy's free-spirited sister shows up with her wimpy fiancé, then an unhappily married couple that Judy and Dave have known for years pop in as well. The movie soon dissolves into an overly talky, emotional joy ride, with Jaglom in the driver's seat for most of the movie and everybody else taking an occasional turn at the wheel.

It's obvious that Jaglom and his ex-wife intend this movie to be another stage of working out their problems, and they should be commended for their public honesty. Certain scenes explore universal sore spots in relationships that only a few filmmakers, such as Woody Allen and Eric Rohmer, have had the guts to confront. But who really cares about all the intimate details of this confused couple's love life? Even though some moments in *Always* are very clever, Jaglom is unable to make his dirty laundry consistently funny or compelling. Most of the bantering is more embarrassing than anything else, and ultimately the only ones who could be truly interested are the parties involved.

RATING: *R for nudity, sex and substance abuse.*

AMARCORD
(Video, dubbed)

★ ★ ★ ★ ★

Coming-of-Age Satire

Italy   Italian

1974   127 Min.   Color

CREDITS: *Directed by Federico Fellini. Written by Federico Fellini and Tonino Guerra. Produced by Franco Cristaldi. Cinematography by Giuseppe Rotunno. Music by Nino Rota. Released by Warner Brothers. Distributed nontheatrically by Films Inc. Starring Bruno Zamin, Magali Noel, Pupella Maggio, Armando Brancia, Giuseppe Ianigro, Nando Orfei, Ciccio Ingrassia and Luigi Rossi.*

The film that popularized Fellini with non–art house audiences, *Amarcord* is a nostalgic look at Fellini's youth and one of his most enjoyable films to date. Set in an Adriatic village during Mussolini's rule, it tells the story of a teenager, a Fellini-surrogate named Titta (Bruno Zamin). Through his eyes, we meet an assortment of characters: his crazy uncle who, on a family outing, has to be talked out of a tree by a midget nun; Titta's perpetually flatulent grandpa; and his bricklayer father, who didactically espouses the virtues of socialism. But the most memorable characters in Titta's life play a role in his adolescent obsession with sex, including his buxom math teacher, whose tight sweaters are an inspiration to her students; the town's prolific prostitute; and the tobacco shop proprietress who nearly smothers Titta with her quadruple-D-cup breasts.

Gloriously photographed by Giuseppe Rotunno and set to an unforgettable soundtrack by Fellini regular Nino Rota, *Amarcord* is full of bittersweet observations on human nature and the tragic political events occuring in Italy at the time. Fellini doesn't gloss over this unfortunate period in Italian history, especially in the scenes of Titta's father being dragged off by Mussolini's soldiers for his political beliefs. But *Amarcord* is predominantly a gentle comedy about Titta's awkward journey into adulthood, his fears about his sexuality, and the wonderful people he observes along the way. In fact, *Amarcord* is the teen comedy to top all teen comedies, with satire so delightfully irreverent and characters so lovable that it's easy to understand why this is Fellini's most popular film.

RATING: R for numerous scenes of bare breasts.
AWARDS: 1974 Academy Award for Best Foreign Film. One of the National Board of Review's 10 Best Foreign Films in 1974.
WARNING: The dubbing is decent on the video version, but because the dialogue is so important the quality of the film is seriously affected.

THE AMERICAN FRIEND
(Video, subtitled)

Psychological Thriller

W. Germany   German, French
                              and English

1977   127 Min.   Color

CREDITS: *Directed by Wim Wenders. Written by Wim Wenders, based on the novel* Ripley's Game *by Patricia Highsmith. Cinematography by Robby Muller. Music by Jurgen Knieper. Released and distributed nontheatrically by New Yorker Films.*

Starring Bruno Ganz, Dennis Hopper, Lisa Kreuzer, Sam Fuller, Nicholas Ray, Gerard Blain, Peter Lilienthal, Daniel Schmid, Jean Eustache, Rudolf Schundler, Sandy Whitelaw and Lou Castel.

Wim Wenders calls *The American Friend* his "entertainment film," and it certainly is a departure from his personally penned films in the past. Based on the novel *Ripley's Game* by Patricia Highsmith, *The American Friend* disguises itself as a murder mystery, but it's really a psychological drama about the unusual relationship between an American art thief named Tom Ripley (Dennis Hopper) and German picture framer Jonathan Zimmermann (Bruno Ganz). The two meet at an art auction in Hamburg where Jonathan snubs Ripley because of his reputation. Ripley is offended, so he devises a plan to get even, in the process taking care of a nasty chore that he has been avoiding.

Jonathan has leukemia, and Ripley spreads the rumor that his cancer is out of remission. When the rumor gets back to Jonathan, he thinks he is about to die and agrees to commit a murder for Ripley in order to make some quick cash to leave to his family after his death. But what's not in Ripley's plan is that in the days leading up to the "hit," he and Jonathan become good friends and he comes to regret the mess he's gotten Jonathan and his family into.

Although *The American Friend* requires more than a little patience to watch because of its intricate, sometimes confusing plot, it's well worth the effort. This film is a brilliantly directed study of alienation in modern society, as well as a homage to American film noir greats Sam Fuller and Nicolas Ray (who both have cameos in the film). Wenders and his cameraman Robby Muller *(Down by Law)* show supercool movement between New York's SoHo, Paris and Hamburg, and an attention to detail that sets the mood perfectly for the ironies in Ripley's and Jonathan's lives. The movie's rock-and-roll soundtrack is great, but it's really Hopper and Ganz who make this film so remarkable. They both give commanding performances, as their characters take us through a whole range of feelings about friendship, desperation, betrayal and greed. In fact, there is so much going on under the surface in them, and in the story itself, that *The American Friend* is actually more rewarding with each additional viewing.

RATING: R for violence and language.

AND THE SHIP SAILS ON
(Video, subtitled)

Social Satire

Italy	Italian
1984	138 Min.	Color

CREDITS: *Directed by Federico Fellini. Written by Federico Fellini and Tonino Guerra. Produced by Franco Cristaldi. Cinematography by Giuseppe Rotunno. Music by Gianfranco Plenixio. Released by Columbia Pictures/Triumph Films. Distributed nontheatrically by Swank Motion Pictures. Starring Freddie Jones, Barbara Jefford, Victor Poletti, Peter Cellier, Janet Suzman, Elisa Marinardi, Norma West, Paoulo Paolini, Sarah Jane Varley and Florenzo Serra.*

Fellini is a master at parading bizarre characters in front of the camera, but in *And the Ship Sails On*, there's little else happening. The time is 1914, and a group of dancers, musicians and aristocrats are on an ocean liner called the *Gloria N* to pay tribute to the late opera singer Edmea Tetua by scattering her ashes at sea. With them is Orlando (Freddie Jones), a journalist doing a story on the dead diva; he also doubles as the film's narrator.

Orlando introduces us to the Grand Duke of Austria, his blind companion, a romantic homosexual, a fat Egyptian, and various other lunatics who roam around the ship quarreling, singing, and passing the time of day. Most of them share a love for the dead opera star and a dislike of each other. Meanwhile, the *Gloria N* picks up a a group of Serbo-Croation freedom fighters trying to escape the clutches of the Austro-Hungarian Empire. When their enemy's battleship approaches the *Gloria N* and demands that the captain turn them over, the life of everybody on the ocean liner is suddenly threatened.

And the Ship Sails On has more than its share of obnoxious aristocrats, musicians, artists and royalty. Although some of them are humorous in a bizarre sort of way, none of them ever rise above the level of caricature, and most of the time Fellini seems content to let their display of idiosyncracies take the place of a conventional narrative. Fortunately, the subplot concerning the refugees adds some life, and there is a hilarious miniplot concerning a rhinoceros down in the ship's hold who's stinking up the ship. Also, Gianfranco Plenixio's music is quite good, as are the film's costumes. But as a post–World War I political drama, and as a satire on the frivolities of the upper class, *And the Ship Sails On* is only mildly entertaining.

RATING: No MPAA rating, with nothing objectionable.

ANGELO, MY LOVE
(Video, partially subtitled)

Cultural Drama

U.S.A.	English and Gypsy
1983	115 Min.	Color

CREDITS: *Directed and written by Robert Duvall. Produced by Gail Youngs. Cinematography by Joseph Friedman. Music by Michael Kamen. Released by Cinecom. Distributed nontheatrically by New Yorker Films. Starring Angelo Evans, Michael Evans, Ruthie Evans, Tony Evans, Debbie Evans, Steve "Patalay" Tsigonoff, Millie Tsigonoff, Frankie Williams, George Nicholas, Katerina Ribraka, Timothy Phillips, Lachaln Youngs and Jennifer Youngs.*

Robert Duvall discovered a young Gypsy boy named Angelo Evans hustling on the streets of New York and was so taken by this macho and precocious eleven-year-old kid that he decided right then and there to make a movie about him. Although *Angelo, My Love* is a fictionalized story, Duvall convinced Angelo, his family, and dozens of other Gypsies to play themselves in a mostly improvised narrative. The result is a fascinating glimpse at the morals, superstitions and life-styles of New York City Gypsies. The plot wanders all over the place, but it basically concerns Angelo's attempt to recover a family ring stolen by a Russian Gypsy named Stevie (Angelo and his family are Greek). Aimless and uncompelling, the story can be ignored, but the characters and settings in this movie command your attention like a fast-talking Gypsy con artist.

Duvall takes us to a Gypsy court, a wedding and a feast in Canada, and introduces us to a wide range of proud Gypsies who tell fortunes, lie and hustle whenever they get the chance. To act the trickster is part of the Gypsy way of life, and nobody exemplifies this more than Angelo. He looks, acts and talks like a combination of a pre-pubescent John Travolta and a pimp. His shirt is unbuttoned down to his navel, his pants are tight and he can never pass a mirror without primping in it. When he's not hustling money for clothes or hitting on females of all ages, he's shooting off his foul mouth in somebody's face. Yet Angelo is also as loving and emotional as any eleven-year-old boy. It only takes about thirty seconds of watching Angelo in action to realize why Duvall was so captivated by him.

RATING: R for language.
FILMNOTE: Robert Duvall spent seven years raising money and doing research before the filming began. He then had the added problem of dealing with Gypsies from all over the country who'd heard about the project and showed up on the set, aggressively competing for his attention.

ANGRY HARVEST
(Video, subtitled)

Psychological Drama

West Germany   German

1985   102 Min.   Color

CREDITS: Directed by Agnieszka Holland. Written by Agnieszka Holland and Paul Hengge. Produced by Artur Brauner. Cinematography by Josef Ort-Snep. Music by Jorg Strass Burger. Released by Filmunst. Distributed nontheatrically by European Classics. Starring Armin Mueller-Stahl, Elisabeth Trissenaar, Kathe Jaenicke, Hans Beerhenke, Isa Haller, Margit Carstensen and Wojciech Pszioniak.

Once an assistant to Andrzej Wajda *(Man of Marble)*, Polish filmmaker Agnieszka Holland shares her mentor's interest in the dynamics of repression and dependence. Set in Poland during World War II, Holland's *Angry Harvest* chronicles the relationship between Leon (Armin Mueller-Stahl), a lonely Polish farmer, and Rosa (Elisabeth Trissenaar), a beautiful Viennese Jewess who escapes into the countryside near his home from a train bound for the death camps.

When Leon discovers Rosa, hungry and wounded, he impulsively hides her from the Gestapo. But what appears to be a humane gesture turns out to have darker motives. Widowed, Leon is so starved for companionship that he demands affection and obedience from Rosa in return for his charity. Rosa, for her part, recognizing Leon's desperation, threatens to desert him if he doesn't yield to her wishes. The story quickly becomes an emotional tug-of-war, a battle complicated by the Nazis who are combing the woods near Leon's home.

Angry Harvest explores the basest level of human desires. Leon and Rosa come together out of dependence, not love. But each has such a primal need to dominate the other that their union is doomed from the start. While little background is given to make Rosa and Leon wholly sympathetic characters, both Mueller-Stahl and Trissenaar are powerfully convincing in their roles and carry the film over the rough spots of a sometimes stifling story line. But Holland's sparse narrative style only works in the context of Leon and Rosa's relationship. Her attempts to include the townspeople and Nazis around Leon's farm are often tensionless. And though the dynamic of Leon and Rosa's relationship can be quite compelling, toward the end of *Angry Harvest* even their struggle becomes a little flat.

RATING: No MPAA rating, with violence and brief nudity.
AWARDS: 1985 Academy Award nomination for Best Foreign Film.

ANOTHER COUNTRY
(Video)

★ ★ ½

Coming-of-Age Drama

England

1984   90 Min.   Color

CREDITS: Directed by Marek Kanievska. Written by Julian Mitchell, based on his novel. Produced by Alan Marshall. Cinematography by Peter Biziou. Music by Michael Storey. Released by Orion Classics. Distributed nontheatrically by Films Inc. Starring Rupert Everett, Colin Firth, Michael Jenn, Robert Addie, Anna Massey, Betsy Brantley, Rupert Wainwright, Tristan Oliver and Cary Elwes.

Guy Burgess and Donald Maclean were two friends from well-to-do families who became Russian spies. When the two upstanding British citizens defected to the Soviet Union in 1951, the mystery of their betrayal obsessed all of England. The premise of *Another Country*, a fictionalized treatment of the story, is that their repressive years at boarding school in the thirties planted the seeds for their treasonous acts later on.

From the moment we are introduced to them at school (in this movie, Guy and Donald are called Guy and Judd), it's obvious that neither fits into a system that seems to value only money, class and status. Judd (Colin Firth) is already an avowed Communist with a disdain for the bourgeoisie, and Guy (Rupert Everett) is a wide-eyed idealist who picks his last year at school to let everybody know he is a homosexual. The other students and teachers are ruthless in rebuking Judd for his politics and Guy for his sexual preference.

Despite its efforts, *Another Country* doesn't convince us that Judd and Guy turned into spies thirty years later because of mean-spirited schoolmates and teachers, Guy's homoeroticism, and Judd's early Marxist beliefs. What it does do is overportray the stifling life in a British boarding school. Firth and Everett deliver strong performances, but if they aren't going through rigorous scholastics or taking verbal and physical abuse from their fellow classmates, they are looking up the noses of their stern and ruthless teachers. With little compelling action and the school's atmosphere so repressive, it's hard to breathe in *Another Country*.

RATING: PG, with sexual innuendos.
AWARDS: Best Artistic Contribution Award for Cinematography (Peter Biziou) at the 1985 Cannes Film Festival.

APARAJITO . . . THE UNVANQUISHED
(Video, subtitled)

★ ★

Cultural Drama

India   Bengali

1958   113 Min.   B&W

CREDITS: Directed and produced by Satyajit Ray. Written by Satyajit Ray, based on the novel Pather Panchali by Bibhutibhusan Bandapaddhay. Cinematography by Subroto Mitra. Music by Ravi Shankar. Released by Epic/Aurora Films. Distributed nontheatrically by Films Inc. Starring Pinaki Sen Gupta, Smaran Ghosal, Karuna Banerji, Ramani Sen Gupta, Charu Ghosh, Subodh Ganguly, Kali Charan Ray and Santi Gupta.

Aparajito is the second in Satyajit Ray's Apu trilogy and continues where *Pather Panchali* left off. Apu (Pinaki Sen Gupta) is now an adolescent, and his parents are aging. They move to the city hoping to escape the poverty and tragedy that plagued them in their Bengali village. They don't. Apu's father (Karuna Banerji) soon becomes ill and dies, and Apu and his mother (Karuna Banerji) are forced to work as house servants for a wealthy Indian family.

Although both mother and son are determined that Apu have a better future, they differ on what path he should take. Mom wants her boy to grow up to be a Brahman priest like his father, but Apu is eager to become Westernized and educated. Eventually he earns a scholarship to attend Calcutta University, and for the rest of the film, we see Apu (now a different actor, Smaran Ghosal) with bags under his eyes from exhaustion, obsessively working and studying, as he rejects tradition and the wishes of his mother. When he goes home for one of his infrequent visits, Apu doesn't notice that his mother is lonely, heartbroken and becoming quite ill.

Although the relationship between mother and son serves as a striking indictment of the loss of traditional values in India today, Ray drives this theme home to the point of tedium in *Aparajito*. The same scenes of Apu rebuking his mother are replayed over again in different settings. The acting is quite good, particularly Karuna Banerji's performance as Apu's despairing mother. The film's lyrical cinematography and mystical Ravi Shankar soundtrack add a great deal of cultural texture. But *Aparajito* suffers from a static story line and sparse, ineffective dialogue. As Apu drifts away from his mother in scene after scene in this movie, it's easy for us to drift as well.

RATING: No MPAA rating, with nothing objectionable.
AWARDS: Golden Lion for Best Film at the 1957 Venice Film Festival.

THE ASSAULT
(Video, dubbed)

★   ★   ½

Political Drama

Holland   Dutch

1986   150 Min.   Color

CREDITS: *Directed and produced by Fons Rademakers. Written by Gerard Soeteman, based on the novel by Harry Mulisch. Cinematography by Theo Van De Sande. Music by Jurriaan Andriessen. Released by Cannon Films. Distributed nontheatrically by Swank Motion Pictures. Starring Derek De Lint, Marc Van Uchelen, Monique Ven De Ven and John Kraaykamp.*

The surprise 1986 Oscar winner for Best Foreign Film, *The Assault* begins powerfully as the small Dutch village of Haarlem struggles to survive during the last few days of Nazi occupation in 1945. When the Resistance shoots a notorious local collaborator, the Nazis react by murdering forty-five prisoners, as well as destroying the house at which the murdered collaborator's body was inexplicably discarded. Only twelve-year-old Anton (Marc Van Uchelen) survives this attack on his home; the rest of his family is killed while Anton is held in a detention cell for the night, then shipped off to his uncle's home in Amsterdam the next day. But before he is released, the confused boy is confronted in the dark by his cellmate, a beautiful, anonymous woman who tries to comfort the boy by telling him that his family was sacrificed for the good of his country.

The film follows the adult Anton (Derek De Lint) through the next forty years of his life, stopping at ten-year intervals to examine his struggles to cope with the tragic loss of his family. On the surface, Anton adjusts well, studying to become a doctor and marrying a good woman. But his practice and family are only temporary barriers against his increasingly fragile emotions, which are haunted by those monumental events many years before.

The Assault works best at the beginning. Director Fons Rademakers and his cinematographer Theo Van De Sande skillfully shoot scenes of Anton as a boy in a blue light that gives the film a chill, eerie sense of foreboding. This extended prologue is tension-filled, and then tender, as Anton's cellmate gently explains the facts of war to the confused little boy. Unfortunately, what follows is much less interesting, a flaccid psychological drama that awkwardly switches gears at the end to become a political diatribe. Rademakers is too ambitious in trying to show how events forty years before affect the political and personal life of Anton today. The older Anton gets, the more impenetrable and repressed his character becomes, while the questions Rademakers raises so passionately in the film early on are lost in Anton's brooding and self-pity.

RATING: PG, with mild violence.
AWARDS: 1986 Academy Award for Best Foreign Film.

ATLANTIC CITY
(Video)

Social Thriller

U.S.A./Canada

1981   104 Min.   Color

CREDITS: Directed by Louis Malle. Written by John Guare. Produced by Dennis Heroux. Cinematography by Richard Ciupka. Music by Paul Anka and Robert Goulet. Released by Paramount. Distributed nontheatrically by Films Inc. Starring Burt Lancaster, Susan Sarandon, Kate Reid, Hollis McLaren, Robert Joy, Al Waxman, Robert Goulet, Wallace Shawn and Michel Piccoli.

When leading men like Burt Lancaster creep into their late sixties, American audiences tend to write them off and the entertainment industry assigns them to a ghetto of bit parts in exploitation and television movies. But in Louis Malle's *Atlantic City,* Lancaster shows that a graying lion can still roar. He plays Lou, an aging, two-bit hustler who is fond of reminiscing about the old days when he was a bodyguard for a big-time gangster and Atlantic City was alive with flashy limos and high rollers.

Those times are long past for Lou and Atlantic City. Now he spends his time sleeping with a dead mobster's neurotic widow, making a few bucks running numbers, and watching a beautiful woman (Susan Sarandon) through his apartment window. Through a seris of mishaps, he and the woman get involved in romance, murder and drug dealing. Along the way they meet up with dangerous gangsters, the police and a pregnant, vacuous flower-child abandoned by her "old man." But more important, the adventure gives Lou the chance to remake his life, to become the big-time mobster he never was while acting as savior for a woman he comes to love.

Atlantic City works well on several different levels. Although it begins slowly, it builds into a jaw-grinding thriller complete with a surprise ending. As a comedy, it has an assortment of characters who deliver some outrageously funny lines. But at the heart of *Atlantic City* is a social drama about society's losers, people who have little to show for their lives but who never let go of their dreams. French director Louis Malle *(My Dinner with Andre)* does a remarkable job getting to the core of the lonely, desperate underclass of Americans who are drawn to a place like Atlantic City. And Lancaster gives one of the best performances of his illustrious career as the self-deluded king of the roost—a slightly crazed hustler who never stops dreaming that he'll make it to the big time.

RATING: R for nudity, drugs and violence.
AWARDS: Golden Lion for Best Film at the 1980 Venice Film Festival; 1981 British Academy Awards for Best Director (Louis Malle) and Best Actor (Burt Lancaster); 1981 New York Film Critics Awards for Best Screenplay (John Guare) and Best Actor (Lancaster); 1981 Academy Award nominations for Best Picture, Best Director (Malle), Best Actor (Lancaster), Best Actress (Susan Sarandon) and Best Screenplay.

THE ATOMIC CAFE
(Video)

Anti-Nuke Documentary

U.S.A.

1982   88 Min.   Color

CREDITS: *Directed, written and produced by Kevin Rafferty, Jayne Loader and Pierce Rafferty. Edited by Jayne Loader and Pierce Rafferty. Archival research by Kevin Rafferty. Sound by Margie Crimmins. Music by Orick Eaker. Released by Almi Pictures. Distributed nontheatrically by New Yorker Films.*

When it comes to nuclear war or radioactive fallout, it's better not to be caught with your pants down—at least that's the prophetic advice given from the "selling of the bomb" propaganda in the *The Atomic Cafe*. The result of over five years of combing through archives from all over the country, this hilarious and frightening documentary is a collection of newsreels and U.S. government films from the late forties and fifties warning of the Communist threat, placating fears about nuclear war and educating citizens on how to respond if a bomb were actually dropped.

The film's most notorious clip features Bert the Turtle instructing youngsters to "duck and cover" when they see the flash of a nuclear explosion. Other perversely funny segments include a father advising his family to stay in their air raid shelter for at least one minute after the explosion; an officer at a nuclear test site reassuring soldiers they won't be harmed so long as they cover their eyes; and an Air Force pilot casually commenting that dropping the hydrogen bomb on Nagasaki was "perfectly routine." Also, for nuclear holocaust paraphernalia freaks, *The Atomic Cafe* shows all kinds of atomic war consumer goods, including air-raid-shelter kits and survivalist tools.

Until Claude Lanzmann's *Shoah, The Atomic Cafe* was probably the most thoroughly researched documentary ever produced. The filmmakers' hard work definitely shows in the staggering amount of misinformation they came up with. Although several scenes in *The Atomic Cafe* are uproariously funny, the film's comedy is overshadowed by its sobering warnings about the dangers of nuclear war and the nature of propaganda and deception.

RATING: *No MPAA rating, with some graphically violent footage.*
FILMNOTE: *The filmmakers Kevin and Pierce Rafferty and Jayne Loader started out making a documentary about propaganda films made for the government and industry. The enormity of their research forced them to narrow their focus to propaganda surrounding the bomb.*

AU REVOIR LES ENFANTS (GOODBYE, CHILDREN)

★ ★ ★ ★ ★

Coming-of-Age Drama

France   French

1987   100 Min.   Color

CREDITS: *Directed, written and produced by Louis Malle. Cinematography by Renato Berta. Released by Orion Classics. Distributed nontheatrically by The Samuel Goldwyn Company. Starring Gaspard Manesse, Raphael Fejto, Stanislas Carre de Malberg, Francine Racette, Francois Negret and Peter Fitz.*

Based on Louis Malle's childhood memories of the Nazi occupation of France, *Au Revoir les Enfants* is the bittersweet story of the friendship between two eleven-year-olds at a Catholic boarding school. When Julien Quentin (Gaspard Manesse) first meets Jean Bonnet (Raphael Fejto), he is curious about this dark-skinned newcomer to his school who his classmates make fun of. Jean is different from the others—intelligent, clever and sensitive. As they become friends, Julien discovers that Jean is also half Jewish—a secret that must be kept hidden from the Nazi occupiers and their French collaborators. While the two boys struggle with the normal childhood problems of homework, peer pressure and puberty, the potential danger to Jean is never far from the surface as the frightened boy has to deny his past and naive Julien must resist his childish urge to tell others the secret he's discovered about his friend.

Set in the idyllic French countryside near the village of Fontainebleau, *Au Revoir les Enfants* is photographed to look softly beautiful, almost dreamlike. The contrast between the pleasant setting and the ugly behavior of the humans who inhabit it is very effective, yet at times, the lush cinematography mutes some of the film's more heartfelt emotions.

What's never muted are the moral questions that arise from everyday life for these children caught in an adults' war. Both main characters are likeably imperfect, yet Malle is careful not to oversimplify their emotions or make them into overly sentimental vehicles. With his alter ego Julien, Malle brilliantly symbolizes the innocence that could be so dangerous during this dark time in French history.

RATING: PG, with nothing objectionable.
FILMNOTE: Like Julien, Louis Malle as a child attended a Catholic boarding school near Fontainebleau whose headmaster hid Jewish boys from the Gestapo. While Malle was at the school, the Nazis discovered the Jewish boys and sent them and the headmaster to concentration camps.

AUTUMN SONATA
(Video, dubbed)

Psychological Drama

Sweden	Swedish
1978	93 Min.	Color

CREDITS: Directed and written by Ingmar Bergman. Produced by Lew Grade and Martin Starger. Cinematography by Sven Nykvist. Released by New World Pictures. Distributed nontheatrically by Films Inc. Starring Liv Ullmann, Ingrid Bergman, Lena Nyman, Halvor Bjork, Gunner Bornjstrand, Erland Josephson, Linn Ullmann, Georg Lokkeberg and Knut Wigert.

Ingmar Bergman's *Autumn Sonata* explores a mother/daughter relationship with the same intensity that his *Scenes from a Marriage* grappled with marriage. It's a wrenching story of the rage that Eva (Liv Ullmann) has harbored toward her mother, Charlotte (Ingrid Bergman), for thirty years. Her anger finally explodes when Charlotte comes for an extended stay at her daughter's country home.

Charlotte is a cold, egotistical pianist who neglected Eva throughout her childhood to advance her own musical career. She hasn't seen Eva for seven years because she's simply been too busy performing. When Charlotte first arrives, Eva keeps her feelings inside and dotes on her mother like any loving daughter. But when the mother learns Eva has taken in Charlotte's youngest daughter, Helena (Lena Nyman), a terminally ill paraplegic Charlotte abandoned in a nursing home years before, the ice breaks. Charlotte exorcises her guilt by angrily denouncing Eva. Eva responds with a wrath of her own—an entire lifetime of rage. And for the rest of the film, Eva confronts Charlotte with her failures as a mother and a human being, while Charlotte denies the charges or makes accusations of her own.

Nothing ever gets resolved in *Autumn Sonata*, which is both realistic and frustrating. In the end, Ingmar Bergman is telling us that you can't heal a lifetime of wounds—you can only learn to live with them. For both of these women, it's a hard lesson to learn.

The acting is extraordinary, with Ullmann giving an intense performance as a daughter severely damaged by her repressed anger. In her last motion picture performance, Ingrid Bergman is also tremendous as the unfeeling mother. In her sixties and ill herself at the time, Bergman knew this was to be her last screen role. It is a fitting end to her illustrious career that she acts so superbly in her own language, directed by Sweden's most accomplished filmmaker.

RATING: PG, with nothing objectionable.
AWARDS: 1978 New York Film Critics Award for Best Actress (Ingrid Bergman); the National Board of Review's Best Foreign Film, Best Actress (Ingrid Bergman) and Best Director (Ingmar Bergman) in 1978.

L'AVVENTURA
(Video, subtitled)

Psychological Drama

Italy	Italian
1960 145 Min.	B&W

CREDITS: Directed by Michelangelo Antonioni. Written by Michelangelo Antonioni, Elio Bartolini and Tonino Guerra. Produced by Cino Del Duca. Cinematography by Aldo Scavarda. Released by Janus Films. Distributed nontheatrically by Films Inc. and Kino International. Starring Monica Vitti, Gabriele Ferzetti, Lea Massari, Dominique Blanchar, James Addams, Renzo Ricci and Esmeralda Ruspoli.

A mystery surrounding Michelangelo Antonioni's *L'Avventura* is how it earned the honor of being rated the seventh greatest film of all time in *Sight and Sound* magazine's 1982 poll of international movie critics.

The story takes place in the late fifties and follows a group of young upper-class Italians who take a day trip to an island on a yacht. Among them are Anna (Lea Massari) and Sandro (Gabriele Ferzetti), a mannequinlike couple who never express emotion to one another, even when they are making love. En route to the island, Anna jumps off the moving yacht, then cries "Shark!" After she is rescued, she confides, to the disgust of her best friend Claudia (Monica Vitti) that the whole scene was a charade. When the group finally reaches the island, Anna vanishes. Claudia is convinced that Anna is up to more mischief, but after extensive searching, it seems as though her disappearance is authentic. Finally, even the police give up searching, but Claudia convinces Sandro that they must continue to look for Anna in nearby villages. As the two travel from town to town, they also drift into an affair. Sandro seems to feel no sadness that Anna could be dead, while Claudia is plagued by guilt for becoming involved with her best friend's lover.

Like Buñuel, Antonioni skillfully captures the emptiness and arrogance of the privileged class. But the director's self-conscious attempts to obscure the plot's meaning in a web of intrigue and metaphoric camera work, plus his slow pacing, create one of the greatest snoozers of all time. It would be a gross understatement to say that *L'Avventura* is devoid of tension. Most of the film's action sequences include solitary figures walking, eating, standing and sleeping. The film's few patches of dialogue over a minute long are full of the broadest clichés, reflecting the alienation of the main characters. In fact, there are so many blanks to fill in this epic vacuum that the experience of watching it resembles one giant daydream. The only saving grace is Aldo Scavarda's breathtaking cinematography, capturing in crisp black-and-white shots the beautiful panoramas of lifeless landscapes.

RATING: No MPAA rating, with nothing objectionable.
AWARDS: Special Jury Prize to Michelangelo Antonioni for his Artistic Contribution to Language, at the 1962 Cannes Film Festival (even though L'Avventura was notoriously booed by the audiences).

BABETTE'S FEAST
(Video, subtitled)

Social Satire

Denmark	Danish and French
1987 105 Min.	Color

CREDITS: Directed by Gabriel Axel. Written by Gabriel Axel, based on the "Anecdotes of Destiny" short stories by Isak Dinesen (Karen Blixen). Produced by Just Betzer and the Danish Film Institute. Cinematography by Henning Kristiansen. Edited by Finn Henriksen. Music by Per Norgard. Released by Orion Classics. Distributed nontheatrically by New Yorker Films. Starring Stephane Audran, Birgitte Federspiel, Bodil Kjer, Vibeke Hastrup, Hanne Stensgard, Jarl Kulle, Gudmar Wivesson, Jean-Philippe Lafont and Bibi Andersson.

The first Danish movie to win the Academy Award for Best Foreign Film, *Babette's Feast* is a true banquet for the senses. Shot against the bleak landscapes of Denmark's Jutland peninsula in the late 1800s, the film begins by framing the dutiful lives of two deeply religious sisters, Martine (Vibeke Hastrup) and Filippa (Hanne Stensgard), who sacrifice everything to serve their Lutheran faith and their pastor father. After he dies, the story skips to show them as elderly spinsters (now portrayed by Birgitte Federspiel and Bodil Kjer), directing Bible meetings, cooking boiled meals and knitting endlessly by the fire.

Into their incredibly stagnant lives comes Babette (Stephane Audran), a Frenchwoman they hire to cook and take care of the house so they can devote more time to their religious charity. At first quite accommodating, Babette eventually slips an exotic French meal onto the suspicious sisters' dinner table. They are elated, and before long Martine and Filippa discover that Babette is an ex-masterchef, one of the most famous in France. Babette turns their lives upside-down when she inherits 10,000 francs, and decides to spend every last penny of it creating an elaborate feast for Martine, Filippa and their important friends in town.

Babette's Feast begins slowly; Danish director Gabriel Axel does perhaps too thorough a job of portraying the emptiness and stiffness in the two sisters' lives. But once Babette enters the scene, the film is filled with humor, social comment and delightfully quirky characters. Axel and his editor Finn Henriksen rhythmically build the scenes of Babette's dinner preparation into an orgasmically scrumptious eight-course feast that ranks as one of the most sensual film experiences since the food orgy scene in *Tom Jones*. The close-ups on the expressions of the aging, lifeless Danish villagers are wonderfully captured by cinematographer Henning Kristiansen, as are the gray, austere landscapes of the Danish countryside. But it's Stephane Audran as the radiant Babette who makes this film so enjoyable. Every moment she is on the screen, she creates appetizing treats for the body, mind and soul.

RATING: No MPAA rating, with nothing objectionable.

BADLANDS
(Video)

Crime Docudrama

U.S.A.

1974   95 Min.   Color

CREDITS: Directed, written and produced by Terrence Malick. Cinematography by Bryan Probyn and Steve Larner. Music by Carl Orff, Erik Satie, Nat King Cole and George Tipton. Released by Warner Brothers. Distributed nontheatrically by Swank Motion Pictures. Starring Sissy Spacek, Martin Sheen, Warren Oates, Romon Bieri, Alan Vint, Gary Littlejohn, John Carter, Bryan Montgomery, Gail Threlkeld and Charles Fitzpatrick.

In 1958, a nineteen-year-old ex-garbageman named Charles Starkweather and thirteen-year-old Caril Ann Fugate went on a shooting spree in the northern United States that resulted in eleven deaths. Once the two were caught, Americans were shocked to learn that they had no explanation for the killings and showed no remorse. In *Badlands*, director/writer Terrence Malick *(Days of Heaven)* tells their story.

The film is narrated by Holly (Sissy Spacek), an unremarkable girl who lives with her father (Warren Oates) in Fort Dupre, South Dakota. Until she meets Kit (Martin Sheen), Holly spends most of her time reading *True Romance* and *Modern Screen* and twirling her baton. Almost overnight, Kit turns her drab existence into a real-life adventure similar to the fantasies she lives through her magazines. Holly falls in love with this James Dean look-alike, but when her father finds out, he forbids her to see Kit again and punishes Holly by shooting her dog. Kit responds by shooting Holly's dad. When they hide out in the woods and three bounty hunters come after them, Kit shoots them too. The rest of the film follows Kit and Holly as they drive through the desolate West, stealing food and gas, while Kit casually takes more innocent lives and Holly watches passively.

Spacek and Sheen give outstanding performances as the film's insipid, vacuous protagonists. They seem to murder because they have nothing better to do. When Kit shoots an acquaintance in the stomach and then politely holds the door open so the dying man can step outside, Holly asks him: "Is he upset?" Kit responds: "He didn't say anything to me." This kind of deadpan dialogue is a perfect complement to Holly's cliché-ridden narration, which is the key to the real reason for their indifference: their inability to understand anything that isn't mass-produced and media-inspired. The blood they witness can't be real, it looks too much like ketchup. Although Malick drives home Kit and Holly's desperate need to glamorize their empty lives to the point that he risks boring the audience as well, *Badlands* stands as a harrowing comment on modern amorality. And the film's naturally lit cinematography of the vast western expanse is breathtaking.

RATING: *PG, with mild violence*
FILMNOTE: Badlands *was Terrence Malick's first film. Before making it, he was a Rhodes scholar, a professor of philosophy at MIT, and later an assistant to Arthur Penn during the filming of* Bonnie and Clyde.

LE BAL

(Video)

Dance Musical

France/Italy

1984   112 Min.   Color

CREDITS: *Directed by Ettore Scola. Written by Ettore Scola, Jean-Claude Penchenat and Ruggero Maccari, based on the play by Penchenat. Produced by Giorgio Slivagni. Cinematography by Ricardo Aronovich. Music conducted by Vladmir Cosma. Production design by Luciano Ricceri. Costume design by Ezio Altieri and Françoise Tournafond. Released and distributed by Almi Pictures. Starring Christopher All-wright, Regis Bouquet, Jean-François Per-*

rier, Marc Berman, Chantal Capron, Danielle Rochard, Nani Noel and Azis Arbia.

Adapted for the screen by Italian director Ettore Scola *(A Special Day, We All Loved Each Other So Much)* and based on Jean-Claude Penchenat's successful French stage play by the same name, *Le Bal* tells its own version of fifty years of French history—from 1936 to the present—without one word of spoken dialogue and without ever leaving the setting of a French ballroom. Instead, it relies on pantomime, dance, makeup and clothing to express the joy, despair, fear and optimism of the Great Depression, Nazi Occupation and Liberation, the carefree fifties, the rebellious sixties and the materialistic seventies.

While the twenty or so characters in this movie aren't classically attractive, each has a quirky quality that distinguishes him or her from the next. Every time-frame has its introvert, nerd, show-off, sex kitten, pervert, etc. Scola and his costume designers take great care to dress each player in clothes that are as faithful to the personality as they are to the era. *Le Bal's* musical score is terrific, with familiar songs by Glenn Miller, Edith Piaf, Count Basie, The Beatles and The Platters, to name just a few. And production designer Luciano Ricceri's sets are very well crafted.

But even with so much going for it, *Le Bal* ends up becoming tedious. The film's characters are so stereotypical and stylized, they'd fit right into a Merry Melodies cartoon. Although it could be fascinating to notice the differences in time periods, Scola dilutes this effect by lingering too long on each one before going to the next. No matter where we are in French history, every vignette has so little going on in it that each period begins to feel the same as the others.

RATING: *No MPAA rating, with nothing objectionable.*
AWARDS: *1984 French Caesars for Best Film and Best Director (Ettore Scola); Special Jury Prize for Best Director (Scola) at the 1984 Berlin Film Festival; 1984 Academy Award nomination for Best Foreign Film.*

LA BALANCE
(Video, dubbed)

Police Thriller

France	French
1982 102 Min.	Color

CREDITS: *Directed by Bob Swaim. Written by Bob Swaim and M. Fabiani. Produced by Georges Dancigers and Alexandre Mnouchkine. Cinematography by Bernard Zitzermann. Released by Spectrafilms. Distributed nontheatrically by New Yorker Films. Starring Nathalie Baye, Philippe Leotard, Richard Berry, Christophe Malavoy, Jean-Paul Connart, Bernard Freyd and Albert Dray.*

Winner of French Caesars (Oscar equivalent) for Best Picture, Actor and Actress, Bob Swaim's *La Balance* is a hard-hitting cop story set in the tough immigrant neighborhoods of Paris. At the start of the film, we learn that drugs have gotten so out of hand that the police have formed "territorial brigades" that control a complex network of informers. One of the officers operating such a network is Foxy (Richard Berry), a dedicated vice detective whose main informer is murdered by a vicious kingpin named Massina. Foxy vows to do whatever it takes to get Massina, and an innocent prostitute, Nicole (Nathalie Baye), and her recently paroled pimp boyfriend, Dede (Philippe Leotard), are caught up in his scheme.

Despite their professions, Nicole and Dede are passionately in love, but when Foxy forces Nicole to be his new stool pigeon, their relationship takes a turn for the worse. Although Dede will hate her for it, Nicole reluctantly helps Foxy because he threatens to turn her boyfriend in for violating his parole. The whole situation is complicated by a disastrous manhunt as the police chase Dede, together with the murderous Massina and his gang of thugs.

Director Swaim is an American making movies in Europe, and his roots definitely show. The actors, sets and language mark *La Balance* as a foreign film, but with a cops-and-robbers story line, fast-paced editing and graphic violence, it is a clone of an American crime thriller. Still, as a French version of an American cops-and-criminals story, *La Balance* works well on many levels. The performances are strong from the three main characters, with Baye particularly engaging as the vulnerable and love-smitten prostitute. There are also plenty of well-shot action scenes that place *La Balance* in a class with Dirty Harry flicks. But what makes this film so interesting is the dynamics of betrayal and blackmail. Director Swaim turns his three characters into victims who tug at our heartstrings as they betray each other's trust.

RATING: *R for sex and a lot of graphic violence.*
AWARDS: *1983 French Caesars for Best Film, Best Actor (Philippe Leotard) and Best Actress (Nathalie Baye).*
WARNING: *The dubbing on the video version is not good, but because the film is filled with action and not dialogue, this only mildly detracts from the film's quality.*

THE BALLAD OF GREGORIO CORTEZ
(Video, partially subtitled)

Political Western

U.S.A.	English and Spanish
1983 99 Min.	Color

CREDITS: *Directed by Robert Young. Written by Victor Villasenor, based on the song "The Ballad of Gregorio Cortez" and the novel With His Pistol in His Hands by Americo Paredes. Produced by Michael Hausmann at Robert Redford's Sundance Institute. Cinematography by Ray Villalobos and Robert Young. Released by Embassy Pictures. Distributed nontheatrically by Films Inc. Starring Edward James Olmos, James Gammon, Tom Bower, Alan Vint, Tim Scott, Pepe Serna, Brion James, Barry Corbin and Rosana DeSoto.*

In *The Ballad of Gregorio Cortez*, as in his prison film *Short Eyes*, director Robert Young displays a talent for exposing racism without mincing words. This time his canvas is an old-fashioned American Western, complete with strapping cowboys, posses itching for a lynching, and wild horse chases.

Set in the Texas Territory of the late 1800s, the film tells the true story of a poor Mexican farmer named Gregorio Cortez (Edward James Olmos, Lt. Castillo on "Miami Vice"). In a fit of rage, Gregorio kills a white sheriff after the sheriff murders his brother in cold blood. Gregorio flees to a neighbor's house where a posse tracks him down, and two more whites are killed in the ensuing shoot-out. Gregorio escapes a second time, but his wife and kids are thrown in jail and a $10,000 bounty is put on his head. A huge posse finally catches Gregorio, and though some want a lynching, he's brought back to trial before an all-white jury clearly out for Mexican blood.

Based on a Mexican-American folk ballad, *The Ballad of Gregorio Cortez* is presented in documentary style through flashbacks sparked by testimony at the trial. The old West isn't glamorized, as the film's sets are gritty, and the clothes and mannerisms are very authentic. But in striving for realism, Young gives us a surplus of long chase scenes that nearly bring his narrative to a halt. Still, he creates a drama that plunges right into the heart of the deep-set racism of the white settlers without resorting to stereotyping. While he portrays the extreme poverty and degradation of the Mexicans, he also gives them a strong cultural identity and self-dignity. Only with the character of Gregorio's white lawyer, and in the film's tearful ending, are our sympathies manipulated.

RATING: *PG for violence.*
FILMNOTE: *The jail and courthouse in this film were the ones used during the trial and incarceration of the real Gregorio Cortez.*

THE BALLAD OF NARAYAMA
(Video, subtitled)

Cultural Drama

Japan		Japanese
1983	128 Min.	Color

CREDITS: *Directed by Shohei Imamura. Written by Shohei Imamura, based on the stories "Narayama Bushi-ko" and "Toho-ku No Zunmatachi" by Scichiro Fakazawa. Produced by Goro Kusakaba and Jiro Tomoda. Cinematography by Masao Tochizaga. Music by Shin'ichiro Ikebe. Released by Toei/Shochiku. Distributed nontheatrically by Kino International. Starring Ken Ogata, Sumiko Sakamoto, Takejo Aki, Tonpei Itidari, Shoichi Ozawa and Kaoru Shimamori.*

When *The Ballad of Narayama* opens with several long, quiet shots of a Japanese mountain village covered in snow, you get the feeling that you're in for a couple of hours of peasant nobility, an Oriental *Tree of Wooden Clogs.* But an early scene, in which a spring thaw reveals a discarded baby's bluish corpse, quickly shatters this first impression.

The film is set in the mid-1800s in a small village at the base of the Narayama Mountains, where a brutal code of behavior has been created to compensate for the villagers' extreme poverty. Unable to feed a surplus of children, the villagers often sell infant girls to a passing salt dealer, while unwanted boys are simply murdered. If a man is caught stealing, he and his family are buried alive. And when village elders reach the age of seventy, their sons must carry them to the summit of Narayama and leave them to die in front of the gods.

One elder nearing this fate is Orin (Sumiko Sakamoto). Orin has long been the object of envy in the village, because she is healthy and has a mouthful of strong teeth. As her time draws near, she bravely accepts her destiny, preparing her family for her departure by seeking out mates for her younger sons, "Stinker" (Kaoru Shimamori) and Tatsuehi (Ken Ogata of *Mis-*

hima). But most important, Orin must help her reluctant Tatsuehi accept his duty to carry her off to Narayama.

Much of *The Ballad of Narayama* is harsh and difficult. Even the comic subplots are brutally frank. In one, a widow tries to remove a curse on her husband by sleeping with every man in the village, making them pray between her splayed legs before mounting her. This crudity is typical of director Imamura's style, but in this film he also finds a balance between the gentleness of the beautiful landscapes and the clear-eyed determination of the villagers. The entire cast is extraordinary, as is Masao Tochizaga's cinematography and Shin'-ichiro Ikebe's music. Unlike other farm movies suggesting that forces of nature can be conquered, *The Ballad of Narayama* shows peasants working in concert with nature, recognizing its power and struggling to create a niche in its shadow.

RATING: No MPAA rating, with graphic violence
AWARDS: Golden Palm for Best Film at the 1983 Cannes Film Festival.
FILMNOTE: The commitment of the cast and crew to authenticity in this film was enormous. Sumiko Sakamato, for example, actually had her front teeth surgically removed to make one particularly brutal scene more realistic. Another actress, vying for the same part, had her teeth removed as well. Also, during the spring, when a freak snowstorm buried the village, Imamura, his cast and crew shoveled the whole village virtually snow-free so they could continue filming.

BARFLY
(Video)

Social Drama

U.S.A.

1987   100 Min.   Color

CREDITS: Directed by Barbet Schroeder. Written by Charles Bukowski. Produced by Barbet Schroeder, Tom Luddy and Fred Roos. Cinematography by Robby Muller. Edited by Eva Gardos. Production design by Bob Ziembicki. Released by Eric Rohmer Films. Distributed nontheatrically by Swank Motion Pictures. Starring Mickey Rourke, Faye Dunaway, Alice Krige, Jack Nance, J. C. Quinn, Frank Stallone, Joe Rice, Julie (Sunny) Pearson, Sandy Martin, Roberta Bassin and Gloria LeRoy.

Whether you enjoy *Barfly* will depend on your propensity for extreme alcoholic antics. Now infamous poet-alcoholic Charles Bukowski wrote the script for this tale of two severe alcoholics, Henry (Mickey Rourke) and Wanda (Faye Dunaway), struggling through their daily rituals of finding money to drink themselves into a stupor.

The movie opens with a classic barroom brawl as Henry and the bartender Eddy (Frank Stallone, Sylvester's brother) from Henry's favorite watering hole, punch it out in the back alley. What seems to be a brutal one-time fight turns out to be a recurring bloodfest—one that Henry always loses. As the story develops, we find out that there is more to Henry than drinking himself into a frenzy and his macho bluster. Henry is also a poet and is discovered and then seduced by Tully (Alice Krige), a rich and beautiful young publisher. But the real change in Henry's life comes when he meets Wanda. Wanda turns out to be the perfect match for Henry because she can drink, barf, pass out and espouse philosophical recantations on life and society just as excessively as Henry.

The major glitch in *Barfly* arises when the sexy Tully seduces Henry. Henry is constantly sick from overdrinking, and his face cut and swollen from his brawls. He doesn't bathe, brush his teeth or change his clothes. Only another street person (like Wanda) would be able to stand getting within six feet of Henry, let alone into bed with him. But the rest of Bukowski's script is almost too believable. He understands the finer points of revolting, desperate alcoholic behavior, and as daily diary of that behavior, *Barfly* is too true to life for comfort. German director Barbet Schroeder and his cameraman Robby Muller (Wenders's cinematographer) bring Bukowski's story to life with swirling shots and close-ups that will make even hard-core moviegoers squirm.

Although neither Rourke nor Dunaway is an appealing or likeable character, they are very convincing in their roles—tragic and repulsive, but often hilarious as well.

RATING: R for brief nudity and a lot of profanity and violence.

THE BASILEUS QUARTET
(Video, dubbed)

 ½

Social Drama/Musical

Italy/France	French
1984 118 Min.	Color

CREDITS: *Directed and written by Fabio Carpi. Produced by Arturo La Pegna. Cinematography by Dante Spinotti. Music by Schubert, Debussey, Ravel, Beethoven, Wagner and Bellini. Released and distributed nontheatrically by Almi Pictures. Starring Pierre Malet, Hector Alterio, Omero Antonutti, Michel Vitold, Alain Cuny, Gabriele Ferzetti and Lisa Kreuzer.*

The Basileus Quartet opens as four distinguished-looking, elderly gentlemen perform an intricate chamber piece, their music sweetened by the strength of the close personal bonds they have from playing together for many years. But once offstage, the violinist collapses and dies, setting off a chain of events that will alter the lives of the surviving partners forever.

At first, the three—Diego (Omero Antonutti of *Night of the Shooting Stars*), Alvaro (Hector Alterio of *The Official Story*) and Guglielmo (Michel Vitold)—agree to a trial separation, anxious after thirty years on the road together to get a taste of "real life." But a short time later, when a brilliant young violinist named Eduardo (Pierre Malet) insists on auditioning, the bored musicians jump at the chance to perform again. Eduardo's presence in the quartet proves disruptive. His partners jostle for his affections, their jealousy creating deep rifts in their friendships. Eduardo also sleeps with an endless procession of beautiful women, smokes marijuana and gleefully shows his partners the possibilities for a life that has passed them by. Eventually, Eduardo's actions force Diego, Alvaro and Guglielmo to question their own lives, while they begin to lose interest in the one thing that once made them all happy—their music.

The Basileus Quartet is far too schematic to be successful. Director/writer Fabio Carpi sets up his conflicts in the most obvious ways, and then films them flatly, with little interest in creating depth of emotion. Also, the handsome Malet gives a stiff performance as Eduardo, and a plot twist involving a hitchhiking terrorist he picks up is absurdly unbelievable. Yet *The Basileus Quartet* is blessed with beautiful musical interludes, and Carpi very effectively directs the chamber music scenes with fluid tracking shots that convey the richness and beauty of the music. The three older actors turn in fine work, distinguished and controlled throughout the film.

RATING: No MPAA rating, with brief nudity and homosexual themes.
WARNING: The dubbing is okay, but it slightly affects the quality of the movie.

LE BEAU MARIAGE
(Video, subtitled)

Psychological Drama

France	French
1982 97 Min.	Color

CREDITS: *Directed and written by Eric Rohmer. Produced by Margaret Menogoz. Cinematography by Bernard Lutic, Romain Winding and Nicolas Brunet. Music by Roman Gure and Simon Des Innocents. Released by United Artists. Distributed nontheatrically by Films Inc. Starring Beatrice Raymond, Andre Dussollier, Feodor Atkine, Hugette Faget, Arielle Dombasle, Thamila Mezbah, Herve Duhamel and Sophie Renoir.*

Le Beau Mariage is the second in Eric Rohmer's "Comedies and Proverbs" series

(*The Aviator's Wife* is the first), and he once again gets right to the core of the female psyche. His heroine is Sabine (Beatrice Raymond), a woman who, after years of living a Bohemian life-style, decides she needs to get married and have children. But with nobody particular in mind, she blindly chooses a kind and stodgy lawyer named Edmund (Andre Dussollier) whom she barely knows, and who isn't very interested in her. But that doesn't stop Sabine. She is so confident in her abilities to snag Edmund, and so rigid in her desire to marry, that she pursues him even after he bluntly refuses to even be seduced by her. By the film's end, Sabine has embarrassed herself in every way imaginable, while her pigheaded drive toward marriage has completely shattered her confidence.

Although there are several funny moments in *Le Beau Mariage*, it's an intense psychological drama with characters and situations so real they are unnerving. For most of the film Sabine is either arguing with her friends and family, hounding Edmund or wallowing in self-pity. The times she and Edmund spend together are excruciating because he is so repressed and painfully fragile. All of the acting in *Le Beau Mariage* is excellent, particularly Raymond's performance as the neurotic young seductress. Some of her most humiliating moments are also the film's most powerful, while Rohmer shows his skills at opening up her vulnerabilities in nearly every scene.

RATING: *R for brief nudity and sexual situations.*

BEAU PÈRE
(Video, dubbed)

Sex Farce

France	French
1981	120 Min.	Color

CREDITS: *Directed and written by Bertrand Blier. Produced by Alain Sarde. Cinematography by Sacha Viermy. Music*

by Philippe Sarde. Released and distributed nontheatrically by New Line Cinema. Starring Patrick Dewaere, Ariel Besse, Maurice Ronet, Nicole Garcia, Nathalie Baye, Maurice Risch, Macha Meril, Pierre Lerumeur and Yves Gasc.

Bertrand Blier (*Get Out Your Handkerchiefs, Menage*) is often regarded as the bad boy of international cinema for his tasteless sex farces, of which *Beau Père* is a toned-down example. It's the story of Remi (Blier regular Patrick Dewaere), a failed pianist who ekes out a living playing background music in cocktail lounges. Although his marriage is troubled, Remi is crushed when his wife is killed in a car accident, leaving him to raise his fourteen-year-old stepdaughter, Marion (Ariel Besse), by himself. In his state of confusion and despair, he blindly complies when the girl's real father, Charly (Maurice Ronet), arrives to take her away, despite her objections.

Soon Marion runs from her overbearing father back to Remi. He is delighted to be reunited with her again until the tempestuous nymphet announces that she is sexually attracted to him. At first, he indignantly refuses her charms, yet Marion is so persistent that the lonely Remi can't resist. Tortured by guilt after they have sex, he tries to resume his paternal role. Marion responds by throwing parties and flirting with teenage boys, driving Remi into a jealous funk and back into Marion's bed. But as their love deepens, the couple must avoid detection by the outside world, especially a watchful and angry Charly, who would love to have Marion back in his clutches.

Although the surface story is perverse, *Beau Père* is sweet in tone, and ultimately quite moral. Blier wants to scandalize, but he places everything back on the middle-class shelf before the end, which makes the film less shocking than some of his other movies. The tension created by Remi's fear of being caught in an affair with his stepdaughter is sustained throughout, with certain scenes culminating in nail-biting suspense. Like John Hughes, Blier sets up the teen characters to be wiser than the adults, with much of the humor coming from the manner with which the self-assured Marion outsmarts her unwitting stepfather. At times, these situations are clever. But at other moments, Remi is too neurotic to be believable or funny, and Marion's character is scheming to the point of seeming lifeless.

RATING: No MPAA rating, with nudity and sex.
WARNING: The dubbing on the video version is mediocre.

BEAUTY AND THE BEAST
(Video, subtitled)

Fantasy

France   French

1946   90 Min.   B&W

CREDITS: Directed by Jean Cocteau. Written by Jean Cocteau, based on the fairy tale by Mme Leprince de Beaumont. Produced by Andre Paulve. Cinematography by Henri Alekan. Music by Georges Auric. Art direction by Christian Berard. Makeup by Hagop Arakelian. Released by Lopert Films. Distributed nontheatrically by Films Inc. Starring Jean Marais, Josette Day, Marcel Andre, Mila Parley, Michael Auclair and Nane Germon.

Although Jean Cocteau's *Beauty and the Beast* is a film adaptation of the famous fairy tale, it is a movie for adults. In case you've forgotten the story, Beauty (Josette Day) lives in a modest country cottage with her kindly father and her two wicked sisters. One day, her father (Marcel Andre) stumbles upon a strange mansion, and an angry, ugly sorcerer named Beast (Jean Marais) threatens to kill the intruder unless one of his daughters comes to live with him. The terrified father returns home, and Beauty sneaks away that evening to save her father's life. Although Beauty can barely look at this beast, with his hairy body and smoke pouring out of his fingertips, he is so kind to her that eventually she sees through his horrendous exterior to the beauty inside him.

Although made before the days of special effects wizardry, *Beauty and the Beast*'s supernatural trickery makes it a visual masterpiece. The makeup by Hagop Arakelian in this filmed fairy tale is exquisitely detailed, and Christian Berard's sets (allegedly designed to imitate Vermeer paintings) are enchanting. Cocteau *(Blood of a Poet, Orpheus)* and his cinematographer Henri Alekan achieve powerful images inside Beast's highly stylized mansion, with candelabras held by human arms and gargoyles with live human heads. Slow pans and grainy lighting make the tone in these scenes magically surreal and haunting. What's surprising about *Beauty and the Beast* is that even its predictable story is surprisingly compelling. Marais's Beast, so lonely and insecure about his looks, is a completely sympathetic character, while Beauty's evil sisters are a riot.

RATING: No MPAA rating, with nothing objectionable.

BEING THERE
(Video)

Social Satire

U.S.A.

1980   130 Min.   Color

CREDITS: Directed by Hal Ashby. Written by Jerzy Kosinski, based on his novel. Produced by Andrew Braunsberg. Cinematography by Caleb Deschanel. Music by John Mandel. Released by Lorimar/United Artists. Distributed nontheatrically by Swank Motion Pictures. Starring Peter Sellers, Melvin Douglas, Shirley MacLaine, Jack Warden, Richard Basehart, Richard Dysart, Ruth Attaway and Dave Clenon.

Peter Sellers is usually associated with the slapstick Pink Panther series, but in Hal Ashby's *Being There,* he's given the opportunity to show enormous skills as a dramatic actor. Sellers plays Chance, the gardener—a mentally underdeveloped, fiftyish man who's literally spent his whole life taking care of a millionaire's garden and watching TV. When his employer dies, Chance is told he must leave the estate. Dressed in one of his deceased master's impeccably tailored suits, he walks out to face the real world for the first time.

Naturally, Chance responds to everything by relating it to TV or gardening, but the people he encounters are amazed by him. Here is a well-dressed and distinguished-looking gentleman who stares you straight in the eye and confidently makes statements such as "When you water the plants in the spring, they grow in the summer." Several people Chance encounters mistake his simplemindedness for prophecy, including a dying billionaire industrialist (Melvin Douglas), his horny wife (Shirley MacLaine), and the president of the United States (Jack Warden). Chance even becomes a celebrity on television talk shows, and there are some who think he should run for president.

The plot of *Being There* occasionally suffers from the repetition of the film's single joke. Shirley MacLaine overplays the sex-crazed billionairess; her scenes with Sellers are the most contrived moments in the film. But these excesses are minor compared to the power of Sellers's performance. Walking a thin line between broad satire and dramatic impenetrability, Sellers never falters in the difficult role. A cross between John Sayles's farcical "Brother" from another planet and Werner Herzog's more serious Kaspar Hauser, Chance is like a wide-eyed and curious child who hasn't learned to play by society's rules. Through Chance's innocent and unspoiled eyes, the rest of us can see our own startling reflections.

RATING: PG, *with nothing objectionable.*
AWARDS: *1979 Academy Award for Best Supporting Actor (Melvyn Douglas); 1979 Academy Award nomination for Best Actor (Peter Sellers).*

BELIZAIRE THE CAJUN
(Video)

Cultural Western

U.S.A.

1986   114 Min.   Color

CREDITS: *Directed and written by Glen Pitre. Produced by Glen Pitre and Allan L. Durand. Music by Michael Doucet. Cinematography by Richard Bowen. Creative consultant, Robert Duvall. Released by Skouras Pictures. Starring Armand Assante, Gail Youngs, Michael Schoeffling, Stephen McHattie, Will Patton, Nancy Barrett, Loulan Pitre, Andre deLaunary, Jim Levent, Paul Landry, Ernest Vincent and Paul Harchy.*

One of the best things about the movies is that they can expose us to times, cultures and places we would otherwise never experience. *Belizaire the Cajun* is a good example. Set in Louisiana in 1859, it's the story of French refugees forced to deal with growing white resistance to their presence.

Belizaire (Armand Assante) is a healer who's not very well accepted by the whites, particularly wealthy Matthew (Michael Schoeffling), whose common-law Cajun wife, Alida (Gail Youngs), depends on Belizaire for medicine. Matthew leads a raid on Belizaire's Cajun settlement, ordering twenty families to clear out of the state. Belizaire's young cousin resists, and when Matthew turns up dead the next day, the boy becomes the object of a murderous posse. Belizaire, who has long been in love with Matthew's wife, must now juggle his pursuit of her with an effort to save his cousin from lynching. Instead, he ends up casting suspicion on himself.

Director/writer Glen Pitre seems to know Cajun culture well, investing each scene with deep feeling for these people and their strange and magical customs. An upbeat score of Cajun music adds even more color, and Assante is beguiling as the healer, con man, lover and thief. But many of the other performances in *Belizaire the Cajun* don't equal his. The other Cajuns are barely developed, so that there is little sense of what kind of people they are or how they are affected by the tragic events in their lives. Most of the settlers are broad stereotypes, and their conflict with the Cajuns is, at times, too obvious and clichéd. But if these faults in *Belizaire the Cajun* can be overlooked, much of it is lighthearted good fun, as well as a fascinating glimpse into a different culture.

RATING: R for nudity and sex.

BELLISSIMA
(Video, subtitled)

Social Satire

Italy		Italian
1951	130 Min.	B&W

CREDITS: *Directed and produced by Luchino Visconti. Written by Luchino Visconti and Francesco Rosi* (Christ Stopped at Eboli), *based on the story by Cesare Zavattini. Cinematography by Piero Portalupe. Music by Franco Mannino. Released by CEL-INCOM. Starring Anna Magnani, Walter Chiari, Alessandro Blasetti, Tina Apicella, Gastone Renzelli, Arturo Bragaglia, Tecla Scarano and Linda Sina.*

Luchino Visconti's *Bellissima* is about the determination of a working-class mother in post–World War II Rome to make her unremarkable six-year-old daughter a star, no matter what the cost. The film begins when Magdalena (Anna Magnani) enters her darling Maria (Tina Apicella) in the "prettiest girl in Rome" contest sponsored by Stella Films, an Italian film company looking for a girl to be in a famous director's movie. Magdalena is so excited about the contest she forces Maria to take acting and dancing lessons, then drags her to the seamstress, the hairstylist and the photographer. But Magdalena's husband, Spartico (Walter Chiari), doesn't make enough money to waste on such nonsense, and when his daughter comes home exhausted several nights in a row he finally

blows a fuse. Even that doesn't stop Magdalena from trying to get Maria the part.

Visconti *(Death in Venice, The Damned)* must have been assaulted by nervous stage mothers and their bewildered children at some point in his career, because he knows the territory well. Every scene in this movie is rich with believable performances—from the annoyed husband to the nosy neighbors to the rival stage moms. Visconti also skillfully captures the frustrations and dreams of Italians rebuilding their lives after a devastating war. But *Bellissima* is really Magnani's show. She is magnetic as the pushy mother who drags her bland Maria through one embarrassing situation after another, driving everybody crazy along the way.

RATING: No MPAA rating, with nothing objectionable.

BERLIN ALEXANDERPLATZ
(Video, subtitled)

Psychological Drama

West Germany		German
1980	921 Min.	Color

CREDITS: *Directed by Rainer Werner Fassbinder. Written by Rainer Werner Fassbinder, based on the novel by Alfred Doblins. Produced by Bavaria Ateller Films. Cinematography by Xaver Schwarzenberger. Music by Peter Raben. Released by Teleculture Films. Starring Gunter Lamprecht, Barbara Sukowa, Hanna Schygulla, Elisabeth Trissenaar, Hark Bohm, Volker Spengler, Gottfried John, Brigitte Mira, Karin Baal and Ivan Desny.*

In a career distinguished by several feature film triumphs, director Rainer Werner Fassbinder ironically created one of his finest and most personal works for television—the fifteen-and-a-half-hour *Berlin Alexanderplatz*.

Set in 1929, it tells the story of Franz Bieberkopf (Gunter Lamprecht), a lumbering, bearish man determined to go straight after four years in prison. Upon his release,

Franz reconnects with his friend Eva (Hanna Schygulla), a prostitute who tries to calm the volatile ex-con by finding him a girlfriend. But Franz is tricked by a psychotic gangster named Reinhold (Gottfried John) into taking part in a burglary, and immediately after, Reinhold coolly pushes his angry accomplice out of the car and into the path of oncoming traffic. Franz loses his arm, and then drifts deeper into alcoholism and despair, until Eva finds him and nurses him back to health. But even after he falls in love with Miege (Barbara Sukowa), a beautiful prostitute who briefly leads him on a stable path, Reinhold reenters his life to destroy Franz's happiness with one stroke.

All the performances in *Berlin Alexanderplatz* are excellent, with Lamprecht's Franz always remaining likable and sympathetic despite being the brunt of society's cruel jokes. Fassbinder and cinematographer Xaver Schwarzenberger combine their skills to present his personal struggles as dark and claustrophobic, in scenes lit only by flashes of neon. Yet the tone lightens up at times for brief scenes of happiness that have a fairy-tale quality to them.

Although a movie of epic length and impressive cinematographic ambition, there isn't a complex message at the center of *Berlin Alexanderplatz*. Quite simply, it's the story of a man struggling to be good while fate perverts his best intentions. Obviously, the scenario was close to Fassbinder, whose own life was cut short by cruel demons. He adapts Alfred Doblin's book with remarkable faithfulness, while taking the story a step further by including a series of elaborate surreal dream sequences. The final two and a half hours of *Berlin Alexanderplatz* are nothing but a dream interpretation of Franz's memories of his troubled past. Conceived by Fassbinder from his own dreams, these scenes are perhaps the strongest vision of the human subconscious ever put on the screen.

RATING: No MPAA rating, with violence.

BETRAYAL
(Video)

Black Comedy/Sex Farce

England

1983   95 Min.   Color

CREDITS: Directed by David Jones. Written by Harold Pinter, based on his play. Produced by Sam Spiegel. Cinematography by Mike Fash. Music by Dominic Muldowney. Released by 20th Century Fox. Distributed nontheatrically by Films Inc. Starring Jeremy Irons, Ben Kingsley and Patricia Hodge.

Harold Pinter is known for his deadpan characterizations and sparse dialogue, and his screenplay for *Betrayal* is a typical example of his work. It's about a love triangle that goes as follows: Robert (Ben Kingsley) and Emma (Patricia Hodge) are married; Robert and Jerry (Jeremy Irons) are best friends; and Jerry and Emma have been lovers behind Robert's back for seven years. There's nothing unusual here—best friends betray husbands all the time in movies—but what's different about this film is how the story is told.

Betrayal begins at the end. In the opening scene, Emma and Robert have finally split up, and the next day Emma tells Jerry that she told Robert about their affair. The rest of the movie traces the events leading up this critical juncture in reverse. First, there is the scene in which Jerry and Emma break up their affair, then we watch Emma tell Robert she has been seeing Jerry. Next, Emma and Jerry rent a secret flat together. At the end of the movie we see where it all began, as Jerry corners Emma at a party and nervously exclaims he is madly in love with her.

In each vignette, only two characters at a time talk about the affair, the betrayal, Robert and Jerry's friendship, and Robert and Emma's marriage. Their conversations are full of innuendos and double meanings, and their true feelings are always just below the surface. Kingsley is the perfect deadpan Pinter hero, and Irons and Hodge are intelligent and witty characters as well. Although it can be frustrating to watch the three conversing, because none of them ever really says what he or she means, their acting is so extraordinary and the sequence of events so clever that if you're a patient viewer *Betrayal* can be enormously satisfying.

RATING: *R for language and sexual situations.*
AWARDS: *1983 Academy Award nomination for Best Screenplay Based on Material from Another Medium (Harold Pinter).*

BETTY BLUE
(Video, subtitled)

Psychological Drama

France	French
1986	117 Min.	Color

CREDITS: *Directed by Jean-Jacques Beineix. Written by Jean-Jacques Beineix, based on the novel by Phillipe Djian. Produced by Jean-Jacques Beineix and Claude Ossard. Cinematography by Jean-François Robin. Released by Alive Films. Distributed nontheatrically by New Yorker Films. Starring Beatrice Dalle, Jean-Hugues Anglade, Gerald Darmon and Consuelo de Havilland.*

Immediately following the credits in *Betty Blue*, there is an incredibly intense and erotic sex scene. When we meet the couple, Betty (Beatrice Dalle) and Zorg (Jean-Hugues Anglade), we learn that they have known each other for only a week. Betty and Zorg show the same passion out of bed as well, continually playing practical jokes on one another, laughing and making out. But sometimes their playful world is interrupted by Betty's mysterious temper tantrums that seem to go on longer than the situation warrants. At first, these outbursts are funny, but then they occur more frequently, and as her physical feelings toward Zorg change as well, Betty begins to show

signs that she is having a mental breakdown.

Betty Blue is really two separate movies—a fast-paced, entertaining love story and a slower-paced, violent psychological drama. The first part works extremely well, as the playfulness and chemistry between these two lovers is lighthearted and amusing, and Betty and Zorg attain a level of uninhibited sexuality and spontaneity that is remarkable. But Betty's gradual slide into insanity irrevocably changes the tone of the story. Although it's not really clear why she falls apart, and her self-destructive behavior is a little too graphically detailed, director Jean-Jacques Beineix cleverly captures how Betty uses sex as a way to express her feelings about Zorg and herself.

As in *Diva*, Beineix and his cinematographer Jean-François Robin create a richly textured atmosphere in *Betty Blue*. The three main indoor sets—a cozy cottage, a cozy Paris apartment and a cozy house in a mountain village—are all warmly furnished and lit.

RATING: *R for plenty of nudity, sex and violence.*
AWARDS: *1986 Academy Award nomination for Best Foreign Film.*

BETWEEN THE LINES
(Video)

Political Comedy

U.S.A.

1977	101 Min.	Color

CREDITS: *Directed by Joan Micklin Silver. Written by Fred Barron. Produced by Raphael D. Silver (Joan's husband). Cinematography by Kenneth Van Sickle. Released by Midwest Films. Distributed nontheatrically by New Yorker Films. Starring John Heard, Jeff Goldblum, Marilou Henner, Lindsay Crouse, Jill Eikenberry, Bruno Kirby, Michael J. Pollard, Gwen Welles and Stephen Collins.*

Although *Between the Lines* is not without flaws, Joan Micklin Silver's mid-seventies political comedy has enough humor and social commentary to make it well worth watching. The film focuses on the staff of a failing underground Boston weekly, the *Back Bay Guardian*. The paper's once-idealistic, socially conscious reporters are now groping for relevant issues to write about and, in the process, compromising their integrity for the sake of profit. This ambivalence carries over into their personal lives as well. Some of the couples on the staff are in the throes of breaking up, while old lovers give it another go and new pairs get together. But few of these serious issues of relationships and politics are explored for long in *Between the Lines*, as the film's assortment of degenerate characters resort to practical jokes and wisecracking, excessive drugs and drinking to carry them through their "heavy" times.

Between the Lines shows some insight into issues of sex, politics and changing values, while capturing that gray period just after the turbulent sixties, before the apathy of the seventies really set in. Yet Silver *(Hester Street)* skips back and forth so quickly between the dozen or so *Back Bay* staffers that character development gets lost in the confusion. Also, the film's romantic interludes evolve into petty bickering, and some of the "meaningful" conversations between the friends come across as contrived. But Silver and her screenwriter, Fred Barron, are more successful with the comedy in the film. Many scenes are filled with hilarious satire, particularly the ones with Jeff Goldblum as the fast-talking, con-man rock critic.

RATING: R for profanity, substance abuse, nudity and sex.

BEYOND THE WALLS
(Video, subtitled)

Prison Drama

Israel		Hebrew and Arabic
1984	103 Min.	Color

CREDITS: *Directed by Uri Barbash. Written by Uri Barbash, Benny Barbash and Eran Pries. Produced by Rudy Cohen. Cinematography by Amnon Salomon. Music by Ilan Virtzberg. Released by Warner Brothers. Starring Amon Zadok, Muhamad Bakri, Assi Dayan, Rami Danon, Boaz Sharaabi, Adib Jahashan, Roberto Polak and Haim Shinar.*

Beyond the Walls sparked a great deal of controversy when it was released in Israel, for its often brutal portrayal of life inside a Jewish prison and for its indictment of the violent country outside the walls.

Set in a modern-day Israeli maximum security prison, the film's central conflict involves a Jew imprisoned for helping the PLO. Spurned by the other Jews for being a traitor, he is rejected by the Arabs because he's Jewish. His mere presence causes racial tensions to build to explosive levels, as the charismatic leader of the Jews, Uri (Amon Zadok), and the leader of the Arabs, Issam (Muhamad Bakri), galvanize their fellow inmates for a big showdown. When the situation ends in tragedy, the two leaders come to realize that the guards, the prison administration and the society of which they are a product are their real enemies—not each other.

Director Uri Barbash doesn't pull any punches when it comes to portraying the homosexual rapes and vicious knifings that are everyday occurrences inside prison. He is also quick to emphasize that these inmates are human beings who deserve their basic rights, regardless of their crimes. Although the scenes of the two factions joining together in a hunger strike are powerful, several earlier confrontations are too stagey to seem credible. Fortunately, Barash's main protagonists, Zadok and Bakri, give controlled and compelling performances throughout the film, as they both come to symbolize Jews and Arabs, alike, fighting for peace in a violent society.

RATING: R for violence and sex.
AWARDS: 1984 Academy Award nomination for Best Foreign Film.

THE BICYCLE THIEF
(Video, subtitled)

Social Drama

Italy		Italian
1948	90 Min.	B&W

CREDITS: *Directed and produced by Vittorio de Sica. Written by Vittorio de Sica, based on the novel by Gennarino Bartolini. Cinematography by Carlo Montuori. Music by Allesandro Cigognini. Released by Mayer-Burstyn Productions. Distributed nontheatrically by Corinth Films. Starring Lamberto Maggiorani, Enzo Staiola, Linanella Carell, Elena Altieri, Victorio Antonucci, Gino Saltamerenda and Fausto Guerzoni.*

The plot and characters of a movie don't have to be complicated to be emotionally powerful, and Vittorio de Sica's *The Bicycle Thief* is about as simple and touching as they come.

Told through the eyes of young Bruno (Enzo Staiola), *The Bicycle Thief* is the story of his father Antonio's struggle to provide for his family in post–World War II Rome. When the film begins, Antonio (Lamberto Maggiorani) hasn't worked for over two years, but he is suddenly hired to paste up advertising posters. This downtrodden, broken man completely changes when he gets the job. Bruno watches his proud father showing off his new uniform while dressing for work in the morning, and after his first day at work, he treats Bruno to a wonderful meal at Trattoria. But then disaster happens. The only requirement for the job is having a bicycle, and the next day, somebody steals it. Antonio desperately tries to find his bike, a search that not only

leads him into the bowels of Rome but also forces him to question his most important values as well.

The Bicycle Thief has been touted by many critics to be the masterpiece of post–World War II Italian neorealism. Antonio is one man pitted against an entire city of nameless and insensitive faces, his plight even more tragic when seen through the tear-filled eyes of his little son, Bruno. De Sica's direction is brilliant, particularly in how he raises the film's issues of morality and corruption. Maggiorani and Staiola give tremendous performances as Antonio and Bruno. They were essentially playing themselves, since Maggiorani was an unemployed factory worker desperate for work and Staiola an impoverished street kid de Sica discovered hanging around the set on the first days of the filming. De Sica and his cinematographer Carlo Montuori's deceptively simple black-and-white camera work keeps us rooting for them every step of the way.

RATING: *No MPAA rating, with nothing objectionable*
AWARDS: *1949 New York Film Critics Award for Best Foreign Language Film; 1949 British Academy Award for Best Film from Any Source; the National Board of Review's 10 Best Films, Best Director (Vittorio de Sica) in 1949; 1949 Honorary Academy Award for Best Foreign Film (this was not a category until 1956).*
FILMNOTE: *Although in need of money to make* The Bicycle Thief, *de Sica turned down American backing when the producers would only give him money if Cary Grant played the lead role.*

BIRDY
(Video)

Psychological Drama

U.S.A.		
1985	120 Min.	Color

CREDITS: *Directed by Alan Parker. Written by Sandy Kroopf and Jack Behr, based* on the novel by William Wharton. Produced by Alan Marshall. Cinematography by Michael Seresin. Music by Peter Gabriel. Released by Tri Star Pictures. Distributed nontheatrically by Films Inc. Starring Matthew Modine, Nicolas Cage, John Harkins, Sandy Baron, Karen Young, Bruno Kirby, Nancy Fish, George Buck and Delores Sage.

In *Birdy*, as in his films *Midnight Express* and *Fame*, British director Alan Parker demonstrates a remarkable insight into America's youth. An adaptation of William Wharton's novel, it's the story of two friends from Philadelphia who are reunited after experiencing the horrors of the Vietnam war. The film begins in a mental ward where the traumatized Birdy (Matthew Modine) sits naked, crouched on the edge of his bed like a bird, occasionally chirping while staring out of a window in the ceiling. His lifelong buddy, Al (Nicolas Cage), himself traumatized by shrapnel wounds that have disfigured his face, has been asked to help bring Birdy out of his trance. As Al reminisces with his catatonic friend, flashbacks lead us through the history of their unusual friendship.

Even as boys, Al was always trying to bring Birdy back to reality. Extremely sensitive and withdrawn, Birdy has been obsessed with birds from the time the two first met. His bedroom was like an aviary, and he was so consumed by his feathered friends that he even ditched his prom date to rush home for a fantasized erotic tryst with his favorite canary. As protective of his friend as he is fascinated by him, Al has always been able to reach Birdy—until now.

Director Alan Parker skillfully develops Birdy's character, and in the process touches upon several important issues of war, self-image and conformity. The film's hard-driving musical score by Peter Gabriel is perfect, and Modine and Cage both give excellent performances, particularly in the hospital scenes. Modine mimics a bird flawlessly, while Cage's Al is a sympathetic foil to Birdy's silence, even as he comes to terms with his own war scars. As a plus, one also comes away from *Birdy* with a whole new appreciation for birds. The bird photography is stunning and the delicate little universe they inhabit is brought to light in fresh and innovative ways.

RATING: R for nudity and language.
AWARDS: Special Grand Jury Prize at the 1985 Cannes Film Festival.

BLADE RUNNER
(Video)

Science Fiction

U.S.A.

1982 118 Min. Color

CREDITS: Directed by Ridley Scott. Written by Hampton Fancher and David Peoples, based on the short story "Do Androids Dream of Electric Sheep?" by Philip K. Dick. Produced by Michael Deeley. Cinematography by Jordan Cronenweth. Music by Vangelis. Special Effects by Douglas Trumball, Richard Yuricich and David Dreyer. Released by Warner Brothers. Distributed nontheatrically by Swank Motion Pictures. Starring Harrison Ford, Rutger Hauer, Daryl Hannah, Sean Young, M. Emmet Walsh, Edward James Olmos, William Sanderson, Brion James, Joe Turkel and Joanna Cassidy.

Blade Runner is a futuristic film noir that takes place in Los Angeles in 2019. Undercover cop Deckard (Harrison Ford) is assigned to find and destroy four renegade Replicants, androids who are virtually indistinguishable from normal humans, but who are responsible for many murders throughout the city. Hard-bitten and cynical, Deckard displays a knack for tracking and killing them. But when he falls in love with a beautiful woman (Sean Young) who may be a Replicant, Deckard becomes an increasingly vulnerable target for those Replicants who want to dispose of this threat to their existence.

The plot of *Blade Runner* is a typical love story mixed in with the "stop the androids before they kill innocent people" theme prevalent in many science fiction movies. Ford gives a good dramatic performance, and Rutger Hauer *(Soldier of Orange)* is particularly sinister as one of the most powerful Replicants.

But what's best about *Blade Runner* is the atmosphere, not the action. Writer/director Ridley Scott *(Alien)* has created a world unlike any you have ever experienced. This Los Angeles of the future is heavily polluted, and the noise level is at times deafening. Tall buildings dominate most of the airspace, billboards clutter the rest. Technology has invaded every crevice of this society, and privacy is a thing of the past. *Blade Runner* is an Orwellian prophecy if there ever was one, and Scott's cinematography and set design bring it to life in remarkable ways. Even if you don't typically enjoy science fiction action movies, *Blade Runner* is worth it for Scott's and writer Philip K. Dick's prophetic vision of what our society can become.

RATING: R for brief nudity and violence
AWARDS: 1983 British Academy Award for Best Production Design/Art Direction (Lawrence G. Paull) and Best Costume Design (Michael Kaplan, Charles Knode); 1982 Academy Award nominations for Best Visual Effects (Douglas Trumball, Richard Yuricich and David Dreyer) and Best Art Direction (Lawrence G. Paull, David Snyder and Linda De Scenna).

BLISS
(Video)

Black Comedy

Australia

1985   112 Min.   Color

CREDITS: Directed by Ray Lawrence. Written by Ray Lawrence and Peter Carey, based on Carey's novel. Produced by Anthony Buckley. Cinematography by Paul Murphey. Music by Peter Best. Released by New World Pictures. Distributed nontheatrically by Swank Motion Pictures. Starring Barry Otto, Lynette Curran, Helen Jones, Miles Buchanan, Gia Carides and Tim Robertson.

In the opening scene of *Bliss,* an advertising executive named Harry Joy (Barry Otto) shares a wonderful dinner with family and friends and then keels over from a heart attack. As the paramedics struggle to get his heart pumping again, Harry's spirit leaves his body and he becomes a spectator to his whole life flashing before his eyes. But these memories are more than a little distorted. Harry sees his wife having sex with his business partner as hundreds of slimy little fish slither out of her vagina. The stomachs of several friends and family members spontaneously split, allowing cockroaches to escape. Harry's son, envisioned now as a Nazi, rapes his daughter, to her apparent enjoyment. In a final vision, Harry has an eight-year courtship with an abusive hooker in the wilderness.

Each scene in *Bliss* begins with a certain amount of normalcy, as writer/director Ray Lawrence creates situations grounded in everyday, middle-class experience. Then, without warning, insects, vermin, blood, death, pain, torture, insanity, and fascism invade the set to pervert Harry's "normal" desires. The camera lingers on all the gory details, then bounces on to Harry's next degenerate fantasy.

The cinematography and sets are certainly original in *Bliss.* Some scenes are absurdly funny for their shock value, while others contain a generous amount of social commentary. But none of them make the slightest bit of sense. When you combine *Bliss*'s jumbled story line with the fact that some of the film's most grotesque scenes are repeated several times, you could rank *Bliss* as one of the longest 112 minutes you'll ever experience at the movies.

RATING: R for nudity, sex and graphic violence.
AWARDS: 1985 Australian Academy Awards for Best Picture, Best Director (Ray Lawrence), and Best Adapted Screenplay (Lawrence and Peter Carey).

BLOOD SIMPLE
(Video)

Film Noir Satire

U.S.A.

1985   96 Min.   Color

CREDITS: Directed by Joel Coen. Written by Joel Coen and Ethan Coen. Produced by Ethan Coen. Cinematography by Barry Sonnenfeld. Music by Carter Burwell. Released by Circle Films. Distributed nontheatrically by Corinth Films. Starring M. Emmet Walsh, John Getz, Frances McDormand, Dan Hedaya, Samm-Art Williams, Deborah Neumann, Rev. William Preston Robertson and Racquel Gavia.

Blood Simple is a murder mystery—black comedy masterpiece. Set in a small town in Texas, the bloody web of misunderstandings begins when a bar owner named Ray (Dan Hedaya) hires a lowlife detective (M. Emmet Walsh) to kill his wife, Abbey (Frances McDormand), for having an affair with his bartender, Julian (John Getz). But the detective has his own ideas, and so do Abbey and Julian. Miscommunications, double crossings and coincidental meetings pile atop each other in every scene in Blood Simple, until the main characters eventually dig themselves deep into holes they can't get out of, while leaving behind dozens of fatal clues with every shovel of dirt.

In Blood Simple, the Coen brothers (Raising Arizona) use the conventions of film noir ingeniously. Slightly overdramatized jazz frames the most crucial scenes, grainy lighting stylizes the film's atmosphere, and the now trademark Coen telescopic camera angles keep the audience right in the middle of the action. Hedaya and Walsh turn in appropriately sleazy performances, while McDormand and Getz are dupes deluxe. Although there is plenty of graphic violence in Blood Simple, it's hard to take it seriously because mostly it's done in jest. In fact, each time the plot takes a violent twist, the film becomes more absurdly funny. Blood Simple will make you jump with fright, but your gasps will also be mixed with laughter.

RATING: R for violence and language.
FILMNOTE: The song "I Can't Help Myself" by the Four Tops is playing in the background during a crucial scene in Ray's bar. Because Motown Records wanted too much money for the royalties, the video version substitutes the much less soulful "I'm a Believer" by the Monkees.

BLOOD WEDDING
(Video, subtitled)

★　★　½

Documentary

Spain   Spanish

1981   72 Min.   Color

CREDITS: Directed by Carlos Saura. Written by Alfredo Manas, based on the play by Federico Garcia Lorca. Music by Emilio de Diego. Choreography by Antonio Gades. Cinematography by Teo Escamilla. Edited by Pablo de Amo. Released and distributed nontheatrically by Almi Pictures. Starring Christina Hoyos, Antonio Gades, Juan Antonio Jimenez, Marisol, Pilar Cardenas and Carmen Villena.

In his three collaborations with famed flamenco dancer—choreographer Antonio Gades (Carmen and El Amor Brujo are the other two), director Carlos Saura has created an innovative new combination of dance and film, in which the dramatic story is expressed through flamenco. Blood Wedding is the first of the trilogy, and though it's a strong introduction to the flamenco tradition, it's not as dramatically complex as the other two.

The film begins as Gades and his dance company file into a rehearsal hall and prepare to perform a flamenco ballet adaptation of Federico Garcia Lorca's play by the same name. Most of these early sequences take place in the dressing room and consist of Gades reminiscing about his beginnings as a dancer, while he's putting on his makeup, then leading his dancers into the rehearsal hall for a brief run-through of the ballet. The final half of the film is a bare-stage performance of the piece, in which Gades plays a lover who steals a bride on her wedding day and then dances a duel to the death with the spurned groom as their families look on in dismay.

Unlike the trilogy's other two films, which try to intertwine dance and drama, *Blood Wedding* is a simple record of a performance. The section that introduces Gades drags on too long, since only those who revere the great choreographer would be interested in all of his anecdotes, but the performance of *Blood Wedding* itself is worth waiting for. The dancing is an intricate blend of athletic power and delicate grace. Cinematographer Teo Escamilla's camera work is a simple combination of long shots that frame the dancers in a stark tableau and close-ups that capture the intensity of concentration in each performer's face. In the end, this performance is a testament to the joy of flamenco.

RATING: No MPAA rating, with nothing objectionable.

BLUE COLLAR
(Video)

Social Drama

U.S.A.

1978　　　　　114 Min.　　　　　Color

CREDITS: *Directed by Paul Schrader. Written by Paul Schrader, Leonard Schrader and Sidney Glass. Produced by Don Guest. Cinematography by Bobby Byrne. Music by Jack Nitzche and Ry Cooder. Released by Universal. Distributed nontheatrically by Swank Motion Pictures. Starring Richard Pryor, Harvey Keitel, Yaphet Kotto, Harry Bellaver, Ed Begley, Jr., George Memmoli, Lucy Saroyan, Lane Smith and Cliff De Young.*

Paul Schrader's directorial debut, *Blue Collar*, is a powerful indictment of working-class repression. Set in Detroit in the mid-seventies, its heroes are best friends—two blacks and one white who work on an auto plant's assembly line. Zeke (Richard Pryor), Smokey (Yaphet Kotto) and Jerry (Harvey Keitel), called "The Oreo Gang" by their fellow workers, have their lousy work, mixed-up family lives, and inability to get ahead financially in common. Seeing a way out, they rob their union's safe. Instead of finding a lot of cash, they discover a ledger that shows their union's illegal dealings. The book spurs another scheme—blackmail—but this one turns out to be a deadly mistake.

Writer/director Schrader *(Mishima)* goes right for the jugular vein of big business, big unions and the middle class in *Blue Collar*. All three characters express various degrees of rage at a system they are helpless to change. Bobby Byrne's camera work in the auto plant scenes looks so real you can almost smell the fumes and feel the grime. And the monotony and dehumanization on the line will give even those unfamiliar with factory life a sense of its claustrophobia.

To his credit, Schrader doesn't give *Blue Collar* a pat Hollywood ending, nor does he oversentimentalize his characters. Zeke, Smokey and Jerry are fallible human beings capable of betraying each other and themselves. That's why their struggles are so real and what happens to them so compelling. The first half of *Blue Collar* is a working-class comedy that suffers from a few two many scenes of Pryor nervously double-talking to his wife and bosses. But once the three pull the heist, this film turns deadly serious and powerful. The acting throughout the film is outstanding. Pryor gives one of his most controlled performances to date, and Keitel and Kotto are equally convincing.

RATING: R for one hauntingly violent scene, profanity and drugs.

BLUE VELVET
(Video)

Film Noir

U.S.A.

1986   120 Min.   Color

CREDITS: *Directed and written by David Lynch. Produced by Richard Roth. Cinematography by Frederick Elmes. Production design by Patricia Norris. Music by Angelo Badalamenti. Released by De Laurentis Entertainment Group. Distributed nontheatrically by Swank Motion Pictures. Starring Kyle Maclachlan, Dennis Hopper, Laura Dern, Isabella Rossellini, Dean Stockwell, Hope Lange, George Dickerson, Brad Dourif and Priscilla Pointer.*

Some viewers love David Lynch's *Blue Velvet*, others loathe it, but everyone is strongly affected by this film. Set in a small North Carolina town, it's the story of two suburban teenagers, Jeffrey Beaumont (Kyle Maclachlan) and Sandy Williams (Laura Dern). Looking for excitement, they get themselves inadvertently involved in an extortion and murder scheme plotted by the villainous Frank Booth (Dennis Hopper) and his gang of thugs. Dorothy Vallens (Isabella Rossellini), a sexy singer at a local nightclub, is right in the thick of it and so is Ben (Dean Stockwell), a drag queen–drug dealer. Eventually everybody collides, and the danger for Jeffrey and Sandy builds to a harrowing climax. As a subplot, Jeffrey becomes obsessed with Dorothy's masochistic sexual charms. When he's not sleuthing with Sandy, he sneaks up to Dorothy's for some action that is often too hot for him to handle.

Maclachlan, Dern and the supporting cast give strong performances, but it's Hopper's character of Frank Booth that makes *Blue Velvet* into a surrealistic nightmare. Whenever he is on the screen, you have to remind yourself that this is just a movie and that he isn't real. As in *Eraserhead,* Lynch seems to relish making the audience squirm—particularly in the maso-chistic sex scenes involving Rossellini, and with the film's grotesque violence. But *Blue Velvet* is disturbing because it is grounded in real emotions and real fears. Lynch not only very cleverly satirizes teen romances and "slice-and-dice" flicks but also gives us a large dose of nail-biting suspense. The cinematography, lighting and sets are highly stylized and stunning, and an upbeat soundtrack lends a special absurdity to the film's most frightening scenes.

RATING: *R for violence, sex and profanity*
AWARDS: *1986 Academy Award nomination for Best Director (David Lynch).*
FILMNOTE: *Director David Lynch wrote the lyrics to many of the songs in* Blue Velvet.

BOAT PEOPLE

Political Drama

Hong Kong   Mandarin

1983   106 Min.   Color

CREDITS: *Directed by Ann Hui. Written by K. C. Chiu. Produced by Miranda Yang and Chui Po-Chu. Cinematography by Chung Chi-Man. Music by Law Wing-Fai. Released by Bluebird Movies. Distributed nontheatrically by New Yorker Films. Starring Lam Chi-Cheung, Season Ma, Andy Lau, Cora Miao, Paul Ching, Wong Shau-Him, Qi Mengshi and Jia Metying.*

Based on a true story, *Boat People* focuses on a Japanese photographer (Chi-Cheung) who witnessed the fall of Saigon and returned to Vietnam five years later to see for himself the changes brought about by the revolution. At first impressed by the schools and happy peasants in the model economic zones outside the city, the photographer quickly sees beyond the façade built by the young regime. He befriends a beautiful fourteen-year-old girl (Season Ma) and her wisecracking young brother (Andy Lau), who are forced to search cadavers' mouths for gold fillings to sell on the black market and ravage the garbage dump for food. He witnesses firsthand peasants being dragged off and shot by the police for no apparent reason and visits economic zones that are really slave labor camps. Eventually, the photographer must make a choice: to remain a neutral observer, or risk his own safety by trying to aid a seemingly endless stream of victims.

Devoid of the sentimental ploys that exploit a Westerner's guilt in *The Killing Fields*, Ann Hui's *Boat People* is a more satisfying examination of a people's revolution gone sour. The acting is first-rate, particularly from Ma and Lau, and the cinematography powerful. This new Vietnam is a terrifying betrayal to its original intentions and its people, and Hui (who was born in China and lives in Hong Kong) portrays the mistakes without composing a laundry list of horrors committed by the Communist regime. Instead, she creates a real world, inhabited by people, that works as an indictment by virtue of its quiet emotional authority. *Boat People* builds to a harrowing climax—an explosion that shouts at the audience the assertion that despite a government's ability to oppress the individual, a defiant mass can never be silenced.

RATING: R, with brief nudity and violence.
FILMNOTE: Cora Miao, who plays the madam who entices the children's mother into prostitution, is married to Wayne Wang, the director of Chan Is Missing and Dim Sum.

BOB LE FLAMBEUR
(Video, subtitled)

Film Noir

France		French
1955	99 Min.	B&W

CREDITS: Directed, written and produced by Jean-Pierre Melville. Cinematography by Henri Decae. Music by Eddie Barclay and Jean Boyer. Art direction by Jean-Pierre Melville and Claude Boxin. Released by Columbia Pictures/Triumph Films. Distributed nontheatrically by Swank Motion Pictures. Starring Roger Duchesne, Isabel Corey, Daniel Cauchy, Howard Vernon, Guy Decomble, Andre Garet, Claude Cerval, Colette Fleury, Gerard Buhr and Simone Paris.

Until his death in 1973, Jean-Pierre Melville was a leading French film noir director, and *Bob le Flambeur* is one of his most acclaimed works. Set in the 1940s in Paris, it's the story of Bob "the gambler" (Roger Duchesne), an aging ex–bank robber whose main joy in life is playing the odds. But Bob's not your ordinary track rat. He's a distinguished-looking gentleman loved by everybody from the dead-end barmaids to his tinhorn cronies, and even the cops.

When the story begins, Bob is down to his last franc when a friend offers him a chance to make some quick cash by robbing the safe of a large casino on the night of the Grand Prix. Bob is quickly enlisted, and he and his cohorts cook up an elaborate scheme complete with financial backers, casino blueprints and dress rehearsals. Meanwhile, a burgeoning young streetwalker (Isabel Corey) in whom Bob has taken a fatherly interest shoots her mouth off about the plan, prompting the typical moral of thrillers from the fifties: "Never tell a dame anything."

The part of *Bob le Flambeur* that drags is the scheming leading up to the heist. Melville lays out so many intricate details that after a while you just wish they'd rob the safe and get it over with. The performances are excellent in this film, full of well-drawn, fiendishly appealing lowlifes. Duchesne is captivating as the debonair gambler who adds grace to an otherwise gritty group, and Corey is enchanting as the femme fatale. But what's most remarkable about *Bob le Flambeur* is the way it looks and feels. The film is made up of carefully composed shots in high-contrast black and white, a jazzy forties soundtrack by Eddie Barclay and Jo Boyer, and some wonderful sets and costumes to add to its slickness. The ultimate effect is a dreamy, noirish quality that is so sensual it dazzles.

RATING: No MPAA rating, with mild violence.

FILMNOTE: Bob le Flambeur *wasn't released in the United States until 1982, after it received a rave response at the 1981 New York Film Festival.*

DAS BOOT (THE BOAT)
(Video, dubbed)

World War II Adventure

West Germany	German
1982	150 Min.	Color

CREDITS: *Directed by Wolfgang Petersen. Written by Wolfgang Petersen, based on the autobiographical novel by Lothar-Guenther Buchheim. Produced by Gunter Rohrach and Michael Bittims. Cinematography by Jost Vacano. Released by Bavaria Atelier/Columbia. Distributed nontheatrically by Swank Motion Pictures. Starring Jurgen Prochnow, Herbert Gronemeyer, Klaus Wennemann, Hubertus Bengsch, Martin Semmelrogge, Bernd Tauber, Erwin Leder and Martin May.*

Das Boot begins with a title card claiming that "of the 40,000 German soldiers who served in U-boats, over 30,000 never returned from the sea." This note lays the groundwork for the sense of doom that pervades the entire film.

The story opens as a U-boat prepares to ship out from France. It's only 1941, but even before the mission, the captain (Jurgen Prochnow) is already disillusioned with Hitler's war. Once at sea, though, he and his crew are caught up in the thrill of the hunt. After forty-five days underwater, the battle-itchy Germans attack a seemingly unescorted convoy, only to realize too late that they've been lured into a fleet of Allied destroyers. Reeling from a depth-charge attack, the captain decides to stagger back to port, but he's overruled by the high command. The U-boat is instead sent on a suicide mission through the heavily fortified Straits of Gilbraltar. The captain's attempt to maneuver through the perilous water is a disaster. The boat is severely damaged and trapped on the bottom of the ocean,

so he and his crew must devise a plan to avoid suffocating in an underwater coffin.

Produced on a budget of over $12 million (at the time of its release, the most ever spent on a German film), *Das Boot* is an amazing technical achievement. Director Wolfgang Petersen *(Enemy Mine)* creates an intensely claustrophobic atmosphere in the corridors of the submarine, while cinematographer Vacano's tracking shots through the port of the boat are exhilarating. But as good as these details are, the strength of the film is the story it tells. The acting is excellent across the board. And *Das Boot* challenges popular notions that all Germans were rabid racists during the war, while effectively dramatizing the sanctity of human life.

RATED: *R for violence and profanity.*
AWARDS: *1982 Academy Award nominations for Best Director (Wolfgang Petersen), Best Screenplay Adaptation (Petersen), Best Cinematography (Jost Vacano), Best Film Editing (Hannes Nikel), Best Sound (Milan Bor, Trevor Pyke, and Mike LeMare) and Best Sound Editing (LeMare).*
FILMNOTE: *Cinematographer Jost Vacano had to practice running with his cameras from compartment to compartment on the submarine for weeks before filming the movie's tracking shots.*

THE BOSTONIANS
(Video)

Literary Drama

U.S.A.	
1984	120 Min.	Color

CREDITS: *Directed by James Ivory. Written by Ruth Prawer-Jhabvala, based on the novel by Henry James. Produced by Ismail Merchant. Cinematography by Walter Lassey. Music by Richard Robbins. Costume design by Jenny Beavan and John Bright. Released and distributed nontheatrically by Almi Pictures. Starring Vanessa Redgrave, Christopher Reeve, Madeleine Potter, Jessi-*

ca Tandy, Linda Hunt, Wallace Shawn and Nancy Marchand.

One common problem in adapting literature to film is that character development often suffers in the transition. This Merchant-Ivory-Jhabvala version of Henry James's *The Bostonians* is a prime example. It's the story of Verena Tarrant (Madeleine Potter), a beautiful suffragette in turn-of-the-century Boston who has to choose between two very different suitors. Although Basil Ransom (Christopher Reeve) typifies the arrogance and sexism of the Southern male, he is too charming and handsome for Verena to resist. Olive Chancellor (Vanessa Redgrave), on the other hand, is a middle-aged suffragette leader whose attraction to Verena goes beyond admiring the girl's oratory skills. Both she and Basil become increasingly possessive of Verena and jealous of one another. Poor Verena is forced to choose sides at every turn in this movie.

The Bostonians explores several important women's issues, especially in the relationship of Basil and Verena. The performances are outstanding, and the filmmakers deftly portray the stifling atmosphere of Victorian Boston, as well as the lavish dress and décor of the era. But the movie fails to get across the reason why Basil and Verena have such a strong attraction for one another in the first place. Though more time is spent on Verena's relationship with Olive, again, only surface emotions are explored. Redgrave's Olive is so nervous and repressed, so one-dimensional almost from the start, it's hard to understand why Verena idolizes her.

RATING: PG, with nothing objectionable. AWARDS: 1984 New York Film Critics Award for Best Actress (Vanessa Redgrave); 1984 Academy Award nominations for Best Actress (Redgrave) and Best Costume Design (Jenny Beavan and John Bright).

A BOY AND HIS DOG
(Video)

Futuristic Black Comedy

U.S.A.

1975   87 Min.   Color

CREDITS: Directed by L. Q. Jones. Written by L. Q. Jones and Alvy Moore, based on the novella by Harlan Ellison. Produced by Alvy Moore. Cinematography by John Arthur Morrill. Music by Tim McIntyre. Released by L. Q. Jones Productions. Distributed nontheatrically by Films Inc. Starring Don Johnson, Susanne Benton, Tiger, Jason Robards, Tim McIntyre, Charles McGraw and Alvy Moore.

Based on Harlan Ellison's Nebula Award–winning novella, *A Boy and His Dog* is set in the year 2024, after World War III, in a barren wasteland once known as Arizona, where bands of men roam the countryside raping women and scrounging for food. The story's hero is Vic (Don Johnson from TV's "Miami Vice"), a young man traveling solo. His only companion is a telecommunicating dog named Blood (Tiger, with a voice by Tim McIntyre), who sniffs out danger and potential women for Vic in exchange for food. One day, Blood discovers a particularly beautiful victim for Vic at a ramshackle outdoor movie theater. Vic trails her to an abandoned YMCA, where he plans to accost her. But she disarms Vic with beauty and friendliness, and instead of raping her, they make love.

The woman's name is Quilla (Susanne Benton), and she is from an underground "civilized" community called Topeka. The men are sterile there, and she has been sent aboveground to lure a healthy young stud back home to impregnate virgins. A willing specimen, Vic gladly follows Quilla beneath the earth, until he realizes that the governing committee, led by Lew (Jason Robards), plans to extract his sperm artificially and then kill him when they have enough.

Vic and the other men aboveground violate and kill women as casually as they might shoot a game of pool. Although it's meant to be a comment on how twisted values can become, it's not an appealing premise upon which to build a film. Only if you can ignore these scenes is *A Boy and His Dog* an entertaining story. The film's sets are elaborately detailed, and director L. Q. Jones effectively contrasts the devastation of postnuclear anarchy aboveground and the sterility of a mind-control civilization below, while throwing in several sharp jabs at consumerism and middle America as well. But it's Blood who makes this film so special—he's the best talking animal to hit the screen since Mr. Ed. His sarcastic and witty remarks to Vic, combined with his worried and aloof expressions, will make even feminists forgive this movie for its frequent lapses.

RATING: *R for multiple rapes, language, nudity and violence.*
AWARDS: *1975 Patsy (deservedly won by Tiger from TV's "The Brady Bunch"), the highest honor paid to an animal in a movie.*
FILMNOTE: *Although a sequel was planned for* A Boy and His Dog, *Tiger died before the production could get off the ground.*

BRAZIL
(Video)

Futuristic Black Comedy
England/U.S.A.

1985   131 Min.   Color

CREDITS: *Directed by Terry Gilliam. Written by Terry Gilliam, Tom Stoppard and Charles McKeown. Produced by Arnon Milchan. Cinematography by Roger Pratt. Special Effects by George Gibbs. Production design by Norman Garwood. Released by Universal. Distributed nontheatrically by Swank Motion Pictures. Starring Jonathan Pryce, Robert De Niro, Michael Palin, Ian Holm, Katherine Helmond, Bob Hoskins, Ian Richardson, Peter Vaughn, Kim Greist, Barbara Hicks and Charles McKeown.*

Brazil is set "somewhere in the twentieth Century," in a metropolis of tall gray buildings with cumbersome ductwork running through and connecting every structure. These monoliths are crowded with huge, clunky machines and 1940s-style furnishings. The human inhabitants are clonelike office workers required to fill out forms to account for their every action. Terrorist bombings and sudden arrests by a brutal police force occur daily in this decaying society. But the real crime against the state is carried out by repairmen who fix machines without the approval of the bureaucracy; these clandestine free-lancers are the society's most-wanted criminals.

Smack dab in the middle of this insanity is the hero of our story, a low-level bureaucrat named Sam Lowry (Jonathan Pryce). Sam's first mistake is to let a hooded repairman (Robert De Niro) fix his furnace without authorization. Then he falls for a beautiful woman who happens to be a terrorist. As Sam begins to spend time with her, he becomes a wanted man.

Each character and physical detail in *Brazil* represents an extreme stereotype of what our society could or has become. With their ideas and characterizations, director Terry Gilliam *(Time Bandits)* and his writers ingeniously satirize uncontrolled bureaucracies, police states and over-technology. The thought that went into their sets alone is astonishing. But there is little to hold on to in *Brazil* except the visuals. The story line is confusing, and the dialogue is mostly inane. Virtually no depth is invested in the citizens of this futurist quagmire, and each vignette is so similar to the next that they begin to blend together. Most viewers have a love-hate relationship with *Brazil*, as happy to have seen the movie as they were anxious for it to end.

RATING: *R for violence and language.*
AWARDS: *1985 British Academy Award for Best Production Design (Norman Garwood); 1985 Los Angeles Film Critics' Award for Best Picture.*
FILMNOTE: *Originally, Universal executives were so unhappy with the finished product that they didn't want to release* Brazil. *Director Terry Gilliam then secretly showed the film to a group of Los Angeles film critics. Their re-*

sponse was so positive that they bullied Universal into releasing the picture.

BREAKER MORANT

(Video)

Docudrama

Australia

1979   107 Min.   Color

CREDITS: *Directed by Bruce Beresford. Written by Bruce Beresford, Jonathan Hardy and David Stevens, based on the play by Kenneth Ross. Produced by Matt Carroll. Cinematography by Don McAlpine. Music by Phil Cunneen. Released by New World Pictures. Distributed nontheatrically by Films Inc. Starring Edward Woodward, Jack Thompson, John Waters, Bryan Brown, Rod Mullinar, Vincent Ball, Frank Wilson, Terence Donovan and Russell Kiefel.*

Breaker Morant is based on the actual records of a 1901 court-marital of three Australian soldiers accused of atrocities in the Boer Wars in South Africa. The film begins when Lt. Harry Morant (Edward Woodward) and two of his men are arrested for killing a group of escaped unarmed black prisoners and the missionary who helped them. None denies the killings, but each claims that he was acting under specific orders from his commanding officer. Despite elegant testimony by Morant and a valiant effort by their defense lawyer (Jack Thompson), they are railroaded into a conviction because it is politically beneficial to the Commonwealth that they are found guilty as charged.

Director Bruce Beresford *(Tender Mercies)* lets us know from the start that the trial is an outrage because these men were only acting in the line of duty. The narrative is effectively recreated through flashbacks so that in the beginning, we aren't sure what has really happened. As we learn more details, the tension builds until the film's inevitable but emotion-packed conclusion. Yet the morality of the murders is

an issue the film never resolves, and one that has caused many to accuse it of having racist undertones.

One of the first films to popularize Australian cinema in America, *Breaker Morant* is a riveting courtroom drama. The acting is first-rate, from Woodward's Morant and the immensely appealing Australian chaps to the hypocritical British officers. It is also well-edited and photographed, sharply pointing out the class differences between common Aussies and arrogant Brits, and how the motherland used its colonial volunteers as pawns in some of her most ruthless games.

RATING: *PG, with mild violence.*
AWARDS: *1981 Academy Award nomination for Best Screenplay Based on Material from Another Medium (Bruce Beresford, Jonathan Hardy and David Stevens).*

BREATHLESS

(Video, subtitled)

Social Drama

France   French

1959   90 Min.   B&W

CREDITS: *Directed by Jean-Luc Godard. Written by Jean-Luc Godard and François Truffaut. Produced by Georges de Beauregard. Cinematography by Raoul Coutard. Music by Martial-Solal. Art direction by Claude Chabrol. Released by Imperira Films. Distributed nontheatrically by New Yorker Films. Starrring Jean-Paul Belmondo, Jean Seberg, Daniel Boulanger, Jean-Pierre Melville (the director of* Bob le Flambeur), *Lilliane Robin, Henri-Jacques Huet, Van Doude, Lilian David, and cameos by directors Jean-Luc Godard, François Truffaut, Philippe de Broca (King of Hearts) and Claude Chabrol (Violette).*

Breathless is a movie of firsts. It's the debut feature of famed French director Jean-Luc Godard, it became the seminal film of the French New Wave movement, and it's the movie that turned Jean-Paul Belmondo into an international sex symbol.

Belmondo plays Michel, a handsome, two-bit gangster who chain-smokes Luckies, wears his fedora at a tilt, and idolizes Humphrey Bogart. At the start of the film, he's stopped by a cop while driving too fast in a stolen car and casually kills the policeman. He then goes to Paris where he hooks up with his American girlfriend, Patricia (Jean Seberg), an expatriate who sells *The Herald Tribune* on the streets of Paris. Although Michel's a hit with the ladies, this tomboy Yankee is his favorite, and he tries to talk her into fleeing the country with him. Patricia is more interested in Mozart and becoming a famous journalist than she is in Michel, but she spends a few days with him anyway, hiding out from the authorities. During their flight, we learn that she's as alienated as her handsome lover. Underneath everything they do is a blatant disregard for society's conventions.

Breathless has a loosely constructed narrative, consisting of fast-moving vignettes strung together with no transitions. Some of the film's conversations continue from one scene to the next, others are repeated within the same scene. In other words, Godard breaks several rules of conventional filmmaking, many for the first time, and he gets away with it masterfully. *Breathless* is as fresh and innovative today as it was when it was released. The film's dialogue alternates between the snappy and the philosophical. Several scenes are clever parodies of American B movies or pay homage to famous directors and actors. And the performances by Belmondo and Seberg are extraordinary. The scenes of them together, although not explicitly sexual, are so hot that they practically steam the screen.

RATING: No MPAA rating, with profanity and violence.

AWARDS: Silver Bear for Best Direction (Jean-Luc Godard) at the 1960 Berlin Film Festival.

WARNING: Since the quality of the video version isn't good, and the film's visuals are very important, you should do your best to see this on a big screen.

FILMNOTE: Godard was persuaded to direct his first feature by François Truffaut and Claude Chabrol, who were impressed by some short films Godard had made. Truffaut went on to be Godard's co-screenwriter on Breathless *and Chabrol to be its art director. After the film's release, Godard became France's most discussed and sought-after filmmaker.*

BRIMSTONE AND TREACLE
(Video)

Mystery/Black Comedy

England

1982   85 Min.   Color

CREDITS: Directed by Richard Loncraine. Written by Dennis Potter (Pennies from Heaven). Produced by Kenneth Todd. Cinematography by Peter Hannan. Music by Sting. Released by United Artist Classics. Distributed nontheatrically by Films Inc. Starring Sting, Denholm Elliot, Joan Plowright and Suzanna Hamilton.

If there's a movie that will convince you of Sting's talent as an actor, *Brimstone and Treacle* is it. He plays Martin Taylor, a dark, sinister mystery man who enters the house of a middle-class couple, Thomas and Norma Bates (Denholm Elliot and Joan Plowright) by saying he's an old, good friend of their daughter Patricia (Suzanna Hamilton). Patricia can't confirm his story because, severely traumatized from a car accident, she doesn't speak. Although the deeply religious matron of the house can't remember him from her daughter's past, Martin seems like such a nice young Christian that she invites him to spend the weekend with them. As his stay stretches into a week, Thomas, who doesn't believe Martin's story from the start, tries to catch him in some sort of slip so he can ask Martin to leave. Meanwhile, Norma feels that her atheist husband is being unfair to the polite young man because of his religious beliefs.

Dennis Potter's script is full of intelligent and satirical commentary on religion, class and morality in middle-class England, while director Kenneth Todd does an outstanding job unraveling the personal repression of each member of the Bates family. The film's setting inside their tidy home is appropriately claustrophic, and all the performances are excellent. But it's Sting's Martin Taylor that is the most captivating. He's an enormously charismatic con man who has a hidden purpose behind everything he does, yet on the surface is quite affable. Without giving away the film's shocking ending, it's safe to say it's one of the most unsettling scenes in recent cinema. This whole creepy mystery is so cleverly laid out you'll get sucked into it whether you want to or not.

RATING: R for disturbing sex and violence.

BRITANNIA HOSPITAL
(Video)

Social Satire

England

1982   115 Min.   Color

CREDITS: Directed by Lindsay Anderson. Written by David Sherwin. Produced by Davina Belling and Clive Parsons. Cinematography by Mike Fash. Music by Alan Price. Released by EMI/Universal. Distributed nontheatrically by Films Inc. Starring Leonard Rossiter, Graham Crowden, Malcolm McDowell, Joan Plowright, Marsha Hunt, Frank Grimes, Jill Bennett, Robin Askwith, John Bett, Peter Jeffrey and Fulton Mackay.

If there was ever any doubt that the British sense of humor is quite different from that of their American cousins, one need only to see Lindsay Anderson's *Britannia Hospital.*

The film records a day in the life of Britannia Hospital, where labor strikes and political protesters threaten to ruin the impending visit of the Queen Mother to celebrate the institution's 500th anniversary. First, picketers block the delivery of the Royal gourmet lunch. Then Potter

(Leonard Rossiter), Britannia's chief administrator, must negotiate with union leaders willing to trade their loyalty for lordships, while the Palace's security head, a tuxedoed dwarf sent ahead to ensure Royal etiquette at the banquet table, badgers Potter with nitpicky details. At the same time, Milar (Graham Crowden), an egocentric biologist, plans his own tribute to the Queen Mum—the unveiling of an artificially constructed man—even if it means sawing off the head of a nosy journalist (Malcolm McDowell) for needed spare parts.

Britannia Hospital is full of jabs at England's growing welfare economy of the seventies, plagued by unemployment, strikes and burdensome bureaucracy while the Royal family flaunted its opulence. But the film's humor is much too obvious for its own good. There's so little subtlety in the jokes that what's meant to be clever satire is often flat and joyless. Many good performers, including Malcolm McDowell, are wasted by a script that takes an easy out whenever it sees an opportunity. Only Graham Crowden's Milar is consistently entertaining, choosing body parts for his creation as if shopping for slices of pie at the Automat. His character is stinging and fresh, qualities that are lacking elsewhere in the disappointing *Britannia Hospital.*

RATING: No MPAA rating, with violence.

THE BROTHER FROM ANOTHER PLANET
(Video)

Social Satire

U.S.A.

1984   110 Min.   Color

CREDITS: Directed and written by John Sayles. Produced by Peggy Rajski and Maggie Renzi. Cinematography by Ernest Dickerson. Music by Mason Daring and John Sayles. Released by A-Train. Distributed nontheatrically by Cinecom. Starring Joe Morton, Maggie Renzie, Fisher Stevens,

John Sayles, Darryl Edwards, Steve James, Leonard Jackson, Rosette Le Noire, Ren Woods and Bill Cobbs.

The Brother (Joe Morton) from outer space is only a "brother" because he is black. Otherwise, he is very different from the people he runs into after his spaceship crashes and he's cast adrift in Harlem. He has three huge toes on both of his feet. He can't talk, yet he seems to have an understanding of what others are saying to him. He also has the power to repair machines by the laying on of hands—a useful skill in Harlem where nothing ever seems to work.

The Brother hangs out at a neighborhood bar where the patrons think he is a little strange, although they welcome his ability to fix the video game. Besides the bar's regulars, he encounters a couple of white Indiana conventioneers who get lost in Harlem, a fast-talking young man on the subway, several junkies, and two dangerous men in overcoats from his own world who are out to kill him. It's a world of racism, sex, drugs, hustling and poverty, and the Brother innocently takes it all in, wondering why humans behave the way they do.

Written and directed by John Sayles (The Return of the Secaucus Seven), the only weak moments in this film come when the Brother wanders around New York alone observing inanimate objects and buildings. With no other person to act as a sounding board for his thoughts, these scenes amble on listlessly. But most of The Brother from Another Planet is a hilarious commentary on modern urban life. The idea of using a mute alien as a naïve observer in Harlem is ingenious in itself, and Morton plays the Brother as the consummate straight man, always bewildered and yet fearlessly getting into precarious situations. The supporting cast of typically pushy and tough New York personalities is a perfect contrast to the Brother's innocence. Most of them are so convincing in their roles that it's as if Sayles plucked them off the streets of Harlem to play themselves.

RATING: No MPAA rating, with substance abuse and profanity.
FILMNOTE: Sayles came upon his film's title by accident. While filming in Harlem, he overheard an interested observer ask the then TV soap-opera star Joe Morton: "Hey, man, aren't you the brother from 'Another World'?"

BROTHER SUN, SISTER MOON
(Video)

Religious Drama

U.S.A.

1973   121 Min.   Color

CREDITS: Directed by Franco Zeffirelli. Written by Franco Zeffirelli, Lina Wertmuller, Suso Cecchi d'Amico and Kenneth Ross. Produced by Luciano Perugia. Cinematography by Ennio Guarniere. Music by Donovan. Art direction by Gianni Quaranta. Set design by Carmelo Patrono. Released by Paramount. Distributed nontheatrically by Films Inc. Starring Graham Faulkner, Judi Bowker, Alec Guinness, Leigh Lawson, Kenneth Cranham, Michael Feast, Nicholas Willatt, Valentina Cortese, Lee Montague and John Sharp.

In the Middle Ages, St. Francis of Assisi rejected the tyrannical Catholic Church that launched the Crusades, and founded his own reform movement that he felt more purely practiced the teachings of Christ. In Brother Sun, Sister Moon, Italian director Franco Zeffirelli (Romeo and Juliet) retells St. Francis's story as a parable to flower children in the sixties.

The film opens as young Francesco (Graham Faulkner) returns home from the Crusades, feverish and disillusioned. But as soon as he gets on his feet again, he's skipping through the fields of wildflowers, or he's off with Claire (Judi Bowker), a blonde-haired maiden who gives her freshly baked bread to the lepers. As idyllic as it sounds, this life isn't enough for Francesco, and he decides that he wants to serve God. He shuns all of his worldly possessions, takes a vow of celibacy and attempts to rebuild an old abandoned church outside of Assisi all by himself. Before long, the cream of Assisi's youth shave their heads and join Francis in his reform movement.

The message of brotherly love and peace is admirable in *Brother Sun, Sister Moon*. But with some screenwriting help from Lina Wertmuller (of all people) and a soundtrack by the father of syrupy folk music, Donovan, Zeffirelli lays on the schmaltz so thick that it can give you kidney stones. With her long, flowing hair and peasant dress, Judi Bowker's Claire is an unadulterated sixties cliché. When she gives food to the downtrodden like a flower child, it's unintentionally comical. Faulkner's Francesco, on the other hand, comes across as too self-conscious, particularly when he is espousing the saint's philosophies. None of *Brother Sun, Sister Moon*'s characterizations are helped by the story's tediously slow pacing. Visually, however, it's a Zeffirelli feast of beautiful cinematography and well-constructed sets.

RATING: PG, with nothing objectionable.

THE BUDDY HOLLY STORY

Rock Docudrama

U.S.A.

1978   113 Min.   Color

CREDITS: Directed by Steve Rash. Written by Robert Gittler, based on Holly's biography by John Coldrosen. Produced by Fred Baur. Cinematography by Steven Lamer. Music by Joe Renzetti and Buddy Holly and the Crickets. Released by Columbia Pictures. Distributed nontheatrically by Twyman Films, Swank Motion Pictures, Kit Parker Films and Westcoast Films. Starring Gary Busey, Charles Martin Smith, Don Stroud, Maria Richwine, Conrad Janis, Albert Popwell, Amy Johnston, Jim Beach and John Goff.

Although Buddy Holly is not as well-known as other rock-and-roll figures, his influence on music is still being felt today. After viewing *The Buddy Holly Story*, it's easy to understand why. This semibiographical portrait follows Holly from his roots in Lubbock, Texas, in the early fifties to his tragic death at the age of twenty-one in a plane crash with two other rock-and-roll greats, Richie Valens and The Big Bopper.

At the film's start, Holly (Gary Busey) and his band, the Crickets (Charles Martin Smith and Don Stroud), switch from playing country music to rock-and-roll at a dance in Lubbock that is being broadcast live over a local radio station. The kids love it, but the adults respond as if the music is turning their children into wild animals. The following Sunday, the minister at Holly's church warns his parishioners that "this jungle music is one of the biggest threats to Christian morals and the American way we have had in the last fifty years." What he's really saying is that Holly's music is too black for a white band to be playing and for white children to be listening to. But that doesn't stop Holly. Through great perseverance, Holly and the Crickets become enormously successful and even appear on "The Ed Sullivan Show."

Although most of *The Buddy Holly Story* is a sentimental "rising star" story, it's still a thoroughly entertaining movie because of Busey's performance and Holly's music. From the moment he appears on the screen, Busey takes us on an emotional joy ride, as if we're right there in the passenger's seat beside him, struggling in his relationships and fighting for what he believes. Busey does a tremendous job with Holly's music. He actually sings (instead of lip-syncs) great songs such as "Peggy Sue," "It's So Easy to Fall in Love" and "That'll Be the Day" to Holly's original studio soundtracks. Most of the supporting performances are also very good, particularly the chipmunk-faced Charles Martin Smith (*Never Cry Wolf*) as Holly's bass player. Best of all, director Steve Rash gets at the heart of why rock-and-roll was so threatening to the complacency of the Eisenhower years, and why Holly played an important part in the music that still dominates popular culture today.

RATING: PG, with nothing objectionable.
AWARDS: 1978 Academy Award for Best Musical Score (Joe Renzetti); 1978 Academy Award nominations for Best Actor (Gary Busey) and Best Sound (Tex

Ruddoff, Joel Fein, Curly Thirlwell and Willie Burton).

FILMNOTE: Before and after he starred in The Buddy Holly Story, Gary Busey was a singer and guitar player who actually performed on stage with several big-name musicians such as Bob Dylan and The Band.

BURDEN OF DREAMS
(Video)

Film Documentary

U.S.A.

1982   94 Min.   Color

CREDITS: *Directed and produced by Les Blank. Cinematography and editing by Les Blank and Maureen Gosling. Sound by Maureen Gosling. Narrated by Candace Laughlin. Released by Teleculture Films. Distributed nontheatrically by Flower Films. Starring Werner Herzog, Klaus Kinski, Jason Robards, Claudia Cardinale and Mick Jagger.*

Burden of Dreams, Les Blank's film on the making of Werner Herzog's *Fitzcarraldo,* is actually more compelling than the movie it documents.

Fitzcarraldo is the story of a nineteenth-century madman who wants to finance an opera house in the Amazon by starting a rubber empire. To get to his land, however, he must drag a steamship across a mountain to an inaccessible river.

Burden of Dreams begins in November 1979 when Herzog started filming this story in the dense jungles of Peru and Ecuador. Months into the production, he is caught in a border dispute between the two countries, and one night the entire camp is burned to the ground. As soon as Herzog moves the production to a safer location 1,200 miles away, his starring actor, Jason Robards, becomes deathly ill with dysentery and has to leave the film. When his other star, Mick Jagger, pulls out because the film runs over schedule, Herzog convinces Klaus Kinski *(Aguirre, the Wrath of*

God) to help him out, but they must reshoot the entire movie.

At this point, Herzog's troubles really begin. Despite warnings from his engineer, Herzog insists on dragging a real steamship over a mountain to make his film authentic, and an Indian extra is severely injured in the process. Then, three crew members are attacked by Indians with real arrows, while others die in a tragic plane crash. The tragedies go on and on until Herzog, like his fictional protagonist, seems driven by madness in an effort to make his vision a reality.

Les Blank captures all these events with remarkable honesty, taking great care to get everyone's point of view—from the Indians to the actors to Herzog. The footage of Herzog is particularly powerful. Charismatic and obsessive, mumbling about the power of the jungle, his expression captures all the stress of the production's ill-fated progress. By the end of the documentary, he is disgusted with himself for the suffering he has caused and is on the verge of a nervous breakdown. Even if you didn't enjoy *Fitzcarraldo,* you'll find *Burden of Dreams* an extraordinary film in its own right. It's a superbly shot and edited documentary about one of the most difficult films ever made. It's also a fascinating portrait of a director consumed by his dreams.

RATING: *No MPAA rating, with mild profanity, nudity and violence.*
AWARDS: *1982 British Academy Award for Best Documentary Feature.*

BURROUGHS
(Video)

Documentary

U.S.A.

1984   86 Min.   Color

CREDITS: *Directed by Howard Brookner. Produced by Howard Brookner and Alan Yentob. Cinematography by Richard L. Camp, Cathy Dorsey, James Lebovitz, Mike Southon, Tom Dicillo, Howard*

Brookner, Larry Shlu and Anthony Balch.
Released and distributed nontheatrically by
Cinecom. Starring William Burroughs,
Allen Ginsberg, Patti Smith, Jackie Curtis,
Billy Burroughs, Lauren Hutton and Greg-
ory Corso.

One might expect a documentary of an
American novelist to be a stuffy production
with a bearded, pipe-smoking professor
narrating the author's story. But William S.
Burroughs is not a typical American writer,
and Howard Brookner's film about his life
is anything but dry and literary.

William Burroughs is one of the original
cadre of Beat writers that includes such
legends as Jack Kerouac, Allen Ginsberg
and Lawrence Ferlinghetti. He first became
famous for his controversial novel Naked
Lunch, because its profanity, violence and
black humor outraged many. But as we
quickly learn from this film, Burroughs has
thrived on controversy his whole life. His
homosexuality drove his family to ostracize
him at an early age (he was an heir to the
Burroughs adding machine fortune). A het-
erosexual exception was his wife, Joan,
whom he loved dearly, but whom he
accidently shot and killed during a drunken
frenzy. Burroughs also adores drugs, alcohol and weapons, both in his personal life
and in his books. He was a junkie for many
years, and at age sixty, he still enjoys getting high and drinking rum and coke.

All of this is bit surprising when you see
the man. His hair is short, he almost always
wears a conservative suit and tie, and he
talks in a polite manner. If you met him on
the street, you might assume that he was on
his way to an Elks meeting. But when he
reads from his works, you know that William S. Burroughs is no lodge brother.

Occasionally, this film gets bogged down
by too many mundane details of Burroughs's everyday existence. Documentary
filmmaker Howard Brookner followed him
around for four years, and some of what he
captured will interest only Burroughs devotees. There are also a couple of dramatizations of his writings that appear contrived.
What's best in Burroughs are his readings
and his wry observations on life. Fortunately there are plenty of both in this film. Out
of this delicate, prim man comes a roar of
dry narrative, deadpan wit and hilariously

shocking metaphors to make Burroughs as
fascinating, humorous and enlightening as
the man himself.

RATING: No MPAA rating, with profanity and substance abuse.

BYE BYE BRAZIL
(Video, subtitled)

Cultural Satire

Brazil		Portuguese
1980	110 Min.	Color

CREDITS: Directed and written by Carlos
Diegues. Produced by Marcos Altberg.
Cinematography by Lauro Escorel Filho.
Music by Chico Buarque, Roberto Menes-
cal and Dominguinhos. Set and costume
design by Anisio Medeiros. Released and
distributed nontheatrically by New Yorker
Films. Starring Jose Wilker, Betty Faria,
Fabio Junior, Zaira Zambelli, Principe
Nabor, Jofre Soares, Marcos Vinicius, Jose
Maria Lima and Emanoel Cavalcanti.

Director Carlos Diegues once stated that
"Bye Bye Brazil is a film about a country
which is about to come to an end, in order
to give way for another which is about to
begin." This colorful story of a carnival
troupe traveling from town to town in Brazil shows both the difficulties and the
humor of old Brazil struggling to become
Westernized.

The film focuses on a young accordian
player named Cico (Fabio Junior) and his
pregnant wife, Dasdo (Zaira Zambelli).
They join a ramshackle traveling carnival,
Caravana Rolidei, in search of adventure.
The other troupe members include Lord
Gypsy (Jose Wilker), King of Magicians
and Clairvoyants, and Swallow (Principe
Nabor), the muscle king. But of special interest to Cico is Salome (Betty Faria),
Queen of Rumba, who also is the carnival's
prostitute. Soon Cico falls under her spell
even as his wife loyally stands by his side.
But Salome and the rest of the troupe have
more important things on their minds than

love. They are on their way to Altamira, a "paradise" in the Amazon where trees are supposed to grow as big as skyscrapers and precious stones litter the ground.

Bye Bye Brazil is more a series of skits than a traditional narrative. Although Cico's love for Salome and the troupe's search for adventure are entertaining sub-plots, at the film's core are the assimilation of isolated villages into the modern world, and the contrast of traditional culture versus new. As this motley group ventures from village to village, they encounter various sad and comical signs of the great changes overtaking Brazil: a band of displaced Indians chanting "bye bye" to the age of magic when jets fly overhead, an Indian chief's wife drinking Coca-Cola for the first time, and a large gathering of small-town compesinos who are glued to a TV set watching an American B movie.

Diegues and his crew logged over 9,000 miles to make this film, and the scenery, costumes and music are as rich and varied as its characters. But the movie works so well because Diegues captures so many precious moments of the Brazilians in the back country who are steeped in magic and superstition and at the same time frightened and amazed by civilization.

RATING: R for nudity and sex.

LA CAGE AUX FOLLES—THE MAD CAGE: BIRDS OF A FEATHER

(Video, dubbed)

Gay Sex Farce

France/Italy		French
1979	99 Min.	Color

CREDITS: *Directed by Edouard Molinaro. Written by Edouard Molinaro, Marcello Danon, François Veber and Jean Poiret, based on Poiret's play. Produced by Marcello Danon. Costume design by Piero Tosi and Ambra Danon. Released by United Artists. Distributed nontheatrically by*

Films Inc. Starring Ugo Tognazzi, Michel Serrault, Michel Galabru, Claire Maurier and Luisa Maneri.

Based on Jean Poiret's long-running play, *La Cage aux Folles* is the second largest-grossing foreign film ever released in the United States (*The Gods Must Be Crazy* is first). The story involves Albin (Michel Serrault) and Renato (Ugo Tognazzi), two middle-aged men who've been living together for twenty years. Renato owns a nightclub that features female impersonators, and Albin is his star singer, Zaza. Although they fight about little things, Albin and Renato are reasonably happy until Renato's son, Simone (Claire Maurier), announces his engagement to Andrea (Luisa Maneri), and she insists that the in-laws-to-be meet.

Naturally, Andrea lied to her parents about Renato and Albin; they think Renato is a cultural attaché happily married to a woman. To add to the confusion, Andrea's father (Michel Galabru) is head of the anti-gay, anti-pornography Union of Moral Order. You can guess what happens next: Albin dresses up like a respectable wife and mother, trying to keep up the façade, but fails miserably.

Gays have mixed feelings about *La Cage aux Folles,* and for good reason. Although it's one of the first films to portray a gay man (Renato) who is more than a limp-wristed stereotype, there is also plenty here that perpetuates biases. Much of the film's humor revolves around Albin and the other drag queens acting ludicrously effeminate, while the film's "comic" climax occurs when the reactionary father has to dress up in drag to avoid his supporters when they storm the club. Also, there isn't much believable affection displayed between Renato and Albin, even though they are supposedly very much in love. In fact, the only vaguely sexual scene in the whole film involves Renato and his ex-wife.

But if you can ignore the less than desirable politics of *La Cage aux Folles,* it's an entertaining and lighthearted comedy. Many of the situations Renato and Albin get themselves into with the best of intentions turn out to be disastrously funny, while both Tognazzi and Serrault give strong and energetic performances.

RATING: PG, with nothing objectionable.
AWARDS: 1979 French Caesar for Best Actor (Michel Serrault); 1979 Academy Award nominations for Best Director (Edouard Molinaro), Best Screenplay Based on Material from Another Medium (Francis Veber, Edouard Molinaro, Marcello Danon and Jean Poiret) and Best Costumes (Piero Tosi and Ambra Danon); the National Board of Review's award for Best Foreign Film in 1979.
FILMNOTE: The success of this film, which grossed more than $50 million, encouraged two sequels. Unfortunately, these aren't nearly as fresh or funny as the original.

CAL
(Video)

Political Drama

Ireland

1984   104 Min.   Color

CREDITS: Directed by Pat O'Conner. Written by Bernard McLaverty, based on his novel. Produced by Stuart Craig. Cinematography by Jerzy Zielinski. Music by Mark Knopfler (of Dire Straits). Released by Warner Brothers. Distributed nontheatrically by Swank Motion Pictures. Starring John Lynch, Helen Mirren, Donald McCann, John Cavanagh, Ray McAnally, Stevan Rimkus and Kitty Gibson.

It's hard to imagine any movie about Northern Ireland not being depressing, but Pat O'Conner's Cal is as gloomy as they come.

Cal (John Lynch) is a young Catholic man caught dead center in Ireland's civil war. He lives with his father in a Protestant neighborhood, where local toughs bully him and threaten to burn down his house. At the same time, the IRA forces him to be a driver for a policeman's execution. One year later, Cal is still consumed by guilt for his part in that murder, unable to erase the stain of his actions even as he falls desperately in love with the policeman's widow (Helen Mirren).

Cal's torment is a constant in this movie. He is sensitive and painfully shy, and always has a frightened look about him. Though watching him is sometimes agonizing, his character is compelling and true to life. Aside from its slow tempo, the major problem with Cal is its sound. Much of the dialogue is difficult to understand, either because of the accents of the actors or because the main characters mumble. But director O'Conner does an excellent job of portraying the hopelessness of living in Northern Ireland. The weather is damp, soldiers are standing on every street corner and many frightened people like Cal want out but remain trapped in circumstances beyond their control. Mirren, Lynch and the other actors in Cal give outstanding performances, weighed down and demoralized by Ireland's despairing history.

RATING: R for one sex scene and violence.
AWARDS: Best Actress award (Helen Mirren) at the 1984 Cannes Film Festival.

CAMILA
(Video-subtitled)

Historical Romance

Argentina   Spanish

1984   105 Min.   Color

CREDITS: Directed by Maria Luisa Bemberg. Written by Maria Luisa Bemberg, Beda Docampo and Juan Bautista Stagnaro. Produced by Angel Baldo and Hector Gallardo. Cinematography by Fernando Arribas. Set design by Miguel Rodriguez. Music by Luis Maria Serra. Released and distributed nontheatrically by European Classics. Starring Susu Pecoraro, Imanol Arias, Hector Altiero, Elena Tastito, Carlos Munoz, Hector Pellegrini and Claudio Gallardou.

Based on the real events in the tragic life of a young Argentine woman in 1847,

Maria Luisa Bemberg's *Camila* is filled with characters as repressed as the times in which they live.

The heroine of the story is Camila (Susa Pecoraro), the rebellious and beautiful daughter of a conservative Buenos Aires landowner (Hector Altiero of *The Official Story*). Camila is more interested in reading foreign literature and being chummy with the servants than in marrying the man her father has chosen for her. But she isn't the only rebel in town. A young Jesuit priest named Father Gutierrez (Imanol Arias) uses his pulpit to condemn the repression of the harsh provincial governor and wealthy landowners like Camila's father. Camila listens intently to his sermons every Sunday and gradually falls in love with the priest, as she embraces his politics. She uses her time in the confessional to express her feelings toward him, and eventually, impure thoughts enter his mind as well. The two have a torrid affair and run away together. But Camila's father, the provincial governor and the church can't accept a scandal of such magnitude, and the lovers are hunted like criminals.

Director Maria Luisa Bemberg does an excellent job depicting the sexual repression of the day. When Camila confesses her love, she and the father sizzle with passion. Reminiscent of movies such as *Tess* and *Barry Lyndon*, the film's cinematography, costumes and sets are also stunning. Unfortunately, though, Bemberg places too much emphasis on the look of *Camila* and not enough on developing her characters. There is little dialogue in the entire narrative, and though we are supposed to feel the star-crossed couple's politics through their expressions, it's not always easy. The same is true for the subplots involving the exploited peasants. In the end, *Camila* is a nineteenth-century costume drama that lacks the substance it needs to bring it life.

RATING: R for nudity and sex.
AWARDS: 1984 Academy Award nomination for Best Foreign Film.

CAN SHE BAKE CHERRY PIE?
(Video)

 ½

Screwball Comedy

U.S.A.

1983   90 Min.   Color

CREDITS: Directed and written by Henry Jaglom. Produced by M. H. Simonson. Cinematography by Bob Fiore. Music by Karen Black. Released by International Rainbow/Jaglom Productions. Starring Michael Emil, Karen Black, Michael Margotta, Frances Fisher, Martin Harvey Friedberg and Robert Hallack.

Although Harry Jaglom is concerned with troubled romance in his other features, *Sitting Ducks* and *Always,* in *Can She Bake Cherry Pie?* this focus is so narrow that he nearly ruins an otherwise entertaining story.

The film begins when Z (Karen Black), a distraught musician recently abandoned by her husband, wanders into a Manhattan café where she compulsively orders the entire dessert menu between uncontrollable sobs. Creating a commotion, she attracts the attention of Eli, a balding, divorced social worker sitting with his friend at the next table. Eli dries her eyes with his tie, and though he and Z soon become lovers, both of them are so filled with self-doubt and various neuroses that their relationship turns into a circus. Eli, for example, quickly loses patience with Z's paranoid conviction that her ex-husband is having them followed, while she resents his overpossessiveness and insistence on measuring his pulse with an electronic meter to gauge the strength of his ardor as they make love. As their inane relationship develops, everything from jealousy and mistrust to the fear of marriage and commitment are thrown into the stew.

Although there are supporting characters in *Can She Bake Cherry Pie?*, they contribute little. Basically, the film is a two-person show, and whether or not you enjoy it will depend on how the main characters rub you. Michael Emil (Einstein in *Insig-*

nificance and Jaglom's brother in real life) is very funny as the stuffy, whiny Eli, whose officiousness masks feelings of warmth and tenderness. Karen Black, on the other hand, wildly overdoes the daffy blonde routine she has played so many times in the past, twitching and gurgling as if she were undergoing shock therapy. As with Jaglom's other work, *Can She Bake Cherry Pie?* is technically crude, with improvisation that leaves the viewer bored and uncomfortable in several scenes. Yet, Emil is very charming, and his offbeat charisma may make this film for some a blind date worth keeping.

RATED: *R for nudity and profanity.*
FILMNOTE: *For most, Karen Black is known only as an actress, and for good reason. She wrote the music and lyrics to the miserable songs she sings in the film.*

CARAVAGGIO
(Video)

Docudrama

England
1986   98 Min.   Color

CREDITS: *Directed and written by Derek Jarman. Produced by Sarah Radclyffe. Cinematography by Gabriel Beristain. Released by Cinevista. Distributed nontheatrically by Kino International. Starring Nigel Terry, Sean Bean and Tilda Swinton.*

Michelangelo Merisi de Caravaggio was one of the most influential Baroque painters, best known for his innovative use of light and shadow. He also had a scandalous personal life involving prostitutes, homosexuals and murder. If you judge him by Derek Jarman's *Caravaggio*, he was more interested in sex than anything else.

Jarman begins Caravaggio's story as the artist lies on his deathbed. Through flashbacks, we see him first as a sensuous-lipped, pubescent teenager, already adept at seducing men; then as a statuesque adult (Nigel Terry) who purchases a pretty young mute boy to be his house-slave and lover; and

finally, as an accomplished artist who's the darling of the aristocracy and the church but also the subject of juicy gossip. Caravaggio has a voracious sexual appetite, and he uses pimps and prostitutes to model for him and satisfy his hunger. When his models aren't posing in provocative positions or having sex with him and each other, they're playing with knives. It's this that eventually gets Caravaggio into big trouble.

The real star of *Caravaggio* is its cinematography. The sets are beautifully framed and colored. The lighting is often extraordinary, as certain scenes are composed to copy lighting effects in Caravaggio's own paintings. But, shot in six weeks for less than half a million pounds, *Caravaggio* has an unfinished feel to it. Director Jarman places so much emphasis on the art direction, and so little on character development, that all the scenes in *Caravaggio* blend together after a while. He also goes to great lengths to show us that Caravaggio and his entourage have dynamite bodies and sexual desires to match, with their burning stares and lustful kisses at the center of every scene. Their lives seem so empty that even with all the exquisite visuals, the excitement in *Caravaggio* gives way to drowsiness.

RATING: *No MPAA rating, with nudity, sexual content and violence.*
AWARDS: *Silver Lion for Visual Achievement at the 1986 Venice Film Festival.*
FILMNOTE: *Caravaggio isn't Derek Jarman's only period piece. After being the art director on several of Ken Russell's films, Jarman made* Sebastiane, *the only movie about Roman times made in Latin.*

CAREFUL, HE MIGHT HEAR YOU

(Video)

Coming-of-Age Drama

Australia

1984   116 Min.   Color

CREDITS: *Directed by Carl Schultz. Written by Michael Jenkins, based on the novel by Sumner Locke Elliot. Produced by Jill Robb. Cinematography by John Seale. Set design by John Stoddard and John Carroll. Released by 20th Century Classics. Distributed nontheatrically by Films Inc. Starring Wendy Hughes, Robyn Nevin, Nicholas Gledhill, Peter Whitford, John Hargreaves, Isabelle Anderson, Geraldine Turner, Colleen Clifford and Julie Nihill.*

Winner of eight Australian Academy Awards, including Best Picture, Best Director and Best Actress, *Careful, He Might Hear You* is about a six-year-old boy whose mother dies, and who is then caught in a custody fight between his two aunts. Appropriately named P.S. since his feelings in the situation are considered only as an afterthought, the boy (Nicholas Gledhill) wants to live with his Aunt Lila (Robyn Nevin), who is kind, honest and loving. But his rich and conniving Aunt Vanessa (Wendy Hughes) hates Lila. When she bribes the boy's alcoholic father (John Hargreaves) into signing a statement saying that he prefers Vanessa to care for the boy, P.S.'s nightmare begins.

Careful, He Might Hear You is a touching story told almost exclusively from P.S.'s point of view. Nicholas Gledhill is an extraordinary young actor who has the look of childhood anguish and delivers his lines with depth of feeling. Robyn Nevin is wonderfully sweet as Aunt Lila, but it's Wendy Hughes who's the star of the film. As the cold, sexually repressed matron, Hughes gives a powerful performance, particularly in the scenes when she tries to express her stilted feelings toward P.S. This marvelous ensemble acting is framed by cinematographer John Seale's luxuriously detailed camera work, although too much time is spent on long pans from P.S.'s perspective, and artsy shots of Aunt Vanessa's mansion. As well done as they are, they slow the narrative and detract from this movie's more sensitive emotional conflicts.

RATING: *PG for one disturbing incest scene.*
AWARDS: *1983 Australian Academy Awards for Best Film, Best Director (Carl Schultz), Best Actress (Wendy Hughes), Best Supporting Actor (John Hargreaves), Best Photography (John Seale) and Best Adapted Screenplay (Michael Jenkins).*

CARMEN

(Video, subtitled)

Musical Romance

Spain   Spanish

1983   95 Min.   Color

CREDITS: *Directed by Carlos Saura. Written by Carlos Saura and Antonio Gades, based on Bizet's opera. Produced by Emiliano Piedra. Cinematrography by Teo Escamilla. Choreographed by Antonio Gades. Music by Paco De Lucia. Released by Orion. Distributed nontheatrically by Films Inc. Starring Antonio Gades, Laura Del Sol, Paco De Lucia, Christina Hoyosm, Juan Antonio Jiminez, Sebastian Moreno, Jose Yepes and Pepe Flores.*

This *Carmen* is a modern adaptation of Bizet's famous opera, with flamenco guitar in place of classical music and flamenco dancing instead of ballet. But the underlying story is the same—a seductive and fiercely independent woman uses her power to drive her jealous lover insane.

Updated to present-day Spain, *Carmen* stars Laura Del Sol as a young woman who gets the lead role in a flamenco production of *Carmen* starring and choreographed by Antonio (portrayed by Antonio Gades, also the movie's choreographer). It doesn't take long for Antonio to succumb to the charms of his leading lady, but when she refuses to be possessed by him, he becomes insanely jealous. In time, Antonio's and Carmen's feelings begin to parallel those of the characters in the story they are rehearsing and the passion of their dancing is fueled by their off-screen romance.

Director Carlos Saura cunningly pieces together the story-within-a-story so that you don't know what is real and what is play-acting. But beyond this clever device, the plot in *Carmen* amounts to little more than a tale of a macho Latin lover making a fool of himself. The story and characters unfortunately become incidental to the music and dancing. Yet even if flamenco isn't your favorite, you can't help but come away from *Carmen* with a new appreciation for the art form. Paco De Lucia plays the music for all of the rehearsals, and it's obvious why he's considered one of the world's foremost flamenco guitarists. Gades does an outstanding job as the choreographer, and all of the 'dance numbers emanate a power and a rhythm that practically steal your breath away.

RATING: R, with one sex scene and a lot of sensual dancing.
AWARDS: 1983 Academy Award nomination for Best Foreign Film; Best Artistic Contribution award at the 1983 Cannes Film Festival.
WARNING: There are at least five other films titled Carmen, *so be careful when selecting this at your video store.*

CHAN IS MISSING

Cultural Comedy

U.S.A.	English and Chinese
1982 80 Min.	B&W

CREDITS: Directed and produced by Wayne Wang. Written by Wayne Wang, Isaac Cronin and Terrel Seltzer. Cinematography by Michael Chin. Released and distributed nontheatrically by New Yorker Films. Starring Wood Moy, Marc Hayashi, Laureen Chew, Peter Wang, Judi Nihei, Presco Tabios and Frankie Alarcon.

Made on a miniscule budget of $22,000, this first film by Chinese-American filmmaker Wayne Wang *(Dim Sum)* was a surprise success at art houses. Set in San Francisco's Chinatown, the story follows a middle-aged Chinese-American cab driver named Jo (Wood Moy) and his wisecracking young nephew (Marc Hayashi) in their attempts to locate a friend named Chan, who disappeared with $4,000 of their savings. The two amateur detectives, who pretend to be Charlie Chan and his Number-One Son, discover that Chan could be either a murderer, a communist, a thief, a computer scientist, a loving father, an honest friend, or all of the above. But, mostly, their sleuthing becomes an excuse to talk to an assortment of Chinese-Americans about what they think of life in the United States.

Chan is Missing is loosely structured as a mystery—the only truly scary scene happens when a Chinese fry cook (Peter Wang, the director of *A Great Wall*) throws noodles into a wok full of boiling grease. The film's soundtrack is also tinny, and some of the film's improvised dialogue rambles on a little too long. As cultural document of Chinese Americans at various stages of assimilation, though, *Chan Is Missing* works well. Director Wang skillfully homes in on his characters' offhanded remarks, and his camera has an eye for catching mannerisms unique to Asian Americans. Some of Jo and his nephew's spiels are humorous, especially their impressions of Americans. And there are several insightful situations that bring out the clashing between the two cultures. If you can ignore its student film appearance, *Chan Is Missing* is a fascinating treatise on Chinese-American life.

RATING: No MPAA rating, with nothing objectionable.

CHICKEN RANCH
(Video)

★ ★ ★ ★

Social Documentary

U.S.A.

1982   84 Min.   Color

CREDITS: *Directed by Nick Broomfield and Sandi Sissel. Produced by Nick Broomfield. Cinematography by Sandi Sissel (the first union camerawoman in the United States). Sound by Nick Broomfield. Edited by Julian Ware. Released by Central Television. Distributed nontheatrically by First Run Features.*

Shot at Nevada's famous Chicken Ranch brothel, which inspired Broadway's *The Best Little Whorehouse in Texas, Chicken Ranch* is anything but a musical comedy. Located fifty miles outside of Las Vegas, this legal whorehouse features attractions including the Bianca Blast, the Creme de Menthe Frappe and an assortment of ladies who operate these pleasure-giving devices. Although they can earn up to $2,000 a week, it doesn't take long to realize that these working women despise their male clients and don't enjoy sex in the slightest. We also learn that most were badly abused in their pasts.

There's nothing fancy about this documentary technically. The camera work is direct and uninteresting, the sound is often poor, and the editing is choppy and confusing. But the subject matter is so strong, and the filmmakers present it in such a straightforward manner, that these technical failings are only slightly bothersome.

Without nudity or titillation, directors Nick Broomfield *(Lily Tomlin)* and Sandi Sissel show us the everyday lives of prostitutes as if presenting a tour of an art museum. We see their paraphernalia, their daily television watching and birth control rituals. They casually talk about work-related subjects, such as the art of five-minute blow jobs or how they defend themselves against sadists. Chicken Ranch comes to seem almost like a prison, with the middle-aged male owner of the establishment setting strict house rules for "his girls' " behavior. Ironically, if there is an underlying message in *Chicken Ranch*, it's that this repressive atmosphere and the profession's degradations and abuses constantly reinforce these women's friendships and trust in one another.

RATING: *No MPAA rating, with profanity and skimpy lingerie.*
FILMNOTE: *Directors Sandy Sissel and Nick Broomfield lived at the Chicken Ranch for three months during production. One night on a bet, the prostitutes forced Sandy to join their lineup. To her amazement, everyone who came in immediately selected her. It turned out to be a prank arranged beforehand by the women.*

CHILLY SCENES OF WINTER
(Video)

★ ★ ★ ★

Psychological Romance

U.S.A.

1979   92 Min.   Color

CREDITS: *Directed by Joan Micklin Silver. Written by Joan Micklin Silver, based on Ann Beattie's novel. Produced by Mark Metcalf, Amy Robinson and Griffin Dunne (the star of* After Hours*). Cinematography by Bobby Byrne. Music by Ken Lauber. Released by United Artist Classics. Starring John Heard, Mary Beth Hurt, Peter Riegert, Kenneth McMillan, Griffin Dunne, Gloria Grahame, Nora Heflin, Ann Beattie, Jerry Hardin, Tarah Nutter and Allen Joseph.*

Joan Micklin Silver's *Chilly Scenes of Winter* is a quintessential baby boomer love story that explores "modern" relationships.

The story takes place in Utah in the 1970s. When Charles (John Heard), a lonely, bored civil service employee, meets an attractive secretary named Laura (Mary Beth Hurt), his drab existence changes drastically. Before long, Charles and Laura are living together and their relationship is the center of his life. But Laura is married, though separated, and she begins to miss her husband as her new boyfriend smothers her with affection. It also becomes clear that Laura feels she doesn't deserve Charles's exuberant adoration. Charles, for his part, is so afraid of losing the woman he can never really possess that he drives her away. Ultimately, his worst fear becomes a reality, and Laura goes back to her husband.

Based on an Ann Beattie novel (the author plays a small role as a waitress in the film), the first half of *Chilly Scenes of Winter* is told through flashbacks. Director Silver *(Hester Street)* cleverly structures Charles's memories to reflect how profoundly this short-lived relationship has affected him. The final half is a linear narrative portraying Charles's sometimes engaging, sometimes pathetic attempts to spy on Laura and win her back. The acting is excellent throughout, with Heard and Hurt giving natural performances. There are also plenty of comical supporting characters, such as Charles's crazy mom and his unemployed best friend–roommate, who consumes inordinate amounts of cheap wine. Although the humor in these characters softens the film's drama, *Chilly Scenes of Winter* is still packed with the pain of broken relationships.

RATING: PG, with nothing objectionable.
FILMNOTE: The film was originally released as Head Over Heels *in 1979 at ninety-nine minutes long.*

CHOOSE ME
(Video)

Romantic Black Comedy
U.S.A.

1985   106 Min.   Color

CREDITS: *Directed and written by Alan Rudolph. Produced by Carlyn Pfeiffer and David Blockner. Cinematography by Jan Kiesser. Released by Island Alive. Distributed nontheatrically by Corinth Films.*

Starring Lesley Ann Warren, Genevieve Bujold, Keith Carradine, Rae Dawn Chong, Patrick Bauchau, John Larroquette and John Considine.

Although there is little nudity or explicit sex in Alan Rudolph's *Choose Me*, it hums with sexual energy. Most of the film takes place in Eve's Lounge—a smoke-filled pickup bar where the movie's assortment of libidinous characters hang out. Eve (Lesley Ann Warren) herself is incurably promiscuous, yet is so desperate for a lasting relationship that she often calls Dr. Nancy Love (Genevieve Bujold), a radio talk show host who dispenses advice on relationships with the authority of an old pro. One would never guess that Dr. Love is terrified of men and has had virtually no sexual experiences outside her active imagination.

The two women's lives become even more intertwined when, not knowing each other's telephone identities, they become roommates. Then Mickey (Keith Carradine) appears on the scene. A handsome mystery man who is either an escaped mental patient or an extraordinarily capable hero, Mickey claims he wants to marry every woman he kisses. He ends up kissing both Dr. Love and Eve, and they both fall in love with him. To add to the confusion, Pearl (Rae Dawn Chong), a regular at Eve's Lounge, also falls under Mickey's spell. She's married to Zack (Patrick Bauchau), a brutal and jealous French gangster who is having an affair with Eve, but who is also interested in seducing Dr. Love.

In a whirl of mixed messages, dumb misunderstandings and coincidental encounters, everyone collides with one another sooner or later in *Choose Me*, and the results are absurdly hilarious. The performances here are excellent, with each character taking a turn inadvertently delivering punch lines laced with double meanings.

Yet this film has a dark side as well. Zack is an affable but frightening gangster, and Eve, Mickey and Dr. Love are driven dangerously close to suicide by their romantic desperation. *Choose Me* takes a sharp look at casual sex, broken marriages and the loneliness of singles bars. Rudolph's narcissistic characters are slaves to their own desires, and, with dreamlike cityscapes and prostitutes slinking in the background, the mood is always set for hot and self-destructive passion.

RATING: *R for adult content with little nudity*
FILMNOTE: *For how great* Choose Me *looks, it is remarkable that the film was produced for under a million dollars.*

THE CLOCKMAKER
(Video, subtitled)

Political Mystery

France		French
1973	105 Min.	Color

CREDITS: *Directed by Bertrand Tavernier. Written by Jean Aurenche, based on the novel* The Clockmaker of Everton *by Georges Simenon. Cinematography by Pierre William Glenn. Released by Lira Films. Distributed nontheatrically by Joseph Green Pictures. Starring Philippe Noiret, Jean Rochefort, Jacques Denis, William Sabatier, Andrée Tainsy and Sylvain Rougerie.*

French director Bertrand Tavernier (*Round Midnight*) is a master at creating alienated characters whose inner strength is tested by intense personal crises. *The Clockmaker* tells the story of Michael (Philippe Noiret), a Lyon watchmaker whose heart has grown cold after a broken marriage and the subsequent death of his estranged wife. His main preoccupations now are halfhearted debates with leftist friends, and his son, Bernard (Sylvain Rougerie), a wild, unfocussed boy who dabbles in leftist politics as a release for his aggression.

Michael's drab existence is abruptly destroyed when Police Inspector Guiband (Jean Rochefort) informs him that Bernard and his girlfriend are wanted for the murder of a wealthy local industrialist. As Guiband organizes a national manhunt for the couple, Michael numbly tries to reason out his son's motive for the murder. The press decides that the crime was politically inspired

and, hoping to capitalize on this angle during an election year, hounds Michael for interviews. When Michael's leftist friends take up Bernard's case as cause célèbre, he breaks away from them as well. In the end, his sole companion becomes Guiband, as both men attempt to make sense of what really happened.

Tavernier works slowly in *The Clockmaker,* gradually building mood and establishing characters in a seemingly ambiguous direction. Then near the end the emotional force that has been gaining momentum explodes in one cathartic burst of reconciliation. The narrative, however, can amble too slowly toward this critical juncture. Many questions raised early are never answered, nor is the central relationship between Michael and Guiband resolved in a satisfying way. But Noiret's character of Michael is believable and empathetic throughout the film. With his jowly, bewildered expressions, Noiret gives the perfect reaction to his son's crime. Then his emotions—angry, despairing and finally hopeful—turn his situation into an engrossing study of personal upheaval.

RATING: *No MPAA rating, with violence.*
AWARDS: *Special Jury Prize for Best First Film and Silver Bear for Best Director (Bertrand Tavernier) at the 1976 Berlin Film Festival; One of the National Board of Review's 5 Best Foreign Films in 1976.*
FILMNOTE: *Bertrand Tavernier was a film critic and scholar until this, his first film.*

A CLOCKWORK ORANGE
(Video)

Futuristic Drama

England		
1971	137 Min.	Color

CREDITS: *Directed and produced by Stanley Kubrick. Written by Stanley Kubrick, based on the novel by Anthony Burgess. Cinematography by John Alcott. Music by Walter Carlos. Released by Warner Broth-*

ers. *Distributed nontheatrically by Swank Motion Pictures. Starring Malcolm Mc-Dowell, Patrick Magee, Michael Bates, Warren Clark, John Clive, Adrienne Corri, Carl Duering, Paul Farrell, Clive Francis and Michael Gover.*

Stanley Kubrick's *A Clockwork Orange* is one of those movies that often sparks heated debates at parties. Some think it is a masterpiece, and others loathe it. There are strong arguments for both sides.

Set in England in the year 2000, the story centers on the anti-hero Alex (Malcolm McDowell), the charismatic leader of a ruthless youth gang called The Droogs. For laughs, he and his droogies terrorize innocent people, beating up elderly men and raping women. But one night, Alex is arrested when he inadvertently kills one of his victims. In prison he's used as guinea pig in an experimental brainwashing program to rehabilitate violent criminals, called the Ludvico Treatment. The treatment works, and Alex is transformed into a spineless man who is nauseated by the thought of sex or violence; he can't even listen to his once-favorite composer Beethoven without becoming seriously ill.

A Clockwork Orange is jammed full of outrageous humor, fast action and snappy dialogue. The film's visuals are extraordinary, and the performances are excellent, particularily McDowell's Alex. But there are two reasons why some viewers hate this film. First is the violence. The movie is filled with abhorrent, graphic violence, the kind that gives you nightmares. The second is that Kubrick tells this story completely from Alex's perspective. Even though he commits horrible crimes, he is the only sympathetic character in the whole film, and we sympathize with him. When Alex has to go through the Ludvico Treatment, it's tortuous, and the sight of Alex no longer able to have sex or listen to his beloved Beethoven is almost too much to bear.

Kubrick twists our moral sensibilities around so much in this film that it's easy to resent him for it. Yet no matter how manipulative, Kubrick and Alex force us to think about how far we are willing to permit personal freedom.

RATING: Although this film was originally rated X, Kubrick edited a few risqué scenes so the MPAA could give it an R for nudity, profanity, sex and plenty of violence.
AWARDS: 1971 New York Film Critics Award for Best Director (Stanley Kubrick); 1971 Academy Award nominations for Best Picture, Best Director (Kubrick), Best Screenplay Based on Material from Another Medium (Kubrick) and Best Film Editing (Bill Butler).
FILMNOTE: The pregnant wife of Anthony Burgess, the author of the novel A Clockwork Orange, *was raped and killed by AWOL American soldiers during a blackout in World War II London.*

CLOSELY WATCHED TRAINS
(Video, subtitled)

Coming-of-Age Comedy

Czechoslovakia	Czech
1966 89 Min.	B & W

CREDITS: Directed by Jiri Menzel. Written by Jiri Menzel and Bohumil Hrabal. Produced by Zdenek Oves. Cinematography by Jaromir Sofr. Music by Jiri Cvrcek. Released by Sigma Films. Distributed nontheatrically by Films Inc. Starring Vaclav Neckar, Jitka Bendova, Vladimir Valenta, Jiri Menzel, Vlastimi Brodsky and Josef Somr.

Jiri Menzel's *Closely Watched Trains* is a sometimes slapstick, sometimes serious film about the winding down of the German occupation of Czechoslovakia in World War II, as seen through the eyes of a young soldier. The film opens with Milos (Vaclav Neckar) looking off into space as his mother proudly adjusts his new military uniform. She tells him to live up to the family name, but Milos knows better, since in order to avoid fighting, his grandfather had hypnotized his commanding officer, and his father had finagled a desk job during the war.

Taking his first assignment, as a dispatcher in a train station, Milos runs into characters just as wacko as dad and gramps. His superior officer is a pigeon-loving simpleton, one co-worker is a sex fiend who tries to seduce every woman he encounters and another is a young train conductress who has her sights on Milos. Despite this lunacy, Milos also takes notice of some of the tragedies of war, watching the German army retreating in defeat and processing a train car full of corpses.

Closely Watched Trains was one of the first of the absurdist tragicomedies to emerge from Eastern Europe in the sixties. More like a series of anecdotes than a traditional narrative, the plot in this movie goes off in so many directions that it's hard to follow. But the characters are funny and interesting, and Menzel *(My Sweet Little Village)* skillfully captures Milos's struggle to come to terms with his painful shyness with women and his need to prove himself a man. In occupied and war-torn Czechoslovakia, his naïve character is also a fitting vehicle through which to observe his country's suffering.

RATING: No MPAA rating, with brief nudity, sex and violence.
AWARDS: 1966 Academy Award for Best Foreign Film.

THE CLOWNS
(Video, subtitled)

Documentary

Italy/France	French and Italian
1971	90 Min. Color

CREDITS: *Directed and produced by Federico Fellini. Written by Federico Fellini and Bernardino Zapponi. Cinematography by Dario di Palma. Distributed nontheatrically by Films Inc. Starring Pierre Etaix, Gustav Fratellini, Annie Fratellini, Anita Ekberg and Federico Fellini.*

The Clowns is Fellini's homage to the profession that affected him in his youth and greatly influenced his directing. The film begins as a young boy (presumably Fellini) becomes curious and frightened by the strange and wonderful people he sees when the circus comes to his town, especially the clowns. The scene then abruptly switches to a room where the real Fellini and his film crew are making a documentary about clowns. For the remainder of the film, we follow them as they travel around Italy and France interviewing famous clowns, leafing through their scrapbooks and screening footage of these performers in action. At the same time, Fellini horses around with his crew in an attempt to show that documentary filmmaking can be just as filled with slapstick as the lives of clowns.

The short-lived sequence of the boy at the circus is Fellini doing what he does best. We see with the boy an assortment of weird and magical characters, and the whole segment is set to the hauntingly beautiful music of Nino Rota. But when *The Clowns* turns into a documentary, the entertainment level of the film plummets. Fellini is overly concerned with the everyday routines and chores of his subjects, and unless you happen to be a great fan of clowns, the details given about their lives won't be interesting. Although it is fun to watch Fellini on film, the "life imitating art" slapstick Fellini stages isn't entertaining. The only truly successful scenes in *The Clowns* are the dramatizations and film clips of the master clowns in action. Unfortunately, there aren't enough to carry the film.

RATING: No MPAA rating, with nothing objectionable
AWARDS: One of the National Board of Review's 10 Best Foreign Films in 1971.
FILMNOTE: The Clowns was originally made for Italian TV. If it weren't for Fellini's popularity in the United States at the time, the film probably never would have been released in American theaters.

THE COCA-COLA KID
(Video)

Social Satire

Australia

1985   94 Min.   Color

CREDITS: Directed by Dusan Makavejev. Written by Frank Moorhouse, based on his short stories "The Americans," "Baby" and "The Electrical Experience." Produced by David Roe and Sylvie Le Clezio. Cinematography by Dean Semler. Music by William Motzing. Released and distributed nontheatrically by Cinecom. Starring Eric Roberts, Greta Scacchi, Bill Kerr, Chris Haywood, Kris McQuade, Max Giles, Tonny Barry, Paul Chubb, David Slingby and Tim Finn.

In The Coca-Cola Kid, Eric Roberts strays from the psycho roles he's known for (Star 80, Runaway Train) to play the comic character of Becker, a Coke troubleshooter from Atlanta sent to help increase Australia's sales.

The Australian Coke employees don't quite know how to handle this corporate dynamo from Georgia. For Becker, the soft drink, "God's miracle from America," represents a way of life. For the Australians, Coke is just a way to make a living. When Becker learns that not one bottle of Coke has been sold in a sparsely populated area of Australia called Anderson Valley, because it has a locally owned soft-drink company, he becomes obsessed with seeing that change. But T. George (Bill Kerr), Anderson Valley's powerful soft-drink mogul, is equally committed to keeping Becker and Coke out of his territory.

When Becker confronts T. George in the field, The Coca-Cola Kid begins to lose some of its fizz. Kerr plays T. George as an Australian version of Colonel Sanders. The caricature is overdone, and the humor in the scenes involving him doesn't quite work. But, for the most part, The Coca-Cola Kid is a lighthearted comedy populated by an assortment of hilariously offbeat characters, reminiscent of the films by Scottish director Bill Forsyth. Greta Scacchi (Heat and Dust) is particularly zany as Becker's secretary, more interested in getting him into bed than upholding the corporate honor. And her estranged husband (Max Giles) is a riot when he drops by the office to taunt her. Yugoslav director Dusan Makavejev (Montenegro) and screenwriter Frank Moorhouse cleverly use Coke as a symbol for U.S. imperialism and put Becker in situations that lend themselves to all kinds of pointed jabs at the American way. Roberts plays this cheerleader from the moral majority as intensely as he did the killer in Star 80.

RATING: R, with some nudity and sex.

COLONEL REDL
(Video, subtitled)

Docudrama

Hungary/W. Germany/Austria   German

1985   144 Min.   Color

CREDITS: Directed by Istvan Szabo. Written by Istvan Szabo and Peter Dobai. Produced by Manfred Durinok. Cinematography by Lajos Koltai. Music by Zolenko Tamassy and Johann Strauss. Released by Orion Classics. Distributed nontheatrically by Films Inc. Starring Klaus Maria Brandauer, Armin Mueller-Stahl, Gudrun Landgrebe, Jan Niklas, Hans-Christian Blech, Laszlo Mensaros and Andras Balint.

On May 25, 1913, Colonel Alfred Redl, one of the most powerful intelligence officers of the Austro-Hungarian Empire, was found shot to death in his Vienna home, a victim of self-inflicted gun wounds. Istvan Szabo's Colonel Redl is an attempt to recreate the events leading up to this surprising and controversial suicide.

Klaus Maria Brandauer stars as the infamous Redl, who rises from poverty through the ranks of the military and into the heart of the aristocracy. So driven for power that he has little concern for others who get hurt along the way, Redl becomes the victim of his own arrogance when an enemy betrays his secret homosexuality to the Russians. The Russians threaten to expose Redl unless he becomes a spy for them, and he reluctantly agrees. As he becomes involved in increasingly dangerous deceptions, Redl is driven past the point of madness and despair.

Since director Szabo and Brandauer worked together so brilliantly in *Mephisto,* you'd expect *Colonel Redl* to have the same intensity and emotional firepower. It doesn't. Brandauer gives a strong performance as the film's protagonist, particularly in the final moments of his breakdown. But for most of the film, his character is so repressed and emotionless that we feel detached from him, while the supporting characters are similarly stiff and lifeless. Szabo skillfully captures the garish atmosphere of the period; some of the film's sets and costumes are stunning, and the cinematography is impeccable. But nearly two and a half hours of this repressed power monger's rise through the military and the upper class is often more yawn producing than entertaining.

RATING: R for nudity and brief sex.
AWARDS: 1985 British Academy Award for Best Foreign Film; 1985 Academy Award nomination for Best Foreign Film.

COME BACK TO THE FIVE AND DIME, JIMMY DEAN, JIMMY DEAN
(Video)

Psychological Drama

U.S.A.

1982   110 Min.   Color

CREDITS: *Directed by Robert Altman. Written by Ed Graczyck, based on his play (which Altman produced off-Broadway). Produced by Scott Bushnell. Cinematography by Pierre Mignot. Released by Sandcastle 5/Viacom. Distributed nontheatrically by Cinecom. Starring Sandy Dennis, Cher,* Karen Black, Sudie Bond, Kathy Bates, Marta Heflin, Mark Patton, Caroline Aaron and Ruth Miller.

Robert Altman's *Jimmy Dean* is the first in his series of stage plays adapted to the screen. Based on Ed Graczyck's off-Broadway show, it's a bizarre tale of a twenty-year reunion of the members of a James Dean fan club founded in a small Texas town near where the movie *Giant* was filmed. Meeting in the old Woolworth's, they begin the afternoon by reminiscing about the good old days. Soon, though, the sweet nostalgia turns to bitterness, self-doubt and anger, as these misplaced souls reveal dark secrets about their lives, both back then and in the present.

The main members of the group are Joanne, Mona and Sissy. Joanne (Karen Black) isn't recognized at first by the others, yet she mysteriously seems to know all about them. Mona (Sandy Dennis) insists that she had Dean's child. Though nobody else can verify this claim, she flaunts her alleged affair with the screen legend like a gold medal. Then there is Sissy (Cher), who looks, acts and talks like a walking love machine but, by the day's end, reveals tremendous insecurities about her sexuality. Their reunion quickly degenerates into a biting satire on small-town mentality, hero-worship, sex and religion.

The acting in *Jimmy Dean* is excellent, with the three main characters giving particularly intense performances. Although there are some wildly funny moments, these women are more tragic than amusing. If you combine their over-the-edge personalities with the movie's claustrophobic setting, the five-and-dime store becomes a suffocating yet fascinating psycho ward from which neither these characters nor the audience can escape. Altman tries to overcome the staginess of this filmed play by using visual aids such as mirrors to shift in and out of time frames. But in the end, *Jimmy Dean, Jimmy Dean* never has a life of its own as a film.

RATING: PG, with mild profanity.
FILMNOTE: Jimmy Dean was shot in less than three weeks.

COMFORT AND JOY
(Video)

★ ★ ½

Screwball Comedy

Scotland

1984   90 Min.   Color

CREDITS: *Directed and written by Bill Forsyth. Produced by Davina Belling and Clive Parsons. Cinematography by Chris Menges. Music by Mark Knopfler (of Dire Straits). Released by Universal. Distributed nontheatrically by Swank Motion Pictures. Starring Bill Paterson, Eleanor David, C. P. Crogan, Alex Norton, Patrick Malahide, Rikki Fulton, Roberto Bernardi and George Rossi.*

Comfort and Joy is a comedy filled with delightfully whimsical characters, the trademark of Scottish director Bill Forsyth *(Local Hero)*. The hero is a popular Glasgow disc jockey named Dickie Bird (Bill Paterson) who tries to stay chipper despite the fact that his kleptomaniac girlfriend, Maddy (Eleanor David), has left him, taking everything in his apartment with her.

One day, while stopped at a light, Dickie spots an attractive young woman driving a Mr. Bunny ice cream truck. She smiles at him, so he follows her until she stops, and then he saunters over to buy a cone and make conversation. But before he can choose chocolate or vanilla, a group of hooded thugs attack the truck, smashing its windows with metal pipes. Dickie's curiosity is aroused by this incident, and with a little detective work he learns that Mr. Bunny and its competition, Mr. McCool, are locked in a life-and-death territorial struggle for the Glasgow ice cream market. Still entranced by the beautiful vendor, and hopeful that an involvement might ease his heartbreak, Dickie becomes the mediator between the two warring groups, and nearly loses his job and his sanity in the process.

Before the ice cream war becomes the focus of the film, *Comfort and Joy* has enough offbeat performances to keep it entertaining. Paterson is an affable character throughout the film, and the scenes of

him on the radio are particularly humorous. But once Mr. Bunny and Mr. McCool go at it full force, *Comfort and Joy*'s plot breaks down. The ice cream opponents take their feud to unbelievable extremes, and most of their characters are overplayed to the point of absurdity. Although some of the material in *Comfort and Joy* is humorous, it's ultimately just a staging ground for Forsyth to parade an assortment of wacky Scottish personalities.

RATING: *PG, with nothing objectionable.*

THE COMPANY OF WOLVES
(Video)

★ ★

Psychological Fantasy

England

1985   95 Min.   Color

CREDITS: *Directed by Neil Jordan. Written by Neil Jordan and Angela Carter, based on her short story. Produced by Stephen Wolley. Cinematography by Bryan Loftus. Art direction by Stuart Rose. Set design by Tony Common. Costume design by Elisabeth Waller. Special effects by Peter MacDonald, Alan Whibley and Ronald Holland. Makeup by Christopher Tucker. Released by Cannon Films. Distributed nontheatrically by Swank Motion Pictures. Starring Angela Lansbury, David Warner, Sarah Patterson, Micha Bergese, Stephen Rea, Tusse Silberg and Graham Crowden.*

Neil Jordan's *The Company of Wolves* gives Little Red Riding Hood an artsy, Freudian spin. Rosaleen (Sarah Patterson), a young, sexually repressed virgin, has a recurring nightmare about a man changing into a wolf. When she goes to visit her Granny (Angela Lansbury) in a dark and mysterious forest full of slithering snakes and dangerous animals, the raspy old matron fuels her fears by warning her about the dangers of men—particularly those whose eyebrows connect (the sign of a werewolf). But that doesn't stop Rosaleen from becoming strangely drawn to a handsome hunter (Micha Bergese) with suspiciously bushy eyebrows. Eventually, her nightmares and Granny's warnings become a terrifying reality.

Superstition and sexual symbolism lurk in *The Company of Wolves*'s sets and landscapes, since they are brimming with creeping spiders, giant mushrooms and the ever-present wolf howling in the background. The film's makeup and costumes are fantastic, and the transformation of the hunter into a wolf is an example of first-rate special-effects magic. But even though director Jordan (*Mona Lisa*) tantalizes us with all these interesting visuals and psychosexual undertones, it amounts to little more than a tease because Patterson's Rosaleen is so cold and unexpressive. It's hard to feel her fears or attraction to the strange, mystical world of her dreams and the forest, while the fantastic visuals only emphasize the lifelessness of her character. There also isn't much driving action in *The Company of Wolves*. Adapted from the twelve-page short story by Angela Carter, it seems that Jordan and Carter try too hard to stretch the thin plot into feature length.

RATING: R for very graphic images of men turning into wolves.

LES COMPÈRES
(Video, subtitled)

Caper Comedy

France	French
1983	92 Min.	Color

CREDITS: *Directed and written by Francis Veber. Produced by Jean-Claude Bourlat. Cinematography by Claude Agostini. Music by Vladimir Cosma. Released and distributed nontheatrically by European Classics. Starring Pierre Richard, Gérard Depardieu, Annie Duperey, Michel Aumont, Stephane Bierry and Jean-Jacques Scheffler.*

As *Les Compères* begins, Lucas (Gérard Depardieu) and Pignon (Pierre Richard) find themselves in an uncomfortable predicament. An old girlfriend, Christine (Annie Duperey), phones them out of the blue and announces to each that he is the father of her seventeen-year-old son, François. Christine is lying through her teeth, fully aware that her son's real father is her husband, Paul, but she has an important reason for carrying out this charade. François has run away from home, and Christine is convinced that her husband and the police aren't doing enough to locate him. In desperation, she lies to her old boyfriends to enlist them in the search. This situation becomes more absurd when Lucas and Pignon run into each other, and when they figure out they are both looking for the same François, they call Christine, who tells them that either of them might be his father. From this point on, they become sometimes reluctant, often belligerent partners in trying to find their "son."

The plot of *Les Compères* is predictable French farce stock. Few situations are believable, and Lucas and Pignon are naïve to the point of absurdity. But their characters give *Les Compères* a vitality despite its story. Depardieu and Richard are a rough-and-tumble comedy team, humorously clashing and colliding while following a trail of clues. Depardieu is the affable, self-confident straight man, while Richard plays the lovable buffoon. The two pull off enough original stunts in this film to sustain a certain comic energy, at least until the story lurches to a conclusion. When they finally find François and all three instantly become soulmates, *Les Compères* trades in its humorous edge for sentimental mush.

RATING: PG, with mild profanity and violence.

CONFIDENTIALLY YOURS

(Video, subtitled)

Mystery

France	French
1983 111 Min.	B&W

CREDITS: *Directed by François Truffaut. Written by François Truffaut, Suzanne Schiffman and Jean Aurel, based on the sixties pop novel* The Long Saturday Night *by Charles Williams. Produced by Armand Barbault. Cinematography by Nestor Almendros* (Days of Heaven). *Music by Georges Delerue. Released by Spectrafilms. Distributed nontheatrically by New Yorker Films. Starring Fanny Ardant, Jean-Louis Trintignant, Philippe Laudenbach, Caroline Sihol, Philippe Morier-Genoud, Xavier Saint Macary and Jean-Pierre Kaflon.*

François Truffaut's final film is an intriguing whodunnit that soars above typical murder mysteries because of a superb performance by his last lover, Fanny Ardant. It's also an affectionate homage to French film noir, a genre Truffaut himself helped to create twenty-five years earlier.

Confidentially Yours opens when a hunter is shot at point-blank range. It doesn't take the police long to find their suspect, a real estate broker named Vercel (Jean-Louis Trintignant of *The Conformist*) who was at the scene of the crime and left his fingerprints on the victim's car. The dead man turns out to be the lover of Vercel's wife, who is murdered a scene later. For the police it's an open-and-shut case, but Vercel pleads his innocence to his ex-secretary, Barbara (Fanny Ardant of *The Woman Next Door*), and she offers to help him find the real killer. Barbara may have been a lousy secretary, but she makes one hell of a detective. The rest of the film follows Barbara in action, as she assumes a number of identities and tries to sort out a labyrinth of clues. She goes to all this trouble for her irascible ex-boss because she is a mystery buff waiting for an opportunity to do some amateur sleuthing. What she didn't plan on was falling in love with Vercel.

Some reviewers criticized *Confidentially Yours* because Truffaut's characters don't have that existential edge found in many of his early films. But as an entertaining comedy and suspenseful Hitchcockesque murder mystery, this film is thoroughly satisfying from start to finish. While Truffaut always keeps the action moving, he never loses sight of the human element. The story line has a good balance of sex, humor and danger. Nestor Almendros's crisp black-and-white cinematography makes this movie beautiful to look at, and where you least expect it, offbeat characters and situations pop up to give extra texture. But it's Ardant's performance as Barbara that steals the show. She cons with such style and finesse, and is so attractive and engaging, that any excuse to have her on the screen in *Confidentially Yours* is just plain fun.

RATING: *PG for one brutal murder scene.*

THE CONFORMIST

(Video, dubbed)

Political Thriller

Italy	Italian
1970 112 Min.	Color

CREDITS: *Directed by Bernardo Bertolucci. Written by Bernardo Bertolucci, based on the novel by Alberto Moravia. Produced by Maurizio Lodi-Fe. Cinematography by Vittorio Storaro. Music by Georges Delerue. Released by Paramount. Distributed nontheatrically by Films Inc. Starring Jean-Louis Trintignant, Dominique Sanda, Stefania Sandrelli, Pierre Clementi, Pasquale Fortunato, Gastone Moschin, Enzo Tarascio and Jose Quaglio.*

Although Italian director Bernardo Bertolucci is best known to American audiences for *Last Tango in Paris, The Conformist* is a richer and more complex film. Set in Rome and Paris during Mussolini's Fascist regime, the protagonist of the story is Marcello (Jean-Louis Trintignant), a thirty-three-year-old Italian aristocrat whose response to a childhood marred by abusive parents and a traumatic homosexual experience is to conform—both personally and politically.

He marries Julia (Stefania Sandrelli), an unremarkable woman he doesn't love, and becomes an avid Fascist, even though, deep down, he hates Mussolini's politics. Marcello's choices come back to haunt him when he is ordered by the Party to assassinate his old philosophy professor, Quadri (Enzo Tarascio), a resistance fighter now living in Paris. When he and his new wife pay a visit to the unsuspecting professor, Marcello is surprised to discover that Quadri is married to Anna (Dominique Sanda), a beautiful woman Marcello fell in love with years before when she was a prostitute. Marcello's loyalty to his wife comes into question with his renewed lust for Anna, while his burgeoning subconscious morality conflicts with his obsession to carry out Party orders.

Visually, *The Conformist* is a masterwork. Shot from odd camera angles with strange lighting by cinematographer Vittorio Storaro, and accented with Georges Delerue's haunting soundtrack, several scenes in the film have the feeling of a Kafkaesque nightmare. The film's performances are intense and captivating, particularly Trintignant's. Bertolucci loads his plot with religious, sexual and political themes, and weaves so many conflicting emotions into Marcello that his character can be very intense. Although Marcello's torment is meant to symbolize Fascists all over Italy who blindly followed Mussolini, *The Conformist* remains a harrowing personal portrait of one man trapped by his subconscious.

RATING: *R, with violence and nudity.*
AWARDS: *One of the National Board of Review's 10 Best Foreign Films in 1970.*
WARNING: *Although the dubbing is decent, the quality of the film is still lessened on video.*

COUP DE GRACE
(Video, subtitled)

Political Drama

West Germany/France		German
1976	96 Min.	B&W

CREDITS: *Directed by Volker Schlondorff. Written by Genevieve Dormann, Margarethe von Trotta and Jutta Bruckner, based on the novel by Marguerite Yourcenar. Cinematography by Igor Luther. Music by Stanley Meyers. Released by Cinevista. Distributed nontheatrically by Almi Pictures. Starring Margarethe von Trotta, Matthias Habich, Valeska Gert, Rudiger Kirschstein, Matthieu Carriere and Marc Eyraud.*

Before the gifted Margarethe von Trotta began writing and directing her own films *(Sisters or the Balance of Happiness, Sheer Madness),* she collaborated with her husband, Volker Schlondorff *(The Tin Drum).* She both co-wrote the screenplay for and starred in his *Coup de Grace.*

In war-torn Latvia, at the end of World War I, the beautiful Sophie (von Trotta), her bizarre aunt (Valeska Gert) and her brother (Rudiger Kirschstein) take refuge in a rundown country estate that German troops have converted into a rebel retreat. Sophie is a breath of fresh air to these men—she tends their wounds and sings and dances for them. Although she secretly sympathizes with the Bolsheviks, politics aren't important to her until she becomes infatuated with the rebels' leader, Erich (Matthias Habich), a brooding, self-absorbed man consumed by anti-Communist politics. When Sophie realizes that Erich is more interested in her brother than he is in her, she takes revenge by betraying him to the enemy and then running off to join the Bolshevik army.

Most of the characters are so taciturn and their dialogue so spare that Sophie and her demented aunt are more than welcome in this picture. In the midst of bombings and death, hollow ideals and frustated love, both give life, passion and energy to every scene, creating characters you're not likely to forget. Director Schlondorff also does an excellent job creating the mood of post-war chaos. The film's cinematography is good, and the decaying country estate, gray weather and barren landscapes add to the atmosphere of this bleak time in Russian history. But even though *Coup de Grace* is intellectually challenging, its narrative touches upon too many different issues of politics, history, war and sex to realize any of them fully.

RATING: No MPAA rating, with violence.

COUP DE TORCHON (CLEAN SLATE)
(Video, subtitled)

Black Comedy

France		French
1981	128 Min.	Color

CREDITS: *Directed by Bertrand Tavernier. Written by Bertrand Tavernier and Jean Aurenche, based on the novel* Pop. 1280 *by Jim Thompson. Produced by Adolphe Viezzi and Henri Lassa. Cinematography by Pierre William Glenn. Music by Philippe Sarde. Released by Film de la Tour. Distributed nontheatrically by Films Inc. Starring Philippe Noiret, Isabelle Huppert, Guy Marchand, Jean-Pierre Marielle, Stephane Audran, Eddy Mitchell, Irene Skobline, Michel Beaune, Jean Champion and Victor Garrivier.*

Bertrand Tavernier's dark, existential version of this *Arsenic-and-Old-Lace*–like story is set in a downtrodden French colonial village in Africa in 1938. The film's central character is Lucien (Philippe Noiret), the town's gutless and drunken police official who ends up becoming everyone's dupe. His bitchy wife, for example, constantly insults him and then has an incestuous affair with her brother right before his eyes. His lover, Rose (Isabelle Huppert), berates him for not standing up to her abu-

sive husband (Guy Marchand), and two gangsters humiliate Lucien whenever they get the chance. But then the spineless Lucien accidentally kills a village lowlife. Suddenly he views himself as a Christlike figure who should do the town and himself a favor by killing off his enemies one by one. Nobody suspects he is responsible for this rash of murders because he was previously such a coward and, after all, he's the peace officer. Slowly, though, the kindly constable degenerates into lunacy.

The main problem with *Coup de Torchon* is its length. At over two hours long, it's slow going for some of the way, especially toward the end. But Noiret's performance as the bumbling executioner makes the film a success. With his week-old beard, weepy eyes and sardonically offhanded remarks, he looks and acts the part perfectly. Tavernier doesn't spare us any of the gruesome details of Lucien's murders, and instead of laughing at the victims for getting their due, we are disgusted at the brutality of Lucien's actions. Noiret nevertheless remains enormously sympathetic. The supporting cast in this film is also quite good, particularly Isabelle Huppert as Lucien's mistress and Guy Marchand as her abusive husband.

RATING: No MPAA rating, with nudity, sex, violence and profanity.
AWARDS: 1982 Academy Award nomination for Best Foreign Film.

COUSIN, COUSINE
(Video, subtitled)

Sex Farce

France		French
1976	95 Min.	Color

CREDITS: *Directed by Jean-Charles Tacchella. Written by Jean-Charles Tacchella and Daniele Thompson. Produced by Bertrand Javal. Cinematography by Georges Lendi. Music by Gerard Anfosso. Released by Gaumont. Distributed nontheatrically by Almi Pictures. Starring Marie-Christine*

Barrault, Victor Lanoux, Marie-France Pisier, Guy Marchand, Ginette Garcin, Sybil Maas and Jean Herbert.

The term *French sex farce* could have been invented for *Cousin, Cousine*, the story of Marthe (Marie-Christine Barrault) and Ludovic (Victor Lanoux), cousins by marriage, whose intimate friendship escalates into a torrid love affair as the rest of their relatives look on in dismay. The couple becomes a scandal because both are still married yet make no attempt to hide their fling. Still, their spouses aren't exactly victims, as they both have been less than faithful themselves. Furthermore, their respective children observe Marthe's and Ludovic's adultery with an uninhibited glee.

A surprise box office success in the United States, *Cousin, Cousine* is pure fluff. Most the film's humor comes from the kissing cousins' casual attitudes about sex. At first it's funny to observe their irreverently blatant affair and the outraged reaction of everyone around them. But after it's replayed a dozen times, the joke finally loses its punch. Lanoux and Barrault are appealing characters throughout the film though. It's refreshing that they aren't hot young sex symbols but adults in their mid-thirties, with bulging waistlines and world-weary senses of humor.

RATING: R for tasteful sex, nudity and language.
AWARDS: One of the National Board of Review's 5 Best Foreign Films in 1976; 1976 Academy Award nomination for Best Foreign Film and Best Screenplay Written Directly for the Screen (Jean-Charles Tacchella and Daniele Thompson).

CRIES AND WHISPERS
(Video, dubbed)

Psychological Drama

Sweden	Swedish
1973	106 Min.	Color

CREDITS: Directed, written and produced by Ingmar Bergman. Cinematography by Sven Nykvist. Music by Chopin and Bach. Released by New World Pictures. Distributed nontheatrically by Films Inc. Starring Harriet Andersson, Kari Sylwan, Liv Ullmann, Ingrid Thulin, Erland Josephson, Henning Moritzen and George Arlin.

Death and the meaning of religion are integral parts of Ingmar Bergman's films, but in *Cries and Whispers* he tackles the subjects head-on. Set in Sweden at the turn of the century, the focus of the story is Agnes (Harriet Andersson), a woman in her early thirties dying of cancer and in a great deal of pain. With Agnes in her last days is her loyal servant, Anna (Kari Sylwan), and two sisters, Karin (Ingrid Thulin) and Maria (Liv Ullmann). The specter of her death serves as a catharsis for the four women to reflect on their lives, the nature of death, and what kind of God would put them through so much suffering.

From flashbacks and their conversations, we learn, for example, that Agnes had an abusive childhood and now questions the very existence of God as she lays on her deathbed. Karin has so much underlying rage at men that she dreams constantly of castrating her husband, while Maria is tormented by guilt because she once had an affair that caused her husband to commit suicide. Only Agnes's servant, Anna, seems to be at peace with herself. She lost a child when she was a much younger woman and, unlike the others, can now accept death as a natural part of life.

With his usual intensity of purpose, Bergman leads us through a whole range of depressing emotions—agony, rage, fear, despair and guilt. There are some gruesome scenes, such as Karen's explicitly detailed castration fantasy, but also a few uplifting ones, such as a scene with the four women basking in the sun together. *Cries and Whispers* is a showpiece for the talents of Bergman's cinematographer, Sven Nykvist. His close-ups of these women's faces and long pans of the starkly furnished room in which Agnes lies in agony, her rasping breath filling our ears while her sisters and Anna stand by, are some of the most powerful work he has done to date. Although Anna is the only likable one of the bunch, all four characters are presented as so complex and full of emotions that if you don't have an anxiety attack first, these magnificent performances can't help but affect you deeply.

RATING: R for violence and brief nudity.
AWARDS: 1972 New York Film Critics Awards for Best Film, Best Actress (Liv Ullmann), Best Direction (Ingmar Bergman) and Best Screenwriting (Bergman); one of the National Board of Review's 10 Best Foreign Films in 1973; 1973 Academy Award for Best Cinematography (Sven Nykvist); 1973 Academy Award nominations for Best Picture, Best Director, Best Screenplay and Best Costume Design (Marik Vos).

CROSS CREEK

(Video)

Women's Drama

U.S.A.

1983　　　　122 Min.　　　　Color

CREDITS: *Directed by Martin Ritt. Written by Dalene Young, based on* Cross Creek *by Marjorie Kinnan Rawlings. Produced by Robert Radnitz. Cinematography by John Alonzo. Music by Leonard Rosenman. Released by Universal. Distributed nontheatrically by Swank Motion Pictures. Starring Mary Steenburgen, Rip Torn, Peter Coyote, Dana Hill, Alfre Woodard, Joanna Miles, Ike Eisenmann, Gary Guffey, Toni Hudson and Malcolm McDowell.*

Based on the life of Marjorie Kinnan Rawlings, *Cross Creek* is a touching yet overwrought drama of a young woman trying to discover herself and make it on her own in the wilderness.

The film is set in an isolated part of Florida in the 1930s. Marjorie (Mary Steenburgen) moves to a run-down orange farm to become a writer. It's not easy, what with fixing up the house, planting vegetables and fighting frost in her groves. But she elicits help from a poor black woman named Geechee (Alfre Woodard), whom she hires on as a domestic servant, and from Paul (Ike Eisenmann), a white moonshiner who tends her crops. Her neighbor, Marsh (Rip Torn), and his daughter, Ellie (Dana Hill), also drop by to give her advice, and Marjorie strikes up a remarkable friendship with Ellie. Although Marjorie will ask for help when she really needs it, she's a fiercely independent woman who won't tolerate men trying to protect her. When the charming and sensitive Norton (Peter Coyote), from a town near her farm, proposes to her, she's unwilling to sacrifice her autonomy, even if it means losing the man she has grown to love.

Cross Creek is like an old-fashioned Walt Disney adventure with a feminist twist. Steenburgen's character is believably strong-willed, but director Martin Ritt (*Norma Rae*) peppers her struggles with too many clichés, from dewy-eyed children and a mischievous yearling to po' folk struggling to survive. Leonard Rosenman's syrupy musical score adds to the film's sentimentality. Yet there's enough magnificent scenery and first-rate acting in *Cross Creek* to overlook its sappiness. Rip Torn gives a moving performance as Marjorie's explosive neighbor, Marsh, while Alfre Woodard earned a well-deserved Oscar nomination for her gutsy role as Marjorie's helper. It's because of the rich characterizations in *Cross Creek* that screenwriter Dalene Young's adaptation of Rawlings's book has the feel of a rich and descriptive novel—one that you get hooked on at first glance and don't want to put down until you've finished.

RATING: PG, with brief violence.
AWARDS: 1984 Academy Award nominations for Best Supporting Actor (Rip

Torn) and Best Supporting Actress (Alfre Woodard).

FILMNOTE: *Mary Steenburgen's real-life husband, actor Malcolm McDowell (A Clockwork Orange), has a brief cameo as Marjorie's editor Maxwell Perkins.*

CROSSOVER DREAMS
(Video, partially subtitled)

Musical Drama

U.S.A.	English and Spanish
1985	85 Min. Color

CREDITS: *Directed by Leon Ichaso. Written by Leon Ichaso, Manuel Arce and Ruben Blades. Produced by Manuel Arce. Cinematography by Claudio Chea. Music by Ruben Blades, Maurico Smith, Conjunto Libre, Andy and Jerry Gonzales and the Ballistic Kisses. Released by Crossover Films. Distributed nontheatrically by New Yorker Films. Starring Ruben Blades, Shawn Elliot, Tom Signorelli, Elizabeth Pena, Joel Diamond and Frank Robles.*

Salsa is upbeat Hispanic-American music that combines pop, mariachi and rock. In *Crossover Dreams,* one of the hottest salsa performers in the country today, Ruben Blades, plays Rudy, a popular Spanish Harlem singer who gets his big break when a sleazy gringo record producer signs him to a contract. Almost overnight, Rudy turns into an obnoxious success. He drops his best friend and trumpet player from his act, cheats on his beautiful girlfriend, and won't have anything to do with his old manager. Easy credit, cocaine, fancy cars and groupies take hold of Rudy's life. But when his record flops, his producer dumps him. Rudy is not only saddled with debts from some dangerous loan sharks, but his attempts to reclaim his old lover and friends turn into disaster.

If the plot of *Crossover Dreams* sounds familiar, that's because it's identical to dozens of other "rising star" movies. Rudy gets so drunk with money and fame that you know he's bound to crash sooner or later.

His demise happens too soon, so the scenes of an arrogant and then desperate Rudy drag on a little long to sustain our interest. But made with a mostly Hispanic cast and crew, and shot in New York, *Crossover Dreams* does have some authentic dialogue and humorous scenes scattered throughout. Although not perfect technically, director Leon Ichaso *(El Super)* and his cinematographer Claudio Chea team up to capture the glitter and neon of life in New York's fast lane. What really makes this film work, though, is Blades's music. He is so charismatic singing and strutting his stuff on stage, and his music is so rich with upbeat Afro-Cuban rhythms, that *Crossover Dreams* brings to life the enormous power of salsa music in the same way that *The Harder They Come* does for reggae.

RATING: *PG-13 for substance abuse, language and brief nudity.*

FILMNOTE: *There were actually two endings produced for* Crossover Dreams. *It was first shown at press screenings with an ending where Rudy gets killed, but the critical response was so negative that the producers released it at the theaters with a less tragic ending.*

CUTTER'S WAY
(Video)

Political Thriller

U.S.A.	
1981	109 Min. Color

CREDITS: *Directed by Ivan Passer. Written by Jeffrey Alan Fiskin, based on the novel* Cutter and Bone *by Newton Thornburg. Cinematography by Jordan Cronenweth. Music by Jack Nitzche. Released by MGM/UA. Distributed nontheatrically by Films Inc. Starring John Heard, Jeff Bridges, Lisa Eichhorn, Ann Dusenberry, Stephen Elliot, Arthur Rosenberg, Nina Van Pallandt and Patricia Donahue.*

When Alex Cutter (John Heard) comes home from the Vietnam war, he's lost an arm, a leg, an eye and many of his army buddies. Pointed sarcasm, cantankerous insults and explosive tantrums make up Alex's personality a good portion of the time, and he is particularly hard on his wife, Mo (Lisa Eichhorn), and his best friend, Richard (Jeff Bridges). Not that Richard and Mo are models of mental stability themselves. Mo mopes around the house all day in her bathrobe, feeling sorry for herself and drinking too much vodka, while Richard has a hard time dealing with responsibility of any kind. He spends his days roaming the beach, sleeping with married women for money and trying to put the make on Mo.

As if these three don't have enough problems, their lives become endangered when Richard witnesses J. J. Cord (Stephen Elliot), a wealthy and powerful Santa Barbara oilman, stuffing a local cheerleader's dismembered body into a garbage can. Richard and Mo don't want to get involved, but Alex becomes obsessed with bringing Cord to justice because he sees the industrialist as a symbol of the corrupt system responsible for sending him to Vietnam.

As a mystery, *Cutter's Way* leaves a lot to be desired. The actual moment Richard sees Cord get rid of the cheerleader's body happens so quickly it's hard to tell what's going on. The scanty evidence Alex and Richard come up with is slurred over in confusing conversations, and the criminal himself remains an enigma throughout the film. Fortunately, the interactions between these three walking wounded are often moving, and Bridges, Heard and Eichhorn each gives a commanding performance. Also, director Ivan Passer *(Creator)* gives this film a rich, noirish atmosphere. Although a Czech émigré, he perceptively captures the scars many Americans carried with them into the post-Vietnam era.

RATING: R *for violence, profanity, substance abuse and nudity.*
AWARDS: *Best Picture, Best Director, Best Actor (John Heard) and Best Screenplay (Jeffrey Alan Fiskin) awards at the 1981 Houston Film Festival.*
FILMNOTE: Cutter's Way *was originally released as* Cutter and Bone, *like Thornburg's book title, but MGM/UA didn't*

feel that the title had commercial appeal. They rereleased it as Cutter's Way *after its success at the 1981 Houston Film Festival.*

DANCE WITH A STRANGER
(Video)

  ½

Psychological Docudrama

England

1985   101 Min.   Color

CREDITS: *Directed by Michael Newell. Written by Shelagh Delaney. Produced by Roger Randall-Cutler. Cinematography by Peter Hannan. Released by Film Four International and 20th Century Fox. Distributed nontheatrically by The Samuel Goldwyn Company. Starring Miranda Richardson, Rupert Everett, Ian Holm, Tom Chadbon, Jane Bertish, Matthew Carroll, David Troughton, Paul Mooney, Stratford Johns, Joanne Whalley, Susan Kyd, Leslie Manvile and Sallie-Anne Field.*

In 1955, bar manager Ruth Ellis murdered her rich and handsome lover outside of his favorite pub and was convicted and hung within three weeks of the start of her trial. Ellis was the last woman executed in England. Though Michael Newell's *Dance with a Stranger* is an attempt to recreate the events leading up to one of the most notorious murder trials ever to hit the London tabloids, his movie isn't nearly as juicy as the real story was reported to be.

At the start of the film, Ruth (Miranda Richardson) and her pubescent son, Andy (Matthew Carroll), live with Desmond (Ian Holm), an older man who wants to be Ruth's lover. Desmond follows her around like a puppy with his tail between his legs, grateful for any scrap from her table. But Ruth is in love with David Blakely (Rupert Everett), a spoiled, aristocratic race-car driver who rapes her in alleys and beats her repeatedly, while shunning her at his high-society social functions because she's lower class. Ruth keeps coming back for more, all the while treating the loyal Desmond like trash. It's only when Ruth becomes pregnant with Blakely's child and he coldly rebuffs her that Ruth goes over the edge.

Using smoke-filled pubs and Desmond's suffocating apartment for much of the film's setting, director Newell does a skillful job creating a brooding, dark atmosphere in *Dance with a Stranger*. The acting is generally good, particularly Marilyn Monroe look-alike Richardson as the alcoholic Ruth, and Holm as her spineless older suitor. But little else about this film is out of the ordinary or well done. The sound is so poor that it's often difficult to understand the dialogue. The film's editing is jumpy, and the narrative is hard to follow. More important, the three main characters aren't developed enough to understand why they are so self-destructive and affected by each other in the first place. Newell makes them so unappealing and driven by their weaknesses that, in the end, the unfortunate fates of this demented trio seem perversely justified.

RATING: R for violence, sex and language FILMNOTE: A few years after his mother's hanging, Ellis's son in real life committed suicide.

DANCING IN THE DARK

(Video)

Psychological Drama

Canada

1986   98 Min.   Color

CREDITS: Directed by Leon Marr. Written by Leon Marr, based on the novel by Joan Barefoot. Produced by Anthony Kramreither. Cinematography by Vic Sarin. Music by Tom Berner and Kelly Hall. Released by New World Pictures. Starring Martha Henry, Neil Munro, Rosemary Dunsmore, Richard Monette, Elena Kudaba, Brenda Bazinet, Anne Butler and Vince Metcalfe.

Edna (Martha Henry) is a forty-year-old housewife who has no children, no interests and no friends. Her whole life revolves around her house chores, which she meticulously organizes, and her distant husband (Neil Munro), with whom she can barely communicate. One day she discovers her husband has been having an affair and she goes over the edge. When he comes home from work that night, she stabs him to death in her clean, well-lit kitchen and then calmly rinses the blade while her husband lies cold on the linoleum.

Dancing in the Dark attempts to explain the circumstances that drove Edna to her violent madness. We see her at the mental hospital where she has been committed, narrating her story while writing in her journal. Interspersed with flashbacks of Edna the housewife, reveling in the repetition of her daily routine, are scenes of Edna the mental patient, intently writing while refusing to feed or bathe herself. Meanwhile, the nurses and doctors cajole her into talking about her crime.

Edna's narration is the film's main problem. Her comments appear stilted and contrived, and her commentary mummifies the intensity of the powerful scenes in the early going of this movie. The other weak link in *Dancing in the Dark* is Edna's final dance—her breakthrough in the hospital. Although it's supposed to be a metaphor for feminist empowerment, this scene comes off as self-conscious and pretentious. But the events leading up to that final image are quite compelling. Martha Henry is riveting as Edna the "ideal wife" who not only finds herself trapped by a loveless marriage but also by her own stifling perfection. She is so thoroughly involved with her character that it's frighteningly real, difficult to watch, yet arresting at the same time. Director Leon Marr (in his first feature), with the help of his excellent cameraman Vic Sarin, does an outstanding job framing Edna's decline into madness with minimal, striking cinematography.

RATING: No MPAA rating, with violence.

DANGEROUS MOVES
(Video, dubbed)

★ ★ ½

Political Drama

Switzerland   French

1984   100 Min.   Color

CREDITS: *Directed and written by Richard Dembo. Produced by Arthur Cohen. Cinematography by Raoul Coutard. Music by Gabriel Yared and César Frank. Released by Spectrafilm. Starring Michel Piccoli, Alexandre Arbatt, Leslie Caron, Liv Ullmann, Daniel Olbrychski, Michel Aumont and Pierre Michael.*

The surprise winner of the 1984 Oscar for Best Foreign Film, *Dangerous Moves* is about a championship chess match between an ailing Russian master named Liebskind (Michel Piccoli) and Fromm (Alexandre Arbatt), a young Soviet expatriate now living in France. The elderly Liebskind suffers from heart disease but is so driven to win that he goes to Geneva for the match against his doctor's advice. Accompanying him is his devoted wife, Henia (Leslie Caron), and a whole entourage of Soviets. Fromm is the John McEnroe of chess—a handsome and ill-mannered superstar the press follows around asking why he defected and how he feels about his wife not being permitted to leave Russia. At the start of their twelve-game match, the two masters are neck and neck. Then each begins trying every dirty trick imaginable to ruin the other's concentration, including hiring hypnotists to distract his opponent and swiping good luck charms. Liebskind's advisers finally resort to flying in Fromm's mentally ill wife, Marina (Liv Ullmann), to fluster him.

With Marina's entry into the story, *Dangerous Moves* delves briefly into cold war politics, as her illness was brought on by her confinement in a Soviet mental hospital. There are other subplots concerning both Liebskind's wife and his doctor, but both come too late in the story to have much meaning. *Dangerous Moves* is really a film with a single concern—the players'

obsession with winning. They are so wrapped up in their superstitions and go to such immature extremes to foil each other's concentration that they both end up looking like children. Piccoli and Arbatt turn in excellent performances, and the sterile setting in Geneva is a perfect backdrop to highlight their insane competition. But because *Dangerous Moves* is so cerebral, the plot feels as stagnant as a chess match.

RATING: *No MPAA rating, with nothing objectionable.*
AWARDS: *1984 Academy Award for Best Foreign Film.*
WARNING: *Although the dubbing is decent, this film is so verbal the dubbing lessens the film's effect.*

DANTON
(Video, subtitled)

★ ★ ½

Historical Drama

France   French

1982   136 Min.   Color

CREDITS: *Directed by Andrzej Wajda. Written by Andrzej Wajda, Jean-Claude Carriere, Agnieszka Holland (the director of* Angry Harvest*), Jacek Gasirowoski and Boleslaw Michalek, based on the play* The Danton Affair *by Stanislawa Przybyszewska. Cinematography by Igor Luther. Music by Jean Prodromides. Set design by Allan Starski. Costume design by Yvonne Sassinot de Nesle. Released by Triumph Films. Distributed nontheatrically by Swank Motion Pictures. Starring Gérard Depardieu, Wojciech Pszoniak, Patrice Chereau, Angela Winkler, Boguslaw Linda, Roland Blanche, Anne Alvaro, Serge Merlin, Roger Planchon and Lucien Melki.*

Many filmmakers and novelists love to glorify the French Revolution, but in *Danton* Polish director Andrzej Wajda portrays the dirty side of the historic era. Loosely based on fact, the story dramatizes the vicious power struggle between two founding members of the Revolutionary Committee that overthrew Louis XVI.

Danton (Gérard Depardieu) is an impassioned and popular idealist who loves wine and women and hates the corruption of the post-Revolutionary government. Robespierre (Wojciech Pszoniak), the new government's leader, was a man of principles but is now preoccupied with preserving his power no matter what the cost. With bread lines and poverty spreading discontent throughout France, Robespierre realizes that the charismatic Danton is a serious threat and arrests him for treason when he hears that Danton has been plotting his demise. During the trial in which Danton faces the guillotine, each makes public accusations about how the other has betrayed the Revolution.

Although *Danton* is well acted and has gorgeous sets, it is basically a two-hour political/philosophical talkfest. All the rhetoric becomes tedious, especially because there's little background to explain why Danton and Robespierre both feel so strongly about their beliefs. The film's characters are also barely developed outside of the context of their politics. Danton's womanizing, for example, stretches the story unnecessarily while not adding much substance. Writer/director Andrzej Wajda *(Man of Marble, A Love in Germany),* a Polish filmmaker in exile, does effectively parallel the lost ideals of the French Revolution with those in his own country's recent political history. He also did his homework on French history, as much of the film's dialogue consists of well-informed and passionate orations on the Revolution and the Reign of Terror that followed.

RATING: PG, with mild sexual situations.
AWARDS: 1983 British Academy Award for Best Foreign Film; 1983 French Caesar for Best Director (Andrzej Wajda).
WARNING: The subtitles whiz by so fast in this film that you have to speed-read to catch them all.

DAY FOR NIGHT
(Video, dubbed)

Social Docudrama

France	French and English
1973	120 Min.	Color

CREDITS: Directed by François Truffaut. Written by François Truffaut, Suzanne Schiffman and Jean-Louis Richard. Produced by Marcel Berbert. Cinematography by Pierre-William Glenn. Music by Georges Delerue. Released by Columbia Pictures. Distributed nontheatrically by Swank Motion Pictures. Starring François Truffaut, Jacqueline Bisset, Jean-Pierre Leaud, Jean-Pierre Aumont, Valentina Cortese and Alexandra Stewart.

Although François Truffaut's *Day for Night* is a fictional narrative about filmmaking, it is also a whimsical autobiographical story about Truffaut's own experiences as a director.

Truffaut stars as Ferrand, the director of *I Want You to Meet Pamela,* a feature he is filming in Nice. It's a sappy romance about a newly married bride (Jacqueline Bisset) who falls in love with her father-in-law (Jean-Pierre Aumont). But the real story in *Day for Night* is the drama of producing a film and the personal lives of the actors and crew involved. Each player behind the scenes has his or her own set of problems, ranging from alcoholism to lovesickness to family troubles. The director has recurring nightmares, difficulties with nervous producers and, yes, he does shoot night scenes during the day (a common practice in film production).

Day for Night demystifies the art of filmmaking. We see stuntmen taking hard knocks, experience the tedious repetition of shooting and reshooting scenes, and witness the torment that actors' spouses and children have to endure during the production process. There are also fascinating moments of special-effects magic, and funny scenes in which the production seems to dissolve into utter chaos. But mostly, *Day for Night* is about the unique and often tragic relationships of the production's stars and crew. They are a diverse group of people who must live in close quarters and withstand countless pressures. Some of them are lovable and others insane, but by the end of *Day for Night,* we have gotten to know them all intimately. The performances are so convincing that it's hard to believe the actors and actresses aren't playing themselves in this film.

RATING: PG, with nothing objectionable.
AWARDS: *1973 Academy Award for Best Foreign Film; 1973 Academy Award nominations for Best Supporting Actress (Valentina Cortese), Best Director (François Truffaut) and Best Screenplay (Truffaut, Jean-Louis Richard, Suzanne Schiffman); 1973 New York Film Critics Awards for Best Picture, Best Director (Truffaut) and Best Supporting Actress (Cortese); 1973 British Academy Awards for Best Film, Best Supporting Actress (Cortese) and Best Direction (Truffaut).*
FILMNOTE: *Truffaut claimed that every event and character in* Day for Night *is based on actual events and characters he has come across as a filmmaker.*

DAYS OF HEAVEN
(Video)

Social Drama

U.S.A.

1978   95 Min.   Color

CREDITS: *Directed and written by Terrence Malick. Produced by Bert and Harold Schneider. Cinematography by Nestor Almendros and Haskell Wexler. Music by Ennio Morricone. Released by Paramount. Distributed nontheatrically by Films Inc. Starring Richard Gere, Brooke Adams, Sam Shepard, Linda Manz, Robert Wilke, Jackie Schultis, Stuart Margolin, Tim Scott, Gene Bell and Doug Kershaw.*

Watching *Days of Heaven* is like eating at a restaurant that has great atmosphere and service but only mediocre food. Every-

thing in Terrence Malick's film looks great and is well executed, but the film's content and characters aren't always satisfying.

The time is 1915, the place is the Texas panhandle. Bill (Richard Gere), his girlfriend Abbey (Brooke Adams), and his twelve-year-old sister, Linda (Linda Manz), are migrant workers who take jobs with a wealthy bachelor farmer (played by Sam Shepard, in his first movie role). For no apparent reason, Bill and Abbey pretend to be brother and sister instead of lovers, a deception that works out well for the farmer because he takes a fancy to Abbey. When Bill finds out that his boss is sick and may die soon, he encourages Abbey to respond to the farmer's advances so Abbey and the farmer can marry, and she can inherit his wealth when he kicks the bucket. What neither of them planned on is that she would fall in love with the farmer, and that he would discover Bill and Abbey's scam.

Days of Heaven is told through voiceovers by Bill's wisecracking sister, Linda. Although her wry comments can be entertaining, writer/director Malick leaves too many gaps in the rest of his characters. You get little, if any, information on Bill's, Abbey's or the farmer's pasts, and few explanations of their present actions as well. Several scenes lack any sort of traditional resolve, petering out or merely rambling into the next. Unfortunately, this fuzziness detaches us from the emotions the characters are trying to express.

But visually, *Days of Heaven* is a masterpiece. With the help of two noted cinematographers, Nestor Almendros and Haskell Wexler, Malick captures the enormous power of golden wheat fields shimmering in a light breeze and beautiful 180-degree skies of the plains of the Texas panhandle. The contrast of the tiny downtrodden figures working in immense, strangely lit landscapes brilliantly demonstrates the rootlessness and alienation that this film embraces as its theme.

RATING: PG, with nothing objectionable.
AWARDS: *1978 Academy Award for Best Cinematography (Nestor Almendros); 1978 Academy Award nominations for Best Costume Design (Patricia Norris), Best Original Score (Ennio Morricone) and Best Sound (John Wilkinson, Robert*

W. Glass, John Reitz and Barry Thomas); 1979 National Board of Review's award for Best Film; Mise-en-Scene (Best Cinematography) Award at the 1979 Cannes Film Festival; 1979 British Academy Award for Best Original Film Music (Morricone).

FILMNOTE: Although the Texas setting is integral to its story, Days of Heaven was actually shot in Canada. Malick wanted to capture in the film that "very weird light" of the long days of a Canadian summer.

THE DEAD
(Video)

Literary Drama

U.S.A.

1987   83 Min.   Color

CREDITS: Directed by John Huston. Written by Tony Huston (John's son), based on the short story by James Joyce. Cinematography by Fred Murphy. Music by Alex North. Released by Vestron Pictures. Distributed nontheatrically by Kino International. Starring Anjelica Huston (John's daughter), Donal McCann, Helena Carroll, Cathleen Delaney, Donal Donnelly and Marie Kean.

Director John Huston always had a taste for literary adaptations (from The Maltese Falcon to Prizzi's Honor and many in between), so it's no surprise that his last film is translated from fiction. What is startling is that even though James Joyce's story "The Dead" is mostly one character's internal monologue, in a very subtle way, Huston actually makes it work as a film.

The Dead takes place entirely at a dinner party hosted by two elderly sisters, Aunt Julia (Cathleen Delaney) and Aunt Kate (Helena Carroll) on a cold, winter night in Dublin, Ireland. Very little happens throughout the course of the evening. One guest (Donal Donnelly) frets over a toast he will make during dinner. Another drinks himself into a rambling stupor to the con-

sternation of his mother and his dinner companions. Aunt Julia, once a great performer, sings in a voice that is a mere shell of its former greatness and then embarrassingly mocks herself. No one seems to talk about anything important, instead swapping anecdotes about great and now-dead singers. Only after the party, when two of the guests (Anjelica Huston and Donal McCann) return to their hotel room, does it become clear that this evening will have tragic repercussions.

The catchword for The Dead is subtle. The very ill Huston (his emphysema was so bad the production often had to be delayed) took a gamble in structuring the film very similarly to Joyce's story, hoping the interplay among his sharply defined characters would sustain a viewer's interest until the film's powerful climax. It doesn't always work; he does lose our attention during quiet stretches by not revealing what's at stake until the very end. But the gamble ultimately pays off because the actors, particularly Anjelica Huston, are so good at establishing their characters' relationships with one another without the benefit of explicit motivation. Huston, with the help of his cinematographer Fred Murphy, also keeps us engaged with first-rate camerawork. He makes even a small townhouse seem open and dynamic, while his shots of a snow-covered Dublin in the film's final scenes will send chills up your spine.

RATING: PG, with nothing objectionable.

DEATH IN VENICE
(Video, dubbed)

Psychological Drama

Italy/France   Italian and English

1971   130 Min.   Color

CREDITS: Directed and produced by Luchino Visconti. Written by Luchino Visconti and Nicola Badalucco, based on the novella by Thomas Mann. Cinematography by Pasquale de Santis. Art direction by Ferdinando Scarfiotti. Set design by Nedo Az-

zini. Music by Gustav Mahler. Released by Warner Brothers. Distributed nontheatrically by Swank Motion Pictures. Starring Dirk Bogarde, Mark Burns, Marisa Berenson, Bjorn Andresen, Silvana Mangano, Romolo Valli, Nora Ricci, Carol Andre, Masha Predit, Leslie French and Franco Fabrizi.

Luchino Visconti's adaptation of Thomas Mann's novella is a bleak yet powerful story of an aging man desperately trying to regain his youth.

The film is set in the late 1800s when cholera was breaking out all over Europe. Gustav (Dirk Bogarde) is a German composer in poor mental and physical health who goes to Venice for a rest cure. At first, Gustav shows nothing but disdain for the frivolousness of the other guests at his resort hotel. He spends his days writing and sunbathing alone, and when others approach him, he shuns their advances. But then he notices Tadzio (Bjorn Andresen), a beautiful, blond prepubescent boy who is at the hotel vacationing with his family.

Gustav becomes fascinated with the androgynous-looking boy—a fascination that quickly turns into infatuation and then obsession. He follows Tadzio through the streets of Venice, on the beach and around the hotel. He wants the boy more than he has wanted anything else his whole life and clings to the hope that the boy will notice him. He even pathetically tries to look and dress like a young man, yet Gustav knows very well he'll never be able to regain his youth or possess the boy.

Death in Venice is simply too drawn out to be successful. At over two hours, with little dialogue or action, much of what takes place on the screen begins to resemble a still life of a bowl of fruit—beautiful to look at, yet stiff and two-dimensional. Bogarde gives a haunting performance as the composer clinging to a thread of self-delusion. Although the character is distasteful and irritable, his shield is so transparent that it's hard not to feel for him. Director Luchino Visconti *(The Damned)* and his crew masterfully construct the film's visuals to accentuate Gustav's torment, and to contrast the frolicking rich with the rest of the population of Venice, which is devastated by disease and poverty.

RATING: PG, with nothing objectionable.
AWARDS: Grand Prize at the 1971 Cannes Film Festival; 1971 British Academy Awards for Best Cinematography (Pasquale de Santis), Best Art Direction (Ferdinando Scarfiotti), Best Costume Design (Piere Tosi) and Best Soundtrack (Guiseppe Muratoni); one of the National Board of Review's 10 Best Foreign Films in 1971; 1971 Academy Award nomination for Best Costume Design (Tosi).

DEATHWATCH
(Video)

Political Science Fiction

France/West Germany		English
1980	128 Min.	Color

CREDITS: Directed by Bertrand Tavernier. Written by Bertrand Tavernier and David Rayfiel, based on the novel The Continuous Katherine Mortenhoe *by David Compton. Produced by Gabriel Boustiani and Janine Rubeiz. Cinematography by Pierre-William Glenn. Released by Selta Films—Little Bear. Distributed nontheatrically by Joseph Green Pictures. Starring Romy Schneider, Harvey Keitel, Harry Dean Stanton, Therese Liotard, Bernhard Wicki and Max von Sydow.*

Bertrand Tavernier's first film in English imagines a future world whose inhabitants are ruthlessly voyeuristic about the dying. In industrial Scotland of the not-too-distant future, dying becomes "the new pornography," in the words of Vincent Ferriman (Harry Dean Stanton). Ferriman, a director of the state communications network, NTV, is anxious to take advantage of the public's morbid fascination with the mechanics of death by creating a show that will follow a terminally ill "star" from diagnosis to the final stages of life.

The show's name is "Deathwatch," and the subject Ferriman finds is Katherine (Romy Schneider), a beautiful authoress who is stricken with cancer and has only two months to live. At first, she accepts the celebrity status and the $600,000 Ferriman wants to give her for her cooperation. But the money and notoriety quickly lose their importance for Katherine. One day she skips out on her NTV guard and disappears into the countryside.

Ferriman sends his secret weapon, Roddy (Harvey Keitel), after her. Roddy is a lonely and broken man who allows NTV scientists to plant a light-sensitive camera in his brain, to be used to film Katherine secretly. He finds and befriends the vulnerable woman, and while they travel together throughout the countryside, Roddy surreptitiously films material that is broadcast to a waiting nation each night. Unaware that her last stages of life are becoming a smash hit, Katherine becomes more dependent on her new friend, while Roddy realizes that he is betraying Katherine and stripping her of her dignity.

Deathwatch is a prophetic vision of how our media-enamored society could evolve to the point that "everything is of interest, but nothing matters." Tavernier *(Round Midnight, Coup de Torchon)* plays his story both ways; we, like the "Deathwatch" audience, morbidly follow the progress of Katherine's illness, while becoming engrossed in the growing relationship between her and Roddy. Tavernier keeps the high-tech elements of this science fiction story to a minimum, underscoring how close this distorted future is to our present. All of the performances are first-rate, particularly Romy Schneider. Soon to die of cancer herself, Schneider turns in a gutsy performance as a woman who is willing to fight for her dignity with every last ounce of her strength in a society that wants to exploit her.

RATING: R for profanity and sexual situations.

THE DECLINE OF THE AMERICAN EMPIRE
(Video, subtitled)

Social Drama

Canada		French
1986	95 Min.	Color

CREDITS: Directed and written by Denys Arcand. Produced by Rene Malo and Roger Frappier. Cinematography by Guy Dufaux. Music by François Dompierre. Released by Cineplex Odeon. Distributed nontheatrically by Films Inc. Starring Dominique Michel, Dorothee Berryman, Louise Portal, Genevieve Rioux, Pierre Curzi, Remy Girard, Yves Jacques, Daniel Briere and Gabriel Arcand.

Touted as a *Big Chill* for intellectuals, *Decline* is about four men and four women who get together for a vacation at a lake in Canada. All but one are either history professors or students at a Quebec university, and most have secretly slept with each other's partners or wives.

The film starts out lighthearted and frivolous. The women go to a health club to work out while the men spend the day preparing an elaborate meal for dinner. The conversations at both locations are humorous and intimate, the women revealing their feelings about men in general and their partners in particular, while the men brag about their sexual exploits. These heart-to-heart talks are quite a buildup for dinner. The evening explodes with waves of anger, jealousy and betrayal. But there is also a great deal of affection and respect among the friends around the dinner table, as they reflect on the state of their lives.

All the performances in *Decline* are convincing, but none of them stand out above the rest. The script is written so that each character takes a turn opening up, and flashbacks to the actual events illustrating their conversations spice up the talking. Director Denys Arcand wisely adds these flashbacks to break up all the intellectualizing, but it doesn't always help. Parts of

Decline are still too verbose, but many scenes work extremely well, sensitively bringing up feminism, aging and sexual preference. By the movie's end, you have a strong sense of who these people are, their personal dreams and failures, and what is now important in their lives.

RATING: R, with brief nudity and sex
AWARDS: 1986 Academy Award nomination for Best Foreign Film.

DECLINE OF WESTERN CIVILIZATION

(Video)

  ½

Rock Documentary

U.S.A.

1981   100 Min.   Color/B&W

CREDITS: *Directed and written by Penelope Spheeris. Produced by Penelope Spheeris, Jeffrey Prettyman and Gordon Brown. Cinematography by Steve Conant. Released by Spheeris Productions. Distributed nontheatrically by Corinth Films. Starring Lee Ving, Darby Cash, Alice Bag Band, Black Flag, Catholic Discipline, Circle Jerks, Fear, Germs and X.*

A chronicle of L.A.'s hard-core punk music scene in the early 1980s, *Decline of Western Civilization* is aptly titled. It is a morbid record of a violent, nearly valueless culture.

Director Penelope Spheeris produced Albert Brooks's "Saturday Night Live" shorts and his film *Real Life* before she went on to make this, her first feature. In it she follows several bands, including club circuit stars X, Fear, and The Circle Jerks, as well as lesser-known groups such as The Germs, Black Flag, Alice Bag Band, and Catholic Discipline. Although the level of notoriety varies, the musicians all share anarchism and rage, both on- and off-stage. For instance, The Germs' lead singer, Darby Crash (who died of a drug overdose before the film was released), picks fights

with his fans and ends up finishing most of his sets battered and bloody. Another group, Fear, aggressively insults their audience, spitting and calling them "fags from Frisco" until the crowd charges the stage. Spheeris also interviews a few teen fans, journalists and club owners about the punk craze, but these people offer few explanations for the violent subculture of which they are a part.

Certain segments of *Decline* are as entertaining as they are shocking. When Crash and his girlfriend proudly describe posing for pictures with a corpse, it's absurdly funny and disturbing. In another instance, Lee Ving, the lead singer of Fear (who went on to play supporting roles in films such as *Clue*), is actually very clever at taunting his audience into a fury. But these moments aren't enough to carry the film through the earsplitting music of bands such as Catholic Discipline, who drone on endlessly with little to say and even less talent. And though *Decline* is definitely the best documentary to date on the punk music scene, it suffers because director Spheeris doesn't develop enough of a point of view, refusing to delve into her subjects' pasts and avoiding personal questions in the film's interviews. Even if we are meant to take the nihilistic musings of these musicians seriously, their self-importance is laughable and never questioned.

RATING: *No MPAA rating, with substance abuse, violence and profanity.*
WARNING: *The lyrics to the film's songs are difficult to understand. For the worst, though, Spheeris has provided helpful subtitles.*
FILMNOTE: Decline of Western Civilization *was reportedly made for under $100,000, an astoundingly low figure considering the quality of the sound and visuals.*

DERSU UZALA
(Video, subtitled)

Wilderness Adventure

Japan/Russia   Russian

1975   140 Min.   Color

CREDITS: *Directed by Akira Kurosawa. Written by Kurosawa and Yuri Nagibin, based on the journals of Vladimir Arseniev. Cinematography by Asakadru Nakai, Fyodor Dobronavov and Yuri Gantman. Released by Toho and Mosfilm. Distributed nontheatrically by Films Inc. Starring Maxim Munzuk and Yuri Solomin.*

Directed by Akira Kurosawa and filmed in the Soviet Union with an entirely Russian cast, *Dersu Uzala* begins in 1902 Russia when Captain Arseniev (Yuri Solomin) and his men are sent to Siberia to draw maps of the wilderness. In their travels, they meet a gentle little Mongol named Dersu Uzala (Maxim Munzuk) hunting for gold. At first they don't know what to make of this strange character. But when the captain hires Dersu as their guide and he is able to read animal tracks and sense impending danger, the captain and his men begin to develop great respect for him. Eventually Dersu teaches them that living in harmony with nature is the only way to be at peace with oneself, a lesson the captain remembers well when he goes back to civilization. Five years later, the captain returns to Siberia to find old Dersu losing his sight and having a hard time surviving on his own. He convinces Dersu to come back with him to his home in the city, where he becomes a grandfatherly sage to the captain's wife and son. But as you might imagine, city life is difficult for Dersu.

The first Japanese-Russian co-production, *Dersu Uzala* would have made a wonderful hour-long children's adventure, but it's too simple and slowly paced to be a successful two-and-a-half-hour epic. Dersu and the captain are unusual and interesting characters, but often several minutes pass between their short lines of dialogue. Although there are some frightening and

haunting scenes of man battling the forces of nature, most of *Dersu Uzala* is filled with beautiful shots of the mysterious Siberian wilderness. The cinematography is extremely powerful, a Kurosawa trademark that makes this film worth the effort.

RATING: *No MPAA rating, with violence toward animals.*
WARNING: *Because the visuals are so important in* Dersu Uzala, *the quality of the film is decreased on video.*
AWARDS: *1975 Academy Award for Best Foreign Film.*

DESERT BLOOM
(Video)

Coming-of-Age Drama

U.S.A.

1986   104 Min.   Color

CREDITS: *Directed by Eugene Corr. Written by Eugene Corr, based on a story by Linda Remy and Corr. Produced by Michael Hausman. Cinematography by Reynaldo Villabos. Music by Brad Fiedel. Released by Columbia Pictures. Distributed nontheatrically by Swank Motion Pictures. Starring Jon Voight, Annabeth Gish, JoBeth Williams, Ellen Barkin and Allen Garfield.*

Desert Bloom is the story of a thirteen-year-old girl growing up in Las Vegas in 1950, during the height of the Atomic Age. In the film's opening scene, Rose (Annabeth Gish) sums up her outlook on life: "I love movies, books, Wonder Woman and grandmother, in that order. But real life is another story." The reason for her pessimism is her stepfather, Jack (Jon Voight), a World War II veteran with deep mental scars. He's now a violent alcoholic her mother (JoBeth Williams) and younger sisters merely tolerate. But Rose refuses to take his abuse, and everything comes to a head when she catches Jack and her favorite Aunt Starr (Ellen Barkin) smooching during an afternoon of drinking. This domestic drama is set against the backdrop of an impending nuclear test the government is launching near Las Vegas, complete with duck-and-cover drills at Rose's school and protective glasses being handed out to the citizens of Las Vegas so that they can watch the explosion.

Desert Bloom is a movie full of wonderful moments, but the sum isn't quite as strong as its individual parts. One of the main problems is its deliberate pacing. Director Eugene Corr's view of the fifties is almost too realistic: Certain scenes seem as lifeless as the era that frames them. Also, the issues concerning the looming nuclear test, which the film so promisingly raised in the beginning, are disappointingly slurred over by the end.

Nevertheless, *Desert Bloom* is an unusual coming-of-age story. It not only realistically depicts a teenager struggling with puberty and an alcoholic parent, but also attempts to show her in the context of this social and political era. Voight gives a tremendous performance as a tortured drunk, and Gish is a complex and sensitive thirteen-year-old every moment she is on the screen. Shot mainly in Utah and Nevada, the film's cinematography is also magnificent, and the period dress and decor are well rendered.

RATING: PG, *with nothing objectionable.*
FILMNOTE: Desert Bloom *is the first feature released from Robert Redford's Sundance Institute.*

DESERT HEARTS

(Video)

★ ★ ½

Lesbian Romance

U.S.A.

1986   91 Min.   Color

CREDITS: *Directed and produced by Donna Deitch. Written by Natalie Cooper, based on the novel* Desert of the Heart *by Jane Rule. Cinematography by Robert Elswit. Released and distributed nontheatrically by The Samuel Goldwyn Company.*

Starring *Helen Shaver, Patricia Charbonneau, Audra Lindley, Andra Akers, Dean Butler, Jeffrey Tambor, Gwenn Wells and James Staley.*

In the fifties, a "quickie" divorce meant going to Nevada for a minimum of six weeks to establish temporary residency. When Vivian Bell (Helen Shaver), a thirty-five-year-old English professor from New York, stays on a dude ranch outside of Reno to do just that, she also finds love and sexual fulfillment for the first time in her life—with a woman.

The other woman is Cay Rivers (Patricia Charbonneau in her first film role), a sexy twenty-five-year-old casino waitress who loves fast cars, loud music and attractive women. She wins Vivian over by taking her horseback riding and buying her studded cowboy shirts. When they finally make love, it is the best sexual experience in Vivian's life. But Vivian also fears that her reputation will be tarnished by the relationship. When they are found out by the ranch's whiskey-drinking proprietress, Vivian is ousted from the ranch.

Although made for less than a million dollars, *Desert Hearts* is rich with well-shot scenes of neon-lit casinos and arid landscapes. Director Donna Deitch, fresh from UCLA Film School, makes an honest attempt to portray the most important issues surrounding lesbian relationships, in some ways more authentically than any American film to date. The lovemaking scenes in particular are sexy and very convincing. But it's obvious that *Desert Hearts* is Donna Deitch's first feature. The country-girl-meets-sophisticated-woman theme is overplayed, as are the scenes of Cay and Vivian discussing ambition and love. Vivian and Cay are types and not real people, and ultimately their characters lack the intensity to be engaging.

RATING: R *for explicit sex and mild profanity.*
AWARDS: *Bronze Leopard for Best Actress (Helen Shaver) at the 1985 Locarno Film Festival.*

DESPAIR
(Video)

World War II Drama

West Germany   English

1979   119 Min.   Color

CREDITS: *Directed by Rainer Werner Fassbinder. Written by Tom Stoppard, based on the novel by Vladimir Nabokov. Produced by Peter Marthesheimer. Cinematography by Michael Ballhaus. Music by Peer Rabin. Released by Swan Diffusion. Distributed nontheatrically by New Line Cinema. Starring Dirk Bogarde, Andrea Ferreol, Volker Spengler, Klaus Lowitsch, Alexander Allerson, Bernhard Wicki, Peter Kern, Gottfried John and Roger Fritz.*

With Rainer Werner Fassbinder's direction and Tom Stoppard's screenplay adaptation of a novel by Vladimir Nabokov, *Despair* (Fassbinder's thirty-second feature and his only film in English) is the collaboration of three brilliant, if slightly twisted, minds.

The film's setting is Berlin right before the start of World War II. The American stock market has crashed, Jewish shops are being vandalized and the National Socialists are firmly in power. Smack in the middle of these tumultuous times lives Herman (Dirk Bogarde), a candy manufacturer who is oblivious to the bedlam around him, ignoring politics in search of the perfect chocolate bar. He wears blinders at home, too, where his dim-witted, voluptuous wife (Andrea Ferreol) carries on a hardly clandestine affair with her cousin. As both his business and personal affairs deteriorate, so does Herman's mental health. He begins to be haunted by frightening hallucinations that drive him to the edge of madness. Eventually, Herman devises a plan to involve an unsuspecting bum in a plot that will allow him to escape from it all and start his life over with a new identity.

As in many of Fassbinder's other films, *Despair*'s melodramatic story acts as a metaphor—this time for the moral decline of the German bourgeoisie, which allowed Hitler to gain power. "I don't think," Herman says as his friends discuss politics, "I just insure my life." Bogarde's Herman is the perfect symbol of European decay. The screen is often entirely filled with Herman's intense, rigid face, and much of the film is shot through glass partitions that highlight Herman's alienation from himself and others. *Despair*'s off-kilter classical soundtrack and unusual camera angles further enhance this dark mood. Although Bogarde is outstanding as the sullen, cerebral chocolatier, his emotions are often buried in a wall of atmosphere that it takes some patience to dig through. But once you do, the political and personal issues his character touches upon make it well worth the effort.

RATING: *No MPAA rating, with nudity and violence.*

DESPERATELY SEEKING SUSAN
(Video)

Caper Comedy

U.S.A.

1985   104 Min.   Color

CREDITS: *Directed by Susan Seidelman. Written by Leora Barish. Produced by Sarah Pilsbury and Midge Sanford. Cinematography by Edward Lachman. Music by Thomas Newman and Madonna. Edited by Andrew Mondshein. Released by Orion. Distributed nontheatrically by Films Inc. Starring Rosanna Arquette, Madonna, Aidan Quinn, Mark Blum, Robert Joy, Laurie Metcalf, Anna Levine, Will Patton and Anne Carlisle.*

Ever find yourself scanning the personals looking for that one special person? In *Desperately Seeking Susan,* Roberta (Rosanna Arquette) does just that. She's a bored New Jersey housewife who goes to the beauty parlor once a week, cooks with the help of a Julia Child video cassette and religiously reads the personals looking for the excitement she lacks in her own life. One day her curiosity gets the best of her. Especially fascinated by Susan (Madonna) and Jimmy (Robert Joy), two lovers who send messages to each other in the personals, Roberta spies on one of their scheduled rendezvous, accidentally gets a bump on the head and, through a series of mishaps, ends up assuming Susan's identity and experiencing her world of sleazy bars, hustling, promiscuity, drugs and murder.

Desperately Seeking Susan is a suspenseful mystery and a hilarious farce. It pokes fun at chauvinism, punks, casual sex and the good life with an assortment of Lower East Side and New Jersey suburban stereotypes. Thomas Newman and Madonna's soundtrack is upbeat, the editing by Andrew Mondshein is fast-paced and all the performances from its ensemble of character actors are quite strong. But it's Madonna in her acting debut who steals the show. She cons with such style and finesse that it's disappointing whenever she leaves the screen. The only problem with the film is that the coincidences in the plot pile up a little too conveniently, and some are hard to swallow. But for the most part, *Desperately Seeking Susan* is a good mix of scary fun and sharp satire—the kind of film with one-liners you'll remember long after you watch it.

RATING: *PG-13 for brief nudity, mild profanity and marijuana smoking.*
AWARDS: *1985 British Academy Award for Best Supporting Actress (Rosanna Arquette).*

LES DIABOLIQUES
(Video, subtitled)

Film Noir

France		French
1954	110 Min.	B&W

CREDITS: *Directed and produced by Henri-Georges Clouzot. Written by Henri-Georges Clouzot, Jerome Geronimi, Frederic Grendel and René Masson, based on the novel* The Woman Who Was No More *by Pierre Boileau and Thomas Narcejac. Cinematography by Armand Thirard. Music by George Van Parys. Released by Vera Films. Distributed nontheatrically by Corinth Films, Kit Parker Films, Tamarelle Films and Films Inc., among others. Starring Simone Signoret, Vera Clouzot, Paul Meurisse, Charles Vanel, Jean Brochard, Noel Roquevert, Georges Chamarat and Michael Serrault.*

For pure nail-biting suspense, Henri-Georges Clouzot's *Les Diaboliques* ranks right up there with the best of Hitchcock. The story is set in a dilapidated French boarding school run by a tyrannical headmaster named Michel (Paul Meurisse). Michel terrorizes his pupils, as well as his weak-hearted wife, Christina (the director's real-life spouse, Vera Clouzot), and his ex-mistress, Nicole (Simone Signoret), who teaches at the school. Finally, Nicole and Christina can't take his torment anymore and devise a plan to drown him in a bathtub and leave him floating in the boarding school's pool to disguise the death as an accident. Everything goes as planned, until no one notices the body in the leaf-filled pool, and then the corpse suddenly vanishes. Needless to say, the mysterious disappearance is tough on Christina's ticker.

Although Clouzot *(Wages of Fear)* keeps us riveted up to *Les Diaboliques*'s final scene, unlike a typical Hitchcock, there's no dashing hero, beautiful seductress or clever sleuth. The main characters in *Les Diaboliques* are darker and more sinister. Michel is despicable from the moment he's introduced, but Nicole is also cold and calculating, and Christina, the only seemingly warm character, turns out to be capable of committing a ruthless murder. All of the acting is outstanding, with Signoret and Meurisse giving particularly intense performances. Clouzot very skillfully handles the film's lighting, sets and camera angles to accentuate the ominous tone of the narrative.

RATING: *No MPAA rating, with nothing objectionable.*
AWARDS: *1955 New York Film Critics Award for Best Foreign Film.*

WARNING: Most American public domain video and film prints of Les Diaboliques *are in poor shape, unfortunately, so some of the movie's most effective nuances are lost.*

DIARY OF A COUNTRY PRIEST

(Video, subtitled)

Psychological Drama

France	French
1954	120 Min.	B&W

CREDITS: *Directed and written by Robert Bresson, based on the book by George Bernanos. Produced by Leon Carre. Cinematography by Leonce-Henry Burel. Music by Jean-Jacques Grunenwald. Distributed nontheatrically by Films Inc. Starring Claude Laydu, Jean Riveyre, Andre Guibert, Nicole Maurey, Nicole Ladmiral, Marie-Monique Arkell, Martine Lemaire and Antoine Balpetre.*

Robert Bresson is a director with a unique visual style, filming scenes with emotionally distanced shots broken by occasional close-ups of his characters' frozen faces. *Diary of a Country Priest* is an excellent example of his visual genius.

The film opens as a young man (Claude Laydu) journeys to Ambricant, a small French village where he is to serve as the parish priest. Strangely, though, the quiet newcomer who eats only bread and wine for sustenance is not welcomed by his flock. The children of the village taunt him mercilessly, and several other villagers reject his attempts to convert them to the path of Christ. Doing his best to serve God, the priest becomes embroiled in the turmoil of a countess (Marie-Monique Arkell) who is being driven mad by the philanderings of her husband (Jean Riveyre). Although he convinces her to let go of her anger and accept faith, a tragedy befalls the countess that further drives the priest into depression. Eventually, his inner demons not only

torture him mentally but threaten his physical health as well.

Bresson gives us few clues about how we should interpret this subtle story of a priest's suffering. There are no monologues of explanation, and his cinematography only emphasizes the barrenness of the plot. Still, a careful viewer will find a bed of wasps beneath this seemingly calm surface. As in his other films, Bresson records the struggles of a man's journey to his state of grace. In Bresson's world, he must suffer completely, and often needlessly, in order to find salvation. And despite the plainness of Bresson's camera work, he weaves a complex web of cuts and close-ups that create a hypnotic rhythm. His cast of mostly nonprofessional actors, purposely emotionless and understated, make small but heartfelt quivers in a placid but troubled world.

RATING: *No MPAA rating, with nothing objectionable.*
AWARDS: *1954 Grand Prix du Cinema Français; Golden Lion for Best Film at the 1954 Venice Film Festival.*
FILMNOTE: *Bresson and his lead character, Claude Laydu, met every weekend for a year before filming began to talk about Laydu's role and to tour French monasteries.*

DIM SUM: A LITTLE BIT OF HEART

(Video, subtitled)

Cultural Drama

U.S.A.	English and Chinese
1985	88 Min.	Color

CREDITS: *Directed by Wayne Wang. Written by Terrel Seltzer. Produced by Wayne Wang, Tom Sternberg and Danny Yung. Cinematography by Michael Chin. Music by Todd Boekelheide. Released by Orion. Distributed nontheatrically by Films Inc. Starring Laureen Chew, Kim Chew, Victor Wong, Ida F. O. Chung, John Nishio and Cora Miao.*

Dim Sum (little Chinese delicacies) is an appropriate title for Wayne Wang's second feature (*Chan Is Missing* is his first) because he involves us in slices of Chinese-American life that aren't individually substantial, but when combined, they make a satisfying movie.

Set in San Francisco, it's the story of a middle-aged Chinese-American widow named Mrs. Tam (Kim Chew), whose children have all left home except for her youngest daughter Geraldine (Laureen Chew). In her late twenties, Geraldine has been dating a man she wants to settle down with but thinks her mother doesn't want her to leave home. For her part, Mrs. Tam is disgraced by her daughter's continued presence, because Geraldine is past the age where she is expected to marry. Mrs. Tam also spends a lot of time with her bartending brother-in-law, Uncle Tam (Victor Wong), who wants to marry her as soon as Geraldine leaves. She feels she must find a subtle way to push her daughter out of her home without hurting Geraldine's feelings.

Dim Sum is about family responsibilities in the context of Asian experience. It's a slowly paced film, and the issues it deals with might be difficult for some viewers to involve themselves in. But the film's characters and cultural anecdotes make it worthwhile. With his offhanded sarcasm and modern quips, Wong's Uncle Tam is definitely the comedian of the group. Kim Chew's Mrs. Tam and Laureen Chew's Geraldine both express their characters' ambiguous emotions very convincingly. And *Dim Sum* works skillfully as a portrait of the conflict between the old country's values and the second generation's assimilation into the American middle class. Director Wang digs into these situations as someone who knows them very well.

RATING: *PG, with nothing objectionable.* FILMNOTE: *Although director Wayne Wang was born in Hong Kong, his parents were big American movie fans who named him after John Wayne.*

DINER
(Video)

Social Comedy

U.S.A.

1982　　　　　110 Min.　　　　　Color

CREDITS: *Directed and written by Barry Levinson. Produced by Jerry Weintraub. Cinematography by Peter Sova. Music by Bruce Brody and Ivan Kral. Released by MGM/UA. Distributed nontheatrically by Films Inc. Starring Mickey Rourke, Daniel Stern, Kevin Bacon, Ellen Barkin, Steve Guttenberg, Timothy Daly and Paul Reiser.*

Known for launching the careers of Mickey Rourke, Steve Guttenberg, Ellen Barkin and Kevin Bacon, Barry Levinson's *Diner* is definitely a movie for the guys. The story, set in 1959, concerns a group of friends from the same Baltimore high school who are into the Baltimore Colts, scoring with chicks and placing bets. Although some are in college now and others working, their lives still revolve around the diner where they hang out late at night. They have one major flaw in common— their inability to relate to women. Women are great to look at, have sex with, or even marry, but when it comes to discussing important matters such as whose music is better to make out to—Johnny Mathis or Frank Sinatra—that's reserved for the guys at the diner.

Having himself spent his early adulthood in the late fifties in Baltimore, director Barry Levinson *(Tin Men)* knows the territory well. The gang from the diner are just a bunch of semi-intellectual jocks, and Levinson captures their sexist, wisecracking, confused world very authentically. The soundtrack in *Diner* is full of wonderful Golden Oldies, and the film's physical details are superbly rendered. The guys, wearing cardigan sweaters and chinos, eat fried bologna sandwiches and fries with gravy, while the diner parking lot is full of Hudsons and Metropolitans. But it's their conversations that really hit the mark in *Diner*. As they tell each other about their failures and successes in love or the various small-time hustles they get themselves involved in, their remarks can be funny and perceptive or embarrassingly stupid. But nearly all of them are ones that men familiar with the late fifties will fondly remember, and women will want to forget.

RATING: PG for language and many sexual references.
AWARDS: 1982 Academy Award nomination for Best Original Screenplay (Barry Levinson).

EL DIPUTADO (THE DEPUTY)
(Video, subtitled)

Political Thriller

Spain	Spanish
1978 111 Min.	Color

CREDITS: Directed by Eloy de la Iglesia. Written by Eloy de la Iglesia and Gonzalo Goicoechea. Produced by J. A. Perez Giner. Cinematography by Antonio Cuevas. Released by David Whitten Productions and Award Films. Starring Jose Sacristan, Maria Luisa San Jose and Jose L. Alonso.

When it comes to lust, politicians must leave the ranks of those ruled by their desires and stay within the boundaries of "approved" convention. Nobody is more aware of this fact than the protagonist of El Diputado, Roberto (Jose Sacristan). Roberto is an up-and-coming Socialist in post-Franco Spain who is married to an attractive Marxist named Carmen (Maria Luisa San Jose) and gives all the outward appearances of having an acceptable home life. But inside, Roberto is driven by a passion for young boys. Roberto grows especially fond of a tough kid named Juanito (Jose L. Alonso) and finds him a room in his apartment building so that he can enjoy his favors on a regular basis. Soon Carmen discovers Juanito, but instead of exploding in anger, she decides to join the fun, and the three become a ménage, with Roberto and Carmen also serving as the loving parents Juanito never had.

The performances are excellent in El Diputado, while the film's mixture of suspense and political repression is so well-drawn that it often resembles a Costa-Gavras (Z) movie. But once the threesome comes into the picture, the plot of El Diputado becomes a bit absurd. It's particularly unbelievable when Juanito goes through a complete transformation from street urchin to sweet kid after receiving a little affection from his surrogate parents/sex partners. But what writer/director de la Iglesia masterfully conveys is the turbulent politics occurring at this crossroads in Spanish history. Roberto's problems are so devastating because his potential as a leader for social change is sabotaged by his desires. And de la Iglesia shows all too well the failures of post-Franco Spain's promise of freedom, when a politician can still be persecuted for his "aberrant" behavior.

RATING: No MPAA rating, but there is some explicit gay sex and disturbing violence.
FILMNOTE: El Diputado is based on a true story.

THE DISCREET CHARM OF THE BOURGEOISIE
(Video, subtitled)

Black Comedy

France	French
1972 100 Min.	Color

CREDITS: Directed by Luis Buñuel. Written by Luis Buñuel and Jean-Claude Carriere. Produced by Serge Silberman. Cinematography by Edmond Richard. Released by 20th Century Fox. Distributed nontheatrically by Films Inc. Starring Fernando Rey, Stephane Audran, Delphine Seyrig, Bull Ogier, Jean-Pierre Cassel, Paul Frankeur, Claude Pieplu, Michel Piccoli and Julien Bertheau.

Once again, director Luis Buñuel takes a sketch of an idea—three wealthy couples who are continually interrupted as they try to dine—and fleshes it out into a perverse and peculiar story. Most of *The Discreet Charm of the Bourgeoisie* is simply a series of disastrous dinner engagements. One is ruined when the host and hostess attempt a "quickie" that goes on so long their disgusted guests leave. Another is spoiled when a restaurant manager abruptly drops dead. A third is wrecked because the restaurant's kitchen can offer only water to the disappointed patrons. And on two separate occasions, soldiers suddenly appear to disrupt the dinner guests with bizarre, violent descriptions of their dreams. Mixed in with these ill-fated meals are a couple of minor subplots involving a priest, drug smuggling and terrorists.

Using dining as a metaphor, Buñuel effectively lampoons the pretentions of the upper class, and even issues of war, sex and religion in this film. He also throws in his customary surreal dream sequences, although these aren't as richly detailed as in some of his earlier works. Neither are the performances. These three self-admiring, unexpressive couples are excellent vehicles for Buñuel's attack on the hypocrisy of the privileged class, but their characters lack the depth needed to view them as more than caricatures. Eventually, the outrageousness of each spoiled dinner attempt wears thin, and with little character development or action to rescue the film, so does the charm of the movie.

RATING: PG, with marijuana smoking.
AWARDS: 1972 Academy Award for Best Foreign Film; 1972 Academy Award nomination for Best Screenplay (Luis Buñuel and Jean-Claude Carriere); 1972 British Academy Award for Best Screenplay (Buñuel and Carriere); one of the National Board of Review's 5 Best Foreign Films in 1972.

DIVA
(Video, subtitled)

Thriller

France		French
1982	123 Min.	Color

CREDITS: Directed by Jean-Jacques Beineix. Written by Jean-Jacques Beineix and Jean Van Hamme, based on the novel by Delacorta. Produced by Irene Silberman. Cinematography by Philippe Rousselot. Art direction by Hilton McConnico. Music by Vladimir Cosma. Released by Les Films Galaxie and Palace Films. Distributed nontheatrically by Films Inc. Starring Frederic Andrei, Wilhelmenia Wiggins Fernandez, Richard Bohringer, Thuy An Luu, Jacques Fabbri, Chantal Deruaz, Dominique Pinon, Roland Bertin, Gerard Darmon, Jean-Jacques Moreau and Patrick Floersheim.

With its wildly outrageous Pop Art sets, gorgeous cinematography and exciting suspense, Jean-Jacques Beineix's *Diva* provided a needed shot in the arm to many struggling art houses when it was first released, luring viewers back for repeated viewings.

Set in Paris, the story follows a sensitive young postman named Jules (Frederic Andrei) who inadvertently becomes involved in murder and corruption. Living in a loft decorated with wrecked cars and enlarged photographs, Jules voraciously listens to a tape he surreptitiously recorded during a live performance by his idol, famous opera singer Cynthia Hawkins (Wilhelmenia Wiggins Fernandez). Because the diva stubbornly refuses to record her music, a couple of Taiwan record pirates ravage Jules's apartment in search of the tape when they learn of its existence. What neither they nor Jules know is that the mistress of the chief of police slipped another tape, implicating her boyfriend in an international drug ring, into Jules's mail pouch right before she was murdered. Soon the Taiwanese thugs are joined by the police chief's henchman in pursuit of Jules and his tapes, while he hides out with a Vietnamese kleptomaniac and her Buddhist boyfriend.

Writer/director Jean-Jacques Beineix *(Betty Blue)* develops the suspense of his story slowly, introducing an assortment of modern-day weirdos and clumsy punk hoodlums who apparently have little connection to one another. As the characters begin to fit together in an elaborate web of chance encounters and misinterpretations, the violence becomes too real to be humorous. Before you know what hit you, *Diva* turns into a nail-biting thriller. Vladimir Cosma's fast-paced rock and melodic opera soundtrack blends perfectly to match the story line's twists and turns. Even if you're not an opera fan, Fernandez's beautiful voice will make you a temporary convert. American art director Hilton McConnico's New Wave interiors are great fun, while cinematographer Phillipe Rousselot crisply shoots the film's action scenes with high suspense tracking shots and atmospheric colors that make *Diva* a visual feast from beginning to end.

RATING: *No MPAA rating, with violence, sex, profanity and nudity.*

DODES'KA-DEN

(Video, subtitled)

Urban Drama

Japan		Japanese
1970	140 Min.	Color

CREDITS: *Directed by Akira Kurosawa. Written by Akira Kurosawa, Hideo Oguni and Shinobu Hashimoto, based on a book by Shugoro Yamaoto. Produced by Yonkino Kai. Cinematography by Tako Saito and Yasumichi. Set design by Yoshiro and Shinobu Miraki. Released by Toho Films. Distributed nontheatrically by Films Inc. Starring Yoshitaka Zushi, Tomoko Yamazaki, Horishi Akutagawa and Kin Sugai.*

Director Akira Kurosawa once remarked that if he hadn't inserted some humor in *Dodes'ka-den* (meaning "choo choo" in Japanese), nobody would want to go see it. It was also a good idea that he edited down the original four-hour version, because two and a half hours of this surrealistic tragicomedy is unsettling enough.

Set in a modern Japanese ghetto village, *Dodes'ka-den* is filled with weird sets, painted sunsets and wildly colored shacks. Just as bizarre are the film's characters. There's a retarded boy who thinks he's a train conductor, a blind man who hasn't spoken since he caught his wife committing adultery, and two drunks who awkwardly try to swap wives. But perhaps most disturbing are a young girl who makes plastic flowers to support her family, and a father and son who live in a Volkswagen Beetle and fantasize about the wonderful house they will build someday.

Although there is virtually no plot in *Dodes'ka-den,* its cinematography and sets are stunning. Kurosawa purposely drenches several scenes in red, blue and green hues that give everything a fantastic, dreamlike quality. But the visuals only distract us temporarily from the characters. This film's whole motley group give intense performances, and, though some of their situations can be humorously absurd, most are much more tragic and unnerving than entertaining. The two-and-a-half-hour experience is sometimes grueling and monotonous as Kurosawa never lets us forget that poverty can create aberrant behavior. But *Dodes'ka-den* remains a penetrating and important indictment of the hopes and failures of modern life.

RATING: *No MPAA rating, with nothing objectionable.*
AWARDS: *1971 Academy Award nomination for Best Foreign Film.*

LA DOLCE VITA (THE SWEET LIFE)

(Video, subtitled)

Social Satire

Italy	Italian
1960	180 Min.	B&W

CREDITS: *Directed by Federico Fellini. Written by Federico Fellini, Ennio Flaiano, Tullio Pinelli and Bruno Rondi. Produced by Giuseppe Amato and Angelo Rizzoli. Music by Nino Rota. Cinematography by Otello Martelli. Starring Marcello Mastroianni, Walter Santesso, Anouk Aimee, Adriana Moneta, Yvonne Furneaux, Anita Ekberg, Lex Barker and Alan Dijon.*

At 180 minutes, La Dolce Vita stands as Fellini's longest and most elaborate production to date. Set in Rome in the early sixties, the film consists of a series of vignettes about a handsome playboy/reporter named Marcello (Marcello Mastroianni) as he dashes back and forth from various assignments to spend time with his rich, decadent friends. He does cover some serious news, such as the alleged miracle story of the two children who claim to have seen the Madonna; he also encounters personal tragedy when a friend kills his two children and then commits suicide. But most of the news Marcello digs up seems to involve beautiful women, and he usually manages to turn business into pleasure, seducing as many of his subjects as he can.

Take, for example, the voluptuous Hollywood starlet, Sylvia (Anita Ekberg). Forgetting about his interview, Marcello frolics with her in Roman fountains and at an exclusive nightclub, where she reels with unfulfilled passion on the dance floor. And while his photographer friends unsuccessfully hound a striking millionairess (Anouk Aimee of A Man and a Woman), Marcello suavely whisks the heiress away for a one-night stand in a prostitute's flat in the slums. The list of Marcello's sexual conquests goes on and on.

At the three-hour mark, La Dolce Vita will try even the most patient moviegoers,

yet Fellini paints a marvelous portrait of the Bohemian life-style in 1960s Rome in particular, and takes some pointed jabs at the opulence and moral decadence of post–World War II Italy in general. As usual, his camera work is striking, with clean yet metaphorically charged images filling every frame. Fellini regular Nino Rota *(Amarcord)* adds a wonderfully melodic score, but characters take precedence over everything else in La Dolce Vita. The players here are a particularly lively bunch, with the wild Ekberg and mysteriously beautiful Anouk Aimee leading the pack of supporting stars, and Mastroianni is a wry and affable hero whose chauvinism we excuse because he's so lovably naughty.

RATING: *No MPAA rating, with nothing objectionable.*
AWARDS: *1961 Academy Awards for Best Foreign Film and Best Costume Design (Piero Gherardi); 1961 Academy Award nominations for Best Director (Fellini); Best Screenplay Written Directly for the Screen (Fellini, Tullio Pinelli, Ennio Flaiano and Bruno Rondi) and Best Art Direction-Set Decoration (Gherardi).*

DONA FLOR AND HER TWO HUSBANDS

(Video, dubbed)

Sex Farce

Brazil	Portuguese
1978	106 Min.	Color

CREDITS: *Directed by Bruno Barreto. Written by Bruno Barreto, based on the novel by Jorge Amado. Produced by Luiz Carlos Barreto. Cinematography by Maurilol Salles. Music by Chico Buarque. Released by Carnival Films. Distributed nontheatrically by New Yorker Films. Starring Sonia Braga, Jose Wilker, Mauro Mendonca, Denorah Billanti, Nelson Xavier, Rui Rezende and Mario Gusmao.*

Bruno Barreto's *Dona Flor and Her Two Husbands* remains the largest-grossing movie in Brazil today, surpassing *Beverly Hills Cop* and *Ghostbusters* at the box office. Based on Jorge Amado's novel, it's the story of a Bahian woman's marriages to two very different men. Flor's (Sonia Braga) first husband, Vadinho (Jose Wilker), has a voracious sexual appetite for her and every other woman in town. When he's not wildly having sex with Flor or trying to seduce some pickup at the local bars, he stays out for days at a time gambling and drinking. Finally, his life-style catches up with him, and he suddenly keels over from a heart attack. Flor quickly finds a new husband, Teodoro (Mauro Mendonca)—a mature pharmacist who treats her with respect, rarely drinks and pledges fidelity. But he's also boring in bed, and before long Flor's libido longs for her first mate. One day, her dreams come true when Vadinho's ghost returns to satisfy her.

Dona Flor and Her Two Husbands is a fantasy that, at times, is hard to swallow. Not only are the prowling ghost scenes overdone, but Braga isn't convincing when she feebly expresses anger at her scoundrel of a first husband. She is successful, however, at turning into a passionate lover whenever Vadinho is around the house in this film. Certain sex scenes of the two of them are explicit and racy. And though Vadinho isn't socially appealing, he's funny and lovable even when he's being a louse, while just below the surface in his character, director Barreto and author Jorge Amado are wryly commenting on distasteful attitudes he stereotypically symbolizes.

RATING: *No MPAA rating, with sex and nudity.*
WARNING: *The dubbing is poor.*

DON'S PARTY

(Video)

Social Comedy
Australia
1976   91 Min.   Color

CREDITS: *Directed by Bruce Beresford. Written by David Williamson. Produced by* Philip Adams. *Cinematography by Don McAlpine. Music by Leos Jan. Released by Double Head Productions. Starring John Hargreaves, Pat Bishop, Graham Kennedy, Veronica Lang, Harold Hopkins, Candy Raymond, John Gorton, Ray Barrett, Claire Binney, Jeannie Dryan, Kit Taylor and Graeme Blundell.*

It's 1969 in Sydney, and while most Australians are voting on a new government, Don is having one doozy of an election eve party. It's as if he made sure his politically aware guests were on the edge of nervous breakdowns before he invited them to his party. Nearly all five couples try to sleep with each other's wives or husbands before the party's over, and fifteen minutes don't go by without someone wanting to punch somebody else's lights out. They berate, belittle and abuse each other about everything from penis size to feigned orgasms to broken dreams, as this alternately comic and hostile gathering dissolves into an encounter session where all the players end up mentally and physically exposed.

Although the comedy in *Don's Party* probably seemed risqué when the film was released in 1976, today it comes across a little trite and dated. Most of the film's humor involves the party's unhappily married men openly leching after women. It's not very shocking, and when the situation is repeated several times, the joke wears thin. The dramatic scenes in *Don's Party* are much stronger, as director Bruce Beresford *(Breaker Morant, Tender Mercies)* delves into issues of self-image, machismo and aging with an alert eye for universal sore spots. Particularly powerful are scenes of the wives lashing back at their sexist husbands. But visually, the camera rarely leaves the living room in *Don's Party*, and at times the film's atmosphere is so stifling that it dilutes the impact of the intelligent soul-exposing.

RATING: *No MPAA rating, with brief nudity, profanity and sex.*
WARNING: *Some of the Aussie accents in this film are so thick that the dialogue is a little difficult to understand.*

DON'T LOOK NOW
(Video)

Occult Thriller

England

1973 110 Min. Color

CREDITS: *Directed by Nicolas Roeg. Written by Allan Scott and Chris Bryant, based on a short story by Daphne du Maurier. Produced by Peter Katz. Cinematography by Anthony Richmond. Music by Pino Donaggio. Released by Buena Vista. Distributed nontheatrically by Films Inc. Starring Donald Sutherland, Julie Christie, Hilary Mason, Clelia Matania, Massimo Serato, Renato Scarpa and Giorgio Trestini.*

Based on Daphne du Maurier's occult novel of the same name, Nicolas Roeg's *Don't Look Now* is the kind of film you don't want to watch alone late at night.

Donald Sutherland stars as John, an apparently normal art restorer who specializes in religious mosaics. In his English country home one winter day, while he's looking at slides of an ancient Venetian cathedral, he is seized by a frightening psychic vision, a vision that proves all too real when he runs outside and finds his young daughter, Christine, drowned in an icy pond. Two years later, John and his skittery wife, Laura (Julie Christie), are in Venice where he's working on that very same cathedral. At a café, John and Laura meet two English sisters, one of whom, Heather (Hilary Mason), is blind. She tells Laura of a vision she just had about their dead daughter, then warns Laura that the couple must leave Venice right away, that John's life is in danger. But when Laura warns John, he dismisses the whole thing as nonsense. Sure enough, bad luck begins to befall the couple in Venice, and John has more strange premonitions that become real.

Don't Look Now falters only in its dialogue. Although Laura and John are meant to be on different wavelengths, instead of creating an uneasiness their miscommunications can distance us from their characters and the strange events happening to them. But many other elements in *Don't Look Now* add to an overall air of suspense, from a creepy soundtrack by Pino Donaggio to the labyrinth of clues that pop up in nearly every scene. All the acting is strong, but it's Mason's Heather, with her dull bluish eyes and icy gaze, who will haunt your dreams after you've seen this movie. Director Nicolas Roeg's *(Walkabout)* vision of Venice as a frightening maze of dead-end passageways and steamy tunnels, the disquieting tone of the film's lighting, and the surrealistic layering of time sequences and images are very effective.

RATING: *R for nudity, sex and violence.*
AWARDS: *1973 British Academy Award for Best Cinematography (Anthony Richmond).*
FILMNOTE: Don't Look Now *was originally rated X for a very explicit sex scene between Sutherland and Christie. Although slightly cut for an R rating, that scene is so hot it's still one of the most legendary movie sex scenes from the seventies.*

DOWN BY LAW
(Video)

Social Satire

U.S.A.

1986 106 Min. B&W

CREDITS: *Directed and written by Jim Jarmusch. Produced by Alan Kleinberg, Tom Rothman and Jim Stark. Cinematography by Bobby Muller. Music by John Lurie and Tom Waits. Released by Island Pictures. Distributed nontheatrically by New Yorker Films. Starring Tom Waits, John Lurie, Roberto Benigni, Ellen Barkin, Nicoletta Braschi, Billie Neal, Rockets Redglare and Timothea.*

Down by Law is only the third feature by director Jim Jarmusch, but already he has developed quite a following for his deadpan humor and abstract portraits of Americans who live on the fringe. In this film, they are three unlikely cellmates in a Louisiana prison. Zack (Tom Waits) is an ex-deejay in for driving a stolen Jaguar with a dead man in the trunk. Jack (John Lurie) is a pimp who makes an offer to a hot new hooker who turns out to be an underaged setup by the police. And Bobby (Roberto Benigni) is an Italian tourist who, when caught cheating at poker, unintentionally kills one of the players with a pool ball.

If their separate paths to prison seem absurd, wait till you hear their conversations. Jack struts and talks tough, Zack launches into occasional deejay raps, and Bobby, though his English is poor, incessantly spouts clichés such as "If looks could kill, I would be now dead." Bobby is also the brains of the outfit, and before long, he finds a way for them to escape. Outside prison, the three are stranded for days in a swamp, where they develop a strange symbiotic relationship.

Although billed as "part fantasy, part nightmare," *Down by Law* is mostly concerned with how these screwballs interact in confined spaces. Each is individually funny, but the three together are a riot—that is, when they are saying something. There's a little too much silence in this movie for it to be consistently entertaining. Although the lack of dialogue is intentional, as when the characters silently pace and fidget, it's hard not to want to pace and fidget yourself. But visually, *Down by Law* is always interesting. Cinematographer Bobby Muller's camera pans through swamps and lower-class New Orleans neighborhoods capturing remarkable beauty in the desolation. His cleverly arranged shots inside the cell carry the same kind of power. Director Jarmusch (*Stranger Than Paradise*) calls *Down by Law* a "neo-beat-noir-comedy." He forgot to add that it's also a visual masterpiece.

RATING: R for profanity, drugs and nudity.
WARNING: Because the visuals are so important, much is lost watching this film on video.

DREAMCHILD
(Video)

Social Drama

England

1985 93 Min. Color

CREDITS: Directed by Gavin Millar. Written by Dennis Potter. Produced by Rick McCallum and Kenith Trodd. Cinematography by Billy Williams. Set design by Roger Hall. Wonderland creatures designed by Jim Henson. Costume design by Jane Robinson. Music by Stanley Meyers. Released by Universal. Distributed nontheatrically by Swank Motion Pictures. Starring Coral Browne, Ian Holm, Peter Gallagher, Amelia Shankley, Caris Corfman, Nicola Cowper, Jan Asher, Shane Rimmer, Emma King and Imogen Boorman.

Dreamchild begins when eighty-five-year-old Alice Hargreaves (Coral Browne) travels to America for the first time, to receive an honorary degree at Columbia University. As a girl she inspired Lewis Carroll (whose real name was Rev. Charles Dodgson) to write the *Alice in Wonderland* books, but in her old age she is haunted by memories of their relationship together. In the days before the ceremony, Alice has nightmares in which the once-whimsical *Wonderland* characters taunt her. As her dreams and memories lead her through a dark and long-shuttered past, Alice comes to understand that behind Rev. Dodgson's delightful stories were his romantic yearnings for her. Even more difficult for Alice to now accept is her realization that as a child she recognized Rev. Dodgson's attraction and cruelly encouraged it in order to torment him.

Dreamchild takes place on three different levels: Victorian Mrs. Hargreaves's reaction to her first visit to America; young Alice (Amelia Shankley) and her relationship with her shy, stuttering neighbor, Rev. Dodgson (Ian Holm); and the nightmares populated by the fantastic creatures of Wonderland (created by Jim Henson). The first two work well. Mrs. Hargreaves's outrage at the rude, money-grubbing Yankees is hilarious, particularly when she sees her notoriety as a chance to make some extra money herself by doing radio commercials. As a young girl, Alice is delightfully precocious and free-spirited, while Ian Holm gives a tremendous performance as Rev. Dodgson, a man tortured by desires he could never act upon.

Only the dreams don't fit. Although the characters themselves are detailed in the typically wonderful Jim Henson fashion, these sequences feel unconnected to the rest of the story, and their symbolism is unnecessarily ominous. Fortunately, there is something entertaining and provocative going on in nearly every other scene in *Dreamchild*. Director Gavin Millar and screenwriter Dennis Potter *(Brimstone and Treacle)* have created an extraordinary, albeit slightly twisted, interpretation of the real people behind *Alice in Wonderland*. By the film's cathartic ending, you'll have fallen in love with young and old Alice and the man who made her famous.

RATING: PG, with nothing objectionable.

THE DRESSER
(Video)

Literary Drama

England

1984　　　　118 Min.　　　　Color

CREDITS: *Directed and produced by Peter Yates. Written by Ronald Harwood, based on his play. Cinematography by Kelvin Pike. Music by James Horner. Released by Columbia Pictures. Distributed nontheatrically by Swank Motion Pictures. Starring Albert Finney, Tom Courtenay, Edward Fox, Zena Walker, Eileen Atkins, Michael Gough and Cathryn Harrison.*

The saying "all the world's a stage" is a fitting prelude for *The Dresser*, a film about a brilliant but mentally unstable British actor who tours England while the country crumbles under Hitler's bombs. Albert Fin-

ney stars as the aging Shakespearean actor, called Sir by his dresser, Norman (Tom Courtenay). Sir never stops performing even when he is offstage, and has an enormous ego in need of constant attention. He is also an alcoholic who, in drunken rages, verbally attacks those around him, including the loyal Norman upon whom he is completely dependent.

While Norman badgers, cajoles and pleads with Sir, as the old actor resists preparing for *King Lear*, it doesn't take long to figure out that both men have severe self-image problems, although they express them differently. Sir needs to be constantly reaffirmed, while Norman feels that he deserves his master's scorn. Moreover, Norman is gay and doesn't want to be, while Sir has a dangerous heart condition aggravated by his drinking and the Germans' continual shelling of London.

Director Peter Yates *(Breaking Away)* rarely allows his camera to leave the dressing room, where Norman and Sir have their escalatingly neurotic exchanges. This visual strategy makes *The Dresser* excessively stagey, but Finney's and Courtenay's performances often transcend the film's setting. Although separately the two characters are multifaceted, together their relationship is so complex that it's exhausting to try to comprehend it fully. The acting in *The Dresser* can be too much of a good thing. Finney's character rarely stops performing and though some of his Shakespearean quips and theatrical monologues are entertaining, the sheer number of them and their hamminess overpower the script and soften the intensity of his unusual relationship with Norman.

RATING: PG, with nothing objectionable.
AWARDS: Award for Best Actor (Albert Finney) at 1983 Berlin Film Festival; 1983 Academy Award nominations for Best Director (Peter Yates), Best Screenplay (Ronald Harwood) and Best Actor (Finney, Tom Courtenay).

EATING RAOUL
(Video)

Sex Farce

U.S.A.

1983   87 Min.   Color

CREDITS: *Directed by Paul Bartel. Written by Paul Bartel and Richard Blackburn. Produced by Anne Kimmel. Cinematography by Gary Thieltges. Released by 20th Century Fox. Distributed nontheatrically by Films Inc. Starring Paul Bartel, Mary Woronov, Robert Beltran, Buck Henry, Richard Paul, Susan Saiger, Ed Begley, Jr., and Dan Barrows.*

When Paul (Paul Bartel) and Mary (Mary Woronov) Bland realize that they must scramble to raise a down payment on their dream restaurant, Chez Bland, they decide to create their own version of a cottage industry. The couple advertises Mary's kinky sexual favors in the personals of a local paper, and when the johns come over, Paul clunks them on the head with a cast-iron frying pan and steals their money and valuables. Their scheme proceeds smoothly until a burglar named Raoul (Robert Beltran) stumbles onto one of the bodies while he is ripping off their apartment. He demands a cut of the action or he'll turn in the couple to the police. So Paul and Mary reluctantly go into partnership with Raoul—they do the luring and clunking and he hocks the victims' cars and sells their bodies to a factory to be used as dog food. *Eating Raoul* is about as deadpan (excuse the pun) as black comedy gets. Paul and Mary are an extremely boring suburban white couple, but their dullness is exactly what makes them so funny. This film is particularly humorous when they're responding to the "stud," Raoul, and when the glib couple gets involved with swingers who are into the most extreme sexual fetishes. Because of the film's low budget, *Eating Raoul*'s soundtrack can be tinny, and the lighting and camera work are unpolished. And toward the end of the film, the head clunking joke begins to wear thin.

Still, *Eating Raoul* is so full of screwy characters and comical situations that it turns into a clever little satire on libido-driven men and twisted materialism.

RATING: *R for brief nudity and marijuana smoking.*

8½
(Video, dubbed)

Social Satire

Italy   Italian

1963   135 Min.   B&W

CREDITS: *Directed by Federico Fellini, assisted by Lina Wertmuller. Written by Federico Fellini, Tullio Pinelli, Ennio Flajano and Bruno Brunello. Music by Nino Rota. Cinematography by Gianni de Venanzo. Costume design by Pierro Gherardi. Released by Embassy Pictures. Distributed nontheatrically by Corinth Films. Starring Marcello Mastroianni, Anouk Aimee, Sandra Milo, Claudia Cardinale, Barbara Steele, Rossella Falk and Guido Alberti.*

8½ is Federico Fellini's autobiographical film catharsis about everything—the creative process, death, love, fidelity, redemption—you name it, and it takes a turn on screen in this movie.

The story takes place in the sixties at an Italian hot springs resort where a forty-three-year-old filmmaker named Guido (Marcello Mastroianni) tries to relax while planning his next movie. Nearby, set designers are constructing a giant rocket ship, and producers, financial backers and actors are swarming around in anticipation of Guido's film. Everybody's ready but Guido, who has written and rewritten the script yet can't seem to come up with a concrete idea for the film. Meanwhile, his hungry colleagues try to prod him to make decisions about screen tests and shooting schedules, but the director remains disarmingly aloof from all of them. Despite his surface serenity, the whole ordeal has Guido filled with self-doubt. He is hounded day and night by strange visions and nightmares about dying, his work and the women in his life.

Disjointed fantasies, bizarre images and nostalgic memories come hurling at us from all sides in 8½, yet Fellini achieves a balance among the various themes that makes Guido's struggles remarkably compelling. The film's main set—the clammy steam rooms filled with ghostly clientele clad only in white robes—is wonderfully symbolic of the spiritual purgatory in which Guido is suffering. All of the acting is outstanding, particularly by the hilariously deadpan Mastroianni and Anouk Aimee, as Guido's wife, Louisa. The only problem with 8½ is its length. A two-hour-and-fifteen-minute tour of the strange, frenetic reaches of Guido's mind is occasionally too much to handle.

RATING: No rating, with nothing objectionable.
AWARDS: 1963 Academy Awards for Best Foreign Language Film and Best Costume Design (Pierro Gherardi); 1963 New York Film Critics Award for Best Foreign Film; one of the National Board of Review's, 5 Best Foreign Films in 1963; Grand Prize at the 1963 Moscow Film Festival.
FILMNOTE: When asked about the title of the film, Fellini once commented that he had made three short films and six features before 8½. With this film included in the total, it adds up.

84 CHARING CROSS ROAD
(Video)

Literary Docudrama

England

1987   84 Min.   Color

CREDITS: Directed by David Jones. Written by Hugh Whitemore, based on the novel by Helene Hanff and the play by Jameo Roose-Evan. Produced by Geoffrey Hellman. Cinematography by Brian West. Released by Columbia Pictures. Distributed nontheatrically by Swank Motion Pictures. Starring Anne Bancroft, Anthony Hopkins and Judi Dench.

Based on Helene Hanff's autobiographical novel, 84 Charing Cross Road will make you appreciate the literary life. The story begins in New York City in the early 1950s, as the struggling author Helene Hanff (Anne Bancroft) writes to a small London bookshop requesting a particular volume of Pepys's Diaries that is unavailable in New York. To her surprise, the shop not only promptly sends her the volume at a very reasonable price but completes the package with a polite note thanking her for her patronage and entrusting her with the bill as well.

Thus begins a correspondence between the bookshop's manager, Dole (Anthony Hopkins), and Helene that lasts for ten years. As Helene inquires about a range of English literature for her library, she also includes several paragraphs of personal anecdotes and opinions. Her pen pal politely responds with details of his staid existence. Eventually, their shared interest in literature leads to a tantalizing attraction for one another.

84 Charing Cross Road is an ode to a dying breed of book lovers, and your enjoyment of this film may depend on your fondness for literature. As the bookshop manager, Hopkins is thoughtful and introverted—a bookworm inside and out. Dole fits the stereotype of a repressed intellectual so completely that one can't help wondering if he would actually be capable of expressing any feelings to Helene, even if they did meet. Fortunately, just as the scenes in London begin to feel as musty as a shelf full of Milton, director David Jones (Betrayal) switches back to Helene's articulate pontifications in time to revive the film. Bancroft's Helene expresses more than enough for both characters. In her blunt New York way, Helene's narration of letters to Dole (sometimes spoken directly into the camera) is often sardonically witty and bullheaded at the same time. Even though the only real tension in the plot is the overplayed question of whether the two will ever meet face to face, Bancroft's performance breathes enough life into this overly

intellectual babble that *84 Charing Cross Road* is well worth the effort.

RATING: No MPAA rating, with nothing objectionable.

ELENI
(Video)

Docudrama

U.S.A.

1985   117 Min.   Color

CREDITS: *Directed by Peter Yates. Written by Steve Tesich, based on the book by Nicolas Gage. Produced by Nick Vanoff, Mark Pick and Nicolas Gage. Cinematography by Billy Williams. Released by Warner Brothers. Distributed nontheatrically by Swank Motion Pictures. Starring Kate Nelligan, John Malkovich, Linda Hunt, Oliver Cotton, Ronald Pickup, Rosalie Crutchley and Glenne Headly.*

Eleni is based on the true story of journalist Nicolas Gage's mother, who was killed when he was a young boy. When the film begins, Eleni (Kate Nelligan) lives with her children in a small Greek village occupied by the Communists during a brief civil war following World War II. Because Eleni's husband emigrated to America, she is already suspected by the Reds of being a capitalist sympathizer. When she helps her children escape to America after the Communists demand that they be reeducated in Albania, she is convicted of treason and shot by a firing squad.

Thirty years later, her son, Nick (John Malkovich), a *New York Times* reporter, finagles a job as the Athens bureau chief so he can find, and punish, the man responsible for her execution. Through untiring investigation, Nick tracks down several villagers who remember his mother, then bullies the reluctant peasants until he learns the identity and whereabouts of his mother's murderer.

Both stories unfold simultaneously in *Eleni*, with Nick's investigations in the seventies followed by flashbacks of the actual events as they happened in the forties. The transitions between the eras are smooth, the time periods subtly marked by details such as a passing car or donkey, and by beautiful cinematography that contrasts the past and present. Unfortunately, little else holds together in this film.

Malkovich plays Nick as a man too driven by revenge for us to feel compassion for him or even understand why he becomes so obsessed with avenging his mother's death thirty years after the fact. He doesn't express his feelings to anybody in this movie, and after watching his silent, agonized face and tearful eyes in scene after scene, you just wish he'd lighten up. Nelligan, on the other hand, is more expressive as the distraught mother, but she is seriously miscast as a Greek. Malkovich and Linda Hunt (another Communist-battered mother from Eleni's village) don't look or act Greek either. The fact that all their dialogue is in English with no Greek accent only exacerbates the problem.

RATING: PG, with mild violence.
FILMNOTE: Gage's real attempts to find out about his mother's murderer led him to interview over four hundred people in seven countries, producing tens of thousands of pages of transcribed conversations.

THE ELEPHANT MAN
(Video)

Docudrama

England

1980   125 Min.   B&W

CREDITS: *Directed by David Lynch. Written by David Lynch, Christopher De-Vore and Eric Bergren, based on the books* Elephant Man—A Study in Human Dignity *by Ashley Montagu and* A Study of Human Dignity *by Frederick Treves. Produced by Jonathan Sanger and Mel Brooks. Cinematography by Freddie Francis. Music by John Morris and Samuel Barber. Production de-*

sign by Stuart Craig and Hugh Scaife. Makeup and costume design by Patricia Norris. Released by Paramount. Distributed nontheatrically by Films Inc. Starring Anthony Hopkins, John Hurt, Anne Bancroft, John Gielgud, Wendy Hiller, Freddie Jones, Michael Elphick, Hannah Gordon, Helen Ryan, John Standing and Dexter Fletcher.

Based on a true story, David Lynch's The Elephant Man describes a grossly deformed man's struggle for dignity during the last few years of his life in England at the turn of the century. His name is John Merrick (John Hurt), although he is known as "The Elephant Man" in the carnival freak show where he is virtually enslaved in a cage at the start of the film. When Merrick falls gravely ill, a Dr. Treves (Anthony Hopkins) is summoned to the carnival. The doctor discovers that Merrick not only has severe asthma but also scars all over his body from having been beaten by his carnival master.

Treves insists on caring for Merrick in his hospital where he plans to keep him as long as he can. But in his first weeks there, Merrick is too frightened to talk and Treves's chief administrator (John Gielgud) wants to put him in an asylum for the profoundly retarded. Eventually, Treves gets Merrick to open up, and he turns out to be an articulate, artistically talented man. He even becomes a London celebrity when a famous stage actress (Anne Bancroft) comes to visit him. Yet Merrick is still hounded by his former carnival master, who plots to kidnap him back, and some local toughs who sneak into his room and taunt him at night.

This wouldn't be a David Lynch film without fantastic dream sequences, and though they aren't as elaborate as in Eraserhead, they are still quite impressive. Lynch and his designers do an outstanding job recreating an authentic and often darkly gritty, nineteenth-century London. And the acting is first-rate from the entire cast, particularly the immensely appealing Hurt, who is able to convey even the simplest emotions through his fantastic makeup. The film's main flaw is its oversentimentality. Several scenes are staged for optimum tear shedding. It's also unfathomable that even though he spent most of his life in a

cage, Merrick turns out to be a paragon of mental health.

RATING: PG, with nothing objectional.
AWARDS: 1981 French Caesar for Best Foreign Film; 1980 British Academy Awards for Best Film, Best Production Design/Art Direction (Stuart Craig) and Best Actor (John Hurt); 1980 Academy Award nominations for Best Picture, Best Actor (Hurt), Best Director (David Lynch) and Best Film Editing.

ENORMOUS CHANGES AT THE LAST MINUTE
(Video)

Women's Drama

U.S.A.

1983   110 Min.   Color

CREDITS: "Virginia's Story" directed by Ellen Hovde and Muffie Meyer. "Faith's Story" directed by Mirra Bank and Ellen Hovde. "Alexandra's Story" directed by Mirra Bank. Written by John Sayles and Susan Rice, based on the short stories by Grace Paley. Cinematography by Tom McDonough. Released by Ordinary Lives. Distributed nontheatrically by Cinecom. Starring Ellen Barkin, Kevin Bacon, Lynn Milgrim, Maria Tucci, David Strathairn, Ron McLarty, Sudie Bond, Jeffrey DeMun, Zvees Schooler, Fay Bernardi, Eda Riess Merin and John Wardwell.

Enormous Changes is a film adaptation of three faintly connected Grace Paley short stories about women from New York's Lower East Side trying to make it on their own. The first one focuses on Virginia (Ellen Barkin), a young mother of three who's been abandoned by her husband and now finds herself looking forward to Thursday night visits from a frumpy, balding, married man named John (Ron McLarty). The second segment is about Faith (Lynn Milgrim), a lonely divorcée with two children who goes to visit her meddling Jewish mother and poet father in an old-age home on Coney Island. The final section features Alexandra (Maria Tucci), a divorced social worker in her late thirties who becomes pregnant by an immature young cabbie (Kevin Bacon) who's not her choice as a husband.

The first segment in *Enormous Changes* is clearly the best. Barkin is outstanding as the abandoned mother, and her scenes with her pudgy, middle-aged boyfriend are full of awkward and warm moments. The second story is the weakest. It is turgidly paced, but there's a woman confined to a wheelchair in the old folks home (Fay Bernardi) who's the wriest character in the whole film. The acting in all three is natural and believable, and screenwriters John Sayles and Susan Rice do a good job of adapting Paley's stories. Important issues of loneliness, divorce, sex, motherhood, monogamy, aging and death are delved into with sensitivity. *Enormous Changes* is a sort of manifesto for single mothers of the eighties; all that's missing is texture. Probably because of its low budget, the music is ordinary, the cinematography unremarkable and the lighting poor, giving the film a tinny, home-movie feel.

RATING: No MPAA rating, with sexual situations.

ENTRE NOUS
(Video, subtitled)

Women's Drama

France	French
1983	110 Min.	Color

CREDITS: Directed by Diane Kurys. Written by Diane Kurys, based on a book by Oliver Cohen and Kurys. Produced by Ariel Zeitoun. Cinematography by Bernard Lutic. Released by MGM/UA. Distributed nontheatrically by Films Inc. Starring Isabelle Huppert, Miou-Miou, Guy Marchand, Jean-Pierre Bacri, Robin Renucci, Jacques Airic and Jacqueline Doyen.

With surprising box office success, Diane Kurys's semiautobiographical *Entre Nous*

marked the emergence of movies with feminist themes about intense relationships between women. The film begins during the height of World War II at a Vichy camp where the frightened young Lena (Isabelle Huppert) is a Jewish prisoner and handsome Michel (Guy Marchand) is a guard. Although they barely speak to one another, he sends her a note proposing marriage as a way of saving her life, and she accepts. At the same time, a young art student named Madeleine (Miou-Miou) and her boyfriend Raymond (Robin Renucci) are caught in the cross fire of a battle between the Underground and Vichy soldiers. He is shot and tragically dies in her arms.

Ten years later, Lena and Michel have built a traditional but passionless marriage, while Madeleine has married a narcissistic actor named Costa (Jean-Pierre Bacri), even though she still loves her long-deceased boyfriend from the war. Meeting through their children, the two women develop an instant rapport. As if lovers, they stare into each other's eyes, while sharing the realization of the emptiness of their postwar lives.

The main tension in the latter part of the movie comes from their respective husbands' jealous overreaction to their close friendship, and Madeleine's and Lena's responses. Unfortunately, the same scenes are repeated several times in different settings, and the whole situation becomes a bit wearing. Unlike the exciting early war segments, the characters' lives in the fifties are as dull as the era itself. But writer/director Kurys skillfully observes the complacency and coldness of Lena's and Madeleine's marriages, as well as the intensity in their relationship. In the end, *Entre Nous* stands as a testament to that friendship, as well as a bitter indictment of the lack of freedom that made it so important.

RATING: No MPAA rating, with mild violence and brief nudity.
AWARDS: 1983 Academy Award nomination for Best Foreign Film.

EQUUS
(Video)

Psychological Drama

U.S.A.

1977   138 Min.   Color

CREDITS: Directed by Sidney Lumet. Written by Peter Shaffer, based on his play. Produced by Lester Persky and Elliott Kastner. Cinematography by Oswald Morris. Music by Richard Rodney Bennett. Released by United Artists. Distributed nontheatrically by Films Inc. Starring Richard Burton, Peter Firth, Jenny Agutter, Colin Blakely, Joan Plowright, Harry Andrews, Eileen Atkins, John Wyman and Kate Reid.

Occasionally somebody commits a crime so hideous it's difficult for an outsider to comprehend. Adapted from Peter Shaffer's stage play, the movie *Equus* concerns such a crime. Late one fall night, for no apparent reason, eighteen-year-old Alan Strang (Peter Firth) let himself into the riding stables where he worked and repeatedly stabbed six horses in their eyes with a metal spike.

Alan's crime becomes the obsession of his psychiatrist, Martin (Richard Burton). After a number of grueling sessions with Alan, the doctor's obsession borders on madness. He manipulates and bullies Alan, applying all of his skills to get the young man to confess the reason for the mutilations. When all of the pieces of the puzzle are put together, the final revelation is a catharsis that carries a tremendous emotional weight for both patient and doctor.

The events leading up to "that" evening are retold through a series of therapy sessions, flashbacks and interviews with Alan's parents. But there are gaps in Martin's psychological sleuthing that leave questions unanswered. Other critical junctions in the plot are confused by unnecessary background information. The result is that *Equus* is uneven as a psychological mystery, with uninspired camera work (except when Alan blinds the horses) and as many slow moments as there are riveting ones. It's no fault of the main actors,

though. Both Burton and Firth give outstanding performances, particularly in their intense therapy sessions. As an actor's showpiece, *Equus* ranks right up there with films such as *The Dresser* and *Who's Afraid of Virginia Woolf?*

RATING: R for one sex scene and violence.
AWARDS: 1977 Academy Award nominations for Best Actor (Richard Burton), Best Supporting Actor (Peter Firth) and Best Screenplay Based on Material from Another Medium (Peter Shaffer).
FILMNOTE: The scene of Alan blinding the horses is so real that the filmmakers had to assure animal rightists that the horses weren't actually harmed.

ERASERHEAD
(Video)

Black Comedy

England

1978   90 Min.   B&W

CREDITS: Directed, written, produced, edited, set design and special effects by David Lynch. Cinematography by Frederick Elmes and Herbert Cardwell. Released by Libra Films. Starring John Nance, Charlotte Stewart, Allen Joseph, Jeanne Bates, Judith Anna Roberts, Laurel Near and V. Phipps-Wilson.

Director David Lynch calls *Eraserhead* "a dream of dark and troubling things," but that only begins to characterize it. The film is set in an eerie nightmare world of urban landscapes and human refugees. The hero is a young man with an unruly pompadour named Henry Spencer (John Nance), who wears shoddy clothes and lives in a sleazy apartment building full of prostitutes and thugs. Henry's existence is so bleak that for entertainment, he plays records that constantly skip and looks out of his window at the wall of another apartment. His life brightens when his girlfriend Mary X (Charlotte Stewart) moves in with him, until she gives birth to a deformed chicken-baby and deserts them, leaving Henry to care for the premature child. He tries to be a good father, but, bombarded by a constant industrial drone and trapped in a dim, depressing apartment with his screaming baby, Henry is soon swept into a series of perverse nightmares that drive him to the brink of madness.

Everything and everybody is abnormal in *Eraserhead*, but in a twisted sort of way all this sickness is quite funny. Nance, who returned to obscurity after the release of this film, is the perfect deadpan vehicle for Lynch's horrific vision of urban loneliness and fear. The nightmare sequences are brilliant (a bit diluted, they were later incorporated into Lynch's *The Elephant Man*), while other scenes, such as a dinner at the girlfriend's house, where roast chickens come to life, are surrealistic sidesplitters. But as original and brilliant as this film is, it can also test the limits of your movie-watching patience. There's little to hold on to except bizarre images and inane dialogue. In the end, it's as aggravating and tedious as it is worth seeing.

RATING: *No MPAA rating, with nudity and gross, disturbing images.*
FILMNOTE: *It took Lynch five years to make* Eraserhead—*a labor of love the former art student created almost entirely himself.*

ERENDIRA
(Video, subtitled)

Literary Satire

Mexico	Spanish
1983 103 Min.	Color

CREDITS: *Directed by Ruy Guerra. Written by Gabriel Garcia Marquez. Produced by Alain Queffelean. Cinematography by Denys Clerval. Music by Maurice Lecoeur. Art direction by Pierre Cadiou. Released by Miramax Films. Distributed nontheatrically by New Yorker Films. Starring Irene Papas, Claudia O'Hana, Michal Lonsdale, Oliver Wehe, Ernesto Gomez Cruz, Pierre Vaneck, Carlos Cardan and Humberton Elizondo.*

Nobel Prize–winning novelist Gabriel Garcia Marquez originally wrote *Erendira* as a screenplay but then decided to incorporate the material into his *One Hundred Years of Solitude*. That was a wise decision, since *Erendira* works better as fiction than as film.

Director Ruy Guerra, one of the central figures of Brazil's Cinema Novo movement, transforms Marquez's screenplay into a wonderfully visualized but somewhat tedious farce about a beautiful young fourteen-year-old forced into servitude to her grandmother. When Erendira (Claudia O'Hana) accidentally sets fire to her grandmother's house, the vengeful matriarch (played by Greek singer/actress Irene Papas) insists on payment for the damages and turns her granddaughter into a prostitute. In a short time, Erendira's beauty becomes legendary among men of all ages, and her grandmother organizes a whole carnival of sideshows and musicians to travel with the girl on the road. Politicians, soldiers, workers, adolescents—everybody seems to want Erendira. But this lucrative enterprise becomes endangered when Erendira falls in love with a young blond boy named Ulysses (Oliver Wehe) who tries to steal her away from Grandma's clutches.

While some of the imagery in *Erendira* is violent and disturbing, Guerra *(Opera do Melandro)* does a remarkable job of capturing the sensual richness of the myths and magic so dominant in Latin American art and literature. Papas is so convincing as the film's symbol of uncontrolled evil and greed she will make even hardened American moviegoers shudder. But *Erendira* is not an easy film to watch because few of the characters are developed beyond their surface symbolism. Eventually, the story line becomes bogged down in all of its imagery, and there is little else to hold on to. Guerra is obviously more interested in portraying a sexual fable drawn from an exotic mixture of paganism, politics and Catholicism than he is in giving us a traditional linear narrative. In that respect, he succeeds resoundingly.

RATING: R for nudity, sex and violence.
WARNING: Because the visuals are so important in Erendira, much is lost on video.
FILMNOTE: Because the Greek actress Irene Papas didn't know Spanish well at the beginning of the production, she took intensive language lessons and was able to dub in her dialogue successfully at the end of the filming.

EUREKA
(Video)

Social Drama

U.S.A.

1984   129 Min.   Color

CREDITS: Directed by Nicolas Roeg. Written by Paul Mayersberg, based on the book Who Killed Sir Harry Oakes? by Marshall Houts. Produced by Jeremy Thomas. Cinematography by Alex Thompson. Music by Stanley Myers. Released by MGM/ UA. Distributed nontheatrically by Films Inc. Starring Gene Hackman, Theresa Russell, Rutger Hauer, Jane Lapotaire, Mickey Rourke, Ed Lauter, Joe Pesci, Helena Kallianiotes, Cavan Kendall and Corin Redgrave.

Nicolas Roeg's Eureka begins in a surrealistic dreamworld, as prospector Jack McCann (Gene Hackman) wanders the Yukon in search of gold in the 1920s. Drifting into a near-deserted boom town, Jack first witnesses the suicide of a disheartened miner, then encounters a Gypsy fortune-teller and whore (Helena Kallianiotes) who gives him a lucky stone she says will lead him to gold. Driven into a blizzard by this vision, Jack's dream is fulfilled when he literally falls into a pool of liquid gold and becomes the richest man in the world.

Twenty years later, however, his dream has eroded into a nightmare. Trapped in a loveless marriage and distraught because his daughter Tracey (director Roeg's wife, Theresa Russell) has married a money-grubbing French playboy named Claude (Rutger Hauer), Jack paces angrily around his Caribbean island mansion threatening to throw his son-in-law off the estate. His life is further complicated when Claude hooks up with two Miami gangsters (Joe Pesci and Mickey Rourke) who want to buy a chunk of his island to open a casino. Jack's refusal to sell and his escalating battles with Claude result in the billionaire's being marked for murder.

Leave it to Nicolas Roeg (The Man Who Fell to Earth, Walkabout) to take a money-can't-buy-happiness story worthy of a TV melodrama and twist it into a difficult meditation on greed and desire. But with offensive lines such as "Gold smells stronger than a woman" and a murky, jumpy visual style that makes the action a challenge to follow, Eureka is not an evening's light entertainment. In fact, much of this film is simply pretentious and silly. Yet Roeg captures certain scenes, such as Jack's discovery of gold, with striking cinematography. The performances are also very good, particularly Russell when she delivers an incendiary courtroom monologue and Hackman as the bullying billionaire swaggering around his island like a cock of the roost.

RATING: R for profanity and violence.

THE EUROPEANS
(Video)

Literary Romance

England/U.S.A.

1979   90 Min.   Color

CREDITS: Directed by James Ivory. Written by Ruth Prawer-Jhabvala, based on the novel by Henry James. Produced by Ismail Merchant. Cinematography by Larry Pizer. Music by Richard Robbins. Art direction by Jeremiah Rusconi. Costume design by Judy Morcroft. Released and distributed nontheatrically by New Yorker Films. Starring Lee Remick, Robin Ellis, Lisa Eichhorn, Wesley Addy, Tim Woodward, Kristin Griffith, Tim Choate, Nancy New and Helen Stenborg.

The first Merchant-Ivory adaptation of a Henry James novel (*The Bostonians* soon followed), *The Europeans* is a visually lavish production but a tad thin in content. Set in nineteenth-century Boston, it's the story of the romantic adventures of three children from the monied Wentworth family and their two first cousins, all ripe for marriage. When two European cousins, Eugenia (Lee Remick) and Felix (Tim Woodward), show up out of the blue one day for a "visit," the Wentworth household is embroiled in a Victorian soap opera.

The children convince the conservative Wentworth patriarch to let Eugenia and Felix stay in the adjacent country house, although the father is wary of "the peculiar influence" they might have on his children because of their loose Continental morals. His suspicions soon prove to be well-founded when, within a few weeks, fiancés are breaking up with each other and then realigning themselves with past lovers. Even though dad is about to have a nervous breakdown, everybody finds his or her perfect match and lives happily ever after.

The filmmakers succeed masterfully with the film's visuals. The costumes and sets are luxuriously detailed, and the stifling atmosphere of nineteenth-century Boston is captured in all its garish opulence. But who's related to whom, and who's courting whom, is so confusing in the *The Europeans* that you need a scorecard to keep it all straight. Ultimately, it's hard to care about the entire bunch because they don't have a great deal of personality. Director Ivory (*A Room with a View*) treats the Wentworth children and their cousins more like decorated mannequins than real people. Victorian morals aside, the sexual tension in this film is so understated that it barely exists. The dialogue is also predictable, and the ending too pat.

RATING: PG, with nothing objectionable.

EVIL DEAD II: DEAD BY DAWN
(Video)

Horror Satire

U.S.A.

1987   85 Min.   Color

CREDITS: *Directed by Sam Raimi. Written by Sam Raimi and Scott Spiegel. Produced by Robert G. Tapert. Cinematography by Peter Deming. Edited by Kaye Davis. Released by Rosebud and De Laurentiis Entertainment Group. Distributed nontheatrically by Films Inc. Starring Robert Campbell, Sarah Berry, Dan Hicks (of the popular seventies group, Dan Hicks and His Hot Licks), Kassie Wesley and Theodore Raimi.*

Sam Raimi works exclusively in the horror genre, and consequently most of his highly satirical films are packed off to grind houses, where they are undeservedly ignored by art audiences.

Related only by title and location to his much more exploitative *Evil Dead*, *Dead by Dawn* begins when a young man (Robert Campbell) and his girlfriend stumble upon a cabin in the dense woods and decide to spend the night. Finding *The Book of the Dead* on a table in the cabin, the couple chants a few of its incantations, and in short order, the girl is dragged off and killed by a ghostly menace, while the boy fights her severed head and his own possessed hand to stay alive. At the same time, the daughter of a professor, her boyfriend and two hayseed guides arrive at the cabin in search of the young woman's recently disappeared parents. This group, too, is besieged by the evil spirit, and soon only the girl (Sarah Berry) and the battered young man are left standing. Realizing that only reading aloud another incantation from *The Book of the Dead* will vanquish their enemy, the boy and the girl have to fight her mother's spirited cadaver in the fruit cellar for control of these crucial pages, with not only their lives but the fate of the entire world at stake.

Despite gallons of blood shed in service to a rather absurd plot, most of the violence in *Dead by Dawn* is done in such jest that it's not especially gruesome or scary. The fifteen-minute sequence in which the boy fights his own rebellious hand for control of his body is a sidesplitter, while the film's "lone survivor" ending is a clever takeoff on the Mad Max series. Raimi was also obviously inspired by the work of cartoon director Chuck Jones *(Bugs Bunny)*, since many of the film's nonanimated scenes are marked by off-center camera angles, garish lighting and frenetic pacing. But he stumbles when he tries to insert animation sequences, which look amateurish and aren't very effective.

RATING: *No MPAA rating, with a lot of violence and nudity.*
FILMNOTE: *De Laurentiis Entertainment Group, the film's real production company, released* Dead by Dawn *through the independent Rosebud Productions to slip it by the MPAA for fear that it would be rated X.*

EXPERIENCE PREFERRED . . . BUT NOT ESSENTIAL
(Video)

  ½

Coming-of-Age Comedy

England

1983   80 Min.   Color

CREDITS: *Directed by Peter Duffell. Written by June Roberts. Produced by Chris Griffen. Cinematography by Phil Meheux. Music by John Scott. Released by Enigma Films. Distributed nontheatrically by the Samuel Goldwyn Company. Starring Elizabeth Edmonds, Sue Wallace, Geraldine Griffith, Karen Meagher, Ron Bain, Alun Lewis, Robert Blythe, Maggie Wilkinson and Roy Heather.*

Experience Preferred . . . But Not Essential is a mildly entertaining comedy about Annie (Elizabeth Edmonds), a frumpy college student who takes a job as a waitress at a Welsh seaside resort during her summer vacation in 1962. This is the first time Annie's ever been away from home, and during that fateful summer she makes some big steps toward becoming an adult—she smokes her first cigarette, drinks her first beer and, most important, takes her first lover.

But Annie's life at the resort isn't exactly one big sorority party. It's hard work hustling three meals a day for demanding guests and the hotel's imperious restaurant manager. Although she likes the crazy bunch she rooms with in the servants' quarters, they have their problems as well. One worker becomes pregnant by a man twice her age, another has been hurt so often by deceitful men she prefers the safety of one-night stands. Then there's the assistant chef who's gay but afraid to come out of the closet. But luckily, Annie is also courted by Mike (Ron Bain), the hotel's head chef who woos her with delicacies on silver trays and long, satisfying walks on the beach.

For this naïve young woman away from mum and pop for the first time, several of the people she comes to know on her summer vacation would appear to have serious problems. But most of these situations are handled like just another lunch shift in *Experience Preferred*, since the film's important issues of loneliness, personal failure and sexual confusion are introduced briefly and then passed over. As a result, the sometimes comical narrative seems like a series of loosely tied together vignettes, and the characters are unremarkable. Edmond's Annie is the most interesting of them all and has some warm and compelling moments in her coming of age, particularly in how she responds to her first sexual encounter. Director Peter Duffell and his cinematographer Phil Meheux do an excellent job capturing the tranquil beauty of the Welsh shore, while the authentic sixties party dresses and hairdos are great fun.

RATING: *PG for language.*

EXPOSED
(Video)

★   ★   ½

Political Thriller

U.S.A.

1983   100 Min.   Color

CREDITS: *Directed, written and produced by James Toback. Cinematography by Henri Decae. Music by Georges Delerue. Released by MGM/UA. Distributed nontheatrically by Films Inc. Starring Nastassja Kinski, Rudolph Nureyev, Harvey Keitel, Ian MacShane, Bibi Andersson, James Toback, Pierre Clementi and Ron Randell.*

Exposed is a seriously flawed but interesting story of Elizabeth (Nastassja Kinski), a restless Midwestern college student who drops out of school to become a classical pianist in New York City. With her stunning looks, she ends up becoming a model instead when a fashion photographer turns her into a famous cover girl for *Glamour* and *Vogue*.

At a party to celebrate her overnight success (which takes less than fifteen minutes of screen time to achieve), Elizabeth is approached by Daniel (Rudolph Nureyev), an enigmatic, poetry-spouting violinist whose bizarre manner entices her. After he seduces her (accomplished in part with his violin bow), he lures her to Paris, where he confesses that he is the leader of an anti-terrorist group and that he slept with her to enlist her in his cause. Daniel wants Elizabeth to infiltrate the camp of Rivas (Harvey Keitel), a famous terrorist whose army is mostly made up of beautiful women. Elizabeth refuses but somehow finds herself in Rivas's group anyhow and is caught in a deadly tug-of-war between the two men.

By casting Kinski as a Wisconsin farm girl, writer/director James Toback shows that he obviously has more on his mind than a believable narrative. So little about this film fits into the realm of possibility that a viewer is probably better off not even asking questions such as why Kinski joins Keitel's group and why both men are so desperate to have this naïve college dropout on their sides in the first place.

To enjoy this movie, you have to look past the main story line to the film's wonderful small moments and to Kinski's compelling performance. As in his earlier sleeper, *Fingers,* Toback has a knack for creating darkly funny moments in nearly every scene. When Kinski becomes involved in a stakeout, for instance, she is interrupted by an insane beggar who continues to badger her when he deems the one franc she tosses him insufficient. Daniel's violin bow seduction scene is another example of Toback's strangely comical talents. But it's Kinski's character of Elizabeth that holds this film together. Although she gets little support from the rest of the cast (Nureyev is particularly miscast), Kinski is marvelous as the sexually charged young model. A scene of Kinski dancing in front of a mirror is a testament to her raw erotic power, a sexual charisma that, along with Toback's inventive sideshow, makes *Exposed* well worth a look.

RATING: *R for nudity, sex and violence.*

THE EXTERMINATING ANGEL
(Video, subtitled)

Black Comedy

Mexico   Spanish

1962   95 Min.   B&W

CREDITS: *Directed by Luis Buñuel. Written by Luis Buñuel and Luis Alcoriza, based on the play* Los naufragos de la Calle de la Providentia *by Jose Bergamin. Produced by Gustavo Alatriste. Cinematography by Gabriel Figueroa. Music by Alessandro Scarlatti and Pietro Domenico. Released by Altura Films. Distributed nontheatrically by Kit Parker Films. Starring Silvia Pinal, Enrique Rambal, Jose Baviera, Jacqueline Andere, Luis Beristein, Augusto Benedico, Claudio Brook, Antonio Bravo and Cesar Del Campo.*

In *The Exterminating Angel,* Luis Buñuel again makes fun of the rich, this time by condemning them to purgatory. The film begins when a wealthy couple invites several guests over for a dinner party, and after an evening of insincere socializing they inexplicably can't leave the house. Some of the men begin to fight with each other and some of the women become hysterical, but most of the bewildered aristocrats just wander around—lost, depressed and afraid. After being trapped in the house for days, they run out of food and start to go crazy from hunger and claustrophobia. In one hilarious scene, some of these socialites pray to a rubber Virgin Mary. In another, they take a vote on whether to kill their host in order to break the curse. What's just as bizarre is that a group of concerned friends and relatives have gathered outside the mansion and are unable to rescue them.

Typically Buñuelian, *Exterminating Angel* presents a simple but perverse situation that is stretched to its limit. Each scene is rich with outrageous dialogue and symbolism. Simple discussions about clothes, food and money, for example, are really about alienation and redemption in the afterlife. The film takes a certain frame of mind to appreciate. Who the characters are in this film or what they do isn't important; what matters is that they are rich and have little personality or direction in their lives and are enslaved by their Catholic guilt. For what the script requires, the ensemble of players Buñuel selected is convincing. They are sometimes quite funny, and at other moments intentionally aggravating. To add to the absurdity, Buñuel uses surreal filming techniques such as repeating scenes and altering them slightly, or rerunning certain scenes without changing them at all. This effect leaves the already inane characters suspended in space and time.

RATING: No MPAA rating, with nothing objectionable.

THE EYES, THE MOUTH
(Video, subtitled)

Psychological Drama

Italy/France	Italian
1982 100 Min.	Color

CREDITS: *Directed by Marco Bellocchio. Written by Marco Bellocchio and Vincenzo Cerami. Produced by Enzo Porcelli and Enea Ferrano. Cinematography by Giuseppe Lanci. Music by Nicola Piovani. Released by Columbia Pictures/Triumph Films. Distributed nontheatrically by Swank Motion Pictures. Starring Lou Castel, Angela Molina, Emanuelle Riva and Michel Piccoli.*

Since the mid-sixties, Marco Bellocchio *(Fists in the Pocket)* has been one of Italy's most important and prolific filmmakers. Unfortunately, *The Eyes, the Mouth,* his most accessible film to American art house and video store audiences, is not one of his best.

The film begins as a troubled, middle-aged Giovanni (Lou Castel) rushes home from Rome to comfort his mother (Emanuelle Riva of *Hiroshima, Mon Amour)* after the suicide of his brother, Pippo. Long the black sheep of his family because of his failure as an actor, Giovanni helps his mother cope with her grief by convincing her that Pippo's death was the result of an accident, not suicide. He tries to enlist the help of Pippo's estranged lover, Vanda (Angela Molina of *That Obscure Object of Desire),* to corroborate the story, but the impetuous and angry Vanda not only refuses to support Giovanni's assertion but tells Giovanni's mother that Pippo killed himself because of Vanda and that she has his suicide note as proof. To complicate matters, while Giovanni's mother suffers a nervous breakdown, he and Vanda become lovers although she is pregnant with Pippo's child.

The idea for this film—the examination of a family's struggle to cope with suicide as a betrayal—is a good one, but Bellocchio botches the effort superbly. *The Eyes, the*

Mouth is hopelessly boring all the way up to its tensionless climax. Much of the film consists of Castel's Giovanni staring into space, brooding or engaging in shouting matches with Vanda for no discernible reason. When he breaks the pattern and finally goes over the edge, Giovanni behaves so oddly that it's hard to see what possibly could be going on inside of him. In one scene, for example, he eats his food directly from a tray like a dog, naked and on all fours. And in another, he croons the song "Are You Lonely Tonight" directly into the camera. Although it's obvious that Molina is angry and tortured by Pippo's suicide, her emotions are even more hidden than Giovanni's. The bright spots in this film are the performances of Emanuelle Riva as Giovanni's mother and Michel Piccoli as his uncle, plus Giuseppe Lanci's atmospheric cinematography. But the fine acting and good camera work are wasted on this silly, pretentiously self-indugent movie.

RATING: R for nudity, sex and violence.
FILMNOTE: *In one scene of* The Eyes, the Mouth, *Bellocchio makes a plug for his most famous film. Castel and Molina go see his 1965 release* A Fist in His Pocket, *which also stars Castel.*

FANNY AND ALEXANDER
(Video, subtitled)

Coming-of-Age Drama

Sweden	Swedish
1983 197 Min.	Color

CREDITS: *Directed, written and produced by Ingmar Bergman. Cinematography by Sven Nykvist. Art direction by Anna Asp and Susan Linham. Set design by Jacob Tigerskiold. Released by Embassy Pictures. Distributed nontheatrically by Films Inc. Starring Pernilla Allwin, Bertil Guve, Gunn Wallgren, Allan Edwall, Ewa Froling, Jan Malmsjo, Erland Josephson, Harriet Andersson and Anna Bergman.*

In his prolific career, Ingmar Bergman directed over seventy-five feature films,

and most of his works can be described as intense character studies of people on the edge of madness. Although his final venture, *Fanny and Alexander,* does have some of these same elements, it's also a warm, life-affirming movie.

The film explores a few years in the childhood of Fanny (Pernilla Allwin) and Alexander (Bertil Guve), two young children growing up in a provincial Swedish town at the turn of the century. We're first introduced to their family at Christmas dinner. Almost everybody is involved with the theater, which provides Bergman with fertile ground to develop some wonderful, overly theatrical personalities. Some of them are typically Bergmanesque, such as the suicidally depressed uncle and his despondent German wife. But others belong in a French farce, such as a jovial uncle who tries to have sex with every young woman he encounters. For the most part, the two children have a happy and colorful childhood.

But when their father dies suddenly during a play rehearsal, and their mother marries Bishop Vergerus (Jan Malmsjo), the children's lives change for the worse. The vicar's home is prison for them, as their ruthless stepfather shoves religion down their throats and beats them if they disobey his orders. Finally, he becomes unbearable, and Fanny and Alexander hide out with a Jewish antique dealer who is an old friend of the family. His house is mysterious and magical, with forbidden rooms, secret passageways and puppets that come alive in the children's imaginations.

Bergman mixes in a bit of everything in this highly autobiographical grand finale—dark character studies, religious symbolism, fond childhood memories and the mysteries of the unknown. All of it is woven together magnificently, from the performances and script to the sets and cinematography. Although there are some slow sections, such as the father's funeral, *Fanny and Alexander* is so top-heavy with well-drawn characters, lavish sets and beautiful cinematography that you can live with the film's occasional overindulgence.

RATING: *R for brief nudity, profanity and violence*
AWARDS: *1983 Academy Awards for Best*

Cinematography (Sven Nykvist), Best Art Direction (Anna Asp and Susan Linham), Best Foreign Film and Best Costume Design (Marik Vos); 1983 Academy Award nomination for Best Director (Bergman); 1983 French Caesar for Best Foreign Film; 1983 New York Film Critics Awards for Best Foreign Film and Best Direction.

WARNING: The cinematography is so important that the quality is lessened on video.

FILMNOTE: Although Bergman claimed that Fanny and Alexander was going to be his last feature film, the made-for-TV movie After the Rehearsal was released in 1984.

FEMALE TROUBLE
(Video)

Social Satire

U.S.A.

1974   92 Min.   Color

CREDITS: Directed, written, produced and photographed by John Waters. Edited by Charles Roggero. Released by Saliva Films. Distributed nontheatrically by New Line Cinema. Starring Divine, David Lochary, Mary Vivian Pearce, Mink Stole, Edith Massey, Cookie Mueller, Susan Walsh, Michael Potter and Ed Peranio.

It takes a special director to cast a 325-pound transvestite as a giggling ingenue. John Waters (Pink Flamingos) is that sort of filmmaker, and your willingness to follow his most perverse impulses will also measure your enjoyment of this typical Waters film.

Female Trouble concerns Dawn Davenport (the gargantuan Divine), a "bad girl" who progresses from teenage promiscuity to petty burglary and ultimately murder. Set down on an unhappy path after she's raped (using trick photography, Divine "rapes" himself in a dual role), Dawn battles her Aunt Ida (Edith Massey) and tries her hand at fashion modeling and waitress-

ing to support her child, all the while vainly resisting the criminal impulses that draw her ever closer to a fatal confrontation with the electric chair.

Thanks to tireless self-promotion (including an autobiography, Shock Value), John Waters has made a name for himself as an independent filmmaker, even though to say that his films are thinly constructed is certainly an understatement. Female Trouble could head the list. The acting is amateurish, the script is flat, and the direction is soft and visually uninspired. But in Waters's work, these flaws are trivial. The shock gags are meant to carry the load, and sometimes—such as when Dawn bites through the umbilical cord of her newborn child, throws up on her sore-covered penis or lops off the hand of a caged Edith Massey—they do. But an hour and a half of not very funny gross-out jokes is too much for any viewer to handle. In the end, Female Trouble is not only sick, violent and disgusting, it's also boring.

RATING: X for violence, profanity, nudity, sex and vileness.

FILMNOTE: Female Trouble is the ultimate low-budget film. Made for $25,000, Waters did everything but edit the film.

THE FESTIVAL OF CLAYMATION
(Video)

Animation

U.S.A.

1987   90 Min.   Color

CREDITS: Directed and produced by Will Vinton. Written by Will Vinton, Susan Shadburne, Derek Muirden, Doug Aberle and John Morrison. Animation by Will Vinton, Tom Gasek, Barry Bruce, Joan Gratz, Matt Wuerker, Joanne Radmilovich, Mark Gustafson, Craig Bartlett, Bill Fiesterman and Doug Aberle. Music by Peter, Paul and Mary, Marvin Gaye, Ron Walker,

Dave Friesen, John Stowell and Billy Scream. Released and distributed nontheatrically by Expanded Entertainment.

Clay animation has come a long way since the days of Gumby and Pokey cartoons, thanks mostly to Will Vinton. Calling his process Claymation (for which he holds a patent), Vinton basically moves and reshapes clay sets and figures a single frame at a time, the technique long used by other animators in the past. What sets Vinton's work apart is the quality of character and set design, and the painstaking effort he and his staff undertake in order to achieve a desired effect. A showpiece of his work, *The Festival of Claymation* documents how Vinton and his staff of twenty-two create some of the most outrageously funny and visually complex animated figures ever brought to the screen, capturing expressions and movement so subtle that it's easy to forget that these figures aren't really alive. Each shot is enhanced by state-of-the-art lighting and excellent camera work, but it's the detail of the characters and sets themselves that make these shorts so remarkable.

At the start of the film, a short piece introduces Vinton and his motley crew of ex-hippies, explaining the process of Claymation and showing them in action, laboriously sculpting their sets and characters. Then we see the results of their effort—twenty innovative shorts on subjects as varied as children's fantasy stories, clips from his Claymation feature *The Adventures of Mark Twain,* and the now-famous California Raisins commercial featuring soulful raisin-men singing Marvin Gaye's "I Heard It Through the Grapevine." Bookending each short are two dinosaur movie critics resembling Gene Siskel and Roger Ebert, who self-mockingly quarrel about what they have just viewed and introduce the next clip. Although some of the pieces are more entertaining than others, the creativity in each is so intoxicating that even grownups will find themselves laughing hysterically, and oohing and ahhing with each passing delight.

RATING: No MPAA rating, with nothing objectionable.

AWARDS: Various shorts in the film won the following awards: "The Great Cognito" (1982 Academy Award nomination); "Dinosaur" (Gold Hugo at the 1980 Chicago Film Festival); "Legacy" (Best Film at 1985 ASIFA East); "The Creation" (1982 Academy Award nomination).

FITZCARRALDO
(Video, subtitled)

★ ★ ½

Adventure/Drama

West Germany		German
1982	158 Min.	Color

CREDITS: Directed and written by Werner Herzog. Produced by Werner Herzog and Lucki Stipetic. Cinematography by Thomas Mauch. Music by Popol Vuh. Released by New World Pictures. Distributed nontheatrically by Films Inc. Starring Klaus Kinski, Claudia Cardinale, Jose Lewgoy, Miguel Angel Fuentes and Paul Hittscher.

Similar in scope and theme to his earlier masterpiece, *Aguirre: The Wrath of God,* Werner Herzog's *Fitzcarraldo* is a less successful epic about a madman trying to conquer nature.

Fitzcarraldo (Klaus Kinski) is an Irishman who comes to the Amazon consumed by a dream of building a jungle opera house in which the great Caruso can perform. If his dream seems crazy, his method of financing it is even more lunatic. With the help of his lover, Molly (Claudia Cardinale), he plans to transport a steamship over a mountain to a previously inaccessible river, opening hundreds of thousands of square miles to commerce. Fitzcarraldo buys a broken-down ship and brings it upstream on a parallel river, then coerces hostile Indians to drag the thirty-ton ship over a dense jungle incline to the body of water on the other side. But by the time Fitzcarraldo reaches his destination, all but three crew members have abandoned him, and his tribal slaves have united to create their own dark plan for both the ship and its captain.

In Les Blank's revealing documentary, *Burden of Dreams* (see page 83), on the making of *Fitzcarraldo*, we learn that in spite of the advice of experts, Herzog became as obsessed with realizing his complicated artistic vision as Fitzcarraldo was with building an opera house. The film does pay off in its visuals. The terror of the jungle river and the awesome spectacle of the ship being pulled up the mountain are extremely powerful, as is Kinski's performance. We never stop empathizing with him even as he is driven to the point of insanity. But Herzog, too, seems out of control, driven by the movie's physical details. The scenes on the boat and the mountain, which have little dialogue, overwhelm the characters and plot in this movie. By the film's remarkable conclusion, this two-and-a-half-hour epic is simply too leaden to handle.

RATING: PG, with mild violence.
AWARDS: Award for Best Director (Werner Herzog) at the 1982 Cannes Film Festival.

A FLASH OF GREEN
(Video)

Political Thriller

U.S.A.

1984   131 Min.   Color

CREDITS: *Directed, photographed, and edited by Victor Nunez. Written by Victor Nunez, based on the novel by John D. MacDonald. Produced by Richard Jordan. Released by Spectrafilm and shown on PBS's "American Playhouse." Starring Ed Harris, Blair Brown, Richard Jordan, George Coe, Isa Thomas, Joan Goodfellow and Jean De Baer.*

When Jimmy Wing (Ed Harris) drifts back to his hometown, Palm City, in the Florida Keys in the early sixties, he returns mostly because he has nowhere else to go. His wife is permanently institutionalized with a degenerative mental disorder, and

Jimmy is emotionally burned out. He takes a mindless job as a reporter for his small-town paper, covering events such as traffic accidents and flower shows with a sense of bemused detachment. Only Kat (Blair Brown), a newly widowed friend, shakes Jimmy from his moral lethargy.

In this condition, Jimmy is an easy target for Elmo Bliss (Richard Jordan), a corrupt county commissioner who intends to destroy a local bay in order to develop a vacation resort. Mindful of the protests against the project led by Kat and her environmentalist friends, Elmo hires Jimmy to dig up dirt on the activists. Jimmy goes along with the blackmail scheme until Elmo's cohorts nearly beat one of Kat's friends to death. Realizing his mistake, Jimmy must choose between hiding his complicity or confessing, and risk losing the one woman he truly loves.

When Jimmy betrays his friends, it's not because he means them harm as much as he feels he doesn't deserve their affection. But when he realizes his actions have implications he can't possibly live with, his choices become more complex. Brown and Harris turn in outstanding performances as the couple joined by their own desperate needs. This film is also an excellent portrait of one man's descent into a hell of his own making, and his eventual struggle for redemption. But *A Flash of Green* stumbles when director Victor Nunez *(Gal Young 'Un)* introduces too many poorly developed subplots involving the blackmail scheme, plus artsy camera shots and ineffectual noirish touches.

RATING: No MPAA rating, with nothing objectionable.

FOOL FOR LOVE
(Video)

Psychological Drama

U.S.A.

1985   105 Min.   Color

CREDITS: *Directed by Robert Altman. Written by Sam Shepard, based on his play.*

Produced by Menaheim Golan and Yoram Globus. Cinematography by Pierre Mignot. Music by Sandy Rogers and Waylon Jennings. Released by Cannon Films. Distributed nontheatrically by Swank Motion Pictures. Starring Sam Shepard, Kim Basinger, Harry Dean Stanton, Randy Quaid, Martha Crawford, Louise Egolf and Sura Cox.

Although directed by Robert Altman, *Fool for Love* is a Sam Shepard tour de force. He wrote the successful play, adapted it for the screen and stars as Eddie, the central character in the film. When the film opens, Eddie, a cowboy, has just driven 2,048 miles across the barren Southwest to meet with his old sweetheart, Mae (Kim Basinger), who lives in a rundown motel in the middle of nowhere. In an adjacent trailer lives an old man (Harry Dean Stanton) who drinks like a fish and lives like a junkyard dog.

The first half of the film shows Eddie and Mae kissing, fighting, and talking in circles about what went wrong in their relationship, while the amused old man gets soused in the background. When Mae's date for the evening, Martin (Randy Quaid), appears on the scene, the truth of their lives is revealed. We learn that the old man is father to both Mae and Eddie, and that the half-brother and half-sister fell in love as teenagers before either knew what was what. As the three tell their story to the hopelessly dense Martin, a mysterious woman in a Mercedes keeps driving by, trying to kill them all.

Fool for Love is Altman's fourth movie based on a stage play (*Jimmy Dean, Streamers, Secret Honor*), and he has become very adept at taking us into small places and twisted minds. Pierre Mignot's surreal cinematography gives certain scenes a dreamlike, almost poetic, quality, while Altman draws top-notch performances from all four main players in the film. Shepard is particularly strong in his only performance in a movie for which he wrote the screenplay. Basinger's Mae is also a surprise, breaking out of her sex symbol pigeonhole and proving herself to be a serious dramatic actress. Yet *Fool for Love* suffers in translation from the stage. With little action and a camera that crawls from

one claustrophobic setting to the next, this film sometimes moves as slowly as tumbleweed on a windless day.

RATING: *R for language, mild violence and sexual situations.*
FILMNOTE: *The film features eight original country-and-western songs, some of them quite good, that are written and performed by Shepard's sister, Sandy Rogers.*

THE 400 BLOWS
(Video, subtitled)

Coming-of-Age Drama

France		French
1959	99 Min.	B&W

CREDITS: *Directed and produced by François Truffaut. Written by François Truffaut and Marcel Moussy. Cinematography by Henri Decae. Music by Jean Constantin. Released by Janus Films. Distributed nontheatrically by Films Inc. Starring Jean-Pierre Leaud, Patrick Auffay, Claire Maurier, Albert Remy, Guy Decomble, Georges Flamant and Yvonne Claudie.*

The 400 Blows was François Truffaut's filmmaking debut, and it remains one of his best works. It's a semiautobiographical story of the unhappy childhood of an eight-year-old Parisian boy from a lower middle-class family. We meet Antoine (Jean-Pierre Leaud) in the classroom as he passes around a pinup calendar to his classmates at school. Once he is caught by his stern teacher, his misfortunes begin. School is oppressive and humiliating for Antoine, and home is no better. His parents argue constantly and give him attention only to scold him. To make matters worse, while playing hooky from school one day, Antoine accidentally catches his mother (Claire Maurier) with another man. Then he overhears his stepfather (Albert Remy) reacting to the tension at home with plans to shuffle Antoine off to camp to get him out of the way. It's too much for any kid to handle and Antoine rebels by running away from home and stealing to get by. Eventually Antoine is caught by the police and, with his stepfather's approval, is placed in a juvenile delinquent observatory.

In French, "400 blows" is a colloquial expression that means "raising hell," and Antoine does his best to live up to the saying. Although the boy is capable of cruelty himself, Truffaut definitely pounds home the message that he is an innocent victim of abusive parents and a school system that only knows how to punish students for "unacceptable" behavior. All the performances are believable in The 400 Blows, but it's Leaud's Antoine who is at the center of every scene. With his weepy eyes and dourly honest expressions, he's the kind of kid whose problems make you want to yell "That's not fair!" at the screen as Truffaut portrays the terrifying events in his life completely from his perspective. Henri Decae's moody black-and-white cinematography, depicting a bleak and foggy Paris, and the enchanting music by Jean Constantin combine to make this one of the most compelling coming-of-age stories ever put on film.

RATING: No MPAA rating, with mild violence.
AWARDS: Award for Best Director (François Truffaut) at the 1959 Cannes Film Festival; 1959 New York Film Critics Award for Best Foreign Film.
FILMNOTE: After his performance as a young boy in The 400 Blows, Jean-Pierre Leaud went on to star in several more Truffaut films as a teenager and then as an adult.

THE 4TH MAN

(Video, dubbed)

Psychological Thriller

Holland		Dutch
1983	104 Min.	Color

CREDITS: Directed by Paul Verhoeven. Written by Gerard Soeteman, based on the novel by Gerard Reve. Produced by Rob Houwer. Cinematography by Jan De Bont. Music by Loek Dikker. Art direction by Roland De Groot. Released and distributed nontheatrically by New Yorker Films. Starring Jeroen Krabbe, Renee Soutendijk, Thom Hoffman, Geert de Jong, Dolf De Vries, Hans Veerman, Hero Muller, Caroline De Beus and Reinout Bussemaker.

Paul Verhoeven's The 4th Man is a black comedy that's more much more dark than humorous. It's the story of Gerard (Jeroen Krabbe), a bisexual writer from Amsterdam who, after lecturing at a book club in another city, is seduced by the club's treasurer, a beautiful blonde widow named Christine (Renee Soutendijk). They have an erotic night at her exotically decorated house, but in the morning, Gerard recognizes another of Christine's lovers from a photograph on her dresser.

His name is Herman (Thom Hoffman), and this is the same attractive man Gerard became obsessed with the day before, after spotting him on a train. Gerard really prefers men to women, but he feigns affection for Christine so he can meet Herman. When he does, Herman isn't interested in Gerard. Meanwhile, Gerard has recurring nightmares about castration and murder, and then discovers that all three of Christine's husbands had accidental deaths after Christine shot home movies of them. Naturally, she's in the process of shooting footage of both Gerard and Herman.

In The 4th Man, Verhoeven (Soldier of Orange, Robocop) combines wonderfully stylized sets and religious metaphors with fantastic dream sequences reminiscent of Ingmar Bergman. Writer Gerard Soeteman's script sustains a heightened level of suspense all the way to its harrowing climax, while Verhoeven throws in nonstop visual jokes to lighten his characters' intense inner conflicts. Although Gerard's nightmares are almost too graphic to handle, Verhoeven and his cinematographer Jan De Bont cleverly shoot them so it's not clear if they are really happening until Gerard wakes up. Given all the other strange events in this film, they seem within the realm of possibility. Obviously, Verhoeven, like Eraserhead's David Lynch, enjoys making us squirm.

RATING: R for graphic violence, nudity and sex
AWARDS: International Critics Prize at the 1983 Toronto Film Festival.
WARNING: The dubbing is decent on the video version, but it does affect the quality of the film.

FOX AND HIS FRIENDS

Gay Drama

West Germany	German
1975 123 Min.	Color

CREDITS: Directed by Rainer Werner Fassbinder. Written by Rainer Werner Fassbinder and Christian Hohoff. Produced by Christian Hohoff. Cinematography by Michael Ballhaus. Music by Peter Raben. Released and distributed nontheatrically by New Yorker Films. Starring Rainer Werner Fassbinder, Peter Chatel, Karl-Heinz Bohm, Harry Baer, Adrian Hoven, Ulla Jacobsen and Christian Maybeach.

Rainer Werner Fassbinder's *Fox and His Friends* is the first film in which he features himself in the starring role. He plays Fox, The Talking Head at a carnival sideshow, until the master of ceremonies (his lover) is arrested, putting Fox out of a job. But Fox's luck changes when he purchases a lottery ticket and wins 500,000 marks, then falls in love with a handsome printing company executive named Eugen (Peter Chatel). Although Eugen is a cultured man who normally wouldn't have anything to do with a lowlife like Fox, he's able to see beyond Fox's pudgy body and into his fat wallet. Fox is willing to spend any amount on his new lover. He buys Eugen a new apartment and antiques to furnish it, then bails Eugen's financially troubled printing company out of debt on a couple occasions. Meanwhile, Eugen goes out with other guys and humiliates Fox for his bad habits and manners whenever he gets the chance.

Fox is the dupe's dupe. Fassbinder plays him as a man so desperate for his lover's affection and respect that he will grovel in horse manure for it. Eugen is so abusive to Fox that it's infuriating, but it's also a little hard to swallow. Eugen's motives are transparent from the moment they meet, and it's unbelievable that poor Fox doesn't figure them out until the end of the movie. But *Fox and His Friends* works extremely well as a study in masochism and class. Fassbinder never shows Fox experiencing joy, even when he wins the lottery (we learn he won through a snide remark by an acquaintance at a party), and Fox's relationship with Eugen serves as an indictment of bourgeois values, as well as a bleak vision of lower-class doom.

RATING: No MPAA rating, with mild profanity and nudity.
AWARDS: Golden Hugo for Best Film at the 1975 Chicago Film Festival.

THE FRINGE DWELLERS
(Video)

Cultural Drama

Australia	
1987 98 Min.	Color

CREDITS: Directed by Bruce Beresford. Written by Bruce and Rhoisin Beresford (Bruce's wife), based on the novel by Nina Gare. Produced by Sue Milliken and Bruce Beresford. Cinematography by Don McAlpine. Released by Atlantic Entertainment Group. Distributed nontheatrically by Films Inc. Starring Justine Saunders, Kristina Nehm, Bob Maza and Kylie Belling.

Bruce Beresford's *The Fringe Dwellers* is a fascinating but uneven story of the Comeaways, an Aborigine family who live in a shantytown in the conservative province of Queensland. The family's matriarch is Mollie (Justine Saunders), a rotund woman who barely holds the family together. Her husband, Joe (Bob Maza), isn't much help, more intent on drinking and gambling with his friends than on earning money for his family. The eldest daughter, a nurse, chips in her salary, and with some support from their neighbors the family manages to eke out a living. But the youngest daughter, Trilby (Kristina Nehm), isn't satisfied with this life and talks her parents into taking out a government loan to buy a tract house in the suburbs. Once the move is made, Trilby's bright hopes for her family turn into disaster. Then the enraged Trilby becomes pregnant with a child she doesn't want.

The one glaring hitch in *The Fringe Dwellers* involves the fate of this baby and, without giving the scene away, it's so wrong for Trilby's character that it almost ruins the film. Moreover, in keeping too much with Aborigine rhythms, certain scenes are too loosely structured to hold together the plot's driving tensions. But director Bruce Beresford *(Breaker Morant, The Getting of Wisdom)* takes us into the heart of shantytown life in very intimate ways. The Comeaways are believable characters who not only live outside of town but also exist on the fringe of both white and Aborigine cultures. Their lives are rich in family and community bonds, yet they are caught in a subculture of a racist society that dooms them to poverty and exclusion. Beresford addresses several issues of prejudice sensitively, but it's the underlying and subtle racism of well-meaning liberals that hits the mark in *The Fringe Dwellers*.

RATING: PG, with one brief sex scene and nudity.

FROM MAO TO MOZART: ISAAC STERN IN CHINA
(Video)

Music Documentary

U.S.A.	English and Chinese
1980	84 Min. Color

CREDITS: Directed by Murray Lerner. Distributed nontheatrically by Films Inc. Starring Isaac Stern, David Golub and Tan Shuzhen.

In 1979, with the Gang of Four in prison and a new liberalization firmly in place, American violin master Isaac Stern received a special invitation from the foreign minister of China to visit that country. When asked what he planned to do there, Stern replied: "Use my music as a passport." He succeeded, as many doors traditionally closed to Westerners were opened to him. This life-affirming film documents Stern's experiences in China and in doing so crosses cultural boundaries and touches our hearts and minds as well.

In the film, Stern travels to several provinces in China and gets involved in impromptu concerts and lectures at conservatories. But mostly he observes and tutors musicians of all ages. Some of the film's more humorous scenes include an orchestra welcoming him with a classical rendition of "Oh, Susannah" and Stern teaching students so young they can barely hold their violins under their tiny chins. There are also sobering moments, such as when music teachers tell Stern how they were imprisoned and tortured for teaching Western music. If there is a theme to this tightly edited documentary, it's in Stern's observation that Chinese musicians are well-disciplined and proficient but lack a certain emotional depth to their music. The film's most repeated scene is of the animated Stern trying to put soul into his Chinese students, moments that smack of Western condescension.

The cinematography in *From Mao to Mozart* is stunning. Pans of the landscapes—the misty rice paddies and fog-enshrouded mountains—look like Chinese tapestries on film. And, of course, the music is tremendous, both Stern's and that of the Chinese playing their strange and wonderful instruments.

RATING: No MPAA rating, with nothing objectionable.
AWARDS: 1979 Academy Award for Best Documentary Feature.

In *The Tokyo Story*, a father and his daughter-in-law represent the clash of old and new values in post–World War II Japan.

Twelve-year-old Ingemar (Anton Glanzelius) contemplates life with his faithful companion in *My Life as a Dog*, Lasse Hallstrom's bittersweet coming-of-age story.

Carla Dunlap struts her stuff in *Pumping Iron II: The Women*, George Butler's exploration of how women bodybuilders view their sport and their femininity.

Top left: In *Hour of the Star,* Brazilian filmmaker Suzana Amaral's first feature, social outcast Macabea (Marcelia Cartaxo) lives through her romantic fantasies.

Top right: In *Sugarbaby,* Percy Adlon's romantic farce, the heroine (Marianne Sagebrecht) seduces a handsome train conductor with his favorite candy.

Right: The sexual attention of a concentration camp commandant (Shirley Stoler) is just one of the disasters Giancarlo Giannini's Pasqualino must overcome in *Seven Beauties,* Lina Wertmuller's sexual satire.

Below: Frank (Dean Stockwell), an American military advisor, tries to befriend Alsino, a Nicaraguan peasant boy (Alan Esquivel), in *Alsino and the Condor.*

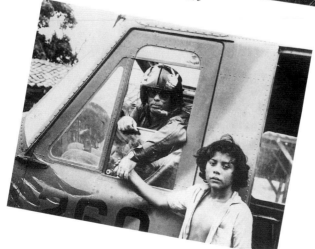

In Nikita Mikalkov's historical satire *A Slave of Love*,
the filming of a Russian
melodrama turns into slapstick comedy.

Sexually obsessed Frank
R.pploh seduces an acquaintance in *Taxi Zum Klo*, a
highly controversial gay film.

Prostitutes get ready for
another day's work in
one of Lina Wertmul-
ler's best political sat-
ires, *Love and Anarchy*.

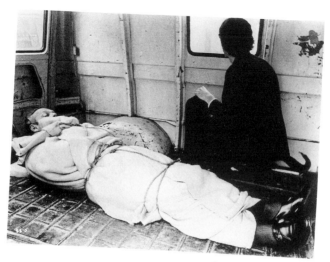

In Constantine Costa-Gavras's political thriller *State of Siege*, South American leftist guerrillas abduct an undercover CIA official.

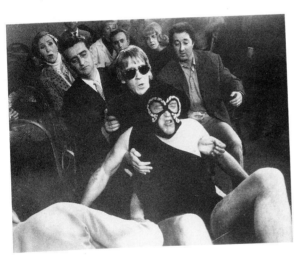

David Warner is a lovable lunatic in *Morgan*, Karel Reisz's sixties satire.

Three unlikely cellmates (John Lurie, Tom Waits and Roberto Benigni) on the lam in *Down by Law*, Jim Jarmusch's comedy.

Italian sharecroppers Grandpa Anselmo (Giuseppe Brignoli) and Bettina (Maria Grazia Caroli) listen as Batisti (Luigi Ormaghi) tells a story in *The Tree of Wooden Clogs*.

In *Pixote*, Brazilian director Hector Babenco spares few gruesome details in his depiction of the lives of homeless teenagers.

Claude (Louis Perryman) and Cowboy (Sonny Carl Davis) discuss life's problems in *Last Night at the Alamo*.

Poles from the town of Auschwitz in *Shoah*, Claude Lanzmann's nine-hour Holocaust
documentary.

In *Aguirre, the Wrath of God*,
Aguirre (Klaus Kinski) realizes
he has gone too far in his quest
for power when his daughter
(Nastassja Kinski) is shot by an
arrow.

In *Parting Glances*, a
gay couple (John Bol-
ger and Richard
Ganoung) struggle
with their relationship
and AIDS.

Odd couple Julius (Heiner Lauterbach) and Stefan (Uwe Ochsenknecht) have a moment of truce in *Men*, Doris Dorrie's lampoon of the modern German male.

Job (Ferenc Zenthe) takes his newly adopted son (Gabor Feher) fishing in *The Revolt of Job*, a story of Hungarian/Jewish peasant life during World War II.

Highway sprawl in Godfrey Reggio's harrowing documentary of "life out of balance": *Koyaanisqatsi.*

In this 1950s Civil Defense photo, Boy Scouts show off their "state of the art" fallout shelter in *The Atomic Cafe*.

In *Mephisto*, Klaus Maria Brandauer stars as an actor in Hitler's Germany, caught between his principles and his beliefs.

A sixty-year-old German widow (Brigitte Mira) and a young Moroccan immigrant (El Hedi Ben Salem) fall in love on the dance floor in *Ali: Fear Eats the Soul*.

FULL MOON IN PARIS
(Video, subtitled)

★ ★ ½

Psychological Romance

France   French

1984   102 Min.   Color

CREDITS: *Directed and written by Eric Rohmer. Produced by Margaret Menegoz. Cinematography by Renato Berta. Music by Elli Jacno. Art direction and costume design by Pascale Ogier. Released by Orion Classics. Distributed nontheatrically by Films Inc. Starring Pascale Ogier, Fabrice Luchini, Tcheky Karyo, Christian Vadim, Virginia Thevenet, Laszlo Szabo and Anne-Severine Liotard.*

In this film (the fourth in his "Comedies and Proverbs" series), Eric Rohmer shows his skills at exploring relationships from a woman's perspective. His heroine in *Full Moon in Paris* is Louise (Pascale Ogier), a designer in her mid-twenties who has been living with Remi (Tcheky Karyo) for quite a while. Feeling suffocated, she gets up the nerve to rent her own apartment so that she can spend a few days a week by herself. At first, Remi overreacts, assuming that she is looking for some action on the side, but Louise convinces him that the separation will allow their relationship to grow. It does, but not exactly in the ways she planned.

It turns out that the person Louise spends most of her time with in her new apartment is Jacques (Fabrice Luchini), a married friend who desperately tries to seduce her and is as possessive and jealous as Remi. Then, with bitter surprise, Louise is forced to choke down a gulp of her own medicine when Remi decides to take advantage of his freedom as well.

Rohmer drums home the message that freedom can look good in theory, but the practice can be a different matter. He also gives us plenty to think about concerning commitment and complacency between lovers. All the characters in *Full Moon in Paris* realistically portray different levels of power and powerlessness in relationships.

Ogier captures Louise's fragile character very naturally, while Luchini and Karyo are equally convincing as her pushy friend and insensitive boyfriend. What's missing are the reasons they are together in the first place. Everything revolves around the structure of the relationships, but little attention is paid to the content. And because the characters never rise above a certain level of mediocrity, they rarely engage us more than players in a mental exercise.

RATING: *R for one brief nude scene and see-through T-shirts*
AWARDS: *Award for Best Actress (Pascale Ogier) at the 1984 Venice Film Festival.*
FILMNOTE: *To the shock of the French film industry, the very talented twenty-four-year-old Pascale Ogier died of a heart attack shortly after completion of* Full Moon in Paris.

GAL YOUNG 'UN
(Video)

★ ★ ★ ★

Women's Drama

U.S.A.

1979   105 Min.   Color

CREDITS: *Directed, produced, photographed and edited by Victor Nunez. Written by Victor Nunez, based on the O. Henry Award–winning story by Marjorie Kinnan Rawlings. Music by Azalea String Band. Released by Nunez Productions. Distributed by First Run Features. Starring Dana Preu, David Peck, J. Smith, Jenny Stringfellow, Gene Densmore and Tim McCormack.*

Like Martin Ritt's *Cross Creek*, Victor Nunez's *Gal Young 'Un* is based on Marjorie Kinnan Rawlings's story about a woman in the backwoods of Florida in the early twenties. But unlike its star-studded, big-budget Ritt counterpart, *Gal Young 'Un* is a completely unsentimentalized exploration of a rural woman's coming of age.

Dana Preu was never in a film before

Nunez cast her as the strong-willed, plain-looking Mattie Siles, "widow of means" who excitedly marries Trax (David Peck), a handsome young ex-con. But the marriage begins to disintegrate as soon as it becomes clear that Trax took her as his wife only because she had the money he needed to set up a lucrative bootlegging business. At first, Mattie chokes down his abuse. But when Trax returns from a business trip with a beautiful young woman (J. Smith) by his side to share their house and his body, his flaccid explanation that she is "a gal young 'un with no place to go" is too much for Mattie to handle. In one of the most satisfying revenge scenes since Newman and Redford's payoff in *The Sting*, Mattie gets back at this sleazy excuse for a husband in some surprising ways.

There isn't a great deal of action in *Gal Young 'Un*. The film's dialogue is terse, the characters are understated, and there is only a smattering of suspense. But this low-budget (under $100,000) frontier woman's story is as authentically realized and soulful as any of its big-budget counterparts because of Preu's performance as Mattie. A Florida A&M University professor who had never acted before, her speech is so straightforward and her manner so unassuming that we never stop feeling for her from beginning to end. Yet director Nunez *(A Flash of Green)* is careful never to allow us to pity her. Although trapped in a terrible marriage, somehow we're always certain that Mattie has the dignity and courage to break away and rebuild her life.

RATING: No MPAA rating, with brief nudity.
AWARDS: Silver Hugo for Best First Feature at the 1979 Chicago Film Festival.
FILMNOTE: Gal Young 'Un was a real labor of love. The crew and most of the cast worked for bare minimum wages, while Nunez took nothing at all and worked as a cameraman on other films during this production to support his family and himself.

GALLIPOLI
(Video)

Coming-of-Age Adventure

Australia

1981   111 Min.   Color

CREDITS: *Directed by Peter Weir. Written by Peter Weir and David Williamson. Produced by Robert Stigwood and Patricia Lovell. Cinematography by Russell Boyd. Music by Brian May and Michel Jarre. Set design by Wendy Weir. Released by Paramount. Distributed nontheatrically by Films Inc. Starring Mel Gibson, Mark Lee, Robert Grubb, Tim McKenzie, David Argue, Bill Kerr, Harold Hopkins, Charles Yunupingu, Heath Harris, Gerda Nicolson and David Argue.*

Although *Gallipoli* is one of Peter Weir's most popular films, it's not one of his most complex. Set during World War I, it's the story of two young Australian runners who meet at a national race and become friends. Archy (Mark Lee) is a naïve eighteen-year-old from a Waltons-type family, who is dominated by his stern grandfather, a former racing champion. Frank (Mel Gibson) is a railroad worker whose friends are ruffians and whose father is a drunk. They both see the 10-guinea prize for the race as a way to escape the repression in their lives. Eventually they do escape, but by enlisting in the army rather than pursuing racing careers.

In the second half of the movie, the racing buddies are reunited at a training camp in Cairo. The British are at war with Turkey, and Frank and Archy proudly train for the time that they may fight for the Crown. That day comes in Gallipoli, but it's not what they expected. They discover that the Brits commonly send Aussie troops into their most unwinnable conflicts.

The senselessness of war and British prejudice toward Australians are points well presented in *Gallipoli,* but it's an arduous journey to get to them. The first part of the film, set in Australia, rambles; subplots are quickly started and dropped, and insignificant characters are introduced. Once overseas, Archy, Frank and the other Aussie soldiers romanticize war so much it's an obvious setup for their impending doom. It's also not very compelling, because we quite simply haven't gotten to know them or their country's history well enough. Still, Gibson and Lee give fine performances with the sparse dialogue they have to work with and are often charming in this film. Russell Boyd's cinematography is stunning, Brian May's music is haunting, and the film's sets and costumes are authentic as well. But none of this texture is enough to keep *Gallipoli* interesting.

RATING: PG, with mild violence.

AWARDS: 1981 Australian Academy Awards for Best Film, Best Director (Peter Weir), Best Actor (Mel Gibson), Best Supporting Actor (Bill Hunter), Best Photography (Russell Boyd), Best Screenplay (Weir and David Williamson), Best Sound (Don Connolly, Greg Bell and Peter Fenton), Best Editor (William Anderson) and Best Art Direction (Herbert Pinter and Wendy Rubin).

THE GARDEN OF THE FINZI-CONTINIS

(Video, dubbed)

World War II Drama

Italy	Italian
1971 103 Min.	Color

CREDITS: *Directed by Vittorio de Sica. Written by Cesare Zavattini, Vittorio Bonicelli, Ugo Pirro and Giorgio Bassani, based on the novel by Bassani (who later criticized and disavowed the finished version of the film). Music by Manuel de Sica (Vittorio's brother). Cinematography by Ennio Guarnieri. Set design by Franco D'Andria. Released by Titanus Films. Starring Dominique Sanda, Lino Capolicchio, Helmut Berger, Fabio Testi, Romolo Valli, Raffaele Curi, Camillo Angelini-Rota and Katin Vigletti.*

During World War II, Mussolini's Fascists carted many Jews off to concentration camps with little public protest, prompting famed Italian director Vittorio de Sica *(The Bicycle Thief)* to exclaim that "all Italians are guilty." *The Garden of the Finzi-Continis* is his attempt to come to terms with his country's persecution of Jews.

The story is set in 1938, in Ferrara, just as Mussolini begins a new campaign against the Jews, banning mixed marriages and barring them from public schools. These restrictions worry a middle-class Jewish college student named Giorgio (Lino Capolicchio) yet are ignored by his rich Semitic friends, the Finzi-Contini family, who choose to avoid the threat by hiding behind the great walls that separate their mansion from the rest of the town. At first, Giorgio follows their lead, joining them in endless games of tennis and flirting with the beautiful Micol (Dominique Sanda), whom he loves. Later, when he travels to France and learns of the existence of the death camps, Giorgio awakens to the horror of the anti-Semitism and tries to warn Micol and her family. But his warnings are dismissed by them, and when Micol rejects him to take another lover, a despondent Giorgio can only watch helplessly as the Finzi-Continis drift naively toward a fatal confrontation with the Fascists.

Although beginning slowly, with the garish life of the Finzi-Continis portrayed in too much detail, *The Garden of the Finzi-Continis* is a powerful story that works as a romantic melodrama and a political tragedy. Giorgio's eye-opening journey to France is masterfully tied together with his involvement with the Finzi-Continis, who mistakenly believe that their money can protect them from anything. Director de Sica combines the two disparate strands of his story brilliantly, creating a sense of loss and despondency that reverberates throughout the entire second part of the narrative. Franco D'Andria's sets and Ennio Guarnieri's cinematography are also consistently exquisite, while the director extracts excellent performances from the entire cast.

RATING: R for nudity and violence.

AWARDS: 1971 Academy Award for Best Foreign Film; 1971 Academy Award nomination for Best Screenplay Based on Material from Another Medium (Ugo Pirro and Vittorio Bonicelli); Golden Bear for Best Film at the 1971 Berlin Film Festival; one of the National Board of Review's 10 Best Foreign Films in 1971.

WARNING: Dubbing on the video version is often out of sync and seriously affects the quality of the movie.

FILMNOTE: Unfortunately, Almi Pictures lost the nontheatrical rights to The Garden. . . . The only way the film can now be seen is on video.

GATES OF HEAVEN
(Video)

Social Documentary

U.S.A.

1978   85 Min.   Color

CREDITS: Directed, produced and edited by Errol Morris. Cinematography by Ned Burgess. Sound by Jay Miracle. Released and distributed nontheatrically by New Yorker Films. Starring Floyd McClure, Joe Allen, Martin Hall, Mike Koewler, Ed Quye, Lucille Billingsly, Zella Graham, Florence Rasmussen and the Harberts.

Errol Morris's Gates of Heaven is a slice of Americana so droll it belongs in a Kurt Vonnegut novel. Filmed in 1977, this documentary concerns two California families who own pet cemeteries and the assortment of customers who use their services. The film's first conflict arises when the Foothill Memorial Gardens pet cemetery goes bankrupt and 450 pet graves have to be exhumed and moved. There are interviews with Foothill's owner Floyd McClure, an old-timer who's been in the pet burial business since his favorite pooch got run over by a Model T, and an outrageous discussion with Florence Rasmussen, one of McClure's customers, who laments the death of her pet, then launches into a monologue on kids today. There is also an outrageous interview with the owner of a plant where they render tallow from dead animals.

Then the action switches to the Bubbling Well Pet Memorial Park in Napa Valley, where the corpses are to be transferred. Bubbling Well is the Hilton of pet cemeteries, featuring elaborate services, piped-in music and undertakers well-versed in comforting bereaved masters. Once we're introduced to Bubbling Well's owners, the Harberts, we realize this is a business involving innovative salesmanship and a good deal of dedication.

Although Gates of Heaven is sometimes unintentionally comical (as when one woman self-assuredly comments, "I wish to have a deep and meaningful relationship with my poodle."), Morris isn't making fun of pet masters or cemetery patrons or owners in this documentary. There aren't leading questions to push the film's subjects into making fools of themselves. In fact, there are few on-camera questions at all. Ned Burgess's camera is almost always stationary as the people interviewed casually express their views and philosophies on a variety of subjects related to dead pets and their lives, while surrounded by their favorite objects. Of course, some ramble on too long about subjects that aren't very interesting, but most of Gates of Heaven is a fascinating look at Americans in a situation that allows them to be surprisingly honest about their failures, successes and dreams, as well as a haunting document of the everyday moments in life.

RATING: No MPAA rating, with nothing objectionable.

FOOTNOTE: If you enjoy Gates of Heaven, you should see "Vernon, Florida," a 60-minute documentary Morris made for PBS about several delightfully eccentric characters from a speck of a town in northern Florida.

GENERAL DELLA ROVERE

(Video)

World War II Drama

Italy/France	Italian
1960　　　160 Min.	Color

CREDITS: *Directed by Roberto Rossellini. Written by Sergio Amidei, Diego Fabri and Indro Montanelli, based on the novel by Indro Montanelli. Produced by Morris Ergas. Cinematography by Carlo Carlini. Music by Renzo Rossellini. Released by Gaumont Films. Distributed nontheatrically by New Yorker Films. Starring Vittorio de Sica, Hans Messemer, Vittorio Caprioli, Guiseppe Rossetti, Sandra Milo, Giovanna Ralli, Anne Vernon and Baronessa Barzani.*

Like Erich von Stroheim before and François Truffaut after, Vittorio de Sica *(The Bicycle Thief)* was a great director who moonlighted as an actor in other people's films. In *General della Rovere*, a political drama made by Roberto Rossellini *(Open City)*, de Sica turns in his finest performance, as Bardone, a con man struggling to eke out an existence in Genoa during World War II.

Because of his extreme poverty, Bardone jumps at a Nazi offer to assume the identity of slain Resistance leader General della Rovere and to infiltrate freedom-fighter operations in prison. But as he funnels out valuable information to his German masters (the other prisoners treat him as the heroic officer they mistake him to be and Bardone feels pressure to meet their expectations), he begins to have second thoughts about being a Nazi spy. Eventually, he must choose between betraying the Nazis and thus sentencing himself to death, or continuing to play his role and destroying the self-respect he has earned for the first time in his life.

Although Rossellini's camera work in *General della Rovere* has elements of the striking images from his neorealistic *Open City,* it appears more intentionally grubby than it does authentic. The film's sets are also crude and many of the supporting performances amateurish. But the biggest problem with *General della Rovere* is its sluggish pacing. Certain scenes drag on until all of their emotional potency is kaput. But even with these flaws, the movie works because of de Sica's performance. At the beginning, de Sica is a flabby, conniving lout, and his transformation to noble leader, despite torture and threat of death, is stunning. Like the players in de Sica's own *Garden of the Finzi-Continis,* his character in this film serves as a powerful example of the moral choices of naïve Italians in the throes of Fascism.

RATING: *No MPAA rating, with nothing objectionable.*
AWARDS: *Golden Lion for Best Film at the 1960 Venice Film Festival.*

GEORGE STEVENS: A FILMMAKER'S JOURNEY

(Video)

Documentary

U.S.A.

1985	113 Min.	Color/B&W

CREDITS: *Directed and written by George Stevens, Jr. Produced by George Stevens, Jr., and Susan Winslow. Edited by Susan Winslow. Music by Carl Davis. Released and distributed nontheatrically by Castle Hill. Starring Alan Pakula, Warren Beatty, John Huston, Frank Capra, Katharine Hepburn, Irwin Shaw, Fred Zinnemann, Joseph L. Mankiewicz, Ginger Rogers, Joel McCrea, Fred Astaire and Rouben Mamoulian.*

Although George Stevens is not a household name as are his filmmaking compatriots John Ford and Frank Capra, his influence on Hollywood was just as great. In this affectionate tribute to his father, George Stevens, Jr., lets us know why.

George Stevens: A Filmmaker's Journey begins with Katharine Hepburn explaining how she gave Stevens his big break by pushing studio producers in 1935 to let this thirty-one-year-old cameraman direct her in RKO's *Alice Adams*. Hepburn adds that he was the one who came up with the idea of teaming her with Spencer Tracy, and he went on to cast and direct their first picture together, *Woman of the Year*. During World War II, Stevens was assigned to film the D-Day invasion in Normandy, and his footage there turned out to be the only color film shot in Europe during the war. He was also the first U.S. filmmaker to record the horrors of the Dachau concentration camp—an experience that stayed with him long after the war and influenced his darker works such as *Shane, Giant* and *The Diary of Anne Frank*.

The only part of this wonderful documentary that goes on too long is the footage of Stevens's melodramas. Academy Award–winning tearjerkers when they were released, these films are pure cornball today. Still, *A Filmmaker's Journey* is full of wonderful personal clips, home movies of the rich and famous. These alone are great fun, but the way they are appropriately mixed with various stages of Stevens's career make this a superbly edited documentary. But what's most remarkable about George Stevens is the respect he commanded from everyone with whom he worked. In one tribute after another, those interviewed praise his brilliance as a director and his integrity as a man.

RATING: PG, with harrowing footage of Holocaust victims.

GET OUT YOUR HANDKERCHIEFS

(Video, dubbed)

Sex Farce

France/Belgium   French

1978   109 Min.   Color

CREDITS: *Directed and written by Bertrand Blier. Produced by Paul Claudon. Cinematography by Jean Penzer. Music by*

Georges Delerue. Released and distributed nontheatrically by New Line Cinema. Starring Gérard Depardieu, Patrick Dewaere, Carol Laure, Riton, Michael Serrault and Eleonore Hirt.

Bertrand Blier's *Get Out Your Handkerchiefs* is as delightfully irreverent as it is insidious. The film opens in a restaurant, with Raoul (Gérard Depardieu) yelling at his vacant-faced wife, Solange (Carol Laure). He tells her that if he can't satisfy her, he'll find somebody who can. Raoul then walks over to Stephane (Patrick Dewaere), another diner whom Raoul mistakenly thinks his wife was staring at, and offers Solange to him. The astonished man accepts the challenge. Stephane tries to share his passion for Mozart and literature, as well as his body, with Solange, but to no avail. Although he can't bring her out of her desultory trance either, this "other man" and the husband eventually become best friends in their struggle to make Solange happy. Finally they come up with the idea that if she could only fulfill her womanly destiny by bearing a child, she would snap out of it. In the end, Solange does have a child, but it's not at all the way Raoul and Stephane had planned.

As there is little visually out of the ordinary in this movie, the aesthetics of *Get Out Your Handkerchiefs* take a backseat to the comedy. Women will find it frustrating because its narrative is told completely from the male perspective. Solange barely speaks in the entire film, and we never know what she is thinking. But her unresponsiveness is the secret to the story's success. In trying to make the stone-faced Solange happy, Depardieu and Dewaere make complete fools of themselves in this sex farce. Both of them are funny, in pathetic and slapstick ways. But they can also be dense and ridiculous to the point of absurdity. The humor isn't derived from believable characters or situations so much as from twists of plot. In this respect, Blier *(Ménage, Going Places)* is very adept at taking modern-day moral conventions and running them through a blender.

RATING: R for nudity, sex and language. AWARDS: 1978 Academy Award for Best

Foreign Film; 1978 French César for Best Musical Score (Georges Delerue).
WARNING: *Dubbing on video version is decent but does affect quality of the film.*

THE GETTING OF WISDOM
(Video)

★ ★ ½

Coming-of-Age Drama

Australia

1977   100 Min.   Color

CREDITS: *Directed by Bruce Beresford. Written by Eleanor Witcombe and Moya Iceton, based on the novel by Henry Handel Richardson. Produced by Phillip Adams. Cinematography by Don McAlpine. Released by Atlantic. Distributed nontheatrically by Films Inc. Starring Susannah Fowle, Barry Humphries, John Waters, Shelia Helpmann, Patricia Kennedy, Julia Blake and Dorothy Bradley.*

There is something about boarding schools that quickens the pulse of Australian directors, for Peter Weir, Fred Schepisi and Gillian Armstrong all used this milieu in their early films. The same is true of Oscar-nominated Bruce Beresford *(Tender Mercies).*

Set in the early 1900s, *The Getting of Wisdom* tells the story of Laura Rambotham (Susannah Fowle), a precocious fifteen-year-old who is sent from her outback home to an exclusive girl's school in Melbourne. At first, Laura is thrilled at the chance to study with the best teachers, but this overdressed yokel sticks out like a cowlick among her wealthy, class-conscious schoolmates. And she is hardly better received by her teachers, who mistake her willfulness and social awkwardness for arrogance. Even when she tries to be accepted by feigning a romance with a handsome young teacher, her attention-grabbing backfires disastrously.

With well-detailed sets and costumes and beautiful shots of Australia at the turn of the century, Beresford demonstrates a keen eye. He also shows an understanding of the pain of adolescence and peer pressure that can be horrifying. But *The Getting of Wisdom* isn't wholly successful, because it's hard to feel for Laura's character. Although Fowle adeptly plays Laura as a teenager willing to trade in her self-dignity for acceptance, she never pays the emotional price for her mistakes in a way that makes us feel her struggles deeply. And just as Laura is strangely unsympathetic, several scenes in this film drift sulkily from anecdote to incident without a clear narrative line or an engaging theme at their core. In the end, *The Getting of Wisdom* is full of sensitive and authentically realized moments, but it settles into a rut.

RATING: *No MPAA rating, with nothing objectionable.*

GINGER AND FRED
(Video, subtitled)

★ ★ ½

Social Satire

Italy   Italian

1986   126 Min.   Color

CREDITS: *Directed by Federico Fellini. Written by Federico Fellini, Tonino Guerra and Tullio Pinelli. Produced by Alberto Grimaldi. Cinematography by Tonino Delli Colli and Ennio Guarnieri. Music by Nicola Piovani. Released by MGM/UA. Distributed nontheatrically by Films Inc. Starring Marcello Mastroianni, Giulietta Masina, Frederick Von Ledenberg, Franco Fabrizi, Martin Blau, Toto Mignone, Antonio Iuro, Augusto Poderosi and Francesco Casale.*

Fellini has his formula down pat: Find a situation in which to present bizarre characters and human fallibility, and exploit it to the max. In *Ginger and Fred,* that situation is an Italian television variety show featuring once-famous acts from years gone by. Invited to participate in the program are Pipo (Marcello Mastroianni) and Amelia (Fellini's wife, Giulietta Masina), a briefly successful dance team nicknamed Ginger and Fred, who have long since broken up and gone their separate ways.

When the film opens, the two elderly dancers check into their own hotel rooms, anxiously awaiting their reunion. Once they meet, however, they are nervous about rehearsing, and by the time they actually perform, they are emotional wrecks. Just as they start their act with millions of Italian TV viewers looking on, there is a blackout. Eventually, the lights come on and their performance is a smash success—a catharsis that makes the neurotic few days of rehearsal worthwhile. Pipo and Amelia realize that not only can they still perform, but the strong romantic feelings that they once had for each other still exist.

The setting—a hotel full of washed-up circus, stage and comedy acts—is a perfect staging ground for Fellini to introduce the unusual array of strange and funny characters. The TV show itself is a production that allows him to mount a lavish musical extravaganza, while throughout *Ginger and Fred* is blessed with a wonderfully bittersweet soundtrack, reminiscent of the score in *Amarcord*. All the crust is here for a Fellini comedy—what's missing is the filling. Amelia's and Pipo's relationship and characters are hardly developed beyond their fits of anxiety, and their feelings of love and affection for each other are barely realized. It's only at the end that Amelia and Pipo settle down enough to express them. But by then it's too late; their characters seem empty, and *Ginger and Fred* does, too.

RATING: PG-13 for adult content.

THE GIRL IN THE PICTURE
(Video)

Screwball Comedy

Scotland

1986   90 Min.   Color

CREDITS: *Directed and written by Cary Parker. Produced by Paddy Higson. Cinematography by Dick Pope. Released and distributed nontheatrically by The Samuel Goldwyn Company. Starring Gordon John Sinclair, Irina Brook, David McKay and Gregor Fisher.*

Cary Parker's *The Girl in the Picture* mimics fellow Scot Bill Forsyth's comedy style, but the film lacks the depth and wackiness of Forsyth's work.

The story's central character is named Alan (Gordon John Sinclair), an aspiring magazine photojournalist working at a photo shop that specializes in wedding pictures. Alan's dissatisfaction with his job carries over into his personal life, and he impetuously decides to dump his live-in girlfriend, Mary (Irina Brook). But before he can get up the nerve, Mary sits him down for a heart-to-heart talk and tells him that she, too, is unhappy with the state of their relationship and wants to break up.

Alan is crushed. He goes out on other dates, but they always leave him wanting Mary even more. Determined to win her back, he begins concocting wild excuses to call or visit her, but either Mary will have nothing to do with him, or her lesbian, man-hating roommates prevent him from seeing her. In a parallel story, Kenneth (David McKay), Alan's nerdy assistant at the photo shop, becomes obsessed with a girl he spots in a wedding picture. He constantly asks Alan for his expert advice, but Alan is so absorbed in his own lovesickness that he quickly loses patience with Kenneth's whining.

As in *Gregory's Girl*, Sinclair plays a heartbroken young man who is awkward and conniving. It's easy to be charmed by him and some of the other offbeat characters, but their charisma alone can't sustain the film's tensionless narrative. Much of *The Girl in the Picture* is a series of skits in which the same situations are repeated in different settings. Alan's relationship with Mary isn't developed enough to explain the depths of his obsession, while McKay's Kenneth is so overdone that he gets on the audience's nerves as much as Alan's. In the end, *The Girl in the Picture* is simply too shallow to be consistently entertaining.

RATING: PG-13, with mild nudity, language and substance abuse.

THE GODS MUST BE CRAZY
(Video, partially dubbed)

★ ★ ★ ★

Cultural Comedy

South Africa	English and Bushman
1980	109 Min.	Color

CREDITS: *Directed, written and produced by Jamie Uys. Cinematography by Buster Reynolds, Robert Lewis and Jamie Uys. Released by 20th Century Fox. Distributed nontheatrically by Films Inc. Starring N!xau, Marius Weyers, Sandra Prinsloo, Louw Verwey, Jamie Uys, Michael Theys and Nic De Jager.*

Although made on a small budget by South African filmmaker Jamie Uys and a crew of six, with virtually no initial publicity from its distributor, *The Gods Must Be Crazy* has become the largest-grossing foreign film ever in the United States, France and Japan.

Set in modern-day Botswana, it's a slapstick comedy involving an isolated tribe called Bushmen from the Kalahari Desert in Africa. At the start of the story, a chipper-voiced narrator explains that the Bushmen are an unusual race of people who have, for the most part, never set foot inside buildings nor seen cars and white people. He goes on to say that they are so much at peace with their world that words for *jealousy, anger* and *hate* don't exist in their vocabulary.

But when a pilot throws a Coke bottle out of his plane and it lands near the Bushman Xi (N!xau) and his family, it becomes a prized object that members of Xi's family fight to possess. This is the first time they have fought about anything, so Xi decides he must take this evil gift back to the gods from whence it came. With bottle in hand, he starts his journey and along the way gets mixed up with Marxist guerrillas, the police, a pretty schoolteacher, a bumbling anthropologist who collects elephant dung, and a crusty old car mechanic.

The Gods Must Be Crazy's low budget is evident in its atrocious dubbing and cheesy Tijuana Brass–style soundtrack. But the main reason this film has become such a word-of-mouth success is its hilarious slapstick. Director/writer Jamie Uys, who has made twenty-two unknown features in thirty-four years, is an avid fan of Jacques Tati, Charlie Chaplin and Buster Keaton movies, and he employs many of the same techniques of speeded up frames and coincidental encounters as sight gags, though some of the slapstick scenes, particularly the ones involving the Marxist guerrillas, are so overdone they belong on a Three Stooges episode. There are also some beautiful shots of the Kalahari and its animals. But the scenes with Bushman N!xau and his family are what make this movie so entertaining and fascinating.

RATING: *PG, with nothing objectionable.*
FILMNOTE: *When director Uys found N!xau roaming the Kalahari with his family, the Bushman had never seen white people or experienced civilization before. That's why his reactions to these "pale, strange" people are so genuine in the film. It took three years to make the film because hyenas kept stealing the production equipment, and every two weeks Uys stopped filming to let N!xau go back to the Kalahari to be with his family for two weeks.*

GOING PLACES
(Video, dubbed)

★

Sex Farce

France	French
1974	117 Min.	Color

CREDITS: *Directed by Bertrand Blier. Written by Bertrand Blier, based on his novel. Produced by Paul Claudon. Music by Stephan Grappelli. Cinematography by Bruno Nuyten. Released and distributed nontheatrically by Almi Pictures. Starring Gérard Depardieu, Patrick Dewaere, Miou-Miou, Isabelle Huppert, Brigette Fossey, Jeanne Moreau and Michael Peurilon.*

Going Places was Bertrand Blier's first popular film, and it laid the foundation for a string of similar irreverent sex farces that have characterized his career. It's also the film that made Gérard Depardieu a star.

Depardieu and Patrick Dewaere (two Blier regulars) are sixties French hippies who have little respect for personal property or propriety. They roam the countryside stealing whatever they can and trying to seduce every female they meet. When the movie opens, the two friends are caught ripping off a car by its angry owner, and in the ensuing ruckus they defiantly respond by taking the owner's wooden girlfriend (Miou-Miou) as hostage, but not before Dewaere takes a bullet below the belt. Next, they force a doctor to treat Dewaere at gunpoint, and then hop a train where they ask a nursing mother to put her baby aside so they can take a turn. Meanwhile, their voluptuous hostage waits obediently in a rented flat so they can periodically drop by to abuse her. Finally, they meet an older woman (Jeanne Moreau), who teaches them both the meaning of love.

Going Places reaches absurd levels of unbelievability in the opening car-theft scene, and continues along the same contrived path all the way to its ridiculous ending. Blier stretches our willingness to be entertained by frenetically staging one outrageous schtick after another. Most of the gags are so poorly set up that they aren't clever or funny, and the same is true of the performances. Depardieu and Dewaere's characters are mean-spirited, abusive and shallow, and the women they meet, with the exception of Moreau, are like Barbie dolls. Although the sexually liberated characters and absurd situations in *Going Places* were probably shocking when the film was first released, today they are not only offensive but boring. Only Stephan Grappelli's jazzy violin soundtrack and Bruno Nuyten's beautiful cinematography save this film from being a bad joke.

RATING: *R for nudity and sexual situations.*
WARNING: *The dubbing on the video version is not good.*

THE GOOD FATHER
(Video)

Social Drama

England

1987   90 Min.   Color

CREDITS: *Directed by Michael Newell. Written by Christopher Hampton, based on a novel by Peter Prince. Produced by Ann Scott. Cinematography by Michael Couter. Music by Richard Hartley. Released by Skouras Pictures. Starring Anthony Hopkins, Jim Broadbent, Harriet Walter, Joanne Whalley, Simon Callow, Mariam Margolyes, Michael Byrne and Harry Gibb.*

Michael Newell's *The Good Father* deals with issues of male rage in our present-day "liberated" society in ways that few movies have delved into as deeply or as sensitively. Anthony Hopkins stars as forty-year-old recently separated Bill, a progressive man whose feminist beliefs soured into bitterness toward women when his wife quickly found another lover. When Bill meets another man separated from his wife, a schoolteacher named Roger (Jim Broadbent), he inappropriately involves himself in Roger's life as a way of venting his own anger.

Roger's estranged wife (Joanne Whalley) left him for another woman. This upsets Roger, but he is able to live with it until she and her lesbian lover decide to move to Australia and take Roger's son with them. Bill vehemently urges his friend to hire a ruthless lawyer (Simon Callow), who unfeelingly slings all the mud he can about Roger's wife's sexual preferences and radical feminist past to make his case. But the situation's resolution ultimately hurts everyone involved, even Bill, whose emotional investment in his friend's case forces him to confront his own deep-seated fears and the real reason he left his own wife and son.

The only problem with *The Good Father* is that with all of the drama surrounding Roger's custody case, and Bill's loss of his own son by separation, neither father-son relationship is developed enough to explain why both fathers are so despondent over losing their sons. But director Michael Newell *(Dance with a Stranger)* cleverly shows us how freedom of choice can affect people who don't always have the emotional tools to deal with nontraditional social values. The performances in *The Good Father* are outstanding, as each of the main characters represents disparate viewpoints realistically and compassionately. The courtroom scenes are particularly powerful, showing all the players to be victims. Except for Roger's overly pompous lawyer, all the main characters in *The Good Father* are sympathetic, engaging and believable.

RATING: R for brief nudity and profanity.

THE GOSPEL ACCORDING TO ST. MATTHEW

(Video, subtitled)

Religious Drama

Italy/France	Italian
1964 135 Min.	B&W

CREDITS: *Directed and written by Pier Paolo Pasolini. Produced by Alfredo Bini. Cinematography by Tonino Delli Colli. Music by Luis Enrique Bacalov, Bach, Mozart, Prokofiev and Webern. Released by Continental Films. Distributed nontheatrically by Films Inc. and Kit Parker Films. Starring Enrique Irazoqui, Margherita Caruso, Susanna Pasolini, Marcello Morante and Mario Socrate.*

As unlikely as it might seem for a Marxist-atheist homosexual to make an epic on the life of Christ, Italian director Pier Paolo Pasolini *(Pigpen)* pulls it off in ways that are as profound as they are difficult. *The Gospel According to St. Matthew* captures all the major Biblical events in Jesus' brief life, with dramatized parables and scenes involving familiar characters—Joseph and Mary, the three wise men, the evil King Herod and John the Baptist. Although the film's dialogue is taken from the Bible verbatim, Pasolini imbues his narrative with his own very personal vision of Christ's life and times.

Unlike the Sunday school picturebooks that bathe Christ and his surroundings in a clean, golden glow, the sets and costumes in *St. Matthew* are gritty and authentic: Notice Mary and Joseph's crude, cavelike dwelling or squirmy baby Jesus' grubby clothes and his adult dirty, rough-woven robes. The violence in this film, such as the beheading of John the Baptist, is frighteningly real. But Pasolini really strays from tradition in his unorthodox depiction of Jesus himself, portraying his harshness and his rebellious spirit.

It's obvious that Pasolini sees the Bible as a political allegory, and several scenes in *St. Matthew* can be interpreted in terms of economics, sex and class. The acting by the cast of unprofessional actors (including Pasolini's mother as Mary in her old age) is strong, while the hand-held camera and constant use of zoom shots give the film the feel of a documentary. But the slow tempo of *St. Matthew* makes the film almost stop. Minutes go by with static shots of hollow faces or an enraged-looking Jesus prodding the tensionless narrative along. Even taking into account Pasolini's unusual analysis of the Biblical past, two hours and fifteen minutes of this film can be as tedious as a Sunday school class on a beautiful spring day.

RATING: No MPAA rating, with nothing objectionable.
AWARDS: Special Jury Prize at the 1964 Venice Film Festival; 1966 Academy Award nominations for Best Costume Design (Danilo Donati), Best Art Direction-Set Decoration (Luigi Scaccianoce) and Best Scoring of Music—Adaptation or Treatment (Luis Enrique Bacalov).
WARNING: The impact of the film's visuals are lessened on video. Subtitles on video print leave a lot to be desired, but film is still watchable.
FILMNOTE: An atheist, Pasolini oddly dedicated this film to Pope John XXIII.

GOSPEL ACCORDING TO VIC
(Video)

Religious Satire

Scotland

1987   92 Min.   Color

CREDITS: *Directed and written by Charles Gormley. Produced by Michael Relph. Cinematography by Jan Pester. Distributed by Skouras Pictures in association with Film Four International. Starring Tom Conti, Helen Mirren, David Hayman, Brian Pettifer, Jennifer Black, Dave Anderson, Tom Busby, Sam Graham and Kara Wilson.*

The Catholic Church has strict rules about requiring proof of at least three miracles before considering a deceased disciple for sainthood. Father Cobb, the saint-obsessed chaplain of Glasgow's Blessed Edith Semple Catholic School, futilely lobbies the Vatican to consider Edith for the honor, although the long-dead nun has but one verifiable miracle to her credit. Ironically, Edith's chances are resurrected by one of Father Cobb's least religious teachers, Vic (Tom Conti).

Prone to dizzy spells, Vic goes to the hospital, where X-rays show that he has a massive brain tumor and not much longer to live. But when he accidentally falls four stories while attempting to rescue a suicidal student, Vic not only lands virtually unharmed but also is cured of his tumor. The newspapers get wind of the story and attribute these miracles to the saintly Edith, whose holiness is being channeled through Vic. Before he knows what's happening, Vic is watching his less-than-articulate students on TV, delivering testimonials to their teacher's "miraculous" ability to transform their dim-witted classmates into brilliant pupils. Vic is infuriated by the interpretation of his hard work as divine will, until he sees his alleged gift as a way to become involved with an attractive, devout teacher (Helen Mirren) who had previously shunned his advances.

Director Charles Gormley is an associate of *Local Hero* director Bill Forsyth, and the similarities between the two filmmakers' styles are striking. *Gospel According to Vic* is laden with offbeat Scots, as well as a generous dose of warmhearted satire of Catholicism, sex and parochial schools. As unfathomable as the miracles of his story might appear to be, Gormley keeps them well within the realm of believability by always hinting at logical explanations for their occurrences, and by not overplaying his hand. In fact, the catchword for this entire film is *subtle. The Gospel According to Vic* is one of those quietly funny movies in which the characters are friendly and genuine. And Conti shines as the nonbelieving miracle worker.

RATING: PG-13, *with mild profanity and brief nudity.*

GREASER'S PALACE
(Video)

Western Farce

U.S.A.

1972   91 Min.   Color

CREDITS: *Directed and written by Robert Downey. Produced by Cyma Rubin. Cinematography by Peter Powell. Music by Jack Nitzche. Released and distributed nontheatrically by Almi Pictures. Starring Allan Arbus, Albert Henderson, Michael Sullivan, Luana Anders, James Antonio, George Morgan, Ron Nealy, Larry Moyer and John Paul Hudson.*

Greaser's Palace was a mid-seventies college circuit and midnight movie hit, more for its sheer outrageousness than anything else. Set in the Old West, it's about a messiah named Zoot Suit (Allan Arbus, photographer Diane Arbus's husband) who parachutes into the town Greaser's Palace and tells everybody he is on his way to Jerusalem to be an entertainer. In between working on his song-and-dance routines, Zoot walks on water and brings dozens of the citizens of Greaser's Palace back to life after Seaweedhead Greaser (Albert Henderson), the town's evil despot, murders them for no apparent reason. Zoot Suit even resurrects Seaweedhead's son, whom his father shot because he suspected him of being a "homo." There are various other characters who cross paths with Zoot Suit, including a cowboy who rapes squaws, a bare-breasted Indian sex kitten and a horny homosexual midget. Eventually, Zoot Suit is crucified by an insane woman who wants to purge herself of the devil.

Greaser's Palace is a bizarre, plotless farce that makes no attempt at explaining who the characters are, how they fit together or why they exist in the first place. For a farce, it isn't very funny either. The film's few good jokes and many predictable ones are run into the ground with an equal fervor. And to say writer/director Downey's humor is in bad taste is being too kind. He manages not only to make fun of, but to utterly degrade, Mexicans, Indians, women, midgets, people with speech impediments, retarded people and homosexuals, to name just a few. Although his satire *Putney Swope* was one of the cleverest comedies to come out of the sixties, *Greaser's Palace* is one of the worst of the seventies.

RATING: R for language, nudity and plenty of violence.

THE GREEN ROOM
(Video, subtitled)

Psychological Drama

France	French
1979	94 Min.	Color

CREDITS: *Directed by François Truffaut. Written by François Truffaut and Jean Gruault, based on the short story by Henry James. Cinematography by Nestor Almendros. Music by Maurice Jaubert. Released by New World Pictures. Distributed nontheatrically by Films Inc. Starring François Truffaut, Nathalie Baye, Jean Daste, Jean-Pierre Moulin, Antoine Vitez, Jane Lobre, Monique Dury, Laurence Ragon and Marcel Berbert.*

One of François Truffaut's favorite subjects in films such as *The Story of Adele H.* and *The Woman Next Door* is the destructive power of obsessive love. In *The Green Room,* he holds a mirror to this theme by directing himself as a character who is consumed by death as well.

Julien Davenne (Truffaut) is a morose man whose only passion is for writing obituaries in a failing literary journal. Still broken by the loss of his comrades during World War I and the death of his beautiful wife, Julie, Julien refuses to let go of his grief. He collects slides of war atrocities and spends each night in his green room, a dreary parlor filled with photographs of Julie. With the assistance of Cecilia (Nathalie Baye), a woman he meets at an auction, Julien tries to channel his obsessions by converting an abandoned chapel into a permanent memorial for the war dead. Although Cecilia shares her own personal grief over the death of her lover, Paul, her fondness for her partner in mourning grows into love.

Nathalie Baye is nothing less than magnificent as Cecilia, giving her character's personal struggles a certain depth of feeling that keeps us involved with her throughout the film. As always, Truffaut knows how to capture powerful small moments, such as the long tracking shot at Paul's funeral that moves away from the grave and rests finally on a weeping and hidden Cecilia. But Truffaut smothers *The Green Room* with such an unrelenting somber tone that what might normally pass for melancholy is simply leaden and bleak. Unfortunately, his own presence in the leading role only adds to this heaviness; he isn't charismatic enough to compensate for Julien's alienation from the other characters. This performance, combined with the film's slow pacing and sparse dialogue, makes *The Green Room* tough going right from its depressing start to its despairing conclusion.

RATING: PG, with nothing objectionable.

GREGORY'S GIRL
(Video)

Coming-of-Age Comedy

Scotland

1981   91 Min.   Color

CREDITS: *Directed and written by Bill Forsyth. Produced by Clive Parsons and Davina Belling. Cinematography by Michael Coultier. Music by Colin Tully. Released by The Samuel Goldwyn Company. Distributed nontheatrically by New Line Cinema. Starring Gordon John Sinclair, Dee Hepburn, Chic Murray, Jake D'Arcy, Clare Grogan and Robert Buchanan.*

The surprise success in 1982 of Scottish filmmaker Bill Forsyth's *Gregory's Girl* helped set the stage for what soon became an onslaught of awkward-adolescent teen comedies from Hollywood. It's also the film that launched Forsyth's career.

The hero of this story is Gregory (Gordon John Sinclair), a gangly teenager who fails to make the starting roster of his high school soccer team, losing out to a girl named Dorothy (Dee Hepburn). His ego shattered, Gregory consoles himself by falling hopelessly in love with her. He soon becomes so obsessed with the girl that he burdens all of his friends with every detail of his botched pursuit of her, and even resorts to soliciting advice on girls from his precocious ten-year-old sister. Finally, in the film's most nerve-racking scene, he asks Dorothy for a date.

Because Gregory's inability to ask Dorothy out is the main tension of *Gregory's Girl*, the situation becomes tiresome. Gregory's character is, at times, too nervous to be believed—a walking jack-in-the-box who bobs his awkward head in adolescent fury at the slightest provocation. Yet Forsyth does a good job of making light of the tender parts in his teenage psyche, and his friends and little sister in particular are quirky and lovable. Unlike the film's American counterparts, *Gregory's Girl* is refreshingly free of mean-spirited characters

and horny young studs bemoaning their virginity.

RATING: *PG, with nothing objectionable.*
WARNING: *The thick Scottish accents and colloquial expressions of Gregory and his friends make this film a little difficult to understand.*

THE GREY FOX
(Video)

Western

Canada

1982   92 Min.   Color

CREDITS: *Directed by Philip Borsos. Written by John Hunter. Produced by Peter O'Brian. Cinematography by Frank Tidy. Music by Michael Conway Baker. Released by Mercury/UA. Distributed nontheatrically by Films Inc. Starring Richard Farnsworth, Jackie Burroughs, Wayne Robson, Ken Pogue, Timothy Webber and Gary Reineke.*

Bill Miner (Richard Farnsworth) used to rob stagecoaches until he spent thirty-three years behind bars for his crimes. By the time he's finally released from prison at the start of *The Grey Fox*, it's the twentieth century (1903 to be exact). There aren't any stagecoaches to rob anymore, and the ex-bandit's reentry into society is an awkward one. But when he happens on the Edwin S. Porter movie *The Great Train Robbery*, the idea of a new career pops into his mind. With the help of his dim-witted assistant, Shorty (Wayne Robson), Miner takes up robbing trains and becomes mildly successful at it.

Miner isn't your typical train robber. A handsome, distinguished-looking man, he's gentle and considerate even when holding up railroad passengers. In fact, he becomes known as a gentleman train robber and develops into a folk hero of sorts, particularly among the ladies. But Miner is interested in just one woman—a suffragette photographer he meets named Kate Flynn

(Jackie Burroughs). Although she suspects that he is the legendary outlaw known as the Grey Fox, they develop a warm and tender relationship.

Loosely based on the real events in the life of Bill Miner, *The Grey Fox* is told simply and without frills. Train robbing isn't glorified, but neither is law enforcement. What little violence there is in this story is harrowing. Cinematographer Frank Tidy portrays the Canadian wilderness with an awesome, overwhelming power, while the indoor sets are gritty, dimly lit and sparsely furnished. But it's the performances of Farnsworth and Burroughs that make this story so compelling. Farnsworth plays Miner as a thoughtful man who chooses his words carefully and conveys a great deal with his expressions. Burroughs's Kate is similarly quiet and genuine. Although some viewers may find them too softly drawn, there is an enormous charm to these two renegades, particularly when they are falling in love.

RATING: PG, with mild violence and sex.
FILMNOTE: A former character actor and stunt man, this was Farnsworth's first lead. Rumor has it that Francis Ford Coppola recommended Farnsworth to Borsos for the role.

HAIL MARY/THE BOOK OF MARY

(Video, subtitled)

Religious Black Comedy

France	French
1985	95/25 Min.	Color

CREDITS: "Hail Mary": Directed and written by Jean-Luc Godard. Produced by Phillipe Malignon and Francois Pelissier. Cinematography by Jean-Bernard Menoud and Jacques Firmann. Music by Bach, Dvorak and Coltrane. Released by Gaumont Films. Distributed nontheatrically by New Yorker Films. Starring Myriem Roussel, Thierry Lacoste, Phillipe Lacoste, Malachi Jara Kohan, Johann Leysen and Anne Gauthier. "The Book of Mary": Directed and written by Anne-Marie Mievelle. Produced by Phillipe Malignon and Francois Pelissier. Cinematography by Jean-Bernard Menoud and Jacques Firmann. Music by Bach, Dvorak and Coltrane. Released by Gaumont Films. Distributed nontheatrically by New Yorker Films. Starring Rebecca Hampton, Aurore Clement, Bruno Cremer and Valentine Mercier.

Ironically, had it not been for the Catholic Church's objection to it, *Hail Mary* would have faded into obscurity. The first movie in history to be officially banned by the Pope, this film sparked worldwide curiosity as angry Catholics picketed outside theaters in protest of its "blasphemous" treatment of the nativity story.

Jean-Luc Godard's "Hail Mary" is about Mary (Myriem Roussel), the teenage star of her high school basketball team, who lives with her gas station–attendant father, while enjoying an innocent romance with a cab-driving boyfriend named Joseph (Thierry Lacoste). Her Uncle Gabriel approaches her one day at the gas station, telling her that she will soon give birth to a very special son. When Joseph learns that she is pregnant, he becomes jealous and hurt, convinced there is another man since he's never been allowed to get past first base with her. But when Mary's gynecologist confirms she is indeed pregnant, yet still a virgin, the two decide to get married. Soon, they both espouse the teachings of Christ, and Mary gives birth to a beautiful baby who grows up to rename his marble-playing friends after the disciples.

The Catholic Church obviously has little sense of humor, because it's hard to take "Hail Mary" seriously. Godard (*Breathless*) is so intent on mounting an absurd modern-day parable of the nativity story that he completely loses sight of story line and characters. The film's plot is confused, unfunny and ultimately boring. Most of the supporting characters are outlined and then never filled in. Although Roussel gives a strong performance as a teenager confused about her sexuality, when she begins to frenetically spout the teachings of Christ, she smothers the film with monotonous dialogue. The film's redeeming quality is its visuals. Cinematographers Jean-Bernard Menoud and Jacques Firmann do a wonderful job juxtaposing sharply composed scenes of the characters with surreal shots of misty fields of wildflowers and dreary rainfall on a stagnant pond.

"Hail Mary" is preceded on tape and film by "The Book of Mary," a 25-minute companion piece by Anne-Marie Mieville. This film is about a precocious and intelligent young girl (Rebecca Hampton), who reacts to her parents' separation by withdrawing into a private world alone in her bedroom, where she listens to classical music, recites poetry and performs improvisational dance. And as her father becomes less of a presence in her daily life, Mary's sexual feeling for him subtly rises to the surface.

"The Book of Mary" is a compelling short story about a young girl's struggle to come to terms with a personal tragedy. Hampton expresses a broad range of emotions, particularly in her cathartic dance of defiance. The scene in which she expresses her sexual feelings toward her father is also very sensitively executed.

RATING: No MPAA rating, with nudity.

HAMMETT
(Video)

Film Noir

U.S.A.

1983   97 Min.   Color

CREDITS: Directed by Wim Wenders. Written by Ross Thomas, Dennis O'Flaherty and Thomas Pope, based on the novel by Joe Gores. Produced by Fred Roos, Ronald Colby and Don Guest. Cinematography by Philip Lathrop, Joseph Biroc and Randy Roberts. Released by Orion/Warner Brothers. Starring Frederic Forrest, Peter Boyle, Marilu Henner, Roy Kinnear, Elisha Cook, Richard Bradford, R. G. Armstrong and Lydia Lei.

Hammett's original producer Francis Ford Coppola thought German director Wim Wenders (The American Friend; Paris, Texas) was a perfect match for this noirish homage to mystery writer Dashiell Hammett. But halfway through the production, Coppola lost his funding and dropped out before he could see this union through. Although Wenders eventually convinced Orion Pictures to back the project after a long delay, the result has the feel of film plagued by difficulties.

Hammett begins as the cynical, alcoholic Dashiell Hammett (Frederic Forrest) finishes a story about a tough detective and the woman who betrays him (his Continental Op stories). As he reads the manuscript with satisfaction, an over-the-hill dick named Ryan (Peter Boyle), Hammett's mentor and inspiration, shows up at Dashiell's doorstep asking for help on a difficult case. Ryan is tracking a mysterious Chinese woman and persuades the reluctant Hammett to assist him. When Ryan disappears in Chinatown, Hammett continues the search himself, despite warnings from the police to lay off and the sudden presence of a menacing gunman on his tail. With the help of the hard-as-nails dame (Marilu Henner) who lives downstairs, Hammett follows the trail left by Ryan's mystery girl into the heart of the Chinese slave market, only to discover a blackmail and murder ring involving some of San Francisco's most powerful men.

Like the best film noir, Hammett is rich in atmosphere. Wenders and his crew of cinematographers create a story played out on smoky sets, with their cameras brilliantly capturing the shadows and the blanket of gray that shrouds a detective's world. Unfortunately, a film can only go so far on mood, and Hammett has little substance to bolster its style. Sluggishly paced, the plot gets bogged down in unimportant details that better films would skim past, while most of the performances, particularly Henner's, are uninspired. Although there are many elements of a good noirish mystery in Hammett, the haphazardness of the narrative and the film's lethargic pacing turn its promising premise into a soggy mess.

RATING: PG, with mild violence and profanity.

HANNA K.
(Video, partially subtitled)

★ ★ ½

Political Thriller

France/U.S.A. English, Hebrew and Arabic

1983   111 Min.   Color

CREDITS: *Directed by Constantine Costa-Gavras. Written by Constantine Costa-Gavras and Franco Solinas. Produced by Michele Ray-Gavras. Cinematography by Ricardo Aronovich. Music by Gabriel Yared. Released by Universal. Distributed nontheatrically by Swank Motion Pictures. Starring Jill Clayburgh, Jean Yanne, Gabriel Byrne, Muhamad Bakri, David Clennon, Oded Kotler, Shimon Finkel and Michael Bat-Adam.*

Costa-Gavras's *Hanna K.* was controversial at the time of its release because it was the first film widely distributed in America to defend the struggle of the Palestinians in modern-day Israel. Jill Clayburgh stars as Hanna Kaufman, a Jewish-American lawyer living in Jerusalem. Hanna is appointed by the court to represent a suspected Palestinian terrorist named Selim (Muhamad Bakri), who tries to sue the state of Israel for the right to return to his Palestinian village now occupied by Jews. To her surprise, Hanna finds that she empathizes with the plight of his people, but her feelings become more confused when she finds herself falling in love with Selim at the same time she begins to suspect he is really a terrorist. Meanwhile, Hanna finds out she is pregnant by her recent boyfriend, Josue (Gabriel Byrne), who also happens to be the attorney representing Israel in Selim's case. Then Hanna's estranged French husband, Victor, shows up, asking her to come back to him.

What a mess Hanna's life turns into—there's the Palestinian situation, her Jewish guilt and three different men tearing at her from all sides. Costa-Gavras clutters up his story with so many political issues, coincidental occurrences and personal concerns that none of it holds much weight. Although Bakri as the impassioned Palestin-

ian and Byrne as Hanna's arrogant ex both give strong performances, there's little chemistry between them and Clayburgh's Hanna. In fact, with all the different calamities in Hanna's life, Clayburgh's character shows little believable emotion in response. Even Costa-Gavras's trademark fast editing doesn't enhance the plot line, and instead defuses the emotions in Hanna's personal life.

But *Hanna K.* does bring to the fore some important, if unpopular, issues about Jewish prejudice against Arabs and the displacement of the Palestinians. Costa-Gavras displays his knack for portraying the effect of political events on people's everyday lives with unpretentious but powerful camera work. Ricardo Aronovich's cinematography of the stark Israeli landscapes pitted against the intense faces of this politically torn country is also quite moving.

RATING: *R for language, brief nudity and violence.*

THE HARDER THEY COME
(Video, partially subtitled)

Musical Drama

Jamaica   English and Patois

1973   98 Min.   Color

CREDITS: *Directed, written and produced by Perry Henzell. Music by Jimmy Cliff, Desmond Dekker and the Slickers. Cinematography by Peter Jassop and David McDonald. Released by New World Pictures. Distributed nontheatrically by Films Inc. Starring Jimmy Cliff, Janet Bartley, Basil Keane, Ras Daniel Hartman, Bobby Charlton, Winston Stona and Carl Bradshaw.*

The hero in *The Harder They Come* is Ivan (Jimmy Cliff), a poor black Reggae singer. Ivan tries to make a better life for himself by taking a job with a preacher (Basil Keane) but is soon fired for fraternizing with one of his altar girls (Janet Bartley). Just as he is about to leave, he catches another of the preacher's flock trying to steal his bike, and in the ensuing scuffle, Ivan knifes the thief and goes to jail. When he's finally released, he's had enough of the Christian path and takes up *ganja* (marijuana) dealing instead. At the same time he's feeling pressure from the police and other dealers, a sleazy producer will only offer him $10 for recording his single, "The Harder They Come." Ivan explodes into rage and guns down a dozen police and drug dealers, acts that turn him into a folk hero and a hit singer.

The Harder They Come is a Jamaican western in which the good guys are the pot-smoking Rastafarians and the bad guys are white and rich. Ivan even carries a couple of six-shooters and is quick on the draw. Although the film's climax is a bit implausible, the events leading up to it are quite real. Cliff gives an outstanding performance as both an innocent young man trying to do good and the angry rebel who realizes he is oppressed. First-time director Perry Henzell skillfully introduces us to the underside of Jamaican poverty and despair that few Americans ever see.

RATING: R for violence, nudity, sex and marijuana smoking

WARNING: The tape quality of The Harder They Come *is poor. Unfortunately, the lyrics of the songs are some of the few nonsubtitled portions of the film that are easy to understand. The English is next to impossible to comprehend.*

FILMNOTE: Jimmy Cliff's original music is so strong that the film's soundtrack has become the largest-selling Reggae album ever to be released in the United States.

HARLAN COUNTY, U.S.A.
(Video)

Political Documentary

U.S.A.

1976   103 Min.   Color/B&W

CREDITS: *Directed and produced by Barbara Kopple. Associate director: Anne Lewis. Cinematography by Hart Perry. Music by Hazel Dickens and Merle Travis. Released and distributed nontheatrically by Almi Pictures.*

In the summer of 1973, impoverished workers at the Brookside coal mine in Harlan County, Kentucky, voted to join the United Mine Workers union. The Eastover Mining Company refused to acknowledge the vote and proceeded to hire scabs to take over the mines. Camera in hand, filmmaker Barbara Kopple went with her crew to Harlan County for a year to document this intense and tragic real-life drama.

Harlan County, U.S.A. is a story that practically tells itself. With no narration and just a few frames of written material as background, the film consists of people talking right into the camera, as casually as if Kopple were a neighbor sitting at the kitchen table with coffee and a donut. But what these people have to say is anything but casual. We meet extremely poor, hardworking miners, desperate to make a better life for themselves. There are old men, incapacitated by black lung disease, who proudly talk about similar struggles in the old days when unions were in their infancy, and courageous miners' wives who organize right alongside their husbands, never flinching at the outbreak of company-instigated violence.

Kopple takes us all around Harlan County—to miners' shacks, jail cells and picket lines. We see mining company thugs terrorize strikers, and there is frightening footage of the company foreman indiscriminately firing into a crowd of strikers (an action that later results in his on-camera arrest). Kopple adds to the film's authority by capturing scenes of the striking miners singing UMW songs, and inserting some black and white footage of an early Brookside strike in the 1930s, where five miners were killed. But when *Harlan County, U.S.A.* leaves Kentucky to investigate corruption in the UMW leadership and the Yablonski murders, the movie drifts away from what it does best—capturing the daily struggles of miners. The UMW investigation, an unplanned detour that just happened to occur during the filming, is a subject far removed from Harlan County, and Kopple does an incomplete job of documenting it. When the film finally does get back to the Brookside strike in Kentucky, the main story has lost some of its impact.

RATING: PG, with violence.
AWARDS: 1977 Academy Award for Best Documentary Feature. Blue Ribbon at the 1977 United States Film Festival. One of the National Board of Review's 10 Best Films in 1977.
FILMNOTE: Harlan County, U.S.A. is required viewing for all masters candidates at Harvard's Business School.

HAROLD AND MAUDE
(Video)

Social Satire

U.S.A.

1972   90 Min.   Color

CREDITS: Directed by Hal Ashby. Written by Colin Higgins (from his graduate thesis at UCLA Film School). Produced by Colin Higgins and Charles Mulvehill. Music by Cat Stevens. Cinematography by John Alonzo. Released by Paramount. Distributed nontheatrically by Films Inc. Starring Ruth Gordon, Bud Cort, Vivian Pickles, Cyril Cusack, Ellen Geer, Charles Tyner and Eric Christmas.

Harold (Bud Cort) is not exactly the kind of twenty-one-year-old an upper-class mother would always be proud of. When Mrs. Chasen (Vivian Pickles) invites nice girls from a computer dating service over to

meet her boy, he responds by plunging a fake knife into his stomach or pretending to set himself on fire. Besides staging fake suicides, Harold's other pleasure is attending funerals—any funeral, no matter whose, so long as several mourners are in attendance. At one such service Harold meets Maude (Ruth Gordon), a seventy-nine-year-old woman who shares the boy's passion for mourning strangers. They become fast friends, and Maude encourages Harold to enjoy life before it's too late by showing him how to sing and dance, teaching him how to play the banjo and taking him for rides on the back of a motorcycle they steal from a cop. Although there is a sixty-year difference in their ages, they also become lovers.

Harold and Maude is a film people go back to see so many times that, like *The Gods Must Be Crazy*, it's almost an art house cliché. There are several good reasons for this popularity, including the film's irreverent attitude toward holy institutions such as marriage and funerals, and an upbeat Cat Stevens soundtrack so integrated with the plot you imagine scenes from the movie whenever you hear the songs again. But it's really Ruth Gordon's performance that gives *Harold and Maude* life. As an elderly woman with ten times the energy of most teenagers, she embodies the word *spunk*. Although there are too many overly sentimental moments in *Harold and Maude,* it's hard not to fall in love with her as much as Harold does.

RATING: PG, with only simulated violence.

HEART LIKE A WHEEL
(Video)

Women's Drama

U.S.A.

1983   113 Min.   Color

CREDITS: Directed by Jonathan Kaplan. Written by Ken Friedman. Produced by Charles Roven. Cinematography by Tak

Fujimoto. Music by Laurence Rosenthal. Released by 20th Century Fox. Distributed nontheatrically by Films Inc. Starring Bonnie Bedelia, Leo Rossi, Beau Bridges, Hoyt Axton, Bill McKinney, Anthony Edwards, Dean Paul Martin, Paul Bartel (Eating Raoul), Missy Basile and Michael Cavanaugh.

In the sixties, Shirley "Cha Cha" Muldowney became the first woman to break into hot rod racing, and she went on to be one of the biggest money-makers on the circuit. *Heart Like a Wheel* tells her story.

The film begins when Shirley (Bonnie Bedelia) wins a drag race against a rich kid from her high school. From that moment on, racing is in her blood. Although she marries her high school sweetheart, Jack (Leo Rossi), and tries to settle into becoming a housewife and mother, after a few years, she wants to race. At first, Shirley is able to convince her reluctant husband to let her drag professionally, and, after overcoming The National Hot Rod Association's ban on women, she quickly becomes a national champion. But Jack becomes threatened by his wife's success and eventually gives her an ultimatum: racing or him. She chooses racing but then gets involved with a womanizer named Connie (Beau Bridges) who takes her for a ride that's more emotionally exhausting than her championship races.

Bedelia gives a strong performance as a woman who can be as tough with her husband and the other men who try to stop her as she is tender with her son. Japanese cinematographer Tak Fujimoto's camera work during the race scenes is exhilarating, while Shirley's relationship with Jack subtly captures how she becomes trapped by his fragile male ego. But as soon as Connie becomes Shirley's boyfriend, *Heart Like a Wheel* spins its wheels. The same scenes of Connie's infidelity and Shirley's jealousy and anger toward him are replayed over and over again. Shirley's important struggles from the first half of the film get lost in all their repetitive bickering.

RATING: PG, with nothing objectionable.

HEART OF THE STAG
(Video)

Psychological Thriller

New Zealand

1984   91 Min.   Color

CREDITS: Directed by Michael Firth. Written by Michael Firth, Neil Illingsworth, Martyn Sanderson and Bruno Lawrence. Produced by Michael Firth and Don Reynolds. Cinematography by James Bartle. Music by Leonard Rosenman. Released by Southern Light. Distributed nontheatrically by Swank Motion Pictures. Starring Bruno Lawrence, Mary Regan, Terence Cooper, Anne Flannery, Michael Wilson and Susanne Cowie.

Heart of the Stag is New Zealand filmmaker Michael Firth's profoundly disturbing thriller about incest. Bruno Lawrence *(Smash Palace, The Quiet Earth)* stars as Peter, who is hired as an extra hand at Robert Jackson's (Terence Cooper) 14,000-acre ranch. Before long, he realizes something is amiss.

Jackson's wheelchair-bound wife (Anne Flannery), who has suffered a stroke, tries desperately to tell Peter something that he can't understand. The wife is cared for by her lovely daughter, Cathy (Mary Regan), who rarely speaks and always runs away when Peter tries to talk to her. Another ranch hand (Michael Wilson) warns him that "Mr. Jackson doesn't like anybody touching what's his," which Peter assumes means he shouldn't hunt the numerous prize stags on the owner's property. But he realizes the ranch hand was referring to Cathy after she finally confesses to Peter that her father forces her to have sex with him every night. When Jackson learns of Peter's concern for Cathy, it's Peter, and not the deer, he hunts.

The performances are very convincing in *Heart of the Stag,* and that's why the suspense is so spine-chilling and the incest scenes so disturbing. Juxtaposed with Cathy's and Peter's terror and Jackson's insanity are cinematographer James Bartle's exquisite shots of the New Zealand countryside: The expansiveness of the sky, mountains and lush green hills make their personal claustrophobia all the more powerful. Director Firth and his writers also deserve credit for portraying this difficult subject matter so sensitively. Instead of exploiting Cathy's situation for sympathy, they aren't afraid to show typical incest patterns such as Cathy hating her father and yet feeling responsible for his actions, or Cathy being extremely distrustful of all men, including the nonthreatening Peter.

RATING: R for profanity, violence and sexual situations.

HEARTBREAKERS
(Video)

Psychological Romance

U.S.A.

1984   98 Min.   Color

CREDITS: Directed and written by Bobby Roth. Produced by Bobby Roth and Bobby Weiss. Cinematography by Michael Ballhaus. Music by Tangerine Dream. Released by Orion. Distributed nontheatrically by Films Inc. Starring Peter Coyote, Nick Mancuso, Carole Laure, Max Gail, Carol Wayne, Jamie Rose, Kathryn Harrold and James Laurenson.

The scars of broken relationships and one-night stands are everywhere in *Heartbreakers,* and the film's two heroes, Eli and Blue, are the most battle-weary of all. Best friends, they are attractive men in their thirties who wholeheartedly embrace the singles life-style. Blue (Peter Coyote) is an angry young artist who puts his work ahead of Syd (Kathryn Harrold), the woman he's lived with for five years. But when she leaves him for a colleague (Max Gail of TV's "Barney Miller") Blue envies professionally, he is crushed. Eli (Nick Mancuso), on the other hand, is a wealthy young businessman who rarely gets beyond

casual affairs with women. The one woman he is infatuated with, Liliane (Carole Laure), is so afraid of commitment she prefers to have sex in the car.

Some of the women characters in *Heartbreakers* fit too easily into stereotypes. Liliane, for example, doesn't walk and talk as much as she slinks and coos, and a model (Carol Wayne) who poses for Blue's Andy Warholesque paintings, overplays her Marilyn Monroe routine. The other annoyance is the film's technopop soundtrack by Tangerine Dream. Still, *Heartbreaker's* artists' lofts, jazzercise clubs and singles bars are stylishly photographed by cinematographer Michael Ballhaus (a Fassbinder regular), and the film's dialogue is intelligent and snappy. Although Roth treads on some difficult turf in *Heartbreakers,* in the end, he artfully portrays young singles who are desperate for involvement but sabotage every opportunity, and others who are so afraid to lose their freedom they wall themselves into a circle of loneliness. Blue and Eli represent both sides of the spectrum, but all the characters live it in *Heartbreakers.*

RATING: R for language, nudity and sex.

HEARTLAND
(Video)

Cultural Drama

U.S.A.

1980   96 Min.   Color

CREDITS: Directed by Richard Pearce. Written by Beth Ferris, based on the letters of Elinore Randall Stewart. Produced by Beth Ferris and Michael Hauseman. Cinematography by Fred Murphy. Music by Charles Gross. Released by Women's Wilderness Production. Distributed nontheatrically by Twyman Films. Starring Rip Torn, Conchata Ferrell, Barry Primus, Lilia Skala, Megan Folsom, Amy Wright, Jerry Hardin and Mary Boyland.

Made by documentary filmmaker Richard Pearce, *Heartland* authentically depicts a homesteading couple's life in Wyoming in 1910. But when art imitates life this closely it's not all that interesting at times.

The film's heroine is Elinore (Conchata Ferrell), a strong-spirited woman who travels to godforsaken Burnt Fork with her ten-year-old daughter. She plans to work as cook for a Scottish rancher named Clyde (Rip Torn) to earn enough money to homestead her own ranch, and soon discovers her new boss is short on conversation and long on expectations. For a mere seven dollars a week she has to cook, clean house and care for the chickens. Eventually, with moral support from an eccentric neighbor and one of the few other women living in those parts (Lilia Skala), Elinore is able to buy a piece of land. But the harsh winter that comes to Burnt Fork that year dooms Elinore's efforts from the start, and she and her daughter have to move back in with Clyde. Soon after, Clyde proposes and they marry just in time to struggle to save Clyde's ranch, and themselves, from the ravages of the winter.

Made on a budget of only $600,000, *Heartland* has the look a big-budget production. The sets and photography are so real that you won't doubt for a second you're in Wyoming in the middle of winter (when most of this film takes place). But director Pearce seems more concerned with cosmetics than content, as the film's plot and character development are as sparse as its setting. Torn and Ferrell are convincing as indomitable spirits who survive against all odds. But because their feelings for each other are never expressed beyond the simplest friendly gestures (they barely have conversations over two sentences long in the entire film), it's hard to feel their emotions. In contrast to their stoicism, Pearce's depiction of animals suffering is brutally graphic. Brought to you in living color are scenes such as a cow being branded, a pig shot in the head and a starving horse covered with sores. It's certainly real, but it isn't pleasant.

RATING: *Rated PG, with graphic violence toward animals.*
AWARDS: *Golden Bear for Best Film at the 1981 Berlin Film Festival.*

HEAT AND DUST
(Video)

  ½

Women's Drama

England

1983　　　　130 Min.　　　　Color

CREDITS: *Directed by James Ivory. Written by Ruth Prawer Jhabvala. Produced by Ismail Merchant. Cinematography by Walter Lassally. Music by Richard Robbins. Production design by Wilfred Shingleton. Costume design by Barbara Lane. Released by Universal. Distributed nontheatrically by Swank Motion Pictures. Starring Julie Christie, Greta Scacchi, Christopher Cazenove, Zakir Hussain, Shashi Kapoor, Julian Glover, Susan Fleetwood, Madhur Jaffrey and Nickolas Grace.*

Heat and Dust is a Merchant-Ivory-Jhabvala (*A Room With a View*) collaboration about upper-class British morals and the clashing of two cultures. This film begins in London when Anne (Julie Christie) becomes obsessed with a scandal involving her great-aunt Olivia (Greta Scacchi) after reading letters Olivia wrote from India as a young woman sixty years before. Because Anne has little direction in her own life, she travels to India to learn more about Olivia's. In retracing her aunt's steps, she discovers that in the 1920s her great-aunt was the beautiful wife of a British consul stationed in Satipur who caused a stir with the other colonials when she refused to participate in their racism and cattiness. But her main offense was having a not-so-secret affair with the region's charming Indian Prince Newab (Shashi Kapoor). By becoming pregnant and then aborting the child, Olivia finally disgraced herself in the eyes of the colonials and the Indians.

Interspersed with flashbacks to Olivia's past are scenes in the present of Anne getting involved with an Indian man herself and, yes, also becoming pregnant. But that's about all the two women have in common. Anne is as cold and repressed as Olivia is warm and free-spirited. Trying to parallel the two women's lives was an unwise move, for Anne's portion of the film is lifeless in comparison to Olivia's. But the Olivia flashbacks are very well executed in *Heat and Dust*. The chemistry between Olivia and Newab is electric, and the social issues her character brings up are handled compassionately. As has come to be expected in a Merchant-Ivory production, the filmmakers take a great deal of care with the film's sets, costumes and music so that, particularly in the flashbacks, you get a real feel for India's strange, rich culture.

RATING: *R for sex and nudity.*
AWARDS: *1983 Academy Award for Best Adapted Screenplay (Ruth Prawer Jhabvala).*

HEAVEN
(Video)

Documentary

U.S.A.

1987   75 Min.   Color

CREDITS: *Directed and written by Diane Keaton. Produced by Joe Kelly. Cinematography by Fredrick Elmes and Joe Kelly. Production design by Barbara Ling. Edited by Cole Barns. Music by Howard Shore. Released by Island Pictures.*

Diane Keaton became an audience darling and Oscar winner by playing Annie Hall, a slightly ditsy, good-hearted woman with her head in the clouds. Keaton has kept her sights on this same ethereal plane for her directorial debut, *Heaven,* a ditsy documentary exploration of our perceptions of the Great Beyond.

Using both archival footage from old Hollywood films and interviews with an assortment of oddballs and anonymous passersby, Keaton seeks answers to questions such as "What does heaven look like?" and "Is there sex in heaven?" The old clips poke fun at the Hollywood vision of the afterlife, first showing winged black angels floating through a pork chop orchard, then presenting a heavenly chorus joyously

belting out an angelic tune conducted by God himself. Yet the live interviews in the film are hardly less perverse, as a bag lady, a couple encased in gaudy Polynesian robes, and even Keaton's sweet old grandmother relate their own eccentric, self-serving visions of heaven, which aren't far removed from Hollywood's.

Although Keaton makes the interesting suggestion that our ideas of faith and heaven have been coopted by a shallow movie industry, it's hard to imagine a crueler, less interesting treatment of the subject. The weird array of Hollywood clips are often used out of context or with little point. Scenes from Fritz Lang's *Metropolis,* for example, have nothing to do with heaven at all, and the novice director simply lays these and other clips out in hopes that their bizarre qualities will entertain us. They don't, and neither does the documentary's interview footage.

Keaton seems to have gone out of her way to find pathetic, emotionally unstable participants as her live subjects, and she exploits them at every opportunity. Visually, she highlights their defects by recording them with odd camera setups, obscuring their faces in shadows or scrunching them into corners of the frame. These techniques are not only heavyhanded and unflattering but also give the project an air of smugness. In fact, the whole tone of *Heaven* smacks of the director's condescension and self-indulgence.

RATING: *PG, with nothing objectionable.*

HESTER STREET
(Video, partially subtitled)

Cultural Drama

U.S.A.   English and Yiddish

1975   92 Min.   B&W

CREDITS: *Directed by Joan Micklin Silver. Written by Joan Micklin Silver, based on the story "Yekl" by Abraham Cahan. Produced by Raphael D. Stewart. Cinematography by Kenneth Van Sickle. Released and distributed by Almi Pictures. Starring Steven Keats, Carol Kane, Mel Howard, Dorrie Kavanaugh, Doris Roberts, Stephen Strimpell, Lauren Frost, Paul Freedman and Zvee Scooler.*

Hester Street is the promising first feature by Joan Micklin Silver (*Chilly Scenes of Winter, Between the Lines*). Set in the crowded Jewish ghettos, tenements and sweatshops on New York's Lower East Side at the turn of the century, it tells the story of a Russian-Jewish immigrant named Jake (Steven Keats) who is anxious to become Americanized. But when his wife, Gitl (Carol Kane), arrives from the old country to join him, Jake's past comes back to haunt him. Gitl represents everything about the old country he has tried to forget. Although she is a good wife and mother, he no longer desires to be with such an old-fashioned woman. Eventually, Jake takes up with a modern Jewish woman and Gitl is not only forced to deal with the ungodly ways of this new country, she has to face her husband's blatant infidelity as well.

Hester Street is so loaded with Jewish stereotypes that you almost expect Abe and Harry from the local deli to pop onto the screen to extol the virtues of herring and sour cream and bagels with a shmeer. The accents of many of the film's characters sound more like modern Jewish New Yorkers than European immigrants who barely know English. And Silver's portrait of ghetto life is too happy and prosperous for this difficult time in Jewish-American history. Still, Silver seems to have done her homework when it comes to portraying Jewish traditions and Yiddish expressions. The film's sets and costumes are quite authentic, while it ruefully captures Jewish immigrants at various stages of coming to terms with who they are in America. Jake and Gitl's marriage is the biggest casualty in the film, but all of *Hester Street*'s characters pay a price for starting over in America.

RATING: PG, with nothing objectionable. AWARDS: 1975 Academy Award nomination for Best Actress (Carol Kane).

THE HIDDEN FORTRESS
(Video, subtitled)

 ½

Samurai Comedy

Japan		Japanese
1958	137 Min.	B&W

CREDITS: Directed by Akira Kurosawa. Written by Akira Kurosawa, Ryuzo Kikushima, Shinobu Hashimoto and Hideo Oguni. Cinematography by Ichio Yamasaki, filmed in Cinemascope. Music by Masaru Sato. Art direction by Yoshiro Muraki and Kohei Ezaki. Released by Albex. Distributed nontheatrically by Films Inc. Starring Toshiro Mifune, Misa Uehara, Takashi Shimura, Minoru Chiaki and Kamatari Fujiwara.

Akira Kurosawa's The Hidden Fortress is a samurai adventure-comedy set in sixteenth-century Japan. It follows two bumbling peasants who get mixed up with a beautiful young princess and the brave general who tries to protect her.

Princess Yukihime (Misa Uehara) and General Rokurota (Toshiro Mifune) are hiding behind a waterfall when Tahei (Minoru Chiaki) and Matashichi (Kamatari Fujiwara) accidentally stumble upon them and their cache of gold. Instead of killing them, Rokurota very cleverly decides to use these two fools, promising them more gold if they help transport the princess and her wealth to a safe territory. Along the way, the group is attacked by the princess's enemies, but each time it is the general who gets them out of the jam. By the end, the cowardly Tahei and Matashichi betray him and the princess for their gold.

The Hidden Fortress marks Kurosawa's first use of Cinemascope (Tohoscope), and he's obviously so taken by the visuals that the film's content suffers in the process. Although Ichio Yamasaki's cinematography is spectacular, certain scenes seem to drift on aimlessly as the camera captures expansive, barren landscapes. Mifune is excellent as the brave warrior—a wry and deadpan persona that can be quite humorous. Kurosawa also breaks with Japanese dramatic tradition with Misa Uehara's Princess Yukihime, creating a defiant, strong-willed character that even the general has a hard time handling. The weak links in this film are the idiots. At the slightest provocation, they whine and whimper. These characters are overdone, not really as funny as they are irritating and repetitive.

RATING: No MPAA rating, with nothing objectionable.
AWARDS: Silver Bear for Best Direction (Akira Kurosawa) at the 1959 Berlin Film Festival.
WARNING: The video print has black borders at the top and bottom, so the Cinemascope is reflected well on tape, while the subtitles show brilliantly on a black background, yet the image is smaller than you may be used to.
FILMNOTE: George Lucas acknowledges The Hidden Fortress as his primary inspiration for Star Wars.

HIROSHIMA MON AMOUR
(Video, subtitled)

Psychological Drama

France	French
1959	91 Min.	B&W

CREDITS: Directed by Alain Resnais. Written by Marguerite Duras. Produced by Samy Halfon. Cinematography by Sacha Vierny and Michio Takahashi. Music by Georges Delerue and Giovanni Fusco. Released by Zenith Films. Distributed nontheatrically by Tamarelle Films, New Yorker Films and Kit Parker Films. Starring Emmanuelle Riva, Eiji Okada, Bernard Fresson, Stella Dassas and Pierre Barbaud.

Alain Resnais's first feature is one of the most important films of the French New Wave, a disturbing story that involves a twenty-four-hour affair between a French actress (Emmanuelle Riva) and a Japanese architect (Eiji Okada). The two meet in a Hiroshima café and learn very little about each other, not even each other's names,

before sleeping together that night and falling in love. For the remainder of the film, the two of them lie in the darkness of the bedroom or sit in dim cafés, as the woman confides the tragic events of her first romance. All the while, images of the Hiroshima bombing aftereffects flash on the screen.

The actress's personal tragedy occurred just before the end of World War II. Living with her family in Nevers, France, the eighteen-year-old girl had a passionate affair with a young Nazi soldier. When the soldier was killed the day the war ended, she was accused of being a Nazi collaborator and was disgraced in her village. The villagers shaved her head, and her ashamed parents locked her in a cellar, where she went crazy.

The images of Hiroshima bomb victims and flashbacks of the actress's confinement are combined with cryptic, alienating scenes of these two strangers talking and making love, creating a clear sense of the effect of war on its innocent victims. The shots of bomb survivors are particularly painful to watch, but almost every scene in the film has a heightened level of intensity. Resnais's direction is quite innovative, resisting a linear narrative by using jump cuts and repetitive imagery. The film's lighting is eerie, and the disturbing soundtrack by Georges Delerue and Giovanni Fusco further enhances the film's dark mood. And the performances by Riva and Okada are riveting. In the end, it all comes together with themes so complex and emotions so raw that Hiroshima Mon Amour ranks as a masterpiece.

RATING: No MPAA rating, with well-concealed bed scenes.
AWARDS: International Critics Award and Film Writers Award at the 1959 Cannes Film Festival; 1959 New York Film Critics Award for Best Foreign Film; 1960 Academy Award nomination for Best Screenplay Written Directly for the Screen (Marguerite Duras).

THE HIT
(Video)

Psychological Thriller

England

1984   97 Min.   Color

CREDITS: *Directed by Stephen Frears. Written by Peter Prince. Produced by Jeremy Thomas. Cinematography by Mike Molloy. Music by Paco de Lucia and Eric Clapton. Released by Island Alive. Distributed nontheatrically by New Yorker Films. Starring Terence Stamp, John Hurt, Tim Roth, Laura del Sol, Bill Hunter, Fernando Rey, Carlos Lucena, Freddie Stuart and Ralph Brown.*

Although best known for his art house smash *My Beautiful Laundrette*, director Stephen Frears's earlier thriller *The Hit* is also worth serious attention. The story opens when a small-time criminal named Willie (Terence Stamp) turns state's evidence against his bank robbery partners in exchange for money and a new life in Spain. Ten years later, the men he sent up the river hire a seasoned hit man, Braddock (John Hurt), to fetch Willie to Paris to be executed. Traveling to Spain with an obnoxious punk kid named Myron (Tim Roth), Braddock not only abducts Willie but, through a series of mishaps, a voluptuous Spanish woman named Maggie (*Carmen's* Laura del Sol) as well. She soon becomes an obstacle in the plan. Myron fancies her, while Braddock insists that she be killed.

The emotional dynamics of the two hit men and their intended victims traveling in a car together on their way to France is what makes *The Hit* so intriguing. The most curious attitude is Willie's. He accepts his fate as if it's "a natural phase of life" and is not afraid of, or angry at, his potential executioners. He just seems content to make his last few days in life as harmonious as possible. Eventually, Willie gains the respect of even the hardened Braddock, who begins to balk at the notion of killing him.

All the acting is excellent in *The Hit,* with the cold yet tortured Hurt and his dim-witted assistant giving particularly intense performances. But it's the enigma of Willie's character that makes *The Hit* soar above the ordinary thriller. Stamp is thoroughly convincing as the Zenlike snitch, quickly seducing the audience with the same ease that charms his car companions. Except for its unbelievable ending, *The Hit* works well, both as a nail-biting thriller and a psychological drama. The film's violence is brutally real, while Mike Molloy's cinematography of the expansive Spanish countryside juxtaposed with the claustrophobic intensity of the four in a car together is quite powerful. Director Frears also cleverly involves us in the gray morality of their relationships in such a way that nearly every scene contains a betrayal, a double meaning or an uncertain choice.

RATING: *R for violence and brief nudity.*
WARNING: *The power of the film's cinematography is lessened on video.*

HOLLYWOOD SHUFFLE
(Video)

Social Satire

U.S.A.

1987   82 Min.   Color

CREDITS: *Directed by Robert Townsend. Written by Robert Townsend and Keenen Ivory Wayans. Produced by Robert Townsend and Carl Craig. Music by Patrice Rushen and Udi Harpaz. Released and distributed nontheatrically by The Samuel Goldwyn Company. Starring Robert Townsend, Anne-Marie Johnson, Helen Martin, John Witherspoon, Starletta Dupois, Craigus R. Johnson, Domenick Irrera, Paul Mooney, Lisa Mende and Keenen Ivory Wayans.*

When actor Robert Townsend, fresh from supporting roles in *A Soldier's Story* and *American Flyers,* encountered problems finding work in anything but exploitation pictures, he took matters into his own hands by writing, producing and directing *Hollywood Shuffle.*

It's the story of Bobby Taylor (played by Townsend himself), a middle-class black actor who works at a Los Angeles hot-dog stand while breaking his back to land any role in Hollywood, even as a drug addict, street hustler or psycho killer—the only choices for most black actors. The film begins as the clean-cut Bobby practices a monologue for an audition to play a pimp, contorting his body, grabbing his crotch and whining, "Why you be pulling a knife on me? I be got no weapon." This awkward burlesque is typical of the humiliation Bobby must go through pandering to white casting agents and directors. But while he suffers through these auditions, Bobby daydreams about the possibilities of the black actor. In one scene, he plays a hard-boiled detective who cracks a case by destroying the processed hairdo of a key informer, and in another, he and a friend host "Sneakin' in the Movies," a crude parody of Siskel and Ebert that takes the black view of traditional Hollywood releases.

These and several other daydreams are the funny moments in *Hollywood Shuffle*, which carry the film after the rest of the plot has long since collapsed. Townsend has little use for subtlety in these gags, going straight for the comic jugular with the bluntest instrument he can find. But despite their crudity, they work because Bobby himself is so genuine and appealing.

Unfortunately, the narrative that frames these extended riffs is an awkward, shallow exploration of a subject that demands a deeper approach. Townsend's slapstick style haunts him, as he creates white director and writer targets who are too easily and humorlessly shot down. And an underlying problem is Townsend's attitude toward other blacks. He portrays both poor and rich blacks with the same disdain as does the white entertainment industry, suggesting that only a middle-class black like his character in the film is the ideal representation of black America.

RATING: R for profanity.
FILMNOTE: Hollywood Shuffle's trailer shows Townsend begging audiences to attend because he ran up thousands of dollars on his credit cards that he has to pay off. He meant it. On a tiny budget, the film took two and a half years to
make (although the total shooting time added up to be just over fourteen days). The actor who plays his kid brother grew so much that you'll notice him sitting down a lot in the second half of the film.

THE HOME AND THE WORLD
(Video, subtitled)

Cultural Drama

India		Bengali
1986	130 Min.	Color

CREDITS: Directed by Satyajit Ray. Written by Satyajit Ray, based on the novel by Rabindranath Tagore. Produced by The National Film Corporation of India. Cinematography by Soumendu Roy. Music by Satyajit Ray. Released and distributed nontheatrically by European Classics. Starring Victor Banerjee, Swatilekha Chatterjee, Soumitra Chatterjee, Copa Aich, Jennifer Kapoor, Manoj Mitra and Indrapramit Roy.

Satyajit Ray's *The Home and the World* is a penetrating cultural drama that takes place on the turbulent ground where social revolution and personal desires intersect.

Set in India in 1907, the film begins as Bimala (Swatilekha Chatterjee) reflects on her extraordinary marriage to Nikhil (Victor Banerjee), a gentle nobleman who owns a marketplace. Unlike other Indian men, Nikhil refuses to seclude his wife in a small room with the servant women, urging her instead to speak English and read, and treating her like an equal. When an old schoolmate named Sandip (Soumitra Chatterjee) visits their home, Nikhil insists that his wife become friends with their houseguest. Sandip tries to enlist Nikhil into the Swadeshi movement to expel foreign products from Indian markets, but Nikhil resists, not wanting to harm the poor tenants at his market who depend on foreign goods. But Bimala is captivated by the activist's charisma and volunteers to pressure her husband to reconsider. Soon, Bimala's political passion turns into a personal one, as she not only adopts Sandip's cause, but she falls in love with him as well.

The Home and the World succeeds both as a spirited melodrama and a political thriller. Director Ray *(Distant Thunder)* suggests that personal and political emancipation come at no small cost, while he skillfully captures the social rebellion festering below the surface of an Indian society imprisoned by colonialism. Soumendu Roy's cinematography superbly brings to life Bimala's indecision and isolation with close-ups of Chatterjee's face against stark backgrounds. And *The Home and the World*'s acting is uniformly excellent, particularly Banerjee's performance as a man of conscience whose quiet strengths eventually drive his wife from a strict patriarchal tradition into her betrayal of their marriage.

RATING: No MPAA rating, with mild violence.

THE HONEYMOON KILLERS
(Video)

Crime Docudrama

U.S.A.

1970   108 Min.   B&W

CREDITS: *Directed by Leonard Kastle and Oliver Wood (whom cast members acknowledge as the real director). Written by Leonard Kastle. Produced by Warrn Steibel. Cinematography by Oliver Wood. Music by Gustav Mahler. Released by Roxanne/Cinerama. Distributed nontheatrically by Almi Pictures. Starring Shirley Stoler, Tony LoBianco, Mary Jane Higby, Doris Roberts, Kip McArdle, Marilyn Chris and Dortha Duckworth.*

The Honeymoon Killers is one of those unknown gems—an alluring dramatization of the shocking real-life "Lonely Hearts" murders that took place in the sixties. It tells the story of Martha (Shirley Stoler), an unattractive, heavyset Alabama nurse whose hatred of others is equaled only by her appetite for chocolates. Realizing that she needs to make a change in her life, and coerced by a friend who believes love might cure her repellent personality, Martha joins Aunt Carrie's Friendship Club, a pen-pal dating service that specializes in matching middle-aged singles.

She soon catches the attention of Ray (Tony LoBianco), an oily Spanish Lothario from New York who makes his living seducing Aunt Carrie's clients and stealing their money. But when Ray travels to Alabama and rips off Martha, she follows him back to New York where she threatens to expose his scheme unless she can get a piece of the action. So Ray and Martha pose as brother and sister, while Ray marries lonely spinsters and robs them. But Martha becomes jealous of the attention he gives his victims, and after she accidently murders one of them with an overdose of sleeping pills, she finds it easier to kill Ray's new wives than compete with them. Ray, for his part, grows to depend on Martha's love and is willing to go along with anything, including murder, to be with her.

After the young Martin Scorsese was removed from his first directorial assignment after only a week of production, the job of finishing *The Honeymoon Killers* fell into the hands of novice screenwriter/composer Leonard Kastle (who up until that point had been an opera composer) and several other members of the cast and crew. The confusion in this creation by committee shows as certain shots are poorly lit, and the camera angles often obtrusively call attention to themselves.

On the other hand, this lack of polish gives *The Honeymoon Killers* the appearance of a documentary, which underlines both the horror and the black comedy inherent in the story. The violence is particularly gruesome and realistic. But more important, this film shines because of the rich performances by the entire cast. The supporting cadre of spinsters are wonderfully absurd characters who still hang on to their elemental dignity. Stoler, also unforgettable as the demanding commandant in *Seven Beauties,* is perfect as a cold and ruthless murderess, while LoBianco matches her performance as the slightly dense con man who slips and falls in love with her.

If you enjoyed Terrence Malick's *Badlands*, you should love *The Honeymoon Killers*.

RATING: *R for violence.*
FILMNOTE: *François Truffaut once stated that this was his favorite American film.*

HOUR OF THE STAR
(Video, subtitled)

Women's Drama

Brazil	Portuguese
1987	96 Min.	Color

CREDITS: *Directed by Suzana Amaral. Written by Suzana Amaral and Alfredo Oroz, based on the novel by Clarice Lispector. Produced by Assuncao Hernandez. Cinematography by Edgar Moura. Music by Marcus Viunicius. Released and distributed nontheatrically by Kino International. Starring Marcelia Cartaxo, Jose Dumont, Tamara Taxman, Fernanda Montenegro and Umberto Magnani.*

At the age of fifty-two, after raising nine children, Brazilian housewife Suzana Amaral put herself through NYU Film School and went on to make *Hour of the Star* in four weeks for $150,000. It's a remarkable first achievement.

The film is about Macabea (Marcelia Cartaxo), a homely, slightly retarded nineteen-year-old from a poor Brazilian province who moves to the big city of São Paulo. Sharing a room with several other impoverished women, she finds a job as a secretary working for less than minimum wage. Macabea is more than shy—she is inept at talking to people and has body odor and several disgusting habits. Because of her looks, clothes and the way that she carries herself, men are always making fun of Macabea behind her back.

But one day in the park, she meets a man who asks her on a date. He's a slaughterhouse worker named Olympico (Jose Dumont), who epitomizes the worst qualities in men, constantly bragging and bla-

tantly sexist. Macabea puts up with his machismo, although she hardly understands him.

Director Amaral adds her astutely observed glimpses of the urban poor, and ironic situations in every scene in *Hour of the Star*. Although not much happens and some viewers might find it frustrating because none of the characters are wholly sympathetic, Amaral does a remarkable job portraying Macabea's loneliness and alienation, as well as showing us the humor in her situation without making fun of her. All the acting in *Hour of the Star* is very convincing, particularly Cartaxo's Macabea, who plods through her dull existence with only her fantasy world bringing her to life. She is truly one of the most memorable characters to appear on the screen for a long time. As the newspaper ad so aptly puts it: "Everybody who's seen *Hour of the Star* is talking about Macabea."

RATING: *No MPAA rating, with one sexual situation.*
AWARDS: *Winner of the Best Film Award at the 1986 Brazilian Film Festival. Winner of the Best Film Award at the 1986 Havana Film Festival. Winner of the award for Best Director (Suzana Amaral) at the 1986 Women's Film Festival. Winner of the award for Best Actress (Marcelia Cartaxo) at the 1986 Berlin Film Festival. Winner of the award Best Actress (Cartaxo) at the 1986 Venice Film Festival.*
FILMNOTE: *Marcelia Cartaxo came from a similar background to that of her character in the film and experienced many of the same problems as Macabea when she moved to São Paulo to act in the theater.*

I MARRIED A SHADOW
(Video, dubbed)

Psychological Thriller

France	French
1982	110 Min.	Color

CREDITS: *Directed by Robin Davis. Written by Robin Davis and Patrick Laurent, based on the novel* No Man of Her Own *by Cornell Woolrich. Produced by Alain Sarde. Cinematography by Bernard Zitzermann. Music by Philippe Sarde. Released by Spectrafilm. Distributed nontheatrically by New Yorker Films. Starring Nathalie Baye, Francis Huster, Richard Bohringer, Madeleine Robinson, Guy Trejan, Victoria Abril, Veronique Genest, Maurice Jacquemont, Solenn Jarniou, Humbert Balsan and Marcel Roche.*

Based on a Cornell Woolrich novel (he wrote many noir mysteries, including *Rear Window*), *I Married a Shadow* is a deliciously complex thriller, tightly plotted and thoroughly satisfying. Nathalie Baye *(The Return of Martin Guerre)* stars as Helen, a woman struggling to deal with her abusive husband, Frank (Richard Bohringer), while she is pregnant with his child. When he abruptly leaves her, the despondent Helen aimlessly boards a Bordeaux-bound train, where she befriends Patricia (Veronique Genest), another expectant mother, traveling with her husband to meet his wealthy family for the first time.

That night, while Helen is napping in Patricia's cabin, the train suddenly derails. Patricia and her husband are killed, and Helen is mistaken for the dead heiress. When she's invited to live with Patricia's in-laws, Helen tries to tell them the truth. But when she realizes her importance to the dying mother-in-law and sees the chance to raise her son with a future, she decides to stay. Helen is quite happy in her new home, growing to love Patricia's in-laws as if they were her own family. But Helen's comfort is complicated first by her attraction to Patricia's brother-in-law, Pierre (Francis Huster), and later by anonymous notes she receives in the mail accusing her of being a fraud.

Director Robin Davis deftly handles several plot threads in *I Married a Shadow*, weaving them together with twists and turns that keep the audience transfixed. Davis also proves adept at creating an atmospheric visual style to match the film's dark script. But the film's real trump card is Nathalie Baye's performance. Long one of the most underrated French actresses, Baye is immensely sympathetic as a woman trapped in a dilemma of her own making.

At the base of her character is love and decency, but when she is threatened with the loss of everything she holds dear, Helen is willing to go to any extreme to protect herself and the family she has grown to love. It's her character and a tightly executed script that make *I Married a Shadow* an entertaining mystery all the way to its smashing final scene.

RATING: No MPAA rating, with nothing objectionable.
WARNING: Although most video copies say "Subtitled" on the box, don't be misled—the Miravision video versions are all dubbed. The dubbing is good, but because much of the film's dialogue is meant to be subtle, it does affect the quality of the film.

IF . . .
(Video)

Coming-of-Age Drama

England

1969   111 Min.   B&W/Color

CREDITS: Directed by Lindsay Anderson. Written by David Sherwin and John Howlitt. Produced by Lindsay Anderson, Michael Medwin and Roy Baird. Cinematography by Miroslav Ondricek. Released by Paramount. Distributed nontheatrically by Films Inc. Starring Malcolm McDowell, David Wood, Richard Warwick, Christine Noonan, Rupert Webster, Robert Swann and Hugh Thomas.

At the time of its release, Lindsay Anderson's *If . . .* was enormously popular with the sixties counterculture because of its portrayal of youth in rebellion.

Set in an ultraconservative English boarding school, the film's hero is Travis (Malcolm McDowell), a rambunctious sixteen-year-old who hates to study, likes to drink, and pins up posters of naked women and Che Guevara on his dorm room wall. Travis's school, College House, is out of the nineteenth century, with strict rules and harsh discipline from its sadistic teachers. But just as brutal is an unspoken hierarchy among the students themselves that includes the seniors' harassment and humiliation of College House's younger students. Travis and his friends are long-haired juniors who don't take kindly to authority, either of their peers or of the system, and try to escape it by drinking profusely and sneaking off to town for sexual rendezvous. Eventually, when Travis and his friends are severly beaten by a senior with the school headmaster's sanction, they explode in to violence.

If . . . is separated into eight sections, each announced by a title card. These breaks are more disruptive than anything else, since the titles don't necessarily relate to the ensuing action and only serve to distance us from the narrative. Anderson also uses surrealistic devices that are very effective, such as beginning a scene in black and white and then reverting to color, and arbitrarily inserting wild fantasies throughout the film. In addition to mixing entertaining comedy and wild surrealism, If . . . works well as a coming-of-age story that explores themes of disenchantment, homosexuality and immorality. College House, with its pecking order and strict rules for behavior, is an excellent societal microcosm exposing the twisted moral values that fostered the anarchy of the sixties.

RATING: Originally rated X for a nude shower scene, which Anderson cut out to get the film an R rating for milder nudity, profanity and violence.
AWARDS: Golden Palm at the 1969 Cannes Film Festival.

IKIRU (TO LIVE)
(Video, subtitled)

Psychological Drama

Japan		Japanese
1952	140 Min.	B&W

CREDITS: Directed by Akira Kurosawa. Written by Akira Kurosawa, Hideo Oguni and Shinobu Hashimoto. Cinematography by Asaishi Nakai. Music by Fumio Hayasaka. Art direction by So Matsuyama. Released by Toho Films. Distributed nontheatrically by Films Inc. Starring Takashi Shimura, Nobuo Kaneko, Miki Odagiri, Kyoko Seki, Kamatari Fujiwara and Makoto Kobori.

Although best known for his lavishly staged samurai epics, director Akira Kurosawa has a genius for capturing small moments as well.

In Ikiru, Takashi Shimura (the aging leader in Seven Samurai) stars as Watanabe, the head of a minor Tokyo government division, who is so serious about the piles of useless paper on his desk that he is sarcastically nicknamed "The Mummy" by his staff. An embittered widower, Watanabe wallows in self-pity at home, allowing his son to take advantage of him whenever he gets the chance. But everything changes for Watanabe when he learns that he has stomach cancer and only six months to live. At first, he stays out all hours, drinking and geisha-hopping. But he quickly tires of the fast lane and tries to give his life new vitality by spending money on Toyo (Miki Odagiri), an attractive young worker in his office. Finally, he becomes obsessed with building a park for impoverished children, a project that has long been buried in a mound of city government red tape.

From the moment that the poor mothers approach Watanabe with their petition, we know that the park project will buy him peace of mind. With such an obvious message at its center, Ikiru skirts the edge of falling into cliché. But the film's execution more than compensates for its predictability. Kurosawa brilliantly weaves themes of impersonalization of bureaucracies and alienation within families into Watanabe's tortured character. Shimura gives a subtle yet intense performance as the emotionless bureaucrat whose entire personality changes as he journeys toward death. Kurosawa's stark cinematography, voice-over narration and unique juxtaposition of images powerfully frame the last stages of Watanabe's life, creating one of the most moving characters to come out of cinema in the fifties.

RATING: No MPAA rating, with nothing objectionable.
WARNING: The video version of this film is uneven at best, with some subtitles difficult to read, although the film has so little dialogue it is still easy to follow.

IMPROPER CONDUCT
(Video, subtitled)

Politcal Documentary

France	Spanish and French
1984	115 Min.	Color

CREDITS: Directed and written by Nestor Almendros (cinematographer of Days of Heaven) and Orlando Jimenez-Leal. Cinematography by Dominique Merlin. Narration by Jeoffry Lawrence. Released by Cinevista. Distributed nontheatrically by New Yorker Films. Starring Reinaldo Arenas, Susan Sontag, Armando Valladares, Caracol, Fidel Castro, Cuillermo Cabrera Infante, Ana Maria Simo and Juan Goytisolo.

The first mention of Castro's campaign of terror against his own people in *Improper Conduct* comes from a group of exiled ballet dancers who complain that Cuba lacks artistic freedom. Their stories are mild compared to what follows in this documentary. The harrowing details of torture by secret police, false trials, brutal interrogations, forced labor and reeducation are discussed by dozens of Cuban expatriates of all ages and from all walks of life. Some of their crimes included having long hair, listening to the Beatles and dressing like an American. Others were considered counter-revolutionary for being feminists, Jehovah's Witnesses, artists, writers or intellectuals. And Castro seemed particularly hard on gays.

From a filmmaking point of view, *Improper Conduct* leaves a lot to be desired. The number of interviews presented makes the movie visually tiresome, while the tone of *Improper Conduct* smacks of anti-Castro propaganda. The pre-Revolution conditions in Cuba are barely discussed by the film's subjects and narrator; neither are the gains Castro has made for his people in health, education and living standards.

But even with these omissions, so many of the film's subjects reveal the same horrific details of their lives in Cuba that it is undeniable that much of what they say did, and probably still does, occur. Their testimony is heart-wrenching and frightening. Those who revel in the glories of Castro's Revolution are in for a rude awakening with *Improper Conduct*, while the ones who have been criticizing Castro all along will certainly have their suspicions confirmed.

RATING: No MPAA rating, with graphic descriptions of torture.

THE INHERITORS
(Video, subtitled)

Social Drama

Austria	German
1983	89 Min.	Color

CREDITS: Directed, written and produced by Walter Bannert. Cinematography by Hanus Polak. Music by Gustav Mahler. Released by Island Alive. Distributed nontheatrically by Corinth Films. Starring Nikolas Vogel, Roger Schauer, Anneliese Eberhard, Jaromir Borek, Klaus Novak and Ed Stavjanik.

Most of modern Germany remembers the Nazi era humbly, apologizing for the atrocities committed in the name of racial "purity." Yet not all Germans today share this guilt, as this controversial story of the German neo-Nazi movement attests.

The Inheritors begins as an awkward and unhappy teenager named Thomas (Nikolas Vogel) is invited to join a youth club by Charlie (Roger Schauer), a young hoodlum who makes his way stealing motorcycles. The group watches old Nazi propaganda films and listens to their graying sponsors reminisce about the "good old days," but these kids aren't just political underachievers—they're the youth arm of a Fascist right-wing movement. Wearing uniforms and jackboots, Thomas and Charlie are the muscle at party rallies, beating hecklers into silence. Soon, Thomas's involvement escalates beyond crowd control. As he quarrels with his suspicious middle-class parents and endures the taunts of his classmates, the boy joins a secret paramilitary army and moves even closer to dangerous violence.

The Inheritors touched off an explosion of controversy (including demonstrations and theater bombings) when it was released, both for suggesting how vital neo-Nazism still is in Europe today, and for its often brutal depiction of the movement. In one frightening scene, for example, Thomas and his friends gleefully play at executing Jews, painting a Star of David on a boy's back and holding a revolver to his head. In this and other moments, writer/director Walter Bannert suggests the appeal of neo-Nazism to directionless young thugs who are enjoying power for the first time in their lives. But as disturbing as these individual scenes can be, the whole of the film has little punch outside of shock value. Most of Bannert's explanations for Thomas's actions, including sexual rejection, scholastic failure and abusive parents, are melodramatic and clichéd. The film's overdone subplot involving the fight for control of the new Fascist party isn't very credible either. Although the performances are good, *The Inheritor*'s predicatable story line and shallow characterizations may not sustain your interest.

RATING: *R for sex and violence.*
FILMNOTE: *After being beaten by a neo-Nazi group in a Vienna café, writer/ director Walter Bannert infiltrated neo-Nazi groups over a two-year period to research this film.*

INSIGNIFICANCE
(Video)

Cultural Satire

England

1985   105 Min.   Color

CREDITS: *Directed by Nicolas Roeg. Written by Terry Johnson, based on his play. Produced by Jeremy Thomas. Cinematography by Peter Hannan. Music by Paul Le Mare. Set design by David Brockhurst. Released by Island Alive. Distributed nontheatrically by New Yorker Films. Starring Theresa Russell, Michael Emil, Gary Busey, Tony Curtis and Will Sampson.*

Nicolas Roeg's *Insignificance* is a fictionalized account of an evening in which Marilyn Monroe (Theresa Russell) and Albert Einstein (Michael Emil) meet and share their own personal views on life and the universe. Marilyn instigates the get-together—she thinks they have a lot in common because they're both victims of a society that exploits its celebrities. At 3:00 A.M. she invites herself into Einstein's hotel room, where they have a bizarre conversation on subjects as diverse as sex symbols, Hitler and relativity. But during the course of the evening and the next morning, Joe McCarthy (Tony Curtis) keeps showing up to bait the scientist with accusations of "Communist" connections, while Marilyn's jealous husband, Joe DiMaggio (Gary Busey), also comes by to cause more trouble.

At several points in *Insignificance,* Roeg inserts flashbacks of Einstein's and Monroe's pasts that relate to the present, as well as some violent dream sequences concerning nuclear war and the Holocaust. These scenes zoom by so quickly that it's hard to catch what's going on, and they often disrupt the flow of the narrative. But what we learn from them is that both Einstein and Monroe are who they are because of painful events they experienced early in life.

Although some of the actors don't physically resemble the famous characters they portray in *Insignificance*, their performances are so good we don't need look-alikes to transport us into their worlds. Roeg's cinematography is crisp and innovative, and much of the film is set to a wonderfully upbeat big-band soundtrack. Even if the almost nonstop miscommunications in this film are frustrating (Einstein and Monroe are the only ones who are ever on the same wavelength), *Insignificance* is a wildly entertaining, intelligent look at the nature of American icons and the political and sexual repression of the fifties.

RATING: R for brief nudity and violence.
AWARDS: Grand Prix for Technical Excellence at the 1985 Cannes Film Festival.

JEAN DE FLORETTE
(Video, subtitled)

  ½

Historical Drama

France	French
1987	122 Min.	Color

CREDITS: Directed and produced by Claude Berri. Written by Claude Berri and Gérard Brach, based on the novels Jean de Florette and Manon of the Spring by Marcel Pagnol. Cinematography by Bruno Nuytten. Music by Jean-Claude Petit. Production design by Bernard Vezat. Released by Orion Classics. Distributed nontheatrically by Films Inc. Starring Yves Montand, Gérard Depardieu, Daniel Auteuil, Elizabeth Depardieu, Ernestine Mazurowna, Marcel Champel and Armand Meffre.

The largest grossing foreign film in the U.S. in 1987, *Jean de Florette* is a well-crafted but emotionally empty adaptation of the first volume of Marcel Pagnol's 1963 novel. The story begins during the aftermath of WWI, as Jean de Florette (Gérard Depardieu), a hunchbacked soldier, brings his wife, Aimée (Elizabeth Depardieu), and daughter Manon (Ernestine Mazurowna) to a village in the French countryside. But Jean's dream of raising rabbits puts him in conflict with an aging land baron, Cesar Soubeyran (Yves Montand), and his dim-witted nephew, Ugolin (Daniel Auteuil); they covet a spring on the hunchback's land that could water the Soubeyran vineyards. When Jean refuses to sell them his water, the two villains secretly cap Jean's spring at its source, then sit back and wait as the hunchback heroically hauls water for miles in a futile effort to keep his family and farm together.

Cosmetically, *Jean de Florette* has much to recommend it. The cinematography of the lush countryside is breathtaking, and the sets and costumes are richly detailed. The acting is outstanding, particularly Yves Montand as the villain and Daniel Auteuil as his skittish accomplice. But *Jean de Florette*'s acting and lovely physical details can't save it from its clichéd, soap opera story line. Depardieu's Jean should be sympathetic, but he is too noble to be compelling. Worst of all, the film's main conflict involving Jean refusing to sell Cesar his water is so poorly established that the reasons for all the fuss aren't initially clear. Instead of explanations, we get endless scenes of poor Jean toting water intercut with Cesar cackling malevolently. In the end, there is little that is engaging below the surface of *Jean de Florette*.

RATING: PG, with mild violence.
FILMNOTE: Although the sequel Manon of the Spring ties together all the loose ends set up in Jean de Florette, it is even more melodramatic than the first film.

A JOKE OF DESTINY, LYING IN WAIT AROUND THE CORNER LIKE A BANDIT
(Video, subtitled)

Political Satire

Italy	Italian
1984 105 Min.	Color

CREDITS: *Directed by Lina Wertmuller. Written by Lina Wertmuller, based on a story by Wertmuller and Silvia D'Amico Bendico. Produced by Giuseppe Giovannini. Cinematography by Camillio Bazzoni. Released and distributed nontheatrically by The Samuel Goldwyn Company. Starring Ugo Tognazzi, Pier Degli Esposti, Gastone Moschin, Renzo Montagnani, Roberto Herlitzka, Valeria Golino, Livia Cerini, Enzo Jannacci and Massimo Wertmuller.*

After gaining a well-deserved reputation in the late sixties and early seventies for her scathing satires on sex and class, Lina Wertmuller hit the skids. *A Joke of Destiny* is an example of her decline in the eighties.

The film has several different subplots going on at once, but all mean misfortune for the hero, Vincenzo de Andreiis (Ugo Tognazzi of *La Cage aux Folles*). His troubles begin when his boss, the Italian minister of the interior, gets locked in a high-security Fiat after the car's computer system malfunctions. The car happens to be near Vincenzo's house, so the petty bureaucrat and a couple of policemen push it into his garage to cover up the embarrassing incident until help can arrive. Meanwhile, Vincenzo's seductive fifteen-year-old daughter (Valeria Golino) decides that one of the cops guarding the minister is just the man to take her virginity and manages to handcuff herself to him and throw away the key. Soon after, Vincenzo discovers that his wife has hidden her lover, an escaped Red Brigade terrorist, in their basement. Finally, Vincenzo's dope-dealing mother-in-law (Livia Cerini) drops by to add a little extra bitter spice to this already disastrous day.

After a long absence from comedy, Wert-

muller returned to it with a passion, throwing everything she could think of into this frenetic stew—sexual politics, a horny virgin, a marriage that's mostly a shouting match, corrupt politicians, incompetent cops, a pot-smoking grandmother and bumbling leftists and rightists. Yet her political satire is largely lost on non-Italian audiences, and most of the jokes are predictable and humorless. The funniest scene in the film is one of the minister locked in his Fiat. His expressions alone are hilarious, and the idea of a minister held captive in a car designed to protect him from terrorist kidnapping is a clever sight gag that becomes funnier each time Wertmuller returns to it.

RATING: *PG, with sexual situations.*

JULES AND JIM
(Video, subtitled)

Psychological Drama

France	French
1961 104 Min.	B&W

CREDITS: *Directed by François Truffaut. Written by François Truffaut and Jean Gruault, based on the novel by Henri-Pierre Roche. Produced by Marcel Berbert. Cinematography by Rauol Coutard. Music by Georges Delerue. Released by Janus Films. Distributed nontheatrically by Films Inc. Starring Oskar Werner, Jeanne Moreau, Henri Serre, Marie Dubois, Vanna Urbino, Sabine Haudepin, Boris Bassiak, Kate Noelle, Anny Nelsen and Christine Wagner.*

Rated one of the top movies ever made by *Sight and Sound* magazine's prestigious poll of international film critics, François Truffaut's *Jules and Jim* is a bittersweet story of two friends and the extraordinary femme fatale they both love. The story begins just before World War I in Paris. The introverted Austrian Jew, Jules (Oskar Werner), and the gregarious Parisian, Jim (Henri Serre), become such good friends that they share everything, from poetry and art to wine and even women. This changes when they meet the very beautiful Catherine (Jeanne Moreau). For the first time, Jules tells his friend, "Not this one." Jim agrees, but that doesn't stop him from falling in love with Catherine anyway.

The three rent a country house and spend a glorious summer together laughing, running through the woods and living in carefree harmony. Although Catherine is ostensibly attached to Jules, she has both men following her every whim and fancy and loves every minute of it. This idyllic time comes to an end when World War I is declared, and Jules and Jim go off to fight on opposite sides. When the story picks up again after the war, Jules and Catherine are now married, have a daughter and are living in Austria. But it's not an easy time for Catherine, because her monogamous life with Jules makes her unhappy and restless. After doing everything in his power to regain her love, Jules figures that if he can't make her happy, maybe his best friend can. Jim comes to stay with Jules and Catherine, but it's too late to recapture the feelings the three once felt.

Although it's easy to find metaphors for France before and after World War I in *Jules and Jim,* at the center of the film is the simple need that these three characters have for each other. Jules and Jim are best friends down to their very core, while Catherine is not a real person for them so much as she is an ideal. Catherine can't live without their adoration, although in the end she is smothered by it as well. Truffaut captures these subtle emotions without sentimentality, yet still makes the three of them sympathetic. Werner, Serre and Moreau all give outstanding performances, while Coutard's lyrical black-and-white photography and Georges Delerue's music add just the right amount of magic and eeriness to their emotional seesaw.

RATING: No MPAA rating, with mild violence.

KAGEMUSHA (THE SHADOW WARRIOR)
(Video, subtitled)

Samurai Drama

Japan		Japanese
1980	179 Min.	Color

CREDITS: *Directed by Akira Kurosawa. Written and produced by Akira Kurosawa and Masato Ide. Cinematography by Takao Saito, Shoji Ueda, Kazuo Miyagawa and Asaishi Nakai. Set design by Yoshiro Muraki. Presented in the United States by Francis Ford Coppola and George Lucas. Released by 20th Century Fox. Distributed nontheatrically by Films Inc. Starring Tatsuya Nakadai, Tsutomu Yamazaki, Kenichi Hagiwara, Kota Yui, Hideji Otaki, Hideo Murata, Kaori Momoi and Daisuke Ryu.*

When Akira Kurosawa made *Kagemusha* in 1980, its $6 million price tag made it the most expensive film ever produced in Japan. The money and effort definitely show.

This epic drama begins when a powerful clan leader, Lord Shingen, is killed by an assassin's bullet. As two other warring clans join forces to overtake Shingen's fortress, it becomes clear to Shingen's men that their lord's death must remain a secret if they are to stay in power. With a stroke of good fortune, they find a petty thief who looks so much like the slain leader that he can pass for him. But Kagemusha (Tatsuya Nakadai) has spent his entire life in poverty and lacks the manners, background and education to impersonate Shingen easily. With a great deal of coaching, he not only learns to feel comfortable in the role but becomes a strong ruler as well. The fact that others show him respect for the first time in his life and are even willing to die for him in battle profoundly affects this shadow warrior.

Kurosawa and his staff of cinematographers give us more than our money's worth of long battle sequences and lavish ceremonies of feudal Japan. Although every detail in these scenes is visually stunning, the cinematography and costumes alone are often not enough to keep them interesting. But the famed director is very adept at less theatrical moments in this film, such as Kagemusha's touching scenes with Lord Shingen's grandchild, and the various moments in which Kagemusha nervously impersonates the slain leader in the company of the late lord's unsuspecting warriors and mistresses. Nakadai gives a compelling performance as the sleazy misfit who turns into a brave ruler.

RATING: PG, with mild violence.
AWARDS: Golden Palm for Best Film at the 1980 Cannes Film Festival; 1980 French Caesar for Best Foreign Film; 1980 British Academy Award for Best Direction (Akira Kurosawa); 1980 Academy Award nominations for Best Foreign Film and Best Art Direction-Set Decoration (Yoshiro Muraki).

KAMIKAZE '89
(Video, subtitled)

Science Fiction Satire

West Germany	German
1983 106 Min.	Color

CREDITS: Directed by Wolf Gremm. Written by Wolf Gremm and Robert Katz, based on the novel Murder on the 31st Floor *by Per Wahloo and Maj Sowall. Produced by Regina Ziegler. Cinematography by Xaver Schwarzenberger. Music by Tangerine Dream. Released by Trio-Oase. Distributed nontheatrically by New Line Cinema. Starring Rainer Werner Fassbinder, Gunther Kaufmann, Boy Gobert, Arnold Marquis, Richy Mueller, Brigitte Mira, Frank Ripploh and Franco Nero.*

Wolf Gremm's *Kamikaze '89* is a confused, low-budget science fiction story that's blessed by an outrageous performance by filmmaker Rainer Werner Fassbinder in his last screen role.

Set in 1989, this film's Germany has become a world economic power no longer plagued by inflation, unemployment or pollution. The country's population is kept docile by The Information Combine, a Big Brother media power that programs television shows meant to keep most of the viewing public anesthetized. But The Combine and its leader, Blue Panther (Boy Gobert), are being undermined by a shadowy resistance group that calls itself Krysmopompus. When the group warns that a bomb has been planted in The Combine's headquarters, a top Berlin detective named Jansen (Fassbinder) is called to the scene. Jansen, a bearish man in a leopard-skin suit who's never left a case unsolved, immediately gets down to work. But then the initial evidence and a too-coincidental murder make Jansen wary of the Blue Panther and his cohorts.

Although world-renowned as a director *(The Marriage of Maria Braun)*, Fassbinder also worked steadily as an actor in his own and other filmmakers' movies. In *Kamikaze '89*, he turns in an absurdly undisciplined performance that is well-suited to the ragged film it dominates. Fassbinder is most of the show here, preening ridiculously before every mirror he finds and bullying his way through every scene. He doesn't work well with the supporting players (including Gunther Kaufmann, Fassbinder's roly-poly real-life lover, who plays his assistant), but as a one-man show, he is perversely entertaining.

Director Gremm and cinematographer Xaver Schwarzenberger also distinguish themselves with delirious, drunken camera work—including circle tracking, odd angles and garish color schemes—that is as original as it is distracting. But all this innovative work is swallowed up by an impenetrable story that becomes progressively more boring as it gets harder to follow. Gremm never makes it clear what Krysmopompus is, what The Combine does to keep people in line, or what its connection is to the government. So much of what passes for mystery in the plot is just a lot of running around and shouting. In the end, *Kamikaze '89* is an ineffectual, disjointed mood piece with Fassbinder's boozy performance creating all the atmosphere.

RATING: No MPAA rating, with violence.

KANGAROO
(Video)

Literary Drama

Australia

1987   105 Min.   Color

CREDITS: *Directed by Tim Burstall. Written by Evan Jones, based on the novel by D. H. Lawrence. Produced by Ross Dimsey. Cinematography by Dan Burstall. Released by Cineplex Odeon Films. Distributed nontheatrically by Films, Inc. Starring Colin Friels, Judy Davis, John Walton, Hugh Keays-Byre and Julie Nihill.*

Set in 1922, this adaptation of D. H. Lawrence's semiautobiographical *Kangaroo* is about British novelist Richard Somer's (Colin Friels) experiences when he and his wife, Harriet (Judy Davis), briefly immigrate to Australia (Lawrence wrote the novel in only six weeks, during a brief attempt to settle in Australia in 1922). Their reasons for leaving England seem solid at the time: Richard is disgusted by Britain's participation in World War I and the mislabeling of his writings as pornographic, and both are fed up with the constant harassment of Harriet because of her German descent.

Moving into a Sydney suburb, the couple befriends their neighbor, Jack Calcott (John Walton), a fiery young man who tries to seduce Harriet and lure Richard into his Fascist politics. Harriet rebuffs Jack's advances, but Richard, unable to resist opening a Pandora's box, is drawn to Jack's clandestine organization. Eventually, Richard is introduced to a white supremacist leader—Kangaroo (Hugh Keays-Byrne). Kangaroo is so impressed by Richard's writing talents and intelligence that he furtively tries to enlist him in his cause. Although enamored of Kangaroo as well, Richard is already politically aligned with Kangaroo's enemies—the Socialists and the Wobblies.

A common mistake directors make in adapting literature to the screen is sacrificing character development to advance a novel's plot. In *Kangaroo*, the opposite is true. Director Tim Burstall gives us too little background on the Fascists and Socialists in pre–World War II Australia, and it's never clear why Kangaroo is so desperate for Richard's loyalty and writing skills. But Burstall does an excellent job portraying D. H. Lawrence's emotionally and politically complex characters. Walton is particularly captivating as the likeable young neighbor who turns out to be a virulent racist and vicious Red-hater. And Davis is outstanding as Richard's strong-willed spouse who won't stand for his attempts to make her into a dutiful housewife, or even pay lip service to the ridiculous self-importance of his male-dominated political beliefs.

RATING: *R for sexual content and violence.*

KEROUAC
(Video)

★ ★ ½

Documentary

U.S.A.

1984   73 Min.   B&W/Color

CREDITS: *Directed by John Antonelli. Written by John Antonelli, John Tytell and Frank Cervarich. Produced by John Antonelli. Cinematography by Jerry Jones. Edited by Will Parrinello. Released by Day-Break Films. Starring Jack Coultar, David Andrews, Jonah Pearson, John Rosseau, Jack Kerouac, Lawrence Ferlinghetti, Allen Ginsberg, William S. Burroughs, Steve Allen and William F. Buckley.*

Jack Kerouac was admittedly one of the most talented and influential American Beat novelists in the fifties, but in *Kerouac*, director John Antonelli makes him into a saint.

This part-documentary, part-docudrama tries to portray Kerouac through dramatizations of the author (played by Jack Coultar), narrations of his work, interviews with his friends and colleagues, and footage from Kerouac's television appearances on

"The Steve Allen Show" and William Buckley's "Firing Line." Antonelli starts out by giving background information on Kerouac at Columbia University (where he dropped out), in the navy (where he was kicked out), and struggling through a couple of marriages (which end in divorce). He goes on to show Kerouac roaming the United States and Mexico with his friend Neil Cassidy and eventually descending into alchoholism.

Some of the documentary footage in *Kerouac* is very entertaining, particularly Kerouac's inebriated television monologues and the interviews with his outrageous Beat cohorts Allen Ginsberg and Lawrence Ferlinghetti. But several other interviews, like the film itself, are limited to chronicling events without explaining how they affected his life. Important issues such as Kerouac's inability to handle success and his alcoholism and arch-conservatism in the years before his suicide are barely addressed. The dramatizations in *Kerouac* are a disaster. Jack Coultar doesn't look or act like the author we see in the film's real footage because his performance is overly theatrical. Antonelli tries to obscure these problems by giving the dramatizations a grainy, dreamlike look, but unfortunately, he only accentuates how poorly executed these scenes are.

RATING: No MPAA rating, with mild profanity and substance abuse.

THE KING OF COMEDY
(Video)

Black Comedy

U.S.A.

1984   109 Min.   Color

CREDITS: *Directed by Martin Scorsese. Written by Paul Zimmerman. Produced by Arnon Milchan. Cinematography by Fred Schuler. Music by Robbie Robertson (of The Band). Released by 20th Century Fox. Distributed nontheatrically by Swank Motion Pictures. Starring Robert De Niro, Jer-*ry *Lewis, Sandra Bernhard, Diahanne Abbott, Ed Herlihy, Lou Brown, Whitey Ryan, Cathy Scorsese, Catherine Scorsese, Martin Scorsese and Doc Lawless.*

In Martin Scorsese's *The King of Comedy*, Rupert Pupkin (Robert De Niro) is one hell of a joker. He wears loud clothes, and nearly everything that comes out of his mouth is a snappy one-liner. In fact, Rupert dreams of becoming a famous comedian like his idol, Jerry Langford (Jerry Lewis), a Johnny Carson–style TV talk-show host whom Rupert watches religiously. Rupert is thrilled when, after forcing himself into Jerry's limo one night after a show, he runs through a routine and is rewarded by Jerry with an offhanded invitation to audition for the show. Rupert spends hours practicing his best stuff, and then marches up to Jerry's office, where, of course, Jerry's staff won't let Rupert near the star. Hurt and angry, Rupert becomes a desperate man, willing to do anything to get on "The Jerry Langford Show."

De Niro plays Rupert to perfection. He is loud, obnoxious and dense. His jokes will make you cringe with embarrassment, and he is so persistent and pushy it's hard to feel much sympathy for him. Watching him and his neurotic friend Masha (Sandra Bernhard), who is obsessed with dreams of seducing Langford, is like observing a used-car salesman sell a car to a carnival barker. It's hard to stand either one of them, and yet they are fascinating. Scorsese has created a powerful scenario of what desire for fame can do to a person. Parts of the film are unnerving and tragic, others are suspenseful and funny, but with the exception of its unfathomable ending, all of it is extremely real.

RATING: PG-13 for brief nudity.
AWARDS: 1983 British Academy Award for Best Original Screenplay (Paul Zimmerman).

KING OF HEARTS
(Video, subtitled)

 ½

Social Satire

France   French

1966   102 Min.   Color

CREDITS: *Directed by Philippe de Broca. Written by Daniel Boulanger and Maurice Bessy. Produced by Philippe de Broca. Cinematography by Pierre L'Homme. Music by Georges Delerue. Released by United Artists. Distributed nontheatrically by Films Inc. Starring Alan Bates, Genevieve Bujold, Pierre Brasseur, Jean-Claude Brialy, Françoise Christophe, Adolfo Celi, Micheline Presle and Julien Guiomar.*

In the sixties, *King of Hearts* had cult classic status almost equal to *Harold and Maude* for its ability to draw audiences back for repeated viewings.

Set in France toward the end of World War I, it's the story of a peace-loving, scatterbrained Scottish infantryman, Private Charles Plumpick (Alan Bates), who is ordered into a small town to locate a bomb the Germans have left behind. All of the town's inhabitants have fled except for the abandoned patients of an insane asylum. Having assumed a variety of different roles (both real and imaginary), the patients are now running the town. At first, Plumpick doesn't know what to think of these lunatics, but he is soon taken with the quirky, lovable bunch. His affections make him all the more frantic to locate the soon-to-explode bomb. Yet he worries about the fate of his new friends, because once he locates the bomb, the others will return to their homes, and the inmates will have to go back to the asylum.

King of Hearts takes pointed jabs at institutions such as war, religion, money and class. In some scenes, the patients mock society by imitating the so-called normal people, while in others, the absurdity of the events is enough to make sharply critical statements. But *King of Hearts* is primarily a comedy about eccentricity, as the psychotics dress up in outrageous outfits and launch into off-the-wall monologues on all kinds of nonsensical subjects. Unfortunately, the costumes and theatrics only go so far in *King of Hearts*. Director Philippe de Broca *(Dear Inspector)* and screenwriter Daniel Boulanger *(That Man from Rio)* seem more concerned with how their players look and act than with making them into believable characters. Because there is little plot or action aside from acting out of the inmates' fantasies, *King of Hearts* can eventually grow tiresome.

RATING: *No MPAA rating, with brief nudity*

KIPPERBANG
(Video)

Coming-of-Age Comedy

England

1984   85 Min.   Color

CREDITS: *Directed by Michael Apted. Written by Jack Rosenthal. Produced by Chris Griffin and David Puttnam (Chariots of Fire). Cinematography by Tony Pierce-Roberts. Released by MGM/UA. Distributed nontheatrically by Films Inc. Starring John Albasiny, Abigail Cruttenden, Maurice Dee, Alison Steadman, Garry Cooper, Robert Urquhart and Mark Brailsford.*

"P'tang P'tang, Kipperbang" is an expression the fourteen-year-old boys in this movie use instead of "What's happening?" or "Take it easy." It's 1950 in England and the hero of this story, Ducksworth (affectionately nicknamed "Quack Quack" by his classmates), has an important matter on his mind—kissing Anne, the pretty young girl in his class about whom he daydreams constantly. In guilt-laden prayers every morning, the boy practically begs God to make his dream come true. But Ducksworth isn't the "dishiest" boy in their class, and Anne doesn't seem interested in returning his affections until Ducksworth inadvertently proves worthy of her luscious lips by committing a brave deed.

Cleverly using a cricket match announcer to narrate the boy's struggle, director Michael Apted *(Coal Miner's Daughter, 28/Up)* equates Ducksworth's battle with puberty to all of the excitement of a championship match between the Aussies and the Brits. In these and many other moments in the film, Apted exaggerates those forbidden urges that permeate every corner of an adolescent's mind. Ducksworth does some embarrassing things in this movie, but for the most part he is a bright and levelheaded kid. Because he is intelligent, likeable and somewhat believable, *Kipperbang* is much more satisfying than most of its American teen comedy counterparts.

Unfortunately, a problem with this film is simply understanding it. Much of the dialogue is colloquial or clipped, nearly impossible for us Yankees to understand. Still, what is comprehensible in this film is comical, entertaining and well worth experiencing.

RATING: PG, with nothing objectionable.
FILMNOTE: Kipperbang was produced for Britain's independent Channel 4 on a small budget of only $700,000, and the whole film was shot in less than three weeks.

KISS OF THE SPIDER WOMAN
(Video)

Political Thriller

U.S.A.

1985   119 Min.   Color

CREDIT: Directed by Hector Babenco. Written by Leonard Schrader, based on the novel by Manuel Puig. Produced by David Weisman. Cinematography by Rodolfo Sanchez. Music by John Nechling. Released by Island Alive. Distributed nontheatrically by New Yorker Films. Starring William Hurt, Raoul Julia and Sonia Braga.

Hector Babenco's award-winning adaptation of Manuel Puig's *Kiss of the Spider Woman* is a savage exploration of the limits of both personal and political repression. Placed together in a cell somewhere in South America, Molina (William Hurt) is an effeminate, apolitical window dresser imprisoned for his homosexuality, and Valentin (Raoul Julia) a homophobic leftist held without trial as a suspected guerrilla. In the beginning, Valentin views Molina with disgust. With torture wounds all over his body and lofty political philosophies burning in his brain, Valentin has more important things on his mind than the frivolities of this gay man's life. Molina, on the other hand, could care less about social issues, passing each day recounting scenes from a Nazi propaganda film and a ridiculous romantic thriller about a Spider Woman (Sonia Braga) who ensnares her men. But as they begin to share their innermost secrets, their animosity toward each other turns into an ultimately fatal love.

Although the turgid Spider Woman dream and movie sequences are more confusing than enriching, and the clips of the Nazi love stories are as boring as the real propaganda probably was, these are minor quibbles compared to the intensity of Hurt and Julia's performances and the issues their characters bring up. Hurt is brilliant as Molina. There are subtleties to his expressions and a reach to his performance that make his Molina one of the most involving characters to appear on the screen for a long time. Julia's part is less theatrical, but his performance is no less captivating. And though the film is a brutal indictment of South American dictatorships and political repression, what's most interesting about it is how director Hector Babenco *(Pixote)* skillfully has Molina and Valentin switch roles. Whereas Valentin is angry at the injustice in the world and seems to live only for his politics, he is out of touch with his own emotions and can be coldly insensitive to Molina. Molina appears narcissistic but in reality is very selfless and caring. Few moments go by when he isn't thinking about Valentin, and it is Molina's kindness and love that is the emotional core of this movie.

RATING: R for language, gay and straight sex and brief nudity.

AWARDS: *1985 Academy Award for Best Actor (William Hurt); 1985 Academy Award nominations for Best Picture and Best Director. Award for Best Actor (Hurt) at the 1985 Cannes Film Festival.*

KNIFE IN THE WATER
(Video, subtitled)

Psychological Drama

Poland	Polish
1963 94 Min.	B&W

CREDITS: *Directed by Roman Polanski. Written by Roman Polanski, Jerzy Skolimowski and Jakub Goldberg. Produced by Stanislaw Zylewicz. Cinematography by Jerzy Lipman. Music by Kryzystof Komeda. Released by Janus Films. Distributed nontheatrically by Films Inc. Starring Leon Niemczyk, Jolanta Umecka and Zygmunt Malanowicz.*

Knife in the Water was Roman Polanski's first feature and the only film he made in his native Poland. It is therefore not surprising that it's much closer to the Polish cinema of his roots than the Hollywood horror and crime genre he was later to embrace in films such as *Chinatown* and *Rosemary's Baby.*

Co-written by Jerzy Skolimowski (*Moonlighting*), the film is a claustrophobic story of one twenty-four-hour period in the lives of a cultured couple and a lower-class drifter they pick up hitchhiking. Andrez (Leon Niemczyk) and his much younger wife, Christine (Jolanta Umecka), are on vacation when they nearly run over a young man (Zygmunt Malanowicz) who darts in front of their car. Andrez angrily confronts him, and the young man responds with scorn for the upper class. Strangely enough, Andrez and Christine then invite him to join them on an overnight trip on their sailboat, and the young man accepts. For the rest of the film, the three live in close quarters on the boat, where the two men compete fiercely as Christine stays outside of their verbal fencing matches, cynical and amused. Finally, the stakes of the game become deadly, with Andrez playing for the drifter's life, while the young man sets his sights on his adversary's wife.

Although Niemczyk and Malanowicz give intense performances in difficult roles, Umecka's Christine is too aloof and wooden to be continually interesting. Polanski also leaves much of the story line open to broad interpretation, the film's dialogue-weak narrative can be slow and there's little action outside of the infantile challenges Andrez and the stranger construct to prove their manliness. Yet in its own understated way, *Knife in the Water* is a fascinating exploration of class, sex and power in male and female relationships. Using mostly a hand-held camera, cinematographer Jerzy Lipman exquisitely composes each shot to reveal the oppression and conflicts among these characters, while Polanski cleverly constructs metaphors to express the emptiness of their lives. Although *Knife in the Water* takes some patience to sit through, there is plenty in the film to make it worth the effort.

RATING: *No MPAA rating, with mild profanity.*
AWARDS: *International Film Critics Award at the 1963 Venice Film Festival; 1963 Academy Award nomination for Best Foreign Film.*
WARNING: *The video version of this film is a public domain print that isn't the best quality, with subtitles that are sometimes hard to read. Luckily, there isn't much dialogue in the film.*

KOYAANISQATSI
(Video)

Documentary

U.S.A.	
1983 87 Min.	Color

CREDITS: *Directed by Godfrey Reggio. Written by Godfrey Reggio, Ron Fricke and Michael Hoenig. Produced by Godfrey Reggio. Cinematography by Ron Fricke. Music by Philip Glass and Michael Hoenig.*

Released and distributed nontheatrically by New Yorker Films.

The word *koyaanisqatsi* means "life out of balance" in Hopi, and Godfrey Reggio, with his feature film debut, shows us how our world has gone off-kilter with a collage of images set to an extraordinary soundtrack by Philip Glass.

The film begins with shots of the earth's wonders—volcanoes, waterfalls, dunes, geological formations and clouds—accompanied by slow choral music and a low bass chanting of *koyaanisqatsi*. These segments are beautiful and meditative, lulling you into a hypnotic trance. Slowly you are brought back to reality, as the scenes switch to modern civilization. Humans appear like ants, busily running from place to place, tearing down the environment, building monoliths and acting in strange ways. Bombs and rockets shoot through the sky; rivers of people stream out of skyscrapers and factories; and herds line up on escalators and subways. In one scene a woman sunbathes next to an industrial plant, while in another, workers level a housing project in the South Bronx. The score in this section is composed of frenetic drones and irritating atonal noise. The images are surreal, metaphoric and very disturbing.

Although there's no spoken dialogue, and much of *Koyaanisqatsi* is repetitious, it's certainly not boring. In fact, too much happens in images that whiz by so fast that they're hard to grasp. But what Reggio and cinematographer-editor Ron Fricke manage to express with meticulous editing and the juxtaposition of visual and audio rhythms is quite remarkable, making *Koyaanisqatsi* a feast for those intrigued by cinematic wizardry. Without preaching, Reggio also shows us how we are destroying the delicate balance of the universe and the natural forces within ourselves. It's as fascinating as it is overwhelming.

RATING: No MPAA rating, with mildly violent and disturbing images.
FILMNOTE: Reggio, formerly a member of a Catholic Brothers Teaching Order, conceived Koyaanisqatsi in 1974. It took seven years to complete.

THE LACEMAKER

Psychological Drama

Switzerland		French
1977	108 Min.	Color

CREDITS: *Directed by Claude Goretta. Written by Claude Goretta and Pascal Laine, based on Laine's novel. Produced by Yves Peyrot and Yves Gasser. Cinematography by Jean Boffety. Music by Pierre Jansen. Released by Citel/Action Films. Distributed nontheatrically by New Yorker Films. Starring Isabelle Huppert, Yves Beneyton, Florence Giorgetti, Anne-Marie Duringer, Renata Schroeter, Michel de Re, Monique Chaumette and Jean Obe.*

Claude Goretta's third film features the best performance of Isabelle Huppert's career to date. Huppert stars as Beatrice, a plain, timid young woman who lives with her mother in a Normandy town and works at a local beauty shop. She and her vivacious friend Marylene (Florence Giorgetti) go to the beach for a vacation, where Marylene quickly shacks up with a man she meets in their hotel. Poor Beatrice spends days alone trying to pass the time, until a handsome young man approaches her in a café and introduces himself as a student of great literature.

His name is François (Yves Beneyton), and after a few days, she agrees to have sex with him, even though she has never before slept with a man. In short order they are living together in his Paris apartment and her entire life is consumed by her new lover. But it's soon clear that he isn't satisfied by her, and when he explains that they are different and that it would be best for them to break up, she agrees without emotion. A few days later, she has a complete nervous breakdown.

Goretta takes us into Beatrice's dark, lonely world without relief in *The Lacemaker*. The gray skies of Normandy set the mood for her self-torment, and the film's bittersweet music adds to the oppressive atmosphere. Even when Beatrice and François are together, Beatrice's unconditional love is too desperate to contain any passion or joy. It's obvious what's going on inside of Beatrice from the moment we meet her, although she rarely speaks at all. Beatrice's body language reveals a great deal, while her relationship with the overly intellectual François tells the rest of her story. Huppert gives a brilliant performance, and you never stop feeling for Beatrice. But you also wish that she would snap out of it. She never does, and the final nervous breakdown is a fitting conclusion to a powerful and depressing film.

RATING: No MPAA rating, with nudity and sex.
AWARDS: Ecumenical Prize at the 1977 Cannes Film Festival.

THE LAST MÉTRO
(Video)

 ★ ★

World War II Thriller

France   French

1980   133 Min.   Color

CREDITS: Directed by François Truffaut. Written François Truffaut, Susan Schiffman and Jean-Claude Grumberg. Cinematography by Nestor Almendros. Music by Georges Delerue. Art direction by Jean-Pierre Kohut-Svelko. Editing by Martine Barraque. Released by United Artists. Distributed nontheatrically by Films Inc. Starring Catherine Deneuve, Gérard Depardieu, Jean Poiret, Heinz Bennent, Andrea Ferreol, Paulette Dubost and Jean-Louis Richard.

When The Last Métro was released in 1980, it won ten French Caesars (their Oscar equivalent), including Best Picture, Actor, Actress, etc., which makes it one of the most overrated films in French history.

Set in Paris during the height of World War II, The Last Métro focuses on a troupe of theater people struggling to keep their craft alive during Nazi occupation. Maria Steiner (Catherine Deneuve) is director of a popular Paris theater formerly run by her exiled Jewish husband. But Maria harbors a

secret: Her husband, Lucas (Heinz Bennent), is actually hiding out in the theater's cellar, where he listens to play rehearsals through heating ducts and then gives her detailed instructions when she steals visits with him each evening. But Maria soon grows weary of listening to and having to care for him, and her dissatisfaction deepens when she is attracted to the new young actor, Bernard (Gérard Depardieu), who's playing the lead role opposite her in her husband's play. Bernard, meanwhile, has his own secret: He is dangerously involved with the Resistance. The sexual tension between Maria and Bernard is further complicated when local Nazis zero in on Lucas's whereabouts, and Maria has to depend on Bernard to save her husband's life.

Truffaut gathered all of the technical talent he could for The Last Métro, including famed cinematographer Nestor Almendros (Days of Heaven) and musical director Georges Delerue (Shoot the Piano Player). Unfortunately, they are not at their best in this film. The camera work is so stylized that certain scenes appear lifeless, while Delerue's overdone soundtrack is obtrusive rather than enhancing. But the biggest problem with The Last Métro is its uneven writing. At nearly two and a quarter hours, many scenes drag on too long, and right from the start there are big gaps in the narrative that don't make sense in the context of the story or the historical events that are taking place. In addition, the suspense leading up to the climax demands far more attention than the confused and unresolved ending deserves.

RATING: R for mild violence and sex.
AWARDS: Ten French Caesars including awards for Best Picture, Actor (Gérard Depardieu), Actress (Catherine Deneuve), Supporting Actor (Jean Poiret), Supporting Actress (Andrea Ferreol), Art Direction (Jean-Pierre Kohut-Svelko), Editing (Martine Barraque), Music (Georges Delerue), Screenplay (François Truffaut, Jean-Claude Grumberg and Suzanne Schiffman) and Cinematography (Nestor Almendros); 1980 Academy Award nomination for Best Foreign Film.

LAST NIGHT AT THE ALAMO
(Video)

Social Drama

U.S.A.

1984   80 Min.   Color

CREDITS: *Directed by Eagle Pennell. Written and produced by Eagle Pennell and Kim Henkel. Cinematography by Brian Huberman and Eric A. Edwards. Music by Chuck Pennell and Wayne Bell. Released and distributed nontheatrically by Cinecom. Starring Sonny Carl Davis, Louis Perryman, Steven Matilla, Tina-Bess Hubbard, Doris Hargrave, Amanda LaMar, Peggy Pinnell, J. Michael Hammond, Henry Wideman and George Pheneger.*

All of Eagle Pennell's second feature on Texans takes place on a single night at the Alamo, a bar that will close down the next day to make way for a high-rise. On this evening, the regulars assemble to lament the bar's passing. A few women hang out at the Alamo, but most of the patrons are an assortment of alcoholic men who brag about their sexual exploits and taunt each other with fifth-grade machismo.

The cock-of-the-roost is a strapping hunk called Cowboy (Sonny Carl Davis). When Cowboy enters the bar, he tells the others to relax, that his good friend, a state representative, will save the Alamo before the night is over. But while waiting for salvation, Cowboy holds court, winning a chug-a-lug contest and starting a couple of ridiculous brawls. As the night wears on, the motive for Cowboy's foolishness becomes obvious. He has the most to lose if the Alamo closes, for the Alamo is the only place where people think anything of him. In the outside world, he's a loser.

If you were driving through Houston looking for refreshment and came upon a raunchy bar filled with alcoholic rednecks, would you want to spend an hour and a half listening to the clientele's petty arguments and drunken tirades? In *Last Night at the Alamo,* you have no choice. Stifling, with no variation in sets or pacing, each scene is filled with cursing, infantile conversations and blatant sexism. Still, the performances are intense, often frighteningly authentic, and co-writers Pennell and Kim Henkel *(Texas Chain Saw Massacre)* effectively dismantle feigned machismo and the fragile male ego. By the end of this evening of debauchery, we have come to know several of the Alamo's regulars a little too intimately for comfort.

RATING: *No rating, with a lot of profanity and brief violence.*
FILMNOTE: The Whole Shootin' Match, *Eagle Pennell's first film about Texas men, has characters similar to those in* Last Night at the Alamo, *only its narrative isn't as well developed.*

LAST TANGO IN PARIS
(Video, paritially subtitled)

Psychological Drama

France/Italy   English and French

1973   129 Min.   Color

CREDITS: *Directed and produced by Bernardo Bertolucci. Written by Bernardo Bertolucci and Franco Arcalli. Edited by Franco Arcalli. Music by Gato Barbieri. Cinematography by Vittorio Storaro. Distributed nontheatrically by Films Inc. Starring Marlon Brando, Maria Schneider, Jean-Pierre Leaud, Massimo Girotti, Catherine Allegret and Darling Legitimus.*

Although Bertolucci's *Last Tango in Paris* caused quite a stir when it was originally released, because it featured Oscar-winner Marlon Brando in supposedly sensational X-rated sex scenes, those moments in the film would only earn an R by today's MPAA standards. But that fact doesn't render them any less disturbing.

When we meet Paul (Marlon Brando), he is looking at an apartment to rent in Paris. A beautiful young woman named Jeanne (Maria Schneider) is looking at the same apartment, and within minutes of their coincidental encounter, they are making love in the large empty space. From that moment on, the two strangers become regular lovers, albeit strange ones, because Paul refuses to reveal anything about his past and shows no interest in getting to know his new partner. She isn't happy with this arrangement but continues to meet him at the apartment, addicted to sex with Paul as if it were a drug. The more obsessed she becomes, the more brutally he mistreats her while she tearfully submits to his abuse. When they aren't making love, Paul often lies in a fetal position on the bare floor of the unfurnished apartment, crying, as his young lover does everything she can to get him to pay attention to her. Gradually, we learn the dark and tragic secrets that have driven Paul to this cold, inhuman sanctuary.

There are very few actors who could portray the depth of feeling needed to pull off Paul's complicated character, but Brando manages it brilliantly. His Paul is sleazy and brutal, tortured by his past but also extremely charismatic. The film is well worth seeing for his performance alone, although Schneider is also quite good as the confused and obsessed young woman. Director Bertolucci (1900, The Conformist) with the help of cinematographer Vittorio Storaro imbues every scene with atmospheric lighting and powerful camera work, and Gato Barbieri's melancholy jazz score further enhances the mood. Be forewarned that this film contains a lot of raw language and sexual abuse, women aren't portrayed favorably, and several scenes contain little dialogue or action. But as a portrait of two people tortured by their twisted sexual desires, it ranks with Nagisa Oshima's In the Realm of the Senses as one of the most disturbing and compelling visions of eroticism ever filmed.

RATING: X for nudity, sex, language and violence.
AWARDS: 1973 New York Film Critics Award for Best Actor (Marlon Brando); 1973 Academy Award nominations for Best Actor (Brando) and Best Director (Bernardo Bertolucci).

THE LAST WALTZ
(Video)

Rock Documentary

U.S.A.

1978   117 Min.   Color

CREDITS: Directed by Martin Scorsese. Cinematography by Michael Chapman, Vilmos Zsigmond, Laszlo Kovacs and David Myers. Released by MGM. Distributed nontheatrically by Films Inc. Starring The Band (Robbie Robertson, Levon Helm, Garth Hudson, Richard Manuel and Rick Danko), Joni Mitchell, Bob Dylan, Van Morrison, Eric Clapton, Martin Scorsese, Muddy Waters, Neil Young, Ronnie Hawkins, Dr. John, The Staple Singers, Ringo Starr, Paul Butterfield, Emmy Lou Harris and Neil Diamond.

After nearly twenty years of performing, The Band decided to call it quits on Thanksgiving in 1976 with a farewell show at San Francisco's Winterland that included some of the most important performers of the day. They also arranged for Martin Scorsese (Taxi Driver and editor of Woodstock) and his top-notch crew of cinematographers and sound experts to film the concert. The result is an amazingly clear portrait of a rock-and-roll event that captures the raw power and energy of the performances as well as the subtle emotional moments of the performers themselves.

Interspersed with the concert footage are interviews with The Band members, in which they tell stories and try to put their experiences into perspective. This material is less effective, both because Scorsese as interviewer asks too many leading questions, and because some of The Band try too hard to characterize themselves as jaded survivors of the road. Still, pianist Richard Manuel (who later committed suicide) shines in these sections, self-deprecatingly mocking sixties pychedelia as a time of "chocolate stockings and marshmallow overcoats" and suggesting that The Band should be appreciated primarily for their music. His attitude is consistent with the film itself as, musically, *The Last Waltz* delivers a soulful celebration that only a handful of other music documentaries, such as *Stop Making Sense* and *Heartland Reggae*, have been able to do.

RATING:PG, *with nothing objectionable.*
FILMNOTE: *The interview scenes in* The Last Waltz *are notoriously lampooned in Rob Reiner's* This Is Spinal Tap.

THE LAST WAVE

(Video, partially subtitled)

Occult Thriller

Australia	English and Aborigine
1977	106 Min. Color

CREDITS: *Directed by Peter Weir. Written by Peter Weir, Tony Morphett and Peter Popescu. Produced by Hal and James McElroy. Cinematography by Russel Boyd. Music by Charles Wain. Released by World Northal. Distributed nontheatrically by Kit Parker Films. Starring Richard Chamberlain, Olivia Hamnett, David Gumpilil, Frederick Parslow, Nanjiwarra Amagula, Walter Amagula and Vivean Gray.*

As Peter Weir's *The Last Wave* begins, a blue sky and shining sun are abruptly replaced by deafening thunder and a torrential storm of rain and hail. As the rain pours down, David (Richard Chamberlain), a lawyer in Sidney, is haunted by a bizarre dream of two Aborigine men holding medallions carved with symbols. David has no idea how these characters from his dream will affect his life until one of them, Chris (*Walkabout*'s David Gumpilil), turns up as one of four Aborigines he is hired to defend in a murder case. As David works on the case, he not only discovers highly peculiar facts about the murder but also finds out the frightening reasons for his own nightmares.

Although the first half of *The Last Wave* develops slowly, by the film's apocalyptic conclusion, you are riveted to your seat. Richard Chamberlain's performance is ex-

cellent, and director Peter Weir (*Witness, The Year of Living Dangerously*) skillfully creates a supernatural aura by the constant drip, flow and gush of water throughout. His chilling score of Aboriginal music, which sounds like a chorus of frogs, is also very effective. Perhaps better than any film in recent memory, *The Last Wave* enters that "other" dimension of psychic phenomena. Yet even more frightening are David's experiences in tribal Aborigine culture—a secret and ancient world different from anything we've ever experienced.

RATING: PG, *with disturbing images.*

LAST YEAR AT MARIENBAD

(Video, subtitled)

★ ★ ½

Psychological Drama

France/Italy	French
1962	94 Min. B&W

CREDITS: *Directed by Alain Resnais. Written by Alain Robbe-Grillet, based on his novel. Produced by Pierre Courau and Raymond Froment. Cinematography by Sacha Viermy, filmed in Cinemascope. Music by Francis Seyrig. Released by Silver Films. Distributed nontheatrically by New Yorker Films and Kit Parker Films. Starring Giorgio Albertazzi, Delphine Seyrig, Sacha Pitoeff, Françoise Bertin and Luce Garcia-Ville.*

Most of Alain Resnais's films (*Mon Oncle d'Amerique, Hiroshima mon Amour*) take some patience to penetrate, but *Last Year at Marienbad* is virtually impossible. The story begins simply. A bachelor (Giogio Albertazzi) and a married woman (Delphine Seyrig) meet in the ancient Roman garden of a resort chateau. The man insists that they had a passionate affair one year before and that she had agreed to meet him a year later at this same chateau to run away with him. The woman claims to have no idea what he is talking about and in fact denies ever meeting him. The two go back and forth for hours. She accuses him of making the whole thing up, while he becomes obsessed with having her for his own.

Although their dialogue never seems to connect on any level, something about the situation strangely compels both to continue beyond any hope of resolution. At the same time, the woman's husband (Sacha Pitoeff) turns up at various intervals in the story, and it soon becomes obvious that he neither knows nor loves his wife. Also mixed in with the disjointed conversations of the present are several surreal flashbacks (or fabrications) of the supposed sexual rendezvous the year before.

In *Last Year at Marienbad*, Resnais and his screenwriter Alain Robbe-Grillet abandon a traditional story line for pure stream-of-consciousness. It's never clear if the main characters are really conversing or if the whole episode is a creation of the man's imagination. The film's intentionally jumpy editing and surreal images further confuse the narrative, while little of the plot fits into a traditional time sequence. But buried in all of the jumble is a fascinating portrait of the subconscious workings of the two lead characters.

The film's allegorical dialogue and richly detailed metaphors suggest a strong message about the inevitability of loneliness and the futility of intimacy. Cinematographer Sacha Vierny superbly captures a dreamlike tone using slow pans of the two conversing in the garden and the mistily shot flashbacks, while the atmosphere is further enhanced by a dissonant organ score. The performances by the two leads are excellent as well. But none of these qualities can save *Last Year at Marienbad* from its incessant claustrophobia. Although the stage is set for suspense early on, the conversations and flashbacks grow increasingly incomprehensible and the entire film evolves into an exercise in futility.

RATING: No MPAA rating, with nothing objectionable.
AWARDS: 1962 Academy Award nomination for Best Screenplay Written Directly for the Screen (Alain Robbe-Grillet).
WARNING: Subtitles on the video version are hard to read at times and can also whiz by too fast to catch unless you are a speed reader.

LATINO
(Video, partially subtitled)

Political Drama

U.S.A.   Spanish and English

1985   105 Min.   Color

CREDITS: Directed and written by Haskell Wexler. Produced by Benjamin Berg. Cinematography by Tom Sibet. Music by Diane Louie. Released and distributed nontheatrically by Cinecom. Starring Robert Beltran, Annette Cardona, Tony Plana, Ricardo Lopez and Julio Medina.

Those of us who loved cinematographer Haskell Wexler's 1968 directorial debut, *Medium Cool*, were anxiously awaiting his next release. We had to wait seventeen years for *Latino*, and it's a disappointment.

The film's central character is Eddie Guerrero (Robert Beltran of *Eating Raoul*), a Chicano lieutenant in the Special Forces whose assignment is to secretly instruct Nicaraguan Contras in guerrilla tactics. Since Eddie is a veteran of four stints in Vietnam, this mission is all in a day's work for him. But it doesn't take him long to realize the Contras are carrying out a brutal war of rape, torture and murder against many innocent civilians in Nicaragua. Although he got used to such treatment against "gooks" in Vietnam, it's hard for him to watch the same thing happen to these Nicaraguan villagers, because he too is Hispanic.

On an action-adventure level, there is enough going on in *Latino* to keep the plot moving, and the sets in Nicaragua and Honduras give the film an authentic look. But the acting is generally uninspired, and the themes come across more like a Sandinista propaganda film than a believable political drama. While the Contras are about as evil as human beings can get, the Sandinistas are happy people who cheerfully work on cooperative farms and espouse the virtues of the revolution. There is even upbeat indigenous music in the background for the scenes with the Sandinistas and a sinister soundtrack for the Contras. Wexler (co-cinematographer for *Days of Heaven*) overstates his case every step of the way. Although he makes some important points about the brutality of the Contra war in the process, his lack of objectivity will doom *Latino* to audiences who are already converted to what he is trying to preach—and even they won't appreciate the movie, because it is poorly made.

RATING: No MPAA rating, with nudity, violence and profanity.

LAW OF DESIRE
(Video, subtitled)

Gay Drama

Spain	Spanish
1987	100 Min.	Color

CREDITS: *Directed and written by Pedro Almodovar. Produced by Miguel A. Perez Campos. Cinematography by Angel Luis Fernandez. Costume design by Jose Mario Cossio. Set design by Javier Fernandez. Released by Cinevista. Distributed nontheatrically by New Yorker Films. Starring Eusebio Poncela, Carmen Maura, Antonio Banderas, Miguel Molina, Manuela Velasco, Bibi Andersson, Fernando Guillen, Nacho Martinez and Helga Line.*

If there's a Spanish filmmaker who has benefited from the new freedoms of the censorship-free post-Franco era, it's Pedro Almodovar. With his highly irreverent *What Have I Done to Deserve This* and *Law of Desire*, he flaunts Fascist and Catholic conventions in ways that are as entertaining as they are shocking.

Set in a modern-day Madrid of flashy sports cars, discotheques and cocaine, the film explores the price people pay for obsessive love. The story's main casualties are Pablo (Eusebio Poncela), a gay filmmaker in his early forties, and his transsexual sister, Tina (Carmen Maura). Tina can never manage a satisfying relationship, while Pablo is in love with Juan (Miguel Molina), a pretty young boy who adores Pablo but

isn't attracted to men. Pablo is so enamored of the boy that he forges love letters to himself to fuel his fantasies while Juan is away at the beach. In seeking a small diversion, he has a one-night stand with Antonio (Antonio Banderas), a handsome young man who, with one taste, becomes obsessed with possessing Pablo. The more Pablo rejects Antonio, the more insane Antonio becomes. Eventually, when Antonio stumbles across a love letter "from" Juan, he is pushed to do anything to force Pablo to recognize the depth of his desire.

Law of Desire's weak link is its story line. Certain plot twists land far outside the realm of possibility; director Almodovar even resorts to having Pablo develop amnesia as a way out of an unlikely situation. But visually, *Law of Desire* is a feast, containing sets and cinematography reminiscent of Jean-Jacques Beineix's *Diva*. The raw passions among the men are handled with a directness that greatly enhances the story. And all of the performances are outstanding, with Maura's work as the voluptuous, transsexual Tina particularly captivating. In the end, the three main players are desperate for love they can never attain, and Almodovar is able to carry their obsessions to absurdly funny levels without sacrificing the intensity of their hurt and betrayal.

RATING: No MPAA rating, with nudity, substance abuse, violence and gay sexual situations.

LETTER TO BREZHNEV
(Video)

Romantic Drama

England	
1986	95 Min.	Color

CREDITS: *Directed by Chris Bernard. Written by Frank Clark. Produced by Janet Goddard. Cinematography by Bruce McGowan. Released by Britain's Channel 4. Distributed nontheatrically by Circle Releasing Corp. Starring Margi Clarke,*

Alexandria Pigg, Peter Firth and Alfred Molina.

Elaine (Alexandria Pigg) and Teresa (Margi Clarke), the pretty young heroines of *Letter to Brezhnev,* face slim pickins in the desirable men department. Their problem is largely where they live—dingy, depressing Liverpool, where the men are either punks with rotting teeth and swastikas for jewelry, or working-class toughs driven solely by their libidos. But Elaine and Teresa still get dolled up and cruise nightclubs for their masculine dream. Finally, they strike pay dirt, meeting Sergei (Alfred Molina) and Piotr (Peter Firth), two sailors on leave from a Russian freighter. They pair off—Teresa with Sergei, Elaine with Piotr—and the two excited couples get adjoining hotel rooms, where their emotions are fanned into raging fires.

Although they have a hard time relating verbally because Sergei barely speaks a word of English, he and Teresa have no trouble communicating with their bodies. Elaine and Piotr, on the other hand, just lie in bed, holding each other and talking. By the end of the night, Teresa and Sergei are sexually spent, and Elaine and Piotr are very much in love. The only problem is that Sergei and Piotr have to be back to their ship by 5:00 that night and will probably never again return to England. After weeks of desperately missing Piotr, Elaine writes a letter to Brezhnev explaining her situation, and to her surprise, he responds with a one-way ticket to Russia. Now Elaine is faced with the decision of whether or not she can leave everything for a man she barely knows, who lives in a dark and ominous country.

Letter to Brezhnev is a small story about simple people who live through their dreams. Elaine and Teresa are men-obsessed because they are looking for a way out of their dull, lower-middle-class lives. Produced in association with England's independent Channel 4 television (as was *My Beautiful Laundrette*), *Letter to Brezhnev* is not a big-budget production. But director Chris Bernard skillfully makes everything about Liverpool, including the people, gray and edgy. Although at times Elaine's romance with Piotr can be overly sentimental, the Madonnaesque Clarke and good-girl

Pigg are so compelling and humorous as men-hungry heroines, it's easy to overlook the film's occasional lapses into sappiness.

RATING: R for sexual content, language and brief nudity.
AWARDS: 1985 British Academy Award nomination for Best Actress (Alexandria Pigg).
WARNING: A good portion of the dialogue is so thick with Liverpudlian accents that the film is often hard to understand.

LIANNA
(Video)

Lesbian Drama

U.S.A.

1983   110 Min.   Color

CREDITS: *Directed and written by John Sayles. Produced by Jeffrey Nelson and Maggie Renzi. Cinematography by Austin de Besche. Music by Mason Daring. Released by United Artists. Distributed non-theatrically by Films Inc. Starring Linda Griffiths, Jane Hallaren, Jon DeVries, Jo Henderson, Jessica Wight MacDonald, Stephen Mendillo and John Sayles.*

Although it seems a little incongruous that a male filmmaker could create a compelling film about a housewife coming out of the closet and accepting her homosexuality, John Sayles does just that in *Lianna*.

Lianna (Linda Griffiths) is a thirty-one-year-old mother of two children stuck in an unhappy marriage with an arrogant, selfish college professor (Jon DeVries). To get out of the house, she takes a child psychology course from an attractive professor named Ruth (Jane Hallaren) and finds herself looking for excuses to stay after class. Finally, one night it happens—they have an affair. Although it's her first time sleeping with a woman, Lianna loves it. The next day she tells her husband, and in a matter of hours, her life completely changes. She has to leave her kids and home and find a way to support herself. It's quite a shock for Lianna, especially when her best friend drops her, her kids don't want to see her and then Ruth tells her she is still involved with an old lover and is wary of a serious commitment to Lianna.

Sayles handles *Lianna*'s delicate subjects well. Although her husband is certainly a schmuck, the main reason Lianna becomes a lesbian is because she is attracted to Ruth. It's easy to understand that attraction right from the start because Ruth is an intelligent, sensitive person. When she and Lianna open up to each other, and then make love, it's not only soft and caring, but it makes perfect sense. Even when confronted with her friend's and family's narrow-mindedness, Lianna doesn't buckle under the pressure and atone for her "sins." She rightfully tries to get them to understand that she is the same person she always was, and they are the ones who have to accept her. Although *Lianna* is not without some bothersome technical problems because of limitations in its budget, and some imperfections in plot and character development, Sayles manages to create a film about real people whose struggles come through loud and clear.

RATING: R for nudity and sex.

LIQUID SKY
(Video)

 ★ ★

Futuristic Black Comedy

U.S.A.

1983   112 Min.   Color

CREDITS: *Directed and produced by Slava Tsukerman. Written by Slava Tsukerman, Anne Carlisle and Nina Kerova. Cinematography by Yuri Neyman. Music by Slava Tsukerman, Brenda Hutchinson and Clive Smith. Special effects by Yuri Neyman. Released and distributed nontheatrically by New Yorker Films. Starring Anne Carlisle, Paula Sheppard, Susan Doukas, Otto von Wernherr, Bob Brady, Elaine Grove, Stanley Knap and Jack Adalist.*

Despite its surprise success on the college cult and midnight movie circuit, Slava Tsukerman's *Liquid Sky* usually drives a good third of its audience toward the exits after the first fifteen minutes.

The bizarre plot concerns the exploits of a New Wave model named Margarette (Anne Carlisle), who is used by a pickle-sized alien who needs a chemical produced in the brain at the moment of orgasm in order to survive. A stiking woman, Margarette is a perfect surrogate; her constant companions are junkies, punks and lecherous men and women, all of them eager to have sex with her. An endless stream of admirers visit her rooftop Manhattan apartment, shoot heroin and then rape her, dying at the moment of orgasm as the alien feeds off their brains. They have to force themselves on Margarette because she hates sex, men and practically everything else save her professor boyfriend and her junkie lesbian roommate. But these two aren't safe for long either.

Tsukerman takes an obscene and absurd situation and stretches it to the limits of good taste. Most of the dialogue is profane, often delivered with a sneer, and barely five minutes go by without a rape. (There is one especially unpleasant vignette in which Margarette's roommate rapes a dead boyfriend.) None of the sex abuse or violence is explicit, and Tsukerman intersperses low-budget psychedelic effects and pulsating, synthesized punk music with the film's action. Some of these techniques are original, particularly the ones that resemble twisted Peter Max drawings. In other scenes, Tsukerman cleverly captures the degradation and disillusionment of the punk experience. But most of *Liquid Sky* is tedious, vacuous and offensive, and ultimately the film has a limited appeal beyond college audiences who enjoy the outrageousness.

RATING: R for plenty of substance abuse, profanity and sex.
WARNING: The visuals are so important in this film that watching it on video lessens the experience.

LOCAL HERO
(Video)

Social Satire

Scotland

1983   111 Min.   Color

CREDITS: *Directed and written by Bill Forsyth. Produced by David Putnam. Cinematography by Chris Menges. Music by Mark Knopfler (of Dire Straits). Released by Warner Brothers. Distributed nontheatrically by Swank Motion Pictures. Starring Peter Riegert, Burt Lancaster, Fulton MacKay, Denis Lawson, Norman Chancer, Jenny Seagrove, Peter Capaldi, Rikki Fulton and Alex Norton.*

Bill Forsyth's *Local Hero* spawned a series of imitations, creating a whole new genre of film—the wacky Scottish comedy. It follows the exploits of MacIntyre (Peter Riegert), a young acquisitions executive from a Houston-based oil company who is ordered to buy out the entire village of Ferness, Scotland, where his company hopes to build an oil refinery.

In the course of a few days, though, Mac falls in love with the North Shore town and its assortment of offbeat inhabitants. He becomes so enamored of Ferness, in fact, that he can't decide between carrying out his mission, thus destroying what's so precious about the town, and sabotaging both the project and his career. Ferness's citizens, though, are actually anxious to have the money, but play hard to get in hopes that Mac's company will raise the stakes. The double charade gets even more complicated when an elderly beach owner refuses to sell his crucial tract of land, and Mac's eccentric boss (Burt Lancaster) from Houston must fly in to close the deal.

Built on a mountain of metaphysics, *Local Hero* demands a few leaps of faith that are a bit difficult to make. But the premise of a yuppie from Texas traveling to an isolated town in Scotland to make poor but savvy fishermen wealthy is hilarious in itself, while the inhabitants of Ferness are a pack of daftly entertaining comedians. For-

syth also superbly contrasts the warmth of Scotland's North Shore with the impersonalization of supermodern Houston. As isolated as life in the village seems, Forsyth is clearly as taken by the simplicity and beauty of the place as Mac is. *Local Hero*'s scenery shots are breathtaking, as Forsyth and his cinematographer Chris Menges capture the serenity of the expansive beach and the power of the ocean and the stars as effectively as any filmmaker in recent memory.

RATING: *PG, with nothing objectionable.*
AWARDS: *1983 British Academy Award for Best Direction (Bill Forsyth); 1983 New York Film Critics Award for Best Screenplay (Forsyth).*

LOLA
(Video, subtitled)

Psychological Drama

West Germany   German and English

1982   114 Min.   Color

CREDITS: *Directed by Rainer Werner Fassbinder. Written by Rainer Werner Fassbinder, Peter Marthesheimer and Pea Froehlich. Produced by Horst Wendlandt. Cinematography by Xaver Schwarzenberger. Music by Peer Raben. Released by United Artists. Distributed nontheatrically by Films Inc. Starring Armin Mueller-Stahl, Barbara Sukowa, Mario Adorf, Rosel Zech, Matthew Fuchs, Helga Feddersen, Karin Baal, Ivan Desny and Karl-Heinz von Hassel.*

Lola, the third in Fassbinder's post–World War II trilogy (also including *The Marriage of Maria Braun* and *Veronika Voss*), is about a rebellious cabaret singer–prostitute named Lola (Barbara Sukowa) who lives in a small German city rebuilding after the war. The man who uses her services the most is a corrupt contractor named Schukert (Mario Adorf), who also owns the mayor, the police commissioner and many of the city's prominent citizens

But Schukert runs into a wall when the mayor hires the conservative Von Bohn (Armin Mueller-Stahl) as his new building commissioner. Von Bohn falls in love with Lola, and then discovers that she is Schukert's personal playmate. With the help of a socialist colleague who hates Schukert for his own reasons, he tries to destroy the developer, only to have his plan thwarted by his love for Lola and her drive for power and money.

Visually, *Lola* is a masterpiece. Fassbinder and his cinematographer Xaver Schwarzenberger brilliantly capture the moodiness of the film's characters, as well as the austerity of a ravaged city rebuilding after the war. Armin Mueller-Stahl and Mario Adorf give particularly outstanding performances, and all of the characters in *Lola* come to symbolize how postwar Germans were willing to compromise their morals for personal gain. In weaving an intricate web of his players' self-deception, Fassbinder strikes at the false promises of capitalism and socialism, the impersonalization of Germany's growing bureaucracy, and the shortsightedness of fast redevelopment. There are also many humorous scenes in this film, which help balance the intensity of the characters and settings and make *Lola* one of the most satisfying films of Fassbinder's prolific career.

RATING: R for nudity and language.
FILMNOTE: *Although actually filmed before* Veronika Voss, Lola *was released afterward and was meant to be the third film in the trilogy.*

LONELY HEARTS
(Video)

Psychological Romance

Australia

1981   95 Min.   Color

CREDITS: *Directed and written by Paul Cox. Produced by John B. Murray. Cinematography by Yuri Sokol. Released and distributed nontheatrically by The Samuel Goldwyn Company. Starring Wendy Hughes, Norman Kaye, Julia Blake, Jonathan Hardy, Irene Inescort, Vic Gordon and Ted Grove-Rogers.*

Paul Cox's *Lonely Hearts* is an Australian version of *Marty* about two shy and lonely misfits who overcome great personal barriers to become romantically involved. Peter (Norman Kaye) is a withdrawn, fifty-year-old piano tuner who wears a toupee and plays bingo once a week. Although it seems out of character, he also shoplifts whenever he gets the chance. Patricia (Wendy Hughes) is an office worker in her mid-thirties who has lived most of her life with her domineering parents. When they meet for the first time, through a dating service, they are nervous. When they try to have sex a couple of months later, they are downright anxious. It's a long, hard struggle as they twitch, stutter and fumble their way into a relationship, but eventually they fall in love.

With virtually no plot, slow pacing and most scenes revolving around their anxieties about each other, *Lonely Hearts* is a difficult movie to watch. But Kaye's and Hughes's performances are so outstanding and the emotions their characters get across so heartfelt, it's well worth the effort. Director Paul Cox *(Man of Flowers, My First Wife)* reveals the inner workings of his two main characters in very intimate ways. The camera becomes their eyes and ears, and what's unspoken between them is just as important as what they verbalize. In the end, Cox's sensitive direction and the principals' acting keep us involved with the characters and this movie every unnerving step of the way.

RATING: R for brief nudity.

THE LONG GOOD FRIDAY
(Video)

Gangster Thriller

England

1980   105 Min.   Color

CREDITS: *Directed by John MacKenzie. Written by Barrie Keefe. Produced by Barry Hanson. Cinematography by Phil Meheux. Music by Francis Monkman. Released by Embassy Pictures. Starring Bob Hoskins, Helen Mirren, Pierce Brosnan, Eddie Constantine, David King, Bryan Marshall, George Coulouis and Stephen Davies.*

Long before his 1987 Oscar nomination for *Mona Lisa,* British actor Bob Hoskins had made a splash with American art house audiences with his performance in *The Long Good Friday.*

He plays Harold Shand, the leader of a London crime syndicate, a gravelly voiced bulldog whose greed is matched only by his lust for power. As the film opens, someone is taking aim at Harold's empire. His assistant is knifed in a gay bath, while the car in which his mother is riding to Good Friday mass is booby-trapped with a bomb. At first, Harold assumes the attacks are an effort to discredit him as he prepares to meet with an American mobster named Charlie (Eddie Constantine) to talk about buying into a casino. He rounds up his enemies and, hanging them by their heels in a deserted meat locker, tries to torture confessions out of them but learns nothing. When a restaurant he and Charlie are going to is bombed, Harold becomes nearly paralyzed by this challenge to his authority. With the help of his resourceful lover, Victoria (Helen Mirren), Harold learns that one of his betrayers has been in earshot of his bellowing mouth all along.

The Long Good Friday falters sporadically. The American gangster subplot, although a necessary red herring, is poorly done, particularly due to Constantine's clichéd performance as Charlie. Also, the gay bath knifing is graphic to the point of being exploitive. Still, director John Mac-

Kenzie handles most of the action sequences with an adept hand, and the plot has enough suspense to keep us thoroughly involved until the movie's surprise ending. But most important, the two leads, Hoskins and Mirren, are nothing short of brilliant. Mirren (who won the Best Actress prize at Cannes for *Cal*) does a remarkable job as Harold's calm and sensual mistress. In contrast, Hoskins is terrifying as an angry man who doesn't comprehend his own self-destructive need for revenge. Ramrod straight, eyes always darting, Hoskins simply breathes corruption as Harold, and his tour de force performance makes this film a fine, offbeat gangster thriller.

RATING: *R for violence.*

THE LOST HONOR OF KATHARINA BLUM
(Video, subtitled)

Political Drama

West Germany   German

1975   104 Min.   Color

CREDITS: *Directed by Volker Schlondorff and Margarethe von Trotta. Written by Margarethe von Trotta, based on the novel by Heinrich Böll. Produced by Willim Benninger and Eberhard Junkersdorf. Cinematography by Jost Vacano. Music by Hans-Werner Henze. Released by Paramount/Orion. Distributed nontheatrically by Films Inc. Starring Angela Winkler, Mario Adorf, Dieter Laser, Heinz Bennent, Hannelore Hoger, Jurgen Prochnow and Harald Kuhlmann.*

Volker Schlondorff and Margarethe von Trotta's *The Lost Honor of Katharina Blum* is a frightening vision of police and the press run amok. The nightmare begins for Katharina (Angela Winkler), a quiet maid, when she uncharacteristically picks up a stranger (Jurgen Prochnow) at a party and spends the night with him. In the morning, after he is gone, an army of police overrun her apartment in search of her lover, who turns out to be a bank robber and a leftist terrorist. Hoping to flush out the fugitive, Inspector Beizmenne (Mario Adorf) makes Katharina the focus of public attention by announcing that she is part of the terrorist's gang. But instead of leading Beizmenne to the fugitive, Katherina returns to her destroyed apartment where she becomes the victim of threatening letters and obscene phone calls. Soon the press makes her a public pariah, investigating her failed marriage and fabricating quotes from her dying ex-husband that become front-page news. As her troubles deepen, Katharina becomes genuinely politicized and begins seeking retribution against a system to which she has always meekly subscribed.

The Lost Honor of Katharina Blum is a clear-eyed indictment of the sleazy methods of both the German police and newshounds desperately hunting for a story. The acting is solid throughout the film, with Winkler *(Sheer Madness)* giving a particularly strong performance as a woman who is transformed from a disinterested follower into a strong and defiant rebel. The script argues passionately from Katharina's point of view, while giving the police and the press a fair shake for their actions as well. Schlondorff and von Trotta pace their narrative briskly, deepening the conflicts among the various characters until the film's inevitably tragic conclusion. In the end, *The Lost Honor of Katharina Blum* is as well reasoned as an editorial, yet as passionate as a barroom brawl.

RATING: *R for sex and violence.*
FILMNOTE: *Directors Volker Schlondorff and Margarethe von Trotta are husband and wife.*

LOVE AND ANARCHY

(Video, subtitled)

Political Satire

Italy		Italian
1973	108 Min.	Color

CREDITS: *Directed and written by Lina Wertmuller. Produced by Herbert Stein-* mann. *Cinematography by Giuseppe Rotunno. Music by Nino Rota. Released by Peppercorn Films. Distributed nontheatrically by Almi Pictures. Starring Giancarlo Giannini, Mariangela Melato, Lina Polita, Eros Pagni, Pina Cei and Elena Flore.*

Love and Anarchy was the first commercial success in the United States for Lina Wertmuller and still stands as one of her best films. The anarchy of the film involves a country peasant named Tunin (Giancarlo Gianinni) who comes to the city to assassinate Mussolini. He could care less about politics but wants to kill Il Duce because the Fascists murdered a family friend. Tunin's contact in the city is Salome (Mariangela Melato), an anarchist who was politicized when her fiancé was also brutally murdered by the Fascists.

Here's where love comes into the story. Salome is a prostitute at a Rome bordello, and in the days leading up to the assassination attempt, Tunin frequently visits her whorehouse. Tunin is like a kid at the circus. Everywhere he looks, beautiful women are frolicking before him in skimpy lingerie. But he takes a special interest in one, Tripolina (Lina Polita). Despite her profession and his impending political action, they fall madly in love.

Wertmuller's trademark battle of the sexes consumes much of *Love and Anarchy*, although it's less vicious and much more humorous than in some of her other films. There's combat among the sexes too, as Salome and the other prostitutes verbally assault each other whenever they get the chance, and these scenes are entertaining as well. But Tunin is the real lifeblood of the film. This big-eyed, freckle-faced bumpkin is so pathetic and lovable at the same time that it's easy to understand why the girls at the bordello are so easily charmed by him.

In a greater sense, Tunin and Salome represent the powerlessness of common people in Mussolini's Italy in the thirties, and Wertmuller fashions that political climate very effectively. But she gets carried away with the film's long and graphically violent conclusion. The ending is consistent with the rest of the story, but most of *Love and Anarchy* is so sweet and funny it's disconcerting and unpleasant to have to leave the theater in shock.

RATING: R for nudity, violence and profanity.
AWARDS: Award for Best Actor (Giancarlo Giannini) at the 1973 Cannes Film Festival.

A LOVE IN GERMANY
(Video, subtitled)

World War II Romance

West Germany	German
1984　　　110 Min.	Color

CREDITS: Directed by Andrzej Wajda. Written by Andrzej Wajda, Boleslaw Michalek and Agnieszka Holland (Angry Harvest), based on the book by Rolf Hochhuth. Produced by Arthur Brauner. Cinematography by Igor Luther. Released by Stand Art/Triumph Film. Distributed nontheatrically by Swank Motion Pictures. Starring Hanna Schygulla, Marie-Christine Barrault, Armin Mueller-Stahl, Elisabeth Trissenaar, Piotr Lysak, Daniel Olbrychski and Bernhard Wicki.

Although exiled filmmaker Andrzej Wajda has long been considered one of Poland's best directors, A Love in Germany is not a movie that adds luster to his reputation. The film begins when a young German man returns to the town of his youth, anxious to learn the details of his mother's death there thirty years before. Through flashbacks, sparked by interviews with villagers, the young man begins piecing together the details of her life, learning how she struggled to support her young son by running the general store while her husband served in Hitler's army.

Lonely and isolated, Pauline (Hanna Schygulla) becomes attracted to a young Polish prisoner of war named Stani (Piotr Lysak), who assists her around the shop. The attraction heats quickly into a passionate affair, as the two star-crossed lovers sneak kisses and more behind the counter, in the cellar and wherever else they can steal a few moments alone. Their desire makes them less discreet than they should be, however, because before long the entire village knows about their steamy romance. At this hateful period in German history, when Poles were considered only a step above Jews and homosexuals, Pauline's infidelity carries more dangerous consequences than either she or Stani could have anticipated.

Forbidden love in Hitler's Germany is a plot often used in World War II movies, and there's little about Wajda's A Love in Germany that makes it stand above the rest. The acting is uninspired, the dialogue is flaccid and Schygulla and Lysak seem to come alive only when they are in bed. The film's few attempts at slapstick involving the town's ridiculous mayor are not only misplaced but are not particularly funny either. Still, Wajda superbly captures warstricken Germany's paranoid and oppressive atmosphere. With his usual astute camera work, sets and lighting, the director sets the tone for the tragedy that's to befall Pauline and Stani. Unfortunately, all the atmospheric skills Wajda musters aren't enough to keep A Love in Germany interesting.

RATING: R for nudity, sex and violence.
WARNING: A Love in Germany is actually oversubtitled, with titles like "horse neighs" and "man hums" that would be useful only for the hearing impaired.

LOVE STREAMS
(Video)

Psychological Drama

U.S.A.

1984	122 Min.	Color

CREDITS: Directed by John Cassavetes. Written by John Cassavetes and Ted Allan, based on Allan's play. Produced by Menahem Golan and Yoram Globus. Cinematography by Alan Ruban. Music by Bo Hardwood. Distributed nontheatrically by Films Inc. Starring John Cassavetes, Gena Rowlands, Diahnne Abbott, Risa Martha Blewitt, Seymour Cassel, Margaret Abbott, Michele Conway and Jakob Shaw.

Many critics feel that *Love Streams* is John Cassavetes's best work to date. He wrote and directed it and stars in it as Robert, a writer of trashy novels who has never been able to love.

Robert fills up his life with vacant starlets, gambling, casual sex and too much booze. His sister, Sarah (Cassavetes's real-life wife, Gena Rowlands), is his opposite: a clinging housewife who loved her husband (Seymour Cassel) and daughter so much that she drove them away. Going through an ugly divorce, she now lives with her brother in his California mansion and is on the verge of mental breakdown. Gradually, the siblings begin to exchange roles. Coming to realize that without love his life is meaningless, Robert tries to connect with his depressed sister. But Sarah has decided that it's time to love herself over others.

Using his familiar techniques of long takes and improvisation, Cassavetes gets astounding performances from all of his leads (including himself). His Robert is decadent to the point of absurdity, and Rowlands is powerful as the neurotic Sarah. Although many scenes in this film seem ragged at first, they often build in intensity to explosive climaxes. But *Love Streams* also suffers from sluggish pacing and repetition. Cassavetes tries our patience with the film's long takes, talky narrative and length. Robert's excessive debauchery and Sarah's hysteria are replayed over and over again. Even though many of these scenes are emotionally potent, the sheer number will unsettle even Cassavetes's biggest fans.

RATING: PG-13 for profanity.
AWARDS: Silver Bear for Best Director (John Cassavetes) at the 1984 Berlin Film Festival.
FILMNOTE: This is the first film that Cassavetes directed in which he also appeared.

LOVES OF A BLONDE
(Video, subtitled)

Coming-of-Age Romance

Czechoslovakia		Czech
1966	88 Min.	B&W

CREDITS: *Directed by Milos Forman. Written by Milos Forman, Jaroslav Papon-sek, Ivan Passer* (Cutter's Way) *and Vaclav Sasek. Cinematography by Miroslav Ondri-cek. Music by Evzen Illin. Released by CBK. Distributed nontheatrically by Films Inc. Starring Hana Brejchova, Vladimir Pucholt, Vladimir Mensik, Jan Vostrcil, Jiri Hruby and Ivan Icheil.*

Before Milos Forman immigrated to the West to make blockbusters such as *Amadeus* and *One Flew Over the Cuckoo's Nest*, he directed small comedies about the lives of simple villagers in Czechoslovakia, such as *Loves of a Blonde*.

In a remote Bohemian town after World War II, a young blonde, Andula (Hana Brejchova), works in a shoe factory and lives with her female co-workers in a dormitory. Brought there to work in the town's factory, the women outnumber eligible men sixteen to one. This sexual imbalance becomes so critical that the factory's foreman convinces the army to station soldiers nearby. At an army dance, Andula meets Milda (Vladimir Pucholt)—a piano player from Prague hired to perform there. Milda diligently convinces Andula to spend the night with him in his hotel room—her first sexual experience. Yearning for him a week later, she impulsively hitches to Prague and not only surprises Milda but also causes Milda's old-fashioned parents to have a conniption.

The dialogue in *Loves of a Blonde* is deceptively simple, almost banal, but for the most part, this is what makes the movie so wonderful. Forman used mostly non-professional actors who share their characters' backgrounds, and their performances are quirky, appealing and authentic. He is especially successful showing the humor in their everyday lives. When Andula and Milda have sex in his hotel room, for instance, there is a hilarious scene of Milda trying to close some uncooperative window shades. And Milda's nervously puritanical mother is a riot not because her reactions are overdone but because they are so real. Forman mixes together dozens of similarly flavored slices of Czech peasant life to create a cache of plain and affable characters who are as funny as they are touching.

RATING: No MPAA rating, with brief nudity and sex.
AWARDS: 1966 Academy Award nomination for Best Foreign Film.

LOYALTIES
(Video)

Women's Drama

Canada

1986　　　　　97 Min.　　　　　Color

CREDITS: Directed by Anne Wheeler. Written by Anne Wheeler and Sharon Riis. Produced by William Johnston and Ronald Lillie. Cinematography by Vic Sarin. Music by Richard Comnay. Distributed by Norstar Releasing. Starring Susan Wooldridge, Kenneth Welsh, Tantoo Cardinal, Vera Martin, Diane Debassibe, Tom Jackson, Jeffrey Smith, Meredith Rimmer and Yolanda Cardinal.

Loyalties is a wrenching drama that attempts to peel back the veneer of respectability from a typical housewife to reveal the deep well of anger and frustration beneath.

The film is set in a small village in northern Canada, where the very proper Lily Sutton (Susan Wooldridge) and her two young children arrive to join her English husband, David (Kenneth Walsh), the town's doctor. Lily's aloof manner alienates the village's more down-to-earth residents, and her relationship with her unemotional husband is mysteriously strained as well. In a short time, Lily finds herself friendless, alone and increasingly depressed in this desolate place. But just when she appears to be on the verge of a breakdown, David hires an Indian woman, Roseanne (Tantoo Cardinal), to help Lily settle in. Roseanne's nononsense manner gradually thaws Lily's reserve, and they develop a friendship. Yet Roseanne's presence in the household also ignites a dark side of David, the brutal flaw in his character that Lily had tried to forget but now must confront once again.

The conflict involving David in Loyalties is too contrived. At the thirty-minute mark in this movie, it's obvious how Lily's relationship with her husband will evolve. But Lily's predictable relationship with David doesn't dilute the power of her remarkable friendship with Roseanne. That friendship is at the center of this film, as it's through Roseanne that Lily learns to confront the unpleasant facts of her life, regardless of past loyalities and present consequences. Both Wooldridge and Cardinal turn in natural, unadorned performances. Lily's repressed hysteria is artfully juxtaposed with Roseanne's casual acceptance of life on her own terms.

RATING: No MPAA rating, with violence.

McCABE AND MRS. MILLER
(Video)

Romantic Western

U.S.A.

1971　　　　　121 Min.　　　　　Color

CREDITS: Directed by Robert Altman. Written by Robert Altman and Brian McKay, based on the novel McCabe by Edmund Naughton. Produced by David Foster and Mitchell Brower. Cinematography by Vilmos Zsigmond. Distributed nontheatrically by Swank Motion Pictures. Starring Warren Beatty, Julie Christie, Shelley Duvall, Keith Carradine, Rene Auberjonois, Hugh Millais, Michael Murphy and John Schuck.

Even though McCabe and Mrs. Miller could be classified as a western, it only fits the genre in its external trappings. Otherwise, this Robert Altman near masterpiece is as much about interpersonal relationships and sex roles as any drama set in modern times.

McCabe and Mrs. Miller takes place in a damp, ramshackle mining town in the Northwest at the turn of the century. The hero of the story is a gambler-entrepreneur named McCabe (Warren Beatty) who considers himself a he-man but in reality is a bumbling fool. When he drifts into the desolate mining town, McCabe stumbles into a lucrative business venture—opening a whorehouse to service the sex-starved miners, who jump at the chance for affection, whatever the cost. But intent on a more meaningful relationship, McCabe himself looks to the whorehouse's cold-hearted, opium-smoking madam, Mrs. Miller (Julie Christie), as more than his business partner. McCabe is so taken with her that he goes to tremendous lengths to win her affection, but nothing seems to work. Mrs. Miller has an inner world that she is not willing to share with anybody, including McCabe.

The only crack in what would otherwise be a perfect movie is its tempo. Altman throws in a few too many pans of the damp woods in the middle of winter, with little more than the frozen landscape to sustain our interest. But Altman and cameraman Vilmos Zsigmond give other scenes so much texture that they practically ooze off the screen. The settings, characters and dialogue in *McCabe and Mrs. Miller* do nothing to glamorize the West: The mining town, the miners and the violence in this film are gruesome. But what's most remarkable about the film is the way Altman handles the relationship between McCabe and Mrs. Miller. McCabe is a romantic disguised as a two-bit hustler, and Mrs. Miller a feminist who uses her only tool, her body, as a weapon. Both are appealing and repulsive at the same time. Their interaction is as tough and believable as the film's setting.

RATING: R for brief nudity, substance abuse and violence.
AWARDS: 1971 Academy Award nomination for Best Actress (Julie Christie).

MAD MAX
(Video)

 ★ ★ ½

Science Fiction Adventure

Australia

1979   89 Min.   Color

CREDITS: *Directed by George Miller. Written by George Miller, James McCausland and Byron Kennedy. Produced by Byron Kennedy. Cinematography by David Eggby. Music by Brian May. Production design by Jon Dowding. Special effects by Chris Murray. Released by Filmways. Distributed nontheatrically by Swank Motion Pictures. Starring Mel Gibson, Joanne Samuel, Tim Burns, Roger Ward, Hugh Keays-Byrne, Steve Bisley, Vince Gil, Geoff Parry, Paul Johnstone and John Ley.*

Mad Max is the first of George Miller's post-nuclear road flicks and serves as good background for the others *(The Road Warrior, Mad Max: Beyond Thunderdome)*. Set after World War III in Australia, it tells the story of Max (Mel Gibson), a motorcycle policeman who, with his raunchy partner Goose (Steve Bisley), chases ruthless biker gangs that torture and kill innocent civilians. He is happily married to Jessie (Joanne Samuel) and has a wonderful little girl.

During one especially hard day at work, Max and Goose kill the leader of a notorious gang. The rest of the gang avenges his death by trapping Goose in the cab of a truck and setting it on fire. After Max visits his severely burned buddy in the hospital, he decides to quit the force and enjoy his life before it's too late. But when he goes on vacation with his family to Jessie's mother's house in the country, the same gang shows up to take revenge on Max and his whole family.

For action fans, *Mad Max* has plenty of high-speed chase scenes, complete with spectacular stunts and violence. And the world-gone-crazy that Miller creates is just as heartless and vicious in this film as in the rest of the trilogy. But where *Mad Max* suffers by comparison is in its sets, costumes and post-nuclear metaphors. There are no punks and gas-hoarders, and few souped-up vehicles or homemade weapons. Miller inserts a family love melodrama to create extra tension, but without all the bizarre characters and paraphernalia of the sequels, *Mad Max* comes across like any cop-and-criminal story, with a futuristic set its only distinction.

RATING: *R for sex, violence and profanity.*
FILMNOTE: *Enormously popular in Australia when it was released,* Mad Max *went on to outgross even* Star Wars *at the box office there.*

MALCOLM
(*Video*)

Screwball Comedy

Australia

1986   90 Min.   Color

CREDITS: *Directed by Nadia Tass. Written by David Parker. Produced by Nadia Tass and David Parker. Cinematography by David Parker. Released and distributed nontheatrically by Vestron Pictures. Starring Colin Friels, John Hargreaves, Lindy Davies, Chris Haywood, Charles Tingwell, Beverly Philips, Judith Stratford, Heather Mitchell and Katerina Tassopoulos.*

Malcolm is a small but enjoyable Australian film about a socially retarded mechanical genius. Colin Friels *(Kangaroo)* stars as Malcolm, whose house is full of his wild inventions, which make his life more convenient and fun. He has a toy car that goes down to the corner store for milk, and a miniature train that picks up the mail. He's even constructed his own replica of an old-fashioned trolley car, which he takes for joy rides on the city's tracks when public transportation shuts down at night.

But as brilliant as he is with machines, he is lost with people. Malcolm remains alone in his world of gadgets until he loses his job and must take in boarders to make ends meet. At first, it's difficult for Malcolm to adjust to having others in the house, and the couple to whom he rents aren't exactly easy to live with. Frank (John Hargreaves) is an ex-con with the temperament of an aging Hell's Angel, and Judith (Lindy Davies) is embittered after years of waitressing in pubs full of lecherous men. But she quickly grows fond of the nonthreatening Malcolm, and after a while, so does Frank. Eventually, the three not only get on marvelously as roommates but also become partners in robbing banks, using Malcolm's remote-control inventions to pull off the jobs.

Directed by novice Australian filmmaker Nadia Tass, this low-budget, low-key comedy is quietly entertaining. Friels plays Malcolm as a shy, soft-spoken Pee Wee Herman type whose material world is filled with toys, but whose emotional life is slightly off-kilter. Although his character is at times overly cute, most of the confrontations between Malcolm and macho Frank are comical, while Judith's quips to the ass-pinching men at her pub are as sharp as razors. But the gadgets steal the show in this movie. Each invention Malcolm comes up with tops the next, and director Tass makes sure that every scene in this film has plenty of Malcolm's entertaining wizardry.

RATING: *PG-13 for one brief nude scene.*

A MAN AND A WOMAN
(*Video, dubbed*)

Romance

France   French

1966   102 Min.   B&W

CREDITS: *Directed, produced and photographed by Claude Lelouch. Written by Claude Lelouch and Pierre Uytterhoeven. Music by Francis Lai. Released by Allied Artists/Warner Brothers Classics. Starring Anouk Aimee, Jean-Louis Trintignant, Pierre Gauthier, Valerie Lagrange and Pierre Barouth.*

Claude Lelouch's *A Man and a Woman* was the first international "art" film to have widespread success in the United States. Not only did it set American box-office records for a foreign film and win two Academy Awards, its soundtrack album and theme song became best-sellers. But that was in 1966. Now *A Man and a Woman* comes across as interminably sappy.

It's the story of the budding romance between a scriptwriter-widow named Anne (Anouk Aimee) and a race car driver–widower named Jean-Louis (Jean-Louis Trintignant). The two have "serious" talks while driving back and forth to their children's boarding school. First Anne asks Jean-Louis about his past, and after a moment's hesitation, there's a long flashback to the events leading up to his spouse's tragic death. When the scene returns, Anne gives him an understanding glance, then he asks about her past, and the sequence is repeated. This soul-exposing leads to outings with the kids in which everyone, including the little boy and girl, gets along famously. The romance is clinched, however, when Anne watches Jean-Louis win the Grand Prix on television. Jean-Louis is not only kind, brave and handsome, but he's also a national hero. The only obstacle is that Anne can't forget her deceased husband.

A Man and a Woman was unique to American audiences for its artsy camera angles and lighting—much of the film was shot through filters and switches (for no apparent reason) from black and white to color. The performances by Aimee and Trintignant are generally good, and the chemistry between them can be quite intense. But the story is so sickeningly sweet, it's like putting hot fudge on chocolate-chocolate chip ice cream. From the two of them embracing on the beach with a gorgeous sunrise in the background to her watching him become a hero on TV, *A Man and a Woman* is overflowing with predictable clichés. And the Francis Lai music that was so popular in the sixties is grating today.

RATING: *No MPAA rating, with one mild sex scene.*

AWARDS: *Grand Prize for Best Film at the 1966 Cannes Film Festival; 1966 Academy Awards for Best Foreign Film and Best Screenplay Written Directly for the Screen (Claude Lelouch and Pierre Uytterhoeven); 1966 Academy Award nominations for Best Actress (Anouk Aimee) and Best Director (Lelouch); 1966 British Academy Award for Best Actress (Aimee).*

FILMNOTE: *This film spawned a sequel, A Man and a Woman: 20 Years Later. It has all of the problems of the original, plus the characters have grown not only older but more stiff and lifeless.*

MAN FACING SOUTHEAST
(Video, subtitled)

Political Drama

Argentina		Spanish
1986	108 Min.	Color

CREDITS: *Directed and written Eliseo Subiela. Produced by Lujan Pflaum. Cinematography by Ricardo De Angelus. Music by Pedro Aznar. Released by Cinequanon and Film Dallas. Distributed nontheatrically by Films Inc. Starring Lorenzo Quinteros, Hugo Soto, Ines Vernengo and Christina Scarmuzza.*

In 1985, *The Official Story* heralded the reemergence of Argentine filmmaking. Though most of the films now coming from Argentina directly involve the country's turbulent political past, *Man Facing Southeast* tackles the subject through a science fiction allegory.

The film takes place in a Buenos Aires mental hospital, where a disillusioned staff psychiatrist, Dr. Dennis (Lorenzo Quinteros), drifts aimlessly through the halls, resigned to the fact that he's really unable to help his patients. But Dennis is shaken from his lethargy when a patient who calls himself Rantes (Hugo Soto) suddenly appears in his ward, claiming to be an extraterrestrial. Dennis is at first skeptical, but when Rantes fervently sticks to his story, the doctor gradually becomes intrigued. Rantes does seem to have some strange powers; he is telekinetic, and every day he stands facing southeast, where he claims to receive messages from his faraway planet. Then Rantes's female friend, dubbed "The Saint" (Ines Vernengo), shows up, saying that she is also an alien, and the doctor is attracted to her. Eventually, her presence forces him to choose to believe what he cannot rationally understand or deny the one person in his life who can help him break out of his emotional shell.

Director Eliseo Subiela leans on Christian imagery and ponderous dialogue that make *Man Facing Southeast* intellectually challenging but also turgidly paced. Since little background is given to explain Dr. Dennis's decline, he eventually seems to be more alienated than he has earned the right to be, and by the film's unresolved ending his character becomes too aimless.

But director Subiela combines political allegory with science fiction very effectively in the first half of the film, particularly in the scenes of Rantes claiming his alien powers and the reactions of those around him to his remarkable claims. The acting is outstanding throughout, and though the characters have no regional or national identity, what they symbolize clearly reflects Argentina's recent political history. Rantes, for example, represents the "abhorrent" behavior that was so harshly rebuked during years of dictatorship; the hospital is the status quo that has to censor and ultimately punish any challenge to its normalcy; and Dr. Dennis is the ambiguous middle class, which was willing to tolerate injustice for its own personal safety.

RATING: R for nudity, sex and violence.

MAN OF FLOWERS
(Video)

Psychological Drama

Australia

1983   91 Min.   Color

CREDITS: Directed by Paul Cox. Written by Paul Cox and Bob Ellis. Produced by Jane Ballantyne. Cinematography by Yuri Sokol. Music by Gaetano Donizetti. Released by Spectrafilms. Distributed nontheatrically by New Yorker Films. Starring Norman Kaye, Alyson Best, Chris Haywood, Sarah Walker, Julien Blake, Bob Ellis, Barry Dickens, Patrick Cook and Werner Herzog.

Perhaps one of the strangest movies to come out of Australia in the last several years is Paul Cox's *Man of Flowers*, a story about a middle-aged millionaire named John (Norman Kaye) who has a unique sexual problem. He only gets aroused by pure aestheticism—looking at beautiful things such as flowers, paintings and women in elegant clothing undressing in front of him. One such woman is Laura (Alyson Best), a young artist's model he hires to come to his house once a week to strip for him. She enjoys her work and eventually grows fond of John—so fond, in fact, that she wants to leave her junkie boyfriend and become John's lover. But the idea of having sex with her terrifies John. So when things get hot, he retreats to a nearby church and relieves his tension by playing the organ.

In home movie–style flashbacks of John's childhood, we are given the key to his sexual idiosyncracies. When big-breasted women would come over to his parents' house, the boy would stare at them until, with his whole family watching, he was driven to cop a feel. Punished severely by his father (Werner Herzog) for such outlandish behavior, John learned that looking was okay, but touching was not.

The story of *Man of Flowers* is at times quite comical, and the acting is top-notch, as writer-director Paul Cox *(My First Wife)* unveils John's disturbed world in a slow, methodical way. Each scene is presented as if it were a beautiful painting—the lighting is exquisite, the sets are rich and luxurious and the photography is handsome. Because John is an aesthete, Cox realizes the best way to portray his world is with shots that linger over the objects that John himself enjoys. In a sense, you get to know this man through his material world in dozens of beautiful moments that you have to let seep in instead of embrace. Some viewers may not find John's world always interesting or entertaining, but it's difficult not to appreciate it.

RATING: R for nudity and language.

MAN OF MARBLE

Politcal Drama

Poland		Polish
1977	160 Min.	Color/B&W

CREDITS: *Directed by Andrzej Wajda, assisted by Agnieszka Holland. Written by Aleksander Scibor-Rylski. Produced by Polish Film Group X. Cinematography by Edward Klosinski. Music by Andrzej Korzynski. Edited by Halina Purgarowa. Released and distributed nontheatrically by New Yorker Films. Starring Kyrstyna Janda, Jerzy Radziwilowicz, Tadeusz Lomnicki, Jacek Lominicki, Michal Tarkowski, Kyrstyna Zachwatowicz, Piotr Cieslak and Wieslaw Wojcik.*

Andrzej Wajda's *Man of Marble* is a movie within a movie within a movie. In it, an aggressive young Polish film student struggles to make a movie about the man who was the subject of a once-famous 1950s Party propaganda film that attempted to make him into a working-class hero.

The student's name is Agnieszka (Krystyna Janda) and the subject of her film is Birkut (Jerzy Radziwilowicz), a bricklayer who once placed a record 10,000 bricks in an eight-hour shift. A propaganda film of his feat made him an overnight national hero, and Birkut was promoted to super-

visor of a housing development. But Birkut soon "abused" his power in the eyes of the Party by procuring housing for "common" citizens, and by publicly protesting the arrest of his best friend. Birkut lost his job and was sent to a reeducation camp, where all traces of this former "exemplary" worker quickly disappeared.

Man of Marble switches from Agnieszka's interviews in the present to black-and-white propaganda footage, to color dramatizations of Birkut's life. The portions of the film dealing with Agnieszka are intense. She is so obsessed with her project that she treats her film crew miserably and is obnoxious to anybody who stands in her way. Through her passion we also see the promises and failures of Stalinism all too well. The acting is excellent from the entire cast, and the story unfolds like a political documentary, one whose conclusion makes sense in the context of recent Polish history yet is fair to the system it criticizes. The fact that Wajda was permitted to make a film so critical of the Party is remarkable, although the flow of the narrative does suffer slightly from the censor's scissors. But the vast majority of *Man of Marble* is a piercing look into post–World War II Polish history, the art of documentary filmmaking and the nature of propaganda.

RATING: No MPAA rating, with nothing objectionable.
AWARDS: International Critics Prize at the 1978 Cannes Film Festival.
FILMNOTE: Although banned there today, Man of Marble *became the highest-grossing film in post–World War II Poland after its initial release, even though the name of its assistant director, Agnieszka Holland* (Angry Harvest), *was stricken from the credits because she was in disfavor with the government.*

THE MAN WHO FELL TO EARTH

(Video)

Science Fiction

England

1976   117 Min.   Color

CREDITS: *Directed by Nicolas Roeg. Written by Paul Mayersberg, based on the novel by Walter Tevis. Produced by Michael Deeley and Barry Spikings. Cinematography by Anthony Richmond. Music by John Phillips. Special effects by Paul Elleshaw. Released and distributed by Almi Pictures. Starring David Bowie, Candy Clark, Buck Henry, Rip Torn, Bernie Casey, Jackson Kane, Rick Riccardo, Tony Mascia and Linda Hutton.*

David Bowie's strange, androgynous looks are well-suited for playing an alien, and in Nicolas Roeg's *The Man Who Fell To Earth* his role as Thomas is a perfect fit. Thomas is a frail and sickly space traveler who falls to earth and arranges a meeting with a gay patent lawyer named Oliver Farnsworth (Buck Henry), to whom Thomas shows nine technologically advanced industrial patents. He wants Farnsworth to use them to create a corporation that will earn enough money for Thomas to finance transporting water back to his own drought-stricken planet. While waiting for Farnsworth to amass millions, Thomas moves to New Mexico. There the bleak American landscape drives him to become an alcoholic, watch a dozen TVs at once, and get involved with a spacy hotel maid (Candy Clark) and a lecherous college professor (Rip Torn).

The Man Who Fell to Earth is not an easy movie to watch. Its plot doesn't always make sense, its dialogue is intentionally vague, and the script is full of characters as bizarre as Bowie. The few fast-paced suspenseful scenes are heavily outnumbered by slower, more deliberate ones. Though Roeg pulls off some satirical jabs at popular culture, he also captures the aimlessness and

alienation of our earthly existence too well to be consistently entertaining.

But the acting is excellent in *The Man Who Fell to Earth,* particularly Bowie as the mysterious stranger and Clark as his ditsy girlfriend. And on a purely aesthetic level, the film is a masterpiece. The soundtrack, special effects and lighting work together to create one powerful image after another, as Roeg and his cameraman Anthony Richmond show our planet completely from Thomas's perspective. It's through his frightened, confused and then vacant eyes that we see how warped it is.

RATING: *R for nudity and sex.*
WARNING: *Because the film's visuals are so important, watching on video decreases the quality of the film.*

THE MAN WHO LOVED WOMEN

(Video, dubbed)

Sex Farce

France   French

1977   119 Min.   Color

CREDITS: *Directed by François Truffaut. Written François Truffaut, Michel Fermaud and Suzanne Schiffman. Cinematography by Nestor Almendros. Released and distributed nontheatrically by Almi Pictures. Starring Charles Denner, Brigette Fossey, Nelly Borgeaud, Leslie Caron, Genevieve Fontanel and Nathalie Baye.*

Throughout his career, François Truffaut displayed an unusual aptitude for understanding women, creating memorable, complex female protagonists in films such as *Jules and Jim* and *Confidentially Yours.* But in *The Man Who Loved Women,* he slips into stereotypical portrayals of shallow sex objects for one man's incorrigible womanizing.

Bertrand (Charles Denner), an aerodynamics engineer and a voracious reader, is easily distracted by a shapely leg or pretty face, willing to go to any length to trap a woman who captures his eye. He bashes in the front end of his car, for instance, in order to trace a potential liaison's license number through her insurance company. Every attractive woman he meets becomes an immediate obsession, and he has affairs with a variety of women. But when an aging lingerie store owner rejects him, Bertrand begins to question his future as a lover. In an attempt to put his life in order, he writes his romantic memoirs, unearthing memories that draw him closer to discovering the real motive for his promiscuity.

The Man Who Loved Women is told through a series of flashbacks as Bertrand writes his memoirs. The film's funniest scenes involve his elaborate schemes to meet and seduce beautiful strangers and his public escapades with Delphine (Nelly Borgeaud), a neurotic housewife who thrills at the risk of discovery, insisting that Bertrand make love to her in his car and even in a department store. But Truffaut doesn't explore the male-female dynamic with much depth, and none of the women characters in the film are developed to any satisfying degree. Bertrand loves women's bodies and the process of enticing them, but he has few discussions with his lovers beyond telling them how sexy and alluring they are. In the end, the film may be a celebration of seduction with all the trimmings, but it is a degrading and joyless one.

RATING: No MPAA rating, with some nudity and adult situations.
AWARDS: One of the National Board of Review's 5 Best Foreign Films in 1977.
WARNING: The dubbing is okay on the video version, but it detracts slightly.
FILMNOTE: Blake Edwards remade this film in 1983 starring Burt Reynolds, but the remake is just as offensive as the original.

MARLENE
(Video, partially subtitled)

Documentary

West Germany English and German

1983   96 Min.   Color-B&W

CREDITS: Directed by Maximilian Schell. Written by Maximilian Schell and Meir Dohnal. Produced by Zev Braun and Karel Dirka. Cinematography by Ivan Slapeta. Sound by Meir Dohnal, Norbet Lill and Maximilian Schell. Released by Alive Films. Distributed nontheatrically by New Yorker Films. Starring Marlene Dietrich and Maximilian Schell.

Marlene Dietrich was so known for her gutsy, tough-talking performances in movies such as *The Blue Angel* that it always seemed she would be the same kind of person in real life. Maximilian Schell's documentary *Marlene* leaves no doubt. Now in her seventies, Dietrich governs this documentary like a master sergeant—ordering Schell around and attempting to make most of the movie's decisions, while retaining control of a carefully groomed image.

Her first demand is that Schell not film her—so the Marlene in *Marlene* is off-camera throughout the film, present only as a disembodied voice. Although that voice is magnetic, carrying on about a range of subjects from feminism and love to Hollywood and Hitler, this creates a problem with the visuals. Schell very cleverly combines footage from Dietrich's movies and newsreels with what she is talking about in the present, but there aren't enough of these clips. The rest of the time, the camera lethargically wanders around rooms in her apartment, struggling to fill the space left by her physical absence. It can also become aggravating that she and Schell bicker so often. More like a married couple than a filmmaker and his subject, the two of them go at it in nearly every scene.

Still, as Marlene gossips about famous actors and directors and bluntly reveals personal details about her life, she is sometimes hilarious, sometimes emotional, and almost always fascinating. As a result, this documentary is not only a compelling tribute to an important actress, but it reveals a great deal about the nature of the celebrity and how a former sex symbol comes to terms with her own aging process.

RATING: No MPAA rating, with slight profanity.
AWARDS: 1986 Academy Award nomination for Best Documentary Feature.

THE MARRIAGE OF MARIA BRAUN
(Video, subtitled)

Psychological Drama

West Germany	German and English
1978	120 Min.	Color

CREDITS: Directed by Rainer Werner Fassbinder. Written by Rainer Werner Fassbinder, Peter Marthesheimer and Pia Frohlich. Produced by Michael Fengler. Cinematography by Michael Ballhaus. Music by Peer Raben. Released and distributed nontheatrically by New Yorker Films. Starring Hanna Schygulla, Klaus Lowitsch, Ivan Desny, Gottfried John, George Bryd, Gisela Uhlen, Gunter Lamprecht, Hark Bohm, Elisabeth Trissenaar and Rainer Werner Fassbinder.

The Marriage of Maria Braun is the first of Rainer Werner Fassbinder's trilogy about postwar Germany in decline (*Lola* and *Veronika Voss* are the other two). Set in the rubble of post–World War II Berlin, the story begins with Maria (Hanna Schygulla) desperately trying to locate her husband, Hermann, who hasn't returned from the war. When she is told that Hermann is still missing in action, Maria becomes a prostitute, eventually seducing a black GI named Bill (George Byrd), who becomes her steady boyfriend after she is told that Hermann is dead. She soon becomes pregnant. But then, out of the blue, Hermann (Klaus Lowitsch) shows up. In a display of her love for her husband, Maria kills the unsuspecting soldier. She is arrested and tried, but during the trial, Hermann confesses to the murder and is sent to prison in her place, while Maria promises to wait for him until he gets out. Later, Maria becomes the mistress and business associate of a German financier and is obsessively driven to become wealthy, all the time holding on to her love for Hermann.

Schygulla is magnificent as the cold, calculating Maria—even during her most dramatic crises she looks as if she is wearing an impenetrable mask. But the most fascinating aspect of Maria's character is what it symbolizes. On a personal level, Maria is a woman who controls men by seducing them; it's the only way she can maintain her power. Her unrealized love for Hermann keeps her from relinquishing that control, using him as an excuse to avoid intimacy with anyone else. On a more universal level, Maria stands for West Germany's single-minded drive for economic gain after World War II, and its refusal to feel guilt for its war crimes. Fassbinder brilliantly frames the intricacies of Maria's character with striking sets and cinematography. In the end, *The Marriage of Maria Braun* is an intense, enormously satisfying movie and a Fassbinder masterpiece.

RATING: R for sex and nudity.
AWARDS: Silver Bear for Best Actress (Hanna Schygulla) at the 1979 Berlin Film Festival; one of the National Board of Review's 5 Best Foreign Films in 1979.

MASCULIN-FÉMININ
(Video, subtitled)

Social Satire

France	French
1966	103 Min.	B&W

CREDITS: Directed and produced by Jean-Luc Godard. Written by Jean-Luc Godard, based on the stories "Paul's Mistress" and "The Signal" by Guy de Maupassant. Cinematography by Willy Kurant. Music by Francis Lai and Jean-Jacques Debout.

Released by Royal Films. Distributed nontheatrically by Corinth Films and Tamarelle Films. Starring Jean-Pierre Leaud, Chantal Goya, Marlene Jobert, Michel Deborb, Catherine Duport, Eva-Britt Strandberg, Elsa Leroy, and a cameo by Brigitte Bardot.

Loosely based on two Guy de Maupassant short stories, Jean-Luc Godard's *Masculin-Féminin* was one of the first films to attempt to capture the political and social chaos of the sixties.

Set in Paris during the infant stages of the student movement and the sexual revolution, this loosely structured story follows the exploits of Paul (Jean-Pierre Leaud), a twenty-one-year-old who is discharged from the army and takes a job interviewing people about their personal habits for a consumer magazine. An avid Marxist, Paul spends his spare time spray painting anti-Vietnam slogans on buildings and police cars. Paul likes the excitement of rebellion more than the nuts-and-bolts mechanics of revolution, but his real desire is to settle down with a beautiful young folk singer named Madeleine (Chantal Goya). He eventually moves in with her, but the pair comes to realize the extent of the gulf that lies between desire and happiness.

Godard refers to this film as his exploration of the "children of Marx and Coca-Cola." He turns Leaud's Paul into a rhetorical sounding board for several important issues of politics, sex and war in the sixties. The scene in which he mockingly interviews Miss Nineteen for his magazine is so clever that it's worth watching the entire movie for those few minutes. But much of *Masculin-Féminin* is as uneven and confusing as the time it portrays. Several moments are self-conscious in their social commentary, while Godard's and his cinematographer Willy Kurant's use of free-floating camera techniques further jumbles the lives of his characters. Yet Godard isn't interested in developing a narrative in the traditional sense. What one gets instead in *Masculin-Féminin* is a collage of impressions, small glimpses that come together to form an atmosphere.

RATING: *No MPAA rating, with brief nudity and sex.*

AWARDS: *Silver Lion for Best Male Performance (Jean-Pierre Leaud) at the 1966 Venice Film Festival.*
FILMNOTE: *In France Masculin-Féminin was restricted to audiences over eighteen, which distressed Godard since moviegoers under eighteen were just the audience he was trying to reach.*

MATEWAN
(Video)

Political Drama

U.S.A.

1987   132 Min.   Color

CREDITS: *Directed and written by John Sayles. Produced by Peggy Rajski and Maggie Renzi. Cinematography by Haskell Wexler. Released and distributed nontheatrically by Cinecom. Starring Chris Cooper, Will Oldham, Jace Alexander, Ken Jenkins, Bob Gunton and James Earl Jones.*

John Sayles's name has become synonymous with American independent film because of his willingness to take chances with the content and characters in his movies. With *Matewan*, he has finally matured into a first-rate director.

Based on the real events that led up to a famous coal miners' strike in Matewan, West Virginia, in the 1920s, the story begins when Joe Kenehan (Chris Cooper), a union organizer, arrives in the town. He finds that the conditions in the Stone Mountain Coal Company mine are dangerous, and many of the miners suffer from black lung disease. The company owns Matewan's homes, stores and mining equipment, and it pays such small wages that every family in town has been heavily in debt to it for years. But with Joe's help, the impoverished people of Matewan finally realize their only hope is to organize a union and strike. Naturally, Stone Mountain will stop at nothing to break the strike, including hiring vicious thugs, pitting black, white and Italian miners against one another, and trying to frame Joe.

Although *Matewan* is similar to movies like *The Grapes of Wrath* and *Norma Rae*, Sayles's characters aren't brave warriors and sentimentalized clichés put on the screen to open our tear ducts. One moment they are hopeful and willing to fight for their basic human dignity. The next they are scared, angry and so frustrated about their situation they often forget who their real enemy is. Sayles has done his home-work on these simple, desperate West Virginia miners and their families, and his cine-matographer Haskell Wexler *(Days of Heaven)* brings them to life so vividly that *Matewan* has the feel of a tightly edited documentary. With the exceptions of James Earl Jones and Sayles himself (who plays a "hell-baiting" preacher), few of the cast members are known. But the quality of acting from the entire cast is as good as any film in 1987.

RATING: PG-13, with mild violence.

A MATTER OF HEART
(Video)

Documentary

U.S.A.

1986   107 Min.   Color/B&W

CREDITS: *Directed by Mark Whitney. Written and conceived by Suzanne Wagner. Produced by Michael Whitney (Mark's brother). Released and distributed nonth-eatrically by Kino International. Original music by John Adams. Featuring Carl Gus-tav Jung, Dr. Emma Jung, Dr. Marie-Louise von Franz, Sir Laurens van der Post (on whose life story* Merry Christmas, Mr. Lawrence *was based), Barbara Hannah, Dr. Liliane Frey, Professor C. A. Meier, Dr. Gerhard Adler and Joseph Henderson, M.D.*

Constricted by the arbitrary limits of its feature length and overwhelmed by the enormous complexity of the man who is its subject, this documentary on Carl Jung is both frustrating and fascinating. Writer Suzanne Wagner and director Mark Whit-ney try to jam as much as they can into the 107 minutes of *A Matter of Heart*, with interviews of twenty-one people who were Jung's friends, associates and neighbors. They explain his theories through quotes from Jung that appear on flashcards, and also present archival footage, stills, home movies and filmed interviews with Jung himself.

Before Jung died in 1961 at the age of eighty-six, he wrote dozens of books and lectured all around the world on subjects as diverse as the collective unconscious, arche-types, alchemy, dreams, animus and anima (masculine and feminine), psychic phe-nomena, Eastern religion, and Armaged-don. His teachings shook the foundations of psychotherapy and Western philosophy to their core, and many in those fields today still devote their lives to understanding and interpreting Jung's theories.

Of Jung's disciples interviewed in this movie, Dr. Marie-Louise von Franz is per-haps the most eloquent. With stern posture and careful delivery, she remembers how Jung altered the course of her life when she was a young woman, teaching her to dis-cover through her dreams subconscious feelings buried deep inside. Several of Jung's patients share memories of his tech-niques and mannerisms in therapy, while others talk about his love affair with Toni Wolff and his stormy relationship with Sig-mund Freud. One chord that rings through all those interviewed is that these people feel blessed to have had Jung touch their lives.

A Matter of Heart is so full of the genius of Jung's thinking and the enormous charis-ma of the man himself, that it's well worth seeing, for Jung scholars and novices alike. But the built-in problem with a movie like this is that filmmakers can't introduce a whole lifetime of personal history and visionary philosophy without merely skimming the surface on every level. Although the interview footage has plenty of interesting and enlightening moments, it's almost always evident that what the subjects reveal is out of context and chopped to the point of confusion. Jung's quotes on flashcards further scatter the narrative.

RATING: No MPAA rating, with nothing objectionable.

FILMNOTE: It took Mark Whitney and Suzanne Wagner ten years to complete their research for A Matter of Heart.

MAURICE
(Video)

Gay Drama

England

1987　　　135 Min.　　　Color

CREDITS: *Directed by James Ivory. Written by James Ivory and Kit Hesketh-Harvey, based on the novel by E. M. Forster. Produced by Ismail Merchant. Cinematography by Pierre Lhomme. Edited by Katherine Wenning. Music by Richard Robbins. Released and distributed nontheatrically by Cinecom. Starring James Wilby, Hugh Grant, Rupert Graves, Denholm Elliot, Simon Callow, Billie Whitelaw, Ben Kingsley, Judy Parfitt, Phoebe Nicholls, Mark Tandy and Barry Foster.*

After the spectacular success of *A Room with a View,* the producer/director team of Ismail Merchant and James Ivory tried to repeat their winning formula with *Maurice,* another adaptation of an E. M. Forster novel.

Set in repressed Edwardian England, the film begins with Clive's (Hugh Grant) careful seduction of Maurice (James Wilby), his good friend and classmate at Cambridge. The quiet and middle-class Maurice is slow to respond to Clive's advances. Eventually, though, Maurice embraces his true feelings and is consumed by his desire for Clive. The affair ends abruptly, however, when Clive, fearing detection, marries and settles into a false and comfortable life. Heartbroken, Maurice seeks solace in brief homosexual affairs that leave him emotionally unsatisfied and dangerously open to exposure.

Maurice is a disappointment to many because it works over the same territory as *A Room with a View,* but it lacks the humor

and witty dialogue to drive it past its stuffy atmosphere and stylized theatrics. Perhaps this is where the absence of Merchant and Ivory's longtime collaborator, screenwriter Ruth Prawer Jhabvala, is most noticeable. The other big problem with the film is that it is at least thirty minutes too long. Several scenes creep along too deliberately without the narrative tension to keep them interesting. As in every Merchant/Ivory production, the cinematography and sets are lush and beautiful. The acting from the mix of newcomers and veterans is proficient and at times engaging. And the filmmakers do an outstanding job of showing the horrible cost of being gay during this repressive time in history, where every moment of the ill-fated lovers' tenderness is undercut by the threat of ruin.

RATING: R for gay sexual situations and nudity.

MEAN STREETS
(Video)

Cultural Drama

U.S.A.　　　　　　　　　English

1973　　　110 Min.　　　Color

CREDITS: *Directed by Martin Scorsese. Written by Martin Scorsese and Mardik Martin. Produced by Jonathan Taplin. Cinematography by Kent Wakeford. Edited by Sid Levin. Released by Warner Brothers. Distributed nontheatrically by Swank Motion Pictures. Starring Robert De Niro, Harvey Keitel, Amy Robinson, David Proval, Richard Romanus, Cesare Danova, Victor Argo, George Memmoli, Lenny Scaletta, Jeannie Bell, Murray Mosten, Robert Carradine and David Carradine.*

Although not a commercial success, *Mean Streets* is the film that introduced Robert De Niro and director Martin Scorsese to critics and laid the groundwork for their burgeoning careers.

Set in the Little Italy section of Manhattan, it tells the story of Charlie (Harvey

Keitel), a small-time hood who wants to be taken in by a powerful mafia family headed by Giovianni (Cesare Danova). Giovianni likes Charlie and is willing to let him run one of his nightclubs, but he doesn't like Charlie's girlfriend, Teresa (Amy Robinson), and best friend since childhood, Johnny Boy (Robert De Niro). Giovianni wants Charlie to stop hanging around with Teresa, because she's epileptic and considered "sick in the head," and Johnny Boy, because he's a two-bit hustler who owes money to everybody in town. But Charlie sees them anyhow. When Johnny Boy gets into trouble way over his head and Teresa fetches Charlie to bail him out, Charlie is forced to choose between his own advancement and his feelings for them both.

Writer/director Martin Scorsese (Taxi Driver, After Hours) doesn't glorify the lives of his characters or make them appealing. Charlie, Johnny Boy and their friends argue constantly, while degrading women and blacks. Appealing or not, these characters are extremely real. The acting from the entire cast is extraordinary. Many critics think that De Niro's Johnny Boy is his best performance to date, while Keitel is compelling as the film's central character. Scorsese, who grew up in Little Italy, is obviously quite familiar with the turf. The back alleys, bars and restaurants he creates are so alive you can practically smell the olive oil and prosciutto. In Mean Streets, he was also one of the first American filmmakers to risk striving for authenticity at the expense of snappy dialogue and fast-paced action. Although the film's violence is gruesome, and at the end borders on being excessive, the payoff is enormous.

RATING: R for brief nudity and a lot of profanity and violence.
FILMNOTE: Mean Streets wasn't shot on location in New York, because it was actually cheaper for Scorsese to create his sets in a studio and shoot them in Los Angeles. Although the film looks great, it was made for a budget of under $600,000 and shot in six days.

MEN
(Video, dubbed)

Social Satire

West Germany	German
1986 99 Min.	Color

CREDITS: Directed and written by Doris Dorrie. Produced by Harald Kugler. Cinematography by Helge Weindler. Music by Claus Barthelmes. Released and distributed nontheatrically by New Yorker Films. Starring Heiner Lauterbach, Uwe Ochsenknecht, Ulrike Kriener, Janna Marangosoff, Dietmar Bar, Marie-Charlott Schuler and Edith Volkmann.

Here's a double standard for you. A wealthy advertising executive named Julius (Heiner Lauterbach) has been cheating on his wife, Paula (Ulrike Kriener), for years, but when he finds out that she is having an affair with a long-haired artist named Stefan (Uwe Ochsenknecht), Julius completely falls apart. First, he's curious about what Stefan has that he hasn't and follows them around watching them kiss and ogle each other. Soon driven mad by jealousy, Julius takes a leave of absence from his job, assumes a different identity and becomes Stefan's roommate. His plan is to sabotage their romance by turning Stefan into a clone of himself. What Julius doesn't expect is that he and Stefan would sit around for hours sharing their troubles about women and their personal failures. After a few days of living together, they become each other's best friend.

Throughout Men, Lauterbach and Ochsenknecht make a hilarious odd couple, particularly during a scene when Paula suddenly drops by the house to meet Stefan's new roommate. But unlike their Italian sex comedy counterparts, Julius and Stefan have more going on inside than their hurt male egos. Julius is a German yuppie who gave up his sixties politics for a comfortable house in the suburbs and a fancy car. Stefan held on to his sixties ideals and now wonders if the real pleasures in life are passing him by. They are fascinated with each other because each of them sees in the other something that he has given up. Writer-director Doris Dorrie *(Straight Through the Heart)* has an eye for finding soft spots in their characters and chipping away at them. But because she isn't preachy about her women's politics in *Men,* the important points she makes about the modern male are much easier to appreciate.

RATING: *No MPAA rating, with brief nudity and profanity.*
WARNING: *Although the dubbing on the video is decent, it ruins the timing of much of the film's more subtle humor.*
FILMNOTE: *Dorrie claims that most of the dialogue in* Men *was taken from actual conversations she has overheard from men in various social situations.*

MEPHISTO
(Video, dubbed)

Psychological Drama

Hungary/West Germany   German

1981   135 Min.   Color

CREDITS: *Directed by Istvan Szabo. Written by Istvan Szabo and Peter Dobai, based on the novel by Klaus Mann. Produced by Manfred Durniok. Cinematography by Lajos Koltai. Music by Zdenko Tamassy. Released by Cinegate and Kino International. Distributed nontheatrically by Almi Pictures. Starring Klaus Maria Brandauer, Krystyna Janda, Rolf Hoppe, Ildiko Bansagi, Karin Boyd, Christine Harbort and Gyorgy Cserhalmi.*

Based on the novel by Klaus Mann (Thomas Mann's son), *Mephisto* is the true story of Henrik Hofgon, an actor who paid a large personal price in rising to fame in Nazi Germany. Klaus Maria Brandauer plays the Socialist actor whose Jewish, black and gay friends are as varied and freethinking as the German theater to which they are all dedicated. But when the Nazis take power, Henrik trades in his ideals to become the darling of the Third

Reich. As he basks in the glory of center stage, Henrik must close his eyes while his friends are dragged off to concentration camps. Eventually, the conflict between his ambitions and his values drives him to the edge of madness.

Although *Mephisto* develops little beyond the intensity of Brandauer's character, his Henrik is one of the most memorable screen performances of the last decade. As a metaphor for Germans who sold their morality for personal gain, his personality is so multifaceted that it's difficult to comprehend its subtleties the first time you see this film. Director Istvan Szabo *(Colonel Redl)* also does an extraordinary job showing the transition from the freethinking of the twenties and thirties in Germany to the terrifying reality of the Third Reich, while the film's cinematography is rich and elaborately detailed.

RATING: *No MPAA rating, with nudity, sexual content and violence.*
AWARDS: *1981 Academy Award for Best Foreign Film; Award for Best Screenplay (Istvan Szabo and Peter Dobai) at the 1981 Cannes Film Festival; 1981 British Academy Award for Best Foreign Film.*
WARNING: *Because of the subtleties of Brandauer's performance, much is lost in the video's dubbing.*
FILMNOTE: *Klaus Mann committed suicide, allegedly because he couldn't find a publisher for his novel, on which this film was based.*

MERRY CHRISTMAS, MR. LAWRENCE
(Video, partially subtitled)

World War II Drama

England/Japan   English and Japanese

1983   122 Min.   Color

CREDITS: *Directed by Nagisa Oshima. Written by Nagisa Oshima and Paul Mayersberg, based on the autobiographical novel* The Seed and the Sower *by Laurens van der Post. Produced by Jeremy Thomas. Cinematography by Toichiro Narushima. Music by Ryuichi Sakamoto. Released by Universal. Distributed nontheatrically by Swank Motion Pictures. Starring David Bowie, Tom Conti, Ryuichi Sakamoto, Takeshi, Jack Thompson, Johnny Okura, Alistair Browning and James Malcolm.*

Although the Geneva Accord provides rules for the treatment of war prisoners, we all know from World War II movies that whether or not they were obeyed depended on the will of the men in charge of the prison camp. In *Merry Christmas, Mr. Lawrence,* the commanders of a Japanese camp on Java in 1943 have very strange wills indeed. Captain Yonoi (Japanese pop singer Ryuichi Sakamoto) and Sergeant Hara (Japanese comedian Takeshi) are driven by superstition, religion and values of honor more than by outward hatred for their enemy. The odd relationships they develop with two of their British prisoners, Colonel Lawrence (Tom Conti) and Major Celliers (David Bowie), don't seem to follow traditional guidelines. But the two Westerners aren't your typical prisoners of war either.

Colonel Lawrence (Tom Conti) is a benevolent sort who not only speaks Japanese but also has a high regard for Japanese culture. In contrast, Major Celliers is a racist upper-class Brit who is tortured by guilt for the atrocities he committed and is now a little off his rocker. The more Major Celliers displays crazy behavior, the more Yonoi is troubled by him. Eventually, Yonoi believes Celliers to be an evil spirit, and, because Lawrence is Cellier's friend, he thinks Lawrence has betrayed him as well. To complicate matters, there is an unspoken homosexual attraction between Yonoi and Celliers, which Celliers uses to his advantage.

All four protagonists give outstanding performances in *Merry Christmas, Mr. Lawrence,* as the plot touches upon the brutality of war, the nature of authority and Japanese and British codes of honor. The film's moving musical score and striking cinematography add texture, while director Oshima (in his first English-language film) spares us none of the gruesome details of war. But the movie is often confusing.

Celliers can be stark raving mad at one moment and completely lucid the next. Yonoi and Hara display similarly erratic behavior. In some of the most dramatic scenes, the characters appear to be interacting at cross purposes. In the end, *Merry Christmas, Mr. Lawrence* can't decide whether it wants to be a psychological drama, a war movie or a film about the clashing of two cultures. Ultimately, it falters at all three.

RATING: R for violence and profanity.
AWARDS: 1983 British Academy Award for Best Musical Score (Ryuichi Sakamoto).

MIKEY AND NICKY
(Video)

Psychological Thriller

U.S.A.

1978   105 Min.   Color

CREDITS: Directed and written by Elaine May. Produced by Michael Hausmann. Music by John Strauss. Cinematography by Victor Kemper. Released by Paramount. Starring John Cassavetes, Peter Falk, Ned Beatty, M. Emmet Walsh, Rose Arrick, Carol Grace, William Hickey, Sanford Meisner and Joyce Van Patten.

John Cassavetes and Peter Falk fans will revel in *Mikey and Nicky,* because it gives a heavy dose of both of them. They play two small-time hoods who've been through so much together that they are as close as brothers. Yet, like real siblings they carry resentments around with them as if they were overstuffed suitcases bursting at the seams.

Since childhood, Mikey (John Cassavetes) has bullied Nicky (Peter Falk) into various shady schemes, then depended on his friend to bail him out. Such is the case at the start of the film when Mikey rips off his boss, Resnick (played by renowned New York acting coach Sanford Meisner), and holes up in a cheap hotel when the gangster puts a price on his head. By the time Nicky arrives, Mikey is frantic, constantly looking out the window and pacing his room like a caged animal. As much as he needs his friend's help, Mikey doesn't trust even Nicky, and for good reason. Nicky works for Resnick, too, and Mikey can't be sure that his oldest friend isn't the one hired to kill him.

Even though *Mikey and Nicky* is written and directed by Elaine May *(Ishtar)*, it has enough improvised dialogue and jerky editing to be made by Cassavetes himself. The story gradually builds in intensity until it becomes a suspenseful, psychological tug-of-war. We're never sure until the film's ending if Mikey's paranoia is based in reality. While the constant jumbling of loyalties is exhausting, the two actors give outstanding performances. Falk plays a bumbling, compassionate straight man who knows much more than he lets on, and Cassavetes is brilliant as the paranoid fool prone to explosions of violence, laughter and tears. Although there are several moments in *Mikey and Nicky* that may leave you uncomfortable, their acting alone makes it worth the effort.

RATING: *R for sex and violence.*
FILMNOTE: *After the film's completion, Paramount studio executives hated the ending so much they demanded that director/writer Elaine May change it before they would release it. May responded by swiping the original negative and hiding it in her garage for several months, until she ended up getting the rights herself.*

MISHIMA: A LIFE IN FOUR CHAPTERS

(Video, subtitled)

  ½

Literary Docudrama

U.S.A./Japan	English and Japanese
1985	121 Min.	Color

CREDITS: *Directed by Paul Schrader. Written by Paul and Leonard Schrader.*

Produced by Mata Yamamoto and Tom Luddy. Cinematography by John Bailey. Music by Philip Glass. Set design by Eiko Ishioka and Takenaka Kazuo. Released by Zoetrope Studios/Lucasfilm. Distributed nontheatrically by Swank Motion Pictures. Starring Ken Ogata, Mashayuki Shionoya, Hiroshi Mikami and Naoko Otani.

This big-production biography of Japanese author Yukio Mishima begins with his sensational kidnapping of a general at a Japanese army garrison in 1970. Mishima's self-styled soliders hold the general hostage, while Mishima gives an impassioned speech to the garrison's cadets, trying to convince them to reject Westernization and revert to the traditional values of the Samurai warrior. When the confused soldiers begin to make fun of him, he returns to the general's office and undertakes his last public act of honor—seppuku. By delving into his background and presenting stylized dramatizations from three of his novels, *Runaway Horses, Temple of the Golden Pavilion* and *Kyoko's House,* American director Paul Schrader *(Blue Collar)* tries to explain the man behind those explosive events.

Ken Ogata *(Vengeance is Mine)* is captivating as the controlled, quietly mad Mishima. In scenes with his army of followers, he displays an understated yet frightening intensity. And when his speech to the army cadets proves unsuccessful, the depth of his disappointment colors his every expression and movement. Unfortunately, Schrader seems more preoccupied with how Mishima looked, and with the symbolism in his fiction, than he is with the man himself. There are few moments when Mishima expresses his beliefs. The kitchen sink approach to his childhood covers major events, but the characters are too one-dimensional for the audience to empathize with them. Although *Mishima* works as a beautifully constructed abstract of the author, it doesn't have the drama of real life or the depth of character to give it impact.

RATING: *R for violence, sex and nudity.*
AWARDS: *Award for Best Artistic Contribution at the 1985 Cannes Film Festival.*

WARNING: The cinematography and sets are so integral to this story that it is best seen at the theater.

FILMNOTE: Although Schrader wisely left out the gory details in this film, Mishima carried out the usual practice of seppuku: he disemboweled himself, and then one of his followers beheaded him with a samurai sword.

MISSING

(Video, partially subtitled)

Political Thriller

U.S.A.   English and Spanish

1982   122 Min.   Color

CREDITS: *Directed by Constantine Costa-Gavras. Written by Constantine Costa-Gavras and Donald Stewart, based on the book The* Execution of Charles Horman *by Thomas Hauser. Produced by George R. Batcheller* (Midnight Express). *Cinematography by Ricardo Aronovich. Music by Vangelis. Edited by François Bonnot. Released by Universal. Distributed nontheatrically by Swank Motion Pictures. Starring Jack Lemmon, Sissy Spacek, John Shea, Charles Cioffi, Melanie Mayron, David Clennon, Richard Venture, Jerry Hardin and Richard Bradford.*

Missing is a dramatization of the true story of Charles Horman, a young American living in Chile who was one of many to disappear after the military overthrow of Salvador Allende in the early seventies. Through a series of flashbacks, we follow the events leading to Charles's abduction and the attempts of his free-spirited wife, Beth (Sissy Spacek), and conservative father, Ed (Jack Lemmon), to find out what happened to him. Their task isn't easy, as they are forced to battle both Chilean and U.S. red tape at the height of the repression following the coup. But Mr. Horman is a Republican businessman who knows important people in Washington, and the American embassy officials have been instructed to open every door possible for him. With a great deal of threatening from Mr. Horman, they finally do, and he and Beth not only find out what happened to Charles but also learn the reason behind his abduction.

Filmed on location in Mexico, Missing is not only Costa-Gavras's first work in English, but it is also his most accomplished work to date. Though it's a fictional account of real events, it feels like a documentary. François Bonnot's editing is tight, Vangelis's eerie music sets the mood, and the camera work by Ricardo Aronovich commands the audience's attention. There are some harrowing scenes in this film, such as those shot at the infamous National Football Stadium in Santiago where thousands of detainees were tortured and killed. Missing also effectively digs into the "generation gap" that existed in the sixties and early seventies as the Spacek and Lemmon characters confront each other's differing values on sex, politics and money. With superb performances by these actors, who both received Oscar nominations for their roles, few other movies about the era depict these issues as well or as objectively.

RATING: *R for violence and nudity.*
AWARDS: *Awards for Best Film and Best Actor (Jack Lemmon) at the 1982 Cannes Film Festival; 1982 Academy Award for Best Screenplay Adaptation (Costa-Gavras and Donald Stewart); 1982 Academy Award nominations for Best Picture, Best Actor (Lemmon) and Best Actress (Sissy Spacek).*
FILMNOTE: Missing *sparked an official State Department news conference and a several-page condemnation of the film. The State Department also filed a lawsuit against the filmmakers, which backfired when the suit was dismissed because there was too much evidence to support the film's point of view.*

MR. LOVE
(Video)

Romantic Comedy

England

1986   98 Min.   Color

CREDITS: *Directed by Roy Battersby. Written by Kenneth Eastaugh. Produced by David Putnam, Susan Richards and Robin Douet. Cinematography by Clive Tickner. Music by Willy Russell. Released by Warner Brothers. Starring Barry Jackson, Maurice Denham, Christina Collier, Helen Cotterill, Julia Deakin, Margaret Tyzack, Linda Marlowe and Helen Cotterill.*

Mr. Love is one of those small, sentimental English comedies that straddles the fence between being touching and syrupy. It's the story of a wide-eyed, gentle gardener-projectionist named Donald Loveless (Barry Jackson) who, after his tragic death in a car accident at the age of fifty, becomes a legend in his hometown of Southport, England, for his alleged amorous escapades during the last year of his life. Hence, he's dubbed Mr. Love, but we learn from his eccentric old friend's (Maurice Denham) narration that the title isn't necessarily founded on fact.

Donald is looking for the love he never had in his passionless twenty-eight-year marriage, and as he approaches the downside of middle age, he realizes he'd better find it soon before it's too late. So shy, balding, fifty-year-old Donald pursues several of Southport's available women, although he is so unassuming most don't suspect his intentions are romantic. Donald's female friends are an unusual bunch. There's the usherette at a movie theater who is always launching into famous movie monologues because she wants to be a star; an opera singer who spontaneously sings in public; an aging hooker; a divorcee who is obsessed with spiders and an attractive widow who doesn't trust any man but Donald.

Even if the premise of this film is a little farfetched, *Mr. Love* works because of Jackson's Donald. He plays a middle-aged Romeo who's so human and lovable that it's easy to see why his women friends were so easily taken with him. His romantic liaisons also have their entertaining moments in this film. Without giving it away, there's one scene between Donald and the usherette (Julia Deakin) at the theater where they both work that's worth the entire price of a rental to see. Whether you enjoy the rest of *Mr. Love* might depend on your ability to understand British accents and your propensity for cuteness.

RATING: *PG, with some sexual innuendo.*
FILMNOTE: *The theater in which the scene mentioned above takes place is the oldest surviving movie theater still in use in the world.*

MIXED BLOOD
(Video)

★

Urban Black Comedy

U.S.A.

1984   89 Min.   Color

CREDITS: *Directed by Paul Morrissey. Written by Paul Morrissey and Alan Browne. Produced by Antoine Gannage and Teven Fierberg. Cinematography by Stefan Zapasnik. Released by Cinevista. Starring Marilia Pera, Richard Ulacia, Linda Kerridge, Geraldine Smith, Angel David and Ulrich Berr.*

Paul Morrissey's *Mixed Blood* is a raunchy satire about a middle-aged Brazilian named Rita La Punta (Marilia Pera), the matriarch of a family of street urchins in New York's Lower East Side. This isn't the Lower East Side of art galleries, French patisseries and Thai restaurants. It's Alphabet City—the land of junkies, rats, needles and guns. Rita and her family live on top of the garbage heap, controlling a lucrative drug business and murdering anybody who stands in their way. The family's main executioner is Rita's muscle-bound son, Thiago (Richard Ulacia). When he's not plugging a hole through some rival gang member's head or dealing junk to teenagers, he has to share his affections with three different women—a sleazy Brazilian he's been seeing for a while, a new white-bread girl who enters his life (Linda Kerridge), and Rita. An obedient son, Thiago not only kills for his mother but has sex with her as well.

From the deranged mind of Paul Morrissey, the man who gave us *Andy Warhol's Frankenstein* and *Dracula*, *Mixed Blood* is a meant-to-shock black comedy that is far more gruesome than comical. While there are some funny moments in this movie, such as Rita's journey to a store crammed with Menudo artifacts, or Thiago's blonde girlfriend's final apology for her disheveled appearance after being shot in the head, the bottom line in *Mixed Blood* is that it's exploitive.

The majority of the film's characters end up gruesomely murdered, and Morrissey spares us none of the blood-spurting details. With the exception of Pera's Rita, the acting in *Mixed Blood* is uninspired. Ulacia, for example, has the screen presence of a slab of clay. And the film's dialogue consists mostly of profane street jive.

It also should be noted that Hispanic characters in this film are depicted so stereotypically that the film only perpetuates the most obvious kind of prejudice. Unless you enjoy violence and obscenity for their own sake, *Mixed Blood* won't entertain you.

RATING: *R for a lot of violence, sex and substance abuse.*

FILMNOTE: *Because of where* Mixed Blood *takes place, it was supposed to be named* Alphabet City. *But Amos Poe beat Morrissey to the punch by naming his action and violence film after the nickname for New York's Lower East Side avenues A, B, C and D.*

MODERN ROMANCE
(Video)

Romantic Comedy

U.S.A.

1981   93 Min.   Color

CREDITS: *Directed by Albert Brooks. Written by Albert Brooks and Monica Johnson. Produced by Andrew Scheinman and Martin Shafer. Cinematography by Eric Saarinen. Music by Lance Robin. Released by Columbia Pictures. Starring Albert Brooks, Kathryn Harrold, Bruno Kirby, Jane Hallaren, James L. Brooks, George Kennedy, Tyann Means and Karen Chandler.*

In *Modern Romance*, Albert Brooks *(Real Life, Lost in America)*, the most self-absorbed comic around, plays Robert Cole, a film editor who tries to follow his heart while his brain scrambles to dope out what's in it for him. The overly possessive lover of the beautiful Mary Harvard (Kathryn Harrold), Robert is so afraid of how a commitment might change his life that he impulsively breaks up with her, only to change his mind immediately. Meanwhile, Mary accepts his decision a little too easily, and it drives him crazy.

Attempting to rebound from the broken relationship, Robert takes to jogging, dating and gulping handfuls of megavitamins and Quaaludes, but nothing seems to help. As he searches through health food stores and goes on blind dates to cure his broken heart, he is constantly reminded of Mary, and nothing will suffice but his true love. Utterly miserable, he finally tries to win her back with gifts such as Teddy bears and a doll that whines "I'm sorry" when she pulls its string.

As in his other films, Brooks creates for himself a vain, pathetic protagonist and then deftly skewers the character on his own pretentions. *Modern Romance* is not Brooks at his best, in part because the break-up-to-make-up scenario plays too long and becomes wearing, but principally because Brook's character is a little too shrill. Although Brooks is never sympathetic in his films, here the line between satire and self-pity is poorly drawn. Still, there are some uproariously funny bits, such as when Robert goes to a sporting goods store and asks for a "post-relationship jogging outfit" or when he demands that a co-worker join him in a "little male bonding." In these scenes, and many others, Brooks sarcastically recognizes many single men's feelings of self-doubt and loneliness and their feeble efforts to mask those emotions.

RATING: R for sexual content, language and brief nudity.

THE MODERNS
(Video)

Romantic Satire

U.S.A.

1988   126 Min.   Color

CREDITS: Directed by Alan Rudolph. Written by Alan Rudolph and Jon Bradshaw. Produced by Carolyn Pfeiffer and David Blocker. Cinematography by Toyomichi Kurita. Music by Mark Isham. Released by Alive Films. Starring Keith Carradine, Linda Fiorentino, Genevieve Bujold, Geraldine Chaplin, Wallace Shawn, Kevin J. O'Connor and John Lone.

Although Alan Rudolph's *The Moderns* lacks the everything-in-its-place precision of *Choose Me*, it is clearly his most ambitious and heartfelt film to date.

The Moderns begins as a celebration of Paris in 1926, where commerce and art awkwardly intersected, where Gertrude Stein and Alice B. Toklas's turbulent relationship festered, where Ernest Hemingway cadged drinks in cafés while obsessively scribbling his impressions of the moveable feast, where F. Scott Fitzgerald found his inspiration. The protagonist of the story is a less successful expatriate named Nick Hart (Keith Carradine), who draws caricatures for a Parisian gossip columnist (Wallace Shawn) to finance his pas-

sion for creating ambitious oil paintings that hang unsold in the gallery of Valentin (Genevieve Bujold). Hart is so disillusioned with being an artist, he is willing to forge Cezannes in order to earn a fast buck. But his fever for life is reignited when he runs into his ex-lover Rachel (Linda Fiorentino). Rachel is now married to a ruthless industrialist named Stone (John Lone), who made his fortune in condoms. Even though Hart tries to resist Rachel, their verbal sparring at salon parties soon gives way to a passionate reconciliation, leading the couple to a dangerous confrontation with the possessive and violent Stone.

Although the film is not as entertaining as *Choose Me*, Rudolph once again uses goofy ensemble comedy to relay his belief in the power of love. Offbeat, comically eccentric characters bounce through scene after scene, unhappy and alone, searching for the equilibrium that this director finds only in romance. But Rudolph is more ambitious here. *The Moderns* was a work-in-progress for nearly a decade, and the investment certainly shows in the depth of the moral issues he explores. Kevin J. O'Connor's Hemingway seems overly contrived, but the rest of the cast is impeccable, particularly Carradine as the burned-out artist and John Lone as the brutish Stone. Rudolph's fluid, dreamy camera work (now his trademark) and Mark Isham's subtle musical score powerfully underline the film's message that the importance of power and money is dwarfed in the wake of passion.

RATING: No MPAA rating, with profanity, nudity, sex and violence.

MON ONCLE D'AMERIQUE
(Video, subtitled)

Psychological Drama

France   French

1980   125 Min.   Color

CREDITS: Directed by Alain Resnais. Written by Jean Gruault, inspired by the works of Prof. Henri Laborit. Produced by Philippe Dussart. Cinematography by Sacha Vierny. Released by New World Pictures. Distributed nontheatrically by Films Inc. Starring Roger-Pierre, Nicole Garcia, Gérard Depardieu, Nelly Bourgeaud, Gerard Darrieu, Philippe Laudenbach, Maria Dubois and Pierre Arditi.

As a foreshadowing of what's to follow, a voice at the beginning of *Mon Oncle d'Amerique* states, "A being's only reason for being is being." Using this sort of cerebral narration by a professor of behavior modification, director Alain Resnais *(Hiroshima Mon Amor)* tells the story of three loosely connected people who each have serious problems in their careers and in their personal lives.

Jean (Roger-Pierre), the attaché to France's minister of education, risks his strong political aspirations to have an affair with a failed stage actress, Janine (Nicole Garcia), walking out on his family to be with her. Although in love with him, Janine eventually leaves Jean when his wife lies to her, saying she needs her husband to return home because she is dying. Unaware of his wife's scheme, the heartbroken Jean returns to his family and his burgeoning political career.

Meanwhile, Janine has periods of mixed stage success but eventually becomes a fashion designer and takes a position with a clothing manufacturer, where the other protagonist of the story, René (Gérard Depardieu), also works. René hasn't had an easy go of it either. By the time he meets Janine, he has been transferred from several responsible positions, often separated from his wife and children, and now suffers from ulcers and a lack of self-confidence. Janine ironically comes to play a part in deciding the fate of René's career, as she becomes involved with his boss.

Interspersed with the biographical portraits in *Mon Oncle d'Amerique* are the behavior modification professor's observations of the three main characters' "Homo sapien" patterns, pointing out their similarities to the rats in his experiments. During this commentary, we see lab rodents responding to various stimuli such as electric shock. Resnais also intercuts clips of the three characters' favorite movie stars, with expressions on their faces that mirror the emotional states of Jean, Janine and René.

Watching *Mon Oncle d'Amerique* is like reading Thomas Pynchon's *Gravity's Rainbow*—once you make it past the first fifty pages, you can't put it down. Although it takes a while for all the elements of the film to come together, when we get to know the main players well enough to become involved, these seemingly disjointed segments fit together extremely well. The cinematography is excellent throughout, from the shots of animals in and out of the laboratory to richly textured pans of French countryside and cityscapes. Although the themes in *Mon Oncle d'Amerique* are primarily disturbing and depressing, Resnais also throws in some absurdly funny moments such as rats dressed up in suits and ties wandering around a miniature house. And all three characters, with their ordinary personalities and everyday problems, are excellent vehicles for Resnais's bizarre exploration of animal and human behavior.

RATING: PG, with nothing objectionable.
AWARD: 1980 French Caesars for Best Film, Best Director (Alain Resnais) and Best Screenplay (Jean Gruault); 1980 Academy Award nomination for Best Original Screenplay (Gruault); Special Jury Prize at the 1980 Cannes Film Festival; 1980 New York Film Critics Award for Best Foreign Film.

MONA LISA
(Video)

Urban Thriller

England

1986   104 Min.   Color

CREDITS: *Directed by Neil Jordon. Written by Neil Jordon and David Leland. Produced by George Harrison, Stephen Woolley and Patrick Cassavetti. Cinematography by Roger Pratt. Released by Island Alive/Handmade Films. Distributed nontheatrically by New Yorker Films. Starring Bob Hoskins, Cathy Tyson, Michael Caine,*

Robbie Coltrane, Clarke Peters and Kate Hardie.

Although Bob Hoskins isn't exactly a sex symbol, this short, bald, fortyish man is one of those actors, like Dustin Hoffman or Jack Nicholson, who doesn't have to be good-looking to be remembered. Hoskins has screen charisma, and no matter how small the part, he tends to steal every scene in which he appears.

In *Mona Lisa*, he stars as George, a loud-mouthed, short-tempered ex-con who, after serving seven years in prison, bullies himself into a job with Mortimer (Michael Caine). Mortimer is a sharply dressed pimp of the eighties who does his bookkeeping on a computer and whose girls work out of expensive hotels. He hires George to be the chauffeur for one of his most lucrative girls, Simone (Cathy Tyson). At first, George and Simone get on miserably. She's an elegant prostitute who makes fun of George's crude vocabulary and bowling-alley outfits, while he writes her off as too superior for her own good. Before long, they become friends—but for George friendship means more. George falls in love with Simone, and she takes advantage of his affections to pressure him to search for another prostitute, a friend of Simone's who has fallen into the clutches of a dangerous pimp.

Hoskins plays George as a dense, two-bit hustler who desperately puts his faith in love yet ends up as everybody's fool. He's slightly frightening when the pool of rage inside his benevolent mind comes exploding to the surface and is hilariously funny for his bluster. Tyson is also outstanding as the sarcastic hooker who manipulates men as she appears to be abused by them. Because we empathize with them both, the violent, sexually distorted world they inhabit is sometimes difficult to take. But even with all of its hard edges, *Mona Lisa* is an entertaining and gutsy thriller filled with fascinating characters and superbly styled sets. Director Jordon (*A Company of Wolves*) cleverly portrays his two protagonists as mismatched allies who have a hard time dealing with their own confused emotions in a world that requires a shell to survive.

RATING: R for violence, nudity and language.

AWARDS: Award for Best Actor (Bob Hoskins) at the 1986 Cannes Film Festival; 1986 Academy Award nomination for Best Actor (Hoskins).

MONTENEGRO
(PIGS AND PEARLS)

(Video, subtitled)

Black Comedy

Sweden/England   Swedish and English

1981   98 Min.   Color

CREDITS: Directed by Dusan Makavejev. Written by Dusan Makavejev, Bo Jonsson, Donald Arthur and Arnie Gilbert. Produced by Bo Jonsson. Cinematography by Tomislav Pinter. Set design by Eric Johnson. Released by Atlantic. Distributed nontheatrically by Films Inc. Starring Susan Anspach, Erland Josephson, Per Oscarsson, John Zacharias, Svetozar Cvetkovic and Patricia Gelin.

What happens when a wealthy American housewife living in Sweden becomes disillusioned with her husband, restless with taking care of two kids and a grandfather who thinks he's Buffalo Bill, and bored from attending endless women's luncheons? In Dusan Makavejev's *Montenegro*, Marilyn (Susan Anspach) sets her bed on fire, feeds the dog rat poison and then gets involved with a Yugoslav woman trying to smuggle a dead pig, a hitchhiker with a knife in his head and a seductive zookeeper.

Sitting through the first half of *Montenegro* is as anxiety-producing as Susan's life. Director Makavejev (*The Coca-Cola Kid, WR: Mysteries of the Organism*) makes sure we understand why Marilyn goes crazy, as the scenes of her blankly feeding her kids and pacing her meticulous house seem to go on forever. Cinematographer Tomislav Pinter does an outstanding job capturing the claustrophobia of Marilyn's lifeless existence. And Anspach is so controlled it's hard to tell that anything is going on underneath her placid exterior. Then it finally happens. Marilyn liberates herself and *Montenegro* switches from a dark satire into an uproarious story, full of life, music and love. In sharp contrast to the stiffness of her family, the immigrants and working-class characters Marilyn meets on her adventures are like a breath of fresh air. Although some later scenes are a little over-laden with animal symbolism, most are as entertaining as the first part of the film is stifling.

RATING: *R for nudity, sex and violence.*

MONTY PYTHON AND THE HOLY GRAIL
(Video)

Historical Farce

England

1975   90 Min.   Color

CREDITS: *Directed by Terry Gilliam and Terry Jones. Written by Graham Chapman, John Cleese, Terry Gilliam, Eric Idle, Terry Jones and Michael Palin. Produced by Mark Forstater. Cinematography by Terry Bedford. Music by Neil Innes. Released and distributed nontheatrically by Almi Pictures. Starring Graham Chapman, John Cleese, Terry Gilliam, Eric Idle, Terry Jones, Michael Palin, Neil Innes, Connie Booth, John Young and Rita Davies.*

Although the Monty Python troupe already had a small but loyal following from their inventive television show, this first feature became a hit on the art theater circuit and exposed millions of new viewers to their special brand of humor.

Set in England at the time of King Arthur, *The Holy Grail* follows the legendary knights of the Round Table—Lancelot, Ga-wain and Arthur himself. As they strike out in search of the Holy Grail, they encounter a black knight who is anxious to do battle even after their swords have sliced off his arms and legs, an abusive French soldier who guards his castle with a pot of flying excrement, and a passel of gigantic knights who can only say "Ni." But the quest is really just an excuse for the Monty Python regulars to satirize whatever strikes their fancy, including the British upper class, the French, art historians and Arthurian film epics themselves.

The Holy Grail gets the typical Monty Python treatment, complete with non se-quiturs, bawdy word play and a haphazard visual style. Willing to use everything in-cluding a killer bunny rabbit to get a laugh, certain routines are hilarious, though others overstay their welcome on screen. In the worst Monty Python tradition, the film loses direction and steam at the very end. But the pluses far outweigh the minuses in this irreverent farce, because a reasonably cohesive narrative demands restraint from the comics, and several schticks are as sharply sarcastic as they are bawdy. John Cleese is particularly funny as the ex-crement-throwing French knight and bat-tling amputee, but all members of the troupe give strong performances. If you've never been introduced to the Monty Python point of view, this is their best feature film to date.

RATING: *PG, with slight profanity.*

MOONLIGHTING
(Video, partially subtitled)

Cultural Drama

England   English and Polish

1982   97 Min.   Color

CREDITS: *Directed by Jerzy Skolimowski. Written by Jerzy Skolimowski, Boleslaw Sulik, Barry Vince and Danuta Witold Stok. Produced by Jerzy Skolimowski and Mark Shivas. Cinematography by Tony Pierce-Roberts. Released by Universal. Dis-tributed nontheatrically by Swank Motion Pictures. Starring Jeremy Irons, Eugene Lipinski, Jiri Stanislav, Eugeniusz Hack-iewicz and Dorothy Zienciowska.*

When he learned that martial law had been declared in his native Poland, exiled filmmaker Jerzy Skolimowski *(The Shout, The Lightship)* was so affected by the news that he abandoned work on another project and wrote and directed *Moonlighting* in a month's time. The result is a powerful account of political and personal alienation.

The film opens as a Polish tradesman named Nowak (Jeremy Irons) and three assistants arrive in London to remodel a rundown townhouse that belongs to his Warsaw construction supervisor. Nowak plans to make a tidy sum with this moonlighting job, but he and his men have no work permits and must hide their identities from prying neighbors and suspicious store clerks. In addition, Nowak is the only one who speaks English, so he's not only burdened with directing the rigorously scheduled project but with feeding and entertaining his men as well. That responsibility becomes too much to handle when he learns that martial law has been enacted in Poland and that they are trapped in England. Nowak hides the news from the others, but, as they grow homesick and his bankroll dwindles, he's pushed to the brink of madness, tyrannically denying his men entertainment and money and driving them beyond reason.

Moonlighting begins as a comedy of sorts about Nowak's bumbling attempts to provide for his workers and all their responses to life in the West. But as their situation becomes more desperate, Nowak's relationship to his men begins to parallel the tragic events occurring in their native Poland. By progressive denying his assistants more freedom, Nowak becomes, in the end, as vicious as his own government. Irons gives a riveting performance as Nowak. His sense of desperation and alienation from his men and his country is extraordinarily moving. Their response to being trapped by circumstances over which they have no control, combined with British cultural racism toward these "ignorant immigrants," is also frighteningly real.

RATING: *PG, with brief nudity.*
AWARDS: *Award for Best Screenplay (Jerrzy Skolimowski, Boleslaw Sulik, Barry Vince and Danuta Witold Stok) at the 1982 Cannes Film Festival.*

MORGAN (A SUITABLE CASE FOR TREATMENT)
(Video)

Social Satire

England

1966   97 Min.   B&W

CREDITS: *Directed by Karel Reisz. Written by David Mercer, based on his television play "A Suitable Case for Treatment." Produced by Leon Clore. Cinematography by Larry Pizer. Released by Quintra Film. Distributed nontheatrically by Almi Pictures. Starring David Warner, Vanessa Redgrave, Robert Stephens, Irene Handl, Newton Blick, Nan Munro and Graham Crowden.*

Although enormously popular at art houses in the sixties for its blatant disregard of society's conventions, *Morgan* is a bit dated today. The story follows the exploits of Morgan (David Warner), a witty, lovable eccentric full of spontaneity and joy. So why is his wife, Leona (Vanessa Redgrave), divorcing him? Because he is also completely nuts.

Morgan is willing to do anything to win his wife back. He tries to charm her, scare her, terrorize her new boyfriend (Robert Stephens) and even kidnap her, but to no avail. As Morgan's schemes become more elaborate, they also become more dangerous. But Leona is merely amused by her crazy Morgan, while her continued love for him, combined with her insistence on getting a divorce, only fuels his confusion and rage. To further complicate his condition, Morgan views the world literally as a jungle, often "seeing" gorillas, exotic birds and alligators meandering in his direction at every turn.

Although Warner plays Morgan as a man completely likable in his craziness, it's frustrating never to be given an opportunity to understand him. Exiled Czech filmmaker Karel Reisz *(The French Lieutenant's Woman)* doesn't even attempt to explain his actions but focuses only on the surface humor of his character. Still, Warner and Redgrave shine in *Morgan,* as both bring to their comic debuts all their experience and skills as dramatic performers. The film's action is upbeat and moves along at a nice clip, while the one-note premise—Morgan going to fantastic lengths to win Leona back—is ingeniously recreated in scene after scene. But when Reisz tries to show off with some innovative filmmaking techniques, such as speeding up and slowing down the photography, and inserting old Tarzan and African wildlife footage, the film now seems a little hokey.

RATING: *No MPAA rating, with nothing objectionable.*
AWARDS: *1966 British Academy Award for Best Screenplay (David Mercer); 1966 Academy Award nominations for Best Actress (Vanessa Redgrave) and Best Costume Design (Jocelyn Rickards).*

MOSCOW DOES NOT BELIEVE IN TEARS

(Video, dubbed and subtitled)

Cultural Drama

U.S.S.R.	Russian
1980　　　115 Min.	Color

CREDITS: *Directed by Vladimir Menshov. Written by Valentin Tschemych. Produced by V. Kuchinsky. Cinematography by Igor Slabnjewitsch. Music by Sergei Niktin. Released and distributed nontheatrically by International Film Exchange. Starring Vera Alentova, Irina Muravyova, Raisa Ryazonova, Natalia Vavilova and Alexei Batalov.*

Vladimir Menshov's Oscar-winning *Moscow Does Not Believe in Tears* is about modern Soviet life, with a heavy emphasis on the problems of Moscow's single women, who strongly outnumber the city's single men.

The story begins in 1958. Katerina (Vera Alentova) and her best friend, Ludmila (Irina Muravyova), live in a workers' dormitory with other young women. A worried Katerina has flunked her exam, which means that unless she passes it on her next try, she is doomed to remain a factory worker for the rest of her life. Ludmila isn't as concerned about academics—she just wants to find a man. At a party, they each land an eligible bachelor. Ludmila's turns out to be a nice guy she eventually marries, but Katerina's is a rogue who knocks her up and then abandons her. Ten years later, Ludmila's marriage has gone sour, while Katerina's life is more or less in order. She has a wonderful daughter and is the director of a plant at a good salary. But she is still desperately lonely, and so set in her ways that it's hard for her to get involved in a relationship even when the opportunity arises.

Moscow Does Not Believe in Tears is a simple overview of Soviet life. In both the fifties and sixties segments director Menshov takes us into supermarkets, apartments and factories, and introduces us to an assortment of ordinary Russians doing the best they can with problems that arise in their daily lives. Although the supporting actors aren't flashy, they are authentic, while Alentova is compelling both as a woman coming to terms with being a single mother and as a career woman who buries her feelings of loneliness in her work. There is no earth-shattering message in *Moscow Does Not Believe in Tears.* Some scenes are comical in the most obvious ways, while others are slowly paced. But this film is full of fascinating and intimate slices of modern Moscow life little known to Westerners. For that alone it's worthwhile.

RATING: *No MPAA rating, with brief nudity.*
AWARDS: *1980 Academy Award for Best Foreign Film.*
WARNING: *The video versions are a double whammy. The original language video is poorly subtitled and hard to read. The dubbed video is atrocious. My vote by a small margin is the original language video.*

MY BEAUTIFUL LAUNDRETTE

(Video, partially subtitled)

Cultural Drama

England   English and Pakistani

1986   117 Min.   Color

CREDITS: *Directed by Steven Frears. Written by Hanif Kureishi. Produced by Sarah Radclyffe and Tim Bevan. Cinematography by Oliver Stapleton. Released by Orion Classics. Distributed nontheatrically by Films Inc. Starring Gordon Warnecke, Saeed Jaffrey, Roshan Seth, Daniel Day Lewis, Shirley Ann Field and Rita Wolf.*

Stephen Frears *(The Hit, Prick Up Your Ears)* took everybody by surprise when his low-budget (£600,000), stylish *My Beautiful Laundrette* came from nowhere to become a smash hit at the art house box office. It's the story of Omar (Gordon Warnecke), a young Pakistani immigrant who lives with his intellectual papa (Roshan Seth) in a shabby South London flat. Omar is at a crossroads in his life, trying to decide which direction to take. His alcoholic father wants him to "feed his spirit" with an education and to shun the material world. But his Uncle Nassar (Saeed Jaffrey), a wealthy racketeer, thinks the boy should follow in his footsteps. Eventually, Nassar wins out by giving Omar a dilapidated laundrette to manage, and Omar is infected with an entrepreneurial fever.

With help from his white, punk buddy Johnny (Daniel Day Lewis of *A Room with a View*) and some quick cash from stepped-on cocaine, Omar creates a laundrette the likes of which nobody has ever seen. Tropical fish, stereo, overstuffed couches, Art Deco, neon, video machines, you name it, Omar's laundrette has it. It becomes an instant success. Omar takes care of the business end of things, while Johnny the bouncer makes sure undesirables, including his racist punk friends, stay away. The two turn out to be a great combo in more ways than one. About two-thirds of the way through the movie, with little warning, Johnny and Omar become passionate lovers.

Ho hum, just another Pakistani youth and white punk having sex—movies are full of them these days. Or at least that's how director Frears portrays this affair. Given who they are, two lower-class men of different races in a society overly conscious of race, class and sexual preference, it's an unusual approach to romance. Frears uses this same irreverent, sardonic style to delve into all of the film's themes of race and class in London's fringe subcultures, and that's what makes *My Beautiful Laundrette* so refreshing. The movies's performances are very good, particularly from the Pakistani actors in the cast. But the film stumbles a bit in its story line. Starting out with all the makings of a well-developed narrative, about halfway through, the plot begins to wander, and by the final scene, most of the interesting subplots and characterizations in the film have virtually disintegrated. Throughout, however, Frears does an outstanding job creating a richly textured combination of sleaze and dazzle in the film's sets and mood.

RATING: *R for profanity, nudity and heavy straight and gay petting.*
FILMNOTE: My Beautiful Laundrette *is a successful product of British television's Channel 4, one of the big forces in independent filmmaking in England today.*

MY BRILLIANT CAREER

(Video)

Women's Drama

Australia

1980   101 Min.   Color

CREDITS: *Directed by Gillian Armstrong. Written by Eleanor Witcombe, based on the autobiographical novel by Miles Franklin. Produced by Maragaret Fink. Cinematography by Don McAlpine. Music by Nathan Waks. Production design by Luciana Arrighi. Costume design by Anna Senior. Released and distributed by Almi Pictures. Starring Judy Davis, Sam Neill, Wendy Hughes, Robert Grubb, Max Cul-*

len, Pat Kennedy, Aileen Brittain, Peter Whitford and Carole Skinner.

Sybylia (Judy Davis) causes quite a stir among the well-bred in turn-of-the-century Australia. Not only is she cursed with plain looks and a father who is always in debt, but she is a rebel as well.

Sybylia doesn't want to marry into a wealthy family like the other women her age, she wants to be a writer instead. Her mother, grandmother and Aunt Helen think she is "selfish, useless and Godless" and pressure her to get in step. But when an approved friend of the family named Frank (Robert Grubb) lowers himself to ask such a plain girl for her hand, Sybylia pushes him into a sheep pen. Then Sybylia unexpectedly falls for the charms of rich and handsome Harry (Sam Neill); however, she must make a choice between the irreconcilable differences of her heart and her principles.

Based on the real experiences and subsequent novel of Miles Franklin, *My Brilliant Career*'s cinematography stunningly captures the power of the Australian Outback. The film's sets and costumes are equally authentic. But cinematographer Don McAlpine's camera lingers on the landscapes a little too long at times, and certain scenes amble on listlessly. Still Sybylia's enormous strength as a rebel brings every scene to life. Director Gillian Armstrong (*Starstruck*, *Mrs. Soffel*) doesn't romanticize or exploit Sybylia, while Davis's performance is so natural she makes it seem as if it couldn't be any other way. In the end, Armstrong and Davis combine to make a strong feminist statement without posturing.

RATING: No MPAA rating, with nothing objectionable.
AWARDS: 1980 British Academy Awards for Best Actress and Most Promising Newcomer to Leading Film Roles (Judy Davis); 1980 Academy Award nomination for Best Costume Design (Anna Senior).

MY DINNER WITH ANDRE
(Video)

Comedy/Docudrama

U.S.A.

1981   110 Min.   Color

CREDITS: Directed by Louis Malle. Written by Wallace Shawn and Andre Gregory. Produced by George W. George. Cinematography by Jeri Sopanen. Music by Allen Shawn (Wallace's brother). Released and distributed by New Yorker Films. Starring Walllace Shawn, Andre Gregory, Jean Lenauer and Roy Butler.

The premise for this movie—recording two friends having a dinner conversation—seems like it would run out of gas after two minutes, much less two hours. But *My Dinner with Andre* is anything but boring, because of the two remarkable characters having this movie-long talk.

Playwright-actor Wallace Shawn is the narrator. The film begins as Wally expresses his apprehension about his upcoming dinner with an old director friend, Andre Gregory. Gregory has returned to New York after years of drifting on the fringes of society. At the restaurant, these apprehensions are immediately confirmed. An extremely articulate, slightly crazy, self-centered intellectual, Gregory espouses his philosophies on a whole range of subjects, from the existential nature of spiritualism to the decay of Western society. He talks about his experiences performing avant-garde theater in a Polish forest and trekking deep into the mountains of Tibet to talk with a monk. Gregory is an explosive story-teller. Throughout dinner, his face is alive with expression, and words fly off his tongue so quickly that Shawn can hardly get a word in edgewise. Then, when the director finally stops to take a breath, Wally launches into his own cynical and hilarious commentary, skewering everything Gregory has been saying.

Shawn and Gregory are off-screen friends who wrote the movie's script based on real conversations they had after a five-year separation. Although this evening together is ostensibly about the void in their creative lives now that the sixties are over, they touch upon many universal issues of family, love, religion and society.

Visually, *My Dinner with Andre* is stagnant, but it was director Louis Malle's *(Atlantic City)* choice to avoid any distractions from Gregory's mental gymnastics and Shawn's wry commentary. Remarkably, the actors themselves are able to transport us to the forests in Poland and the mountains of Tibet without concrete images. *My Dinner with Andre* is not an easy film to pull off, yet the power of storytelling is demonstrated here more than in any other film in recent memory, with the notable exception of Jonathan Demme's *Swimming to Cambodia*.

RATING: *No MPAA rating, with nothing objectionable.*
FOOTNOTE: *The late comedian Andy Kaufman did a hilarious TV takeoff on this film called "My Breakfast with Blassie" about having breakfast with a wrestler.*

MY FIRST WIFE
(Video)

Psychological Drama

Australia

1984   95 Min.   Color

CREDITS: *Directed by Paul Cox. Written by Paul Cox and Bob Ellis. Produced by Paul Cox and Jane Ballentyne. Cinematography by Yuri Sokol. Released by Spectrafilms. Starring John Hargreaves, Wendy Hughes, Lucy Angwin, Anna Jemison, David Cameron, Julia Blake, Charles Tingwell, Robin Lovejoy, Lucy Uralov and Xenia Groutas.*

After his wife left him, Australian filmmaker Paul Cox *(Man of Flowers)* wanted to make a film that went "for the throat" of divorce. *My First Wife* certainly lives up to his intention.

John (John Hargreaves) is successful as a chamber music composer and disk jockey for a Sydney classical radio station. But his personal life falls apart when, after he experiences a frustrating attempt to make love to his wife, Helen (Wendy Hughes), she nervously confesses that she has been having an affair for months. During the course of the evening, it also comes out that she no longer loves him and wants a divorce. At first refusing to believe her, John becomes so completely unglued when she moves out the next day that he attempts suicide. Luckily, he's unsuccessful, and after his dying father tells him that "in the end, family is everything," John literally begs Helen to give him another chance. But Helen quickly loses patience with his whining and whimpering and insists on her freedom. Finally, he resorts to posturing with Helen's family and friends, and even violence, to get her to change her mind.

Although similar stories of heartbreak and abandonment have been told in movies in the past, few have the emotional firepower of *My First Wife*. Director Paul Cox doesn't waste any time uncovering the raw emotions just below the surface of John's and Helen's characters. John has good reason to feel betrayed, yet Helen's decision to leave him is also easy to understand. And as in real life, they each take turns being victim and victimizer. Both Hargreaves and Hughes give intense and compelling performances, while Cox delicately weaves into their characters issues of ego, loneliness and personal freedom. *My First Wife* is also elegantly photographed, spiced up by super-8 home movie snippets that recreate the times of happiness in their relationship, while they accentuate the devastation when their marriage goes bad.

RATING: *No MPAA rating, with nudity.*
AWARDS: *1984 Australian Film Awards for Best Director (Paul Cox), Best Actor (John Hargreaves) and Best Original Screenplay (Cox and Bob Ellis).*

MY LIFE AS A DOG
(Video, dubbed and subtitled)

Coming-of-Age Comedy

Sweden		Swedish
1985	101 Min.	Color

CREDITS: *Directed by Lasse Hallstrom. Written by Lasse Hallstrom, Brasse Braannsstrom and Pelle Bergluun, based on the story by Reidar Jonsson. Cinematography by Jorgen Persson and Rolf Lindstrom. Released by Skouras Pictures. Distributed nontheatrically by New Yorker Films. Starring Anton Glanzelius, Anki Liden, Tomas von Bromssen and Melinda Kenneman.*

When we think of Swedish movies, we invariably recall Ingmar Bergman's dark, brooding psychological dramas about loneliness and alienation. That's why *My Life as a Dog* is such a surprise. Despite its title, it's a wonderful coming-of-age story that moves us both to tears and to laughter.

The film's hero is thirteen-year-old Ingemar (Anton Glanzelius), a charismatic boy whose inspiration is Laika, a dog the Russians send into orbit during the early days of their space program. Ingemar's enthusiasm for life is undampened even as his beloved mother grows steadily weaker from tuberculosis. Sometimes his energy gets him into minor trouble, and finally, Ingemar is shipped off to live for the summer with his uncle (Tomas von Bromssen) in a remote village so his mother can rest. That summer is magical for Ingemar. He adores his uncle and the rest of the town's inhabitants, and attracts the attention of a pretty young tomboy. Months later, however, when Ingemar returns to the village in winter, he finds that this happy world has changed. His uncle and the rest of the villagers are now caught up in their own lives, and Ingemar must struggle to fit in while trying to come to terms with his own personal tragedies.

My Life as a Dog is a film of tonal shifts, lurching us from tear-ridden drama to slapstick comedy in the same motion. First-time director Lasse Hallstrom seems to be saying that this is real life. The transitions are rough at times, and some of the film's more powerful dramatic moments are defused in the process, yet despite its minor rough spots, *My Life as a Dog* is worth watching because of Glanzelius's Ingemar. He is so charming and captivating that we are willing to follow him in any direction, whether serious or comical. The rest of the cast is also very good, particularly Tomas von Bromssen as Ingemar's droopy-eyed, easygoing uncle. The scenes of Ingemar's first visit to the country in the summer are little gems. They are gently funny and contain a bittersweet sense that life carries on despite all the hardships and obstacles of growing up.

RATING: *No MPAA rating, with brief nudity.*

MY NEW PARTNER
(Video, subtitled)

Caper Comedy

France		French
1985	107 Min.	Color

CREDITS: *Directed and produced by Claude Zidi. Written by Claude Zidi and Didier Kaminka, based on a story by Simon Mickael. Cinematography by Jean-Jacques Tarbes. Released by Orion. Distributed nontheatrically by Films Inc. Starring Philip Noiret, Thierry Lhermitte, Regine, Grace De Capitani, Julien Guiormar and Pierre Frag.*

In *My New Partner,* the common knowledge that big-city cops are on the take is taken to an absurd extreme. René (Philip Noiret), a twenty-year veteran of the Paris detective squad, and his partner, Pierrot (Pierre Frag), can't walk down the street without a vendor slipping them a hundred, a butcher tossing them a leg of lamb or a restaurateur popping open a vintage bottle of wine. Even when René and Pierrot get a tip on a drug deal and they stake out the rendezvous, their intentions aren't necessarily to bust the dealers. But one day their scheming unexpectedly catches up with them, and Pierrot ends up taking the fall for his partner, René.

Enter René's new partner, François (Thierry Lhermitte), an inspector fresh from the academy who is a young French version of Sergeant Joe Friday on "Dragnet." To René's bewilderment, the straight-laced François is more anxious to arrest criminals then solicit bribes. It doesn't take long for François to get on René's nerves. The older cop devises an elaborate plan to change his partner's angelic ways, but the plot backfires every step of the way.

My New Partner has that same rehashed odd-couple plot we all know so well. But what makes this film entertaining are Noiret's hilarious hound-dog expressions and perfect timing. Noiret's delivery is so quick that it's easy to miss one lie rolling off his tongue in order the catch the next. Aside from Noiret, however, the film isn't particularly remarkable. The film's final scene is so thick with sentiment you can get a Jeep stuck in it, and, with the exception of Francois, most of the other characters are overdone. Fortunately, Noiret's antics are at the center of nearly every scene in the film. In *My New Partner,* he reaffirms his place as one of the most clever comic performers in French cinema.

RATING: R for language, substance abuse and brief nudity.
AWARDS: 1984 French Caesars for Best Picture and Best Director (Claude Zidi).

MY SWEET LITTLE VILLAGE

Screwball Comedy

Czechoslovakia		Czech
1986	100 Min.	Color

CREDITS: *Directed by Jiri Menzel. Written by Zdenek Sverak. Produced by Ben Barenholtz. Cinematography by Jaromir Sofr. Music by Jiri Sust. Released and distributed nontheatrically by Circle Films. Starring Janos Ban, Marian Labuda, Ru-*

dolf Hrusinsky, Libuse Safrankova, Petr Cepek, Jan Hartl, Josef Stibich and Marie Jezkova.

Best known for his *Closely Watched Trains,* director Jiri Menzel once again comes up with a colorful and tender portrait of life in a Czech village in *My Sweet Little Village*. The central character is Otik (Janos Ban), a bumbling, small-town simpleton who works with a pudgy, irascible truck driver named Pavek (Marian Labuda). Otik is more than clumsy, he's a walking disaster who fumbles everything he puts his hands on. Finally, Pavek asks his superiors to transfer Otik to another truck. But since none of the other drivers want him either, the party officials decide that Otik will have to be transferred to Prague where there are more jobs. For Otik, who has never left his village, this will mean loneliness and isolation.

Menzel has a remarkable ability of taking us into the lives of simple people and making us feel right at home. His characters in *My Sweet Little Village* are delightfully quirky, yet the best humor comes from their everyday struggles. Labuda and Ban are a hilarious comedy team, a Czech Laurel and Hardy. Every time they get together in this film, you know that Otik will do something for which Pavek will pay later. Although most of their routines are predictable, they are funny nonetheless. *My Sweet Little Village* also contains Menzel's pointed jabs at the impersonalization and inequities of the Czech government. But it's Ban's Otik who makes this movie so special. With his bewildered looks and infectious smile, he can be uproariously funny yet as innocent and helpless as a child.

RATING: No MPAA rating, with brief nudity.
AWARDS: 1986 Academy Award nomination for Best Foreign Film.
FILMNOTE: Ban is a Hungarian who doesn't speak a word of Czech, so his reactions to what's going on around him in this film are quite genuine.

THE MYSTERY OF KASPAR HAUSER—EVERY MAN FOR HIMSELF AND GOD AGAINST ALL

(Video, subtitled)

Psychological Drama

West Germany   German

1975   110 Min.   Color

CREDITS: *Directed, written and produced by Werner Herzog. Cinematography by Jorge Schmidt-Reitwein. Music by Albinoni Pachelbel. Released by Cine International. Distributed nontheatrically by Almi Pictures. Starring Bruno S., Walter Ladengast, Brigitte Mira, Hans Musaus, Willy Semmelrogge and Michael Kroecher.*

Few filmmakers have delved into the problems of society's misfits as many times, and with as much emotion, as Werner Herzog. *The Mystery of Kaspar Hauser* is perhaps his best effort.

Set in 1828, the film tells the story of an odd-looking, speechless man in his early thirties who mysteriously appears in a small German village holding a note that says his name is Kaspar Hauser and that he's spent his entire life chained to a cellar floor with almost no human contact. Kaspar (Bruno S.) is adopted by Daumer (Walter Ladengast), who teaches him how to speak, read, write and even play the piano. Once word spreads about his past, Kaspar becomes a celebrity of sorts. An English nobleman attempts to make him his protégé, and several men of the cloth wonder if he experienced God during his life of confinement. Kaspar disappoints the priests by admitting no religious faith, and in fact most explanations of religion, society or nature make little sense to Kaspar. The more he learns, the less he is able to deal with the disparity between the actions and words of those who try to socialize him.

Although *Kaspar Hauser* is based on a real story of a German boy who was found living in a cave in the 1800s, Herzog takes the story one step further by giving us an intelligent adult who is strong enough to question what he learns. When he expresses these feelings, people are threatened by his honesty, because the society he encounters has no place for a grown man who bluntly says what he thinks. Ex–mental patient Bruno S. (*Strozek*) gives an outstanding performance as the bewildered and frustrated young man. With his wide-eyed stare and curious mind, Bruno's Kaspar begins as a childlike innocent, in touch with feelings most adults have long since buried. Herzog's documentary-style direction keeps Kaspar's experiences immediate, while cinematographer Jorge Schmidt-Reitwein's raw shots of the outdoors powerfully demonstrate man's interference with the delicate balance of nature.

RATING: *No MPAA rating, with nothing objectionable.*
AWARDS: *Grand Jury Prize at the 1975 Cannes Film Festival.*

THE MYSTERY OF PICASSO

(Video, subtitled)

★   ★   ½

Documentary

France   French

1956   76 Min.   Color

CREDITS: *Directed, written and produced by Henri-Georges Clouzot. Cinematography by Claude Renoir, partially filmed in Cinemascope. Music by Georges Auric. Narrated by Henri-Georges Clouzot. Released and distributed nontheatrically by The Samuel Goldwyn Company. Starring Pablo Picasso.*

Originally released in 1956, this documentary quickly faded into oblivion in the United States until its re-release in 1986. It's easy to understand why. The only "mystery" revealed about Picasso in *The Mystery of Picasso* is how he looks with his shirt off.

French director Henri-Georges Clouzot *(Les Diaboliques)* doesn't make much of an effort to uncover the inner workings of his famous subject. There are only a few interviews in this documentary, and most of them come across as incoherent ramblings. Otherwise, *The Mystery of Picasso* consists of the shirtless artist doing fifteen drawings and washes on a transparent surface, shot in fast motion from behind. This elaborate Picasso Etch-a-Sketch is set to a nondescript but loud soundtrack of Georges Auric's jazz and pop music.

Still, watching Picasso draw is fascinating. The first lines he lays down resemble doodles, but as the forms begin to take shape, Picasso's abstract genius powerfully emerges. Then just as we're about to forgive this film's shortcomings and become engrossed in the master's techniques, Picasso ruins each perfectly executed drawing by blotting it out with paint. It's painful to watch this destruction, and, combined with his forked tongue, it's easy to feel that the Picasso in this documentary is not the artist but the public figure who doesn't want us to take him or this movie very seriously.

RATING: *No MPAA rating, with nothing objectionable.*
AWARDS: *Special Jury Prize at the 1956 Cannes Film Festival.*
FILMNOTE: *This film has been declared a French National Treasure because all the pieces Picasso produced in this movie were immediately burned upon completion of the film.*

NATIVE SON
(Video)

★ ★ ½

Social Drama

U.S.A.

1987   112 Min.   Color

CREDITS: *Directed by Jerry Freedman. Written by Richard Wesley, based on the novel by Richard Wright. Produced by Diane Silver. Cinematography by Tom Burstyn. Released and distributed nontheatrically by Cinecom. Starring Victor Love,* Oprah Winfrey, Akosua Busia, Matt Dillon, Elizabeth McGovern and Geraldine Page.

This second film adaptation of *Native Son* is saddled with the same problems as Pierre Chanal's 1950 version of Richard Wright's powerful novel: too many clichéd characters. Set in Chicago in the 1940s, the story focuses on Bigger Thomas (Victor Love), a nineteen-year-old black man who lives with his mother (Oprah Winfrey) and two sisters in an unheated, rat-infested apartment on the South Side. Bigger is alienated and full of rage. But when he's hired to be a chauffeur-houseboy for the Daltons, a wealthy Hyde Park family, he puts a cap on his anger and plays the role of an accommodating "colored" servant.

As soon as Bigger starts his job, the Daltons let him know they're liberals. Their daughter, Mary (Elizabeth McGovern), is the worst. She and her leftist boyfriend (Matt Dillon) ride around with Bigger in their limo, patronizing and humiliating him with their good intentions. His hidden anger finally comes exploding to the surface and lands him in jail for a murder he didn't intend to commit. While waiting for his trial, Bigger finally comes to understand that "fear oppresses everyone . . . including the oppressors."

Certain scenes in *Native Son* suffer from a bad case of Hollywood sentiment, particularly the depiction of Bigger with his family in their one-room ghetto squalor. Director Jerry Freedman uses every opportunity he can to milk the most sympathy out of the tragic situations in Bigger's life. Oprah Winfrey, who turned in a strong performance in *The Color Purple,* is misused as Bigger's mother in this film, her character much too weepy to feel sincere. Matt Dillon and Elizabeth McGovern come off equally as bad as the budding leftist intellectuals who befriend Bigger. Fortunately, Love gives a surprisingly moving performance in his first screen role, resoundingly expressing his rage at the condescension of well-meaning liberals and his despair about his future in the ghetto. Freedman does not sugarcoat the violence in *Native Son* either; certain scenes in this movie are so graphic they are almost unbearable to sit through.

RATING: R for violence.
FILMNOTE: Richard Wright starred as Bigger in the 1950 Native Son.

NIGHT OF THE SHOOTING STARS

(Video, subtitled)

World War II Drama

Italy		Italian
1982	106 Min.	Color

CREDITS: Directed by Paolo and Vittorio Taviani. Written by Paolo and Vittorio Taviani, Giuliani G. DeNegri and Tonino Guerra. Produced by Giuliani G. DeNegri. Cinematography by Franco di Giacomo. Music by Nicola Piovani. Released by United Artists. Distributed nontheatrically by Films Inc. Starring Omero Antonutti, Margarita Lozano, Claudio Bigagili, Massimo Bonetti, Norma Martelli and Enrico Maria Modugno.

The Taviani brothers' *The Night of the Shooting Stars* is a series of vignettes involving simple farmers and shopkeepers from the Tuscan village of San Lorenzo who are caught up in the hysteria and hopes of the last days of World War II. Some are resistance fighters, while others have joined Mussolini's Fascists, but all the villagers are desperately waiting for the Americans to liberate their country from the Germans so they can carry on with their lives.

The film's central conflict involves an order for the town's inhabitants to gather in the safety of the church, while the Germans destroy a select number of homes in anticipation of the Allied advance. About half of the villagers don't trust the Germans and decide to sneak out of town that night to find the Americans. With their neighbors wishing them good luck, this rag-tag group sets out on a journey filled with touching and comical moments, until they run into returning Fascist soldiers and tragedy.

Franco di Giacomo's cinematography of the cultivated landscapes surrounding San

Lorenzo is magnificent in *Night of the Shooting Stars,* reminiscent of Impressionist scenery. There isn't a great deal of dialogue, but the film's performances are so rich that the actors are able to express emotion with few words. In one scene, for example, an anguished father displays his grief over his son's death by simply rubbing his face in dirt. The Taviani brothers also do a remarkable job of emphasizing that there are no villains or heroes in war, as the citizens of San Lorenzo are just as foolish, unlucky and fearful as the soldiers who finally alter their lives. And though their follies and foibles provide some absurdly funny comedy, the film's underlying message involves the travesty and senselessness of war.

RATING: R for violence and brief nudity.
AWARDS: Special Jury Prize at the 1982 Cannes Film Festival.
WARNING: The video version has excellent subtitles, but the cinematography is so important to the film that it is best seen on a large screen.

90 DAYS

(Video, partially subtitled)

Romantic Comedy

Canada		English and Korean
1986	90 Min.	Color

CREDITS: Directed by Giles Walker. Written by Giles Walker and David Wilson. Produced by Giles Walker and David Wilson. Edited by David Wilson. Cinematography by Andrew Kitzanuk. Music by Richard Gresko. Released and distributed by Cinecom. Starring Stefan Wodoslawsky, Christine Pak, Sam Grana and Fernanda Tavares.

90 Days follows the romantic misadventures of two Montreal bachelors and good friends, Blue and Alex. Blue (Stefan Wodoslawsky) is an office worker so desperate for a mate that he imports to Montreal a Korean woman he discovers in a mail-order bride magazine. Immigration gives them only ninety days to decide if they want to get married, but that's only the beginning of their problems. Blue and Hyank-Sook (Christine Pak) are very different from each other. He is frustrated when she refuses to sleep with him before marriage, and confused by the strange customs that have her waiting on him hand and foot. For her part, Hyank-Sook is puzzled by Blue's "womanly" affection for cooking and other chores, at the same time she feels trapped and bored in his apartment. After a series of nearly disastrous miscommunications, Blue and Hyang-Sook begin to understand each other, but by then the Immigration time clock is ticking away, and the bureaucratic red tape that they must unravel to keep Hyank-Sook in Canada becomes overwhelming.

Meanwhile, Alex (Sam Grana) is thrown out of the house by his wife for having a girlfriend on the side, and then hounded by a voluptuous lawyer representing a client looking for an Italian sperm donor for a $10,000 price. Alex doesn't care about the money, but he sure likes the looks of the lawyer (Fernanda Tavares). Of course, he hopes that he will have a chance to donate his sperm to her directly, but he soon discovers that a test tube is the only receptacle she has in mind.

The two plots—marriage-by-mail and money-for-sperm—both show how impersonal two life processes can become, yet director-writer Giles Walker handles these subjects very intimately. Much of the film's dialogue is improvised. The main characters stammer through their lines as if they are playing themselves and the camera is incidental. That's what makes 90 Days so special. Aside from the obtrusive, carnival-like music and some flat sex gags involving Alex's sperm donations, it is believable throughout. The characters, caught in embarrassing and uproarious faux pas, are consistently entertaining, while Walker builds his comedy naturally, simply allowing these ordinary people to react as any of us would in similar circumstances.

RATING: No MPPA rating, with sexual situations.

EL NORTE
(Video, partially subtitled)

Political Drama

U.S.A.   English and Spanish

1983   141 Min.   Color

CREDITS: Directed by Gregory Nava. Written by Gregory Nava and Anna Thomas. Produced by Anna Thomas for PBS's "American Playhouse." Cinematography by James Glennon. Music by Mahler, Verde, Samuel Barber, and The Folkloristas. Released by Island Alive. Distributed nontheatrically by Cinecom. Starring David Villalpando, Zaide Sylvia Gutierrez, Ernesto Gomez Cruz, Alicia del Lago, Enaclio Zepeda and Trinidad Silva.

One of the few American films to personalize the plight of Central American refugees, Gregory Nava and Anna Thomas's El Norte is the story of two teenaged Guatemalans, Enrique (David Villalpando) and his sister Rosa (Zaide Sylvia Gutierrez), who flee their homeland after their mother and father are killed by a right-wing death squad. En route to the United States, the frightened pair endure many difficulties traveling through Mexico, and when they finally arrive at the border, a guide they hire to take them across steals their money. In one of the most harrowing scenes of modern cinema, Enrique and Rosa end up crawling through sewer pipes full of snakes and rats to get to the States. Once they make it, however, their dreamed-of "land of opportunity" soon becomes a land of harassment and degradation.

El Norte takes place in three separate segments: in Guatemala, on the trip through Mexico and across the border, and finally in the United States. The first section is a rich look at the cultural life of Guatemalan villagers. The cinematography in this segment is particularly breathtaking, and the children's family is portrayed as loving and good. In contrast, the Mexico section is a jolting mixture of drugs, street crime and extreme poverty. And finally in America, Enrique and Rosa experience prejudice against Hispanics and illegal aliens and, for the first time, come to recognize the broad differences between rich and poor.

El Norte is not without its orchestrated sentiment, as certain scenes are set up to demand our sympathies. Enrique and Rosa can also be unbelievably gentle and naïve amid the terrible circumstances bombarding them. But their reactions don't lessen the impact of their experiences, and these are very real in *El Norte*. Filmmakers Nava and Thomas succeed in taking us to the heart of the daily struggles of Central American refugees in ways that few other filmmakers have attempted. We get to know Enrique and Rosa, and completely understand why they have to leave their homeland to come to the United States. In a broader sense, *El Norte* helps to transform the nameless faces of Central American refugees we see on the evening news into living, breathing human beings who are not immune to pain and suffering. *El Norte* is much more than a movie; it is an overwhelming plea for decency and justice.

RATING: *R for brief nudity, violence and language.*
AWARDS: *Grand Prize at the 1984 Montreal Film Festival.*
FILMNOTE: *Producer/writer Anna Thomas used the profits from her successful* Vegetarian Epicure *cookbooks to help finance* El Norte.

A NOS AMOURS
(Video, subtitled)

    ½

Coming-of-Age Drama

France	French
1984	99 Min.	Color

CREDITS: *Directed and produced by Maurice Pialat. Written by Maurice Pialat and Arlette Langmann. Cinematography by Jacques Loiseleux. Music by Klaus Nomy. Released by Triumph Films. Distributed nontheatrically by Swank Motion Pictures. Starring Sandrine Bonnaire, Dominique*

Besnehard, Maurice Pialat, Evelyne Ker, Anne-Sophie Maille, Christopher Odent, Cyr Boitard and Maite Maille.

Awarded the Caesar (the French Oscar) for Best Film in 1984, *A Nos Amours* is a disturbing exploration of a fifteen-year-old girl's attempts to come to terms with her parents' divorce and her own burgeoning sexuality.

Her name is Sandrine (*Vagabond's* Sandrine Bonnaire, in her first film), and in many ways she is a typical teen, arguing good-naturedly with her mother and chubby older brother while carrying on an innocent, playful romance with a young boy next door. But when her parents' marriage ends abruptly, and she is separated from the father she idolizes (played by director Maurice Pialat), Sandrine gradually falls apart. Her quarrels with her mother and brother turn bitter and violent. She overindulges in drugs and alcohol as she drifts through a series of abusive one-night stands, all the while rejecting the one boy who truly loves her. By the end, her shell is so hard that even her father can't reach the emotionally dead Sandrine.

A Nos Amours is both powerful and difficult. Bonnaire gives an intense performance as the disturbed young woman, and director Pialat *(Lulu, Police)* successfully uses improvisational dialogue and long takes to involve us in her exterior world. Yet, just as Sandrine is unreachable by the other characters in the film, she is also inaccessible to the audience. Sandrine doesn't confide in her friends, write in a journal or give any other clues to what's going on inside. In fact, Sandrine hardly expresses herself at all, except to show her anger, disillusionment or fear. And her relationship with her family simply isn't enough to explain her breakdown. Pialat makes the mistake of showing us too many of the surface symptoms of Sandrine's disease but doesn't dig deeply enough to discover the real causes.

RATING: *R for nudity, substance abuse, profanity and sex.*
AWARDS: *1984 French Caesar for Best Film.*

LA NUIT DE VARENNES
(Video, subtitled)

Historical Drama

France/Italy   French

1983   151 Min.   Color

CREDITS: *Directed by Ettore Scola. Written by Ettore Scola and Sergio Amidei. Produced by Renzo Rosselli. Cinematography by Armando Nannuzzi. Music by Armando Travajoi. Art direction by Dante Ferretti. Costume design by Gabriella Pescucci. Released by Triumph Films. Distributed nontheatrically by Swank Motion Pictures. Starring Harvey Keitel, Marcello Mastroianni, Hanna Schygulla, Jean-Louis Barrault, Jean-Claude Brialy, Daniel Gelin, Jean-Louis Trintignant, Eleanore Hirt and Michel Piccoli.*

La Nuit de Varennes is set in France in 1791, on the night Louis XVI (Michel Piccoli) and Marie Antoinette (Eleanore Hirt) escape arrest in Paris and race by coach to the countryside in hope of reclaiming the throne. When the famous writer Nicolas Restif (Jean-Louis Barrault) catches wind of their flight, he follows the royal couple by boarding another coach en route to Varennes. Joining him in pursuit are Countess Sophie de la Borde (Hanna Schygulla), a friend of Marie whose own future depends on the success of Louis, and Thomas Paine (Harvey Keitel), the American patriot who has come to France to foment another revolution. Along the way, the coach picks up the aging Casanova (Marcello Mastroianni), now a doddering, powdered clown running away from his job as court entertainer for a wealthy German baron.

As Louis and Marie, the four coach-mates, and a troop of soldiers converge on Varennes, the anticipation of an act that will change the course of mankind lies heavy in the air. "Anything could happen," Casanova solemnly suggests at one point, but very little does. *La Nuit de Varennes* is so poorly executed that even combining four famous historical figures with one of the most explosive political situations of the

century isn't enough to sweep us into the drama.

These characters have little chemistry among them, and the actors turn in mostly lifeless performances. Keitel, with his high voice and slight New York accent, stands out like a sore thumb in a role unbefitting his talent, while Schygulla must pitch a screaming fit to capture our attention. Only the two experienced veterans, Barrault and Mastroianni, get the better of the screenplay, delivering with their personal charisma what the script can't, while Scola *(We All Loved Each Other So Much, Le Bal)* also directs the film with typical élan and lavish cinematography. But in the end, his combination of American, French and German stars with a weak script comes across as a piece of romantic fluff in search of strong performances and solid direction.

RATING: *R for profanity and nudity.*

O LUCKY MAN!
(Video)

Social Satire

England

1973   173 Min.   Color

CREDITS: *Directed by Lindsay Anderson. Written by David Sherwin and Malcolm McDowell. Produced by Lindsay Anderson. Cinematography by Miroslav Ondricek. Music by Alan Price. Released by Warner Brothers. Distributed nontheatrically by Swank Motion Pictures. Starring Malcolm McDowell, Ralph Richardson, Rachel Roberts, Arthur Lowe, Helen Mirren, Alan Price, Colin Green, Clive Thacker, Dave Markee and Ian Leake.*

In this three-hour epic early seventies satire, director Lindsay Anderson portrays British class struggles through the misadventures of Mick Travis (Malcolm McDowell)—an ordinary man pitted against the powerful forces of capitalism.

This loosely formed sequel to *If . . .* begins as Travis lands a job as a salesman for

Imperial Coffee. He soon finds himself rubbing shoulders with a corrupt businessman (Arthur Lowe) who invites him to his private sex club, where the naïve Travis witnesses shocking X-rated movies and sex acts. Then, on his way to a business meeting in Scotland, Travis takes a wrong turn in his car and ends up at a top-secret military camp, where he's arrested, tortured and forced to sign a confession stating that he's a terrorist. Luckily, Travis escapes the camp just before it blows up, only to meet a crazed doctor who tries to use him for a dangerous medical experiment. He manages to flee the hospital as well and hitches a ride with a van full of hippies. He quickly falls in love with a flower child named Patricia (Helen Mirren) whose father is Sir Randolph James (Ralph Richardson), one of the wealthiest men in England. But when Travis becomes Sir Randolph's assistant, he becomes the fall guy for a chemical-weapons and slave-labor deal in Africa that lands him in prison.

Director Anderson uses the members of his cast to play several different roles throughout O Lucky Man! and, though this can be confusing at times, it also gives the story a whimsical feel that softens the disastrous events in Travis's life. But so many tragedies befall poor Travis that the narrative would be overwhelmingly depressing and absurdly unbelievable if McDowell weren't such a lovable straight man. As the hapless entrepreneur trying to make an honest living for himself while danger lurks around every corner, McDowell gives one his most entertaining performances. Within a short time span, he is devilish, debonair, naïve and goofy, but mostly he is sympathetic and comical. Alan Price's upbeat, sixties soundtrack frames Travis's predicaments brilliantly. And through Travis's often trauma-shocked eyes, Anderson skillfully shows how the common man is forced to struggle against the military, the government, big business and multinationals in order to survive.

RATING: R for adult situations, nudity and language.
AWARDS: 1973 British Academy Awards for Best Supporting Actor (Arthur Lowe) and Best Original Film Music (Alan Price).

THE OFFICIAL STORY
(Video, subtitled)

Political Drama

Argentina		Spanish
1985	112 Min.	Color

CREDITS: *Directed by Luis Puenzo. Written by Aida Bortnik. Produced by Historias Cinematograficas. Cinematography by Felix Monti. Distributed nontheatrically by Almi Pictures. Starring Norma Aleandro, Hector Alterio, Chunchuna Villafane, Analia Castro, Chela Ruiz, Hugo Arana and Maria Luisa Robledo.*

From 1976 to 1982, the military junta in Argentina abducted, tortured and murdered tens of thousands of its citizens. Many women who "disappeared" were pregnant or had very young infants at the time of their abduction, and the most desirable of their children were given to government supporters looking for children to adopt. "The Official Story" is about Alicia (Norma Aleandro), a middle-class mother who accidently learns that her adopted daughter is one of these children.

The film begins slowly, as the relationships among Alicia, her husband, Roberto (Hector Alterio), and daughter, Gaby (Analia Castro), are developed. Theirs is a stable family, caught up in the mundane details of everyday life. Roberto is a successful businessman and a loving father, while Alicia blindly teaches her high school history students a censored version of Argentina's recent past. But Alicia is jolted out of her complacency when an old friend, Ana (Chunchuna Villafane), returns after years of exile and tells of being tortured. Ana also plants a seed of doubt in Alicia's mind about her own role in the "dirty war" by exposing the junta's practice of giving babies to its right-wing supporters. After Alicia accidently meets a woman who carries a photo of her missing granddaughter that bears a marked resemblance to Gaby, she is plagued by guilt over what happened to her daughter's real mother. In putting the pieces of the puzzle together, Alicia comes to the horrifying realization that her husband has been secretly connected with right-wing death squads and has been lying to her for many years.

The Official Story is derived from real stories now surfacing about the atrocities committed by Argentina's ruling junta. The acting is superb, particularly Aleandro's portrayal of Alicia and Villafane's performance as her tormented friend. First-time Argentine director Luis Puenzo handles the movie's complicated issues of motherhood and betrayal brilliantly; the scene in which Alicia finally confronts her husband about their daughter and his politics is explosive. In the end, Alicia and Roberto's adoption of Gaby not only evolves into terrible personal tragedy, but it also symbolizes Argentina's collective guilt for tolerating, and even benefiting from, a dark time in that country's history.

RATING: No MPAA rating, with violence.
AWARDS: 1986 Academy Award for Best Foreign Film; 1986 Academy Award nomination for Best Original Screenplay (Aida Bortnik); award for Best Actress (Norma Aleandro) at the 1985 Cannes Film Festival; 1986 New York Film Critics Award for Best Actress (Aleandro).

LOS OLVIDADOS (THE YOUNG AND THE DAMNED)
(Video, subtitled)

Urban Crime Drama

Mexico		Spanish
1950	88 Min.	B&W

CREDITS: Directed by Luis Buñuel. Written by Luis Buñuel and Luis Alcoriza. Produced by Oscar Dancigers. Cinematography by Gabriel Figueroa. Distributed nontheatrically by Corinth Films. Starring Alfonso Mejia, Roberto Cobo, Estela India, Miguel Inclan, Jesus Navarro and Alma Delia Fuentes.

Driven to make a movie about abandoned barrio children after observing the wretched poverty in Mexico City's slums, Luis Buñuel barely scraped together a budget of 450,000 pesos to make *Los Olvidados*. The film not only became his own personal favorite, but it is acclaimed by many to be his best.

Based on real case histories Buñuel researched at a Mexico City reformatory, *Los Olvidados* is the story of two young teenagers whose fates fatally intersect. At the start of the film, Jaibo (Roberto Cobo), a vicious gang leader who has just broken out of the reformatory, is looking for the boy who was responsible for landing him in jail. After he finds the snitch, Jaibo coerces the new kid in his gang, Pedro (Alfonso Mejia), into helping him kill the traitor. Pedro is an abandoned child whose mother won't let him return home because she already has too many mouths to feed. But after he helps Jaibo murder the snitch, the gang leader becomes the boy's new master, prodding him to steal and commit other crimes, including beating up a blind beggar and robbing a man with no legs. Soon Pedro is consumed by fear, as he hides from both the police and the murderous Jaibo.

In an interview about *Los Olvidados*, Buñuel stated that he "loathed films that make the poor romantic and sweet." He more than compensated in the other direction in this film. Even though he tries to soften the narrative with love affairs and friendships, there is little about this story that is romanticized. Jaibo, the blind beggar and Pedro's mother may be victims of poverty, but they are also vicious. Even Pedro and other more sympathetic characters are capable of brutal violence.

Realizing that there are no happy endings for these homeless children, Buñuel wisely approaches his subjects with directness and without frills. He found both professional actors and actual slum dwellers to play his characters, and the performances are extremely convincing. He also shot the film in the heart of Mexico City's bombed-out slums, using hand-held camera shots to lend a documentary feel to certain scenes, and surreal, pastoral footage to provide a startling contrast. The result is one of the most frighteningly real portraits of impoverished children ever put on film.

RATING: No MPAA rating, with violence.
AWARDS: Award for Best Director (Luis Buñuel) at the 1951 Cannes Film Festival.
WARNING: Most video prints of Los Olvidados are public domain and unfortunately many have subtitles that are difficult to read.
FILMNOTE: Buñuel shot the entire film on the streets instead of in a studio, which was a rare occurrence during that era of filmmaking.

ONE SINGS, THE OTHER DOESN'T
(Video, subtitled)

Feminist Drama

France   French

1977   105 Min.   Color

CREDITS: *Directed, written and produced by Agnes Varda. Cinematography by Charlie Van Damme, Nurith Aviv and Elizabeth Prouvost. Music by Francois Wertheimer, Orchid and Vagna. Released and distributed by Almi Pictures. Starring Valerie Mairesse, Therese Liotard, Ali Raffi, Robert Dadies, Jean-Pierre Pellegrin and Francois Wertheimer.*

Although touted as a landmark feminist film when it was released in 1977, the once-timely issues touched upon in Agnes Varda's *One Sings, The Other Doesn't* aren't enough to make it compelling today.

The story follows the relationship between two women that spans a decade and a half. In 1962, seventeen-year-old Pauline (Valerie Mairesse) first becomes involved with twenty-two-year-old Suzanne (Therese Liotard) after Suzanne enlists the younger woman's help in raising money for an abortion. After Suzanne's photographer boyfriend hangs himself, the two friends are separated when Suzanne and her two children go to live on her peasant family's farm. They meet again ten years later at a pro-abortion rally in Paris where Pauline is per-forming as a singer for a popular feminist pop group. Suzanne, whose children are now old enough to go to school, works in a health clinic after years of studying, and eventually settles down with a pediatrician. Meanwhile, Pauline falls for a charming but chauvinistic Iranian. But after experiencing firsthand the horrible oppression of women in Iran, Pauline declares her independence as she and Suzanne are reunited by their common fight for women's rights.

Although writer/director Agnes Varda *(Vagabond)* has created some emotionally powerful movies, *One Sings, the Other Doesn't* isn't one of them. The story is extremely simplistic, full of stereotypes instead of real people. The men don't figure at all in the film except as foils for the two heroines fighting for emancipation. We never get to know Suzanne's photographer lover or learn why he commits suicide. The same is true for Pauline's Iranian husband. The choices the women make function more as statement than plot, while the Big Theme burden is joyless and uninvolving. Still, the acting by the two leads is quite good, since both actresses breathe enough life into their performances to make us empathize with their struggles. And it's hard to fault *One Sings, the Other Doesn't* for its intentions, even if they're not very well realized.

RATING: No MPAA rating, with nothing objectionable.

OUTRAGEOUS
(Video)

Social Drama

Canada

1977   100 Min.   Color

CREDITS: *Directed by Richard Benner. Written by Richard Benner, based on the short story "Making It" by Margaret Gibson. Produced by William Marshall and Hendrik J. Van Der Kolk. Cinematography by James B. Kelly. Music by Paul Hoffert. Starring Craig Russell (a Canadian female impersonator), Hollis McLaren, Richard Easley, Helen Shaver, Allan Moyle and David McIlwraith.*

The only outrageous thing about the two friends and roommates from Toronto who are the main characters in *Outrageous* is everyone else's reaction to them. Otherwise, Robin (Craig Russell), a transvestite, and Liza (Hillis McLaren), a schizophrenic, are just doing the best they can with their lives.

A more sincere relationship than Robin and Liza's would be hard to find, as they never hide their true feelings from each other. But because they aren't considered "normal," they are easily misunderstood by the people who have the greatest effect on them. Robin, for example, enjoys being a female impersonator and is very good at it, yet he is scorned by "regular" gays and his boss at the beauty shop. Liza, on the other hand, is sensitive, intelligent and responsible, but because she also has to fight off her other personality at some inappropriate moments, her therapist constantly threatens to recommit her to the mental hospital where she was "imprisoned" for eight years.

If you can ignore its low-budget technical problems—dark lighting, poor sound quality, etc.—*Outrageous* is well worth watching. McLaren's Liza and Russell's Robin are funny, intelligent, enormously appealing characters from the moment we meet them until the film's final scene. They are both so natural in their roles, it's as if they are playing themselves. Although we never stop empathizing with Liza and Robin, director Richard Benner doesn't allow us to pity them. Despite all of their hardships, they have a wonderful sense of playfulness and a unique perspective on what's important in life that is much more sane than that of the "normal" people in this movie. In the end, that's what makes them so outrageous.

RATING: R for nothing objectionable except that the MPAA probably deemed a movie about a transvestite too sensitive for teens.
AWARDS: Silver Bear for Best Actor (Craig Russell) at the 1977 Berlin Film Festival.

FILMNOTE: Spectrafilm released a 1987 sequel called Too Outrageous, *by the same director and featuring the same main actors.*

PADRE PADRONE
(Video, subtitled)

Cultural Drama

Italy		Italian
1977	114 Min.	Color

CREDITS: Directed by Vittorio and Paolo Taviani. Written by Vittorio and Paolo Taviani, based on the autobiographical writings of Gavino Ledda. Produced by Giuliani De Negri. Cinematography by Mario Masini. Released and distributed nontheatrically by Almi Pictures. Starring Omero Antonutti, Saverio Marconi, Marcella Michelangeli, Fabrizio Forte, Marino Cenna, Stanko Molnar and Nanni Moretti.

The Taviani brothers' *Padre Padrone* was the first film to win both the Grand Prize and the International Critics Prize at the Cannes Film Festival, and for good reason.

Based on the autobiographical writings of Italian scholar Gavino Ledda (Saverio Marconi), the film is a compelling story of a young Sardinian boy enslaved by his father's fears and prejudices. Gavino's father (Omero Antonutti) thinks that civilization and education are the work of the devil. When the young Gavino (Fabrizio Forte) is only five, his father storms into the schoolroom and drags away the boy, crying and wetting his pants. That day changes Gavino's life forever, for instead of getting an education, he is forced to spend his days and nights in the fields tending sheep, where he is severely beaten every time he disobeys his father. Soon the boy's spirit is broken to the point that he rarely speaks or shows emotion. At the age of twenty, he finally runs away from his father to join the army and begin his formal education.

Although Gavino breaks the chains of his childhood to become a scholar, there's little about his story that's life-affirming. As an adult, he is as deeply affected by his father as when he was a child, and everything about this film, from its melancholy regional music to its eerie shots of the solitude of nature, echoes Gavino's personal tragedy. As in *The Night of the Shooting Stars,* the Taviani brothers display an enormous talent for capturing raw, emotional moments in the daily existence of simple peasants. But they do too thorough a job presenting the boredom of Gavino's life as a shepherd. Although these beginning scenes are extremely realistic, the film gets bogged down with the sheer number of them. Still, the acting is excellent from start to finish. Antonutti's performance as Gavino's father is so intense that it doesn't take long for us to loathe him as much as Gavino does. With Marconi's Gavino, we live his every moment of pain and anguish, while the issues of love, dominance and powerlessness that consume his character are as complex as they are devastating.

RATING: *No MPAA rating, with mild violence and profanity.*
FILMNOTE: *The Taviani brothers, using both professional and local Sardinians for their cast, originally made* Padre Padrone *for Italian television.*

PARIS, TEXAS
(Video)

Psychological Drama

U.S.A.

1984   145 Min.   Color

CREDITS: *Directed by Wim Wenders. Written L. M. Kit Carson and Sam Shepard, based on Shepard's collection of short stories,* Motel Chronicles. *Produced by Don Guest. Cinematography by Robby Muller. Music by Ry Cooder. Released by Britain's Channel 4 and 20th Century Fox. Distributed nontheatrically by Films Inc. Starring Harry Dean Stanton, Dean Stockwell, Nastassja Kinski, Hunter Carson, Aurore Clement and Bernard Wicki.*

Paris, Texas opens on Travis (Harry Dean Stanton) catatonically stumbling around in the Southwest desert near Big Bend, Texas. A few scenes later he's rescued by his brother Walt (Dean Stockwell), who hasn't heard from him for years. Gradually, Travis snaps back to reality, and one of the first things he has to deal with is his son, Hunter (Karen Black's son, Hunter Carson), who's now living with Walt and his wife, Anne (Aurore Clement). Together, Travis and his son travel to Houston to find the mother.

Travis eventually discovers his wife, Jane (Nastassja Kinski), in a sex parlor in Houston, and in the movie's most powerful scene, she and Travis indirectly discuss their marriage (while she is behind a see-through mirror in a fantasy booth). Tainted with guilt, hurt and anger, the two remember the tremendous mental and physical abuse that occurred during the last months of their relationship. A few days later Jane and her son have a tearful reunion in a Houston hotel.

Even in these emotion-packed moments, only skeletal explanations are given for the couple's separation, desertion of the child and Travis's wandering. That's the intent of the filmmakers. German director Wim Wenders and cinematographer Robby Muller *(Down by Law)* team up with American playwright Sam Shepard to give us the ambiguities and calculated rhythms of a European film, set against the enormous expanse of the Southwest and the seediness of a Houston sex parlor. There is little fast-paced action or dialogue in *Paris, Texas,* and portions of its two and a half hours meander as listlessly as Travis in the desert. Yet powerful metaphors for loneliness, alienation and the impersonalization of modern society are everywhere in this movie, and the acting is tremendous from all the main characters. Although *Paris, Texas* is not a traditional romantic tragedy, as a poetic vision of love gone sour it's a masterpiece.

RATING: *R for nudity and language.*
AWARDS: *Grand Prize at the 1984 Cannes Film Festival; 1984 British Academy Award for Best Director (Wim Wenders).*

FILMNOTE: *Wenders traveled around the Southwest for three months before deciding on the right location to shoot the opening scene for* Paris, Texas.

PARTING GLANCES
(Video)

Gay Drama

U.S.A.

1986 90 Min. Color

CREDITS: *Directed, written and edited by Bill Sherwood. Produced by Yoram Mandel and Arthur Silverman. Cinematography by Jacek Laskus. Music by Brahms, Bronski Beat, Chopin, Strauss and Mahler. Released and distributed nontheatrically by Cinecom. Starring Richard Ganoung, John Bolger, Steve Buscemi, Kathy Kinney, Adam Nathan, Patrick Tull, Yolande Bavan, Richard Wall, Jim Selfe and Kistin Moneagle.*

Parting Glances is one of the most popular films on gay culture made in the United States, as well as one of the first to deal with AIDS. It tells the story of a twenty-four-hour period in the lives of three gay men in New York City. Michael (Richard Ganoung) and Robert (John Bolger) are lovers who have been living together for six years, but Robert abruptly decides to take a job with a world health organization in Africa and is leaving the next day. He tells Michael that his reasons for going are twofold: he's looking for adventure, and their relationship has gotten stale. But we soon learn there is another reason why Robert suddenly wants to leave the country. Michael's best friend is a musician named Nick (Steve Buscemi) who is dying of AIDS. Robert is jealous of how close they are becoming and is anxious to avoid competing for his boyfriend as Nick gets sicker.

Although there are no sentimental scenes of Nick suffering from his illness, *Parting Glances* touches upon many of the issues related to the disease. Perhaps the most important point writer/director Bill Sherwood makes is how many of Nick's friends abandon him at the same time they deny the time bomb that could be ticking inside of themselves. But *Parting Glances* isn't only an AIDS story. It's as much a film about choices gay men have to make concerning independence, commitment and promiscuity within their life-style in the eighties.

Sherwood approaches those subjects so thoughtfully and with so much heart that *Parting Glances* is hard to criticize. Yet his characters are too constantly upbeat, sarcastic and witty, and their nonstop one-liners act as a shield for the film's serious issues. Even though he is dying, Nick is the biggest comedian of all of them, but all the characters take their turns being onstage in this movie. It's particularly frustrating because most are nonstereotyped gays, yet we don't really spend enough serious time with them to get to know them.

RATING: *R for sexual content, nudity and profanity.*
AWARDS: *Grand Prize at the 1986 United States Film Festival.*

THE PASSENGER
(Video)

Psychological Drama

Italy

1975 123 Min. Color

CREDITS: *Directed by Michelangelo Antonioni. Written by Michelangelo Antonioni, Mark Peploe and Peter Wollen. Produced by Carlo Ponti. Cinematography by Luciano Tovoli, filmed in Cinemascope. Released by MGM/UA. Distributed nontheatrically by Films Inc. Starring Jack Nicholson, Maria Schneider, Jennie Runacre, Ian Hendry, Stephen Berkoff, Ambroise Bia, Jose Maria Cafarel and James Campbell.*

Although Jack Nicholson's career is full of Hollywood successes, his foray into the art house genre with director Michelangelo Antonioni *(Blow Up)* in *The Passenger* should be listed as one of his few failures.

Nicholson stars as David Locke, a noted television journalist covering a guerrilla movement in an unstable African country. Frustrated with his work and an unhappy marriage, Locke sees an escape route when a mysterious Englishman named Robertson suddenly dies at a desert hotel where the two men are staying. Switching passports and possessions, and guided by the dead man's appointment book, Locke assumes Robertson's identity as an arms merchant with ties to African rebels. Dutifully following Robertson's path to Barcelona, Locke becomes lovers with a beautiful, enigmatic woman (Maria Schneider of *Last Tango in Paris*) who joins him on his new adventures. Meanwhile, African agents are fast on the couple's trail in hopes of getting rid of this pesky gunrunner, and Locke's grieving and inquisitive wife searches for Robertson to find out what really happened to her "deceased" husband.

With much of *The Passenger* set in hauntingly beautiful northern African landscapes, Antonioni's visual genius is particularly evident in how he relates the film's stark scenery to the emotional barrenness of his characters. But little outside the visuals and settings in *The Passenger* is inspiring. Schneider is blank as Locke's girlfriend, while Jack Nicholson's talents as a volatile, expressive actor are wasted. Antonioni tries to make him into a brooding, detached cipher as he comes to terms with the meaning of life, but Nicholson never pulls it off convincingly. His lack of animation only further mummifies a narrative that too often rambles listlessly during incidental scenes and skims over important ones. Antonioni's structuralist obsessions and Nicholson's blasé performance mix like oil and water, and the result is a brilliantly photographed, soggy unpleasantness.

RATING: *PG, with nothing objectionable.*
WARNING: *The visuals are so important in* The Passenger *that its quality is lessened on video.*

PASSIONE D'AMORE (PASSION OF LOVE)
(Video, dubbed)

Historical Romance

Italy/France	Italian
1982	117 Min.	Color

CREDITS: *Directed by Ettore Scola. Written by Ettore Scola and Ruggero Maccari, based on the novel* Fosca *by Iginio Ugo Tarchetti. Cinematography by Claudio Ragona. Music by Armando Trovajoli. Costume design by Gabriella Pescucci. Released by Putnam Square. Starring Bernard Giraudeau, Valeria D'Obici, Laura Antonelli, Jean-Louis Trintignant, Massimo Girotti, Bernard Blier and Gerardo Amato.*

Passione d'Amore is more an overheated costume drama than the impassioned view of romantic obsession that writer/director Ettore Scola intended it to be.

Set in 1862 at the end of Italy's war with Russia, the film begins as a heroic cavalryman named Giorgio (Bernard Giraudeau) is separated from his beautiful lover, Clara (Laura Antonelli), when he is transferred to a remote mountain outpost. At first, Giorgio feels desperately lonely and isolated, but he soon becomes fascinated with his colonel's cousin, Fosca (Valeria D'Obici), an unattractive, sickly woman who has never experienced love but who emanates a haunting power nevertheless. Warned by the camp doctor (Jean-Louis Trintignant) that a broken heart might kill her, Giorgio is horrified when his offer of friendship is returned by Fosca with obsessive love. Persuaded by the doctor at least to pretend affection in order to save her, Giorgio's life comes unglued as his relationship with Fosca alienates both his lover and his commander and sets him on an ultimately fatal course.

Passione D'Amore is a film that perhaps could only be made in Italy. Sentimental, sweaty and emotionally overwrought, the whole narrative is little more than an Italian version of "As the World Turns." Borrowing from the greatest director of Italian melodramas, Luchino Visconti (*The Innocent*), Scola (*Le Bal*) and his cinematographer Claudio Ragona fill the screen with scenic landscapes; wild, expressive tracking shots; and close-ups, although these techniques can't pump needed emotion into the story. While lavishly costumed by Gabriella Pescucci, Giraudeau and D'Obici are hysterical and exaggerated. Only Trintignant and Antonelli give controlled performances, and their characters leave the most lasting impression. Unfortunately, most of the rest of *Passione D'Amore* is forgettable, right down to its predictably tragic conclusion.

RATING: No MPAA rating, with nothing objectionable.
WARNING: The dubbing on the video version is only fair and does detract from the quality of the movie.
AWARDS: Special Jury Prize at the 1982 Cannes Film Festival.

PATHER PANCHALI (SONG OF THE ROAD)

(*Video, subtitled*)

Cultural Drama

India		Bengali
1956	112 Min.	B&W

CREDITS: Directed and produced by Satyajit Ray. Written by Satyajit Ray, based on the novel by Bibhuti Bannerji. Cinematography by Subrata Mitra. Music by Ravi Shankar. Released by The West Bengali Government/Edward Harrison. Distributed nontheatrically by Films Inc. Starring Karuna Banerji, Subir Banerji, Kanu Banerji, Umas Das Gupta, Chunibali Devi, Reva Devi and Rama Gangopadhaya.

Pather Panchali is the debut feature of Indian director Satyajit Ray, and the first of his famous Apu trilogy (*Aparajito, The World of Apu*). Set in a Bengali village in 1915, the story focuses on Sarbojaya (Karuna Banerji), a woman from an impoverished family who struggles to raise her son and daughter by herself while her husband (Kanu Banerji), a Brahman priest, travels to find work. The mother's life is already made difficult by natural disasters and sickness, but her young son Apu (Subir Banerji) is always running away to observe trains, the theater and any other semblance of culture that finds its way into their simple community. In addition, her daughter, Durga (Umas Das Gupta), turns into a kleptomaniac, and her elderly sister, Indirtharkun (Chunibala Devi), who also lives with them, is the town beggar. Eventually, Saribojaya has to sell her only valuables so that the family can eat and, in what seems like a heartless act, bans her sister from their home for embarrassing the family. But underlying most of these actions is her love for her children, and self-pride because of her Brahman class.

Pather Panchali started a new movement in Hindi filmmaking called "parallel cinema" or Indian neorealism. Several scenes in this film are oppressively authentic, while others are as slow and devoid of action as life probably was in a Bengali village in 1915. But Ray peppers the narrative with delightful slices of life, such as children lost in their own world, or close-ups of water bugs on the surface of a pond. The sets are simple and real, and though the acting is understated, it is excellent. In fact, nothing about this film smacks of pretention. Ray is so adept at capturing Indian village life, complete with its joys and tragedies, that we feel for his characters as if they were our own neighbors, and by the end of *Pather Panchali* we're aching to know what will become of them.

RATING: No MPAA rating, with nothing objectionable.
WARNING: The subtitles on the video version are a little difficult to read. Because of this and the importance of the cinematography, it's best to see this on a large screen.
FILMNOTE: An artist originally hired to illustrate a children's book version of Pather Panchali, Ray was so excited about making the story into a film that he ventured into it with virtually no money and a crew just as inexperienced as he.

PAULINE AT THE BEACH
(Video, subtitled)

 ½

Coming-of-Age Romance

France   French

1983   94 Min.   Color

CREDITS: *Directed and written by Eric Rohmer. Produced by Amanda Langlet. Cinematography by Nestor Almendros. Music by Jean-Louis Valero. Released by Orion. Distributed nontheatrically by Films Inc. Starring Amanda Langlet, Arielle Dombasie, Pascal Gregory, Feodor Atkine, Simon de la Brosse and Rosette.*

The third of Eric Rohmer's "Comedies and Proverbs" series *(The Aviator's Wife, Le Beau Mariage)*, *Pauline at the Beach* follows two cousins on their romantic escapades during a summer vacation. The younger, fifteen-year-old Pauline (Amanda Langlet), has a sweet relationship with a boy her own age (Simon de la Brosse). It is her cousin Marion (Arielle Dombasle) who has the problems. An attractive divorcee in her late twenties, she falls for a debonair, fortyish man (Feodor Atkine), who sneaks out for sexual rendezvous with a sexy candy seller he meets on the beach. Later one of Marion's old boyfriends—a handsome but immature wind surfer (Pascal Gregory)—shows up, practically begging Marion to come back to him.

Billed as a farce, *Pauline at the Beach* has some funny moments when the main characters get caught with their pants down. There are also some warm scenes involving Pauline's coming of age. But *Pauline at the Beach* is mostly a story of misunderstandings, jealousies and anger. Of the six main characters, Pauline turns out to be the most well-adjusted of the bunch, but it's hard to swallow her self-confidence as she and her fifteen-year-old boyfriend unabashedly have sex for the first time in their lives. The character who becomes most tiresome is Marion's old wind-surfing beau. He hounds Marion to the point of boredom. And Marion is so helplessly self-absorbed that it's easy to lose

patience with her as well. But the main problem with *Pauline at the Beach* is that Rohmer doesn't dig as deeply into his characters' vulnerabilities as he has in his other films. This lack of depth makes us care little about the romantic misfortunes that take over their lives.

RATING: *R for nudity and sex.*

PERSONA
(Video, subtitled)

Psychological Drama

Sweden   Swedish

1966   85/90 Min.   B&W

CREDITS: *Directed, written and produced by Ingmar Bergman. Cinematography by Sven Nykvist. Music by Lars-Johan Werle. Released by Lopert Films. Distributed nontheatrically by several companies including Films Inc. and Corinth Films. Starring Bibi Andersson, Liv Ullmann, Gunnar Bjornstrand, Margaretha Krook and Joseph Lindstrom.*

Hailed by many as Bergman's true masterpiece, *Persona* is certainly one of his most meticulously crafted character studies. The film is about Elizabeth Volger (Liv Ullmann), a famous Swedish stage actress who, for no apparent reason, stops talking in the middle of one of her performances. She completely withdraws into herself from that moment on. Finding nothing physically wrong with her, her doctors urge her to rest at a secluded seaside resort with Sister Alma (Bibi Andersson), a young, inexperienced nurse and long-time fan of the actress, who has been hired to care for her.

Isolated from everyone but each other, the two women develop an intense symbiotic relationship. Alma compensates for her patient's silence by talking to Elizabeth all day long. In a rambling monologue, Alma reveals her innermost secrets to the actress, exposing her feelings of alienation and insecurity about her sexuality. Gradually, the two begin to exchange roles, as the silent

Elizabeth tries to comfort her emotionally tortured nurse, while both are hounded by dreams and hallucinations that they are merging into one person.

In *Persona*, as in many of his other films, Bergman displays an uncanny ability to expose the dark reaches of a character's psyche, layer by layer. It's not until after you really reflect on this film that all of the story's implications fully sink in. By combining footage of early cartoons, slapstick silent movie clips and nightmarish visions full of religious symbolism, Bergman deepens our understanding of his two main characters while he gives his film necessary visual punch. The cinematography, by Bergman regular Sven Nykvist, is stunning, as his use of camera angles and lighting makes the two women's resemblance grow stronger as the ending draws near. But it's the performances of Ullmann and Andersson that make this film so captivating. Essentially a two-woman show, both actresses bring to their characters a broad spectrum of expressions and emotions that is very impressive.

RATING: No MPAA rating, with mild violence.
WARNING: Because this is a public domain movie, video versions will vary in quality. The subtitling is so poorly done in Persona *that it is often used as a classic example of how white letters on a white background make it virtually impossible to read subtitles (a problem that subtitlers have fortunately been working to solve in the last few years). During the film's final scenes in which the two women begin to turn into one another, the dialogue is so difficult to read that you better have a Swedish friend with you to interpret.*

PERSONAL SERVICES
(Video)

Sex Farce

England

1986   104 Min.   Color

CREDITS: Directed by Terry Jones. Written by Terry Jones, David Leland and Cynthia Payne. Produced by Tim Bevan. Cinematography by Roger Deakens. Edited by George Akers. Released and distributed nontheatrically by Vestron Pictures. Starring Julie Walters, Shirley Stelfox, Alex McCowen and Danny Schiller.

In *Personal Services,* the director of several *Monty Python* movies (Terry Jones), the producer of *My Beautiful Laundrette* (Tim Bevan) and the screenwriter of *Mona Lisa* (David Leland) team up to make a highly irreverent satire of the sexual exploits of the British upper class.

The story begins in a London slum, where the prudish Christine (*Educating Rita*'s Julie Walters) struggles to eke out a living waitressing at a diner. When her elderly landlord offers an alternative to paying the rent, Christine begins servicing the old man as an agreeable way to make ends meet. But this new moonlighting gets out of hand when Christine is coerced into the call girl business full-time by her two best friends, Shirley (Shirley Stelfox) and Dolly (Alec McCowen), an army man who has taken to transvestism in retirement. Eventually, when a wealthy customer helps them buy a suburban house, the three become partners in a successful brothel specializing in kinky personal services. But this is a mixed blessing, for as a clientele of prominent citizens flock to the house, Christine, Dolly and Shirley must deal with all kinds of weirdos, nosy neighbors and, finally, the obligatory raid by the police.

Based on the highly publicized sexual exploits of Cynthia Payne, a woman known as the "luncheon voucher madam" in British tabloids, *Personal Services* takes some sharp jabs at lecherous men of all kinds, particularly the ruling elite. Much of the humor comes from the ludicrous sexual situations in which Christine and her friends become enmeshed, but because many of the film's characters are caricatures and not real people, this one joke wears thin at times. In scenes of bondage and other perversities, it's not always clear if we are supposed to laugh or be shocked. Also, too many unimportant subplots are introduced that have little connection to the main story and then are never mentioned again. Still, Walters is a wonderful combination of hapless madam and character from a Barbara Cartland novel, and McCowen is so convincing as Christine's transvestite friend that we're as surprised as Christine is to discover his real sex.

RATING: R for nudity, profanity and sexual situations.

PICNIC AT HANGING ROCK

Occult Mystery

Australia

1980   110 Min.   Color

CREDITS: Directed by Peter Weir. Written by Cliff Green, based on the novel by Joan Lindsay. Produced by Jim and Hal McElroy. Cinematography by Russell Boyd. Costume design by Judy Dorsman. Music by Bruce Smeaton. Released by Atlantic. Distributed nontheatrically by Films Inc. Starring Rachel Roberts, Helen Morse, Jackie Weaver, Anne Lambert, Margaret Nelson, Vivean Grey, Dominic Guard and Kristy Child.

Peter Weir's Picnic at Hanging Rock starts out as a promising metaphysical mystery. After a long prologue that introduces us to the students at a turn-of-the-century Australian girls school, we watch four of them go for a walk to the top of Hanging Rock during a school outing on Valentine's Day. Suddenly, a cloud enshrouds them, they all feel the urge to nap and, when they awaken, three of them continue to hike up the rock and are never seen

again. The fourth is so frightened by what has happened that she can never express what she's experienced. Shocked by the girls' disappearance, the teachers and classmates, as well as peace officers from the town near their school, do all they can to find them. But it's as if the girls have simply evaporated.

Many viewers find this movie frustrating because its entire focus is the girls' disappearance—a mystery with few clues and no resolution. And at times, that fateful hike is replayed to the point of tedium. Yet the unsolved mystery is the point of the narrative. Weir uses it to show how the adults and the girls can't stand the fact that they have no answers to why the three girls disappeared, just as they can't stand their lack of control over the wilderness or their less-refined sexual impulses. Weir and his cinematographer Russell Boyd brilliantly capture the Australian boarding school as a prison of manners and unnatural behavior, at the same time as they portray the haunting, uncontrollable beauty of Hanging Rock. The scary and beautiful atmosphere they create gives them license to overstep the bounds of a conventional story.

RATING: PG, with nothing objectionable.

PIXOTE
(Video, subtitled)

Urban Drama

Brazil   Portuguese

1980   127 Min.   Color

CREDITS: Directed by Hector Babenco. Written by Hector Babenco and Jorge Duran, based on the novel Infancia Dos Mortos by Jose Luzeiro. Produced by Sylvia Naves. Cinematography by Rodolfo Sanches. Music by John Neschling. Released by Unifilm. Distributed nontheatrically by New Yorker Films. Starring Fernando Ramos da Silva, Marilia Pera, Jorge Juliao, Gilberto Moura, José Nilson dos Santos, Edilson Lino, Zenildo Oliveira Santos, Claudio Bernardo, Tony Tornada and Jardel Filho.

At the beginning of *Pixote*, director Hector Babenco *(Kiss of the Spider Woman)* tells us there are three million homeless children in Brazil, many of whom will turn to crime to survive. Protected from prosecution until they're eighteen, the worst that can happen to them is incarceration in a reformatory, but when we visit one of these reformatories in the movie's next scene, we discover that boys from ten to seventeen are beaten by guards, raped by other boys, knifed and even killed. Among them is ten-year-old Pixote (Fernando Ramos da Silva), and after what seems like a long and terrifying stay at this prison, Pixote and some of his friends escape. Once they are out on the streets, they fulfill Babenco's prophecy by stealing, pushing, pimping and murdering.

Although often compared to Buñuel's *Los Olvidados, Pixote* isn't as moving because its story simply isn't as complex. Babenco spares us none of the graphic details of these young boys' lives. The screen is full of blood, drugs and perverted sex. And he introduces us to this hell on earth so that we can't help but see their tragic world in ways that makes it a little tougher to pass judgment on the urban poor. Yet, because there is only a sketch of a plot to tie these shocking events together, *Pixote* doesn't always sustain itself for its two-hour duration. Still, the acting is excellent. Many in the cast are children from the slums, and though they are screen amateurs they are experts at expressing suffering and abuse.

RATING: R for violence, nudity and explicit sex.
AWARDS: Special Festival Prize at the 1980 Lucarno Film Festival; 1981 New York Film Critics Award for Best Foreign Film.
FILMNOTE: Fernando Ramos da Silva, the lead character in Pixote, *was killed in August 1987 in a scuffle with Rio police in which, they stated, he pulled a gun on them; other witnesses claim he was shot in the back while fleeing.*

PLAYTIME
(Video, dubbed)

Social Satire

France

1973   108 Min.   Color

CREDITS: *Directed by Jacques Tati. Written by Jacques Tati, Jacques Lagrange and Art Buchwald. Produced by Rene Silvera. Cinematography by Jean Badal and Andreas Winding. Music by Francis Lemarque and James Campbell. Set design by Eugene Roman. Released by Spectrafilms and Janus Films. Distributed nontheatrically by Films Inc. Starring Jacques Tati, Barbara Dennek, Jacqueline Lecomte, Verlerie Camille, Frace Romilly, Frace Delahalle, Laure Paillette and Colette Proust.*

In the 1950s, Jacques Tati made warmly funny comedies such as *Mon Oncle* and *Monsieur Hulot's Holiday,* but twenty years later in *Playtime,* he sees a much crueler world.

Like his other films, *Playtime* is a series of vignettes with virtually no plot line or dialogue. It begins as a busload of American tourists arrives in Paris. While her seatmate happily snaps pictures of skyscrapers, the heroine of the story, Barbara (Barbara Dennek), is saddened by the sameness of the buildings outside the bus. Visiting a trade show, Barbara crosses the path of Mr. Hulot (Tati), a pipe-smoking Frenchman who gets lost in a maze of gray cubicles and corridors on his way to an important business appointment. Later that evening, Barbara and Hulot run into each other again while dining at a brand-new restaurant where the heating system runs amok and pieces of the ceiling fall on unflinching diners. Finally, in one of the film's few optimistic moments, Barbara and Mr. Hulot find happiness in her simple piano playing, and in a shared a moment of friendship.

In *Playtime,* like his other films, Tati constructs a visual world that is rich in texture, sound, rhythm and color. Obviously disheartened by modern Paris, he exaggerates its enormous impersonalization and inefficiency and shows the city's most famous landmarks only as trapped in the reflections of overpowering skyscrapers. Many of the film's set pieces are sharply satirical and clever, yet in portraying such a sterile world, Tati also drains much of the life out of his film. Devoid of any traditional narrative and dialogue, minutes drag by in *Playtime* with little action or character development, leaving only Tati's technical brilliance to sustain our interest. Although it often does, the film could use less flash and more laughs.

RATING: No MPAA rating, with nothing objectionable.
WARNING: Because there is so little dialogue in the film, the dubbing on the video version isn't distracting even to those who prefer subtitles.
FILMNOTE: Tati took over ten years to make this movie. His sets were so costly that he had to hock the rights to three other films to raise desperately needed capital. Unfortunately, Playtime *was a box office failure.*

THE PLOUGHMAN'S LUNCH
(Video)

 ½

Political Romance

England

1984　　　　107 Min.　　　　Color

CREDIT: *Directed by Richard Eyre. Written by Ian McEwan. Produced by Simon Relph and Ann Scott. Cinematography by Clive Tickner. Music by Dominic Muldowney. Released by Greenpoint Films and Britain's Channel 4. Distributed nontheatrically by The Samuel Goldwyn Company. Starring Jonathan Pryce, Tim Curry, Rosemary Harris, Charlie Dore, Frank Finlay, David De Keyser, Bill Paterson, Margaret Thatcher and Nat Jackley.*

Although an English ploughman's lunch consists of simple fare, such as cheese and bread, Richard Eyre's *The Ploughman's Lunch* is anything but a simple movie.

The film opens when BBC journalist James Penfield (Jonathan Pryce of *Brazil*) campaigns on both personal and professional fronts, first pitching his idea for a book on the 1956 Suez Crisis to a publisher, and then wooing a beautiful socialite named Suzy Banington (Charlie Dore). James is relentless in his pursuit of both prizes, ignoring his mother's serious illness to accompany Suzy on a visit to her own mother, Ann (Rosemary Harris), who also happens to be a Suez historian. Prodded by his best friend, Jeremy (Tim Curry), and mysteriously avoided by Suzy, James is soon trapped in a loveless affair with Ann, which he is reluctant to break off because she can give him invaluable help with his book. While covering a Conservative Party Conference where Margaret Thatcher fuels party patriotism, James becomes suspicious of betrayal by Jeremy and Suzy. Realizing that he, like Egypt, is a victim of callous British deceit, James begins scrambling to save his self-respect.

Made at the height of the Falklands war, *The Ploughman's Lunch* is full of references to the crisis England faced at the time. At the conference, for example, when Thatcher exhorts her constituency to close its eyes while she engages in a thoughtless war, director Richard Eyre and screenwriter Ian McEwan draw a parallel between Britain abandoning its allies and the characters in the movie betraying each other. Yet, as powerfully as this point is made, the film doesn't sustain a heightened level of tension or interest. Although we certainly feel James's torment, particularly when he is trapped by Ann, too much energy is wasted on his brooding and on his slow-building relationship with Suzy. This leisurely pace saps the film of the intensity created by its themes of betrayal and deceit, while Pryce's James is often too bland to express consistently the inner turmoil of his character.

RATING: R for nudity and sex.
FILMNOTE: The Thatcher speech at the Party conference is documentary footage shot by director Richard Eyre.

THE PLUMBER
(Video)

Psychological Thriller

Australia

1980   76 Min.   Color

CREDITS: *Directed and written by Peter Weir. Produced by Matt Carroll. Cinematography by David Sanderson. Music by Gerry Tolland. Released by the South Australian Film Corp/Cinema Ventures. Starring Judy Morris, Ivar Kants, Robert Coleby, Candy Raymond and Henri Szeps.*

For anybody who's ever had his or her house broken into, or personal life intruded upon, Peter Weir's *The Plumber* is an all-too-real bad dream. This nightmare begins for Jill Cowper (Judy Morris) when a plumber named Max (Ivar Kants) shows up at her apartment door and insists on checking her pipes. A few minutes later he takes a sledgehammer to her bathroom walls. After every pipe in her bathroom is exposed, Max notifies a stunned Jill that it's going to take him several days to fix her plumbing. With her bathroom completely torn apart, what choice does Jill have? But Max is a pretty strange guy to have around the house.

As soon as he implants himself in her house, Jill's life takes a darker turn. He hints to Jill that he has served time in prison, seems always to be around the corner when she is dressing, and knows a few too many personal details about her life. It doesn't take long for Jill to become wary, but Max interprets Jill's behavior as that of somebody who is too upperclass to have anything to do with a low-life tradesman like him.

Originally made for Australian TV, *The Plumber* is extremely clever and creepy at the same time. The performances by both main characters are intense, and the camera angles and music very effectively contribute to the film's suspense. It's never really clear whether Jill has reason to be afraid, or whether she is overreacting—what goes on between the two of them can be looked at both ways. Weir leads us around with our

arms behind our backs for the entire movie, and as the double entendres and misunderstandings pile up, each one becomes more frightening and humorous than the last. By the end, we are ready to yell "give!"

RATING: *No MPAA rating, with brief nudity.*

POETRY IN MOTION
(Video)

Documentary

U.S.A.

1982   91 Min.   Color

CREDITS: *Directed by Ron Mann. Produced by Ron Mann and John Giorno. Cinematography by Robert Fresco. Released and distributed nontheatrically by Almi Pictures. Starring Helen Adam, Miguel Algarin, Amiri Baraka, Ted Berrigan, Charles Bukowski, William Burroughs, John Cage, Jim Carroll, Jayne Cortez, Robert Creeley, Christopher Dewdney, Diane DiPrima, Kenward Elmslie, 4 Horsemen, Allen Ginsberg, John Giorno, Michael McClure, Ted Milton, Michael Ondantje, Ed Sanders, Ntozake Shange, Gary Snyder, Tom Waits and Ann Waldman.*

Webster's Dictionary defines poetry as "language chosen and arranged to create a specific emotional response." The two dozen poets who read their work in *Poetry in Motion* mean to shock and entertain, as well as to enlighten.

Charles Bukowski begins by saying that he has read all the great poets and they give him a "headache." Others similarly criticize their profession, yet they all give their best in this movie. The lineup reads like a *Who's Who* of modern American poets, as every imaginable style and type of poetry is represented—from straight podium readings to metaphoric political grandstanding to poetry set to music.

Some of them are quite good, others a little pretentious. But each reading or interview lasts only five minutes, and the thought-provoking, entertaining and outrageous ones far outnumber the less interesting ones. Of special note are Helen Adam's "Cheerless Junkie Song," Allen Ginsberg's "Birdbrain" and Tom Waits's rendition of "By the Time I Make New Jersey, You'll Be in Heaven." (Particularly irritating is the 4 Horsemen's loud, screechy noise performance). Mixed in with the performances are director Ron Mann's interviews with the poets about the nature of their work and the direction their lives have taken, and these segments are as fascinating as the readings. If you aren't a student of contemporary poetry, "Poetry in Motion" serves as an excellent introduction. If you are, it's orgasmic.

RATING: No MPAA rating, with poetic profanity.

PRICK UP YOUR EARS
(Video)

Gay Drama

England

1987   111 Min.   Color

CREDITS: Directed by Stephen Frears. Written by Alan Bennet, based on the biography of Joe Orton by John Lahr. Produced by Andrew Brown. Cinematography by Oliver Stapleton. Released and distributed nontheatrically by The Samuel Goldwyn Company. Starring Gary Oldman, Alfred Molina, Vanessa Redgrave, Julie Walters and Wallace Shawn.

Prick Up Your Ears is ostensibly a biography of famed British playwright Joe Orton (Gary Oldman of Sid and Nancy), but the narrative shows little concern for the story of a struggling artist. Instead, the film opens when two dead bodies are discovered in a ramshackle London flat, and then proceeds to recount the events leading up to those deaths by portraying Orton's relationship with Kenneth Halliwell (Alfred Molina), a pudgy, balding man who was Orton's roommate and lover.

At first, the two are very close, with the older Kenneth prodding the raw but talented Joe to read books important to pursuing a writing career. But in the following years, after Kenneth's encouragement inspires Joe to write hits such as Loot, Kenneth becomes an expendable, shrewish housewife who complains while dusting and sulks when he isn't invited to a dramatists' award dinner. Joe also loses interest in Kenneth sexually and zealously pursues quick tricks and casual affairs in public bathrooms and tube stations. Confronted by infidelity and obsolescence, Kenneth is finally driven to madness.

A mostly excellent drama, Prick Up Your Ears is marred only by clunky flashback sequences. In these, Joe's biographer, John Lahr (Wallace Shawn of My Dinner with Andre), tries to piece together the author's life. Even though they give us the charismatic Vanessa Redgrave as Orton's agent, they also bring too many unneeded characters into the movie and infect it with an irritating voice-over narration.

But like My Beautiful Laundrette, this film is blessed with the nearly flawless camera work of cinematographer Oliver Stapleton and the dry, sardonic humor of director Frears. In the opening scene, for example, Stapleton captures the two bodies in shadows, as the shocked expressions of those who discovered the corpses fill the frame and a policeman casually comments, "Someone's been playing silly buggers." Even more impressive is a surreal pickup scene with Joe in a dark public bath. But the soul of the film is in the performances of Molina and Oldman. Although both can be wildly funny, their personalities are tragically flawed and demand our sympathies every moment we observe their bizarre lives together.

RATING: R for nudity, profanity, violence and homosexual sex.

A PRIVATE FUNCTION
(Video)

Social Satire

England

1985   94 Min.   Color

CREDITS: *Directed by Malcolm Mow-bray. Written by Alan Bennet. Produced by Mark Shivas. Cinematography by Tony Pierce-Roberts. Released by Island Alive/Handmade Films. Distributed nontheatrically by New Yorker Films. Starring Michael Palin, Maggie Smith, Denholm Elliot, Liz Smith, Richard Griffiths, John Normington and Bill Paterson.*

Although strict food rationing is in effect in post–World War II England, the wealthy citizens of Yorkshire are saving a pig for a celebration honoring the marriage of then Princess Elizabeth. When Gilbert (Michael Palin), the town's put-upon chiropodist (clipper of toenails), accidentally discovers the pig, he decides to steal it to tweak the snobs who treat him like a nitwit slug.

But when Gilbert gets the pig home, his prize backfires (literally as well as figuratively). Gilbert's shrill wife (Maggie Smith), who had complained when their kitchen was porkless, becomes a screaming maniac with the live pig grunting underfoot. She demands that Gilbert slaughter the pig, but he doesn't have the heart to butcher the little guy. As days pass, it becomes increasingly difficult to hide a squealing pig in their kitchen, particularly when the whole town is looking for it. Then, to make matters worse, the ungrateful porker gets diarrhea.

Some of the gags in *A Private Function* are a little obscure, and you might not find them funny unless you are familiar with British colloquialisms. Also, the film resembles the old "Monty Python" TV show for running its clever jokes into the ground, as several of the movie's funniest routines are ruined when they're given too much time.

But the premise for this movie—well-heeled citizens obsessed with a pig—is an ideal setup for a satire of the class-conscious Brits. In his first outing, director Malcolm Mowbray is skilled at finding the wry humor in the situation, but what makes this movie amusing is its odd assortment of characters. Michael Palin is hilarious as the chiropodist who primps in front of the mirror and carefully rides off on his bicycle to clip rich women's toenails. Maggie Smith epitomizes a status-conscious housewife who desperately wants to rise out of the middle class. And a good number of Yorkshire's townspeople are quite funny as upper-class snobs.

RATING: *R for vileness.*
AWARDS: *1984 British Academy Awards for Best Actress (Maggie Smith), Best Supporting Actress (Liz Smith), and Best Supporting Actor (Denholm Elliot).*

PRIVATE PRACTICES: THE STORY OF A SEX SURROGATE
(Video)

Documentary

U.S.A.

1985   75 Min.   Color

CREDITS: *Directed and produced by Kirby Dick. Cinematography by Christine Burril and Catherine Colson. Edited by Lois Freeman. Released and distributed nontheatrically by Kino International. Starring Maureen Sullivan and Christopher and John (last names are withheld to protect their privacy).*

Private Practices is a documentary about an increasingly common and controversial new therapy—the use of a surrogate (a paid sex partner) for treating sexual dysfunction in adults.

Professional surrogate Maureen Sullivan and two of her clients, Christopher and John, agreed to be interviewed and have several of their sessions filmed over a four-month period. John is a recently divorced forty-five-year-old schoolteacher whose sex life in his marriage had never been fulfilling, and his wife hadn't hesitated to let him know her feelings about his inadequacy. Now he is afraid that any new sex partner will also discover he is inept in bed. Christopher, on the other hand, is a painfully shy twenty-five-year-old who has never had sex at all. He is terrified to be in the company of a woman, let alone touch one.

Although often explicit, *Private Practices* is neither voyeuristic nor exploitive. It honestly portrays issues of love, self-image and sexual problems. Maureen comes across as a seasoned professional in her therapy sessions, handling her clients with strength and compassion, while Christopher and John emerge as courageous men whose experiences reflect the sexual fears of many people. At times, the subjects talk too much about the details of the sessions themselves and not enough about their lives. At other moments, the patients' actions and soul exposing are so personal it can be embarrassing. But over the four-month period of filming, not only do we see positive changes in both Christopher and John and learn a great deal about sexual dysfunction in general, but we also develop a tremendous respect for Maureen Sullivan and her profession.

RATED: *No MPAA rating, with explicit sex and language.*
FILMNOTE: *At the request of Christopher and John, director Kirby Dick chose two women as his cinematographers, directing them from behind a two-way mirror, all of them using microphones and headsets.*

PRIVATES ON PARADE
(Video)

★ ★ ½

Screwball Comedy

England

1985   96 Min.   Color

CREDITS: *Directed by Michael Blakemore. Written by Peter Nichols. Produced by George Harrison and Simon Relph.* *Cinematography by Ian Wilson. Music by Denis King. Released by Orion Classics. Distributed nontheatrically by Films Inc. Starring Denis Quilley, John Cleese, Patrick Pearson, Michael Elphick, Nicola Pagett, Bruce Payne, Joe Melia, David Bamber and Simon Jones.*

An affectionate tribute to the Song and Dance Units of Southeast Asia (SADUSEA) that entertained British troops in Singapore during World War II, *Privates on Parade* is a zestful farce that ultimately becomes mired in uncomfortable, realistic drama.

The story begins as young Sgt. Steven Flowers (Patrick Pearson) arrives at his new post, a SADUSEA unit directed by Capt. Terry Dennis (Denis Quilley), an aging drag queen clad in a leopard turban and a white suit, and commanded by Giles Flack (John Cleese), a humorless, tone-deaf major. While Flowers rehearses in Captain Dennis's ridiculous song and dance revue, "The Jungle Jamboree," he falls in love with Sylvia (Nicola Pagett), a beautiful singer who encourages his advances with the approval of her real lover, Drummond (Michael Elphick). Drummond is a black marketeer who curiously wants to distract the young private. As the troupe prepares for a barnstorming tour of the jungle, Drummond is apparently killed in an explosion, leaving a confused Flowers to console the pregnant Sylvia. Once in the jungle, playing for a handful of natives and barnyard animals, Flowers and the others are threatened by an ominous presence trailing them and their cache of weapons.

Privates on Parade is two movies, one that is very funny and very good, and one that is deadly serious and deadly dull. In the beginning, when the revue and Cleese's Flack are the focus, the story is hilarious in the bitchy, irreverent style that made Monty Python so much fun. Yet as the narrative shifts into the jungle, there is also a pronounced shift in tone, and *Privates on Parade* becomes a corrosive drama of corruption and destruction. This turn may indeed reflect the harsh realities of war, but it's also a harsh and sudden fictional leap that mangles the engaging satire that the first part of the movie sets up. Director Michael Blakemore realizes by the end that he's painted himself into a corner, as he resurrects dead and maimed characters for a sing-along finale. But by then it's too late, and the return to comedy makes the drama seem all the more pathetic.

RATING: R for nudity, sex and violence.

PROVIDENCE
(Video)

Black Comedy

England

1977   104 Min.   Color

CREDITS: *Directed by Alain Resnais. Written by David Mercer. Produced by Yves Gasser. Cinematography by Ricardo Aronovich. Music by Miklos Rozsa. Art direction by Jacques Saulnier. Released by Action Films. Distributed nontheatrically by Almi Pictures. Starring John Gielgud, Dirk Bogarde, David Warner, Ellen Burstyn, Elaine Stritch, Denis Lawson, Cyril Luckham, Kathryn Leigh-Scott and Milo Sperber.*

French director Alain Resnais's first film in English is a romp through the twisted mind of a British novelist named Clive (John Gielgud). He lives in a country mansion by himself and spends his nights cursing his fate (he is dying) as he inserts suppositories, sits on the "throne" and downs bottle after bottle of white wine.

In this state of agony, Clive dreams up his final novel—a nonsensical story whose characters resemble his two sons, Clyde (Dirk Bogarde) and Kevin (David Warner), his daughter-in-law, Sonia (Ellen Burstyn), and his late wife, Molly (Elaine Stritch). Through dramatizations of his novel, we see Clive take vicarious revenge on all four by wreaking havoc on their lives. As perversely funny as these scenes are, they also reveal an assortment of feelings of guilt, anger and jealousy toward all of them. When we meet Clyde, Kevin and Sonia in real life, it's easy to understand why Clive's imagination turned them into such monsters, but it's also a relief to know that they

are only mildly like the characters in his novel.

The weak links in *Providence* are the women. Why Resnais chose two conventional American actresses to play such odd roles is a mystery. Burstyn and Stritch seem uncomfortable with this type of absurdist, surrealistic acting, and their characters come across stiffly. Still, written by *Morgan*'s David Mercer, *Providence* is much more sophisticated than his earlier work although just as outrageous in its satire, while director Alain Resnais *(Hiroshima Mon Amour)* brings his script to life in some perversely hilarious ways. The physical details in this film are dazzling, from the minimal, modern interior of Clyde's Providence home to the beautiful scenery at his seaside manor. Bogarde and Warner give dry, solid performances, and Gielgud's Clive is so wonderfully demented he'll leave you rolling in the aisles.

RATING: R for nudity and sex.

PUMPING IRON II: THE WOMEN
(Video)

Documentary

U.S.A.

1985   130 Min.   Color

CREDITS: *Directed and produced by George Butler. Written by George Butler and Charles Gaines, based on their book* Pumping Iron II: The Unprecedented Woman. *Cinematography by Dyanna Taylor. Music by David McHugh. Edited by Paul Barnes and Susan Crutcher. Released and distributed nontheatrically by Cinecom. Starring Rachel McLish, Bev Francis, Carla Dunlap, Lori Bowen, George Plimpton, Kris Alexander and Lydia Chergo.*

Pumping Iron II: The Women is not just two hours of women flexing their muscles in front of the camera. It's a fascinating look at how several women body-building contestants view their sport, their sexuality and their lives. The setting is the 1984 Women's World Cup Body Building Competition at Caesar's Palace in Las Vegas, where dozens of women are competing for a $25,000 first prize—the largest purse ever given for a men's or women's body-building contest. The contestants run the gamut from the seductive and flirtatious Rachel McLish to Bev Francis, an Australian who has the body of a nose tackle for the Dallas Cowboys.

Bev's entry into the contest raises questions on the definition of a woman body-builder and femininity. Should Bev's use of steroids be rewarded in a sport that measures muscle development? Or is the fact that she looks like a man too much for the judges and fans to handle? Rachel, of course, represents the Phyllis Schafly perspective in the argument, and many of the other contest participants have strong views on that subject as well.

Pumping Iron II is a slickly produced documentary with fast-paced editing, superb camera work and an upbeat musical score. Even if you aren't interested in body building, it's fascinating to see how the contestants, judges and fans view their femininity and role models in a traditionally male-dominated sport. Although *Pumping Iron II* is filmed with cinema verité techniques, there's nothing staged about its subjects. They are bluntly honest and, at times, vicious in their comments about each other. The film's only major fault is that there is too much footage of the women working out before the contest. But about halfway through, when the sweating and grunting stop and the heated discussions begin, *Pumping Iron II* really starts pumping.

RATING: No MPAA rating, with some very revealing bikinis.

QUADROPHENIA
(Video)

Rock Drama

England

1979   115 Min.   Color

CREDITS: Directed by Franc Roddam. Written by Franc Roddam, Dave Humphries, Martin Stillman and Pete Townshend, based on the album by The Who. Produced by Roy Baird and Bill Curbishley. Cinematography by Brian Tufano. Music by The Who. Musical direction by John Entwistle. Released by World Northal. Distributed nontheatrically by Corinth Films. Starring Phil Daniels, Philip Davis, Leslie Ash, Garry Cooper, Sting, Mark Wingett, Toyah Wilcox and Trevor Laird.

Based on the album by The Who, *Quadrophenia* is about the violent clash of the Mods and the Rockers, two British gangs in the late fifties and early sixties, who defined themselves by their dress and taste in music.

The Mods wore stylish clothes, held jobs and rode Italian scooters, while the Rockers were like typical bikers, grungily dressed and stealing to get by. The film's main protagonist is a skinny Mod named Jimmy (Phil Daniels) who loathes his job as a messenger as much as he loathes his parents. Jimmy only feels powerful picking fights with Rockers, taking speed and seducing his attractive girlfriend, Steph (Leslie Ash). But Steph is any Mod's girl, and when Jimmy realizes that she's slept with his idol, the Face (Sting in his first film role), his rebellion turns into rage against everyone, including himself. Eventually, he ends up in the streets in a drug-induced stupor, thrown out of the house by his parents and spurned by Steph, the only person he is capable of loving.

The performers' accents in *Quadrophenia* are so thick and the dialogue so colloquial that the film doesn't travel well across the ocean. To confuse matters more, there is virtually no character development in the first half of the film, so that the constant barrage of fighting and sex scenes grows tiresome long before we understand their meaning.

Once we learn what makes Jimmy tick, however, *Quadrophenia* becomes a stunning portrait of a teenager's hellish descent into drugs, violence and self-hatred. Director Franc Roddam and his crew do an excellent job with the film's sets and cinematography. The outfits and hairstyles of the Mods and Rockers are outrageous, while the gray, steamy shots in the back alleys and bars of London set the atmosphere for doom and aimless violence. But it's the music that makes this film so entertaining. Produced by John Entwistle (bass player for The Who), the classic Who music is such a part of what's happening on the screen that it's virtually impossible to separate the narrative from its soundtrack.

RATING: R for sex, violence, profanity and substance abuse.

QUERELLE
(Video, dubbed)

Psychological Drama

West Germany   German

1982   120 Min.   Color

CREDITS: *Directed by Rainer Werner Fassbinder. Written by Rainer Werner Fassbinder, based on the novel* Querelle de Brest *by Jean Genet. Produced by Dieter Schidor. Cinematography by Xaver Schwarzenberger. Music by Peer Raben. Released by Triumph Films. Distributed nontheatrically by Swank Motion Pictures. Starring Brad Davis, Franco Nero, Jeanne Moreau, Gunther Kaufmann, Hanno Poschl, Rainer Werner Fassbinder, Burkhard Driest and Dietor Shidor.*

Jean Genet scandalized literary circles with his frank and often nihilistic writings on homosexuality. Rainer Werner Fassbinder's adaption of *Querelle de Brest* is every bit as scandalous as the author's novel, and it's also not very accessible.

Much of *Querelle* takes place in Brest, France, and is told through the eyes of Lieutenant Seblon (Franco Nero), the closeted gay commander of a docked French naval vessel who is sexually obsessed with his handsome seaman, Querelle (American actor Brad Davis). When the film opens, the dashing young Querelle drifts into a sleazy nightclub run by Lysiane (Jeanne Moreau) and her husband, Nono (Gunther Kaufmann). There, Querelle is seduced by the hulking Nono and from that moment on explores the limits of his own sexuality, while beginning to view his life in nihilistic, amoral terms. Meanwhile, Lysiane also lusts after Querelle, even as she becomes entangled in a passionless affair with Querelle's brother (Hanno Poschl). But Querelle could care less about anybody's affection, sinking deeper into a dangerous world of drugs, promiscuity and murder.

Querelle was Fassbinder's last film before his death, but unfortunately it's not one of his best. The movie's main characters fight each other like rats in a back alley, their lives consumed with hedonistic desires. These actions quickly become wearing because of a story line that is difficult to follow. Much of the lieutenant's narration is in non sequiturs, while the film's oblique dialogue and segmented plot make little sense. Fassbinder tries to enrich the atmosphere by using bizarre sets and camera tricks, yet these do little but stretch out and confuse the virtually nonexistent narrative. The bright spots in this film are the performances of Moreau as the whimpering Lysiane and Poschl as Querelle's tormented brother, Richard. But Brad Davis is badly miscast as the protagonist. Although he is handsome to look at, he delivers his lines with so little emotion that his character fails to sustain interest beyond Davis's appearance.

RATING: R for violence, homosexual themes and suggestive sexual situations.
WARNING: Although dubbing is decent, it stills detracts from the quality of the film.

A QUESTION OF SILENCE
(Video, subtitled)

Feminist Drama

Holland   Dutch

1984   96 Min.   Color

CREDITS: *Directed and written by Marleen Gorris. Produced by Matthijs van Heijningen. Cinematography by Froms Bromet. Released by Sigma/Quartet Films. Distributed nontheatrically by Films Inc. Starring Edda Barends, Nelly Frijda, Henriette Tol, Cox Habbema, Eddy Brugman and Dolf de Vries.*

Marleen Gorris's first screenplay, based on a newspaper account of a Dutch woman arrested for shoplifting, was so well received by a Dutch film commission that they not only footed the entire bill for *A Question of Silence,* but they allowed the inexperienced Gorris to be its director. The result is a film as thought-provoking as it is shocking.

A Question of Silence is the story of three women—a waitress (Nelly Frijda), a secretary (Henriette Tol) and a housewife (Edda Barends)—who as the movie begins are shopping in a dress store in a small shopping center. After one of them is caught shoplifting by the smug male boutique owner, all three brutally murder the man. What's particularly bizarre about the incident is that none of them had ever set eyes on their victim or each other before, and when arrested the next day, they show no remorse for what they have done. In fact, all three independently celebrate the killing, as if it were a rite of passage.

The events leading up to the murder are seen through the eyes of Jeanine (Cox Habbema), a court-appointed psychiatrist who must determine if the women should plead innocent by reason of insanity. Through a series of interviews, she discovers that each woman possesses an unspoken rage against men. By the time the trial comes around, Jeanine isn't at all convinced that they were "insane" at the time of the murder.

Although certain scenes in *A Question of Silence* are actually quite funny, most of the film packs an emotional wallop. The four main characters give intense performances, and though they are very different from one another, each is convincing in her role. Director Gorris *(Broken Mirrors)* does a superb job of unraveling their complex personalities and giving us four compelling examples of women oppressed by men. But the catchword for her direction is "subtle." Instead of plunging us into their dark psychological depths or showing us extreme instances of men abusing them, small but important clues are revealed as we come to understand how the defendants could commit such a hideous crime. By the film's slightly contrived courtroom finale, it's wrenchingly clear why Jeanine thinks they had good reason to be enraged.

RATING: *R for violence, brief nudity and sex.*

THE QUIET EARTH
(Video)

Political Science Fiction

New Zealand

1984   126 Min.   Color

CREDITS: *Directed by Geoff Murphy. Written by Bill Baer, Bruno Lawrence and Sam Pillsbury. Produced by Don Reynolds and Sam Pillsbury. Cinematography by James Bartle. Released by Skouras Pictures. Distributed nontheatrically by The Samuel Goldwyn Company. Starring Bruno Lawrence, Alison Rutledge and Peter Smith.*

The Quiet Earth opens with a middle-aged New Zealand scientist trying to commit suicide by downing an entire bottle of sleeping pills. Instead of the white light at the end of the tunnel, Zac (Bruno Lawrence) awakens to a world with no inhabitants. Cars are still running on empty streets, shops full of merchandise are wide open and fishless rivers gently flow, but there isn't a living creature in sight.

At first, Zac desperately tries to find signs

of life, but when he fails, he just attempts to live it up. He moves from his apartment into a mansion, drives to the mall for a whirl of a shopping spree and treats himself to an exquisite meal at a deserted French restaurant. But beneath this playful façade, Zac is going insane until, out of nowhere, a pretty young woman named Joanne (Alison Rutledge) appears. Sure enough, Zac and Joanne slowly fall in love. But then a handsome young Maori (the indigenous Polynesian population of New Zealand) named Api (Peter Smith) shows up and takes a fancy to Joanne as well.

The first part of The Quiet Earth is a suspenseful and compelling "Day After" story. Director Geoff Murphy (Utu) very cleverly combines science with fantasy in ways that contain perceptive social comment and humor yet are frightening and prophetic at the same time. Cinematographer James Bartle superbly captures the eerie quiet of the deserted city streets and the living nightmare of Zac's lonely existence. Bruno Lawrence (Smash Palace) gives a riveting performance, particularly in a scene where he charges into a church to dismember a statue of Christ with his shotgun. But when the love triangle comes to the fore, The Quiet Earth takes on the fake gloppiness of a made-for-TV movie. The intrigue of who will go steady with the last woman on earth quickly becomes trite, and as Zac and Api turn into posturing males, it's easy to stop caring about them, and the monumental events that have irrevocably altered their lives.

RATING: R for discreet sex and nudity.
FILMNOTE: The Quiet Earth is the most expensive film produced in New Zealand film to date.

RAISING ARIZONA
(Video)

Caper Comedy

U.S.A.

1987   94 Min.   Color

CREDITS: Directed by Joel Coen. Written by Joel and Ethan Coen. Produced by Ethan Coen. Cinematography by Barry Sonnefeld. Music by Carter Burwell. Released by 20th Century Fox. Distributed nontheatrically by Films Inc. Starring Nicolas Cage, Holly Hunter, Randall "Tex" Cobb, John Goodman, Trey Wilson and William Forsythe.

As was their first feature, Blood Simple, the Coen brothers' Raising Arizona is made with an everything-but-the-kitchen-sink philosophy. The film is narrated by H.I. (Nicolas Cage), a droopy-eyed, molasses-voiced thief whose taste for robbing convenience stores is matched only by his ability for getting caught in the act. During one of his many mug shot sittings, H.I. falls under the spell of a spunky policewoman named Ed (Holly Hunter). After a long courtship interrupted by several stretches in the penitentiary, H.I. finally claims Ed as his bride.

But disappointment stalks the couple when Ed is unable to become pregnant. She orders H.I. "to get me a toddler" from among the quintuplets that Nathan Arizona (Trey Wilson), the Discounted Unpainted Furniture King, has recently sired. Unfortunately, Ed is wrong when she assumes that Arizona won't miss one of his quints, and the kidnapping sets off a chain of catastrophes that climaxes with the appearance of a bounty hunter (Randall "Tex" Cobb) who snatches the baby boy and threatens to claim him as his own.

The Coen brothers direct Raising Arizona with an exciting visual flair, using tracking shots and elaborate set pieces at every opportunity. The filmmakers also show themselves to be clever thieves—borrowing from films such as Mad Max and Altered States to achieve a desired effect. But the main problem with *Raising Arizona* is that the Coens just don't know when to stop. Some of the film's funniest schticks drag on unmercifully, particularly the endless chase scenes. Also, these New York sharpies seem to be having too much fun at the expense of the locals, whom they strip of all but the barest sense of dignity.

But like a fraternity boy at Daytona Beach in the spring, *Raising Arizona* is mostly out for the easy laugh, and to that end, it's successful. Cage's early narration, overwritten and delivered with an air of self-mocking doom, is hilarious. Hunter's Ed is a riot when her face contorts in anger and despair, lashing out at H.I. over the disastrous state of their marriage. And the film's assortment of animated supporting actors can also be entertaining, particularly Wilson's Nathan Arizona, who peddles three-piece living-room sets like an evangelist selling redemption.

RATING: PG-13 for mild violence and profanity.

RAMPARTS OF CLAY
(Video, subtitled)

Cultural Drama

Tunisia/Algeria	Arabic
1970 85 Min.	Color

CREDITS: *Directed and produced by Jean-Louis Bertucelli. Written by Jean Duvignaud. Cinematography by Andreas Winding. Released and distributed nontheatrically by Almi Pictures. Berber songs collected and sung by Taos Amrouche. Starring Leila Schenna and the villagers of Tehouda.*

Ramparts of Clay is the coming-of-age story of both the film's young protagonist and Tunisia, her native country. The film is set in 1962, just after Tunisia's independence from France, in the small village of Tehouda (actually in Algeria). Wedged between the Salt Mountains and the Sahara Desert, Tehouda is a desolate

oasis where the men slave in the salt quarries for meager wages. In this strict Moslem culture, only men are allowed to work and get an education, while women exist solely to cater to the needs of their husbands and brothers.

One nineteen-year-old woman (Leila Schenna) refuses to be subservient. Eager to learn as much as she can, she eavesdrops on the geography classes meant for male students and saves scraps of newspapers used to wrap bottles, to sneak reading lessons from her younger brother. Meanwhile, Leila's frustration is soon echoed by the men in the village, as they realize that they are exploited at the salt quarry. When they go on strike, the quarry's pompous foreman calls in the national guard, and the village is locked in a standoff. The striking workers are surrounded by soldiers while the women respond by wailing and soaking their hands in the blood of a slaughtered lamb. But when Leila refuses to join in these demeaning rituals, she creates a rupture in the village order that is as severe as the men's defiance of government rule.

Although those with patience will find many rewards in *Ramparts of Clay,* a restless moviegoer will certainly be frustrated by the film's slow, deliberate method of storytelling. The opening sequence, introducing life in Tehouda, rambles on endlessly. Before the strike begins, two-thirds of the way through the film, director Jean-Louis Bertucelli laboriously recycles images. After the strike, the film's plot dashes too quickly to its cathartic conclusion.

But shot on location, *Ramparts of Clay* is so authentic you can practically smell and taste this village's oppressive atmosphere. Bertucelli takes great pains to show the difficult life of these impoverished Muslims, while his pans of Tunisia's stark landscapes, combined with the weathered, sullen faces of the nonprofessional actors, can be extremely powerful. Schenna gives a moving performance as a young woman struggling to maintain her dignity in this stifling culture. Based on an actual incident that occurred in Tunisia, the strike and the villagers' climactic standoff are also quite emotional, both as a tension-filled dramatization of workers fighting for their rights and as a subtle mirror of Leila's intense personal struggles.

RATING: No MPAA rating, with nothing offensive.

FILMNOTE: Because of its progressive politics, Ramparts of Clay *was banned in Tunisia and Algeria at the time of its release.*

RAN
(Video, subtitled)

Historical Adventure

Japan	Japanese
1985	160 Min.	Color

CREDITS: Directed by Akira Kurosawa. Written by Akira Kurosawa, Hideo Oquino and Masato Ide. Produced by Serge Silberman and Masato Hara. Cinematography by Takao Saito, Masaharu Ueda and Asaishi Nakai. Music by Toru Takemitsu and the Sapporo Symphony. Art direction by Yoshiro Muraki and Shinobu Muraki. Costume design by Emi Wada. Released by Orion Classics. Starring Tatsuya Nakadai, Akira Terao, Jinpachi Nezu, Disuke Ryn, Mjeko Harada, Yoshiko Miyazaki, Masayuki Yui and Peter.

Akira Kurosawa is a genius at creating powerful moods in his films, and *Ran* is no exception. Loosely based on Shakespeare's *King Lear, Ran* is another Kurosawa epic powered by seething masses and quietly powerful images.

The story takes place during the clan wars of sixteenth-century Japan. Getting on in years, Lord Hidetora (Tatsuya Nakadai) decides to divide up his land among his three sons while he is still alive, enabling him to oversee his empire while his children handle the smaller details. He fully expects them to cooperate, but instead they amass their own armies and not only order him around but greedily battle each other for their bequeathed land. The result is one bloody skirmish after another, and the ultimate ruin of nearly everyone in the family.

The most expensive and elaborately produced film ever to come from Japan, *Ran* is visually overwhelming. The costumes and the sets are exquisite (Kurosawa executed hundreds of drawings to design the sets), and the battle scenes, some of which are filmed in complete silence, are hauntingly beautiful. But because there is little character development beyond the greediness of the brothers and the anger and disappointment of Lord Hidetora, it's difficult to respond to *Ran* as anything more than an elaborate special-effects movie. In the end, you don't enjoy *Ran* so much as you appreciate it.

RATING: R for violence.

AWARDS: 1986 Academy Award for Best Costume Design (Emi Wada); 1986 Academy Award nominations for Best Director (Akira Kurosawa), Best Cinematography (Takao Saito, Masaharo Ueda and Asakazu Nakai) and Best Art Direction (Yoshiro Muraki and Shinobu Muraki); 1986 New York Film Critics Award for Best Foreign Film.

WARNING: Originally filmed in Cinemascope, the video version is clipped so poorly that it practically ruins the film's beautiful cinematography.

FILMNOTE: Ran is the culmination of a ten-year effort by the ailing and nearly blind seventy-five-year-old director.

RASHOMON
(Video, subtitled)

Psychological Drama

Japan	Japanese
1951	88 Min.	B&W

CREDITS: Directed by Akira Kurosawa. Written by Akira Kurosawa and Shinobu Hashimoto, based on two short stories by Ryunosuke Akutagawa. Produced by Masaichi Nagata. Cinematography by Kazuo Miyagawa. Music by Fumio Hayasaka. Released by RKO Pictures. Distributed nontheatrically by Films Inc. Starring Toshiro Mifune, Takashi Shimura, Masayuki Mori, Machiko Kyo, Minoru Chiaki, Kichijiro Ueda, Fumiko Homma and Daisuke Kato.

The first film to popularize Japanese cinema in the West, Akira Kurosawa's *Rashomon* was an exotic and powerful movie when it was released, but comes across a little stagy today. Although the time and place of the story are never mentioned, *Rashomon* is set in Japan when rich women wore veils and men carried swords to guard their wives' honor. At the beginning of the film, one such couple (Masayuki Mori and Machiko Kyo) are attacked while traveling through the woods by a notorious bandit named Tajomaru (Toshiro Mifune). The wife's honor is tarnished and the husband is killed.

What really happened that fateful day depends on whose story you want to believe: the bandit, the wife, the dead husband (speaking through a medium), or a woodcutter (Takashi Shimura of *Ikiru*) who witnessed the crime—all tell investigating police their own versions of the incident. Three out of the four are good liars, because none of their stories jibe.

Taking great pains with the sets, costumes and cinematography, Kurosawa and his crew create stark, striking images of the crime and the four protagonists, giving rich texture to this seemingly simple story. Kurosawa also goes right for the heart of Japanese honor and the nature of truth as the four relay the events of that fateful day. Of course, each version flatters the teller and humiliates the others. Kurosawa manipulates our instincts so that all four seem as if they could be either lying or telling the truth. Mifune gives the strongest performance as the bandit prone to explosive fits of laughter and anger, while underneath his thunder lies a deep self-hatred. Unfortunately, the other characters are less convincing, particularly the wife, who cries often and insincerely, and the constantly brooding woodcutter. Even if Kurosawa intentionally stylized his characters in the tradition of ancient Japanese theater, it nevertheless becomes wearisome.

RATING: *No MPAA rating, with nothing objectionable.*

AWARDS: *Grand Prix at 1951 Venice Film Festival; 1951 Honorary Academy Award for Most Outstanding Foreign Film (awarded before the Best Foreign Film category was established in 1956).*

FILMNOTE: *Even though* Rashomon *was enormously popular in the West, in Japan, surprisingly, it was not very well received.*

REAL LIFE
(Video)

Documentary Satire

U.S.A.

1979   99 Min.   Color

CREDITS: *Directed by Albert Brooks. Written by Albert Brooks and Monica Johnson. Produced by Penelope Spheeris (the director of* Suburbia). *Cinematography by Eric Saarinen. Released by Paramount. Distributed nontheatrically by Films Inc. Starring Albert Brooks, Dick Haynes, Matthew Tobin, Charles Grodin, Frances Lee McCain, J. A. Preston, Mort Lindsey, Joseph Schaffler and James L. Brooks.*

After making a series of funny shorts for the original "Saturday Night Live," Albert Brooks *(Lost in America)* struck out on his own to create *Real Life*—a satire of the PBS "American Family" series.

Brooks stars in this film as an ambitious and idealistic young director who moves in with a typical Arizona family to make a documentary on their lives. As soon as the camera starts rolling, though, the project degenerates into lunacy. His subjects are less than cooperative, while the pushy Brooks seems willing to offer this family as sacrificial lambs to his god of "cinematic realism." The veterinarian father (Charles Grodin), for example, is humiliated when Brooks captures a horse dying during surgery, and the wife (Frances Lee McCain) tries to placate the obnoxious director by actually inviting him to film her appointment at the gynecologist. Every scene that Brooks's director enthusiastically sets up as a cinema verité masterpiece turns into disaster.

Like Woody Allen, Brooks creates for himself a persona (in his case, a self-deceiving, conniving lout) and carries it into all of his films. In this early work, his character is shrill and constantly risks distancing the audience with his whining and wheedling. Yet Brooks is able to temper these quirks by also playing an earnest fool with inexhaustible naïveté. *Real Life* has some brilliantly funny moments, as well as dozens of sharp-edged jabs at how documentary filmmakers exploit their subjects, and the mediocrity of middle-class suburban life. The father sums it up perfectly when he looks over Brooks's shoulder into the camera and mumbles sheepishly, "This isn't what we expected at all." For the most part, *Real Life* is the same sort of surprise.

RATING: PG, with nothing objectionable.

REMEMBER MY NAME
(Video)

Romantic Thriller

U.S.A.

1978   96 Min.   Color

CREDITS: Directed and written by Alan Rudolph. Produced by Robert Altman. Music and vocals by Alberta Hunter. Cinematography by Tak Fujimoto. Released by Lions Gate/Columbia Pictures. Distributed nontheatrically by Kit Parker Films. Starring Geraldine Chaplin, Anthony Perkins, Moses Gunn, Berry Berenson, Jeff Goldblum, Timothy Thomerson, Alfre Woodard and Marilyn Coleman.

In his later films, *Choose Me* and *Trouble in Mind*, director Alan Rudolph distinguished himself as a creator of loopy characters whose lives are driven by romantic obsession. In *Remember My Name*, he explores the darker forces of love but abandons his stock of lovable eccentrics in favor of sinister and frightening ones.

Geraldine Chaplin *(Nashville)* stars as Lucy, a woman who comes to the Northern California hometown of her ex-husband (Anthony Perkins) after a long and mysterious absence. She gets a job and settles into a reasonable daily routine but is still driven by an urge to spy on him, following him as he leaves his construction job and peeking in the windows of his home. Increasingly disturbed, she sneaks over to his house and destroys his garden, then threatens his wife (Berry Berenson) with a knife. Finally, she is so possessed by jealousy that she seems to be capable of anything, including murder. Although Perkins is so enraged by her actions that he would like to be rid of his ex-wife once and for all, he is also strangely drawn to her murderous desires.

Chaplin gives a searing performance as a woman whose little-girl fussiness about clothes and makeup mask her insanity and homicidal rage. The surface details of Chaplin's character—her trembling hands and evasive eyes—not only reveal her instability but also create sinister electricity that follows her around like a magnet. Perkins is also very good as the weasely ex-husband, and Jeff Goldblum is the film's only comic relief as Chaplin's skittish boss. Director/writer Rudolph and Japanese cinematographer, Tak Fujimoto, give several scenes a fragmented, dreamlike quality that makes Chaplin's actions all the more frightening. But the film's secret weapon is its soundtrack—a bluesy, haunting score by Alberta Hunter that is a perfect reflection of Lucy, a woman who can't let go of obsessions despite her awareness that they will destroy her and the one person she loves.

RATING: R for sex and violence.

REPO MAN
(Video)

Social Satire

U.S.A.

1984   92 Min.   Color

CREDITS: Directed and written by Alex Cox. Produced by Jonathan Wacks and Peter McCarthy. Cinematography by Robby Muller. Music by Iggy Pop, The Circle Jerks and The Untouchables. Released by Edge City/Universal. Distributed nontheatrically *by Swank Motion Pictures. Starring Emilio Estevez, Harry Dean Stanton, Tracey Walter, Vonetta McGee, Olivia Barash, Sy Richardson, Susan Barnes and Fox Harris.*

Repo Man became an overnight cult success on college campuses and the midnight movie circuit. The film follows the colorless existence of Otto (Emilio Estevez), an L.A. punk who spends his days doing drugs, eating generic food with his hippie parents and butting heads with friends as a sign of affection. But one day, when he helps a guy named Bud (Harry Dean Stanton) steal a car for twenty bucks, Otto embarks on an exciting new career—car repossession. Bud is a tough, raspy veteran who teaches his insolent partner the ropes, and after repossessing a few cars from assorted toughs from the ghetto, the pair get hot on the trail of a beat-up 1964 Chevy Malibu with a $20,000 bounty on its chassis. What they don't realize is that the Malibu is prized because its trunk contains a dangerous alien waiting to vaporize anybody who pops open the lid.

Set in bleak landscapes of the neon-lit L.A. suburbs, seamy punk rock clubs and car lots, *Repo Man*'s dark humor sneaks up behind you and lands a sucker punch across your jaw. Writer/director Alex Cox *(Sid and Nancy)* has his assortment of seedy and punk characters deliver their lines so seriously that it takes a while to realize they are funny. Some of the film's most memorable moments involve Bud and the other repo men's inane philosophizing between repossessing gigs. It's also a riot when Otto "raps" with his born-again, hippie parents in the suburbs. And though *Repo Man* was obviously made on a low budget, Cox's neo-punk-sleaze sets and Wim Wenders–style cinematography frame it all very stylishly.

RATING: R for a lot of profanity and substance abuse.

THE RETURN OF MARTIN GUERRE
(Video, subtitled)

Historical Mystery

France		French
1983	111 Min.	Color

CREDITS: Directed and produced by Daniel Vigne. Written by Daniel Vigne and Jean-Claude Carriere, based on the book by Princeton history professor Natalie Davis. Cinematography by Andre Neau. Set design by Alain Negre. Costume design by Ann-Marie Marchand. Released and distributed nontheatrically by European Classics. Starring Gérard Depardieu, Nathalie Baye, Bernard Pierre Donnadieu, Roger Plachon, Maurice Jacquemont, Isabelle Sadoyan and Rose Theiry.

Based on a true story, Daniel Vigne's *The Return of Martin Guerre* is an intriguing mystery set in the sixteenth-century French village of Artigat. Young Martin Guerre and his teenage sweetheart, Bertrande (Nathalie Baye), are married, but Guerre takes many long months to consummate the marriage because a spell has been cast on him. The whole village makes fun of Martin, and one day, after a fight with his father, the embittered young man disappears.

Nine years later, Martin Guerre (Gérard Depardieu) returns to Artigat claiming he fought for his country in the war. Though older and beefier-looking, Martin is recognized by the villagers and welcomed back with open arms. Bertrande is ecstatic to have her husband back. He has not only matured physically, but he's now a kinder, more loving husband, and he begins to amass wealth for his family. But as Guerre fights with his uncle over his inheritance, two vagabonds wander into Artigat and claim that this Martin is an impostor. Soon he becomes the rope in an all-village tug-of-war. The case is brought to trial, and if found guilty, Martin will be sentenced to hang.

Depardieu gives one of his strongest performances to date. He is so convincing that one minute we are certain he's a fake, and the next we're sure he couldn't be anybody but the real Martin. The supporting cast is superb, especially Baye as his abused, and then loyal, wife. Andre Neau's cinematography is luminous, with some scenes so beautiful they belong in a Renaissance painting, while Anne-Marie Marchand's costumes are quite authentic. But it's Daniel Vigne's direction and script that keep us riveted to our seats in suspense until the film's surprise ending.

RATING: No MPAA rating, with brief nudity.

THE RETURN OF THE SECAUCUS SEVEN
(Video)

Social Satire

U.S.A.

1981   110 Min.   Color

CREDITS: *Directed and written by John Sayles. Produced by William Aydelott and Jeffrey Nelson. Cinematography by Austin de Besche. Music by K. Mason Daring. Released by Salsipuedes/Libra Film. Distributed nontheatrically by Almi Pictures. Starring Bruce MacDonald, Maggie Renzi, Adam Lefevre, Maggie Cousineau, Gordon Clapp, Jean Passanance, Karen Trott, Mark Arnott, David Strathaim and John Sayles.*

After writing screenplays for horror films such as *Alligator* and *The Howling,* John Sayles created a very different kind of movie in *The Return of the Secaucus Seven* for his directorial debut.

Calling themselves the Secaucus Seven because one of their shared experiences included an arrest in Secaucus, New Jersey, en route to a peace demonstration in Washington, D.C., seven old friends (four women and three men) get together for a summer weekend in New Hampshire. Now

their hair is shorter, their paunches bigger, and their stamina for drugs, drinking and one-night stands is half what it used to be. But that doesn't stop them from trying to relive their past as they drink, dance and play themselves into a frenzy. There are introspective moments during the weekend as well, when the group pairs off to reminisce about the old days and reflect on what their lives have become. In the process, one long-term relationship breaks up, a few casual ones form and all seven realize how important they still are to one another.

Made on a budget of only $60,000, *Secaucus Seven* has some bothersome technical problems, such as a tinny soundtrack and jerky editing. The artsy camera work is also amateurish, and too much attention for the sake of authenticity is focused on the mundane moments of this old gang's weekend together. But even with all of its faults, this movie has more substance than *The Big Chill.* Although not filled with one-liners and snappy retorts, several conversations among the seven eloquently capture the lost idealism of the sixties, while other moments involve us in their everyday fears and frustrations. Unlike *The Big Chill*'s director, Lawrence Kasdan, Sayles takes a chance by having his characters reveal their inner emotions. Though the payoff may be less entertaining, you come away from *Secaucus Seven* thinking that there's more to this misplaced generation than dancing to Aretha Franklin while doing the dishes.

RATING: No MPAA rating, with one brief male skinny-dipping scene and marijuana smoking.

REUBEN, REUBEN
(Video)

Literary Comedy

U.S.A.

1983   101 Min.   Color

CREDITS: *Directed by Robert Ellis Miller. Written by Julius Epstein, based on the* novel *by Peter DeVries and the play* Spofford *by Herman Shumlin. Cinematography by Peter Stein. Released by 20th Century Fox. Distributed nontheatrically by Films Inc. Starring Tom Conti, Kelly McGillis, Roberts Blossom, E. Katherine Kerr, Cynthia Harris, Joel Fabiani, Kara Wilson, Lois Smith and Ed Grady.*

Gowen McLand (Tom Conti) personifies the word *debauchery.* A once-famous poet, he now devotes his time to reading at colleges, getting sloshed and seducing women. He seems to have a special knack for charming married women—which doesn't make him too popular with their husbands. But one day his marriage wrecking comes to a halt when he meets a beautiful young student named Gloria (Kelly McGillis) and falls hopelessly in love. All the poetic talents he can muster come slurring out of his mouth, and though Gloria is half his age, he convinces her to get involved.

But despite this romantic hopefulness, Gowen's fortunes darken when an irate husband of one of his former conquests volunteers to be his dentist. The ever-cheap Gowen agrees, and in a few sessions that rival Lawrence Olivier's work on Dustin Hoffman's teeth in *Marathon Man,* his newly appointed oral surgeon makes tuna fish salad out of his mouth. His life takes a downward slide from the dentist's chair, stumbling from one calamity to the next.

Conti's character is a familiar one—you've seen Peter O'Toole, Dudley Moore and Albert Finney play the role many times. You are supposed to laugh at his alcoholic antics, but these scenes aren't nearly as funny as they are meant to be. Gowen isn't a comical drunk as much as he is an obnoxious and pathetic one. Although Conti gives a strong performance in all stages of Gowen's inebriation, he is much more entertaining when he's sober enough to rattle off sarcastic quips and poetic metaphors. Fortunately, he has plenty of lucid moments in *Reuben, Reuben.* But the good times conclude abruptly at the end. Be prepared for a final scene that will knock that smile off your face so quickly your head will spin.

RATING: R for language and brief nudity. AWARDS: Award for Best Actor (Tom Conti) *at the 1983 Festival International du Film de Comedie; 1983 Academy Award nominations for Best Actor (Tom Conti) and Best Screenplay Adaptation (Julius Epstein).*

THE REVOLT OF JOB

(Video, subtitled)

Cultural Drama

West Germany/Hungary		Hungarian
1984	98 Min.	Color

CREDITS: *Directed by Imre Gyongyossy and Barna Kabay. Written by Imre Gyongyossy, Barna Kabay and Katalin Petenyi. Cinematography by Gabor Szabo. Edited by Katlin Petenyi. Released by Teleculture Films. Distributed nontheatrically by Cinecom. Starring Ferenc Zenthe, Hedi Temessy, Gabor Feher, Peter Rudolph and Letica Caro.*

Job (Ferenc Zenthe) and Rosa (Hedi Temessy) are an elderly Jewish couple living in an East Hungarian village during World War II who have lost all of their children. Knowing that it's only a matter of time before the Nazis come for them, but having no one to leave their possessions or their heritage to, the couple decides to adopt a non-Jewish boy. They trade their two best cows for a frisky, blond four-year-old named Jacob (Gabor Feher), but it turns out that they get much more than they bargained for.

Jacob is as wild and stubborn as a goat, and at one point, Rosa is so frustrated that she complains to Job that she regrets losing their cows. But gradually Jacob becomes fascinated by his new parents' Jewish rituals and learns to respect them, while Job and Rosa grow more attached to the boy with each passing day. As the shadow of anti-Semitism slowly envelops their village, the elderly couple try to share a lifetime's worth of knowledge and traditions with Jacob; more important, they struggle to leave him with their every last ounce of love.

Although there are several emotionally

draining scenes in *The Revolt of Job,* its story isn't wrought with tear-jerking sentimentalism or terrifying footage of anti-Semitic acts. Instead co-directors Imre Gyongyossy and Barna Kabay tell a simple story of peasant life in a Hungarian village. There are several humorous moments when Job and Rosa try to tame Jacob, as well as many insightful observations on human nature. The scenes of the Hungarian countryside are so beautifully photographed they'll take your breath away. The three main characters give compelling performances, with Feher's Jacob ranking as one of the most extraordinary screen children ever. But at the heart of *The Revolt of Job* is a couple whose religion, heritage and son are extremely important to them, and who have to come to terms with tragic political events that threaten to take it all away.

RATING: No MPAA rating, but there is one brief sex scene and mild violence.
AWARDS: 1984 Academy Award nomination for Best Foreign Film.
FILMNOTE: Feher was selected after the directors interviewed over four thousand young boys to play the role of Jacob.

RIVER'S EDGE
(Video)

Psychological Drama

U.S.A.

1987   100 Min.   Color

CREDITS: Directed by Tim Hunter. Written by Neal Jimenez. Produced by Sarah Pillsbury. Cinematography by Frederick Elmes. Released by Island Pictures and Hemsdale Film Corporation. Distributed nontheatrically by New Yorker Films. Starring Crispin Glover, Dennis Hopper, Keanu Reeves, Ione Skye Leitch, Roxanna Zal, Daniel Roebuck, Joshua Miller, Josh Richman, Constance Forslund, Danyi Deats and Tammy Smith.

When sixteen-year-old California high school student Jacques Broussard killed his fourteen-year-old girlfriend in 1981, Americans were shocked to learn that he showed the body to a dozen of his fellow classmates, and nearly two days passed before one of them finally called the police. In *River's Edge,* director Tim Hunter *(Tex)* attempts to explain why.

The story opens with a close-up of a dead girl's naked body, stiff and blue, dumped by the river's edge. Then we meet the killer, John (Daniel Roebuck), a vacant-eyed, beer guzzling giant who brags to his friends that he strangled his girlfriend Jami (Danyi Deats) because "she was talking shit." When he shows the corpse to his friends, none of them are saddened or horrified, even though they were all friends with the dead girl. The pill-popping, wiry ringleader of the group, Layne (Crispin Glover), sees John's situation as an opportunity for them to show their loyalty to each other, and he corrals his friends into taking part in an elaborate scheme to protect John from the police. But members of the group such as Matt (Keanu Reeves) and his girlfriend Clarissa (Ione Skye Leitch) are more interested in smoking pot and cutting classes. The situation gets out of hand when Layne convinces their one-legged dope dealer, Feck (Dennis Hopper), to let John hide out at his place. Feck is happy to accommodate John as a change of pace from his usual companion—a life-sized, blow-up sex doll.

The acting in *River's Edge* is outstanding from the entire cast, except Glover (the father in *Back to the Future*) as the speed-freak Layne, who is so hyper and jumpy he sticks out like a sore thumb in a film characterized by subtle performances. Hopper is great as the psychotic Feck, who alternates between providing the film with needed comic relief and jarring us with his creepiness. But it's not his character, close calls with the police or even Jami's murder that is frightening in *River's Edge;* it's the lack of morality in these ordinary, modern-day adolescents that will send shivers up your spine.

Director Hunter and his twenty-seven-year-old screenwriter, Neal Jimenez, drive home the emptiness in the characters' lives without mincing words. *Blue Velvet*'s cinematographer Frederick Elmes frames these teenage zombies in gray skies and litter-strewn suburban landscapes. The kids themselves are so boring and shallow that even the murder of one their friends doesn't shock them out of their lethargy, while their parents and teachers are just as emotionally bankrupt. Clarissa sums it up perfectly during one of her few moments of self-reflection when she says, "I cried when the guy died in *Brian's Song*. Why can't I cry for Jami?"

RATING: R for sex, drugs, profanity and violence.
FILMNOTE: Ione Skye Leitch (Clarissa) is the daughter of sixties folk singer Donovan.

THE ROAD WARRIOR
(Video)

Science Fiction Adventure

Australia

1982   97 Min.   Color

CREDITS: *Directed by George Miller. Written by George Miller, Terry Hayes and Brian Hannat. Produced by Byron Kennedy. Cinematography by Dean Semler. Art direction by Graham Walker. Costume design by Norma Moriceau. Released by Warner Brothers. Distributed nontheatrically by Swank Motion Pictures. Starring Mel Gibson, Bruce Spence, Emil Minty, Vernon Wells, Mike Preston, Kjell Nilsson and Virginia Hey.*

George Miller's *The Road Warrior* is the second in his Mad Max trilogy *(Mad Max, Mad Max: Beyond Thunderdome)* and is by far the best. Set in Australia after the nuclear holocaust, it follows a distraught Max (Mel Gibson) as he fights to survive in a wasteland that has reduced much of the remaining human flotsam into gas hoarders, murderers, rapists and thieves. Although Max is one of the few good souls left, he gets by the best way he knows how—by hoarding gas and killing anybody who gets in his way. But Max's special skill is driving trucks. In one exhilarating chase scene after another, he outsmarts his op-

ponents like the Ben Hur of the post-nuclear age, his chariot a sixteen wheeler.

Although Gibson is a handsome hero and a talented driver in this movie, as the embittered symbol of good in a world gone awry, there isn't a great deal of depth to his character. In fact, he hardly utters more than a few sentences of dialogue at a time in the entire film. But this picture is built on action, not words. As a post-nuclear cowboy-and-Indian battle between flower children and punks, with an odd assortment of misfits like Max thrown in for extra measure, it sure is fun. On a pure action level, *The Road Warrior* is full of exciting chase scenes and enough hot vehicles to keep your blood pumping for hours after you've viewed the film.

RATING: R for disturbing violence and rape, nudity, and language.
WARNING: This is definitely one of those special-effects movies that is better on a big screen.
FILMNOTE: The Road Warrior's producer, Byron Kennedy, was killed in the gyrokopter used in the film when he and his son went for a ride in it after the production had been completed.

ROCKERS
(Video, partially subtitled)

Musical Drama

Jamaica   Rasta patois and English

1978   99 Min.   Color

CREDITS: *Directed and written by Theodoros Bafaloukos. Produced by Patrick Hulsey. Cinematography by Peter Sova. Music by Burning Spear, Peter Tosh, Bunny Wailor, Jacob Miller, Gregory Issacs, Robbie Shakespeare and Big Youth. Released and distributed by New Yorker Films. Starring Leroy "Horsemouth" Wallace, Richard "Dirty Harry" Hall, Jacob Miller, Winston Rodney, Gregory Isaacs and Robbie Shakespeare.*

The recent popularity of Reggae has given birth to a whole slew of music documentaries from Jamaica, and though *Rockers* does have a narrative, it also records the world behind the music. The plot is simple. A Rastafarian Reggae drummer, Leroy "Horsemouth" Wallace, borrows money to buy a motorcycle so he can become his own record distributor. When it's stolen by a group of Kingston racketeers, he works out a scheme to retrieve it by enlisting the help of dozens of his Rasta brothers. He not only gets his bike back, but he becomes a self-styled Robin Hood by sharing all of the mobsters' stolen goods with the poor people of Kingston.

Most of the film is taken up with Horsemouth hanging out with his Rasta buddies smoking reefer, conversing in patois and playing music. Reggae is everywhere in this movie. When Horsemouth and his friends aren't performing, Reggae still flows in the background. The characters even seem to walk to a Reggae rhythm.

But *Rockers* is also a fun, upbeat and fascinating journey into Rastafarian culture. Director Theodoros Bafaloukos takes us to the slums, back alleys and Reggae clubs in Kingston as well as to beach and mountain locales. The characters are mostly Reggae musicians playing themselves and performing their own music. Although some of their vignettes are a little stagy, most are alive with wit and soul. The problem is understanding them. Bafaloukos wisely subtitles the dialogue in *Rockers;* even so, some of it's hard to understand because the tenses and sentence construction are so unfamiliar. Still, *Rockers* is a film that's not hard to like if you're the least bit interested in Reggae and the Rastafarian philosophies so integral to the music.

RATING: No MPAA rating, with profanity.

A ROOM WITH A VIEW
(Video)

Romantic Comedy

England

1986   115 Min.   Color

CREDITS: *Directed by James Ivory. Produced by Ismail Merchant. Written by Ruth Prawer Jhabvala, based on the novel by E. M. Forster. Music by Richard Robbins. Cinematography by Tony Pierce-Roberts. Production design by Gianni Quaranta and Brian Ackland-Snow. Costume design by Jenny Beavan and John Bright. Released by Goldcrust Films. Distributed nontheatrically by Cinecom. Starring Helena Bonhom-Carter, Denholm Elliot, Maggie Smith, Julian Sands, Daniel Day Lewis, Simon Callow, Judi Dench, Rosemary Leach and Rupert Graves.*

Although producer Ismail Merchant, director James Ivory and screenwriter Ruth Prawer Jhabvala have been collaborating on films together for twenty-six years, few have been successful outside of art houses. Finally, they hit it big with *A Room with a View*.

Based on E. M. Forster's novel by the same name, it is a comedy of manners about a young woman whose prim and proper surface masks a seething sexual piranha underneath. The time is 1907, and the beautiful Lucy Honeychurch (Helena Bonham-Carter) and her Aunt Charlotte (Maggie Smith) are exploring the art treasures of Florence. Lucy emanates virginity and innocence until she witnesses a fierce argument that results in a fatal stabbing and the handsome young George Emerson (Julian Sands) catching her when she faints.

They are immediately attracted to one another, but George lacks the breeding to court her successfully. Like his father (Denholm Elliot), whose honesty takes Lucy's social circle aback, the graceless George isn't acceptable to Aunt Charlotte or the rest of Lucy's family. Despite the boy's intense passion for her, Lucy returns to England and ends up engaged to a rich young man named Cecil (Daniel Day Lewis of *My Beautiful Laundrette*), whom she doesn't love. By the time Lucy recognizes the depth of her feelings for George, it might be too late.

A Room with a View is full of innuendo, sarcasm and social blunders. Maggie Smith is hilarious as Lucy's pontificating Aunt Charlotte, while Elliot steals every scene he's in with his flagrantly irreverent remarks on Victorian mores. The filmmakers exploit Forster well by taking sharp jabs at the British upper class at every turn in this movie. The script is intelligent and literate, and the cinematography, sets and costumes luxuriously detailed. The only minor flaws are the performances of Carter and Sands. Although they are quite appealing to look at, they don't share the burning chemistry that the script suggests. Compared to the delightfully quirky characterizations by old pros like Smith and Elliot, these two newcomers appear stiff.

RATING: *No MPAA rating, but has brief male nudity and mild violence.*
AWARDS: *Eight 1986 Academy Award nominations; 1986 Academy Awards for Best Screenplay Adaptation (Ruth Prawer Jhabvala), Best Costume Design (Jenny Beavan and John Bright) and Best Art Direction (Gianni Quaranta and Brian Ackland-Snow).*
FILMNOTE: *A Room with a View is one of the top three independent films ever produced, grossing over $20 million in the United States alone and $50 million worldwide.*

ROUND MIDNIGHT
(Video, partially subtitled)

Musical Docudrama

France/U.S.A.   English and French

1986   130 Min.   Color

CREDITS: *Directed by Bertrand Tavernier. Written by Bertrand Tavernier and David Rayfiel. Produced by Irwin Winkler. Cinematography by Bruno De Keyser.*

Music by Herbie Hancock. Released by Warner Brothers. Distributed nontheatrically by Swank Motion Pictures. Starring Dexter Gordon, François Cluzet, Martin Scorsese, Gabrielle Haker, Bobby Hutcherson, Lonette McKee, Herbie Hancock, John Berry, Philip Noiret, Alain Sarde and Eddy Mitchel.

The reason Dexter Gordon's performance as the fictional jazz saxophone player Dale Turner carries so much emotional authority in *Round Midnight* is that he's portraying himself. Not as well-known as other saxophone greats, Gordon was the originator of the bebop jazz sound others emulated. Although this story is also based on the real-life experiences of Bud Powell and Lester Young, two other exiles to Paris in the 1950s, Turner's life most resembles Gordon's own.

The film opens in 1959 in Paris, where Turner is a regular at a small jazz club. He has a serious drinking problem, although the fact that he can barely talk or stand up only slightly affects his sax playing and doesn't deter the jazz hounds who pack the room nightly. One of his biggest fans is Francis (Dustin Hoffman look-alike François Cluzet), a struggling single father who stands outside Turner's club for the chance to hear his idol.

When Francis and Dale first meet, the old jazz man sees an easy target for free drinks. Eventually, he and Francis become such good friends that the Frenchman invites Turner to live with him and his young daughter in their run-down Paris apartment. Francis devotes himself to Dale's rehabilitation, and as Dale becomes deeply involved with Francis and his daughter he is persuaded to give up drinking. The change in Turner's life is remarkable. His eyes light up, his face breaks easily into one continuous big grin and, most important, he starts writing and arranging music again.

Despite its good intentions, the plot of *Round Midnight* is a bit tiresome. Turner's alcoholic antics are replayed so many times that these scenes are interchangeable, and his inebriated speech is so slow that it can lull you to sleep. But French director Bertrand Tavernier *(Sunday in the Country)* and cinematographer Bruno De Keyser skillfully portray the smoky atmosphere of small jazz clubs and the squalor of cheap apartments and seedy Paris alleys. The film's supporting characters, particularly Gordon's fire-mouthed business manager (Gabrielle Haker), are excellent, and Gordon's performance as the aging musician is so immediate and touching that it's hard not to fall in love with him as much as Francis does. Also, Gordon plays his heart out in nearly every musical scene in this movie, both solo and with great backup musicians such as Herbie Hancock and Freddie Hubbard. When he rears back, closes his bloodshot eyes and lets sweet tunes flow from his horn, it's obvious that music is not only the lifeblood of this movie but of Dexter Gordon as well.

RATING: R for profanity and substance abuse.
AWARDS: 1986 Academy Award nomination for Best Actor (Dexter Gordon); 1986 Academy Award for Best Score.

THE RULING CLASS
(Video)

Religious Satire

England

1972   154 Min.   Color

CREDITS: Directed by Peter Medak. Written by Peter Barnes, based on his play. Produced by Jules Buck and Jack Hawkins. Cinematography by Ken Hodges. Music by John Cameron. Production design by Peter Murton. Costume design by Ruth Meyers. Released by Avco Embassy. Distributed nontheatrically by New Yorker Films. Starring Peter O'Toole, Harry Andrews, Arthur Lowe, Carol Brown, Michael Bryant, Nigel Green, William Mervyn, Carolyn Seymour, James Villiers and Hugh Burden.

If you are a Peter O'Toole fan, *The Ruling Class* stands as showpiece for his talents. He plays Alex, the 14th Earl of Gurney, a stark raving but lovable madman who inherits a fortune when his father is found hanging off the rafters of his bedroom wearing a ballerina's skirt. Alex's craziness takes on many forms, but the most prominent one is his Christ complex. Dressed in robes, with long hair and a beard, there is some physical resemblance.

Alex's complex creates problems for his aunt, uncle and cousin, who were left out of his father's will and figure that the only way they can control the Earl's wealth is for Alex to have a child, who presumably will be sane and whom they can influence. It's no easy task, however, finding someone willing to marry Alex and vice versa. Eventually they do, and she and the rest of the family gang up to force Alex out of his Christ complex, which turns out to be a serious mistake for all.

Although two and a half hours of clever puns on religion and the British upper class is a little too much to handle, it's worth it for O'Toole. He's at his best in *The Ruling Class* because his character of Alex allows him to whirl around the room, his face bursting with expression, launching into one hilarious monologue after another. The contrast between Alex and his stuffy family is extreme, although that's not to say that they aren't prone to slightly off-kilter behavior themselves. To add to the fun, director Peter Medak throws in vaudeville song and dance routines at the most inappropriate moments. It's all overly theatrical and at times trite, but thoroughly entertaining nonetheless.

RATING: PG, with mild profanity.
AWARDS: 1972 Academy Award nomination for Best Actor (Peter O'Toole); 1972 National Board of Review Award for Best Actor (O'Toole).

THE SACRIFICE
(Video, subtitled)

Psychological Drama

Sweden/France   Swedish

1986   145 Min.   Color

CREDITS: Directed and written by Andrei Tarkovsky. Produced by Anna-Lena

Wibom. Cinematography by Sven Nykvist. Released by Orion Classics. Distributed nontheatrically by New Yorker Films. Starring Erland Josephson, Susan Fleetwood, Allan Edwall, Sven Wollter, Valerie Mairesse, Flippa Franzen, Tommy Kjellqvist and Gudrun Gisladottir.

Russian expatriate Andrei Tarkovsky came up with a fitting title for this movie, because it is a bit of a sacrifice to sit through two and a half intense hours of *The Sacrifice.* Set at a beach house in Sweden, the story begins when friends and family come over to Alexander's (Erland Josephson) house to celebrate his birthday. His wife, daughter and two best friends are all there for what would appear to be a happy occasion. But how happy can it be when Alexander is seriously depressed, and his companions are brooding intellectuals who can't express themselves without delving into the existential meaning of their lives? Before they can even sit down for ice cream and cake, they are swept up in a nuclear war. What started out to be an unnerving little get-together turns into an apocalyptic sideshow of irrationality, alienation and despair.

Tarkovsky made *The Sacrifice* when he knew he was dying of brain cancer. As a last will and testament, the story is darker and more complex than it appears on the surface. There are many elements in this movie that stylistically resemble Ingmar Bergman's later films. The sets are stark and cold, the lighting is almost always white with dark, angular shadows in the background, and religious metaphors are hiding around every corner. The dialogue, at times powerful, is also painfully deliberate. The main characters say a word, then pause, then carefully go on to the next. Although Sven Nykvist's (a Bergman regular) camera work is always superb, it doesn't vary, and after a while, the movie appears to be in slow motion. But action means very little in this narrative, as it's ultimately *The Sacrifice*'s texture, mood and silent moments that are the most revealing.

RATING: *No MPAA rating, with brief nudity and violence.*
AWARDS: *Special Grand Jury Prize and* Best Artistic Contribution award (Sven Nykvist) at the 1986 Cannes Film Festival.

SAINT JACK
(Video)

Cultural Thriller

U.S.A.

1979　　　　112 Min.　　　　Color

CREDITS: *Directed by Peter Bogdanovich. Written by Peter Bogdanovich, based on the novel by Paul Theroux. Produced by Roger Corman and Hugh Hefner. Cinematography by Robby Muller. Released by New World Pictures. Distributed nontheatrically by Swank Motion Pictures. Starring Ben Gazzara, Denholm Elliot, James Villiers, Peter Bogdanovich, Joss Ackland, Rodney Bewes, Mark Kingston, Lisa Lu, Monika Subramaniam and Judy Lim.*

Jack Flowers (Ben Gazzara) is an Italian-American entrepreneur working in Singapore pimping native women to tourists. But Jack isn't an ordinary pimp. He is tough when his clients get out of hand, but to his women he is very gentle. Jack's main desire is to have the classiest whorehouse in the Orient. Unfortunately, Singapore's Chinese Mafia doesn't take to an American inching in on their territory, and after Jack finally creates his dream bordello, his future in the call girl business becomes precarious. Eventually the pressures become too great, and the normally lighthearted Jack grows despondent.

Jack is superbly played by Gazzara. He's intelligent, quick-tongued and, until the last third of the movie, so full of life he practically bounces from one hustle to the next. But when Jack becomes depressed in the final segment of this film, *Saint Jack* also drags. There is little buildup to his emotional breakdown, and Gazzara isn't as convincing in these scenes. Still, most of *Saint Jack* is a fascinating journey into a very different world. As one character aptly remarks, "Singapore has all the mysteries of the East and all the comfort of the West." Director Peter Bogdanovich *(The Last Picture Show)* and crew deliver the same exotic feel with stunning cinematography and sets that deftly juxtapose the seamier side of Singapore with conspicuously consumptive tourists.

RATING: *R for language, sexual content and brief nudity.*

SALVADOR
(Video, partially subtitled)

Political Docudrama

U.S.A.	English and Spanish
1986	123 Min.	Color

CREDITS: *Directed by Oliver Stone. Written by Oliver Stone and Richard Boyle, based on Boyle's writings. Produced by Oliver Stone and Gerald Green. Music by Georges Delerue. Cinematography by Robert Richardson. Released by Hemsdale Film Corporation. Distributed nontheatrically by Cinecom. Starring James Woods, Jim Belushi, Michael Murphy, John Savage, Elepedia Carillo, Tony Plana, Colby Chester and Cynthia Gibb.*

Although *Salvador* is loosely based on the real experiences of journalist Richard Boyle (who co-authored the film with director Oliver Stone), the writers obviously took some liberties in shaping the script. It's so unlikely, for example, that Boyle would convince his deejay buddy Dr. Rock (Jim Belushi) to come to San Salvador in the middle of a bloody war to party, that the film has been sarcastically renamed *Fear and Loathing in El Salvador* by many critics.

James Woods plays Richard Boyle, a free-lance journalist who goes to El Salvador during the height of the death squad repression to make a fast buck, with his friend Dr. Rock coming up along for the ride. The two proceed to ingest cheap booze and hallucinogens while chasing two-dollar whores. But when Boyle becomes involved with a beautiful Salvadoran woman (Elepedia Carillo) and her family, he gradually gives up the fast lane to become a family man. In trying both to protect them and land a Pulitzer Prize–winning story, he also becomes increasingly affected by the tragic events he witnesses.

Boyle has a knack for showing up at the right place at the right time in this movie. The last person to take communion from the murdered Archbishop Romero and the first to arrive when the bodies of the four Catholic nuns are uncovered in a shallow grave, Boyle is also there to comfort the mortally wounded photojournalist John Hoagland (John Savage). Although these events are certainly important in any historical account of El Salvador, the fact that they are randomly inserted with little background development, and that Boyle is present at every one of them, doesn't help the film's credibility.

Still, Woods gives us our money's worth with his performance as Boyle. His drunken sleaziness and self-indulgence aren't always appealing, but Woods's intensity and skill as an actor lend substance to his every scene. Director Oliver Stone *(Platoon)* also does an excellent job depicting the brutality of a Latin American dictatorship. In spite of the film's serious flaws, it's hard not to be affected by vivid portrayals of innocent civilians torn from their families to be tortured and killed by death squads—scenes made more disturbing by the fact that these incidents are still going on today.

RATING: *R for brief nudity, profanity, substance abuse and a good deal of graphic violence.*
AWARDS: *1986 Academy Award nomination for Best Actor (James Woods).*

SAMMY AND ROSIE GET LAID

(Video)

Social Satire

England

1987   100 Min.   Color

CREDITS: *Directed by Stephen Frears. Written by Hanif Kureishi. Produced by Tim Bevan and Sarah Radclyffe. Cinematography by Oliver Stapleton. Production design by Hugo Luczyc Wyhowski. Released and distributed nontheatrically by Cinecom. Starring Shashi Kapoor, Frances Barber, Claire Bloom, Ayub Khan Din, Roland Gift and Wendy Gazelle.*

Despite the risqué title, which kept the film from being advertised on marquees and in newspapers, Stephen Frears's *Sammy and Rosie Get Laid* is anything but a cheap, teen sex comedy.

The loosely structured story begins with the arrival in London of Rafi (Shashi Kapoor), a Pakistani government official who fled the political unrest there with a sack of money and a troubled conscience. The old man holes up with his son Sammy (Ayub Khan Din) and Sammy's wife, Rosie (Frances Barber), hoping to buy their loyalty and a little peace of mind by setting them up in a house far from the mixed-race slum in which they are stranded. Yet Rafi's goal isn't so easily achieved: Sammy and Rosie seem content amid the squalor, callously flaunting their extramarital affairs and reveling in their own decadence. But as their neighborhood explodes in racial violence, Sammy learns that Rafi's fortune comes from his career as a torturer. Finally, the couple must struggle to overcome a moral bankruptcy they have mistaken for political neutrality and sexual freedom.

As in *My Beautiful Laundrette* and *Prick Up Your Ears,* Frears displays a talent for capturing the humorous side of tragedy. But with virtually no narrative structure or coherent plot line, this film is much more difficult to penetrate. As sexual black com-

edy, *Sammy and Rosie Get Laid* succeeds, with the interplay among Sammy, Rosie, Rafi and their various lovers skillfully juggled until it evolves into a delirious and highly original split-screen climax. Yet while several sexual scenes are played for humor, the film is ultimately quite scathing in its denunciation of Sammy and Rosie's nonchalance. The political undercurrent that runs throughout the film, however, is less successful. Screenwriter Hanif Kureishi *(My Beautiful Laundrette)* seems to want to tackle too many issues, and he doesn't delve deeply into any of them. The scenes of Rafi's haunting past are self-conscious, while the racial tensions in Sammy and Rosie's neighborhood are barely explored outside the physical details of the conflict itself.

RATING: *R, with violence, nudity, profanity, sex and drugs.*

SANJURO

(Video, subtitled)

Samurai Comedy

Japan   Japanese

1962   96 Min.   B&W

CREDITS: *Directed and edited by Akira Kurosawa. Written by Akira Kurosawa, Ryuzo Kikushima and Hideo Oguni, based on the short story "Hibi Heian" by Shugoro Yamamoto. Produced by Ryuzo Kikushima and Tomoyuki Tanaka. Cinematography by Fukuzo Koizumi and Kozo Saito, filmed in Cinemascope. Music by Masaru Sato. Released by Toho Films. Distributed nontheatrically by Films Inc. Starring Toshiro Mifune, Tatsuya Nakadai, Takashi Shimura, Yuzo Kayama, Reiko Dan, Masao Shimizu, Yunosuke Ito, Takako Irie and Kamatari Fujiwara.*

Spurred by the success of *Yojimbo,* director Akira Kurosawa created another action-comedy featuring Toshiro Mifune as the loutish, arrogant samurai whose rough exterior hides a good soul.

Sanjuro begins as Mifune's samurai-with-no-name overhears nine young warriors plot to join forces with the Inspector Kikui to oust their ineffectual leader, the chamberlain. Mifune interrupts the meeting, scratching and yawning as he instructs the boys to trust the chamberlain and not the charismatic Kikui. But disgusted with the chamberlain's leadership, the boys angrily ignore Mifune until their cottage is surrounded by Kikui's men and they realize their mistake. With some ingenious trickery, Mifune rescues the young warriors, and then agrees to help them save the chamberlain, who has been kidnapped by Kikui. Mifune infiltrates Kikui's camp and befriends Murato, Kikui's aide who is Mifune's equal with the sword. As the boys discover the chamberlain's whereabouts, Mifune and Murato are driven toward an inevitable showdown, from which only one can survive.

Sanjuro suffers from predictable action sequences and characters we have seen in samurai films of the past. Like Yojimbo, the focus of the suspense is Mifune's switching loyalties, and the one-note joke that Mifune has a gruff exterior but a heart of gold. His flirting with danger in Kikui's camp is uninvolving, while the film's action sequences aren't staged with the customary Kurosawa flair. Still, Sanjuro can be entertaining. The film is particularly funny when Mifune is dogged by the nine naïve followers who trail behind him like ducklings, and when Mifune is tamed by the chamberlain's old wife, a proper lady who calls the blustering samurai's bluff. Mifune, as always, is excellent, letting an unkempt appearance mask an explosive temper that finds its outlet in short bursts of sword play.

RATING: No MPAA rating, with nothing objectionable.

SAY AMEN, SOMEBODY
(Video)

Documentary

U.S.A.

1982   100 Min.   Color

CREDITS: Directed and written by George T. Neirenberg. Produced by Karen and George T. Neirenberg. Distributed nontheatrically by Films Inc. Starring Willie Mae Ford Smith, Reverend Thomas A. Dorsey, The Barret Sisters, Sallie Martin and The O'Neal Brothers.

Whether religious or not, when a whole church explodes into the rhythmic singing, stomping and clapping of black gospel music, anybody can be turned into a temporary convert. Say Amen, Somebody is a documentary about two of the founders of black gospel music—Willie Mae Ford Smith and Reverend Thomas A. Dorsey.

Both of them are getting on in years, but age only slows them down a bit. They still get up there in front of congregations, prayer meetings and old folks' homes to sing their hearts out and talk about how Jesus has changed their lives. They also remember a good many details of the old days when they reigned as king and queen of American gospel music from their respective altars in Chicago and St. Louis.

Unfortunately, rhythm and blues gospel frequently gives way to ballads in Say Amen, Somebody because both singers are too old for some of the up-tempo routines, while Thomas doesn't have much of a voice left for singing or talking. Filmed with few frills, the interview segments of this film can also ramble on as slowly as some of the ballads. Only close friends and relatives would be interested in all the details this movie reveals.

Still, writer/director George T. Neirenberg takes us behind the scenes of a fascinating world few ever experience firsthand. There is plenty of great music scattered throughout, but more important, Neirenberg and his crew are able to capture the commitment Willie Mae and Thomas have to their music and beliefs. Although they don't always express their inner souls with the vitality of youth, the power of their faith still comes shining through. When Willie Mae and Thomas close their eyes and feel the spirit, it is an undeniably moving experience.

RATING: No MPAA rating, with nothing objectionable.

SCENE OF THE CRIME
(Video, subtitled)

Thriller

France		French
1986	90 Min.	Color

CREDITS: Directed by Andre Techine. Written by Andre Techine, Pascal Bonitzer and Oliver Assayas. Produced by Alain Terzian. Cinematography by Pascal Marti. Released and distributed nontheatrically by Kino International. Starring Catherine Deneuve, Wadeck Stanczak, Victor Lanoux, Nicholas Girandi, Danielle Darrieux and Claire Nebout.

After winning the Best Director award at Cannes for *Rendezvous*, a film that was critically acclaimed but financially unprofitable, Andre Techine decided to cast his next film with a box office draw, Catherine Deneuve. The gamble paid off: *Scene of the Crime* was one of the highest-grossing foreign films in America in 1987.

This highly stylized French thriller begins when the rebellious fourteen-year-old Thomas (Nicholas Girandi) stumbles upon a desperate escaped convict named Martin (Wadeck Stanczak) hiding out in an abandoned shack. Martin makes Thomas bring him money that evening, which starts a chain of misunderstandings and dangerous events that involves Thomas's beautiful mother, Lili (Catherine Deneuve), his grandmother (Danielle Darrieux) and a raving mad femme fatale in a red sports car (Claire Nebout). Mixed in with suspense and murder are symbiotic and twisted rela-

tionships among all of the main players.

Aside from its overly coincidental conclusion, *Scene of the Crime*'s main flaw is zealous camera work. Like a woman with too much makeup, the artsy pans of picturesque landscapes stand out in a script that has plenty going on without these extras. Although the film's suspense is gripping, Techine makes its psychological intrigue as involving as the mystery plot. All the characters in the film have deep-set problems with trust and betrayal. The acting is uniformly excellent, with Denueve giving her strongest performance since *The Last Métro*, and Girandi particularly compelling as her rebellious and tormented son. And as the insane woman in the red sports car, Claire Nebout has a remarkable ability to be beautiful in one scene and repulsive in the next.

RATING: No MPAA rating, with brief nudity and violence.

SCENES FROM A MARRIAGE
(Video, dubbed)

Psychological Drama

Sweden		Swedish
1974	168 Min.	Color

CREDITS: Directed, written and produced by Ingmar Bergman. Cinematography by Sven Nykvist. Set design by Bjorn Thulin. Released by Cinemagraph Films. Distributed nontheatrically by Almi Pictures. Starring Liv Ullmann, Erland Josephson, Bibi Andersson, Jan Malmsjo, Anita Wall and Gunnel Linsblom.

Scenes from a Marriage begins with Marianne (Liv Ullmann) and Johan (Erland Josephson) telling a newspaper reporter that they have been happily married for over a decade. Although the writer buys their story, and Johan and Marianne maintain all the pretenses of a wonderful relationship, they haven't really communicated for years.

Their wall of self-delusion comes tumbling down when Johan tells Marianne that he's been seeing another woman. Long submerged feelings of anger, jealousy, hurt and fear come boiling to the surface from both of them, along with harsh words and even physical abuse. He leaves, then they get back together. They get a divorce, but they still see each other. They both remarry, and then sneak away from their new spouses to have a wildly passionate affair. By the end of this nearly three-hour examination of their marriage and breakup, Bergman has lanced every painful abscess related to that relationship.

Although there is a plot in *Scenes from a Marriage,* it takes a backseat to the sheer emotional intensity of Johan and Marianne's characters. Bergman does an outstanding job plumbing the dark psyches of this emotionally repressed couple. Often only Marianne and Johan's grief-stricken faces fill the screen as they sit stiffly in stark, brightly lit rooms, while cinematographer Sven Nykvist does his best to show us their every twitch, stammer and grimace. Ullmann and Josephson give such wrenching performances that the emotional weight of their "talks" is never less than riveting. Although *Scenes from a Marriage* is exhausting, it deals so thoroughly with issues of anger, fear and self-doubt in relationships that it ranks as one of Bergman's most throught-provoking films.

RATING: PG, with mild profanity.
AWARDS: 1974 New York Film Critics Awards for Best Actress (Ullmann) and Best Screenplay (Ingmar Bergman); one of the National Board of Review's 5 Best Foreign Films in 1974.
WARNING: Although the dubbing is good in Scenes from a Marriage *(Bergman actually dubbed the film into English during production), the film is much better subtitled at the theater.*
FILMNOTE: Scenes from a Marriage was originally a five-hour program for Swedish television that Bergman shortened for theatrical release.

SECRET HONOR
(Video)

Political Satire

U.S.A.

1984   85 Min.   Color

CREDITS: Directed by Robert Altman. Written by Donald Freed and Arnold Stone, based on their play. Produced by Robert Altman and Scott Bushnell. Cinematography by Pierre Mignot. Music by George Butt. Released by Sandcastle 5. Distributed nontheatrically by Cinecom. Starring Philip Baker Hall.

One of the more intriguing parts of the Watergate affair was Richard Nixon's last few days in the White House, when he allegedly drank heavily, wallowed in self-pity, and ranted and raved at those close to him. In Robert Altman's fourth and most successful adaptation of a stage play to the screen, he dramatizes what might have taken place during those historic days.

Secret Honor begins immediately after Nixon's resignation and is set in the Oval Office. Nixon (Philip Baker Hall) is dictating some thoughts on Watergate and his career to be used later in his memoirs. He pours himself a Scotch, paces back and forth, then pours another. In a drunken tirade, he talks about "those studs, the Kennedys" and Henry Kissinger selling out to the Shah. His paranoia deepens as he rambles on about the hippies, Alger Hiss and Vietnam. It's as if his unconscious is talking, with familiar names and situations from the sixties and seventies charging to the surface in a flurry of non sequiturs. But how Nixon expresses himself is just as revealing as what he says—anger, paranoia and guilt underlie every sentence.

Based on Donald Freed and Arnold Stone's long-running stage play, *Secret Honor* takes a little patience at first. Philip Baker Hall doesn't look quite like Nixon, and in the beginning he mumbles so many disparate thoughts that it's hard to follow what's really going on. But once you realize that it's not always what he's saying but how he's saying it that's important in *Secret Honor,* this film turns into a masterwork. Hall gives one hell of a performance from start to finish. His Nixon is sadly comical when he laughs uncontrollably, stammers for words or explodes into obscenities, and infuriating in his conceit and self-deception. Altman cleverly varies the camera angles and lighting to keep the narrative from being too claustrophobic. George Butt's haunting musical score frames Nixon's madness perfectly. Even if you are tired of Watergate, Nixon and all the details of his presidency and resignation, as a portrait of a man obsessed with power and the society that created him, *Secret Honor* is powerful and mesmerizing.

RATING: *No MPAA rating, with profanity.*

THE SEDUCTION OF MIMI
(Video, dubbed)

Social Satire

Italy	Italian
1974	89 Min.	Color

CREDITS: *Directed and written by Lina Wertmuller. Cinematography by Giuseppe Rotunno. Released and distributed nontheatrically by New Line Cinema. Starring Giancarlo Giannini, Mariangela Melato, Agostina Belli and Elena Fiore.*

The Seduction of Mimi is another Lina Wertmuller romp through the political landscapes of sex and class in post–World War II Italy. In this film, Giancarlo Giannini *(Seven Beauties)* plays Carmello Mimi, a quarrier who loses his job when the Mafia discovers he voted for the Communist candidate in his Sicilian hometown elections. Afraid of further reprisals, Carmello quickly flees to Northern Italy to seek other employment, leaving his despondent wife behind. There he finds a job in a factory, becomes a union organizer and falls for Fiore (Mariangela Melato of *Swept Away),* a beautiful young Communist Party activist who is also smitten with Carmello.

But just after she has his child, Carmello's troubles with the Mafia begin anew when he accidently witnesses a shoot-out. The Mafia insists that he return to his Sicilian village to ensure his silence. Unable to refuse their "protection," he moves back to his village with Fiore and his son, where he clandestinely lives two lives—refusing to have sex with his wife while sneaking away to be with his mistress. Meanwhile, when he finds out that his wife is pregnant by a Fascist city official, he goes wild with jealousy and decides to avenge her infidelity by impregnating the man's obese wife.

Feminists squirm at the mere mention of this now-famous seduction scene, in which Wertmuller gives us a full-screen, fish-eye view of this woman's cellulite-laden behind, with the diminutive Giannini cowering in the background. In its own uncomfortable way, that scene is also one of the funniest in a film already loaded with absurdly comical situations. Wertmuller throws in plenty of her trademark references to the oppression of the working class, yet the narrative never gets too bogged down in politics. *The Seduction of Mimi*'s performances are excellent, particularly Giannini, who can express so much through those basset hound eyes. Although the way he treats his women is certainly offensive, he is such a lovable rogue that it's easy to forgive him, as well as Wertmuller, for the blatantly sexist content of his character and her movie.

RATING: *R for language, nudity and sex.* AWARDS: *International Critics Prize at the 1974 Cannes Film Festival.*

THE SERPENT'S EGG
(Video)

Psychological Thriller

West Germany/U.S.A.	English
1977	120 Min.	Color

CREDITS: *Directed and written by Ingmar Bergman. Produced by Dino DeLaurentis. Cinematography by Sven Nykvist. Music* by Rolf Wilhelm. Released by Dino De-Laurentiis Films/Paramount. Distributed nontheatrically by Films Inc. Starring Liv Ullmann, David Carradine, Gert Frobe, Heinz Bennent, James Whitemore, Toni Berger, Paula Braend and Edna Bruenell.

One of Ingmar Bergman's only English language films, The Serpent's Egg is also one of his least successful. Set in Berlin in 1923, where Hitler is only a dark rumor gathering momentum on the fringes of a Germany ravaged by World War I, the film begins when a trapeze artist kills himself for no apparent reason. His brother Abel (David Carradine) quickly turns to the bottle to drown his sorrow and seeks out his brother's ex-wife, Manuela (Liv Ullmann), for comfort. Although Manuela, now a cabaret singer and prostitute, takes Abel in, she can't settle him down, and both are evicted from her apartment because of his erratic behavior. Destitute and homeless, Abel reluctantly accepts shelter and a job in a lab controlled by Hans (Heinz Bennent), a mysterious scientist who is also Manuela's part-time lover. In the following days, Abel becomes even more erratic until he realizes that his brother's death and his own instability are connected to deadly experiments conducted by Hans and financed by a powerful group with plans for a new Germany.

Cinematographer Sven Nykvist, who has served Bergman so well throughout his career, does an excellent job creating a dark and moody atmosphere in The Serpent's Egg. But little else about the film works. Ullmann is hopelessly miscast as a singer/prostitute, often looking ridiculous wearing seductive dresses and pounds of rouge. Compared to Carradine, however, she turns in an Oscar-caliber performance. As the film's protagonist, his role consists mostly of silent brooding and delivering his lines so flatly that he seems to be reading them right off the cue cards. Occasionally, he launches into a temper tantrum, but Bergman is so preoccupied with showing us his rage that he neglects to explain the reason behind it. Bergman also ignores the film's more exciting plot twists in a narrative that becomes increasingly uninteresting as its main character grows more impenetrable.

RATING: No MPAA rating, with sexual situations.

SEVEN BEAUTIES
(Video, dubbed)

Social Satire

Italy		Italian
1976	115 Min.	Color

CREDITS: Directed and written by Lina Wertmuller. Produced by Lina Wertmuller, Giancarlo Giannini and Arrigo Columbo. Cinematography by Tonino Delli Colli. Music by Enzo Iannacci. Released and distributed nontheatrically by Almi Pictures. Starring Giancarlo Giannini, Fernando Rey, Shirley Stoler, Elena Fiore, Enzo Vitale, Mario Conti, Piero Di Orio, Ermelinda De Felice and Francesca Marciano.

Although at times uncomfortably violent and sexually controversial, Seven Beauties is a Lina Wertmuller masterpiece. It's the story of Pasqualino (Giancarlo Giannini), a two-bit gangster who lives with his mother and seven fat sisters in a Rome tenement right before the start of World War II. Pasqualino fashions himself a lady-killer, a big shot and a man of honor, but in reality people are always making a dupe of him.

Pasqualino's real troubles begin when he accidentally kills the pimp of one of his sisters and, like a fool, brags about it. He is sent to jail and then to a mental hospital. When he gets out, he's abducted into Mussolini's army, but the army is just one more wrong turn in Pasqualino's life. He deserts, is caught, and ends up in a German concentration camp. All the tragedy that befell him previously is nothing compared to what he has to endure in the concentration camp. But Pasqualino will do anything to survive, even seduce the concentration camp's hideously fat female commandant (Shirley Stoler of The Honeymoon Killers).

As each escape leads Pasqualino into a more disastrous situation, Seven Beauties evolves into darker satire. Giannini is outstanding as Pasqualino. He acts like a grade-school bully one minute and a cowering fool the next, yet his tremendous will to survive usually keeps us rooting for him. Wertmuller brings out various themes of sex, war, Fascism and class in perversely funny ways. Although there are several moments where she pushes us to the edge of discomfort, in scenes like the one of Pasqualino seducing the fat commandant, she keeps us right in the middle of the action with a tight plot and well-drawn characters.

RATING: R for nudity and graphic violence.
AWARDS: 1976 Academy Award nominations for Best Director (Lina Wertmuller), Best Actor (Giancarlo Giannini), Best Screenplay Written Directly for the Screen (Wertmuller) and Best Foreign Film.
WARNING: Dubbing is poor.
FILMNOTE: Shirley Stoler, the commandant in Seven Beauties, also plays Mrs. Steve on the television show "Pee Wee's Playhouse."

SEVEN SAMURAI
(Video, subtitled)

Samurai Comedy

Japan		Japanese
1954	200 Min.	B&W

CREDITS: Directed by Akira Kurosawa. Written by Akira Kurosawa, Shinobu Hashimoto and Hideo Oguni. Produced by Shojiro Motoki. Cinematography by Asaishi Nakai. Music by Fumio Hayasaka. Released by Columbia Pictures. Distributed nontheatrically by Films Inc. and Kit Parker Films. Starring Takashi Shimura, Toshiro Mifune, Yoshio Inaba, Seiji Miyaguchi, Minoru Chiaki, Daisuke Kato, Isao (Ko) Kimura, Kuninori Kodo and Kamatari Fujiwara.

In Seven Samurai, Akira Kurosawa borrowed themes and characters from the American westerns he loved so dearly to create one of the greatest epics ever made, remembered not only for the power of its action sequences but also for the emotional content of its dramatic scenes.

The film is set in nineteenth-century Japan, where samurai warriors, once the guardians of the feudal system, now wander the countryside as free-lance swords for hire. One such warrior, Kambei (Takashi Shimura), is approached by a group of poor villagers in desperate need of his protection from a gang of vicious bandits who raid their village each year. Touched by the villagers' resolve to be victimized no longer, Kambei agrees to help and recruits five other swordsmen as reinforcements. En route to the village, they pick up a seventh, Kikuchiyo (Toshiro Mifune), an emotional, awkward misfit whose raw desire to belong to the group overshadows his lack of ability. When the seven arrive, however, they are not exactly welcomed by the people they have been hired to defend. So Kambei and his men not only have to train the reluctant villagers to defend themselves, but they must win their confidence as well.

Always known for his ability to stage a spectacle, Kurosawa is at his best in Seven Samurai. The final battle, in which the warriors, bandits and villagers seem to be swallowed up by mud and rain, is one of the most beautiful war scenes in the history of cinema. Some of the film's quieter action sequences, such as a master swordsman's duel with a braggart in a barren field, are also quite powerful. But perhaps most impressive are the smaller dramatic scenes among the villagers and the samurai. Mifune turns in a searing performance as a man whose bluster hides insecurities and self-loathing, while Shimura is excellent as the aging warrior whose code of honor demands his participation in battle despite his obsolescence. At 200 minutes, Seven Samurai may seem like an overwhelming time commitment to some viewers, but the film pays off in so many different ways that it's worth every minute.

RATING: No MPAA rating, with mild violence.
AWARDS: 1955 Academy Award for Best Foreign Film; Silver Lion at the 1954 Venice Film Festival.
FILMNOTE: First released in the United

States as The Magnificent Seven, Seven Samurai *was later renamed to distinguish it from the John Sturges (1960) remake of the film.*

THE SEVENTH SEAL
(Video, subtitled)

Psychological Drama

Sweden	Swedish
1958	96 Min.	B&W

CREDITS: *Directed by Ingmar Bergman. Written by Ingmar Bergman, based on his play* Sculpture in Wood. *Produced by Allan Ekelund. Cinematography by Gunnar Fischer. Set design by P. A. Lundgren. Costume design by Manne Lindholm. Released by Det Sjunde Films. Distributed nontheatrically by Films Inc. Starring Max von Sydow, Gunnar Bjornstrand, Bibi Andersson, Nils Poppe, Bengt Ekerot, Ake Fridell and Inga Gill.*

The son of a minister, Ingmar Bergman was so affected by Christianity at an early age that most of his films, including *The Seventh Seal,* are overflowing with religious symbolism.

This story takes place in the Middle Ages, as a battle-weary knight (Max von Sydow) returns home from the Crusades and, observing the ravages of the plague, begins to doubt a God that could cause so much suffering. Soon he too is visited by Death (Bengt Ekerot), but instead of bowing to his fate, he challenges Death to a chess match—willing to forfeit his life if he loses. In a parallel story, a young, optimistic couple, Jof (Nils Poppe) and Mia (Bibi Andersson), travel from village to village with a small acting troupe. During their journey, they see people in the disease-stricken villages living in fear, while religious zealots mount parades of flagellation, and desperate vigilantes burn "devil-possessed" villagers at the stake. When he meets the couple, the tormented knight is reassured by their love for each other, while Death, his sinister adversary, sits benignly nearby, waiting to make the final move that will decide all of their fates.

Although *The Seventh Seal* is stuffed with visions of mankind in the throes of suffering, the film is also strangely comical in places. Certain scenes, such as the knight bantering with Death and the drunken orgies of free-spirited villagers, are actually silly. The film's sets and costumes are outrageously vaudevillian, providing a visual relief from the intensity of the plot and characters. Even the themes of death and the failure of religion are presented with overt and lively metaphors that are absurdly amusing. But rest assured that Bergman inundates this film with plenty of dark, intense characters and complex issues concerning the meaning of life and death. The cinematography by Gunnar Fischer further enhances these concerns with high-contrast black-on-stark-white tableaux, while the performances are excellent across the board.

RATING: *No MPAA rating, with nothing objectionable.*
AWARDS: *Special Jury Prize at the 1957 Cannes Film Festival.*

SHERMAN'S MARCH: AN IMPROBABLE QUEST FOR LOVE
(Video)

Social Documentary

U.S.A.	
1986	155 Min.	Color

CREDITS: *Directed, written, narrated, recorded, photographed and edited by Ross McElwee. Co-narrated by Richard Leacock. Released and distributed nontheatrically by First Run Features. Starring Ross McElwee (the rest of the cast didn't want their last names in the credits).*

In 1981, documentary filmmaker Ross McElwee set out to make a movie about

General Sherman's historic march through the South at the close of the Civil War. But early on his plans changed when he got a "Dear John" call from his lover in New York. Heartbroken and lonely, Ross returned to his parents' home in South Carolina, where his friends and family tried to fix him up with single women they knew. Ross dropped his work on Sherman to make a documentary on the women of the South—using his new aquaintences as his subjects.

There are seven of them to be exact, and about all they have in common is Ross. His first encounter is with an aspiring actress obsessed with her cellulite exercises and Burt Reynolds. Then Ross goes out with a fundamentalist interior decorator who introduces him to her heavily armed survivalist friends. Among the others are a self-styled intellectual writing her doctoral dissertation in linguistics; a gutsy blues singer determined to be a star; a Mormon folk singer; an ex-girlfriend who is a feminist lawyer; and another girlfriend who is an anti-nuke activist.

Some viewers may find this movie a little slow by the two-and-a-half-hour mark, as few of the characters are snappy conversationalists, but Ross's dry-witted commentary about women, his romantic failures, Sherman's march and his obsession with nuclear holocaust livens up this documentary at just the right moments. It is also quite remarkable that these women let Ross film them in the first place. All the time he asks them questions, follows them around on their daily chores and goes out with them, a camera is perched on his shoulder. And for the most part, they act as if the camera is invisible. The result is a funny, touching and somewhat frightening study of women from the South, and a highly personal journal of being single in the eighties.

RATING: *No MPAA rating, with profanity and one brief nude scene.*

SHE'S GOTTA HAVE IT
(Video)

Social Satire

U.S.A.

1986   100 Min.   B&W

CREDITS: *Directed, written, produced and edited by Spike Lee. Cinematography by Ernest Dickerson. Music by Bill Lee (Spike's father). Released by Forty Acres and a Mule. Distributed nontheatrically by New Yorker Films. Starring Tracy Camila Johns, Tommy Redmond Hicks, John Canada Terrell, Spike Lee and Joi Lee (Spike's sister).*

With tongue planted firmly in cheek, the twenty-nine-year-old director/writer Spike Lee pokes fun at black male stereotypes with his three characters—Jamie Overstreet (Tommy Redmond Hicks), Greer Childs (John Canada Terrell) and Mars Blackmon (Spike Lee). Jamie is a traditional man who wears white button-down shirts and whose values are grounded in the middle-class. Greer is a gold chain–wearing, muscle-pumping male model who is the epitome of the word *macho*. And Mars is a jive-talking bohemian who wears high-top tennis shoes even when he is having sex. The three share the same woman, Nola Darling (Tracy Camila Johns), and though each of them wants her to be his, Nola is a free spirit who shares her body with anyone who suits her fancy. The fact that her men can't handle this freedom doesn't faze her at all.

Although set in a black neighborhood in Brooklyn, and filmed with an all-black cast and crew, the jokes in *She's Gotta Have It* could prick any man, black or white. Lee's Mars is hilarious, particularly in his rap-whining to Nola. Terrell's Greer has some funny moments as the superstud, and Hicks's Jamie is quintessentially cool and successful. Unfortunately, Johns's Nola Darling isn't as strongly drawn as the male characters, and at times the story line has an overly improvised feel to it. Still, this film looks great, especially considering its budget ($175,000). And with enough clever and original satire to fill half a dozen of Hollywood's sitcoms, *She's Gotta Have It* has set Lee's career as a comic filmmaker off and running.

RATING: Originally rated X by the MPAA, the film was toned down by Lee for its theatrical release to get an R rating for tasteful sex and profanity.

SHOAH

(Video, mostly subtitled)

Holocaust Documentary

France   French, Polish, German, Hebrew, English, Yiddish and Italian

1985   563 Min.   Color

CREDITS: Directed by Claude Lanzmann, assisted of Corinna Coulmas and Irene Steinfeldt-Levi. Produced by Les Films Aleph Historia with the participation of the French Ministry of Culture. Cinematography by Dominique Chapuis, Jimmy Glasberg and William Lubchansky. Edited by Ziva Postec and Anna Ruiz. Released and distributed nontheatrically by New Yorker Films. Starring Simon Srebnik, Abraham Bomba, Dr. Rudolf Vrba, Richard Glazar, Filip Muller, Franz Suchomel, Dr. Franz Grassler and Jan Karski.

In one of the first scenes of *Shoah*, director Claude Lanzmann and Polish Jew Simon Srebnik casually stroll through a group of deserted buildings outside the sleepy little village of Chelmno, Poland. We hear the sounds of birds chattering, wind rustling through trees and the roar of a rushing stream. At that tranquil moment, it's difficult to believe that Chelmno was the place where the Nazis first used the gas chamber. Over the course of three years, 400,000 men, women and children died there. Srebnik was one of only two prisoners to survive.

The Chelmno scene is typical of *Shoah*. Shots of beautiful scenery serve as a backdrop for victims and witnesses to retell some of the most ghastly experiences in modern history. Lanzmann interviews Jewish survivors, Polish villagers and farmers who lived near and worked in the camps, former SS men and Nazi bureaucrats who oversaw the operation, and freedom fighters from the Warsaw Ghetto Uprising. Lanzmann's approach was to ask small questions, not the larger ones involving how such a travesty could happen. Matter-of-factly, as if presenting a tour, he exposes many of the details involved in the full-scale extermination process at Treblinka, Auschwitz and Chelmno. The film's subjects talk about the timetables and finances of running a death factory, the logistics of transporting and housing thousands of victims before their executions, the manner in which victims were herded into the gas chambers, and the bureaucracy needed to dispose of bodies without letting the outside world discover their solution to "the Jewish problem." These stories are horrifying, and all the more extraordinary because the recanting is accomplished without one frame of archival footage, without shots of dismembered corpses or frightened prisoners being liberated at the end of the war.

Lanzmann shot over 350 hours of film in fourteen different countries and seven languages over an eleven-year duration. The written text of the film alone is over 6,000 pages, and the running time of *Shoah* is nine hours. Of course, a few segments of this film are tedious, while others are too concerned with inconsequential details. But considering the scope of the project, the uninvolving moments are a small problem that doesn't detract from the entire picture. *Shoah* so thoroughly documents one of the most disturbing episodes of recent history and the stories of people who still bear that period's scars that it is not only one of the most compelling documentaries ever made, but it also serves as an overwhelming affirmation of the value of human life.

RATING: No MPAA rating, with disturbing images.
FILMNOTE: Lanzmann did numerous secret interviews and was occasionally caught and beaten up, and once landed in the hospital.

SHOOT THE PIANO PLAYER
(Video, subtitled)

Mystery Satire

France   French

1962   84 Min.   B&W

CREDITS: *Directed by François Truffaut.
Written by François Truffaut and Marcel
Moussy, based on the novel* Down There *by
David Goodis. Cinematography by Raoul
Coutard. Music by Georges Delerue. Art
direction by Jacques Mely. Released by
Astor Films. Distributed nontheatrically by
Films Inc. Starring Charles Aznavour,
Marie Dubous, Nicole Berger, Serge Devri,
Claude Mansard, Albert Remy, Jacques
Aslanian, Michele Mercier, Richard Kanay-
an and Daniel Boulanger.*

Shoot the Piano Player announces its intentions right from the start when the
heavyset Richard (Jacques Aslanian) is
chased down the street by a pair of thugs
and runs into a lamppost. The next thing
we know, he's having an absurd conversation with a stranger about the nature of
love, and then he ducks into a smoky nightclub to ask his brother Charlie (played by
French singer Charles Aznavour) to help
him escape the mobsters he and their other
brother, Chico (Albert Remy), have just
ripped off.

Charlie is hardly capable of dealing with
anyone else's problems since his wife committed suicide. A once-famous concert
pianist who's now a broken-down honky-
tonk player in a Paris dive, Charlie is paralyzed by women, even though several of
them chase after him. Meanwhile, the thugs
who are after his brothers harass him as
well, and when he gets in a tussle with his
boss at the club, he ends up unintentionally
stabbing him to death.

Is *Shoot the Piano Player* a comedy, a
mystery or a psychological drama? The an-
swer is that it is a hybrid of all three.
Although the story line jumps from one
setting to the next with few coherent transitions, Truffaut gives us a series of wonderfully constructed vignettes about love,

success, and the meaning of life and death.
Some of the film's suspense is scary, while
Charlie makes a consummate existential
straight man when he talks to himself about
his failures with women while some beautiful temptress is trying to seduce him. The
whole cadre of offbeat supporting characters is similarly tragic and comical. Visually
the movie is cleverly crafted to express both
the darker sides to the story's characters
and the atmosphere of Hollywood gangster
films.

RATING: *No MPAA rating, with mild violence.*
WARNING: *Some video versions of this
film have the classic white-subtitle-on-
white-background problem.*

THE SHOOTING PARTY
(Video)

Social Drama

England

1984   108 Min.   Color

CREDITS: *Directed by Alan Bridges. Writ-
ten by Julian Bond, based on the novel by
Isabel Colgate. Produced by Geoffrey
Reeve. Cinematography by Fred Tammes.
Music by John Scott. Released and distrib-
uted nontheatrically by European Classics.
Starring James Mason, Edward Fox,
Dorothy Tutin, John Gielgud, Gordon
Jackson, Cheryl Campbell, Robert Hardy,
Ruppert Frazier, Aharon Ipale and Judi
Bowker.*

The Shooting Party is nothing less than a
remake of Jean Renoir's *The Rules of the
Game* transplanted to England in 1913.
Unfortunately, it's also nothing more, a
pale imitation distinguished only by the
performances of James Mason and John
Gielgud.

Mason (in his last role before his death)
plays Sir Randolph Nettleby, an aging lord
with a country estate. He invites a dozen
friends and relatives for a weekend of sport
and parties in celebration of the impending

marriage of his brother (Gordon Jackson) to Olivia (Cheryl Campbell), a beautiful young woman half his age. At first glance, the gathering is quite genteel, yet the guests' surface manners conceal deep conflicts. Olivia is pursued by Lionel Stephens (Ruppert Frazier), a graceful young man who also represents the only challenge to the shooting supremacy of the highly competitive Gilbert (Edward Fox). Throughout the weekend, Olivia and Lionel circle each other discreetly, tempted to have an affair, but Olivia's fiancé is always lurking in the background. At the same time Lionel moves closer to a dangerous confrontation with Gilbert on the hunting ground. The weekend's hunts are also marred by an eccentric animal conservationist (John Gielgud) who is willing to do anything to stop the senseless murder of God's creatures.

Although based on a novel by Isabel Colgate, *The Shooting Party* contains several scenes transparently borrowed from *The Rules of the Game*. A costume party, the bed hopping among Sir Randolph's servants and guests, and even a tragic hunting accident are all contained (and done better) in Renoir's film. But the story's weak execution finally sinks this film. Certain scenes move so lethargically they are practically in slow motion, while most of the characters emanate little intensity, frozen by their careful manners. Only veterans Mason and Gielgud deliver compelling performances. Playing men at opposite ends of the social scale, their interactions eloquently underscore that the fading of their values, and not the war building overseas, will ultimately destroy the British Empire.

RATING: No MPAA rating, with brief nudity and mild violence.

THE SHOP ON MAIN STREET
(Video, subtitled)

World War II Drama

Czechoslovakia		Czech
1965	128 Min.	B&W

CREDITS: Directed by Jan Kadar and Elmar Klos. Written by Jan Kadar, Elmar Klos and Ladislav Grossman, based on Grossman's story "Obchod No Korze." Produced by Ladislav Hanus, Jaromir Lukas and Jorden Balurov. Cinematography by Vladimir Novotny. Released by Prominent Films. Distributed nontheatrically by Films Inc. Starring Jozef Kroner, Ida Kaminska, Hana Slivkova, Frantisek Zvarik, Helena Zvarikov and Martin Holly.

Occasionally a film comes along that allows us to let down our defenses and feel tender emotions buried deep inside. *The Shop on Main Street* is such a movie. Set in 1942 in a Nazi-occupied Czechoslovakian town, the story concerns Tono (Jozef Kroner), an unemployed carpenter hounded by his wife for not making a living. When his Fascist brother-in-law makes him the Aryan controller of a button shop run by an elderly Jewish widow named Rosalie (Ida Kaminska), he jumps at the chance to get his wife off his back.

But when Tono shows up at the shop, Rosalie is so kind to him he doesn't have the heart to take over. Instead, he pretends to be a distant relative and, with the help of a Jewish civic group that pays Tono to keep up the façade, he and Rosalie develop a good working relationship while growing very fond of each other. But anti-Semitism is ever-present in the background and there is a threat of doom in Rosalie's future.

The Shop on Main Street starts out as a comedy, populated by bumbling Fascists and common villagers such as Tono and Rosalie. There are some hilarious scenes of Tono pretending to his wife to be a tough controller, and then, a moment later, accommodating Rosalie like "a good Jewish boy." The acting is extraordinary, the sets simple and real. With so many warm and wonderful people, it seems as if nothing bad could really happen to Rosalie and the other Jews we get to know. But then history intervenes. Many of the characters we have grown to love are ground up in the Nazi machine, and our laughter gradually turns to tears. By the end of *The Shop on Main Street*, this sweet little comedy turns into a haunting tragedy.

RATING: No MPAA rating, with mild violence.
AWARDS: 1965 Academy Award for Best Foreign Film; 1966 Academy Award nomination for Best Actress (Ida Kaminska).

SHORT EYES
(Video)

Social Drama

U.S.A.

1977   104 Min.   Color

CREDITS: *Directed by Robert Young. Written by Miguel Pinero, based on his play. Produced by Lewis Harris. Cinematography by Peter Sova. Music by Curtis Mayfield. Released and distributed nontheatrically by Almi Pictures. Starring Bruce Davison, Jose Perez, Nathan George, Don Blakely, Shawn Elliott, Miguel Pinero, Curtis Mayfield, Tito Goya, Joe Carberry, Kenny Steward, Bob Maroff and Keith Davis.*

Short Eyes is prison lingo for a child molester, someone like Clark Davis (Bruce Davison, the rat man in the movie *Willard*). A tormented, middle-class white man with a wife and kid, Clark is awaiting his child molestation trial in a New York City jail where the other inmates on his cell block don't take too kindly to a short eyes being in their company. To these murderers, arsonists and junkies, Clark's is the one unforgivable crime.

Davis is also one of three white men on the cell block, where racial tensions run high, especially between the blacks and Puerto Ricans. In the course of the few days during which the story takes place, there are rapes, knifings and brutal confrontations among the inmates. Yet despite their battles, these violent men do have one thing in common: a hatred of Clark.

With the exception of a couple of song-and-dance routines that come off as contrived, *Short Eyes* is a shocking exposé of prison life, from the jargon to the homosexuality to the misplaced machismo. The acting is uniformly excellent and the story's focus moves quickly from one inmate to the next so no single character becomes overbearing. Where the movie stumbles is in its sometimes overly talky script and difficult-to-understand prison jive (there should be subtitles). Still, director Robert Young *(The Ballad of Gregorio Cortez)* and writer Miguel Pinero (an ex-con himself) lead us into the inner souls of the characters so convincingly that we never stop feeling the oppression in their lives. Although these inmates commit senseless acts of violence, they are portrayed as human beings, not animals, whose behavior is better understood in the context of the society that created them.

RATING: R for a lot of violence and profanity.
FOOTNOTE: Short Eyes was filmed in the now-closed, infamous New York City jail, The Tombs.

SID AND NANCY
(Video)

★   ★   ½

Social Docudrama

U.S.A./England

1986   111 Min.   Color

CREDITS: *Directed by Alex Cox. Written by Alex Cox and Abbe Wool. Produced by Eric Fellner. Cinematography by Roger Deakins. Music by Joe Strummer, The Pogues, Pray for Rain and Steve Jones. Released and distributed nontheatrically by The Samuel Goldwyn Company. Starring Gary Oldman, Chloe Webb, Drew Schol-*

field, *David Hayman, Debby Bishop, Tony London, Perry Benson and Ann Lambton.*

This fictionalized biography of Sid Vicious from the Sex Pistols and his girlfriend, Nancy Spungen, is less an exciting film portrait of punk rock celebrities than a disturbing chronicle of two tragic lives. *Sid and Nancy* opens as Sid is arrested for stabbing Nancy to death with a hunting knife. Through flashbacks, the film then attempts to re-create the events leading up to her death.

It doesn't take long to realize that the foundation of Sid and Nancy's relationship is heroin. In fact, they meet when Nancy has just been ripped off by a pusher, and to make her feel better the dim-witted Sid gives her all his money to score some more drugs. From then on in this movie, it's smack, smack and more smack. When they aren't shooting up, throwing up or nodding out, they have violent drug-related arguments or rambling exchanges, all the way up to heroin-induced murder.

It's bad enough that Sid and Nancy actually went through the events revealed in this movie, but director Alex Cox's depiction of the most violent and dehumanizing details of their years together is almost exploitive. Even the few scenes of Sid playing with the Sex Pistols are pretty much the same thing set to music, with Sid in a heroin stupor bobbing to the beat.

As he portrays Sid and Nancy as a tragic, star-crossed couple, Cox inadvertently drives home the message that they must have been awful to be around. Gary Oldman and Chloe Webb give intense and convincing performances as the repugnant couple, and the script of this movie certainly exposes the hopelessness and confusion in their lives. But watching their incoherent conversations and heroin antics repeated for nearly two hours becomes as wearisome as it is repulsive.

RATING: *R for excessive substance abuse, language, violence and some nudity.*
FILMNOTE: *In preparing emotionally and physically for his role as Sid, Oldman went from 150 pounds to a mere 110. At one point, the actor was so thin that he collapsed during a London stage performance and had to be hospitalized.*

SILVER CITY
(Video)

Cultural Drama

Australia

1986   110 Min.   Color

CREDITS: *Directed by Sophia Turkiewicz. Written by Sophia Turkiewicz and Thomas Keanally. Cinematography by John Seale. Music by William Motzing. Art direction by Igor Nay. Costume design by Jan Hurley. Released by Limelight Production. Distributed nontheatrically by The Samuel Goldwyn Company. Starring Gosia Dobrowolska, Hvar Kants, Anna Jemison, Steve Bisley, Debra Lawrence, Ewa Brok, Joel Coen, Tim McKenzie and Dennis Miller.*

When nearly two million Europeans emigrated to Australia after World War II in search of a better life, many encountered prejudice and hardship instead. *Silver City* tells the story of two Polish immigrants who try to break the chains of their heritage in a racist society, while trying to come to terms with their passionate yet impossible love for one another.

Nina (Gosia Dobrowolska) and Julian (Hvar Kants) meet in a barren settlement camp called Silver City soon after they arrive in Australia. She's a beautiful unmarried schoolteacher with bright hopes for the future, and he's an aspiring lawyer with deep scars from his imprisonment during the war. Despite the fact that Julian is happily married, their friendship boils into a passionate love. Nina tries to avoid Julian by taking a job as a linen maid in a town far away, but the separation is too painful for both of them, and she eventually moves to the Polish ghetto in Sydney where Julian and his wife, Anna (Anna Jemison), have settled. In a love nest made from packing crates and in their own secret hideaway in a converted garage, Nina and Julian try desperately to be happy. But always looming over them is Australia's anti-Polish racism and Julian's devotion to his wife.

An often moving drama of desire and will, *Silver City*'s principal strength is its performances. Gosia Dobrowolska is radiant as Nina, whose life-affirming spirit is present every moment she is on the screen. Kants and Jemison fill out the triangle powerfully, and all three convey a sense of dignity in dealing with difficult personal and political situations. Writer/director Sophia Turkiewicz (a second-generation daughter of Polish-Australian parents) and co-writer Thomas Keanally (a noted Australian historian) skillfully capture what it must have been like to be unwelcome in a strange society, while the film's sets and costumes authentically reflect the physical details of the era. *Silver City* only stumbles because the love triangle established early on is merely repeated in several different settings. Instead of growing more complex as their struggles evolve, the three main characters in *Silver City* seem to stagnate in the emotionally dangerous predicament framed by a political climate they are powerless to change.

RATING: *PG, with nothing objectionable.*
AWARDS: *1984 Australian Film Awards for Best Supporting Actress (Anna Jemsion).*
FILMNOTE: *Silver City was a real immigrant camp in Australia, so named because of the tin quonset huts into which its inhabitants were crowded.*

SIMON OF THE DESERT
(Video, subtitled)

Religious Satire

Mexico	Spanish
1965 45 Min.	B&W

CREDITS: *Directed, written and produced by Luis Buñuel. Released and distributed nontheatrically by New Yorker Films. Starring Claudio Brook, Silvia Pinal, Mortensia Santovena and Enrique Alvarez.*

Some of Luis Buñuel's movies are one-joke stories that don't sustain themselves for the length of a feature film. Happily, *Simon of the Desert* is not only one of his funniest movies, but its story is well-suited to the film's forty-five minute duration.

The bizarre little narrative is set in the fifth century, when St. Simon Stylites (Claudio Brook), in order to be closer to God, has stood praying on top of a sixty-foot pillar for thirty-seven years. Simon is so sanctimonious that he blesses his own tooth when it falls from his mouth. His devotion is threatened, however, when the Devil (Silvia Pinal) arrives in the desert wearing a low-cut Catholic schoolgirl's uniform, intent on luring this holy disciple from his perch. At first, Simon is able to resist her temptations, even when she returns disguised as a priest and then, bearded and toga-clad, as God himself. But finally, the Devil asserts her power, arriving at the pillar in a slithering coffin and whisking Simon away to hell—a modern disco where café-set trendies dance to the hit "The Radioactive Flesh."

Although *Simon of the Desert* has an unfulfilling ending and lacks the richness and depth of character of some of Buñuel's best work, its pointed single joke carries the film. Claudio Brook plays Simon straight, but his actions and words are so ludicrous ("Blessing is enjoyable, besides being a holy experience," he solemnly intones at one point in the film) that he is funny in spite of himself. Silvia Pinal also gives a tour de force performance as the Devil, a temptress of sin who quickly dissolves into a pouting woman frustrated by a man immune to her charms. And Buñuel directs *Simon of the Desert* with his customary flair for the perverse and surreal, drawing his characters in sharply satirical terms while the rest of the film serves as a fuzzy, otherworldly background.

RATING: *No MPAA rating, with nothing objectionable.*
AWARDS: *Special Jury Prize at the 1965 Cannes Film Festival.*

SISTERS, OR THE BALANCE OF HAPPINESS

Women's Drama

West Germany	German
1981 95 Min.	Color

CREDITS: *Directed by Margarethe von Trotta. Written by Margarethe von Trotta, Martje Grohmann and Luisa Francia. Produced by Eberhard Junkersdorf. Cinematography by Franz Rath and Thomas Schwan. Music by Konstantine Wecker. Released and distributed by Almi Pictures. Starring Jutta Lampe, Gudrun Gabriel, Jessica Fruh, Rainer Delventhal, Konstantin Wecker, Angnes Fink and Heinz Bennent.*

Don't be misled by the title of Margarethe von Trotta's *Sisters, or the Balance of Happiness.* Although the main characters in this film are sisters, there is little about them that is happy or balanced.

Anna (Jutta Lampe of *Marianne and Juliane*) and Maria (Gudrun Gabriel) share an apartment in a large German city. Anna is a cold, calculating woman driven in every aspect of her life, a superefficient executive secretary for the head of a large corporate firm who even relaxes with an intensity of purpose. Her younger sister, Maria, is her opposite. Soft, sensitive and confused, Maria has a difficult time handling everyday pressures, and torments herself for her failures. Maria depends on Anna to help her make even the simplest decisions, while Anna is patient with Maria. But, as we discover toward the end of the film, Anna's control over her sister allows her to avoid her own feelings of self-doubt.

With stunning cinematography from Franz Rath and Thomas Schwan, writer/director Margarethe von Trotta *(Sheer Madness, Marianne and Juliane)* weaves a web of self-deception and emotional depravity that rivals some of Ingmar Bergman's most complex character studies. But unlike Bergman, she keeps *Sisters* immediate, with few flashbacks and no nightmarish dream sequences. The two main characters are so well developed in this film

these devices are unnecessary. Both Lampe and Gabriel give profoundly intense performances. Neither one is an attractive personality, yet there are subtleties to their expressions and conversations that make them extremely compelling. Their characters also raise many issues about women, careers and the impersonalization of modern life. It's exhausting to watch them for an hour and a half, but the emotions the two actresses stir up are heartfelt and true.

RATING: *No MPAA rating, with brief sex and nudity.*

SITTING DUCKS
(Video)

Caper Comedy

U.S.A.	
1980 90 Min	Color

CREDITS: *Directed and written by Henry Jaglom. Produced by Meira Attia Dor. Cinematography by Paul Glickman. Music by Richard Romanus. Released by United Film Distributor. Starring Michael Emil, Zack Norman, Patrice Townsend, Irene Forrest, Richard Romanus and Henry Jaglom.*

You'd expect a film that begins with two guys ripping off the mob for $750,000 to be a tension-filled chase adventure. But in Henry Jaglom's *Sitting Ducks*, this robbery is a prelude to an offbeat road movie featuring two middle-aged eccentrics struggling with their failures in love.

The egocentric Sid (Zack Norman) and his nebbishy partner Simon (Michael Emil) steal a day's take from a bookie operation of the New York syndicate where Simon works as bookkeeper. With the cash in hand, the two hightail it to Miami, where they plan to catch a plane to Costa Rica in four days. Hiding the money in the tires of their rented limo, the two thieves figure they'll get away clean if they can remain unobtrusive on their way south. Yet to the kvetching Simon's horror, Sid not only hires a strange, guitar-playing Italian named Moose (Richard Romanus) to be their chauffeur, but he can't help flashing his bankroll to everyone they meet. To make matters worse, both men fall in love at a roadside Holiday Inn; Sid with the mysterious and beautiful young Jenny (Jaglom's ex-wife and *Always* co-star Patrice Townsend), and Simon with Leona (Irene Forrest), a waitress who habitually bursts into tears. All five hit the road together, as Sid's and Simon's concern about the mob on their tail is soon replaced by worries about getting their reluctant pickups into bed.

Like Jaglom's *Always* and *Can She Bake Cherry Pie?*, *Sitting Ducks'* improvised humor can be inconsistent, and several scenes stay on the screen long after they have worn out their welcome. The film also suffers from its low budget, for certain set pieces are awkwardly shot and poorly paced, and the soundtrack could be from a home movie. But even with all of its faults, *Sitting Ducks* is Jaglom's best film to date. The narrative has a strong caper plot that keeps things moving briskly, and Jaglom embellishes the film with some hilarious scenes and characters. Patrice Townsend is particularly delightful as the flower child Jenny, who actively courts sexual liaisons while refusing to be kissed. Even more entertaining is Michael Emil's Simon. An obsessive vitamin chewer who tries to seduce a woman with a combination of sexual braggadocio and Doris Day movies, Simon is wonderfully idiosyncratic and entertaining.

RATING: *R for nudity and profanity.*
FILMNOTE: *Michael Emil, also the star of Jaglom's* Can She Bake Cherry Pie? *and Nicolas Roeg's* Insignificance, *is director Henry Jaglom's brother.*

A SLAVE OF LOVE
(Video, subtitled)

Historical Romance

U.S.S.R.   Russian

1978   94 Min.   Color

CREDITS: *Directed by Nikita Mikalkov. Written by Nikita Mikalkov and Andrei Konchalkovsky (the director of* Runaway Train*). Produced by Mosfilm. Cinematography by Pavel Lebeshev. Music by Eduard Artemiev. Set design by A. Adabashyan and A. Samulekin. Released and distributed nontheatrically by Almi Pictures. Starring Elena Solovei, Rodion Nakhapetov, Alexandar Kalyagin, Oleg Basilashivili and Konstantin Grigoryev.*

Unlike most of the lumbering, humorless movies that Russia releases in the United States, *A Slave of Love* is a lighthearted tribute to Soviet filmmaking in the silent era, as well as an engrossing revolutionary drama.

The film is set in 1917, as Leninists battle for control of Moscow and the Czar's soldiers brutalize civilians when they search for Red sympathizers. Olga (Elena Solovei), a famous star of silent melodramas, is insulated from the storm of political change engulfing her country until she becomes attracted to Viktor (Rodion Nakhapetov). Viktor is a handsome young Bolshevik cameraman who mysteriously disappears from the set for hours at a time. When he asks for Olga's help in smuggling incriminating film footage to Communists outside of their White-occupied territory, Olga joins his cause on a lark, spurred as much by her passion for Victor as her political convictions. But as her involvement allows her to witness for the first time the atrocities committed by the Czar's army, Olga joins the underground wholeheartedly, willing to risk her career, and even her life, to fight for justice.

Although some humorous slapstick arises from the complications of making a film during a revolution, at the center of *A Slave of Love* is Olga's political responsibility versus her apathy and self-indulgence. In the tranquil setting of the town where they are making the film, nothing seems out of the ordinary about this famous movie star fretting about small problems in the production. But as she becomes increasingly affected by the repression she witnesses, her character signals a coming of age that is a metaphor for her country as a whole. Solovei is brilliant in this role, subtly transforming from a self-centered actress to a politically conscientious freedom fighter. Although director Nikita Mikalkov *(Dark Eyes)* portrays the film's politics in the most obvious blacks and whites (in this case the whites are evil), there is little heavy-handedness or propaganda in his approach. But the events leading up to this historical moment in Russian history are barely examined, so the repression Olga and Viktor fight against appears as only a surface kind of injustice. In the end, *A Slave of Love* works well as a comical, political love story, but it does little to convey the reasons behind those politics.

RATING: No MPAA rating, with violence.
AWARDS: One of the National Board of Review's 5 Best Foreign Films in 1978.

SMALL CHANGE

(Video, subtitled)

Coming-of-Age Comedy

France	French
1976 104 Min.	Color

CREDITS: Directed by François Truffaut. Written by François Truffaut and Suzanne Schiffman. Cinematography by Pierre-William Glenn. Music by Maurice Jaubert. Released by New World Pictures. Distributed nontheatrically by Films Inc. Starring Geory Desmouceaux, Philippe Goldman, Claudio Deluca, Frank Deluca, Richard Golfier, Laurent Devlaeminck, Bruno Staab, Sebastien Marc, Sylvie Grezel and Le Petit Gregory.

François Truffaut's *Small Change* is perhaps the most unassuming and sensitive movie ever made about children. Set in the French village of Thiers, the film is a series of vignettes focussing on a group of boys who attend the same school. The story's serious segments involve Julien (Philippe Goldman) and Patrick (Geory Desmouceaux), two eleven-year-olds who have difficult home lives. Motherless, his father confined to a wheelchair, Patrick is forced to spend much of his time outside school earning the household income. Julien, on the other hand, comes to class each day hungry and wearing dirty clothes that cover cuts and bruises he receives from an abusive mother.

On the lighter side there are two brothers who rack our nerves as they make breakfast for each other by cutting a hard loaf of bread with a long, sharp knife. Then there's the little girl who pretends she's been abandoned by her parents at home, cajoling her neighbors into sending a basket of food up her mother's clothesline. And finally, there is irresistible little Gregory (Le Petit Gregory), a toddler who, after miraculously surviving a seven-story fall, remarks, "Gregory go boom."

In these and dozens of other scenes in *Small Change,* Truffaut exhibits a remarkable gift for bringing out the humor, fears and foibles in the everyday lives of children. The kids themselves are natural hams who seem as entertained in their roles as they are entertaining. Cinematographer Pierre-William Glenn's camera is always at their level, capturing as many quiet, simple moments as humorous ones. Although the self-consciously "meaningful" segments involving Patrick and Julien stand out in a narrative that is mostly full of wonderfully unpretentious moments, there is so much to celebrate about the spontaneity, resiliency and innocence of children that *Small Change* will keep you smiling long after you've seen it.

RATING: PG, with nothing objectionable.
AWARDS: Catholic Office Award at the 1976 Berlin Film Festival.
WARNING: The Warner Home Video version of this film is too dark in places, but the subtitles are still readable.
FILMNOTE: During the screen test for Small Change, Truffaut had the child actors read a speech by Molière.

SMASH PALACE
(Video)

Psychological Thriller

New Zealand

1981   100 Min.   Color

CREDITS: *Directed and produced by Roger Donaldson. Written by Bruno Lawrence and Peter Hanson. Cinematography by Graeme Cowley. Released by Atlantic. Distributed nontheatrically by Films Inc. Starring Bruno Lawrence, Anna Jemison, Greer Robson, Keith Aberdein and Desmond Kelly.*

It doesn't take a student of psychology to realize the breakup of a marriage can bring out in people a certain craziness that lies dormant in their everyday lives. Roger Donaldson's *Smash Palace* makes that point extremely well.

Jacqui (Anna Jemison) and Al (Bruno Lawrence) don't exactly have a model marriage. His time is spent at Smash Palace, a salvage yard he runs, where he also indulges his obsession with racing cars. She hates it that he profits from other people's misery, and feels lonely and isolated living at the yard. They fight constantly, and eventually Jacqui can't take it anymore. She packs up all of her things and, with their daughter, Georgie (Greer Robson), in tow, leaves Al.

The separation devastates Al. He still has strong feelings for Jacqui, and he loves his daughter more than anyone else in the world. When he catches Jacqui shacking up with his best friend, he starts to go over the edge. But after Jacqui gets a court order that forbids Al from seeing Georgie without her permission, his quiet hurt turns into a boiling rage.

Unlike its American counterpart, *Kramer Versus Kramer,* this film doesn't rely on a cute kid and a lovable father to pump our emotions. Al is engaging because his pain is real. Lawrence gives an outstanding performance as a man unaware of his need for love until he has driven it out of his life. The supporting cast is also quite good, their characters rooted in middle-class experi-

ence. That's why *Smash Palace* is so disturbing. As Al cracks up and the others respond, it's obvious that any of us might react in the same way. Writer/director Donaldson *(The Bounty)* addresses several universal truths about relationships, friends and family, creating a lasting empathy for all the players in *Smash Palace.*

RATING: R *for nudity, sex, violence and language.*

SMILES OF A SUMMER NIGHT
(Video, subtitled)

★   ★   ½

Social Satire

Sweden   Swedish

1955   108 Min.   B&W

CREDITS: *Directed and written by Ingmar Bergman. Produced by Allan Ekelund. Cinematography by Gunnar Fischer. Music by Erik Nordgren. Set design by P. A. Lundgren. Released by Rank. Distributed nontheatrically by Films Inc. Starring Gunnar Bjornstrand, Ulla Jacobsson, Eva Dahlbeck, Margit Carlquist, Harriet Andersson, Jarl Kulle, Ake Fridell and Bjorn Bjelvenstam.*

It's ironic that the film that finally brought international recognition to Ingmar Bergman, the master of dark psychological dramas, was one of his "carnal" comedies, *Smiles of a Summer Night.*

The film opens at the turn of the century, during a weekend get-together at a sprawling country estate. There, four upper-class couples gather, switch partners and make fools of themselves with every twist of the complicated plot. The protagonist is Fredrik (Gunnar Bjornstrand), a stodgy lawyer whose sixteen-year-old virgin wife refuses to have sex with him. He, in response, strikes up an affair with his old mistress, although she is already involved with a count who hates Fredrik. Fredrik's suicidal son eventually runs away with his wife, while their servant seduces a family friend who is about to be married. The whole charade becomes progressively more ridiculous until, by the end, you need a checklist to keep track of who belongs to whom.

Although not a knee-slapping comedy, *Smiles of a Summer Night* satirically dismantles the pretensions of the upper class, the pettiness of conniving women, and the conceit of men with giant egos. The men in this film definitely take the worst beating, but each character has his or her turn getting caught in an embarrassing situation. For the most part, Fredrik and the rest of the weekend guests are too one-dimensional to be sympathetic characters, and the messes they get themselves into are too contrived to be believable. Although *Smiles of a Summer Night* is brimming with sophisticated satire and sarcasm, all the cleverness wears thin after a while. An hour and a half of this film can also produce a good many yawns.

RATING: No MPAA rating.
AWARDS: *Winner of the Special Prize for Most Poetic Humor at the 1956 Cannes Film Festival.*
FILMNOTE: *Often compared to Renoir's* The Rules of the Game, Smiles of a Summer Night *was influenced by Shakespeare's* A Midsummer Night's Dream. *In turn, the film was an influence for Woody Allen's* A Midsummer Night's Sex Comedy *and served as the story for Stephen Sondheim's Tony Award–winning musical* A Little Night Music.

SMITHEREENS
(Video)

Social Satire

U.S.A.

1982   90 Min.   Color

CREDITS: *Directed and produced by Susan Seidelman. Written by Ron Nyswana and Peter Askin. Cinematography by Chirine El Khahem. Music by Glenn Mercer and Bill Million. Released and distributed non-theatrically by New Line Cinema. Starring Susan Berman, Brad Rinn, Richard Hell, Roger Jett and Nada Despotovich.*

In the opening scene of Susan Seidelman's *Smithereens*, the heroine, Wren (Susan Berman), pastes up posters of herself saying "Who Is This Woman?" on a New York subway wall. That's the kind of person Wren is—a pushy and spoiled young woman who will do anything to become a star. But Wren has no talent or money, and she dresses like a punk bag lady, so even her poster attracts little attention. In fact, the only person who notices Wren is a rather conservative young drifter from Montana named Paul (Brad Rinn), who lives in his van in a parking lot down by the pier. He follows Wren around like a puppy, but she is more interested in Eric (Richard Hell of the Voidoids), a washed-up punk rock star who treats Wren like trash.

Susan Seidelman's first feature is less slick than her second, *Desperately Seeking Susan*, although both capture that same funky atmosphere of New York's Lower East Side. But unlike the character Susan's trendy and chic world, there's poverty and alienation in Wren's East Village. *Smithereens* also doesn't have much of a plot. Wren meets up with all kinds of Village characters—hustles them, fights them or gets screwed by them (literally and figuratively)—and then it's on to the next. It's a downward and repetitive spiral of sleaze and despair, with only Wren's wisecracking for relief. But in many ways, *Smithereens* is a more accurate depiction of the dreams and failures of young urban punks. Berman is as tough on the outside as she is fragile on the inside, and the success of her performance, and the film, is that no matter how obnoxious and desperate she becomes, we never stop feeling for her.

RATING: *R for language, substance abuse and brief nudity.*
FILMNOTE: *Made on a budget of only $80,000 and originally shot in 16mm, Smithereens was the first low-budget independent American film to be screened at the Cannes Film Festival.*

SMOOTH TALK
(Video)

Psychological Thriller

U.S.A.

1986   92 Min.   Color

CREDITS: *Directed by Joyce Chopra. Written by Tom Cole, based on a story by Joyce Carol Oates. Produced by Martin Rosen and Timothy Marx for PBS's "American Playhouse." Cinematography by James Glennon. Music by James Taylor. Released by Spectrafilm. Starring Laura Dern, Treat Williams, Mary Kay Place, Elizabeth Berridge, Levon Helm, Sarah Inglis, Margaret Welch and Geoff Hoyle.*

Smooth Talk is an indictment of suburbia, a coming-of-age story and a psychological horror movie all in one. The angelic Laura Dern stars as Connie, a typical fifteen-year-old who fights with her domineering mother, sneaking out with her girlfriends to go to the mall or the drive-in to hunt for boys. Although Connie is mentally fifteen, when she puts on a halter top and eye makeup, she has all the sexual power of a mature young woman.

One day, while sauntering around the drive-in wearing a skimpy T-shirt, she attracts the attention of Arnold Friend (Treat Williams). In his mid-twenties, Arnold is extremeley articulate and self-assured, yet there's something off about him, aside from the fact that he's too old to be hanging out with teenagers. When he shows up at Connie's house just after her family leaves her alone to go on a Sunday outing, it's disconcerting. Later, when he bullies Connie into going for a ride in his car, it's downright frightening. In the end, Connie's fears about Arnold Friend turn out to be well founded.

The first half of *Smooth Talk* moves slowly as director Joyce Chopra does too thorough a job portraying the banalities in Connie's life. Although these scenes accurately depict teenage angst and are necessary background for the film's revealing second half, too little happens. But once

Connie meets Arnold, *Smooth Talk* becomes a gripping suspense story with the powerful character of Arnold Friend at its center. Williams's Arnold is simultaneously intense and subtly psychotic, rivaling Dennis Hopper's Frank in *Blue Velvet* for sheer creepiness. The brilliance of his characterization is in its unpredictability. Not even in the film's conclusion is it really clear what's going on behind his smooth-talking exterior. Dern gives a controlled performance as the sexually confused and quietly angry Connie, and there are a couple of scenes with her parents that are more compelling than most kid-parent confrontations in the movies today.

RATING: *R for brief nudity and profanity.*

SOLDIER OF ORANGE
(Video, subtitled)

★ ★ ½

World War II Adventure

Holland   Dutch

1979   165 Min.   Color

CREDITS: *Directed by Paul Verhoeven. Written by Paul Verhoeven, Gerard Soeteman and Kees Holierhoek, based on the autobiography of Erik Hazelhoff Roelfzema. Produced by Rob Houwer. Cinematography by Peter De Bont and Jost Vacano. Music by Rogier Van Otterloo. Released by International Picture Show. Distributed nontheatrically by Westcoast Films. Starring Rutger Hauer, Jeroen Krabbe, Peter Faber, Derk De Lint, Eddy Habbema, Susan Penhaligon and Edward Fox.*

Paul Verhoeven's first feature, *Soldier of Orange,* is an ambitious attempt to document the Dutch experience during World War II. The film opens in 1938, as an apolitical university student named Erik (Rutger Hauer) endures the hazing of a hedonistic fraternity. Befriended by the group's patrician president, Gus (Jeroen Krabbe), Erik becomes a reckless bon vivant. When war breaks out, the frat boys, like their country, remain neutral until Germany invades Holland itself. Even then, Erik and his friends take the war lightly, volunteering for duty clad in tuxedos. But after Rotterdam is destroyed and the Dutch army surrenders, Eric and Gus finally recognize the severity of Hitler's threat and are drawn into the Resistance movement.

Eventually, the danger is too great, and the two friends escape to London, where they meet the exiled Queen Wilhelmina, who asks them to act as couriers between England and the underground in Holland. Gus and Eric agree, but as they've almost completed their mission back in their homeland, the two agents are betrayed by a friend from the university, a German double agent out to save the life of his Jewish girlfriend.

Verhoeven (*Robocop* and *The 4th Man*) simply bites off more than he can chew in *Soldier of Orange*, trying to encapsulate the total Dutch war experience with the stories of six young men. The film goes on much too long, wasting time following the exploits of a Dutch SS officer and the double agent. In addition, there are two unbelievable subplots, involving the double agent's Jewish girlfriend and a woman Erik meets in London, that lead nowhere. But the story of Gus and Erik's indoctrination into the Resistance is engrossing and tension-filled. Hauer and Krabbe give solid performances that capture how war turns youth and enthusiasm into cold determination to fight for a cause. And some of the film's action sequences are extremely well shot by cinematographers Peter De Bont and Jost Vacano.

RATING: R for sex, nudity, profanity and violence.

SOMETHING WILD
(Video)

Social Satire

U.S.A.

1986   113 Min.   Color

CREDITS: Directed by Jonathan Demme. Written by E. Max Frye. Produced by Jonathan Demme and Kenneth Utt. Cinematography by Tak Fujimoto. Music by Laurie Anderson and David Byrne. Released by Orion. Distributed nontheatrically by Films Inc. Starring Melanie Griffith, Jeff Daniels, Ray Liotta, Margaret Colin, John Waters (director of Pink Flamingos*), Leib Lensky and Dana Preu.*

Jonathan Demme's *Something Wild* begins when a Wall Street accountant named Charlie (Jeff Daniels) tries to sneak out on his lunch bill and is caught red-handed by a black-wigged, miniskirted young woman (Melanie Griffith) who embarrasses him into paying for his meal. Lulu, or at least that's what she says her name is, then offers him a ride back to work in her convertible. But instead of taking him to Wall Street, she whisks Charlie away to New Jersey, where she does an assortment of outrageous and highly illegal things. Then it's off to her Pennsylvania hometown, where she suddenly becomes "Audrey" and introduces him to her mom as her husband.

Because Charlie is a yuppie who fancies himself a closet rebel, he loosens up and enjoys the ride until they go to her high school reunion that night and run into her old flame, Ray (Ray Liotta). Ray is a muscle-bound, smily-faced ex-con who's still hot for Audrey, and who's also prone to outbursts of psychotic violence when he doesn't get his way.

Liotta's performance as Ray is clever and frightening. But his presence also brings up a few glitches in the plot. Without giving away specifics, it's safe to say that his extreme violence doesn't always mix well with the light romance in the film. But most of *Something Wild* is a hilarious and fast-paced zigzag across various eighties landscapes, including yuppiedom, New York's East Village, suburbia and interstate highways. Griffith is tremendous as Lulu/Audrey, rivaling Madonna in *Desperately Seeking Susan* with her hustling and outlandish outfits. Daniels makes a convincing straight man, with his preppy looks and golly geewillikers demeanor. When you combine all of this with an upbeat soundtrack of sixties oldies, Reggae, David Byrne and Laurie Anderson, *Something Wild* is an enormously satisfying satire.

RATING: R for nudity, sex and violence.

SOTTO SOTTO (SOFTLY SOFTLY)
(Video, subtitled)

Sex Farce

Italy		Italian
1985	104 Min.	Color

CREDITS: *Directed and written by Lina Wertmuller. Produced by Mario Gori and Vittorio Cecchi. Cinematography by Dante Spinotti. Music by Paolo Conte. Released by Columbia Pictures. Distributed nontheatrically by Swank Motion Pictures. Starring Enrico Montesano, Veronica Lario, Luisa De Santis, Massimo Wertmuller, Mario Scarpetta, Isa Danieli and Elena Fabizi.*

If you've become a loyal Lina Wertmuller fan after watching biting political satires such as *Seven Beauties* and *Swept Away*, her recent releases are simply a litany of disappointment. With *Sotto Sotto*, she seems to have struck bottom.

The film is the story of Oscar (Enrico Montesano), a traditional Italian male who expects his wife, Ester (Veronica Lario), to be at his sexual beck and call. During one such amorous encounter, when she confesses to fantasizing about another person, Oscar jumps to the conclusion that she is having an affair and proceeds to torture her with his jealousy. After several days, Ester

can't take his abuse anymore and shocks him with the truth: The fantasy lover is her best friend, Adele (Luisa De Santis). Ester's confession compounds Oscar's insane jealousy tenfold. He compares two women making love to having sex with a dog, a horse or, worse yet, a Negro. He shouts at her whenever they are together for the remainder of the movie. When he is alone, he buries himself in a coffin of self-pity.

Even though Oscar is meant to be a hapless victim in *Sotto Sotto*, it's hard to laugh at or feel compassion for this sexist, racist, homophobic man. Both when he is yelling at his wife and when he is making a complete fool of himself, his jealousy is overplayed to the point of boredom. Ester and Adele are equally unsympathetic. Virtually no time is spent developing their friendship or attraction; they simply walk through a park full of female statues and smooching lesbians and suddenly emerge at the other end as starry-eyed closet lesbians who feel compelled only to tease each other while tormenting Oscar. Although there are a few clever moments of Wertmuller dismantling the Italian male ego, most of *Sotto Sotto* is dated and not very entertaining.

RATING: R for language and sexual content.

A SPECIAL DAY
(Video, dubbed)

World War II Drama

Italy/Canada		Italian
1977	110 Min.	Color

CREDITS: *Directed by Ettore Scola. Written by Ettore Scola, Ruggero Maccari and Maurizio Costanzo. Produced by Carlo Ponti (Loren's husband). Cinematography by Pasqualino De Santis. Music by Armando Trovaioli. Released and distributed by Almi Pictures. Starring Sophia Loren, Marcello Mastroianni, John Vernon, Françoise Berd, Nicole Magny, Patrizia Basso, Tiziano De Persio and Maurizio De Paolantonio.*

This film takes place on the "special" day Hitler has come to Italy to meet Mussolini. There is a big parade in Rome to celebrate, which nearly all the city's residents excitedly rush off to attend. But for Gabriele (Marcello Mastroianni) and Antonietta (Sophia Loren), two tenants in the same dilapidated apartment building who aren't participating in the festivities, it's also the special day they get to know each other.

Antonietta is a plainly dressed, working-class woman who's a virtual slave to her husband and six kids. She couldn't attend the celebration because she had so much work to do, but she is also glad to be free of her demanding family for the day. She meets Gabriele, a cultured and impeccably dressed radio announcer with his own reasons for not going to the ceremony, when her mynah bird flies into his apartment and she goes over to retrieve it. After several uncomfortable moments in the beginning, they end up spending hours together, laughing, arguing and opening up their deepest secrets to each other. Repressed sexual tensions and Catholic guilt lie so heavy in the air that it enshrouds their surface conversations in a fog. But by the end of their strange afternoon together, they have become very close, although Gabriele has a secret in his past that dooms their feelings right from the start.

A Special Day is basically a two-person show, with Mastroianni and Loren both giving controlled and compelling performances. Mastroianni plays Gabriele as a gentle, thoughtful man prone to hilarious outbursts of spontaneity and joy. Loren's Antonietta is so desperate to break out of her chains that she embodies the burden of enslaved women everywhere with her expressions and actions. Scola's direction is brilliant, capturing subtle emotions in nearly every scene at the same time that he brutally indicts Italians for blindly following Mussolini and Fascism. Even A Special Day's soundtrack, which consists mostly of a radio blaring commentary of the parade and Hitler's and Mussolini's speeches to the Romans, serves as a fascinating historical document, while accentuating the political and personal repression in Gabriele and Antonietta's lives.

RATING: No MPAA rating, with mild sexual scenes.
AWARDS: 1977 Academy Award nominations for Best Foreign Film and Best Actor (Marcello Mastroianni); one of the National Board of Review's 5 Best Foreign Films in 1977.
WARNING: Dubbing is decent on video version, but the impact of the film depends so much on subtle dialogue that the quality is lessened on tape.

STARSTRUCK
(Video)

 ½

Rock Musical

Australia

1982   95 Min.   Color

CREDITS: Directed by Gillian Armstrong. Written by by Stephen MacLean. Produced by David Elfick and Richard Brennan. Cinematography by Russel Boyd. Choreographed by David Atkins. Costume design and art direction by Brian Thompson. Released and distributed nontheatrically by Cinecom. Starring Jo Kennedy, Ross O'Donovan, Ned Lander, John O'May, Pat Evison, Margo Lee, Max Cullen, Melissa Jaffer and Dennis Miller.

After the enormous art house success of My Brilliant Career, Gillian Armstrong developed another story of a woman's attempt to break into a man's world—this time, Sydney's New-Wave rock scene.

Her heroine in Starstruck is Jackie Mullens (Jo Kennedy), a waitress at her mum's working-class pub by day and a singer at a local rock nightclub at night. Although popular at the Lizard Lounge, Jackie is eager to break into the big time, and with the help of her assertive cousin/manager Angus (Ross O'Donovan) she grabs the media's attention. Donning a fake rubber boob top and superman cape, Jackie walks a tightrope between two skyscrapers while conducting interviews with newsmen poking out of tenth-story windows. Soon, Jackie Mullens is a household name, and it's not long before she competes for a large cash prize in a national television talent show. If she wins, she can both launch her career and save mum's pub from creditors.

Although the wisecracking, precocious young O'Donovan is quite funny as Angus, and Kennedy has her spunky moments as the film's pretty young heroine, there isn't much going on with the characters in *Starstruck* except their outrageous costumes (magnificently designed by *Rocky Horror Picture Show*'s Brian Thompson). Armstrong tries to poke fun at Hollywood musicals, but these jokes are too obvious, while the other performances are too exaggerated to be entertaining or believable. Also, for a feature film musical, *Starstruck*'s song-and-dance routines are hit-and-miss affairs. A few numbers are upbeat and interesting, but most are loaded with monotonous lyrics and melodies. David Atkins's choreography is likewise uninspired, as Jackie moves like a mannequin onstage while the audience stiffly sways back and forth in sync.

RATING: *PG, with mild profanity.*
FILMNOTE: *Two songs from* Starstruck, *("He's Got Body" and "The Monkey in Me") rose near the top of the Australian rock-and-roll charts immediately after the film was released.*

STATE OF SIEGE
(Video, dubbed)

Political Thriller

France/U.S.A./Italy	French
1973 119 Min.	Color

CREDITS: *Directed by Constantine Costa-Gavras. Written by Constantine Costa-Gavras and Franco Solinas. Produced by Jacques Perrin. Cinematography by Pierre-William Glenn. Music by Mikis Theodorakis. Released and distributed nontheatrically by Almi Pictures. Starring Yves Montand, Renato Salvatori, O. E. Hasse, Jean-Luc Bideau, Jacques Weber, Evangeline Peterson, Maurice Teynac, Yvette Etievant and Harald Wolff.*

Although not as well-known as *Z* or *Missing,* Costa-Gavras's *State of Siege* has the same political and emotional firepower. The story begins when an AID (read CIA) official in Uruguay, Philip Santore (Yves Montand), is found murdered in an abandoned car. The Uruguayan news describes him as a loving father and husband who was in Uruguay for peaceful purposes. But through a series of flashbacks showing the events leading up to his kidnapping and a mock trial by his Tupamaro (leftist guerrilla) abductors, we learn that Santore's real mission was to advise the military and police in methods of torturing political prisoners. Knowing this, Santore's abductors distribute this evidence to several of their members, and in a secret voting that takes place on a bus, the group decides that he should be executed.

Based on a real abduction and assassination of a USAID official in Uruguay in the early seventies, and filmed in Chile before the overthrow of Allende, *State of Seige* is presented as if it were a documentary. The two parallel stories—Santore's crimes against political progressives and the Tupamaros deciding whether he should be killed—are riveting and disturbing. The flashbacks to Santore's crimes reveal how integral a part American CIA officials play in brutal Latin American dictatorships.

In certain scenes, Costa-Gavras and writer Franco Solinas (*The Battle of Algiers*) take a stance too strong for objective movie journalism, particularly in the favorable ways the Tupamaros are depicted. They also spare us none of the gruesome details of police torture methods, including one horrifying scene where prisoners have cattle prods placed on sensitive parts of their bodies (real training film footage). But to their credit, they depict Santore as the loving father and husband the news reported, which makes his execution no less horrifying than the violence he perpetrated, and ultimately makes the important issues of this movie much more valid.

RATING: *No MPAA rating, with brief nudity and very explicit violence.*
WARNING: *The dubbing on the video version is badly done.*
FILMNOTE: *According to its nontheatrical distributor, Almi Pictures, State of*

Seige *is often rented by the Air Force Academy, West Point and the State Department.*

STEAMING
(Video)

Feminist Drama

England

1985 95 Min. Color

CREDITS: *Directed by Joseph Losey. Written by Patricia Losey, based on the play by Nell Dunn. Produced by Paul Mills. Cinematography by Christopher Challis. Music by Richard Harvey. Released by New World Pictures. Distributed nontheatrically by Swank Motion Pictures. Starring Vanessa Redgrave, Sarah Miles, Patti Love, Diana Dors, Brenda Bruce, Felicity Dean, Sally Sagoe and Anna Tzelniker.*

Stiff when it should be flowing, and both too schematic and didactic for its own good, Joseph Losey's *Steaming* could be used as a textbook example of how certain stage plays don't translate to the screen.

Based on Nell Dunn's stage hit, *Steaming* takes place in a dilapidated Turkish bath in London run by Violet (Diana Dors in her last role before her death), who calls it "a luxury for working ladies that has deteriorated into a shithouse." Now the baths are mostly frequented by lower-class women like Josie (Patti Love), who uses them as a sanctuary from her abusive lover and sexually demanding boss. Yet they also attract two old friends, a wealthy housewife mired in domestic drudgery, named Nancy (Vanessa Redgrave), and her high-powered lawyer friend, Sarah (Sarah Miles). They spend their time together reflecting on the poor choices they have made in their lives. But the one theme that springs from all the women at the baths is their disdain of men, so when "male" developers threaten to close the spa, they join together in a rescue effort that evolves into a symbolic fight to control their own destinies as well.

As an evening of theater, where live performances give most scripts an added charge, *Steaming*'s clunky metaphors for feminist empowerment may carry more weight. On film, though, too much rings false. Each character represents a classic stereotype of a woman struggling in a man's world, but most aren't real enough to engage our sympathies. The men-battering theme becomes overwrought and tiresome, while the closing crisis is too obvious a symbol to be a satisfying plot twist. Although Losey *(Accident)* and his cinematographer Christopher Challis do an excellent job capturing the sweaty faces of the steam-soaked women as they pour out their hearts to one another, some of the film's most powerful scenes are diluted when they unexplainably jump from the person talking to a blank stare from one her mates. Only the performances of Redgrave and Miles save *Steaming* from being a wash. Both quietly draw us into their lives in ways that make their struggles for self-dignity compelling.

RATING: *R for nudity and profanity.*
FILMNOTE: *Losey died just before the film was completed, which possibly accounts for some of its awkward editing.*

STEVIE
(Video)

Literary Drama

England

1978 102 Min. Color

CREDITS: *Directed and produced by Robert Enders. Written by Hugh Whitemore, based on Whitemore's play and Stevie Smith's writings. Cinematography by Freddie Young. Music by Patrick Bowers. Released by First Artists. Distributed nontheatrically by New Line Cinema. Starring Glenda Jackson, Mona Washbourne, Trevor Howard and Alec McCowen.*

Stevie is about the life of famed British poet Stevie Smith and her relationship with her eccentric Aunt (Mona Washbourne). Set almost entirely in Aunt's modest suburban home, the majority of this film shows Stevie (Glenda Jackson) reciting her poetry, reminiscing with Aunt, and narrating the daily events in their lives. There is a suitor named Freddie (Alec McCowen), who tries unsuccessfully to marry Stevie, and another friend (Trevor Howard) who drives her to poetry readings. But Aunt is the one Stevie is content to spend most of her time with, and the two have an extraordinary friendship.

Stevie doesn't have a driving plot or varied sets. It's overly talky, with Stevie and Aunt sometimes so polite and chipper that they get on your nerves, particularly when they've had a few too many sherries after evening tea. But Jackson's Stevie is so pleasantly literary and Washbourne's Aunt so delightful that it's easy to live with this film's shortcomings. Jackson had a lot of practice perfecting her role as Stevie both in the London stage play and on BBC radio, and she gives a sterling performance. Her character's complexities and darker sides pierce through her amiable exterior when she's simply talking to Aunt and when she's reciting Stevie Smith's poetry. While Jackson has a tendency to overdramatize, Washbourne provides needed comic relief. Her Aunt is so humorously idiosyncratic and lovable you know exactly why Stevie cared so deeply for her.

RATING: No MPAA rating, with nothing objectionable.

STOLEN KISSES
(Video, dubbed)

Sex Farce

France

1969   90 Min.   Color

CREDITS: *Directed by François Truffaut. Written by Bernard Revon and Claude de Givray. Produced by Marcel Berbert. Cinematography by Denys Clerval. Music by Antoine Duhamel. Released by Pro-* ductions Artistes Associes. Distributed nontheatrically by Almi Pictures. Starring Jean-Pierre Leaud, Delphine Seyrig, Michel Lonsdale, Claude Jade, Harry Max, Daniel Ceccaldi, Clair Duhamel and Catherine Lutz.

Stolen Kisses is the third in Truffaut's series of films, which began with *The 400 Blows*, about his character Antoine Doniel. In this film, twenty-year-old Antoine (Jean-Pierre Leaud) is dishonorably discharged from the army for insubordination. Upon returning to Paris jobless and directionless, he immediately tries to reclaim his ex-girlfriend, Christine (Delphine Seyrig); at the same time he is shepherded by an old detective (Harry Max) into becoming a private investigator. Both the job and romance go poorly for Antoine; he is an awkward sleuth unable to tail suspects without being seen, and the only kisses he can wrangle from Christine are stolen. But Antoine's life becomes even more complicated when he goes undercover in a shoe store to learn why the shop's glum owner (Michel Lonsdale) isn't liked by his employees, and he falls under the spell of the owner's seductive wife.

Although Truffaut was criticized for making such a light film during the political upheaval of the late sixties, *Stolen Kisses* stands as one of his warmest and funniest comedies. With his darting eyes and an easy smile, Antoine's enthusiasm for life remains undaunted despite the catastrophes that befall him. Truffaut skillfully balances tender moments of Antoine's romantic disappointment with some hilarious slapstick involving his ineptness as a detective. Truffaut also enjoys playing with our expectations, especially in the scenes of Antoine and Christine together in which the romantic music swells and then nothing really happens. But it's Antoine's reverence for and obsession with love that makes his character so endearing and drives *Stolen Kisses* down its bumpy but charming path.

RATING: R for brief nudity.
AWARDS: 1968 Academy Award nomination for Best Foreign Film.
WARNING: Dubbing in video version is fair and detracts from the quality of the film.

STOP MAKING SENSE
(Video)

Rock Documentary

U.S.A.

1985   84 Min.   Color

CREDITS: *Directed by Jonathan Demme. Written by David Byrne. Produced by Gary Goetzman. Cinematography by Jordan Cronenweth. Music by David Byrne and the Talking Heads. Released by Island Alive/Palace Films. Distributed nontheatrically by Cinecom. Starring David Byrne, Chris Frantz, Jerry Harrison, Tina Weymouth, Edna Holt, Lynn Mabry, Steve Scales, Alex Weir and Bernie Worrell.*

Stop Making Sense begins as Talking Heads' lead singer, David Byrne, strolls on-stage with only an acoustic guitar and delivers a searing rendition of "Psycho Killer." After this powerful opening, each band member (Tina Weymouth, Chris Frantz and Jerry Harrison) joins Byrne for a number, until ninety minutes later, surrounded by an army of backup musicians and clad in an outrageous white suit, Byrne expresses the fire of a tent-show evangelist as he growls through a soulful "Take Me to the River."

Director Jonathan Demme *(Something Wild)* records Talking Heads' live performance with clear, crisp cinematography and few frills. Avoiding the often insipid interviews that mar other rock documentaries, he captures an intimate sense of each musician's personality without resorting to personal anecdotes from the band. Several stage props add resonance to the songs, such as a living room of furniture for a version of "Home" and Byrne's monstrously wide white suit. But it's the music itself that makes this film so great. The performances are flawless, as the technique, spirit and stage presence of David Byrne and Talking Heads blend together in a calculated progression from solo intensity to gospel fervor. As *Stop Making Sense* gathers musical momentum and visual power, it turns into an exciting nonstop dance party, which makes it one of the most entertaining concert documentaries ever put on film.

RATING: *No MPAA rating, with nothing objectionable.*

THE STORY OF ADELE H.
(Video, partially subtitled)

Psychological Romance

France   French and English

1975   97 Min.   Color

CREDITS: *Directed by François Truffaut. Written by François Truffaut and Jean Gruault, Suzanne Schiffman and Jan Dawson, based on the book* Le Journal d'Adele Hugo *by Frances V. Guille. Produced by Marcel Berbert. Cinematography by Nestor Almendros. Music by Maurice Jaubert. Released by New World Pictures. Distributed nontheatrically by Films Inc. Starring Isabelle Adjani, Bruce Robinson, Sylvia Marriott, Reubin Dorey, Joseph Blachley, Ivry Gitlis, Sir Cecil De Sausmarez, Sir Raymond Falla and Roger Martin.*

There is no lack of memorable screen characters in François Truffaut's illustrious movie-making career, but Isabelle Adjani's Adele Hugo is arguably one of his most powerful.

The Story of Adele H. begins in 1863, as Adele arrives in Nova Scotia, where she has followed her one-time lover, an English lieutenant named Pinson (Bruce Robinson). Though her father, Victor Hugo, protests her journey, and even she realizes that Pinson is not worth pursuing, Adele is driven. She trails behind him from post to post, writing odes to Pinson in volumes of journals, obsessed by a love she can never attain. Adele vainly tries to win his affections by giving him money and buying him whores. Then she embarrasses him by creating a scene during military maneuvers and destroying his arranged marriage to another woman by claiming to be his wife. Eventually, it becomes clear that Pinson no longer figures into her obsession. It's her passion for love itself that is her madness.

Based on Adele Hugo's diaries, *The Story of Adele H.* is not an easy film to watch, because we are never allowed to escape the madness of Adele's character. But therein lies the story's strength. Even though we are repelled by Adele's mindless obsession with a man who doesn't want her, we also completely understand it. With her haunting stare and stoic face, Adjani is able to create an emotional firestorm in Adele and plays the role to perfection. She is aided by Maurice Jaubert's melancholy musical score, which provides a dark echo of her pain. The cinematography by Nestor Almendros is equally strong in capturing the barrenness of the Nova Scotia shore. And Truffaut directs this romantic tragedy with his usual flare for small moments and heartfelt emotions.

RATING: PG, with nothing objectionable.
AWARDS: 1975 New York Film Critics Awards for Best Actress (Isabelle Adjani) and Best Screenplay (François Truffaut, Jean Gruault, Suzanne Schiffman and Jan Dawson); one of the National Board of Review's Best Foreign Films in 1975; 1975 Academy Award nomination for Best Actress (Adjani).

LA STRADA
(Video, subtitled)

Social Drama

Italy   Italian

1954   115 Min.   B&W

CREDITS: Directed by Federico Fellini. Written by Federico Fellini, Tullio Pinelli and Ennio Flaiano. Produced by Carlo Ponti and Dino De Laurentis. Music by Nino Rota. Cinematography by Otello Martelli. Distributed nontheatrically by Films Inc. and Kino International, among others. Starring Giulietta Masina, Anthony Quinn, Richard Basehart, Marcella Rovere and Lina Venturini.

One of the most famous examples of post–World War II Italian neorealism, Federico Fellini's *La Strada* still holds up as a masterpiece today. It's the story of a socially retarded young woman named Gelsomina (Fellini's wife, Giulietta Masina), so homely with her baggy overcoat and close-cropped blonde hair that nobody would want to marry her.

One day, Gelsomina's desperately poor mother sells her to Zampano (Anthony Quinn), a strongman who travels from town to town doing his famous Iron Lungs act. Gelsomina learns to pass the hat, play drums and do a bit of clowning during the performance, yet Zampano is only cruel to her in return. He frequently beats Gelsomina for mistakes, and then leaves her sitting alone in the streets in tears. But she loyally stays by his side, even when nuns from a convent offer to take her in, and even when she falls in love with a tightrope walker named Fool (Richard Basehart) at a circus they join in Rome. In a strange way, belonging to this brute gives Gelsomina a purpose in life.

Fellini tells Gelsomina's story completely from her point of view from its tragic start to heartbreaking finish. Nino Rota's soundtrack drenches every scene in melancholy, and the film's striking black-and-white photography further heightens the mood, contrasting beautiful shots of the Italian landscape with close-ups of Gelsomina's tormented face. Quinn gives a strong performance, as do Basehart and the rest of the supporting cast. But without a doubt, the best character in *La Strada* is Masina's Gelsomina. She uses every part of her body to express her character, from her comical, shuffling walk to her remarkable facial expressions, which, in a split second, change from frowns to smiles in the best mime tradition. In fact, her performance will remind you of Charlie Chaplin's *The Little Tramp*, standing as one of the most heartbreaking and comical in cinema history.

RATING: No MPAA rating, with mild violence.
AWARDS: 1956 Academy Award for Best Foreign Film; 1956 Academy Award nomination for Best Original Screenplay (Federico Fellini and Tullio Pinelli). 1956

New York Film Critics Award for Best Foreign Film; Grand Prize at the 1954 Venice Film Festival; one of the National Board of Review's 10 Best Foreign Films in 1956.
WARNING: Because this is a public domain movie, the quality of different video versions varies.

STRANGER THAN PARADISE
(Video)

Social Satire

U.S.A.

1984 90 Min. B&W

CREDITS: *Directed, written and edited by Jim Jarmusch. Produced by Sara Driver. Cinematography by Tom Dicillo. Music by John Lurie (of the Lounge Lizards) and Aaron Picht. Released and distributed nontheatrically by The Samuel Goldwyn Company. Starring John Lurie, Eszter Balint, Cecilla Stark, Richard Edson and Danny Rosen.*

Jim Jarmusch's *Stranger Than Paradise* was the surprise winner of the Camera d'Or (best first film) at the 1984 Cannes Film Festival and started a cult following for this NYU Film School graduate from Akron, Ohio.

The story begins when Eva (Eszter Balint), a sixteen-year-old fresh from Hungary, shows up at her cousin Willie's doorstep in New York. Willie (John Lurie) has lived in this country for ten years, working a little and sleeping a lot, but mostly drinking beer and playing poker with his friend, Eddie (Richard Edson). The last thing he wants to do is babysit his uncommunicative cousin. Eva doesn't like him either, but they are stuck with each other in his one-room Lower East Side apartment until her guardian, Aunt Lotte (Cecilla Stark), gets out of the hospital in Cleveland. After ten days of chain-smoking and watching TV, Eva sets out for Ohio, but by this time Willie has grown fond of her and finds that he misses her almost as soon as she leaves. A year later, he borrows a car and, with the easygoing Eddie in tow, follows her to Cleveland, where they convince Eva to travel on with them to a "paradise" in the south called *Florida.*

The dialogue in *Stranger Than Paradise* is as austere as its plot. When the characters do talk in this film, it's usually in non sequiturs, and three or four minutes often roll by with nothing but Willie blowing on his TV dinner peas or Eva yawning to fill the time. Yet their deadpan characterizations create hilarious sequences through their droll expressions alone. When Willie, Eddie and Eva are with Aunt Lotte in Cleveland, for example, a simple monotone comment from one of them concerning his or her impressions of life in the United States can be as humorous as any snappy punchline. Tom Dicillo's cinematography is also very clever. Shot in black and white with a blank screen dividing each scene from the next, this film includes several images so well constructed they appear to be grainy Stieglitz photographs. In the end, the effect of these Hungarian immigrants hanging out in such a stylized setting creates a vision of the American dream that has never been as beautiful or as humorously inane.

RATING: *R for multiple uses of the F word.*
AWARDS: *Camera d'Or at the 1984 Cannes Film Festival.*
WARNING: *Because so much importance is placed on the visuals in* Stranger Than Paradise, *on video it loses some of its effectiveness.*
FILMNOTE: *The idea for* Stranger Than Paradise *came to Jarmusch from a forty-minute piece cut from director Wim Wenders's film* The State of Things. *Wenders had given Jarmusch this footage to edit into a five-minute short. The State of Things evaporated into oblivion, while Stranger became an overnight cult hit.*

STRANGERS KISS
(Video)

Romantic Thriller

U.S.A

1984   93 Min.   Color and B&W

CREDITS: *Directed and produced by Matthew Chapman. Written by Blaine Novak, based on his story. Cinematography by Mikhail Suslov. Music by Gato Barbieri. Released by Orion Classics. Distributed nontheatrically by Films Inc. Starring Peter Coyote, Victoria Tennant, Blaine Novak, Dan Shor, Richard Romanus, Linda Kerridge and Carlos Palomino.*

Over the years, the film industry has been at its most corrosive when exploring its own corruption. The small feature *Strangers Kiss* is one of the most recent entries into this genre.

The story is set in the fifties, as an egomaniacal, ruthless director named Stanley (Peter Coyote) scrapes together just enough money to shoot his first feature, a melodrama about a naïve boxer who becomes involved with a dance-hall girl and the gangster who owns her soul. But Stanley's financing comes with strings attached: The money is parcelled out weekly by L.A. loan shark Frank Silva (Richard Romanus) on the condition that the director use Frank's mistress, Carol (Victoria Tennant), to play the dance-hall girl. At first, Stanley balks at losing control of his production and is further dismayed when Carol and his leading man, Stevie (co-writer Blaine Novak), express zip in the chemistry department. But Stanley devises a plan to encourage an off-screen romance between Carol and Stevie to ignite the on-screen spark he needs, all the while trying to conceal the budding affair from a dangerously jealous Frank.

Like Truffaut's *Day for Night, Strangers Kiss* explores the obsessions involved in making a movie, and the personal struggles of those people whose lives are consumed by that work. Director Matthew Chapman skates artfully between these two levels with a jazzy Gato Barbieri musical score

and striking cinematography that shifts from black and white for the film-within-a-film sequences to rich color tones that give the rest of the film a soft fifties look. Peter Coyote's Stanley bullies his actors and crew as skillfully as he pitches ideas to Frank. His character is the perfect embodiment of a Hollywood con man and filmmaking genius who'll let no one interfere with his vision. Tennant and Romanus are also good, while Chapman not only portrays an image of Hollywood soundstages where love is easily destroyed by temptation, but also creates a wonderful homage to the art of filmmaking itself.

RATING: *R for nudity and sex.*
FILMNOTE: *The plot of* Strangers Kiss *is loosely based on the making of Stanley Kubrick's* Killer's Kiss.

STREAMERS
(Video)

Vietnam Drama

U.S.A.

1984   118 Min.   Color

CREDITS: *Directed and produced by Robert Altman. Written by David Rabe, based on his play. Cinematography by Pierre Mignot. Distributed nontheatrically by Films Inc. Starring Matthew Modine, Michael Wright, Mitchell Lichtenstein, Alan Grier, Guy Boyd, George Dzundza, Albert Macklin, B. J. Cleveland and Bill Allen.*

There's nothing like the fear of dying to loosen up the old tongue. In Robert Altman's *Streamers,* four young infantrymen and two sergeants, waiting to be shipped out to Vietnam, do nothing but drink and talk. In the course of their few days together, these soldiers reveal their innermost feelings on sex, war, sickness and death. But it's homosexuality and racism that are the hot topics of discussion. Expressions like "gook," "whitey," "faggot" and "nigger" fly around the room until gradually their words turn into misplaced rage and, finally, brutal violence.

Altman's second screen adaptation of a stage play (*Come Back to the Five and Dime, Jimmy Dean, Jimmy Dean* was the first), *Streamers* is set entirely in an army barracks. Drab green is the color of the soldiers' clothes and beds, and it even seems to reflect in their faces. Altman obviously didn't want visual distractions from his six GIs' gradual decline into madness. Yet he and his cinematographer Pierre Mignot employ plenty of tricks to project the intensity of their characters. Even though an overly talky script combined with a stagnant setting is an ever present reminder that this story is better suited for theater, this staginess is overshadowed by excellent performances and the film's blunt examination of issues of race, war and machismo.

RATING: R for graphic violence, language and many sexual references.

STREETWISE
(Video)

Urban Documentary

U.S.A.

1985   92 Min.   Color

CREDITS: *Directed by Martin Bell, Mary Ellen Mark and Cheryl McCall. Produced by Cheryl McCall. Cinematography by Martin Bell. Edited by Nancy Baker. Music by Tom Waits. Released by Angelica Films. Distributed nontheatrically by The Samuel Goldwyn Company. Starring Alabama, Baby Gramps, Black Junior, Breezy, Buddha, DeWayne, Drugs, Lulu, Melissa, Munchkin, Peehole, Rat, Red Dog, Smurf, Sparkles, Tiny and White Junior.*

Streetwise is a documentary about nine runaway children, ages thirteen to nineteen, who pimp, whore, deal, hustle and steal to survive on the streets of the Pike district in downtown Seattle. Shooting entirely on location, the film's three directors split up with camera and sound crews to capture the everyday events in the lives of these teenagers. Spur-of-the-moment fighting, hooking, stealing, confrontations with police and parents, eating out of garbage cans and shooting drugs are filmed as they happen. There are many scenes in which these kids play up to the camera, some just as revealing as the spontaneous ones.

The children themselves come from a variety of backgrounds, from extreme poverty to suburban tract-house comfort. Most have been physically or sexually abused as children, but the common ground they all seem to share is feelings of anger at their parents. For the girl who grimaces while her mother chides her for taking drugs (which is mild compared to her hooking and stealing), and for the young boy whose imprisoned father scolds him for smoking cigarettes, life's most brutal moments occur in the presence of their families.

From a filmmaking point of view, *Streetwise* is first-rate. The editing is tight, and the directors skillfully develop each runaway as a character with depth and still keep the narrative moving. Although *Streetwise* is certainly a frightening and depressing look at what often happens to abused children, it is also strangely uplifting. There are as many tender and funny moments in this film as tragic ones. What's amazing about these kids is their underlying sense that they are doing all right under the circumstances. Their anger and frustrations are sometimes tempered by warm feelings for each other and pride in being able to survive on their own.

RATING: No MPAA rating, with a lot of profanity, drug use and violence.
AWARDS: 1986 Academy Award nomination for Best Documentary Feature.
FILMNOTE: The idea for Streetwise *came to co-directors Cheryl McCall and Mary Ellen Mark when they were doing a piece for* Life *magazine on the homeless kids of Seattle and were extremely affected by the kids they interviewed.*

STROSZEK

Social Satire

West Germany   German and English

1977   108 Min.   Color

CREDITS: *Directed and written by Werner Herzog. Music by Chet Atkins and Sonny Terry. Released and distributed nontheatrically by New Yorker Films. Starring Bruno S., Eva Mattes and Clemens Scheitz.*

Though set in modern times, *Stroszek* is thematically similar to Herzog's earlier masterpiece, *The Mystery of Kaspar Hauser,* and also stars the incomparable Bruno S.

The film begins when the childlike Bruno is released from prison. Returning to Berlin, he is grateful that his elderly neighbor, Mr. Scheitz (Clemens Scheitz), has watched his apartment and mynah bird for him while he was away, and pleased that his friend Eva (Eva Mattes) comes to live with him after her pimp beats her up one too many times. But the pimp doesn't leave Eva or Bruno alone, so they decide to join Mr. Scheitz in starting a new life in America. Eva raises the money, and the three move to Railroad Flats, Wisconsin, where they buy a trailer, color TV and station wagon on credit. But the American dream quickly turns sour for them as Bruno starts drinking, Eva takes up prostitution at truckstops, and the bank repossesses everything. Finally Mr. Scheitz and Bruno become so desperate they rob a barber shop.

The only minor problem with *Stroszek* is its ending. Herzog draws out the last fifteen minutes in repetitive and pretentiously photographed scenes that lessen some of the impact of the rest of the film. But ninety-five percent of *Stroszek* is a comical and tragic comment on the absurdity of modern life. All three actors are outstanding, as they each play characters so innocent and honest they couldn't possibly survive the hypocrisy of the world around them. Certain moments, such as Eva walking out on Bruno at a truckstop, are quite sad. Others are filled with sharp satire, such as the scene when a smiling young bank representative comes by to repossess their trailer and wishes them "a nice day" when he leaves. Herzog's direction and camera work are extraordinary, and the Chet Atkins–Sonny Terry Americana soundtrack frames the trio's follies in America perfectly.

RATING: *No MPAA rating, with mild violence.*

SUBURBIA (THE WILD SIDE)
(Video)

Social Drama

U.S.A.

1983   99 Min.   Color

CREDITS: *Directed and written by Penelope Spheeris. Produced by Bert Dragin and Roger Corman. Cinematography by Timothy Suhrstedt. Music by Alex Gibson, the Vandals, the Germs and T.S.O.L. Released by New World Pictures. Distributed nontheatrically by Corinth Films. Starring Chris Pederson, Bill Coyne, Jennifer Clay, Timothy Eric O'Brien, Michael Bayer, Wade Walston and Andrew Pece.*

Penelope Spheeris's documentary *Decline of Western Civilization* was highly praised by some for its frank depiction of L.A.'s punk music scene. In *Suburbia,* she takes this subject a step further by dramatizing the real-life stories of a group of runaways who live together in an abandoned suburban development.

Calling themselves TRs (The Rejects), these directionless punks roam their neighborhood stealing food and vandalizing property, or sit anesthetized in front of the TV, giving each other punk haircuts and crude tattoos. At night, the TRs hang out at a scuzzy punk rock club where racist, foul-mouthed bands play ear-splitting music, and where rapes, fights and stabbings are common occurrences. Meanwhile, back home in their suburban squalor, the TRs dodge the Citizens Against Crime, a gun-toting vigilante group formed to rid the neighborhood of these "lowlifes."

When a baby is brutally mauled by a Doberman pinscher in the first five minutes of the film, *Suburbia* announces that it is as hard-hearted as its subjects. The violent behavior of these L.A. punks is unrelentingly repeated in scene after scene. Although the TRs can be vicious, they are by no means unsympathetic. From the youngest runaway (Andrew Pece), who rides his tricycle and acquires a mohawk, to the TR's handsome and charismatic leader (Chris Pederson), Spheeris takes great pains to show them as victims of a society that thrives on abuse and violence. In fact, most of the runaways in the film are nonprofessional actors found by Spheeris in L.A. clubs, who share the same despairing backgrounds of the characters they play. Some of their performances are extremely moving, but Spheeris trips in her portrayal of the adults in this movie. The TRs' parents and the Citizens Against Crime are mostly shallow characters, too evil to be believed. In addition, *Suburbia*'s story line is uneven, and the film's ending is not very satisfying. But there's still plenty in *Suburbia* that will sober any viewer unfamiliar with today's versions of rebels without a cause.

RATING: R for violence, substance abuse, profanity and nudity.
AWARDS: First Prize at the 1983 Chicago Film Festival.
FILMNOTE: Some say that Penelope Spheeris made Suburbia *so violent at the urging of her executive producer Roger Corman, who has directed scores of horror films over the last thirty years.*

SUBWAY

(Video, dubbed)

Urban Satire

France	French
1985	104 Min.	Color

CREDITS: *Directed by Luc Bresson. Written by Luc Bresson, Pierre Jolivet, Alain Le Henry, Marc Perrier and Sophie Schmit. Produced by Luc Bresson and François*

Ruggieri. Cinematography by Carlo Varini. Music by Eric Serra and Rickie Lee Jones. Production design by Luc Bresson. Art design by Alexandre Trauner. Costume design by Martine Rapin. Released by Island Alive. Starring Christopher Lambert, Isabelle Adjani, Richard Bohringer, Michel Galabru, Jean-Hughes Anglade, Jean-Pierre Bacri, Jean Bouise, Pierre-Ange Le Pogam and Jean Reno.

Subway's epigraph (" 'To be is to do.'—Socrates; 'To do is to be.'—Sartre; 'Do be do be do.'—Sinatra") sums up how seriously director Luc Bresson wants you to take this film.

This light and frivolous story focuses on Fred (Christopher Lambert), a bleached-blond punk who's on the lam because he crashed the party of a wealthy industrialist and took more than extra hors d'oeuvres with him when he left. Holding the industrialist's valuable documents for ransom, Fred arranges a meeting in the Paris métro with the industrialist's beautiful wife, Helena (Isabelle Adjani), who almost talks Fred into returning the booty. But her husband's thugs follow close behind, and when they try to kill Fred, he flees down the subway tracks, ending up inside the enormous infrastructure. There Fred finds himself in the company of a motley group of criminals and homeless people such as the Roller, a crazed pickpocket on skates; an anarchistic drummer named Chopsticks; and the Florist, a hustler who'd sell his own sister for the right price. Meanwhile, as Helena enlists the help of the police to nab Fred before her husband's hit men do, she and Fred fall deeper and deeper in love.

Although twenty-seven-year-old Luc Bresson's *Subway* doesn't have a complicated plot or a deep message at its core, the film has style. Visually, it rivals Beineix's *Diva* for its unusual sets and costumes, brilliant colors and sharp camera work. But the film's writing and performances are also worth noting. Bresson gets away with making *Subway* little more than a polished comic strip, because of his assortment of delightfully quirky and hard-edged characters, from the psychotic pickpocket to the gruff Walter Matthauesque police commissioner. There are even some comical Keystone Kops types nicknamed

Batman and Robin, who are so incompetent they do everything but butt heads. An energetic New-Wave soundtrack by Eric Serra and Rickie Lee Jones adds more style to Fred's adventures, particularly in the film's chase scenes. And both Lambert and Adjani *(The Story of Adele H.)* give well-posed performances as the film's ill-fated lovers. *Subway* may be fluff, but it sure is entertaining.

RATING: *R for nudity, profanity and violence.*
AWARDS: *1985 French Caesar for Best Actor (Christopher Lambert) and Best Art Direction (Alexandre Trauner).*
WARNING: *Dubbing is decent, but it still affects some of the entertaining offbeat dialogue from the film's characters.*

SUGARBABY

(Video, subtitled)

Romantic Satire

West Germany   German

1985   87 Min.   Color

CREDITS: *Directed and written by Percy Adlon. Produced by Eleonore Adlon (Percy's wife). Cinematography by Johanna Heer. Released and distributed nontheatrically by Kino International. Starring Marianne Sagebrecht, Eisi Gulp, Tony Berger and Manuela Denz.*

Sugarbaby is the kind of comedy that makes you laugh in spite of yourself. The film's heroine, Marianne (Marianne Sagebrecht), is an obese, middle-aged woman who works for a mortician and lives in a starkly furnished Munich apartment. After a hard day of embalming, Marianne jumps right into bed, turns on the TV and shovels food into her mouth until she falls asleep. This routine goes undisturbed until Marianne falls in love at first sight with a handsome young subway conductor (Eisi Gulp). Through some persistent investigating, Marianne discovers that his name is Huber and that he goes to the same candy

bar machine for a snack every day. After buying herself a miniskirt and high-heeled shoes, getting her hair done, and putting on tons of makeup, Marianne sets out, candy bar in hand, to seduce her man. After several days of sweet temptation, Huber finally gives in, but their union is endangered by the jealous rage of his vicious wife.

At the beginning of *Sugarbaby*, this overweight woman scheming to seduce a man twenty years her junior seems pretty absurd, but as Marianne's inner beauty surfaces, Huber's love for her makes perfect sense. Director Adlon *(Celeste)* is careful not to exploit Marianne or her moments of disappointment. By the end of the movie, every ounce of flesh on her Rubensesque body has evolved into a testament to the joy of life.

Sagebrecht gives an immensely appealing performance as both couch potato and cherry blossom. Although Gulp's Huber is more understated, his character is a marvelous foil for Marianne's exuberance. Also, Austrian cinematographer Johanna Heer does an outstanding job with the film's lighting and camera work. Like an Abstract Expressionist on film, she colors the beginning scenes of Marianne vegging out in front of the TV in cold greens and yellows. Then, as she begins to flower, she bathes her background in warmer blues, purples and reds.

RATING: *No MPAA rating, with nudity and sex.*
FILMNOTE: *Adlon got the idea for Sugarbaby after watching Sagebrecht (the den mother for avant-garde theater in West Germany) emanate so much life at a party that several much younger men seemed to be genuinely attracted to her.*

SUGAR CANE ALLEY
(Video, subtitled)

Cultural Drama

Martinique	French
1984 103 Min.	Color

CREDITS: *Directed by Euzhan Palcy. Written by Euzhan Palcy, based on the novel* Black Shack Alley *by Jose Zobel. Produced by Michel Louergue and Alix Regis. Cinematography by Dominique Chapius. Music by Group Malavoi. Released by Orion Classics/Artificial Eye. Distributed nontheatrically by New Yorker Films. Starring Garry Cadenat, Darling Legitimus, Douta Seck, Joby Bernabe, Francisco Charles and Marie-Jo Descas.*

One of the few Third World films to enjoy success at the American box office, Euzhan Palcy's *Sugar Cane Alley* is a beautifully detailed journey into another time and another place, as well as a harsh indictment of colonialism. Set in her native Martinique in 1930, its story is told through the eyes of a charming eleven-year-old black boy named Jose (Garry Cadenat).

Jose lives with his pipe-smoking grandmother, M'man Tine (Darling Legitimus), in a small village of sugarcane cutters. Although slavery has been abolished for many years, freedom has changed their lives very little. They work long hours for a racist French plantation owner, receiving meager wages that almost always go straight to the company store's coffers. But M'man Tine is determined that Jose not get trapped in the fields. She encourages him to excel in school, dreaming that he might win a scholarship to the higher school in Fort De France and eventually become a teacher or government worker. Although Jose is bright and motivated, there are many obstacles in his way.

Jose is a dozen kinds of cute, as only an eleven-year-old can be. When a friend breaks his grandmother's only ceramic bowl, the fear of God overtakes the boy's frightened face. Stealing a bite of stolen papaya, his mouth curves into a satisfied and devilish grin. Although a few scenes are set up to open our tear ducts, for the most part director Palcy takes us into the life of this boy and his grandmother in simple and intimate ways. This remarkable first feature shows a magnificently photographed world embroiled in superstition and despair. Yet M'man Tine, Jose and their neighbors always carry themselves with an air of pride and dignity. And no ruthless plantation bosses or racist white colonials can strip them of that in *Sugar Cane Alley*.

RATING: *PG, with nothing objectionable.*

SUMMER
(Video, subtitled)

Psychological Romance

France	French
1986 98 Min.	Color

CREDITS: *Directed and written by Eric Rohmer. Produced by Margaret Menegoz. Cinematography by Sophie Maintigneux. Music by Jean-Louis Valero. Released by Orion Classics. Distributed nontheatrically by Films Inc. Starring Marie Riviere, Lisa Heredia, Vincent Gauthier, Beatrice Raymond, Rosette Carita, Marc Vivas, Joel Comarlot and Irene Skobline.*

Eric Rohmer's *Summer* is one of those movies that takes a while to sink in, but the longer you think about it, the more profound it becomes. It's a film portrait of Delphine (Marie Riviere), an attractive Parisian secretary in her late twenties who has not had a serious relationship for two years. She is alienated, desperately lonely and has so little confidence in herself that she is uncomfortable with almost every facet of her life but pretends nothing is wrong. Now it's summer, she has a two-week vacation, and there's nobody to share it with.

Delphine ends up going to four different places on vacation, and after a few frightening days alone with her thoughts, she goes back to Paris to begin the cycle all over again. Her friends realize something is wrong when she bursts into tears at the slightest provocation. But Delphine rejects all of their overtures because sympathy only seems to make her feel worse.

Summer's ad slicks make it look like a sexy French farce. Don't be misled. There's little about this movie that is sexy, and even with his hopeful ending Rohmer touches upon emotions within Delphine's character that are as real and tender as they ever get in the movies. Basically, *Summer* has two scenes that are replayed over and over again—Delphine alone in natural settings she is too self-absorbed to appreciate, and Delphine unsuccessfully attempting to relate to her peers. Riviere gives a riveting performance as a woman on the edge of a nervous breakdown, so strong at times that her torment is painful to watch. But Delphine's craziness is so compelling that it's hard for us to stop rooting for her every excruciating inch of the way.

RATING: R for one topless sunbathing scene.

A SUNDAY IN THE COUNTRY
(Video, subtitled)

Psychological Drama

France		French
1985	94 Min.	Color

CREDITS: *Directed by Bertrand Tavernier. Written by Bertrand and Colo Tavernier, based on the novel* Monsieur Ladmiral Va Vientot Mourir *by Pierre Bost. Produced by Alain Sarde. Cinematography by Bruno De Keyzer. Music by Gabriel Fauré. Released by MGM/UA. Distributed nontheatrically by Films Inc. Starring Louis Ducreux, Sabine Azema, Michel Aumont, Genevieve Mnich, Monique Chaumette, Claude Winter, Thomas Duval, Quentin Ogier and Katia Wostrikoff.*

The movies of Bertrand Tavernier *(Round Midnight)* are often sparked by small moments, incidents that barely ripple the surface calm but change the course of his characters' lives forever. *A Sunday in the Country* is just such a story.

It's a subtle portrait of Monsieur Ladmiral (Louis Ducreux), an aging Impressionist painter who realizes on a Sunday near the end of his life that his contemporaries have passed him by, and that his work will die with him. Visited by his son, Edouard (Michel Aumont), a conservative businessman who reveres his father, the artist temporarily forgets the pain of his own mediocrity. But when his beautiful and vivacious daughter, Irene (Sabine Azema), arrives unexpectedly, she reminds him of the relationships with his friends and children he has sacrificed for the work that ultimately means little to him. As he visits with his children and struggles with his last canvas, Ladmiral is forced to confront his own mortality, the nature of art and the importance of his friends and family.

Without preaching, and without resolution, *A Sunday in the Country* not only questions how much a person should sacrifice for the sake of his art but also serves as a moving testament to the power of love and family. Although there are no intense confrontations from Ladmiral's children or self-doubting monologues about the artist's life, his sadness and regret are present in nearly every scene. At times, this narrative's tempo is too slow to remain always interesting. But much of its force is a result of Tavernier's deliberate pacing. He and cinematographer Bruno De Keyzer skillfully capture the poignant faces of the characters against carefully composed landscapes that recall the paintings of Auguste Renoir. As always, Tavernier displays a talent for showing believable emotional pain, as well as small moments of joy and comfort. The performances are also first-rate, particularly Sabine Azema, whose presence underscores the unhappy decisions in her father's life.

RATING: No MPAA rating, with nothing objectionable.
AWARDS: Mise-en-Scene at the 1984 Cannes Film Festival; 1984 New York Film Critics Awards for Best Foreign Film and Best Director (Bertrand Tavernier).

SWANN IN LOVE
(Video, dubbed)

Psychological Romance

France/West Germany   French

1984   110 Min.   Color

CREDITS: Directed by Volker Schlondorff. Written by Peter Brook, Jean-Claude Carriere and Marie-Helene Estienne, based on the first and second volumes of Marcel Proust's Remembrance of Things Past. Produced by Margaret Menegoz. Cinematography by Sven Nykvist. Costume design by Yvonne Sassinot de Nesle. Set design by Jacques Saulinier. Music by Hans-Werner Henze, David Graham, Gerd Kuhr and Marcel Wengler. Released by Orion. Distributed nontheatrically by Films Inc. Starring Jeremy Irons, Ornella Muti, Alain Delon, Fanny Ardant, Marie-Christine Barrault, Nathalie Juvent and Charlotte Kerr.

If you're wondering how German director Volker Schlondorff (The Tin Drum) can translate the Swann in Love section of Marcel Proust's Remembrance of Things Past epic into a stimulating film, wonder no further—he can't.

Screenwriter Peter Brook (Meetings with Remarkable Men), Schlondorff and two others condensed the drama into one twenty-four-hour period in Charles Swann's (Jeremy Irons) life. On this particular summer day in Paris in the late 1800s, Swann is gripped with an obsession for an elegant prostitute named Odette (Ornella Muti), whom he has been seeing for a few months. Insanely jealous, he spies on Odette when she is with gentlemen, visiting her house on several occasions to taunt her. The two quarrel bitterly, but Swann always begs his lover's forgiveness. By turning into such a blithering fool over this woman, however, Swann risks ruining his reputation with the Parisian upper class he has worked so hard to earn in light of his Jewish descent.

Swann in Love's principal flaw is Jeremy Irons in the lead role. Although he has given excellent performances as an English lover in movies such as The French Lieutenant's Woman and Betrayal in the past, an obsessed Jewish French lover he's not. His accent alone would make any Parisian cringe, and the film's sluggishly paced script only makes his performance seem all the more stiff and unconvincing. Swann in Love is also repetitive to the point of tedium. Scenes of Swann spying on and fretting over Odette are replayed so many times that what drama there is in these moments is crushed by the sheer number of them. To the good, Sven Nykvist's camera work is stunning, as are the film's costume designs and sets.

RATING: R for sex and nudity.
WARNING: Certain prints that were released in the United States were dubbed, so the dubbing is good on the video as well. But because the sets, costumes and cinematography are so important, a good deal is lost on a smaller screen.

SWEPT AWAY
(Video, dubbed)

Social Satire

Italy   Italian

1974   116 Min.   Color

CREDITS: Directed and written by Lina Wertmuller. Produced by Romano Cardarelli. Cinematography by Giulio Battiferri, Giuseppe Fornari and Stefano Riccioti. Music by Piero Piccioni. Released and distributed nontheatrically by Almi Pictures. Starring Giancarlo Giannini and Mariangela Melato.

What happens when a sexist, Marxist, working-class deckhand and a spoiled, bourgeois woman are stranded on a desert island together? In Lina Wertmuller's most controversial and popular film, Swept Away, they end up ripping at each other's throats while tearing off each other's clothes.

The two characters are Gennarino (Giancarlo Giannini) and Raffaella (Mariangela Melato of Love and Anarchy). On the boat,

Raffaella treated Gennarino like a dog, expecting him to fetch her drink and food, and commenting on his body odor. When she tries to do the same on the island, he not only doesn't take it, he refuses to give her food unless she follows his orders. In scene after scene, he takes out all of his animosity about Fascist "bitches" on her, while she matches his insults with her own. They argue to a standstill, then Gennarino resorts to violence. He hits her repeatedly and withholds food until she becomes his slave. Finally, when her spirit is completely broken, she begs him to have sex with her. At long last the screaming and crying stop, and the two actually have a loving affair.

Even though this film is made by a woman, feminists wince when they see it, and for good reason. Wertmuller points out very clearly in *Swept Away* that all this vicious, shrill-voiced prima donna needs is a "real" man who will batter, demean and make love to her. It's not an appealing message to have at the center of a film and is especially frustrating because the nonsexual politics in *Swept Away* are handled with so much wit and intelligence. Giannini and Melato give hilarious performances, and their impassioned confrontations cover a whole range of timely issues regarding class, sex and money. Cinematographer Giulio Battiferri's beautifully composed shots of the tranquil island are a perfect contrast to Gennarino and Raffaella's intensity. But their almost nonstop screaming is as exhausting as the sexism is offensive.

RATING: R for an onslaught of offensive language, sex and nudity.
WARNING: Dubbing of video version is poor and seriously affects the impact of this talky script.

SWIMMING TO CAMBODIA
(Video)

Social Satire

U.S.A.

1987   87 Min.   Color

CREDITS: Directed by Jonathan Demme. Written by Spalding Gray, based on his performance piece. Produced by R. A. Shafransky. Music by Laurie Anderson. Cinematography by John Bailey. Edited by Carol Littleton (E.T.). Released and distributed nontheatrically by Cinecom. Starring Spalding Gray.

Don't be discouraged from seeing *Swimming to Cambodia* just because it's a one-person monologue on a bare stage by a little-known writer-actor named Spalding Gray. Directed by Jonathan Demme *(Stop Making Sense, Something Wild)*, this film is so thoroughly entertaining from beginning to end that the lack of props and supporting actors makes no difference at all. Conservative in appearance, the fortyish Gray looks like a Boston banker as he mounts the stage of a small New York theater called the Performing Garage. But as he begins speaking in his sly, deliberate cadence, his eyes twinkle, his face comes alive with expression and, before we know what's hit us, a rapid-fire stream of amazing perceptions and metaphors comes flying off his tongue so quickly it takes all of our concentration to follow them. Yet his command of the language is immense, and his vision of the world is so unique we don't want to miss one precious word.

In the course of an hour and a half, he talks about sitting next to a Commie-hating sailor on a train, nuclear annihilation, how anxious he gets after smoking a few hits of strong pot and what it's like to visit a Thai massage parlor. But most of his monologue focuses on the small role he played in Roland Joffe's *The Killing Fields*, his experiences in Thailand during the filming, and the tragic history behind the events in that movie. Gray describes those events with an absurd detachment, a harrowing and logical perception of how it came to be that the United States dropped tons of bombs on some of the "happiest" people in the world. He goes on to describe why a series of misjudgments led to the systemized murder of over two million Cambodians by a group of "bug-eating, back-to-the-land rednecks" called the Khmer Rouge. At the end of one of his most horrific passages, he quietly says "Who needs metaphors for hell, or poetry for hell? This really happened."

These and every other tragic, cryptic, wise, hilarious and wildly inventive perception Gray shares with us are as engrossing to watch as any traditional film narrative. Demme's "let the man speak for himself" direction and austere set offer few visual distractions. The only "special effects" are dramatic light variations, which serve to heighten Gray's verbal crescendos, and offbeat camera angles effectively shot by cinematographer John Bailey *(The Big Chill).* Laurie Anderson's neomodern soundtrack further enhances the surreal images created. The only problem with *Swimming to Cambodia* is its length— eighty-seven minutes of Spalding Gray just isn't enough time to spend with this extraordinarily brilliant personality.

RATING: *No MPAA rating, with mild profanity.*

THE TALL BLOND MAN WITH ONE BLACK SHOE

(Video, dubbed)

Caper Comedy

France		French
1973	88 Min.	Color

CREDITS: *Directed by Yves Robert. Written by Yves Robert and Francis Veber. Produced by Robert and Alain Poire. Cinematography by Rene Mathelin. Music by Vladimir Kosma. Released and distributed nontheatrically by Almi Pictures. Starring Pierre Richard, Mirielle Darc, Bernard Blier, Jean Rouchfort, Jean Carmet, Colette Casel, Paul Le Person, Jean Obe and Robert Castel.*

The Tall Blond Man With One Black Shoe is a light French farce about a violin player named François (Pierre Richard) who gets caught in an internal battle between two competing groups of French secret service agents. François's troubles begin when one faction lets the other know that a top-secret operative is coming to Paris the following day. As the unsuspecting violinist arrives at the airport after a Munich concert, he's mistaken for that spy because he is wearing one black shoe. For the remainder of the movie, bumbling agents follow François's every move. They bug his phone, ransack his apartment and assign a sexy blonde agent to seduce information out of him. When they find out nothing, they conclude that he must be a superagent remarkably clever at deception. Meanwhile, the bumbling François has no idea why all these strange things are suddenly happening to him.

Writer/director Yves Robert *(Pardon Mon Affair)* and his screenwriter Francis Veber (who went on to write and direct a similar comedy, *Les Compères*) are simply trying to do their best to entertain us in *The Tall Blond Man With One Black Shoe.* The film's violence is as harmless as an episode of *Get Smart,* while some of the gags are funny, others so predictable and slapstick they fall flat. Yet there is something enduring about François's character that carries us through the film's predictability. He is a lovable, clumsy, Chaplinesque type who has an uncanny ability to avoid danger at the last possible moment. How much you are charmed by François will determine how much you'll like this movie.

RATING: *PG, with nothing objectionable.*
WARNING: *Dubbing is decent on video, and since much of the film's humor is sight gags, it only slightly detracts from the quality of the film.*
FILMNOTE: *Robert's sequel,* Return of the Tall Blond Man With One Black Shoe, *and an American remake,* The Man With One Red Shoe, *aren't nearly as good this original.*

TAMPOPO
(Video, subtitled)

Cultural Satire

Japan   Japanese

1987   114 Min.   Color

CREDITS: *Directed and written by Juzo Itami. Produced by Yashushi Tamaoki and Seigo Hosogoe. Cinematography by Masaki Tamura. Released and distributed nontheatrically by New Yorker Films. Starring Ken Watanabe, Tsutomu Yamazaki, Nobuko Miyamoto, Koji Yakusho, Fukumi Kuroda and Rikiya Yasuoka.*

Billing itself as the first Japanese noodle western, Juzo Itami's *Tampopo* is one of the funniest celebrations of food ever served up on the screen.

More a series of skits than a traditional narrative, the film's main story involves Tampopo (Nobuko Miyamoto), the owner of a nondescript roadside noodle restaurant patronized by male customers who constantly ogle her. One day, a truck driver named Goro (Tsutomu Yamazaki), who looks like John Wayne, stops in for a bowl of noodles, gets in a fight and the next thing he knows is being nursed back to health by Tampopo. The gruff Goro thanks her by critiquing her noodle soup. Humbled and ashamed by his frankness, Tampopo begs Goro to show her how to improve her recipe. For the rest of the film, Tampopo, Goro and an assortment of gourmet misfits they pick up along the way (à la *Seven Samurai*) search far and wide for the perfect noodle soup ingredients.

As in a Japanese box lunch, director Juzo Itami gives us a little of everything in *Tampopo*, including references to American westerns, gangster flicks and B-movies, and several warm and touching moments as well. But considering himself a chef first and a filmmaker second, Itami takes the Japanese obsession with food to absurd extremes. Some of the vignettes are just plain silly and stay on the screen too long. But so many are hilarious lampoons of modern Japan and Japanese standards of perfection

and honor that you certainly won't be hungry for laughs after *Tampopo*. The timing and expressions of his assortment of offbeat comedians are outstanding, particularly the mousey Miyamoto as the sukiyaki-absorbed Tampopo. But more important, *Tampopo* bestows an insider's glimpse at modern Japanese culture, cuisine and humor that few Westerners have had the opportunity to observe so irreverently.

RATING: *No MPAA rating, with nudity, sexual situations and violence toward animals.*

TAXI DRIVER
(Video)

Urban Thriller

U.S.A.

1976   112 Min.   Color

CREDITS: *Directed by Martin Scorsese. Written by Paul Schrader. Produced by Michael and Julia Philips. Cinematography by Michael Chapman. Music by Jackson Browne and Bernard Herrmann. Released by Columbia Pictures. Distributed nontheatrically by Swank Motion Pictures. Starring Robert De Niro, Jodie Foster, Cybill Shepherd, Peter Boyle, Albert Brooks, Harvey Keitel, Leonard Harris, Martin Scorsese, Diahnne Abbott and Frank Adu.*

This is the film that made Martin Scorsese notorious—perhaps because of its brilliance, or maybe because its graphic violence was so shocking at the time it was released.

The hero of the story is the gruff, slow-witted Travis (Robert De Niro), who drives a taxi around New York in 1973 and witnesses an unending parade of pornography, rip-offs, johns, pimps, prostitutes and hustlers. He becomes obsessed with all the "filth" yet is powerless to do anything about it. He is rebuffed by a beautiful political campaign worker (Cybill Shepherd), and then he decides to protect a thirteen-year-old prostitute (Jodie Foster) from her ruthless pimp—which neither the girl nor her pimp particularly appreciates. Finally, it becomes too much for Travis, and the dangerous fantasies festering in the far reaches of his mind explode into reality.

Scorsese takes the audience on a joy ride through some harrowing mental and physical landscapes in *Taxi Driver*. The constant shrill of sirens, the blinking of cheap neon signs and the garbage that litters the streets of New York combine to create an intense portrayal of urban decay. The film's obtrusive lighting and documentary-style camera work add even more to its realism, while its violence is brutally graphic. But the real power of *Taxi Driver* is that we are forced to view this world completely through Travis's eyes. Right from the start, we experience the same "filth" and decay that affects him so profoundly. By the film's excessively violent ending, we completely understand his decline into madness. De Niro is so intense as Travis that watching him for nearly two hours is exhausting. But it is also extremely rewarding. *Taxi Driver* ranks as one of the best American films ever made, and De Niro gives one of the most powerful performances ever filmed.

RATING: Although originally rated X by the MPAA, Scorsese toned down some of its violence to merit an R rating for brief nudity and a lot of profanity and violence.

AWARDS: Golden Palm for Best Film at the 1976 Cannes Film Festival; 1976 New York Film Critics Award for Best Actor (Robert De Niro); 1976 British Academy Awards for Best Supporting Actress (Jodie Foster) and Best Original Film Music (Bernard Herrmann); 1976 Academy Award nominations for Best Picture, Best Actor (De Niro), Best Supporting Actress (Foster) and Best Original Score (Herrmann).

TAXI ZUM KLO
(Video, subtitled)

Gay Docudrama

West Germany		German
1981	92 Min.	Color

CREDITS: *Directed and written by Frank Ripploh. Produced by Frank Ripploh, Horst Schier and Laurens Straub. Cinematography by Horst Schier. Music by Hans Wittstadt. Released by Promovision International. Distributed nontheatrically by Almi Pictures. Starring Frank Ripploh, Bernd Broaderup, Gitte Lederer, Hans-Gerd Mertens, Irmgard Lademacher, Bete Springer, Ulla Topf, Franco Papadou and Hans Jurgen Moller.*

Frank Ripploh wrote, directed, produced and starred in *Taxi Zum Klo*, an autobiographical exploration of his life as a gay grade-school teacher coming to terms with both his sexuality in a straight profession and his incurable promiscuity.

Frank lives with Bernd (Bernd Broaderup), a movie theater manager who is totally committed to him. Although Frank returns Bernd's affection, he is addicted to cruising public bathrooms and city parks in search of a quick trick, unable to say no to the excitement of sex with strangers. His roving eye is even active when he and Bernd get together with friends at parties. Frank's promiscuity puts a strain on their relationship but is ultimately hardest on himself. When he loses his teaching job for "moral" reasons as he and Bernd are about to break up, Frank nearly has an emotional breakdown.

Taxi Zum Klo was made on a small budget, and the camera work and lighting are uneven, the sound tinny. But the main problem with the narrative is that Bernd and Frank's relationship is never really developed beyond their surface fighting, so it's hard to understand why they are attracted to each other in the first place.

A storm of controversy also surrounds *Taxi Zum Klo*, in large part because of its explicit gay sex. A detailed golden shower sequence, for example, is extremely difficult to watch, and Ripploh generally lingers too long on his amorous encounters for most straight audiences to feel comfortable. But *Taxi Zum Klo* is much more than a gay exploitation film. Ripploh approaches this very personal sexual diary with intelligence, humor and blunt honesty. There is no background score or blurring of the camera to soften his sexual encounters. His obsessions and passions are up there on the screen for everybody to see, as he digs into the psychological ramifications of promiscuity more effectively than any moviemaker to date.

RATING: No MPAA rating, although with its explicit sex, language, substance abuse and nudity, the MPAA would certainly give this movie an X.

TCHAO PANTIN
(Video, subtitled)

Film Noir

France		French
1985	100 Min.	B&W

CREDITS: Drected by Claude Berri. Written by Claude Berri and Alain Page. Produced by Renn Productions. Cinematography by Bruno Nuytten. Music by Charlie Couture. Released and distributed nontheatrically by European Classics. Starring Coluche, Richard Anconina, Agnes Soral and Philippe Leotard.

Claude Berri took a chance when he cast the fat comedian Coluche for the lead in *Tchao Pantin*, but his gamble with the uninitiated serious actor (known as the French Jackie Gleason) pays off in this movie.

Coluche plays Lambert, a former police inspector who mysteriously quit the force years before and now anesthetizes himself with alcohol while working as a night attendant in a Paris gas station. One night, a young Moroccan hustler named Bensoussan (Richard Anconina) ducks into the station to avoid a policeman, and the two become buddies, although Lambert is dis-

appointed to discover that his new friend is a drug pusher. But when Bensoussan is killed by his supplier, Lambert sobers up, gets his gun down from the shelf and vows to take revenge. With Bensoussan's blonde punk girlfriend, Lola (Agnes Soral), as his sidekick, and a sympathetic Paris cop (Philippe Leotard) reluctantly on his tail, Lambert stalks Bensoussan's murderers until it becomes clear that it is not only his friend's death he seeks to avenge, but a dark secret in his past as well.

As is common in other French noir, *Tchao Pantin* is disappointingly obscure and downbeat at the end. Also, Lambert's hidden albatross from the past is too obvious and clichéd an impetus for his actions. But Coluche is the perfect noir hero—self-pitying in the beginning and then reawakened by a deep code of personal honor. *Tchao Pantin* is also filled with excellent supporting performances, as Soral, Leotard and Anconina all have well-developed, involving relationships with Coluche's Lambert. And director Claude Berri *(The Two of Us)* proves an effective stylist in his first noir by elegantly framing Lambert in stark black-and-white surroundings that mirror his emotional barrenness, while the film's suspense and pacing ranks Berri with some of the masters of the genre, including Cluzot and Melville.

RATING: No MPAA rating, with mild nudity and violence.
AWARDS: 1984 French Caesars for Best Actor (Coluche) and Best Supporting Actor (Richard Anconina).

TESTAMENT
(Video)

Anti-Nuke Drama

U.S.A.

1983   90 Min.   Color

CREDITS: Directed by Lynne Littman. Written by Jahn Sacret Young, based on the story "The Last Testament by Carol Amen." Produced by Jonathan Bernstein and Lynne Littman for PBS's "American Playhouse." Released by Paramount. Distributed nontheatrically by Films Inc. Starring Jane Alexander, William Devane, Rebecca De Mornay, Lukas Haas, Philip Anglim, Lilia Skala, Mako, Leon Ames and Lorene Tuttle.

You often hear people comment that if given a choice, they'd prefer to be at ground zero rather than survive a nuclear war. *Testament* is a frightening affirmation of that desire. The film begins on a typical day for the Wetherlys, a suburban San Francisco family. The kids go to school and Dad (William Devane) to work, while Mom (Jane Alexander) does the breakfast dishes. Even that afternoon, when mother and children huddle together after a nuclear attack to watch as their TV loses reception, they act as if everything will be okay once Dad comes home from work and fixes the set. But the father never returns, and as the days wear on, Carol Wetherly and her children are forced to deal with an increasingly devastating situation.

Testament is a much stronger scenario than *The Day After*, the better-known made-for-TV movie. The film thoroughly explores what it would be like to survive an initial nuclear attack unharmed and then deal with isolation and effects of radiation poisoning. Although director Lynne Littman doesn't exploit the scenes of her characters' growing ill and dying, these moments are often too sugarcoated to swallow. There are also some overly sentimental subplots involving a kind elderly couple and a retarded boy and his Asian father that further use up our sympathy quota. But none of these problems alter the final impact of this film. Because the characters are so well developed, what happens to the Wetherlys and their neighbors seems like it could happen to any of us, at any time. By *Testament*'s terrifying conclusion, you can't help but take the warning at its center very seriously.

RATING: PG, with mild violence.
AWARDS: 1983 Academy Award nomination for Best Actress (Jane Alexander).
FILMNOTE: Director Lynne Littman has also made two excellent documentaries with anthropologist Barbara Meyerhoff:

Number Our Days, *which concerns an L.A. retirement recreation center for Jews, and* In Her Own Time, *which concerns Orthodox Jews and terminal illness. Both films often play on PBS.*

THAT OBSCURE OBJECT OF DESIRE

(Video, subtitled)

Sex Farce

France/Spain		French
1977	103 Min.	Color

CREDITS: Directed by Luis Buñuel. Written by Luis Buñuel and Jean-Claude Carriere, based on the novel La Femme et la Pantin by Pierre Louys. Produced by Serge Silberman. Cinematography by Edmond Richard. Released by First Artists. Distributed nontheatrically by Films Inc. Starring Fernando Rey, Carole Bouquet, Angela Molina, Julien Bertheau, Milena Vukotic, Andre Weber, Pieral Carriere, Jacques Debary and Antonio Duque.

Luis Buñuel's final film in his fifty-year career is also one of his most perversely entertaining. *That Obscure Object of Desire* opens on a train with a well-dressed, middle-aged male passenger named Mathieu (Fernando Rey) dumping a bucket of water over a young woman's head. When he returns to his seat, the other passengers in his compartment are curious about his strange behavior. He says it was "either dump the water on her or kill her" and proceeds to tell them about his relationship with the soggy woman, Conchita (played by two actresses, Angela Molina and Carole Bouquet), who claims to be in love with him but refuses to have sex with him.

Through a series of flashbacks, Mathieu remembers how he met Conchita and fell under her seductive powers, and how each time he came close to finally consummating their relationship she inevitably changed her mind. Maybe it was something he said that spoiled her mood, or maybe it was her fear of losing her virginity. Her reasons weren't as important as the fact that his tongue was almost always hanging out of his mouth and his ego was constantly being run through a revolving door.

That Obscure Object of Desire is a wonderfully Buñuelian treatise on the follies and frustrations of the monied class in general and men in particular. Mathieu starts out each attempt to sleep with Conchita with self-assured smugness, only to be manipulated by the beautiful seductress in every way imaginable. Although we, like Rey, can become a little frustrated after the situation is repeated a dozen times, Buñuel has a way of making each new attempt seem like this really could be the time that Mathieu succeeds. With his debonair manner and polished social graces, it doesn't take much to humiliate Mathieu. Rey plays the straight man perfectly and both Conchitas are master humiliators.

RATING: R for violence, sex and language.
AWARDS: 1977 Academy Award nominations for Best Screenplay Based on Material from Another Medium (Luis Bunuel and Jean-Claude Carriere) and Best Foreign Film.
FILMNOTE: Maria Schneider (Last Tango in Paris) was originally cast to play the elusive Conchita, but early on in the shooting Buñuel decided on two other actresses to play the single role.

THAT SINKING FEELING
(Video)

★ ★ ½

Screwball Comedy
Scotland
1979   92 Min.   Color

CREDITS: Directed, written and produced by Bill Forsyth. Cinematography by Michael Coulter. Music by Collin Tully. Released by Minor Miracle Film Cooperative. Distributed nontheatrically by The Samuel Goldwyn Company. Starring Robert Buchanan, John Hughes, Gordon John Sinclair, Janette Rankin, Billy Greenlees, Douglas Sannachan, Alan Love, Danny Benson and Tom Mannion.

Although you can certainly see glimpses of the absurd humor that would soon make him famous, Bill Forsyth's (Local Hero, Gregory's Girl) first effort is a little crude.

That Sinking Feeling focuses on a pack of unemployed Glasgow boys led by Ronnie (Robert Buchanan), a good-natured kid so disheartened by his inability to find work that he tries to drown himself by inhaling a mouthful of cornflakes and milk. But a lightbulb goes off in Ronnie's feeble brain when he notices that stainless steel sinks, the principal product of Glasgow's factories, sell for sixty quid apiece. Pitching the idea to his friends, Ronnie quickly rounds up a gang of pimply-faced bandits to rob a truckload of sinks one night from a local factory. Ronnie is an awkward leader, but his plan rallies the boys. Amazingly enough, they actually pull off the heist, but when they get the sinks, they have no idea how to hock them.

Although unemployed Glasgow youths expecting hot stainless steel sinks to solve their financial problems is a great idea for a comedy, the concept is better than the execution in That Sinking Feeling. Writer/director Bill Forsyth succeeded in Local Hero at combining eccentricity with somewhat believable characters. In That Sinking Feeling, none of the characters is more than a dim-witted, silly boy, while the film's set pieces are too obvious. Also, the acting by the cast members from the Glasgow Youth Theatre is uneven at best, and the film's patchy camera work and editing betray Forsyth's inexperience as a filmmaker. Still, there are several funny moments in That Sinking Feeling that make it worth a look. Like most Forsyth films, the cleverest moments are the small ones that pop up when you least expect them.

RATING: PG, with nothing objectionable.

THÉRÈSE
(Video, subtitled)

Religious Drama

France		French
1986	90 Min.	Color

CREDITS: *Directed by Alain Cavalier. Written by Alain Cavalier and Camille de Casablanca. Produced by Maurice Bernart. Cinematography by Philippe Rousselot (Diva). Edited by Isabelle Dedieu. Sound by Alain Lachassagne. Released and distributed nontheatrically by Circle Films. Starring Catherine Mouchet, Sylvie Habault, Ghislaine Mona, Helene Alexandridis, Clemence Massart, Nathalie Bernart and Beatrice de Vigan.*

In 1897, a twenty-four-year-old Carmelite nun named Thérèse Martin died of tuberculosis. When her journals were published after her death, they had such an effect on the hierarchy of the Catholic Church that she was cannonized. Alain Cavalier's *Thérèse* documents her devotion in some very unusual ways.

At the start of the film, fifteen-year-old Thérèse (Catherine Mouchet) desperately wants to join her two sisters in the Carmelite order, but because of her age, they won't let her in. Finally, in a comical scene, she convinces the Pope to admit her into the order while he tries to give her a Communion wafer. When she does enter, Thérèse goes through an elaborate ceremony in which she fixes herself up as a beautiful bride to marry Christ. Although daily life at the convent is full of arduous chores and repressed sexual feelings, Thérèse's devotion to her "husband" is so strong that, even when she becomes gravely ill, she never stops smiling and expressing her love for him.

Thérèse is a monument to the power and joy of faith, and little else. Nine-tenths of the story takes place in the few rooms of the convent and is filmed on a bare soundstage. The film's main action consists mostly of eating, praying, getting dressed and cropping hair. Most of the dialogue involves faith. In other words, its narrative won't have you on the edge of your pew.

But visually, *Thérèse* is an austere masterpiece. The rooms inside the convent are sparsely furnished, and the walls, floors and ceilings are cloudish white, so every object and person appears suspended in space. The daily chores of the sisters are incredibly real. When Thérèse and another sister gut fish for dinner, the gurgling noises of the guts flopping into the sink will send shivers up your spine. The scene of Thérèse getting her hair cropped with blunt shears resonates into scalp pain. Cavalier reaches new dimensions with visuals and sound in *Thérèse*, and though the story line may evaporate from your thoughts, the images of this film will stay with you.

RATING: *No MPAA rating, with nothing objectionable.*
AWARDS: *Special Jury Prize at the 1986 Cannes Film Festival; 6 1986 French Caesars, for Best Picture, Best Director (Alain Cavalier), Best Screenplay (Cavalier and Camille de Casablanca), Best Cinematography (Philippe Rousselot), Best Editing (Isabelle Dedieu) and Best Newcomer (Catherine Mouchet).*

THIS IS SPINAL TAP
(Video)

Documentary/Satire

U.S.A.

1984	87 Min.	Color

CREDITS: *Directed by Rob Reiner. Screenplay and music by Rob Reiner, Christopher Guest, Michael McKean and Harry Shearer. Produced by Karen Murphy. Cinematography by Peter Smokler. Released by Embassy Pictures. Distributed nontheatrically by Films Inc. Starring Rob Reiner, Michael McKean, Christopher Guest, Harry Shearer, R. J. Parnell, David Kaff, Tony Hendra and Bruno Kirby.*

Anyone familiar with seventies rock-and-roll documentaries should get some chuckles out of Rob Reiner's *This Is Spinal Tap*, a "rockumentary" about a make-believe British rock band named Spinal Tap and the pretentious filmmaker named Marty (Reiner), who is directing a boring movie about their American tour. Marty can't help it— Spinal Tap's music is loud, their staging and costumes are unremarkable and their fans are mostly obnoxious teenyboppers. When the group isn't arguing among themselves or abusing brainless groupies, they attempt to carry on phony "meaningful" conversations with Marty about their music and their lives. They also gradually become unraveled as they plummet to the bottom of the music charts and find their audiences growing smaller and less receptive.

Reiner made the members of Spinal Tap such extreme stereotypes that they are sometimes more insipid than they are funny. There are also too many scenes of their mediocre, ear-splitting music in this movie. Still, Reiner cleverly satirizes the self-importance and machismo associated with rock bands, their entourage and their fans. There are some hilarious moments of Spinal Tap staging outlandishly unsuccessful stunts during their performances, and with his hand-held camera techniques and off-camera questions, Reiner does an excellent job making this movie feel like a documentary and then skewering the genre.

RATING: *R for language and substance abuse.*
FILMNOTE: *There's even an album of Spinal Tap's terrible music, featuring songs such as "Sex Farm Woman," "Tonight, I'm Going To Rock You Tonight," which rose to the top of the charts in Japan, of all places.*

THREE MEN AND A CRADLE
(Video, subtitled)

Screwball Comedy

France		French
1986	100 Min.	Color

CREDITS: *Directed and written by Coline Serreau. Produced by Jean-François Le Petit. Cinematography by Jean-Yves Escossier. Released and distributed nontheatrically by The Samuel Goldwyn Company. Starring Roland Giraud, Michel Boujenah, Andre Dussolier, Jenifer Moret, Philippine Leroy Beaulieu and Gwendoline Moyrlet.*

Three Men and a Cradle has been enormously popular in France, winning numerous French Caesars (their Academy Award equivalent) and surpassing even *Rambo* at the box office in 1986. But then again, the French are also crazy about old Jerry Lewis movies—a dead giveaway of their fondness for slapstick.

The film involves three swinging bachelors whose Paris apartment is a hothouse of sexy women and one-night stands, until a baby in a basket shows up on their doorstep. A note is attached saying that the child is Marie, the six-month-old daughter of one of the roommates, and that her mom has gone to America to model and will be back in touch when she returns. Overnight, the den of love becomes a panic-stricken maternity ward, as these three swingers struggle to solve the mysteries of infant care. Her diapers need constant changing, her food won't stay in her stomach and her nightly crying invariably begins the moment the three sitters fall asleep. By the end of a week with Marie, the men are exhausted, short-tempered, nervous wrecks. But they have also become completely enamored of Marie.

The problems that one baby can cause in three grown men's lives are enormous but quite humorous. Our newly appointed fathers are like yuppie versions of the Three Stooges—constantly colliding with one another and fighting over the right way to raise the kid. At times, the nearly nonstop, odd-couple-style bickering can be too much to handle. But some of the film's funniest situations come from the everyday mini-crises that arise in taking care of a child, as these three proud fathers devise their own disastrous methods of coping. In the end, *Three Men and a Cradle* has enough hilarious commentary on male child-rearing to make any mother feel that she is getting vicarious revenge.

RATING: *PG-13 for brief nudity.*
AWARDS: *1985 French Caesars for Best*

Film, Best Screenplay (Coline Serreau) and Best Supporting Actor (Roland Giraud); 1985 Academy Award nomination for Best Foreign Film.
FILMNOTE: *There were two babies used to portray Marie during the filming. One reason the babies seem so happy in the film is that all three male stars grew fond of them while teaching them how to walk and changing their diapers.*

TICKET TO HEAVEN
(Video)

Psychological Drama

U.S.A.

1981   107 Min.   Color

CREDITS: *Directed by Ralph Thomas. Written by Ralph Thomas and Anne Cameron, based on the book* Moonwebs *by Josh Freed. Produced by Vivienne Leebosh. Cinematography by Richard Leiterman. Music by Micky Erbe. Released by United Artists. Starring Nick Mancuso, Saul Rubinek, Meg Foster, Kim Cattrall, R. H. Thompson, Jennifer Dale, Guy Bond, Dixie Seatle and Paul Soles.*

Ticket to Heaven *dramatizes too effectively what all of us who have been approached in the airport by friendly, flower-laden religious devotees have always suspected: cult religions are dangerous.*

Slightly depressed after breaking up with his girlfriend (Jennifer Dale), David (Nick Mancuso of *Heartbreakers*) visits a friend in San Francisco and agrees to spend the weekend with his group. A pretty young woman named Ruthie (Kim Cattrall) immediately attaches herself to him and leads him through their activities. The super-friendly members sing, meditate and chant, and everybody is constantly touching and hugging. It all seems pleasant enough, but David is more interested in striking up a relationship with Ruthie than anything else. She continues to flirt with him and convinces him to stay longer so he can truly understand her beliefs. When David agrees, his brainwashing begins.

David is given a diet deficient in protein. There always seems to be something going on to deprive him of sleep. The hugging and chanting become more intense, and the cult members never allow David to be alone or leave the house. Finally, the emotionally and physically exhausted David weakens and joins the cult for good. It's not until months later that David's parents are able to find and kidnap him.

Ticket to Heaven *is a frightening account of the methods religious cults use to ensnare their members. Mancuso's character before and during his indoctrination strikes an arresting balance between intelligence and barely controlled emotions. The supporting players are also convincing, and writer/director Ralph Thomas is careful to keep his story within the realm of possibility all the way up to the time of David's kidnapping. Then* Ticket to Heaven *goes over the edge. Thomas has the devotees go to unreasonable lengths to retrieve their lost sheep, complete with Hollywood-style chase scenes. In addition, the methods David's deprogrammer (R. H. Thompson) uses aren't convincing, and the issues they delve into during these sessions only include the superficial reasons that David joined the group in the first place.*

RATING: *R for profanity.*

TIME STANDS STILL
(Video, subtitled)

Coming-of-Age Drama

Hungary   Hungarian

1982   99 Min.   Color/B&W

CREDITS: *Directed by Peter Gothar. Written by Peter Gothar and Geza Beremenyi. Cinematography by Lajos Koltai. Music by Gyorgy Selmeczi. Released and distributed by Almi Pictures. Starring Istvan Znamenak, Henrik Pauer, Sandor Soth, Peter Galfy, Aniko Ivan, Lajos Szabo, Agi Kakassy, Josef Kroner and Maria Ronyecz.*

Time Stands Still is a Hungarian *Rebel Without a Cause*. In this case, though, there are several teenage rebels, all affected by their parents' participation in the Hungarian civil war seven years before.

The film opens amid the chaos of the revolt. A Budapest freedom fighter, who only has ten minutes to escape the Russian troops, pleads with his wife and two young boys to run away with him. They don't. Then the story jumps to 1963. Her husband in America, his wife is now living with another former resistance fighter, and her two sons are now teenagers in a Budapest high school. With flashbacks to the civil war mixed in with the present, the rest of the film centers around the younger boy, Dini (Istvan Znamenak), and his rebellious schoolmates, who fight, smoke and vandalize their school while they come to terms with their awkwardness about sex and becoming adults. They also love anything American and hate the Party.

Writer/director Peter Gothar's constant paralleling of Dini and his friends to their rebellious parents during the time of the civil war doesn't always work in *Time Stands Still*. These kids are more like aimless teenagers anywhere, frustrated by their parents, peers and a bureaucratic system they are powerless to change. They don't express enough of a political point of view for us always to link their present with their parents' past. Still, *Time Stands Still* is an informative historical document and an entertaining coming-of-age story with a great American-oldies soundtrack and several touching and humorous moments scattered throughout. The performances are excellent across the board, and Gothar superbly captures the rigidity of Socialist Hungary in the sixties, creating a perfect backdrop for Hungarian youths in rebellion.

RATING: *No MPAA rating, with nudity, sex and profanity.*
AWARDS: *Grand Prize at the 1982 Venice Film Festival; 1982 New York Film Critics' Award for Best Foreign Film.*

THE TIMES OF HARVEY MILK
(Video)

Documentary

U.S.A.

1985   87 Min.   Color

CREDITS: *Directed and edited by Robert Epstein. Produced by Richard Schmiechen and Robert Epstein. Cinematography by Frances Reid. Music by Mark Isham. Narrated by Harvey Fierstein. Distributed nontheatrically by Cinecom.*

When Harvey Milk became a San Francisco Board Supervisor in the mid-1970s, he was the first openly gay man elected to office in the United States. Until he and San Francisco Mayor George Moscone were assassinated by former Supervisor Dan White in 1978, he was also the most respected and outspoken advocate for gay rights in the country.

Using TV footage as well as interviews with friends and colleagues, *The Times of Harvey Milk* follows Milk from his hippie days in New York through his coming out of the closet in the late sixties, to his eventual rise in San Francisco politics. There are several humorous scenes, such as Jimmy Carter's homophobic, evangelical sister, Ruth, trying to convert Milk to Christ, and there are some extremely emotional moments, such as the huge candlelight parade that spontaneously formed on the evening of his murder. The film also documents Dan White's trial and the riots that followed his controversial conviction for manslaughter; he received a light sentence, despite the fact that he shot Milk and Moscone several times at point-blank range.

The Times of Harvey Milk is a tightly edited, comprehensive tribute to Milk and the ideals for which he stood. Some feel that the film trails off at the end, that it captures the community's sorrow at the loss of Milk better than it does the subsequent rage over White's sentence. Although these observations have some merit, they don't lessen its enormous power. One comes away from *The Times of Harvey Milk* realizing that

Milk was a remarkable man. During his brief time in public service, he was known for his off-the-wall humor, impeccable integrity and strong convictions. But his greatest accomplishment was to urge gays to be proud enough of themselves to risk losing jobs, friends and family in order to come out of the closet. Filmmakers Epstein and Schmiechen help keep that message alive.

RATING: *No MPAA rating, with some profanity.*

AWARDS: *1985 Academy Award for Best Documentary Feature; 1985 New York Film Critics Award for Best Documentary.*

FILMNOTE: *White's defense gained nationwide notoriety as the "Twinkie Defense," because he pleaded temporary insanity as a result of eating too much junk food. He was subsequently released from prison and shortly afterward committed suicide.*

THE TIN DRUM

(Video, subtitled)

★ ★ ★ ★ ★

Literary Black Comedy

Germany/France/Poland/   German
Yugoslavia

1979   142 Min.   Color

CREDITS: *Directed by Volker Schlondorff. Written by Volker Schlondorff, Jean-Claude Carriere and Günter Grass, based on the novel by Grass. Produced by Franz Seitz and Anatole Dauman. Cinematography by Igor Luther. Music by Frederich Meyer and Maurice Jarré. Released by New World Pictures. Distributed nontheatrically by Films Inc. Starring David Bennent, Mario Adorf, Angela Winkler, Daniel Olbrychski, Katharina Tahlback, Charles Aznavour, Heinz Bennent, Andrea Ferreol, Fritz Hakl, Mariella Oliveri, Tina Engel and Berta Drews.*

One of the few films to win both the Grand Prize at Cannes and the Oscar for Best Foreign Film, Volker Schlondorff's *The Tin Drum* can be described as a black comedy, a political epic and a romantic tragedy.

The narrator and star of the story is Oskar (David Bennent), a boy who can trace his roots to his grandmother hiding his grandfather from the police under her flowing skirts—a scheme that not only saved his grandfather's life but brought his mother into the world. From the moment Oskar is born, he has a difficult time with the hypocrisy of adults. In fact, Oskar fights desperately to stay in his mother's womb, and at the age of three, when he receives his coveted tin drum as a birthday present, Oskar decides to have nothing more to do with growing up.

After staging a fall down the basement stairs as an excuse to stunt his growth, Oskar wills himself to be a dwarf. When a doctor tries to take his drum away from him, he discovers that he also has a talent for shattering glass with his high, screechy voice. It's a skill that the conniving Oskar uses to get back at the world, disrupting a Nazi political rally at one point, and shattering the windows of a church after he catches his mother having sex with his uncle (who is probably his real father). Eventually, the only people Oskar finds who really care about him are a group of traveling circus midgets, whom he later joins as a dwarf who can shatter glass.

Based on Günter Grass's popular novel (Grass also helped write the screenplay), *The Tin Drum* is sharpest in its indictment of the rise of Nazi Germany. As Oskar rejects his father and other adults around him for their mindless ambition and hypocrisy, Hitler's Germany is condemned for its betrayal of humanity as well. But *The Tin Drum* is much more than a World War II political drama. It's a perversely funny "coming-of-age" story, complete with Oskar's wry narration, his sexual awakening and a couple of symbolic food scenes that will make even calloused moviegoers squirm. More important, the performances are outstanding in *The Tin Drum*. Each scene is filled with a hodgepodge of offbeat characters who are comical and disturbing because they are so real. Leading the list is the twelve-year-old dwarf, David Bennent, as Oskar. As the sometimes vicious, almost always misunderstood antihero, he commands our attention every moment he is on the screen. Schlondorff and his cinematographer Igor Luther tell Oskar's story completely from his perspective. Even during his birth, we are right there with him in the womb, struggling to stay inside.

RATING: R for sex, vileness and mild violence.

AWARDS: Grand Prize at the 1979 Cannes Film Festival; 1979 Academy Award for Best Foreign Film.

FILMNOTE: Until Das Boot, The Tin Drum was the most elaborate and expensive German production to date.

TOKYO STORY

Cultural Drama

Japan	Japanese
1953	134 Min.	B&W

CREDITS: *Directed by Yasujiro Ozu. Written by Yasujiro Ozu and Kogo Noda. Produced by Takeshi Yamatoro. Cinematography by Yushon Atsuta. Music by Takanori Saito. Released and distributed nontheatrically by New Yorker Films. Starring Chishu Ryu, Chiyeko Higashiyama, Setsuko Hara, So Yamamura, Haruko Sugimura, Nobuo Nakamura and Kyoko Kagawa.*

Yasujiro Ozu's *Toyko Story* is a simple story of an elderly couple from the small town of Onomichi who decide to visit their married children in Tokyo for the first time. Shukishi (Chishu Ryu) and Tomi (Chiyeko Higashiyama) leave their youngest daughter and excitedly travel by train to Toyko, only to find that their doctor son and beautician daughter don't have much time for them in their busy lives. The children pretend to be glad that their parents are visiting, but it doesn't take much for Shukishi and Tomi to see through the veneer. Shukishi and Tomi decide to leave sooner than they planned. On their last night in town, gramps gets blistering drunk with some lecherous men he meets in a bar, while grandma stays with the widow of their deceased third son, because she's the only one who truly cares about them.

Because all the characters in *Toyko Story* are so understated and polite, it takes a while to find their emotions. But once you get into the film's rhythm, the feelings they touch upon are as profound as those in any traditional Western drama. Considered to be "the most Japanese of Japanese filmmakers," Yasujiro Ozu is known for creating deceptively simple characters and plot lines. Ryu and Higashiyama give subtle yet powerful performances as the couple devastated because their children don't respect them, and because they feel they have failed as parents. Their insensitive children bring up many important themes about the impersonalization of post–World War II Japan and traditional versus modern values. And though *Tokyo Story*'s camera rarely moves, the images Ozu captures are so poetic that many have compared him to a Haiku master.

RATING: No MPAA rating, with nothing objectionable.

TRASH
(Video)

Porn Comedy

U.S.A.		
1970	103 Min.	Color

CREDITS: *Directed, written and photographed by Paul Morrissey. Produced by Andy Warhol. Edited by Jud Johnson. Released and distributed nontheatrically by Almi Pictures. Starring Holly Woodlawn, Joe Dallesandro, Andrea Feldman, Jane Forth, Bruce Pencheur, Michael Sklar, Geri Miller, Johnny Putnam and Diane Poldewski.*

Trash opens with a long close-up of a pimply ass, paired with a woman's murmured mumblings of affection. After several minutes, the camera swings around to reveal Holly (transvestite Holly Woodlawn) trying in vain to orally arouse her junkie boyfriend Joe (Joe Dallesandro). This is life in bohemian New York à la Andy Warhol. Unfortunately, it's also boring.

The rest of *Trash* is a porn comedy of manners, detailing Holly's drive to coax an erection from Joe and to land both of them on the welfare rolls. She loses on both fronts, failing to get a rise out of Joe and alienating a welfare worker when she attempts to bribe her with a pair of shoes she found in a garbage can. Before long, Joe is stealing to support his habit and ignoring the offers of several sexually charged women, while Holly seeks solace with a beer bottle substitute for her man.

Obviously, director Paul Morrissey *(Mixed Blood)* and producer Andy Warhol see these drug- and sex-numbed characters as symbols for an entire culture too anesthetized to combat dehumanizing urban pressures. Yet this point is lost in long, meandering and often excruciatingly improvised conversations. To give you an idea of how insipid the dialogue is in *Trash,* one of the strongest lines in the whole film is when Holly lovingly murmurs, "You're better than any bottle, Joe." Some of the most interesting action sequences are dominated by Dallesandro's flaccid penis. The acting is uniformly terrible, the sound is indecipherable, and the camera work is amateurish. In fact, if it weren't for Andy Warhol's imprint on *Trash,* that's exactly where this film would have ended up.

RATING: R for sex, violence, profanity and substance abuse.

THE TREE OF WOODEN CLOGS

Cultural Drama

Italy		Italian
1978	185 Min.	Color

CREDITS: *Directed, written, produced and photographed by Ermanno Olmi. Music by Fernando Germani and Bach. Set design by Franco Gambarana. Released and distributed nontheatrically by New Yorker Films. Starring Luigi Ormaghi, Francesca Moriggi, Teresa Brescianini, Omar Brignoli, Antonio Ferrari, Carlo Rota, Pasqualina Brolis and Massimo Fratus.*

Hailed by many to be one of the masterpieces of Italian cinema, Ermanno Olmi's *The Tree of Wooden Clogs* is a three-hour epic that portrays four sharecropping families at the turn of the century who live together in a cooperative in Lombardy, Italy. Some of the big events in their lives are a widow's cow getting sick, a farmer realizing that chicken droppings are preferable to cow manure as fertilizer for his tomatoes, and a father cutting down a tree to make clogs for his son to walk to school in. What ties them all together is their hard work, family values and God.

Some viewers might be bored from the opening credits on in this movie. A squealing pig about to be butchered gives the longest monologue in the whole film. The main characters are understated. In order to appreciate this film, you have to think small. There's little action beyond the characters' daily chores and struggles, but once you get involved with them, these events take on a great deal of importance.

The scenery and camera work are astounding in *The Tree of Wooden Clogs.* Director Olmi's grasp of the land, the change of seasons, and the lighting and rhythms of nature ranks with the great masters in cinema such as Kurosawa and Renoir. But it's the performances by the nonprofessional actors that make this film so compelling. They're farmers and villagers who are modern-day counterparts to the characters they portray, and they are thoroughly convincing. What Olmi manages to convey in their daily existence is a tremendous sense of community and commitment. On one level this film shows communism in its purest form. On another, it takes us into a special world that encompasses the struggles of peasants everywhere.

RATING: No MPAA rating, with two violent scenes of animals being butchered.
AWARDS: Palm d'Or for Best New Film at the 1979 Cannes Film Festival; 1979

New York Film Critics Award for Best Foreign Film; one of the National Board of Review's 5 Best Foreign Films in 1979; 1979 British Academy Award for Best Feature Documentary.

THE TRIP TO BOUNTIFUL
(Video)

Social Drama

U.S.A.

1985   106 Min.   Color

CREDITS: *Directed by Peter Masterson. Written by Horton Foote, based on his teleplay and stage play. Produced by Sterling Van Wagenen and Horton Foote. Cinematography by Fred Murphy. Released by Island Pictures. Distributed nontheatrically by Swank Motion Pictures. Starring Geraldine Page, John Heard, Carlin Glynn, Rebecca De Mornay, Kevin Cooney and Norman Bennett.*

The Trip to Bountiful is a bittersweet and simple story set in the fifties—a time, according to screenwriter Horton Foote *(Tender Mercies)*, when life was much less complicated.

Geraldine Page stars as Carrie, an elderly woman who is forced to live with her son, Ludie (John Heard), and daughter-in-law, Jessie Mae (Carlin Glynn, wife of the film's director), in a bleak three-room house in Houston. For Carrie, who was born and raised on a farm in Bountiful, Texas, the big city of Houston and her son's small house are prisons. To make matters worse, Jessie Mae treats Carrie either like a little girl incapable of making her own decisions or a servant who should cater to her every whim. Stripped of her dignity, Carrie lives for a dream that one day she will return to Bountiful. Finally, with the help of a young woman she meets on a bus (Rebecca De Mornay), she does, although she finds both less and more than she imagined.

Oscar-winning screenwriter Foote originally wrote *The Trip to Bountiful* as a teleplay for NBC television in 1953. The setting inside Ludie and Jessie Mae's house is so static, and the script so talk-heavy, that the film does have the feel of a network miniseries. But the deliberate pacing also adds a certain texture, while the acting in *The Trip to Bountiful* is so outstanding and the emotions it ultimately delivers so tender and true that it's easy to go with the flow.

Carlin Glynn is tremendous as the overbearing Jessie Mae. She is obnoxious, insensitive and self-centered, and nearly every moment she is on the screen makes you seethe with anger. Heard is a perfect wimpy husband. But it's Page's performance that carries the show. Her portrayal of the deeply frustrated woman will turn even the most hardened moviegoer into a whimpering sentimentalist.

RATING: *PG, with nothing objectionable.*
AWARD: *1985 Academy Award for Best Actress (Geraldine Page); 1985 Academy Award nomination for Best Screenplay Adaptation (Horton Foote).*

TROUBLE IN MIND
(Video)

★   ★   ½

Romantic Black Comedy

U.S.A.

1986   111 Min.   Color

CREDITS: *Directed and written by Alan Rudolph. Produced by Carolyn Pfeiffer and David Blockner. Cinematography by Toyomichi Kurita. Music by Mark Ishahm and Marianne Faithful. Costume design by Tracy Tynan. Released by Alive Films. Distributed nontheatrically by The Samuel Goldwyn Company. Starring Keith Carradine, Kris Kristofferson, Lori Singer, Genevieve Bujold, Joe Morton, Divine, George Kirby, John Considine and Dirk Blocker.*

Spurred by the success of *Choose Me*, Alan Rudolph quickly followed it up with an awkward clone, *Trouble in Mind*. The film's hero is Hawk (Kris Kristofferson), a cop who served time for killing a suspect without obeying police procedures. Released from prison, Hawk drifts back to his hometown of Rain City and takes up residence on a barstool at Wanda's Café.

Although once his lover, Wanda (Genevieve Bujold) now offers Hawk only companionship and a place to stay, tokens the emotionally burned-out Hawk uneasily accepts. But Hawk's quiet exile ends with the arrival of Georgia (Lori Singer), a beautiful young woman who, with her boyfriend Coop (Keith Carradine), camps in a trailer next to the café. Hawk is immediately attracted to Georgia and watches in dismay as her innocence is ruined by the corruption of the big city. In search of an easy buck, Coop gradually falls into sleazy company, becoming a vicious hustler who pushes dope and pulls off petty robberies. When Coop also begins to beat Georgia, Hawk finally steps in to set himself on a collision course with both Coop and violent ghosts from his past.

As is *Choose Me*, *Trouble in Mind* is stocked with love-starved characters who sabotage their own relationships. The films also share a visual style, marked by scenes bathed in surreal lighting, as well as a similar assortment of offbeat and sleazy characters (including Divine of *Female Trouble* as a man). But the writing is much weaker in *Trouble in Mind*. Apart from Coop's thievery, there is little suspense, while the film's social satire is too obvious to be clever. The only consistently humorous character is Coop, whose hairstyles and outfits are outrageously funny. But the other characters are poorly developed and uninspiring, and the love triangles are devoid of chemistry. What Rudolph artfully creates in *Trouble in Mind* is atmosphere. Rain City is a milder version of Ridley Scott's post-nuclear Los Angeles in *Blade Runner*, but just as damp and dreary. You can almost smell the mildew in this movie. But unfortunately, its rich texture doesn't mask *Trouble in Mind*'s lack of substance below the surface.

RATING: R for language and violence.

TRUE STORIES
(Video)

Social Satire

U.S.A.

1986   111 Min.   Color

CREDITS: *Directed by David Byrne. Written by David Byrne, Beth Henley and Stephen Tobolowsky. Produced by Gary Kurfirst. Cinematography by Ed Lachman. Music by David Byrne and the Talking Heads. Released by True Stories Adventures. Distributed nontheatrically by Swank Motion Pictures. Starring David Byrne, Spalding Gray, Swoosie Kurtz, John Goodman, Alix Elias, Annie McEnroe, John Ingle, Jo Harvey Allen, Roebuck "Pops" Staples and Matthew Posey.*

Talking Heads star David Byrne's *True Stories* is a *Singin' in the Rain* or *Hello, Dolly* for rock-and-roll fans. It has entertaining song-and-dance routines and lavish sets, but unlike any conceivable Broadway extravaganza, *True Stories* is a satire on Texas, middle-class America and musicals themselves.

David Byrne is the film's cheerful narrator who drives around Virgil, Texas, in his new red convertible, introducing us to the town's inhabitants. Among them is the computer whiz (Matthew Posey) who expounds the virtues of the microchip, and the developer (*Swimming to Cambodia*'s Spalding Gray) who points to a barren piece of Texas landscape to show us where he will build the next totally modern kitchen and one and a half baths. We also meet The Dancing Bear (John Goodman), who has a brightly lit sign on his front lawn that flashes Wife Wanted, and The Laziest Woman in the World (Swoosie Kurtz), so rich that she never has to leave her bed. Byrne even takes us to a mall, a disco and a parade, complete with Shriners riding around in red go-carts.

Although some of the characters in *True Stories* are clever and funny, the majority are just insipid. The documentary-narrator format only emphasizes this shallowness, wasting so much time on introductions and cloying transitional sequences that character development is only a wished-for dream. Also, there is an air of condescension that pervades the entire narrative. Still, for an evening of light entertainment, there is plenty of musical merriment, dance extravaganza and good-hearted satire in *True Stories*. Aside from his tremendous music, sets and photography, Byrne gives us a dose of middle America, fundamentalist religion, singles bars, Texans, and suburbia thrown into an Osterizer and set on purée. The finished product is as light as club soda, but it's liable to tickle your funny bone going down.

RATING: PG, with nothing objectionable.

LA TRUITE (THE TROUT)
(Video, subtitled)

Thriller

France   French

1982   100 Min.   Color

CREDITS: *Directed by Joseph Losey. Written by Joseph Losey and Monique Lange, based on the novel by Roger Vailland. Produced by Yves Rousset-Rouard. Cinematography by Henri Alekan. Music by Richard Hartley. Costume design by Annalisa Nasilli-Rocca. Released by Columbia Pictures/Triumph Films. Distributed non-theatrically by Swank Motion Pictures. Starring Isabelle Huppert, Lissette Malidor, Jacques Spiesser, Jeanne Moreau, Jean-Pierre Cassel, Daniel Olbrychski, Alexis Smith and Craig Stevens.*

Although American director Joseph Losey did create many first-rate films (particularly *Accident*) after his exile to Europe in the 1950s, *La Truite* is not one of them. A ponderous, pretentious work that traces a young girl's path from a small French fishing village to the world of high finance, *La Truite* says more about the failed ambitions of its director than the human condition it tries to address.

The film opens in a bowling alley, where Frederique (Isabelle Huppert) attracts the attention of Rambert (Jean-Pierre Cassel) and St. Gemis (Daniel Olbrychski), two rich industrialists out with their wives for a night on the town. Both men are so fascinated by Frederique that they allow her and her husband, Galuchat (Jacques Spiesser), to hustle them as an excuse to meet her. Tired of poverty and frustrated by Galuchat's alcoholism and closet homosexuality, Frederique jumps at St. Gemis's offer to join him on a trip to Japan, although she refuses to sleep with him despite his burning infatuation with her. Later, when Galuchat attempts suicide, Frederique quickly returns to Paris to nurse him back to health. Once back in France, Rambert, St. Gemis, Galuchat and a terminally ill Japanese businessman all struggle to possess her, but Frederique has now grown emotionally barren. She shrewdly manipulates these men for her financial gain while ignoring their romantic intentions.

By inserting numerous flashbacks of Frederique's life with Galuchat in a small village, Losey creates a dense, jumbled narrative that often makes little sense. Nothing in the story explains Huppert's coldness and consistently blank expressions. In fact, *La Truite* is filled with bad performances, often from very good actors. Jeanne Moreau appears so briefly as Rambert's wife that her talents are wasted, while Jean-Pierre Cassel is simply aggravating as the twitchy, Frederique-obsessed Rambert. Because the characterizations are so weak in *La Truite*, its plot is further confused by the murder, suicide and screaming arguments that occur throughout the script. Losey is so concerned about whipping the action into a frenzy that he neglects to create characters who convey emotion.

RATING: R for nudity and adult situations.
FILMNOTE: Blacklisted during the McCarthy era, Joseph Losey moved to Europe and remained there until his death.

TURTLE DIARY
(Video)

Social Satire

England

1986   96 Min.   Color

CREDITS: *Directed by John Irvin. Written by Harold Pinter, based on the novel by Russell Hoban. Produced by Richard Johnson. Cinematography by Peter Hannan. Released by Rank Films. Distributed nontheatrically by The Samuel Goldwyn Company. Starring Ben Kingsley, Glenda Jackson, Richard Johnson, Rosemary Leach, Gary Olson, Harold Pinter and Harriet Walter.*

In America, a caper comedy usually involves a bank robbery or a jewel heist, but in the dry world of screenwriter Harold Pinter's *Turtle Diary,* the unlikely booty is three sea turtles.

Bookshop clerk William Snow (Ben Kingsley) and children's novelist Neara Duncan (Glenda Jackson), both self-professed giant-green-sea-turtle "freaks," bump into each other quite frequently when admiring a trio of the graceful, gentle-eyed amphibians at the aquarium of the London Zoo. Both individually approach the aquarium's turtle keeper, Mr. Johnson (Richard Johnson), to ask whether the turtles are happy in their tank and wonder how an admirer might go about setting the creatures free. Being a turtle enthusiast himself, Mr. Johnson gladly answers their inquiries. He doesn't think "they are all that happy" and suggests that if somebody wanted to set them free, only a van, a trolly and some large crates to hold the turtles would be needed to do the job. With Mr. Johnson's coaching, William and Neara toy with the idea of stealing the turtles and, after thirty years of "prison," setting them free.

William and Neara are intelligent, nervous types who lead reclusive lives. Just talking to each other and the turtle keeper is painful, yet they begin to realize that they have to go through with the theft—not only for the turtles but also for themselves.

Metaphors abound in *Turtle Diary:* giant turtles trapped inside a tank are freed by two humans trapped by their own fears; William and Neara must break society's laws to free themselves and abide by nature's; an observant, benevolent zookeeper watches two people watch each other watch the turtles. The whole merry-go-round is fascinating. Kingsley, Jackson and Johnson are extraordinary in their roles—a finer ensemble would be hard to find. Screenwriter Harold Pinter *(Betrayal)* accentuates their eccentricities with his wonderfully droll dialogue, while director John Irvin *(The Dogs of War)* and his crew don't miss an opportunity to catch their peculiar expressions and mannerisms.

RATING: *PG, with nothing objectionable.*

28/UP

Documentary

England

1985   136 Min.   Color

CREDITS: *Directed and produced by Michael Apted. Cinematography by George Jesse Turner. Sound by Nick Steer. Researched by Claire Lewis. Edited by Oral Norrie Otteg and Kim Horton. Released and distributed nontheatrically by First Run Features. Starring Neil Hughes, Lynn Johnson, Tony Walker, Paul Kligerman, Charles Furneaux, Simon Basterfield, Bruce Balden, Peter Davies, Susan Sullivan, Jacki Bassett, Suzanne Dewey, Nicholas Hitchon, Andrew Brackfield and John Brisby.*

In 1963, Michael Apted *(Coal Miner's Daughter)* began filming a documentary for British television featuring interviews with fourteen seven-year-olds discussing their lives and their futures. Funded by British public TV, it was so well-received that he continued the project with the same subjects at ages fourteen, twenty-one and twenty-eight, and then turned it into a feature film. The result is a documentary with enough fascinating information about growing up in post–World War II England to fill a sociology textbook.

The backgrounds of the four girls and ten boys cover a wide spectrum. Some are from the suburbs, others from the country, still others from the city. Economically, they range from poor to upper class. The histories of many of them are predictable: the great hopes of seven-year-olds with their lives ahead of them turn into adolescent confusion, young adult social idealism and twenty-eight-year-old material preoccupation and social complacency. But several of them don't fit the formula, with the most striking example being bright, optimistic seven-year-old Neil growing into a twenty-eight-year-old depressed drifter.

Apted introduces us to one subject at a time at age seven, then jumps back and forth to catch the same person answering the same question in other stages of his or her life. The fourteen appear as if they are in a time warp—growing up in fast motion right before our eyes. Although not all of them are articulate or engaging speakers, it's mesmerizing to try to keep track of who they wanted to be and how they turn out. *28/Up* is only frustrating in that there is no family background outside of the interviews themselves, and for characters such as Neil you want to know more. But it's a minor quibble compared to the enormous rewards in this movie. Even though *28/Up* is over two hours long, by the time you reach the final scene, you won't want to wait another seven years for the next installment.

RATING: No MPAA rating, with nothing objectionable.
FILMNOTE: Apted is planning another installment at thirty-five, and remarkably enough, of the fourteen originals, only two have told him they don't want to be a part of his documentary again.

UNDER THE VOLCANO
(Video, partially subtitled)

 ½

Literary Drama

U.S.A.   English and Spanish

1984   109 Min.   Color

CREDITS: Directed by John Huston. Written by Guy Gallo, based on the novel by Malcolm Lowry. Produced by Moritz Borman and Wieland Shultz-Keil. Cinematography by Gabriel Figueroa. Released by Universal. Distributed nontheatrically by Swank Motion Pictures. Starring Albert Finney, Jacqueline Bisset, Anthony Andrews, Ignacio Lopez Tarso, Katy Jurado and a cameo by famed Mexican director Emilio Fernandez.

Although John Huston's *Under the Volcano* could be used as a what-could-happen-to-you film for Alcoholics Anonymous meetings, it's not as compelling as the Malcolm Lowry novel on which it was based.

The film revolves around a British diplomat's drinking problems in Mexico circa 1938, and the attempts of his ex-wife Yvonne (Jacqueline Bisset) and half-brother Hugh (Anthony Andrews) to help him. Geoffrey Firmin (Albert Finney), the retired vice counsul in Cuernavaca, drinks from the moment he wakes until he passes out in a state that could be described as sleep. While conscious, he is prone to outrageous bouts of anger, self-pity and attention grabbing. All through his antics, Yvonne and Hugh loyally stand by his side to pick him up when he falls and keep him in good company when he is sober enough to walk.

It's remarkable that Hugh and Yvonne stick by Geoffrey as long as they do, and with little background given that develops their relationship with the ex-consul (a gap Lowry's book fills in much better), it's hard to understand why. At times, Finney adeptly portrays the despair and self-destruction of Geoffrey's character. The actor may even have downed a few too many at some point in his life, too, because he stumbles, slurs and staggers like an old pro. But his drinking-himself-into-oblivion routine gets old after a while. And though there are some interesting subplots about the Fascist rise in pre–World War II Mexico and the poverty in Cuernavaca, these are about as relevant to the story line as a green olive is to a double martini. Director John Huston and screenwriter Guy Gallo stay with Finney too long in *Under the Volcano,* and he ultimately drains the life from the film.

RATING: *R for violence and language.*
AWARDS: *1984 Academy Award nomination for Best Actor (Albert Finney).*
FILMNOTE: *After Malcolm Lowry died in 1957 at the age of forty-seven of alcohol-related causes, the rights to film* Under the Volcano *were bought by a series of people, including Gabriel Garcia Marquez, Ken Russell, Joseph Losey and Jerzy Skolimowski, before ending up at Universal.*

UTU

(Video, partially subtitled)

Cultural Drama

New Zealand   English and Maori

1983   104 Min.   Color

CREDITS: *Directed by Geoff Murphy. Written by Geoff Murphy and Keith Aberdein. Produced by Geoff Murphy and Don Blakeney. Cinematography by Graeme Cowley. Released by Glitteron. Distributed nontheatrically by Kino International Films. Starring Anzac Wallace, Wi Kuki Kaa, Bruno Lawrence, Kelly Johnson, Ilona Rogers, Tim Elliott, Tania Bristowe, Merata Mita and Faenza Reuben.*

If movies are a reliable measure of history, it seems that wherever British colonials went, bloodshed followed. New Zealand was no exception. Geoff Murphy's *Utu* takes place in 1870, as the Brits usurp thousands of acres of Maori land (the indigenous Polynesian population of New Zealand), slaughtering anybody who stands in their way. One such destroyed village is the tribal home of Te Wheke (Anzac Wallace), a Europeanized Maori who scouts for the colonials. Although his people were on good terms with the empire, the cavalry storms the village for no apparent reason, killing everyone, including the scout's family, beneath their thundering hooves.

Enraged, the well-educated, piano-playing Te Wheke tattoos the deep lines of a warrior on his face and goes about *Utu,* the ancient Maori ritual of regaining one's honor with revenge. With the help of a few others, he incites a small Maori rebellion. But instead of directing anger at the soldiers responsible for the atrocities, they indiscriminately attack any whites who cross their path. Finally, after murdering many innocent people, Te Wheke is captured and brought to trial. Through a series of flashbacks at that trial, we learn that Te Wheke was affected not only by the tragedy at his village, but by his own shame for kowtowing to the colonials as well.

With much of *Utu* based heavily in Maori culture, the film is not always easy to understand. Mix-and-match flashbacks confuse matters even more because it's hard to find one's bearings in the film's complex plot structure. Still, *Utu* is a fascinating, powerful and even humorous portrait of one man's rage against racism, disguised as a New Zealand western where the man with the biggest gun wins. Wallace gives a compelling performance, and director Geoff Murphy *(The Quiet Earth)* introduces through his character a number of important themes concerning race, degradation and honor.

To his credit, Murphy doesn't take a traditional liberal approach, although he was attacked by the New Zealand press when the film was released. In the beginning, Te Wheke is likable because he is a Westernized Maori who plays the piano and quotes Shakespeare, not a man committed to his own cultural identity. When he reverts back to his tribal ways, he is strange and distant, and finally, he becomes as vicious as the colonials. To add to this dichotomy, Murphy leaves out few gruesome details in his violence, and it's not until the final scenes that Te Wheke's actions are explained.

RATING: *R for graphic violence and brief nudity.*

FILMNOTE: Utu is considered by many international critics to be the best film from New Zealand to date, and it was the first film from that country to be selected for the main agenda at the Cannes Film Festival.

VAGABOND
(Video, subtitled)

Psychological Drama

France	French
1986	105 Min.	Color

CREDIT: Directed, written and produced by Agnes Varda. Cinematography by Macha Meril. Released by Cine-Tamaris and Britain's Channel 4. Distributed nontheatrically by International Film Exchange. Starring Sandrine Bonnaire, Macha Meril, Stephane Freiss, Laurence Cortadellas, Martha Jarnias, Yolande Moreau and Joel Fosse.

Vagabond opens with the French police pulling a pretty young woman's frozen body out of a ditch. What is her story? How could she freeze to death? These are the questions filmmaker Agnes Varda presents to the audience at the start. Yet by the movie's end, after it has methodically recreated the last few months of this woman's life, most answers remain a mystery.

The young woman is Mona (Sandrine Bonnaire), a scruffy but attractive eighteen-year-old drifter who moves from man to man and hustle to hustle—stealing when she gets a chance, turning an occasional trick to make some fast cash, doing anything necessary to survive. But the girl is basically indifferent to other people. An ex–college professor offers her an honest, hard-working life on his farm, for instance, and after a few days of chores, she drifts away. Later, an academic shows compassion for Mona, but she rebuffs her. Haunted by some betrayal that renders her unable to trust, Mona sabotages each relationship as soon as her emotional wall is threatened. Varda *(One Sings, the Other Doesn't)*

tells Mona's story as if it were a documentary. The camera work is simple and direct, and there is no background music or staging to orchestrate our emotions. With few tools, she creates a real and compelling story of a woman so alienated from the rest of the world that her only expression of feeling is misguided anger. Varda also uses Mona as a catalyst who prods those she meets to reflect on their own personal frustrations. Bonnaire gives a powerful performance as Mona, lending subtle expressions to her characterization that are extraordinary for such a young actress. Drab landscapes of the French countryside in the winter further enhance the film's feelings of despair. Some viewers might have a difficult time caring about Mona since Varda gives us no explanation of her past. Still, the apathy, despair and anger at the core of this story will deeply affect you whether or not you enjoy this film.

RATING: No MPAA rating, but the film does contain nudity, substance abuse and profanity.
AWARDS: Golden Lion at the 1985 Venice Film Festival.

VENGEANCE IS MINE
(Video, subtitled)

Psychological Thriller

Japan	Japanese
1979	128 Min.	Color

CREDITS: Directed by Shohei Imamura. Written by Masaru Baba, based on the book by Ryuzo Saki. Produced by Kazuo Inoue. Cinematography by Shinsaku Himeda. Music by Shinichiro Ikebe. Released and distributed nontheatrically by Kino International. Starring Ken Ogata, Rentaro Mikuni, Chocho Mikayo, Mitsuko Baisho, Mayumi Ogawa and Nijiko Kiyokawa.

Based on a true story, Shohei Imamura's *Vengeance Is Mine* is a harrowing examination of the criminal mind. The film opens when a notorious Japanese murderer, Enokizu (Ken Ogata), is captured by the police. During his drive to death row, he reflects on the important events in his life, beginning as a young boy when he witnesses his father's humiliation at the hands of Japanese soldiers. The incident haunts Enokizu, but it hardly shapes him; he's already a juvenile delinquent. Enokizu goes on to spend much of his early adulthood in prison for an assortment of crimes. After he is released and discovers his wife and father having a near-incestuous relationship, Enokizu's rage takes over. He goes into the country, where he ruthlessly kills two truck drivers on a whim and becomes the object of a nationwide manhunt. Eluding the police for eighty days, in part by posing as a professor from a Kyoto university, Enokizu leaves behind a trail of bodies until he holes up with an industrialist's mistress and her shrewish mother.

Even though the narrative leading up to Enokizu's killing spree is meant to place him in the context of the violent world that created him, Imamura *(The Ballad of Narayama)* isn't excusing his protagonist's actions as much as simply explaining them. *Vengeance Is Mine* is a terrifying portrait of a man without a heart, and Imamura spares us none of the graphic details of Enokizu's vicious killings. In fact, he underlines the horror with black humor, showing Enokizu eating his dinner over the still-warm bodies of his victims. His victims are so innocent and unsuspecting that his crimes seem particularly horrendous. But there is something perversely appealing about his character that attracts, rather than repels, our interest. Ogata *(Mishima)* as Enokizu is brilliant, while Shinsaku Himeda's cinematography has a magical, lyrical quality to it that allows the film to leap from a brutal exploration of a criminal to a metaphysical portrayal of the world in which he exists.

RATING: No MPAA rating, with sex and violence.
FILMNOTE: Like the late master Ozu, Imamura has been described as the most "Japanese" of today's filmmakers; and like Ozu's, his films aren't always easy for Westerners to understand.

VERONIKA VOSS

Psychological Thriller

West Germany   German

1982   105 Min.   B&W

CREDITS: *Directed by Rainer Werner Fassbinder. Written by Rainer Werner Fassbinder, Peter Marthesheimer and Pea Frolich. Produced by Thomas Schuhly. Cinematography by Xaver Schwarzenberger. Music by Peter Raben. Released by United Artists. Distributed nontheatrically by Films Inc. Starring Rosel Zech, Hilmar Thate, Annemarie Duringer, Cornelia Froboess, Volker Spengler, Doris Schade, Erik Schumann, Peter Berling and Gunther Kaufman.*

It's no accident that this third film in Fassbinder's trilogy about post–World War II Germany in decline *(The Marriage of Maria Braun, Lola)* concerns a woman hooked on drugs, as Fassbinder was an addict himself when he made it.

Based on the life of Sybille Schmitz, a famous German actress who committed suicide after World War II, *Veronika Voss* is set in Berlin in the fifties. It tells the story of Veronika Voss (Rosel Zech), a washed-up movie star who suffers a mental breakdown and is treated by the noted neurologist, Dr. Katz (Annemarie Duringer). Katz treats her patients by getting them addicted to morphine, and then holding back the drug until they sign over all of their property to her. Veronika is one of her model patients until a sportswriter named Robert (Hilmar Thate) comes into the picture. He meets Veronika in a coffee shop and becomes so infatuated with her that he loans her money, drops the woman he lives with and starts hanging around Dr. Katz's office, where Veronika stays. The doctor and her assistants don't take kindly to Robert, especially when, after some sleuthing, he figures out why Veronika has so many drastic mood swings.

Like the other films in Fassbinder's trilogy, *Veronika Voss* takes loneliness and alienation in modern society and the power struggle that occurs within relationships as its themes. Fassbinder also gives us plenty of metaphors for Germany's single-minded drive for economic gain and instant memory loss after the war. The acting is excellent across the board, with Zech (a dead ringer for Marlene Dietrich) giving a particularly intense performance as the neurotic femme fatale. As a plus, Robert's uncovering of Veronika's mystery gradually builds in suspense to a frightening climax. Visually, *Veronika Voss* is one of Fassbinder's most powerful films, featuring striking black-and-white photography that highlights the cold world inhabited by the characters in this film. Even though Fassbinder was an addict when he made this movie, it remains one the most lucid and coherent works in his prolific career.

RATING: *R for brief nudity and substance abuse.*
AWARDS: *Golden Bear for Best Film at the 1982 Berlin Film Festival.*
FILMNOTE: *Fassbinder died of a heroin overdose at the age of thirty-six in 1982, the year this movie was released.*

VIRIDIANA
(Video, subtitled)

Black Comedy

Spain		Spanish
1962	90 Min.	B&W

CREDITS: *Directed by Luis Buñuel. Written by Luis Buñuel and Julio Alejandro. Produced by Ricardo Munzo Suay. Cinematography by Jose Aguayo. Music by Handel and Mozart. Released by Uninei S.A. Films. Distributed nontheatrically by Corinth Films, Kit Parker Films and Films Inc. Starring Silvia Piñal, Francisco Rabal, Fernando Rey, Margarita Lozano, Victoria Zinny, Teresa Rabal, Jose Calvo, Joaquin Roa, Luis Heredia and Jose Manuel Martin.*

At the start of Luis Buñuel's *Viridiana,* a young Catholic nun visits her uncle Jaime (Fernando Rey). Before arriving, Viridiana (Silvia Piñal) is leery of her wealthy uncle. But he is so gracious that she doesn't suspect his plot to drug and seduce his innocent niece. Once she is unconscious, however, Jaime doesn't have the heart to abuse her, although he still tells her that she is no longer a virgin, to keep her from leaving him to return to the convent. The girl runs away anyhow, but while waiting for the bus to the convent, a messenger tells her that the now-mad Jaime has committed suicide.

Viridiana returns to his villa and decides to transform the estate into a shelter for the homeless. But Jaime's illegitimate son, Jorge (Francisco Rabal), the other heir to her uncle's fortune, has other plans for his inheritance. He pragmatically goes about shaping his father's farmland into a profitable enterprise, while openly carousing with any attractive woman he can get his lecherous hands on. Meanwhile, Viridiana invites street people by the dozens to live on their land. When she and cousin Jorge go away for the weekend, the mischievous waifs take over the estate, throwing a huge, bawdy banquet that erupts into violence.

Once again, the perversities of Buñuel's humor disguise deeper issues bubbling beneath the surface. There are several obviously symbolic scenes, such as a beggar's banquet resembling Da Vinci's *The Last Supper,* and some hilariously blasphemous sexual gesturing by a drunk with Handel's *Messiah* blaring in the background. But Buñuel seems to be saying with more subtlety that the poor will behave fairly well when there's something in it for them, although their disdain for the monied class will explode into reckless abandon when given the chance. *Viridiana* is also beautifully photographed, with luxurious sets and performances to match, particularly Piñal's Viridiana. It all adds up to a wealth of biting satire, religious symbolism and screen poetry.

RATING: *No MPAA rating, with sexual situations.*
AWARDS: *Golden Palm for Best Film at the 1962 Cannes Film Festival.*
WARNING: *Because of its public domain status, you are liable to find both subtitled and dubbed versions of this film, with varying quality of prints.*
FILMNOTE: *After self-imposed exile from*

Spain of twenty-five years, Luis Buñuel was invited back by Franco to make Viridiana, in recognition of his stature as his country's greatest filmmaker. But Franco's gesture exploded when the filmmaker entered his blasphemous work in the Cannes Film Festival without the generalisimo's approval. Franco responded by denying Spaniards the chance of seeing one of Buñuel's richest films.

WAITING FOR THE MOON
(Video)

★   ★   ½

Women's Docudrama

U.S.A.

1987   88 Min.   Color

CREDITS: *Directed by Jill Godmilow. Written by Mark Magill, loosely based on Gertrude Stein's autobiographical writings. Produced by Sandra Schulberg for PBS's "American Playhouse." Released by Skouras Pictures. Starring Linda Hunt, Linda Bassett, Bernadette Lafont, Bruce McGil, Jacques Boudet and Andrew McCarthy.*

Although Jill Godmilow's *Waiting for the Moon* is ostensibly about the relationship between Gertrude Stein and Alice B. Toklas, it fails to capture the passions that made these women famous.

The film takes place in the 1930s, at a French country house where Stein (Linda Bassett) and Toklas (Linda Hunt) have secluded themselves so Gertrude can write. But Gertrude instead spends much of her time espousing her opinions on a variety of subjects, while Alice edits her work, nags her to produce and waits on her hand and foot. It's obvious that if Alice weren't there to organize Gertrude's life, the writer would never get any work done. But Gertrude pays a price for Alice's doting—she has to put up with fits of anger and martyrdom.

Although there are a few minor subplots involving Ernest Hemingway, Apollinaire and a young man the women pick up

hitchhiking on his way to fight in the Spanish Civil War, most of *Waiting for the Moon* focuses on Gertrude and Alice's symbiotic relationship. Both leads give outstanding performances. Basset's one-sided conversations with Alice impart a true sense of Stein's creativity and brilliance, while Hunt brings to her role the same thoughtful expressions and careful speech that distinguished her in *The Year of Living Dangerously.*

Unfortunately, neither actress is given enough to work with in *Waiting for the Moon.* Despite all the artistic liberties taken by writer Mark Magill in embellishing Alice and Gertrude's life together (anyone familiar with the two will notice many inaccuracies in this biography), his script conveys little more than the couple's surface feelings. The two hardly show affection for each other verbally or physically, while scenes of the "impetuous genius" and her "silently enraged saint" are replayed to the point of tedium. Also, director Godmilow relies too heavily on expressions and body language and not enough on meaningful dialogue to convey the film's emotions. Although some of the scenic French countryside is superbly photographed, most of *Waiting for the Moon* takes place in settings as stagnant as the plot.

RATING: *No MPAA rating, with nothing objectionable.*

WALKABOUT

★   ★   ★   ★   ★

Cultural Drama

Australia

1971   95 Min.   Color

CREDITS: *Directed and photographed by Nicolas Roeg. Written by Edward Bond, based on the novel by James Vance Marshall. Produced by Si Litvinoff. Music by John Barry, Billy Mitchell and Rod Stewart. Released by 20th Century Fox. Distributed nontheatrically by Films Inc. Starring Jenny Agutter, Lucien John, David Gumpilil, John Meillon and Peter Carver.*

A fourteen-year-old Australian girl (Jenny Agutter) and her little brother (Lucien John) are taken by their father (John Meillon) for a picnic many miles into the desolate Outback. He stops the car, lays out the food and then takes out a gun and tries to shoot them. Luckily he is a bad shot, and they escape. With little food and water and no idea where they are, the two frightened children walk for days until they're rescued by a young Aborigine boy (David Gumpilil) who speaks no English. He is on his Aborigine rite of passage into adulthood, called a *walkabout*. In the few days they spend together, he not only protects the children but teaches the young girl many important things about life, including what it is like to feel a forbidden sexual attraction for the first time.

On the surface, *Walkabout* is both an exciting adventure film and a sensitive coming-of-age drama. Director Nicolas Roeg uses innovative camera techniques and surreal images to relay the film's emotions, and the cinematography is breathtaking. But underlying the plot in *Walkabout* is the clash of two very different cultures—the tribal Aborigines who live in harmony with nature and the whites who are out of balance. The children's father is an extreme example of white society gone awry, but all things "civilized" are also off kilter in this movie. *Walkabout* has a sad message: although the Aborigine boy's way of life is magical and pure, it doesn't mesh with our own—a fact that will probably doom his ways to extinction.

RATING: PG, *with disturbing violence and one brief nude scene.*

WATER
(Video)

    ½

Screwball Comedy
England
1986   95 Min.   Color

CREDITS: *Directed by Dick Clement. Written by Dick Clement, Ian LaFrenais and Bill Persky, based on the story by Persky. Produced by George Harrison and LaFrenais. Cinematography by Douglass Slocombe. Music by Mike Moran, Eric Clapton, George Harrison and Eddy Grant. Released by Rank Films/Atlantic. Distributed nontheatrically by Films Inc. Starring Michael Caine, Valerie Perrine, Brenda Vaccaro, Billy Connolly, Leonard Rossiter, Maureen Lipman, Dennis Dugan, George Harrison, Ringo Starr and Eric Clapton.*

Michael Caine stars in *Water* as Thornton Thwait, the colonel governor of the poor Caribbean island of Cascara, who is more concerned with developing a new hybrid of marijuana than he is with helping his impoverished constituents. Absorbed by his gardens, Thornton ignores the efforts of a singing revolutionary named Delgado (Billy Connolly) to liberate his island from colonial rule, as well as the renewed presence of Spenco, an oil conglomerate working mysteriously at a long-abandoned well. But when he discovers that Spenco has struck a vein of Perrier-like spring water, he not only sees hopes for his economically depressed people, but he becomes hopeful about his own coffers as well. The mine of carbonated gold, however, proves to be more of a headache than a salvation, as Delgado, a beautiful environmentalist (Valerie Perrine), and Cuban, French and British military advisers all converge on Cascara to wrestle for control of the fountain, leaving only Thornton and a handful of stoned natives to defend the island's honor.

Although nothing more than a lightweight situation comedy, *Water* has a funny premise—oil executives, revolutionaries, environmentalists and even entire countries driven in pursuit of a soft-drink bonanza. With Caine giving an understated yet often funny performance as the befuddled envoy, the story is somewhat entertaining during the first half of the film. But a rash of shootings, kidnappings and bombings mar the second half. By the time producer George Harrison is joined by Eric Clapton and Ringo Starr for cameo appearances at the UN, the film has become bloated and tedious. Even though *Water* starts out as a dry comedy in the best British tradition, it ultimately drowns itself in unbelievable characters and situations.

RATING: PG-13, with profanity, substance abuse and adult situations.

WE ALL LOVED EACH OTHER SO MUCH
(Video, subtitled)

Social Drama

Italy		Italian
1977	124 Min.	Color

CREDITS: Directed by Ettore Scola. Written by Ettore Scola and Age Scarpelli. Produced by Pio Angeletti and Andriano De Micheli. Cinematography by Claudio Cirillo. Music by Armando Trovaili. Released by European Classics. Distributed nontheatrically by Almi Pictures. Starring Nino Manfredi, Vittorio Gassman, Stefano Satta Flores, Aldo Fabrizi, Stefania Sandrelli, Giovanna Ralli, Isa Barzizza, Marcella Michelangeli, Federico Fellini, Marcello Mastroianni and Vittorio de Sica.

In *We All Loved Each Other So Much*, director Ettore Scola *(Le Bal)* traces the relationship of three men over thirty years, examining issues of friendship and success in a warm-spirited comedy/drama that is also a delightful homage to postwar Italian cinema.

The film opens at the end of World War II, as three idealistic resistance fighters return to Rome to rebuild their lives. Antonio (Nino Manfredi) becomes a hospital orderly and quickly falls in love with Lucianna (Stefania Sandrelli), a beautiful aspiring actress. Anxious to show her off to his friend Gianni (Vittorio Gassman), now a struggling lawyer, Antonio watches in dismay as the two immediately become attracted to each other, and Gianni steals his lover away. But Gianni's relationship with Lucianna ends soon, too, when he is courted by a rich industrialist's daughter who can advance his career. Meanwhile,

the third friend, Nicola (Stefano Satta Flores), becomes a radical film scholar obsessed with the movie *The Bicycle Thief*. He first loses his job when he defends the film's socialism, then loses a fortune on an Italian game show when he stubbornly insists that he, and not the show's judges, knows how director Vittorio de Sica made his young star cry.

Although *We All Loved Each Other So Much* is a little long and rambling, most of it is thoroughly engaging. Gassman and Manfredi are particularly involving as the film's complacent lawyer and hot-tempered orderly. The weak link is Flore's Nicola. As the constantly complaining *Bicycle Thief*–obsessed scholar, his one-dimensional role quickly becomes tiresome and is, at times, exaggerated to the point of ridiculousness.

But most of the film is a splendid hybrid of comedy and drama in which Scola captures the complications in these men's lives as they are forced to compromise their drive for success with their personal ideals. Just as impressive is Scola's tribute to his fellow Italian filmmakers. From cameo appearances by Federico Fellini and Marcello Mastroianni in the famed fountain sequence in *La Dolce Vita*, to Nicola's obsession with *The Bicycle Thief*, Scola lovingly recreates an era of Italian moviemaking, while the film leaves us with the message that friendship, and not success, is of real lasting value.

RATING: No MPAA rating, with nothing objectionable.

WE OF THE NEVER NEVER
(Video)

Women's Adventure

Australia		
1983	132 Min.	Color

CREDITS: Directed by Igor Auzins. Written by Peter Schreck, based on the book by Jane Taylor Gunn. Cinematography by Gary Hansen. Music by Peter Best. Released by Triumph Films. Distributed nontheatrically by Swank Motion Pictures. Starring Angela Punch McGregor, Arthur Dignam, Tony Barry, Tommy Lewis, Lewis Fitz-Gerald, Martin Vaughan, John Jarratt and Tex Morton.

Like a delicate Hummel figurine, Igor Auzins's *We of the Never Never* is beautiful to look at but ultimately uncompelling—a precious bauble with little emotional power.

The film is set in Australia at the turn of the century in the Outback, where the newly married Jeannie (Angela Punch McGregor) has come to make her home with her husband, Aeneas Gunn (Arthur Dignam), a ranch manager for a remote cattle station. When they first arrive at the small settlement, Jeannie is determined to play the role of the dutiful and docile wife. But she is immediately overwhelmed by the harsh conditions of daily life in the Outback and shunned by the hard-bitten cowboys who are disgusted by having a cultured woman in their presence. After a great deal of persistence, she wins the respect of her husband's hired hands and comes to love the beauty of the open green countryside, the natural chorus of croaking frogs, and the native Aborigines who work for her husband on the ranch. But when Jeannie begins meddling in the lives of the Aborigines, defending battered wives and sheltering an outcast girl, she creates tensions in their little community that alienate even her husband.

Based on the memoirs of a white woman's experiences in an Outback territory nicknamed Never Never, this film has wonderful visuals. Director Auzins and cinematographer Gary Hansen have an eye for green vistas and radiant sunsets and for capturing stark tableaus. But the visual punch is most of what this film has to offer. At least thirty minutes too long, *We of the Never Never* is pitched at a snail's pace, meandering from scene to scene with little sense of purpose. The main dramatic conflict—Jeannie's fight on behalf of the Aborigines—is not only introduced too late to bring the film desperately needed tension, but it smacks of liberal condescension as this cultured white woman rides into the Outback on her white horse to save the natives. The film is also marred by uninspir-

ing performances. McGregor is unrelentingly bland as Jeannie, and the other players aren't much better. *We of the Never Never* ends up a story of desperate emotions presented with all the force of a ladies' luncheon travelogue.

RATING: G, with nothing objectionable.
AWARDS: 1982 Australian Academy Award for Best Cinematography (Gary Hansen).
WARNING: Because the cinematography is so important in this film, it loses impact when viewed on video.

THE WEAVERS: WASN'T THAT A TIME!
(Video)

Documentary

U.S.A.

1982   78 Min.   Color

CREDITS: Directed by Jim Brown. Written by Lee Hays. Produced by Jim Brown, George Stoney and Harold Leventhal. Cinematography by Jim Brown, Daniel Ducovny and Tom Hurwitz. Released by United Artists Classics. Distributed nontheatrically by Films Inc. Starring Lee Hays, Ronnie Gilbert, Pete Seeger, Fred Hellerman, Holly Near, Studs Terkel, Arlo Guthrie, Don Mclean, and Peter, Paul and Mary.

Although many people haven't heard of The Weavers (Pete Seeger, Ronnie Gilbert, Fred Hellerman and Lee Hays), they were important American folk singers in the fifties, who performed familiar songs such as "Good Night, Irene" and "On Top of Old Smokey." The reason they're largely unknown is that they were blacklisted during the McCarthy era. It wasn't until they held a filmed reunion at elder Weaver Lee Hays's house, in May 1980, that the Weavers decided to get together for one last concert at Carnegie Hall.

Director Jim Brown takes us to that reunion, to their difficult rehearsals after not having sung together for nearly thirty years, and their two performances at Carnegie Hall. He also mixes in some anecdotal reminiscing from all four Weavers and clips from their concerts in the fifties.

The parts of the film that drag are the rehearsals. Typical of most rehearsals, the music is unpolished, but the editing of these sessions is choppy and they go on way too long. The actual performances at Carnegie Hall, however, are magnificent. But *Wasn't That a Time* is much more than a concert film. Still committed to their progressive politics, all of The Weavers are so fond of each other that warmth comes gushing from them in nearly every scene. The one who really gets those tear ducts flowing is Lee Hays. By the time of the Carnegie Hall concert Hays is gravely ill with diabetes, has had both of his legs amputated and is in a great deal of pain. Shortly afterward, he died. This film is not only a tribute to The Weavers, but serves as memorial to Hays's courage and dignity during the last few months of his life.

RATING: PG, with nothing objectionable.

WELCOME TO L.A.
(Video)

  ½

Romantic Black Comedy

U.S.A.

1977   106 Min.   Color

CREDITS: *Directed by Alan Rudolph. Written by Alan Rudolph, based on the song "One Night Stands" by Richard Baskin. Produced by Robert Altman. Cinematography by David Meyers. Music by Richard Baskin. Released by MGM/UA. Distributed nontheatrically by Films Inc. Starring Keith Carradine, Sally Kellerman, Geraldine Chaplin, Harvey Keitel, Lauren Hutton, Viveca Lindfors, Sissy Spacek, Denver Pyle, John Considine and Richard Baskin.*

After gaining notoriety as Robert Altman's assistant director in *Nashville*, Alan Rudolph *(Choose Me)* got the chance to make his own feature—*Welcome to L.A.*

The film's protagonist is Carroll (Keith Carradine), a handsome, self-indulgent songwriter who returns to California for the holidays after a three-year exile in England and immediately gets involved in a romantic tug-of-war. He rekindles a long-dead affair with Susan (Viveca Lindfors), who coerced him to come back to the United States. He quickly hops into the beds of his father's real-estate agent (Sally Kellerman) and his housekeeper (Sissy Spacek), who insists on vacuuming topless. But Carroll becomes obsessed with two unattainable women: his father's mistress, Nona (Lauren Hutton), and Karen (Geraldine Chaplin), a wealthy emotional cripple who rides around L.A. in taxis all day in an effort to ignore the philanderings of her husband (Harvey Keitel). In love with both women but unable to have either, Carroll has feelings of self-doubt that start to get the better of him.

As in his later films, Rudolph invests *Welcome to L.A.* with his own peculiar vision of casual sex and romantic tragedy. He also gives the film a stylish sense of place, portraying L.A. as a softly lit netherworld where neither love nor truth carry a great deal of weight. But unfortunately, he is less effective in establishing *Welcome to L.A.'s* characters. Although Carradine, Keitel and Spacek all give strong performances in a limited amount of screen time, there are too many half-formed personalities in this film, none of the love triangles holds much chemistry, and Chaplin's frazzled Karen is an uninteresting hinge for many of the film's relationships.

RATING: R for nudity, profanity and sexual content.

WETHERBY
(Video)

★ ★ ½

Psychological Thriller

England

1985   97 Min.   Color

CREDITS: Directed and written by David Hare. Produced by Simon Relph. Cinematography by Stuart Harris. Music by Nick Bicat. Set design by Hayden Griffin. Released by Film Four International/MGM Classics. Distributed nontheatrically by Films Inc. Starring Vanessa Redgrave, Ian Holm, Joely Richardson, Judi Dench, Tim McInnerny, Suzanna Hamilton, Tom Wilkinson and Mike Kelly.

David Hare's *Wetherby* is a peculiar story about violence and repression, as a lonely schoolteacher's world is turned upside down when a mysterious stranger commits suicide in her house.

Vanessa Redgrave stars as Jean, a middle-aged spinster who spends most of her time outside of class quietly reading and occasionally having good friends over for French food and a nice bottle of wine. At one such gathering, her guests arrive with a man who introduces himself as John Morgan (Tim McInnerny). Jean and John are immediately drawn to each other at the party, but when he returns for a visit the following morning, Jean is shocked to learn that he came to dinner uninvited. Before she can react to this startling discovery, John whips out a gun, sticks it in his mouth and pulls the trigger. The rest of the film skips between the present and flashbacks of the past in order to try to explain who John is and how his action has irrevocably shattered the calm of Jean's too-ordered life.

Wetherby has all the ingredients of a suspenseful psychological thriller. McInnerny's John Morgan is certainly an intriguing mystery man, spending that fateful evening at Jean's house passionately espousing his philosophies, while never giving the slightest indication of what he intends to do the next morning. Redgrave delivers an excellent performance as the rigid school-marm imprisoned by her middle-class values and then shocked out of her lethargy by Morgan's suicide. Her real-life daughter, Joely Richardson, does a superb job as the younger Jean in flashblacks, while cinematographer Stuart Harris effectively captures the dreary atmosphere of the English countryside to underscore the intense conflicts going on inside the main character.

Yet the details of John's and Jean's pasts are presented in clipped flashbacks that skip so quickly through time and space that they are often more confusing than helpful. The emotions in these segments, as well as the power of the film's beginning scenes, are frittered away because director Hare (the playwright of *Plenty*) fails to bring the various clues and background information together to a satisfying resolution. In the end, *Wetherby* is tantalizing but dissolves into nothingness.

RATING: R for brief nudity and one violent suicide scene replayed a couple of times.

WHAT HAPPENED TO KEROUAC?

★ ★ ★ ★ ★

Documentary

U.S.A.

1985   96 Min.   Color

CREDITS: Directed by Richard Lerner and Lewis MacAdams. Produced by Richard Lerner. Interviews by Lewis MacAdams. Cinematography by Richard Lerner and Nathaniel Dorsky. Music by Thelonius Monk. Released and distributed nontheatrically by New Yorker Films. Starring Jack Kerouac, Neal Cassady, Steve Allen, William Buckley, Allen Ginsberg, William Burroughs, Lawrence Ferlinghetti, Gregory Corso, Gary Snyder, Michael McClure, Ed Sanders, Diane Di Prima, Herbert Huncke, Jan Kerouac, Edie Kerouac Parker, Joyce Johnson, John Clellon Holmes, Fran Landesman and Robert Creeley.

After the publication of *On the Road,* Jack Kerouac became the instant "father of the Beats." This reputation was not only difficult for Kerouac to accept, it may have even destroyed him. *What Happened to Kerouac?* attempts to explain why.

In creating the best documentary on Kerouac to date, Richard Lerner and Lewis MacAdams focus on the time in Kerouac's life when he most sought publicity—the embarrassing last years of his life. The author of dozens of novels and volumes of poetry, Kerouac was known by scholars for his free-floating, stream-of-consciousness writing style, and by the public for his infamous escapades with Neal Cassady, William Burroughs and other literary figures. But in the couple of years before his suicide at the age of forty-seven, Kerouac was an arch-conservative who lived with his mother in Florida, where he spent his days watching TV and drinking heavily.

Most of the footage of Kerouac in this film is culled from TV appearances on "The Steve Allen Show" and William Buckley's "Firing Line" (whose politics he embraced). He is very entertaining in both segments, although not for social commentary as much as the brilliance that peeks through his inebriated ramblings. In one particularly powerful scene, he reads from *On the Road* as Steve Allen plays the piano in the background. But the real heart of this movie is the interviews with people who knew Kerouac best. Here we get plenty of humorous and insightful answers to the question posed in the movie's title, by some of America's most talented writers, including Allen Ginsberg, William Burroughs, Lawrence Ferlinghetti, Gregory Corso and Robert Creeley. It's through their wise and sober eyes (except for Corso) that we come to understand Jack Kerouac and the nature of celebrities and icons in our society.

RATING: No MPAA rating, with some profanity.

WHEN FATHER WAS AWAY ON BUSINESS

Political Drama

Yugoslavia		Serbo-Croatian
1985	144 Min.	Color

CREDITS: Directed by Emir Kusturica. Written by Abdulah Sidran (a noted Yugoslav poet). Produced by "Forum" Sarajevo. Cinematography by Vilko Filac. Released by Cannon Films. Distributed nontheatrically by Almi Pictures. Starring Miki Manojlovic, Moreno D'E Bartolli, Marjana Karanovic, Mustafa Nadarevic, Mira Furlan and Davor Dujmovic.

Made on a small budget by unknown Yugoslav director Emir Kusturica, *When Father Was Away on Business* was the surprise winner of the Grand Prize at the 1985 Cannes Film Festival. Set in Sarajevo in 1950, the film is narrated by Malik (Moreno D'E Bartolli), a chunky, sleepwalking, nine-year-old boy who loves his family first and soccer second. The boy's father, Mesha (Miki Manojlovic), is a minor Party official and devoted family man whose taste for philandering gets him into trouble. His distraught mistress tells Mesha's brother-in-law (a powerful Party bureaucrat) of an anti-Tito remark Mesha made in response to a political cartoon. This slip of the tongue, made in Yugoslavia during the tense months of Tito's break from Stalin, is costly. His brother-in-law turns him in, and Party officials send Papa to a forced labor camp for political reeducation. As it is explained to Malik by his mom, "Father is away on business."

Until Papa is exiled, *When Father Was Away* is a lighthearted romp through a landscape of slightly offbeat Yugoslavs. Malik's passionate family go through their days fighting and making up, slapping each other and kissing, seemingly impervious to any real dangers that might break them apart. But when Papa goes to the labor camp, a dark cloud descends on them.

As with Czech director Jiri Menzel's *My Sweet Little Village,* the magic of *When*

Father Was Away on Business is that Kusturica takes us inside his characters' lives in intimate and affectionate ways. The performances are excellent, and the film's main players are often developed from both personal and political points of view. Because we know them so well, the history that affects their lives seems particularly brutal. Two and a half hours in duration, the film contains some scenes that drag on longer than they should. But *When Father Was Away on Business* is so rich in memorable characters and cultural anecdotes that its length shouldn't keep you away.

RATING: *R for nudity and sex.*
AWARDS: *Golden Palm for Best Film at the 1985 Cannes Film Festival; 1985 Academy Award nomination for Best Foreign Film.*

WHERE THE BUFFALO ROAM
(Video)

Humorous Docudrama
U.S.A.

1980   98 Min.   Color

CREDITS: *Directed and produced by Art Linson. Written by John Kaye, based on Hunter S. Thompson's* Fear and Loathing in Las Vegas *and* Fear and Loathing on the Campaign Trail '72. *Cinematography by Tak Fujimoto. Music by Neil Young. Released by Universal. Distributed nontheatrically by Swank Motion Pictures. Starring Bill Murray, Peter Boyle, Danny Goldman, Bruno Kirby, R. G. Armstrong, Rene Auberjonois, Raphael Campos and Leonard Frey.*

Gonzo journalist Hunter S. Thompson's antics have been immortalized in both his own popular writings and by Garry Trudeau's Doonesbury character, Duke. *Where the Buffalo Roam* follows Thompson (Bill Murray) on the 1972 Presidential Campaign trail doing what he does best—drinking, popping pills, seducing women and indiscriminately firing his gun. What

little story line there is involves Thompson's relationship with his lawyer and partner in debauchery, Karl Lazlo (Peter Boyle), who rescues Thompson from jail and a hospital psycho ward. Later, Thompson covers a trial in which Lazlo defends several students busted for pot, and also goes along for the ride when Lazlo takes up with a Weather Underground–type terrorist organization.

Although Hunter S. Thompson is certainly a fascinating character to base a movie, *Where the Buffalo Roam* isn't an especially interesting story. The main reason is that Murray is seriously miscast as Thompson. His offhanded style and casual delivery are too subtle for such an outrageous character. He's never convincing when he's drunk, stoned or crazy. Although some of the film's jokes are funny, the plot is so repetitive that it's hard to tell when you are out of one set and into the next. As far as the politics of the sixties and early seventies go, the few issues that are touched upon are so oversimplified it would make anybody familiar with the time period cringe with embarrassment. All in all, *Where the Buffalo Roam* misses the mark by a mile.

RATING: *R for profanity and substance abuse in nearly every scene of the movie.*
FILMNOTE: *Although Thompson himself was present during the beginning of production as an adviser, he apparently was so disgusted with the way the film was progressing that he took his drugs and whiskey and left.*

WHO AM I THIS TIME?
(Video)

Romantic Comedy
U.S.A.

1982   60 Min.   Color

CREDITS: *Directed by Jonathan Demme. Written by Morton Neal Miller, based on a story by Kurt Vonnegut, Jr. Produced by Morton Neal Miller. Cinematography by Paul Vom Brack. Music written and per-*

formed by John Cale. Released by "American Playhouse" and Rubicon Films. Starring Christopher Walken and Susan Sarandon.

Although Jonathan Demme's adaptation of a Kurt Vonnegut short story is one of his least ambitious films, it's one of his most fun.

Who Am I This Time? is an odd romance focusing on the burgeoning relationship between Harry Nash (Christopher Walken) and Helene Shaw (Susan Sarandon), the Stanley and Stella of the North Crawford Mask and Wig Club's production of *A Streetcar Named Desire.* Even though in real life he is a bumbling hardware clerk who barely speaks above a whisper, Harry is the company's star, whose personality is completely consumed by every role he takes. Helene, a transient telephone operator who looks the part of Stella, is at first also emotionally empty off-stage and can't project her character's passions during auditions. Yet when confronted with the enormous charisma of Harry's swaggering Stanley, Helene begins to respond with an ardor of her own that evolves into a strong attraction for Harry, both on- and off-stage. As opening night approaches, however, Helene must struggle to solve the problem that has crushed the dreams of many leading ladies: how to keep the Harry she has grown to love from evaporating into thin air with the last curtain call.

At times the film's one joke can wear thin, yet *Who Am I This Time?* is a perfect testament to love's ability to play casting agent. Walken is extraordinary as Harry, whose bravado dissolves beneath the horn-rimmed glasses and baseball cap he wears off-stage. Sarandon is just as strong in a less showy part, eloquently capturing first Helene's isolation, and then her desperation as she fights to keep the man she loves. Demme *(Stop Making Sense)* doesn't clutter the film with unnecessary visual distractions. Now almost Demme's trademark, the background is filled with an assortment of offbeat characters. Also memorable is the haunting musical score by John Cale (formerly of the Velvet Underground), which brilliantly reflects the lovers' inner turmoil.

RATING: No MPAA rating, with nothing objectionable.

WILD STYLE
(Video)

Urban Drama

U.S.A.

1982   83 Min.   Color

CREDITS: Directed, written and produced by Charlie Ahearn. Released and distributed nontheatrically by Films Around the World. Starring Lee Quinones, Sandra "Pink" Fabara, Patti Astor, Fred Brathwaite, Busy Bee, Andrew "Zethir" Wintton. Grand Master Flash, Rock Steady Crew, Fab Five Freddy, The Cold Crush Four Brothers, The Fantastic Freaks, Double Trouble and Rammel Zee.

In the early eighties, visitors to New York were struck by the complex graffiti designs that covered the city's subway cars and by dozens of young rap musicians/break dancers performing on street corners and hustling for change. Preceding the onslaught of mindless Hollywood break-dance releases, the independently made *Wild Style* was the first attempt to dramatize this subculture.

Set in the South Bronx, the film focuses on Ray (Lee Quinones), a young Latino whose only joys in life are sneaking into the transit yard to spray-paint trains and spending time with his girlfriend, Rose (Sandra "Pink" Fabara). When both Rose and his painting style are stolen by the Union, a slick gang of painters who hope to sell graffiti on canvas to downtown galleries, Ray is despondent until he's offered a commission to paint a mural for an upcoming rap convention. But as soon as he begins to work on the bandshell, he becomes paralyzed, both by lack of inspiration and the loss of his lover. Drifting through chic downtown parties, rap contests and attempted reconciliations with Rose, Ray searches for the key image that will shape this important painting, not realizing that his own self-absorption is hindering his work.

Although a leap ahead of most of its Hollywood break-dance movie successors in terms of authenticity and themes, *Wild Style* is betrayed by its low budget and the inexperience of its director and cast. The cadre of break dancers and graffiti artists whom director/writer Charlie Ahearn found on the streets of New York look, paint, sing and dance their roles perfectly. But when they try to talk, gesturing wildly and delivering their awkwardly written lines in monotone voices, it's obvious most have never acted before. The production looks amateurish, too, with many shots poorly lit and composed, while the transitions between scenes are often jumpy and confusing. However, with the exception of the film's twenty-minute break-dance climax that will bore even hard-core fans, the music and art drive the narrative with their propelling energy, while director Ahearn skillfully confronts the issue of white exploitation of black youth culture with few stereotypes or name calling.

RATING: No MPAA rating, with profanity and violence.

WINGS OF DESIRE

(*Video, subtitled*)

Romance

West Germany		German
1988	130 Min.	B&W/Color

CREDITS: *Directed by Wim Wenders. Written by Wim Wenders and Peter Handke. Produced by Wim Wenders and Anatole Dauman. Cinematography by Henri Alekan. Music by Jurgen Knieper. Art direction by Heidi Luidi. Edited by Peter Przygodda. Released by Orion Classics. Starring Bruno Ganz, Solveig Dommartin, Otto Sander and Peter Falk.*

Returning to Germany after years of uneven work in Hollywood, director Wim Wenders *(Paris, Texas)* rediscovered his filmmaking voice in *Wings of Desire*, creating one of the most original and brilliant films of the decade.

Titled in German "The Heaven over Berlin," the film literally begins up in the air, as two angels, Damiel (Bruno Ganz) and Cassiel (Otto Sander) somberly float through the city, listening in to the thoughts of Berliners struggling in their daily lives. Although the angels are sometimes sensed by children and psychic adults, they are only visible to each other. But that doesn't mean they are silent observers. Besides riding the subway, watching kids playing video games and listening to frustrated parents trying to understand their child's ear-splitting rock music, they offer a comforting hand to an accident victim, bear witness to a potential suicide victim's last ramblings, and enjoy the entertainment provided by a small traveling circus. It is at the circus that Damiel is lured into the real world by a beautiful, troubled trapeze artist (Wenders's real-life girlfriend, Solveig Dommartin). Trading in his angel's breastplate for a loud suit and porkpie hat, Damiel scours Berlin to search for the aerialist and the love he believes will transcend life in the heavens.

A film of many rewards, *Wings of Desire* is a masterpiece of romance and hope. In the first half, Wenders portrays the intensity and history of this island/city more powerfully than any of his colleagues, Fassbinder included. Later, when Damiel becomes a human, he creates a comical, romantic tension that builds into an explosively touching climax. Technically, *Wings of Desire* is also a triumph. The cinematography of seventy-nine-year-old Henri Alekan (the cameraman for Cocteau's *Beauty and the Beast* and scores of other famous French films) is exquisite, capturing Berlin in crisp black-and-white and in lurid Technicolor. Shots of the Berlin Library filled with angels and Ganz on the shoulder of a statue are stunningly original. The performances are wonderful throughout, Ganz being particularly memorable as the brooding, compassionate angel transformed into a goofy human by the pangs of unfulfilled love.

RATING: No MPAA rating, with brief nudity.
WARNING: The visuals in this film are so stylized and powerful that their impact is significantly reduced on video.

WINTER KILLS
(Video)

★ ★ ½

Political Thriller

U.S.A.

1979   97 Min.   Color

CREDITS: *Directed by William Richert. Written by William Richert, based on the novel by Richard Condon. Produced by Fred Caruso. Cinematography by Vilmos Zsigmond. Music by Maurice Jarré. Released by Avco Embassy. Starring Jeff Bridges, John Huston, Richard Boone, Belinda Bauer, Anthony Perkins, Toshiro Mifune, Sterling Hayden, Eli Wallach, Ralph Meeker, Dorthy Malone, Tomas Milian and Elizabeth Taylor.*

William Richert's star-studded *Winter Kills* is the story of Nick Kegan (Jeff Bridges), the Kennedyesque son of a rich industrialist (John Huston), who is given information suggesting that his assassinated older brother, a U.S. president, was the victim of an international conspiracy. Although he is immediately interested in the new theory, Nick doesn't become obsessed with the case until he is led to the gun apparently used for the killing. When the gun is stolen and his contact murdered, he follows a string of evidence to the highest reaches of the family industrial complex, only to discover that the mastermind of his brother's murder is dangerously close to home.

Winter Kills is a mixed bag of tricks, often wildly inventive and darkly funny, but hampered by its haphazard plot and the lackluster performances from an all-star cast. Bridges seems to be wandering through the film in a daze, going from one scene to the next with a blank expression on his face. As the main character, his lack of direction infects the entire narrative, and several scenes, such as the romantic interlude with his live-in girlfriend (Belinda Bauer), are extraneous and lifeless.

Still, the film has extraordinary moments, such as an extended vignette of Bridges interviewing a munitions manufacturer (Sterling Hayden) on his private battlefield, Hayden astride a tank and Bridges huddled in a subcompact. Better yet is Huston's portrayal of the industrialist. As a comic figure who personifies sleazy omnipotence, he is the film's one consistent bright spot. In one hilarious scene, he swaggers around Bridges's bedroom clad only in an open robe and red bikini briefs, a moment that, alone, is worth the price of a video rental or movie ticket.

RATING: *R for nudity, violence and profanity.*
FILMNOTE: *The production and release of* Winter Kills *was riddled with money problems. A week before director William Richert finished shooting, Embassy Pictures refused to finance the amount the film had gone over budget. Richert had to shoot another film* (The American Success Company) *in order to raise the money needed to complete* Winter Kills. *Then it bombed at the box office.*

WISE BLOOD
(Video)

★ ★ ★

Religious Black Comedy

U.S.A.

1979   108 Min.   Color

CREDITS: *Directed by John Huston. Written by Benedict Fitzgerald, based on the novel by Flannery O'Connor. Produced by Michael and Kathy Fitzgerald. Cinematography by Gerald Fischer. Music by Alex North. Released and distributed nontheatrically by New Line Cinema. Starring Brad Dourif, Amy Wright, Harry Dean Stanton, Ned Beatty, Daniel Shor, Mary Nell Santacroce and John Huston.*

When the opening credits roll and director John Huston's first name is misspelled three times, it's an indication of strange and unexplainable things to come. *Wise Blood* is an odd little story about Hazel Motes (Brad Dourif), a discharged soldier who returns to the Southern city of Talkingham wearing the dark hat and suit of a preacher. Everybody mistakes him for a man of the cloth, an assumption that infuriates Hazel because he is a fervent atheist. He responds by forming his own religion—the Church of Jesus Christ Without Christ—and preaches his anti-Christ message from the hood of his beat-up red automobile. But the other evangelists in Talkingham don't take kindly to their new colleague, especially Harry Dean Stanton, a venomous street preacher who pretends to be blind for extra sympathy and money.

Hazel's not a nice guy in *Wise Blood*, nor are the other characters in the film. They aren't big in the brains department either. Their sermons and interactions are completely asinine, although what they're missing in intelligence they make up for with volume and enthusiasm. All the shouting and anger in *Wise Blood* gets irritating, particularly when little of it makes sense. The film's narrative alternates between being confusing and rambling, and its pacing is slow. But director John Huston goes right for the throat of street preaching, the South and middle America's religion with an intensity that rivals the Flannery O'Connor novel. Certain scenes are ingeniously funny, others quite disturbing. The acting of the film's assortment of depressing characters is extraordinary, with Dourif's Hazel especially powerful. *Wise Blood* has been described as aggravating, boring, brilliant and hilarious; in the end, it's a blend of all four.

RATING: *PG, with some disturbing violence.*

WOMAN IN THE DUNES
(Video, subtitled)

Psychological Drama

Japan		Japanese
1964	127 Min.	B&W

CREDITS: *Directed by Hiroshi Teshigahara. Written by Kobe Abe. Produced by Kiichi Ichikawa and Tadashi Ohono. Cinematography by Hiroshi Segawa. Music*

by Toru Takemitsu. Released and distributed nontheatrically by Corinth Films. Starring Eiji Okada, Kyoko Kishida, Koji Mitsui, Sen Yano, Hiroko Ito, Ginzo Sekigushi, Kiyohiko Ichiha and Tamutsu Tamura.

Woman in the Dunes is a movie about being confined—confined physically, confined by society and confined by one's own fears. The person trapped in this film is Jumpei (Eiji Okada), an entomologist from Toyko who goes to the desert looking for insects and, while daydreaming about the pressures of life in the city, misses the last bus back. Suddenly, a group of villagers appear and offer him a place to stay: a hut at the bottom of a huge sand pit. He climbs down a rope ladder and finds a pretty widow (Kyoko Kishida) who is pleased to have him as a guest. But the next morning, when he tries to leave, the ladder is gone. Until the film's optimistic final minutes, Jumpei attempts to escape this hellhole, his growing insanity and his increasingly disturbing relationship with the widow.

At times, it seems as if director Teshigahara is content to let the visuals in *Woman in the Dunes* take the place of plot or character development. Much of the story line is taken up with Jumpei struggling to come to terms with the bizarre events shaping his life without a great deal of dialogue or background information to explain his actions. Still, *Woman in the Dunes* is full of powerful metaphors. The obvious one concerns freedom, but there are several others pertaining to East and West, civilization, nature, men and women. Hiroshi Segawa's cinematography creates stark, beautiful scenes composed as abstract paintings, and several poetic examples of the awesome power of nature. Toru Takemitsu's unsettling soundtrack further adds to the film's intensity. Although *Woman in the Dunes* is not an easy film to watch, it's certainly one you won't forget.

RATING: *No MPAA rating, with brief nudity and sex.*
AWARDS: *Special Jury Prize at the 1964 Cannes Film Festival; 1965 Academy Award nominations for Best Director (Hiroshi Teshigahara) and Best Foreign Film.*

THE WOMAN NEXT DOOR

★   ★   ½

Psychological Romance

France   French

1981   106 Min.   Color

CREDITS: Directed and produced by François Truffaut. Written by François Truffaut, Suzanne Schiffman and Jean Aurel. Cinematography by William Lubtchansky. Music by Georges Delerue. Released by United Artists. Distributed nontheatrically by Films Inc. Starring Gérard Depardieu, Fanny Ardant, Henri Garcin, Michele Baumgartner, Veronique Silver, Philippe Morier-Genoud, Roger Van Hool, Olivier Becquaert and Nicole Vauthier.

Obsessive love is one of Truffaut's favorite themes, and in The Woman Next Door, it dominates the entire film. Bernard (Gérard Depardieu) lives with his wife and son in a house outside of Grenoble, France. They have a happy home life until one day the adjacent house is rented by a couple, and the woman turns out to be Bernard's ex-lover Mathilde (Fanny Ardant). Bernard and Mathilde had a stormy breakup eight years before and haven't spoken since. Though it's never explained why they broke up, they are still in love. They can't seem to avoid seeing each other—out of windows, at the tennis club and in town. Soon the glances turn into secret kisses, and then a clandestine affair. They try to break it off but can't; every time they're together their lust comes sizzling to the surface. Finally, their passion consumes Mathilde, and she has a nervous breakdown.

Bernard's and Mathilde's intense feelings for each other permeate every frame in The Woman Next Door. The camera rarely leaves their tortured faces, and their burning desires are transparent from the moment they meet again. It's a sad story, and the acting is excellent, but what's missing is substance. There is too much surface emotion in this movie and not enough depth to make their obsessive love believable. With virtually no background to their original relationship, and no dialogue explaining their love, it's as if they each take a pill that suddenly makes them tortured and sex-crazed. Their rabid urges are all-consuming in The Woman Next Door, but they swallow up the film's plot and characters as well.

RATING: R for sex and nudity.
FILMNOTE: This was Fanny Ardant's first film. She went on to star in Truffaut's Confidentially Yours and was his lover until his tragic death from brain cancer in 1984.

WORKING GIRLS
(Video)

★   ★   ½

Women's Docudrama

U.S.A.

1987   90 Min.   Color

CREDITS: Directed by Lizzie Borden. Written by Lizzie Borden and Sandra Kay. Produced by Lizzie Borden and Andi Gladstone. Cinematography by Judy Irola. Music by Roma Baran and David van Tieghem. Released and distributed nontheatrically by Miramax Films. Starring Louise Smith, Ellen McElduff, Amanda Goodwin, Maruiza Zach, Janne Peters and Helen Nicholas.

Most movie prostitutes fall into two convenient categories: the high-class hooker with a heart of gold or the hard-bitten streetwalker who loathes her johns. Director Lizzie Borden (Born in Flames) tries to create a mixture of both stereotypes in Working Girls.

The film follows Molly (Louise Smith), a bright, attractive Yale graduate who, even though she is a lesbian with no interest in men, supplements her income from photography by taking a couple of shifts each week at an exclusive "dating service." While waiting for appointments, Molly gossips with two fellow working girls, inanely comparing notes about their customers and wrestling with their own distorted notions of propriety. The place is run by a twittering Southern belle named Lucy

(Amanda Goodwin), an always-smiling matron who patronizes her girls and then viciously criticizes them behind their backs. Although Lucy is difficult to take, Molly is willing to put up with her for the $800 she can earn for a day's work. But the hardest part for Molly is having to pretend she enjoys sex with her clients, even though she despises them. Eventually her veneer of composure crumbles when she is unable to separate her self-worth from the degradation and dangers of her work.

Working Girls is at its best when it defies convention. Borden, who spent months interviewing high-priced call girls, does particularly well in the early scenes, when the three hookers simply, and often hilariously, discuss the nuances of their careers. Borden also does a good job defining sex for these women as a commodity, such as the scene when she visually links plastic-wrapped condoms with the packets of ketchup and mustard the women use on their fast-food lunch. Yet as good as these little touches are, Borden relies too heavily on stock characters and predictable conflicts for the emotional impact of her story.

It's expected that Lucy, the smiling madam, as well as the parade of anonymous and neurotic johns, will be painted in the most unattractive blacks and whites. But the other hookers, who share the stage with Molly, are often clichéd as well. Also, Molly's crisis of confidence, which drives the second half of the film, is poorly developed. Established early on as a woman of control, Molly's fall is quick and unbelievable, a self-conscious and unsuccessful attempt by Borden to push the film toward more complex emotional levels.

RATING: R for profanity, nudity and explicit sex.

WR: MYSTERIES OF THE ORGANISM

 ★ ★ ½

Documentary/Satire

Yugoslavia/	Serbo-Croatian,
W. Germany	German and English
1971	86 Min.	Color

CREDITS: *Directed and written by Dusan Makavejev. Produced by Neoplanta Film. Cinematography by Pega Popovic and Alesandar Petkovic. Released and distributed by Almi Pictures. Starring Wilhelm Reich, Milena Dravic, Jagoder Kaloper, Zoran Radmilovic, Vica Vidovic, Tuli Kupferberg, Jackie Curtis and Betty Dodson.*

Watching Dusan Makavejev's *WR: Mysteries of the Organism* is like going through your medicine cabinet and taking one of everything. This part documentary, part fictional narrative, loosely based on the teachings of Wilhelm Reich, delves into subjects such as psychology, sex, body movement, socialism, Red-baiting, propaganda, pornography and orgasms, just to name a few.

Wilhelm Reich was an associate of Freud who felt that sexual and physical repression were tantamount to political repression. If individuals could be liberated from those constraints, he believed, they would truly be free. Reich was hounded his whole life by people who thought his teachings were pornographic. In the fifties, he was declared un-American by McCarthy's committee, his books were burned and he was thrown in prison, where he later died.

Yugoslavian director Dusan Makavejev tries to document these important events in Reich's life and the basic theories behind his teachings. There are interviews with Reich, his wife and his disciples, filmed therapy sessions showing his techniques and footage of his Maine retreat. But most of the film involves Makavejev's "personal response" to Reich, where we are introduced, for example, to a Yugoslavian nymphomaniac, a yippie romping through Manhattan with a toy machine gun, a man having his penis made into a plaster statue, and a transsexual discussing her/his sex-change operation.

Although diector Makavejev (The Coca-Cola Kid) only begins to skim the surface of Wilhelm Reich's teachings in the documentary sections of this film, they are still interesting background to a brilliant thinker and the indignities he had to suffer because of his views. Unfortunately, the nondocumentary portions dominate the film, and here Makavejev turns Reich's philosophies into leftist dogma, sexual didactics and guerrilla theater, which aren't particularly entertaining or interesting. If Makavejev wants to shock us with these scenes, it works, but they are so frenetic and bizarre they also make the film irritating.

RATING: X for graphic sex, nudity and violence.

A YEAR OF THE QUIET SUN
(Video, subtitled)

Psychological Romance

W. Germany/	English, German
Poland/U.S.A.	and Polish
1984	106 Min.	Color

CREDITS: Directed and written by Krzysztof Zanussi. Produced by Regina Ziegler. Cinematography by Slawomir Idziak. Music by Wojciech Kilar. Released by Sandstar. Distributed nontheatrically by Kino International. Starring Scott Wilson, Maja Komorowska, Hanna Skarazanka, Ewa Dalkowska and Jerzy Stuhr.

The "sun" in the title is quiet that year because it's 1946 in Poland, and although Hitler has been defeated, the country has been ravaged by the war. Food and jobs are scarce, and thousands of Poles have lost their loved ones. This oppressive atmosphere is the setting for an unlikely romance between a widowed Polish woman named Emilia (Maja Komorowska) and Norman (Scott Wilson of In Cold Blood), an American officer who stayed behind in western Poland to serve as a member of a Nazi war-crimes commission. There are a number of reasons why their relationship should be doomed from the start. First, both are shy, their reticence complicated by Norman's not speaking Polish and Emilia's unwillingness to learn English. They come from completely different backgrounds. And more important, what will happen to Emilia when Norman returns to the States? Despite these tremendous obstacles, Emilia and Norman fall in love.

Komorowska and Wilson give outstanding performances, and through their complex characters director Zanussi (Ways in the Night) tells the sad history of his native Poland. With an astute eye for small, emotional moments, he paints a picture of postwar Europe far different from Hollywood's version of the story. There are no grateful peasant girls rushing to hand flowers to liberating soldiers, or cheerful citizens busily putting their lives back together. The inhabitants of Zanussi's Poland are sad, desperate and numb from the horrors they have experienced. But in their own understated ways, Norman and Emilia display a great deal of humanity in an environment that's emotionally barren. Although their odd relationship is the only blue sky in this otherwise depressing film, they have so much trouble communicating, and they are so ill at ease with themselves and their sexuality, that it's as unsettling to watch their relationship evolve for two hours as it is rewarding.

RATING: No MPAA rating, with nothing objectionable.
AWARDS: Golden Lion (Best Feature Film) at the 1984 Venice Film Festival.
FILMNOTE: Because of the film's negative depiction of the Polish government (mostly for mistreatment of Germans after World War II), A Year of the Quiet Sun was only briefly released in Poland and then banned after martial law.

YOJIMBO
(Video, subtitled)

Samurai Comedy

Japan		Japanese
1961	110 Min.	B&W

CREDITS: *Directed by Akira Kurosawa. Written by Akira Kurosawa, Ryuzo Kikushima and Hideo Oguni. Cinematography by Kazuo Miyagawa, filmed in Cinemascope. Music by Masaru Sato. Released by Seneca International. Distributed nontheatrically by Films Inc and Kit Parker Films. Starring Toshiro Mifune, Takashi Shimura, Kamatari Fujiwara, Tatsuya Nakadai, Eijiro Tono, Seizaburo Kawazu, Isuzu Yamada and Hiroshi Tachikawa.*

One of Kurosawa's most popular samurai films, *Yojimbo* is nothing more than a western set in seventeenth-century Japan, featuring warriors fighting with swords instead of cowboys with six-shooters. The hero of the story is a crusty samurai warrior named Sanjuro (Toshiro Mifune), who no longer has a lord to serve and now wanders from town to town selling his killing skills to the highest bidder. One town he happens upon is a virtual gold mine. There are two powerful families at war with each other, and once he hears how greedy and gutless they are he decides to rid the town of both clans and make some money for himself in the process. After proving himself by disemboweling some of their best warriors, Sanjuro hires on as a bodyguard *(yojimbo)* for one family and eventually the other. He deceives and betrays both sides, and warriors from both families get knocked off like ducks at a shooting gallery all the way up to the film's final showdown on main street.

Both families and their warriors are nothing but sleazy, two-faced bloodsuckers. The various other townspeople are either spineless or crazy. Sanjuro himself is so brutal that you wonder about him as well. But his courage and skills as a warrior can't be denied.

Kazuo Miyagawa's wide shots (in Cinemascope) of the dusty town with lone figures hovering in corners are magnificent in *Yojimbo*—a style of photography that's now a Kurosawa trademark. The film's assortment of sleazy characters can be quite funny, particularly Mifune as the stoic, opportunistic warrior plotting his next move. Mifune's lightning-fast sword work is also fun to watch, but there's not much other action in the film. There are only half a dozen battle scenes, while the rest of the movie chronicles the predictable exploits of the evil families and Mifune's reactions. Even the battle scenes, despite the buildup, are a little disappointing. But as a showpiece of bizarre characters and a wry comment on human nature, *Yojimbo* has many moments to make it worthwhile.

RATING: *No MPAA rating, with mild violence.*
AWARDS: *1960 Academy Award nomination for Best Costume Design (Yoshiro Muraki).*
FILMNOTE: *Sergio Leone based his plot for* A Fistful of Dollars *on* Yojimbo. *Kurosawa, in turn, based the plot of* Yojimbo *on Dashiell Hammett's* Red Harvest.

YOL
(Video, subtitled)

Cultural Drama

Turkey		Turkish and Kurdish
1982	111 Min.	Color

CREDITS: *Directed by Yilmaz Gurney and Serif Goren. Written by Yilmaz Gurney. Produced by Edi Hubschmid and K. L. Puldi. Cinematography by Erdogan Engin. Released by Triumph Films/Artificial Eye. Distributed nontheatrically by Swank Motion Pictures. Starring Tarik Akin, Serif Sezer, Halil Ergun, Heral Orhonsoy, Necmettin Cobanoglu, Meral Orhousoy and Semra Ucar.*

Although made on a small budget by a virtually unknown Turkish filmmaker, *Yol* shared the 1982 Grand Prize at Cannes with Costa-Gavras's *Missing*. The honor for this impassioned indictment of traditional Turkish life was richly deserved.

The film follows the struggles of five minimum-security prisoners who are given a one-week leave to return to their wives and families. At first, the inmates are deliriously happy at the prospect of temporary freedom, but it isn't long before each is engulfed in a series of disasters. For one of the men, the nightmare is returning home to find his wife chained in a shed by his family, disgraced because she had an affair in his absence. In one of the film's most powerful scenes, he virtually drags his half-starved wife across the snow while their son walks ahead in tears. Another inmate is shunned by everybody in his family, including his wife, for leaving his brother to be killed by the police during a bank robbery. A third watches as his brother is killed by the police for leftist political beliefs, while a fourth is severely beaten by an angry crowd on a train for having sex with his wife in the bathroom.

Although *Yol* is a semifictional narrative, the performances by its nonprofessional actors and the brutally real situations will leave you feeling as if you are watching a documentary. *Yol*'s screenplay was written by co-director Yilmaz Gurney while he was imprisoned for his progressive politics, and was based on actual stories he heard from other inmates. Gurney's script, as well as his instructions to the film's other director, Serif Goren, were smuggled out of prison in bits and pieces and at great risk. Their collaboration spares us none of the shocking details of the oppression of Turkish life, creating a film marked by violence that is sometimes very difficult to stomach. But *Yol* is not just a superbly photographed, disturbing journey into orthodox Muslim culture. It also serves as an important indictment of a patriarchal society that virtually enslaves its women, severely punishing them for any "immoral" behavior.

RATING: No MPAA rating, with violence.

Z

(Video, dubbed)

Political Thriller

France/Algeria   French

1969   128 Min.   Color

CREDITS: *Directed by Constantine Costa-Gavras. Written by Constantine Costa-Gavras and Jorge Semprun, based on the novel by Vassili Vassilikos. Produced by Jacques Perrin and Hamed Rachedi. Cinematography by Raoul Coutard. Music by Mikis Theodorakis. Edited by Francoise Bonnot. Released and distributed nontheatrically by Almi Pictures. Starring Yves Montand, Jean-Louis Trintignant, Irene Papas, Charles Denner, François Perier, Jacques Perrin, Pierre Dux, Julien Guiomar, Renato Salvatori and Bernard Fresson.*

Set in the early sixties as military repression was building before the military coup in 1967 Greece, Z is based on a true story of the 1963 assassination of Greek liberal Gregorios Lambrakis. The film begins when the pacifist (Yves Montand) is killed by two men in a passing truck as he leaves a political rally. The investigating attorney (Jean-Louis Trintignant) assigned to the case is told the official police version, corroborated by dozens of witnesses: The death was caused by a hit-and-run drunk driver. But as the magistrate interrogates the liberal's colleagues, uncoached eyewitnesses, and police and government officials, he learns the real events behind the killing.

Costa-Gavras takes a stance right from the start when the opening credits state "any resemblance to real events or people is intentional." You can close your eyes in this movie and know when the bad guys are on the screen just by the soundtrack. The right-wingers are for the most part dumb and sleazy looking, while the progressives are intelligent and pleasantly dressed. But everything else is so well done in Z, all the way up to the film's surprise ending, it's easy to overlook this orchestration.

Although Gregorios's death and Greek

political repression are no longer timely issues, Z stands on its own as a political thriller and an indictment of right-wing military ideology. Costa-Gavras *(Missing, State of Siege)* treats his narrative like a documentary, with intelligent dialogue, tight editing and several scenes that are brutally real. Raoul Coutard's cinematography keeps the action immediate and suspenseful, while the performances from veterans such as Irene Papas, Yves Montand and Jean-Louis Trintignant are riveting.

RATED: No MPAA rating, with violence.
AWARDS: 1969 Academy Award for Best Foreign Film and Best Film Editing (Francoise Bonnot); 1969 Academy Award nominations for Best Picture, Best Director (Costa-Gavras) and Best Screenplay Based on Material from Another Medium (Jorge Semprun and Costa-Gavras). 1969 New York Film Critics and National Film Society's awards for Best Foreign Film. Jury Prize at the 1969 Cannes Film Festival.
WARNING: Dubbing on video version isn't good and affects the quality of this overly talky film.
FILMNOTE: Costa-Gavras struggled to scrape together his million-dollar budget, with most of the stars accepting a small salary in addition to a portion of the film's profits. The gamble paid off, as Z became one of the largest grossing films in the United States and Europe in 1969, while setting Costa-Gavras's career off and running.

Appendix A

Renting and Purchasing Videos Through the Mail

To the best of my knowledge, there are only four or five companies that specialize in off-Hollywood movies to rent and purchase through the mail:

Facets Cinematheque Video-by-
Mail and Facets Video
Rental-by-Mail
1517 West Fullerton Avenue
Chicago, IL 60614
800-331-6197

Facets has the largest rent-by-mail library. To rent from them, you must pay an annual fee of $20. Each rental costs $10, which includes shipping to you, not the return postage. Cheaper rates are available if you prepay and rent in quantity. You're allowed to keep rented films for three days. Visa and Master Card orders are taken over the phone. Facets' catalogue is free, and it also lists prices for purchasing videos.

Home Film Festival
P.O. Box 2032
Scranton, PA 18501
800-258-FILM (in Pennsylvania,
800-633-FILM)

Membership costs $25 a year. Rentals are $5 for one, $9 for two or $13 for three cassettes ordered and shipped at the same time, plus round-trip shipping ($2 to $3.50 in continental United States). Rental orders are taken over the phone or with their Cassette Rental Form. Payment can be made with Visa, Master Card or check. Their catalogue is free to members or available to purchase for $5. You are permitted to keep the films three nights. Prices to buy are listed in the catalogue.

Movies Unlimited
Northeast
6736 Castor Avenue
Philadelphia, PA 19149
800-523-0823

Movies Unlimited advertises having the largest selection of VHS, Beta and Laserdisc for sale in the country. For $7.95 plus $2 shipping, they will send you their catalogue and quarterly updates. Your money is refunded with a purchase. Payment can be made with credit card, check or money order.

New Video
276 Third Avenue
New York, NY 10010
800-431-2299
(in New York, 212-473-6000)

New Video has the next largest selection of off-Hollywood films for purchase, including many they've released themselves. Their catalogue is $4.50 and comes out quarterly. You can subscribe to the catalogue for $11.95 a year. They accept Visa, Master Card and American Express.

To rent films nontheatrically for a classroom or a film society is as easy as ordering pizza from Domino. Call the company and ask for their nontheatrical salesperson for your state. Explain to them your seating capacity and whether or not you will be charging admission. They will be happy to send you a catalogue and take your money. Often they will give you a reduced rate, sometimes substantially reduced, if you order more than one title. A first-time customer will probably have to pay in advance, and each company has its own particular restrictions and requirements for insurance, shipping and advertising. Depending on what you get, prices range from $50 to $600 per film, with an average of $20 added on for shipping. The following are the major nontheatrical distributors in the United States:

Almi Pictures, Inc.
1900 Broadway
New York, NY 10023
212-769-2255

Castle Hill
1414 Avenue of the Americas
New York, NY 10019
212-888-0080

Cinecom
1250 Broadway
New York, NY 10001
212-239-8360

The Cinema Guild
1697 Broadway
New York, NY 10019
212-246-5522

Circle Releasing
1101 23 Street, N.W.
Washington, DC 20037
202-331-3838

Corinth Films
34 Gansevoort Street
New York, NY 10014
212-463-0305

Direct Cinema Films and Video
P.O. Box 315
Franklin Lakes, NJ 07417
201-891-8240

European Classics
4818 Yuma Street, N.W.
Washington, DC 20016
202-363-8800

Expanded Entertainment
2222 South Barrington Avenue
Los Angeles, CA 90064
213-473-6701

Films Inc
5547 North Ravenswood Avenue
Chicago, IL 60640-1199
800-323-4222
(in Illinois, 312-878-2600)

First Run Features
153 Waverly Place
New York, NY 10014
212-243-0600

International Film Exchange
201 West 52 Street
New York, NY 10019
212-582-4318

Joseph Green Pictures
200 West 58 Street
New York, NY 10019

Kino International
333 West 39 Street
New York, NY 10018
212-629-6880

Kit Parker Films
1245 Tenth Street
Monterey, CA 93940
408-649-5573

Miramax Films
18 East 48 Street, Suite 1601
New York, NY 10017
212-888-2662

New Line Cinema
575 Eighth Avenue (Sixteenth floor)
New York, NY 10018
212-239-8880

New Yorker Films
16 West 61 Street
New York, NY 10023
212-247-6110

The Samuel Goldwyn Company
10203 Santa Monica Boulevard
Los Angeles, CA 90067
800-421-5743
(in California, 213-284-9278)

Swank Motion Pictures
201 South Jefferson Ave
P.O. Box 231
St. Louis, MO 63166
800-325-3344
(in Missouri, 314-534-6300)

Tamarelle's International Films
110 Cohasset Stage Road
Chico, CA 95926
916-895-3429

Twyman Films
P.O. Box 605
Dayton, OH 45401
800-543-9594
(in Ohio, 800-831-FILM)

Westcoast Films
25 Lusk Street
San Francisco, CA 94107
800-227-3058
(in California, 415-362-4700)

UPDATE: Films Inc has bought New Cinema's nontheatrical library, and Miramax has purchased Almi Pictures' nontheatrical library.

Appendix B

Major Off-Hollywood Directors

The following appendix is meant to be used as an abbreviated survey of my own selection of the fifty-four most noteworthy directors represented in this book. Included in each passage (whenever the information was available) is his or her nationality, year of birth (and death), career background, and a brief description of the director's films and why they are important. I also include a filmography of their major work and the date and country in which it was made. When a film listed is reviewed in this book, it is set in **bold**. A [v] appears after the title if it's available on video.

Robert Altman
(U.S.A., b. 1925)

Altman began his show business career as a television director and was forty-five years old before he directed his first feature film. His reputation peaked in the seventies with over a dozen films in which he applied European technique and characterization to distinctively American themes. Hollywood finally tired of him, and he has since busied himself making film adaptations of successful stage plays.

M.A.S.H. (U.S.A., 1970) [v], *Brewster McCloud* (U.S.A., 1970) [v], **McCabe & Mrs. Miller** (U.S.A., 1971) [v], *Images* (Ireland 1972), *The Long Goodbye* (U.S.A., 1973) [v], *Nashville* (U.S.A., 1976) [v], *3 Women* (U.S.A., 1978), *Popeye* (U.S.A., 1980) [v], **Come Back to the Five and Dime, Jimmy Dean, Jimmy Dean** (U.S.A., 1982) [v], **Streamers** (U.S.A., 1983) [v], **Secret Honor** (U.S.A., 1984) [v], **Fool for Love** (U.S.A. 1985) [v], *Beyond Therapy* (U.S.A. 1987) [v].

Lindsay Anderson
(England, b. 1923)

Anderson worked for sixteen years as a film critic and essayist before making his first feature film in 1962. Often using surreal filming techniques and motivated by a disdain for mediocrity in British cinema, Anderson makes sharply satirical and socially relevant films that cross the boundaries of conventional humor to shock the audience as well.

This Sporting Life (England, 1962), *If . . .* (England, 1969) [v], *O Lucky Man!* (England, 1973) [v], *Brittania Hospital* (England, 1982) [v], *The Whales of August* (U.S.A., 1987) [v].

Michelangelo Antonioni
(Italy, b. 1912)

Although Antonioni's existential psychological dramas can be laboriously slow and confused, his cool, sensuous approach to his characters and his starkly elegant visual style have made him one of the most influential and copied filmmakers of the sixties and seventies.

Love in the City (Italy, 1953), *L'Avventura* (Italy, 1961) [v], *The Red Desert* (Italy/France, 1965), *Blow-Up* (England/Italy, 1966) [v], *Zabriskie Point* (U.S.A., 1970) [v], *The Passenger* (Italy/France/Spain/U.S.A., 1975) [v].

Gillian Armstrong
(Australia, b. 1950)

With her internationally acclaimed *My Brilliant Career* in 1979, Gillian Armstrong became the first Australian woman in fifty years to direct a 35mm feature. Formerly an art director, editor and documentary filmmaker, she has thus far made only three other films, which display her cinematographic talents but don't measure up to *My Brilliant Career*'s content.

The Singer and the Dancer (Australia, 1976), *My Brilliant Career* (Australia, 1980) [v], *Starstruck* (Australia, 1982) [v], *Mrs. Soffel* (U.S.A., 1984) [v], *High Tide* (Australia, 1987).

Bruce Beresford
(Australia, b. 1940)

Along with Peter Weir, Bruce Beresford has been responsible for the new prominence of Australian film. A talented stylist with a keen eye for psychological detail, Beresford began making small but well-crafted comedies and has recently combined his Australian sensibilities with distinctly American themes in movies such as *Tender Mercies* and *Crimes of the Heart.*

Don's Party (Australia, 1976) [v], *The Getting of Wisdom* (Australia, 1977) [v], *Breaker Morant* (Australia, 1980) [v], *Puberty Blues* (Australia, 1982) [v], *Tender Mercies* (U.S.A., 1983) [v], *King David* (U.S.A./England, 1985) [v], *The Fringe Dwellers* (Australia, 1986) [v], *Crimes of the Heart* (U.S.A., 1986) [v].

Ingmar Bergman
(Sweden, b. 1918)

Ingmar Bergman is one of the world's most respected, imitated and critically acclaimed film artists. The son of a minister, he specializes in obsessive and often anguished portraits of people struggling with God and the Devil and love and death, which are heightened by his stark, minimalistic cinematographic techniques and surreal dream sequences.

Secrets of Women (Sweden, 1952) [v], *Sawdust and Tinsel* (Sweden, 1953) [v], *Smiles of a Summer Night* (Sweden, 1955) [v], *The Seventh Seal* (Sweden, 1957) [v], *Wild Strawberries* (Sweden, 1957) [v], *The Virgin Spring* (Sweden, 1960) [v], *Persona* (Sweden, 1966) [v], *Cries and Whispers* (Sweden, 1972) [v], *Scenes from a Marriage* (Sweden, 1973) [v], *The Serpent's Egg* (West Germany, 1978) [v], *Autumn Sonata* (West Germany, 1978) [v], *From the Life of the Marionettes* (Germany, 1980) [v], *Fanny and Alexander* (Sweden/France/West Germany, 1983) [v], *After the Rehearsal* (Sweden/West Germany, 1983) [v].

Bernardo Bertolucci (Italy, b. 1940)

Bertolucci was a child prodigy who published poetry at the age of twelve and directed his first internationally acclaimed film at the age of twenty-two. What followed has been an exhilarating stream of films mixing politics and sex, opera and New Wave, high art with near-pornograhic indulgences, culminating with his five-and-a-half hour magnum opus *1900*.

Before the Revolution (Italy, 1964), *Partner* (Italy, 1968), *The Spider's Stratagem* (Italy, 1970), **The Conformist** (Italy, 1971) [v], **Last Tango in Paris** (Italy/France, 1973) [v], *1900* (Italy, 1977). [v], *The Last Emperor* (1987) [v].

Bertrand Blier (France, b. 1939)

Bertrand Blier's name has become synonymous with the genre of the French sex farce. He has consistently shocked audiences and angered feminists by delivering a mix of perverse, irreverent humor, using as his characters sexist male stereotypes who are meant to be humorous for their offensiveness, and brainless women who enjoy being abused.

Going Places (France, 1974) [v], *Femmes Fatales* (France, 1976), **Get Out Your Handkerchiefs** (France, 1978) [v], **Beau Père** (France, 1981) [v], *My Best Friend's Girl* (France, 1983) [v], *Separate Rooms* (France, 1984), *Ménage* (France, 1986).

Robert Bresson (France, b. 1907)

Robert Bresson's formal, painterly approach to cinema abandons conventional plots and "professional" acting, and favors a stark visual style, subtle acting and deliberate pacing. He is considered a filmmaker's filmmaker, although his work has never reached a broad audience.

The Ladies in the Park (France, 1945), **Diary of a Country Priest** (France, 1950) [v], *Pickpocket* (France, 1959), *Mouchette* (France, 1967), *Lancelot of the Lake* (France/Italy, 1975), *L'Argent* (France/Switzerland, 1983).

Albert Brooks (U.S.A., b. 1947)

Often compared to Woody Allen because of his choice of subject matter and because he always stars in his own comedies, Brooks has cultivated a growing audience for his irreverent, hyperparanoid, unnerving vision of yuppiedom, ill-fated love and the hostile modern world.

Real Life (U.S.A., 1979) [v], **Modern Romance** (U.S.A., 1981) [v], *Lost in America* (U.S.A., 1985) [v].

Luis Buñuel (Spain, 1900–1983)

Buñuel is one of cinema's most original and controversial auteurs. He enjoyed three separate careers as a filmmaker: first, as a surrealist in Paris in the twenties and thirties; second, as an exile in Mexico in the forties and fifties, cranking out cheap melodramas to finance personal artistic statements; and last, as a internationally acclaimed satirist of the upper class and of Catholicism, working in several different countries. Through his long career, his dark humor, sharp wit and surrealistic vision always found the beautiful in the bizarre.

Un Chien Andalou (France, 1928), *L'Age D'Or* (France, 1930), **Los Olvidados** (Mexico, 1950) [v], *Robinson Crusoe* (Mexico, 1952), *El* (Mexico, 1952), *Wuthering Heights* (Mexico, 1953), **Viridiana** (Spain, 1961) [v], **The Exterminating Angel** (Mexico, 1962) [v], *Belle de Jour* (Italy/France, 1967), **Simon of the Desert** (Mexico, 1966) [v], *Tristana* (France/Spain, 1970), **The Discreet Charm of the Bourgeoisie** (France, 1972) [v], *The Phantom of Liberty* (France, 1974), **That Obscure Object of Desire** (France/Spain, 1977) [v].

John Cassavetes (U.S.A., 1929–1989)

An intense actor unhappy with the material that Hollywood was providing him, Cassavetes turned to directing in 1960. He gave his mature psychological dramas, dealing with social problems such as marital strife, race relations and middle-age angst, an improvisational, actor-oriented feel.

Faces (U.S.A., 1968), *Husbands* (U.S.A., 1970), *Minnie and Moskowitz* (U.S.A., 1971), *A Woman under the Influence* (U.S.A., 1974), *Gloria* (U.S.A., 1980) [v], **Love Streams** (U.S.A., 1984) [v], *Big Trouble* (U.S.A., 1986) [v].

Constantine Costa-Gavras (Greece, b. 1933)

Using his camera to indict oppressive regimes the world over, Greek-born Costa-Gavras is known for exciting and sometimes violent political thrillers featuring documentary-style camera work, realistic performances, quick-tempo editing and a strongly leftist political viewpoint.

The Sleeping Car Murders (France, 1966) [v], *Shock Troops* (France/Italy, 1968), **Z** (France/Algeria, 1969) [v], *The Confession* (France, 1970), **State of Siege** (France/Chile, 1973) [v], *Special Section* (France/Italy/Germany, 1975), *Clair De Femme* (France/Italy/Germany, 1979), **Missing** (U.S.A., 1982) [v], **Hanna K.** (France/U.S.A., 1983) [v], *Conseil de Famille* (France, 1986), *Betrayed* (U.S.A., 1988) [v].

Alex Cox (England, b. 1954)

Influenced by rock and roll, kitsch, TV and B-Hollywood, Alex Cox eschews the cool and controlled style that's currently popular, instead serving up frenetic, obsessive stories about hard-edged urban dwellers out of sync with the world around them.

Repo Man (U.S.A., 1984) [v], **Sid and Nancy** (England, 1986) [v], *Straight to Hell* (U.S.A., 1987) [v].

Paul Cox (Holland, b. 1940)

Dutch-born Cox received his education in Australia and eventually settled there to become one of the country's leading cinematographers and documentary filmmakers until, in 1982, he directed his first feature, *Lonely Hearts*. His intensely realistic, emo-

tionally wrenching psychological dramas are about ill-fated love, loneliness and alienation, and are characterized by splendid production values.

Lonely Hearts (Australia, 1982) [v], **Man of Flowers** (Australia, 1983) [v], **My First Wife** (Australia, 1984) [v], *Cactus* (Australia, 1986) [v].

Jonathan Demme (U.S.A., b. 1944)

Demme has emerged as America's leading independent filmmaker. Although he has gained the respect of Hollywood, he has retained his lower Manhattan sensibilities. Whether shooting off-the-wall chase movies, rock and roll documentaries or one-man shows, Demme's later movies consistently illuminate the quirkiness of his subjects, cleverly satirize modern America and challenge his audience.

Caged Heat (U.S.A. 1974) [v], *Crazy Mama* (U.S.A., 1975), *Last Embrace* (U.S.A., 1979), *Melvin and Howard* (U.S.A., 1980) [v], **Who Am I This Time?** (U.S.A., 1982) [v], *Swing Shift* (U.S.A., 1983) [v], **Stop Making Sense** (U.S.A., 1984) [v], **Something Wild** (U.S.A., 1986) [v], **Swimming to Cambodia** (U.S.A., 1987) [v], *Married to the Mob* (U.S.A., 1988) [v].

Vittorio de Sica (Italy, 1923–1974)

De Sica, an Italian matinee idol in the twenties, became a leading director in the Italian neorealist movement, which emphasized low-budget, socially conscious films shot on location. His always superbly photographed releases (four of which won Oscars for Best Foreign Film) included light mass-appeal fare and powerful humanist portraits of Italy during and after World War II.

Sciuscia (Italy, 1946), **The Bicycle Thief** (Italy, 1949) [v], *Miracle in Milan* (Italy, 1950), *Umberto D* (Italy, 1952) [v], *Two Women* (Italy, 1960), *Woman Times Seven* (U.S.A./France, 1967), **The Garden of the Finzi-Continis** (Italy, 1971) [v].

Rainer Werner Fassbinder (West Germany, 1946–1982)

Postwar Germany's most visually gifted, outrageous and complex filmmaker, Fassbinder was also the most prolific. Before his untimely drug-related death at the age of thirty-six in 1982, and working with a loyal troupe of actors and technicians, he created over forty films about Germany's moral decline during and after World War II, which often mirrored his own conflicts with drugs, alcoholism, sexual identity and power struggles in relationships.

Katzelmacher (West Germany, 1969), *The Bitter Tears of Petra von Kant* (West Germany, 1972), **Ali: Fear Eats the Soul** (West Germany, 1974), **Effi Briest** (West Germany, 1974), **Fox and His Friends** (West Germany, 1975), **The Marriage of Maria Braun** (West Germany, 1978) [v], *In the Year of Thirteen Moons* (West Germany, 1978), **Berlin Alexanderplatz** (West Germany, 1979) [v], **Despair** (West Germany, 1979) [v], *Lili Marleen* (West Germany, 1981), *Lola* (West Germany, 1982), *Veronika Voss* (West Germany 1982), *Querelle* (West Germany, 1982) [v].

Federico Fellini (Italy, b. 1920)

Fellini started in the entertainment field as a circus performer and cartoonist and brought his background into his films. Especially in the fifties and sixties, Fellini was known for mixing social comment with surrealism, and humor with humanism. He created so many unforgettable films and outrageously bizarre characters that his name has become synonymous with art house movies.

I Vitlelloni (Italy, 1953) [v], **La Strada** (Italy, 1954) [v], **La Dolce Vita** (Italy, 1959) [v], *8½* (Italy, 1963) [v], *Juliet of the Spirits* (Italy/France/Germany, 1965) [v], *Fellini's Satyricon* (Italy/France, 1970), **The Clowns** (Italy/France/Germany, 1971) [v], *Fellini's Roma* (Italy/France, 1972) [v], **Amarcord** (Italy, 1974) [v], *City of Women* (Italy/France, 1981), **And the Ship Sails On** (Italy/France, 1984) [v], **Ginger and Fred** (Italy/France/Germany, 1986) [v], *Fellini's Scrapbook* (Italy, 1987) [v].

Bill Forsyth (Scotland, b. 1947)

In the early eighties, Bill Forsyth created a whole new genre of film—the wacky Scottish comedy. His films feature delightfully quirky misfits, deadpan dialogue and inventive sight gags. While he enjoys a fiercely loyal art house audience in the United States, ironically Forsyth has yet to find much success in his native Great Britain.

That Sinking Feeling (Scotland, 1979) [v], **Gregory's Girl** (Scotland, 1982) [v], **Local Hero** (England/Scotland, 1983) [v], **Comfort and Joy** (England/Scotland, 1984) [v], *Housekeeping* (Canada, 1987) [v].

Stephen Frears (England, b. 1931)

A leader among British independent filmmakers, Frears's greatest virtues are his bold choice of material, first-rate camera work and a nonexploitative and sardonically humorous handling of society's outsiders—especially homosexuals and London's Pakistani subculture.

Gumshoe (England, 1971), **The Hit** (England, 1984) [v], **My Beautiful Laundrette** (England, 1985) [v], **Prick Up Your Ears** (England, 1987) [v], **Sammy and Rosie Get Laid** (England, 1987) [v], *Dangerous Liaisons* (1988) [v].

Jean-Luc Godard (France, b. 1930)

With François Truffaut, Godard cofounded French New Wave with his first feature, *Breathless*, in 1959. He has imprinted his boldly experimental ideas on every aspect of film language—cinematography, sound, editing, acting and narrative. Audiences in the sixties and early seventies were divided by his intentionally confusing, improvised style, but so great is his influence that many critics refer to European cinema before Godard and after Godard.

Breathless (France, 1959) [v], *Contempt* (France/Italy, 1964), **Alphaville** (France, 1965) [v], *The Married Woman* (France, 1966), **Masculin-Féminin** (France/Sweden, 1966) [v], *Weekend* (France/Italy, 1967), *Every Man for Himself* (Switzerland/France, 1980), *Passion* (France/Switzerland, 1983), *First Name: Carmen* (France/Switzerland, 1983), **Hail Mary** (France/Switzerland, 1985) [v], *Detective* (France, 1985).

Werner Herzog
(Germany, b. 1942)

Herzog, Fassbinder and Wenders formed the nucleus of the German New Wave movement of the sixties and seventies to give voice to the anguish and confusion young Germans felt over their inherited guilt. Herzog's approach has been to use allegory—lost souls trying to cope with society and stories of the *Übermensch* (superman)—to convey his own personal vision of what went wrong and what lies ahead. His cinematography of the powers of nature is some of the most hauntingly beautiful ever filmed.

Even Dwarfs Started Small (West Germany, 1971), *Land of Silence and Darkness* (West Germany, 1972), **Aguirre, the Wrath of God** (West Germany/Mexico/Peru, 1973) [v], **The Mystery of Kaspar Hauser—Every Man for Himself and God Against All** (West Germany, 1974) [v], *Heart of Glass* (West Germany, 1976), *Stroszek* (West Germany, 1977), *Fata Morgana* (West Germany, 1978), *Woyzeck* (West Germany, 1979), *Nosferatu the Vampire* (West Germany/France/U.S.A., 1979), *God's Angry Man* (West Germany, 1980), **Fitzcarraldo** (West Germany, 1982) [v], *Where the Green Ants Dream* (West Germany, 1984) [v].

John Huston
(U.S.A., 1906–1987)

Reared in a show business family, Huston was at various times in his life a boxer, soldier, reporter, equestrian, singer and painter before turning to writing, directing and acting in movies. Huston's Hollywood films include some of the classics of American cinema. His last years were marked by a fierce determination to use his craft to display his own perverse humor and colorful, nontraditional characterizations.

The Maltese Falcon (U.S.A., 1941) [v], *The Treasure of the Sierra Madre* (U.S.A., 1948) [v], *Key Largo* (U.S.A., 1948) [v], *The Asphalt Jungle* (U.S.A., 1950) [v], *The African Queen* (U.S.A., 1952) [v], *The Night of the Iguana* (U.S.A., 1964) [v], *The Man Who Would Be King* (England, 1975) [v], **Wise Blood** (U.S.A., 1979) [v], **Annie** (U.S.A., 1982) [v], **Under the Volcano** (U.S.A., 1984) [v], *Prizzi's Honor* (U.S.A., 1985) [v], **The Dead** (U.S.A., 1987) [v].

Shohei Imamura
(Japan, b. 1926)

Unlike the master Ozu, with whom he apprenticed, Imamura's distinctively Japanese style features aggressive camera movement, harrowing realism and wide-screen images packed with information. He is equally bold in his choice of material, often focusing on characters caught in absurd social conflicts fueled by primitive sex and violence.

Pigs and Battleships (Japan, 1961), *The Insect Woman* (Japan, 1963), *The Pornographer* (Japan, 1966), *Karayuki-san, the Making of a Prostitute* (Japan, 1975) [v], **Vengeance Is Mine** (Japan, 1979) [v], **The Ballad of Narayama** (Japan, 1983) [v], *Lord of the Brothels* (Japan, 1987).

James Ivory (U.S.A., b. 1928)

Ivory was raised and educated in the United States but got his start as a filmmaker shooting documentaries in India. There, in 1959, he met Indian-born producer Ismail Merchant and German-born writer Ruth Prawer Jhabvala. Together they have collaborated on a long succession of exotic, well-crafted films that deal with the clash between Indian and British cultures, and women's sexual coming-of-age in repressive environments.

Bombay Talkie (India, 1970), *Sweet Sounds* (U.S.A., 1976), *The Europeans* (England, 1979) [v], *Quartet* (England/France, 1981) [v], *Heat and Dust* (England, 1983) [v], *The Bostonians* (U.S.A., 1984) [v], *A Room with a View* (England, 1986) [v], *Maurice* (England, 1987) [v].

Jim Jarmusch (U.S.A., b. 1954)

Art audiences and critics alike have marveled at Jarmusch's hypercontrolled, stripped-down cinematographic images and his droll characters who embody out-of-date lower-middle-class American stereotypes and deliver campy fifties-style dialogue. This NYU Film School protégé has become something of a cult figure, thus far resisting Hollywood's numerous offers.

Permanent Vacation (U.S.A., 1982) [v], **Stranger Than Paradise** (U.S.A., 1984) [v], **Down By Law** (U.S.A., 1986) [v].

Akira Kurosawa (Japan, b. 1910)

One of the most highly regarded and imitated filmmakers ever, Kurosawa single-handedly opened the West to Japanese cinema. Known for staging elaborate and beautifully shot samurai battle scenes, he is also skilled at capturing small slices of Japanese life. Although his films deal with subjects as varied as urban poverty and the samurai warrior, his boundless creative energy and powerful visual style are present throughout his prolific career.

No Regrets for Our Youth (Japan, 1946), **Rashomon** (Japan, 1950) [v], *Ikiru* (Japan, 1952) [v], **Seven Samurai** (Japan, 1954) [v], **The Hidden Fortress** (Japan, 1958) [v], **Yojimbo** (Japan, 1961) [v], *Sanjuro* (Japan, 1962) [v], *High and Low* (Japan, 1963) [v], *Red Beard* (Japan, 1965), **Dodes'ka-den** (Japan, 1970) [v], *Dersu Uzala* (Japan/Russia, 1975) [v], *Kagemusha* (Japan, 1980) [v], **Ran** (Japan/France, 1985) [v].

David Lynch (U.S.A., b. 1946)

Catapulted to international fame by his visually extraordinary, haunting film *Eraserhead,* Lynch's claustrophobic, surrealistic and sharply ironic films make audiences squirm and provoke discussion like no one else's.

Eraserhead (U.S.A., 1978) [v], *The Elephant Man* (England, 1980) [v], *Dune* (U.S.A., 1984) [v], *Blue Velvet* (U.S.A., 1986) [v].

Dusan Makavejev (Yugoslavia, b. 1932)

Makavejev surfaced in 1965 with a remarkably competent first feature, *Man Is Not a Bird,* and within a decade he fled the confines of the Eastern Bloc to make his own subversive brand of cinema. Makavejev's ambitious style mixes often wildly frenetic pacing with black humor and sex to create films about personal and political liberation. His detractors complain that his movies are simply ambiguous and vulgar.

Man Is Not a Bird (Yugoslavia, 1965), *Love Affair: Or the Case of the Missing Switchboard Operator* (Yugoslavia, 1966), *Innocence Unprotected* (Yugoslavia, 1968), **WR: Mysteries of the Organism** (Yugoslavia, 1971), *Sweet Movie* (France/Canada/Germany, 1975), **Montenegro (Pigs and Pearls)** (Sweden/England, 1981) [v], **The Coca-Cola Kid** (Australia, 1985) [v], *Manifesto* (Yugoslavia, 1988).

Louis Malle (France, b. 1932)

Malle got his early training making documentaries with Jacques Cousteau, then earned an international reputation with a series of intelligent and controversial films starring Jeanne Moreau and Brigitte Bardot. Later Malle moved to the United States, where the wry and observant Frenchman has, with his best films, favored us with a penetrating outsider's glimpse into our own exotic culture.

Frantic (France, 1957) [v], *A Very Private Affair* (France/Italy, 1962), *The*

Thief of Paris (France/Italy, 1967), *Calcutta* (France, 1969), *Phantom India* (France, 1969), *Lacombe Lucien* (France/Italy/Germany, 1974), *Black Moon* (France, 1975), *Pretty Baby* (U.S.A., 1978) [v], **Atlantic City** (U.S.A., 1981) [v], **My Dinner with Andre** (U.S.A., 1981) [v], *Crackers* (U.S.A., 1984) [v], *God's Country* (U.S.A., 1985), *Alamo Bay* (U.S.A., 1985) [v], **Au Revoir les Enfants** (France, 1987).

Nagisa Oshima (Japan, b. 1932)

Challenging the formal and restrained approach of his fellow Japanese filmmakers Ozu and Mizoguchi, Oshima combines experimental film techniques with non-Western ways of perception. A fine stylist, he frequently mixes violence, politics and eroticism with dynamic cinematography and perceptive social commentary.

Cruel Story of Youth (Japan, 1960), *The Sun's Burial* (Japan, 1960), *Night and Fog in Japan* (Japan, 1960), *Boy* (Japan, 1969), *The Ceremony* (Japan, 1974), *In the Realm of the Senses* (Japan, 1976), *Empire of Passion* (Japan, 1980), **Merry Christmas, Mr. Lawrence** (England/Japan, 1983) [v], *Max Mon Amour* (France, 1986).

Yasujiro Ozu (Japan, 1903–1963)

One of the grand masters of cinema, Ozu is considered the most Japanese of all Japanese directors. His unique and widely imitated style—characterized by a static camera, low-angle shots and long scenes—perfectly compliments his subtle yet emotionally powerful stories of tradition-bound, middle-class Japanese families.

A Story of Floating Weeds (Japan, 1934), *Late Spring* (Japan, 1949), *Early Summer* (Japan, 1951), **Tokyo Story** (Japan, 1953), *Early Spring* (Japan, 1956), *Late Autumn* (Japan, 1960), *An Autumn Afternoon* (Japan, 1962).

Pier Paolo Pasolini (Italy, 1922–1975)

A renowned novelist, poet and Marxist scholar, Pasolini's style was sometimes erratic and laborious and sometimes extremely engaging, switching from elegant cinematography to gritty neorealism. The excessive sex and violence of his later films was perhaps a foreshadowing of his own brutal death—at the hands of a teenager who claimed Pasolini made homosexual advances toward him.

The Gospel According to St. Matthew (Italy, 1964) [v], *Oedipus Rex* (Italy, 1967), *Pigpen* (Italy, 1969), *Medea* (Italy, 1970), *Decameron* (Italy, 1970), *Canterbury Tales* (Italy, 1971), *The Arabian Nights* (Italy, 1974), *The 120 Days of Sodom* (Italy, 1975).

Maurice Pialat (France, b. 1925)

Maurice Pialat is one of the most respected directors working in France today. In the tradition of the classic French directors, Pialat's emphasis is on character development. His complex, dynamic and often brutal portraits of people living on the edge, however, are anything but traditional.

Me (France, 1968), *Passe Ton Bac d'Abord* (France, 1979), *Loulou* (France, 1979), **A Nos Amours** (France, 1983) [v], *Police* (France, 1985) [v].

Satyajit Ray (India, b. 1921)

India has the world's largest film industry, but, ironically, Satyajit Ray is the only director of international acclaim. The father of the Indian neorealistic "parallel cinema movement," Ray uses lyrical camerawork and deceptively simple stories to reveal wisdom in the harsh realities of everyday Indian life, and the clash of "old" and "new" values.

Pather Panchali (Song of the Road) (India, 1955) [v], **Aparajito . . . The Unvanquished** (India, 1956) [v], *The World of Apu* (India, 1957) [v], *Days and Nights in the Forest* (India, 1970), *The*

Inner Eye (India, 1973), *Distant Thunder* (India, 1973) [v], *Sadgati* (India, 1982), *The Home and the World* (India, 1984) [v].

Alain Resnais (France, b. 1922)

Resnais worked for years making documentaries and short films before coming into prominence in the French New Wave. One of the medium's most influential experimentalists, Resnais deftly subverts conventional plot and characterizations, creating his own cinematic language to illuminate his characters' personal alienation in the context of sociopolitical history.

Hiroshima, Mon Amour (France, 1959) [v], *Last Year at Marienbad* (France/Italy, 1961) [v], *Stavisky* (France, 1974), *Providence* (France/Switzerland/U.S.A., 1977) [v], *Mon Oncle d'Amerique* (France, 1980) [v], *Life Is a Bed of Roses* (France, 1983), *L'Amour a Mort* (France, 1984), *Melo* (France, 1986).

Nicolas Roeg (England, b. 1928)

Nicolas Roeg distinguished himself as one of Britain's leading cinematographers before becoming a director, and he brings to his films his own particular visual style, mixing realism, the occult and near-hallucinogenic allegory. Although his films have drawn mixed reviews for their thematic unevenness, he has distinguished himself as a director who is willing to take chances.

Performance (England, 1970), *Walkabout* (England/Australia, 1971), *Don't Look Now* (England/Italy, 1974) [v], *The Man Who Fell to Earth* (England, 1976) [v], *Bad Timing/A Sensual Obsession* (England, 1980), *Eureka* (England, 1984) [v], *Insignificance* (England, 1985) [v], *Castaway* (England, 1986) [v], *Track 29* (U.S.A., 1988).

Eric Rohmer (France, b. 1920)

Another French film critic turned filmmaker, Rohmer creates breezy, low-budget dramas about characters struggling to understand themselves and the nature of love and intimacy. He has a way of digging into fragile male and female psyches as no other director has, with sensitive dialogue and an assortment of offbeat characters.

My Night at Maud's (France, 1970), *Claire's Knee* (France, 1971), *Chloe in the Afternoon* (France, 1972), *Perceval* (France, 1978), *The Aviator's Wife* (France, 1981), *Le Beau Mariage* (France, 1982) [v], *Pauline at the Beach* (France, 1983) [v], *Full Moon in Paris* (France, 1984) [v], *Summer* (France, 1985) [v], *The Adventures of Rainette and Marabelle* (France, 1986), *L'Ami de Mon Amie/Boyfriends and Girlfriends* (France, 1987).

Alan Rudolph (U.S.A., b. 1943)

A Robert Altman protégé, Rudolph is hailed by many as a leading voice in American independent film. His hard-edged, insightful black comedies on the nature of love and fortuitous desires are filled with delightfully quirky characters, dazzling visuals and upbeat soundtracks.

Welcome to L.A. (U.S.A., 1977) [v], *Remember My Name* (U.S.A., 1979) [v], *Return Engagement* (U.S.A., 1983), *Choose Me* (U.S.A., 1984) [v], *Songwriter* (U.S.A., 1984), *Trouble in Mind* (U.S.A., 1985), [v], *Made in Heaven* (U.S.A., 1987) [v], *The Moderns* (U.S.A., 1988) [v].

Carlos Saura (Spain, b. 1932)

While the grand wild man of Spanish cinema, Luis Buñuel, exiled himself from Fascist Spain, Saura, a generation younger, stayed and struggled with censorship and harassment. Saura's films are warm and witty but often brazen critiques of Franco's and post-Franco Spain. Recently he has made several beautifully filmed and nostalgic movies celebrating the song and dance of the Gypsy—flamenco.

Cousin Angelica (Spain, 1974), *Cria!* (Spain, 1976), *Blood Wedding* (Spain, 1981) [v], *Sweet Hours* (Spain, 1982), *Carmen* (Spain, 1983) [v], El Amor Brujo (Spain, 1986) [v].

John Sayles (U.S.A., b. 1950)

A leading American independent filmmaker whose early films were financed personally both by writing novels and writing scripts for B-movies, Sayles creates films with a raw, improvisational quality that often distracts from his well-meaning stories about social injustice. Yet he has established himself as a sensitive social critic, opting for believable characterizations over snappy conversationalists and fast-paced action.

Return of the Secaucus Seven (U.S.A., 1980) [v], **Lianna** (U.S.A., 1983) [v], Baby It's You (U.S.A., 1983) [v], **The Brother from Another Planet** (U.S.A., 1984) [v], **Matewan** (U.S.A., 1987) [v], Eight Men Out (U.S.A., 1988) [v].

Volker Schlondorff (Germany, b. 1939)

Schlondorff apprenticed with directors Alain Resnais and Louis Malle before cofounding the German New Wave. Primarily focusing on Germany's chaotic recent history, Schlondorff has distinguished himself with his cinematographic craftsmanship, mature sensibilities and sometimes perverse sense of humor.

The Lost Honor of Katharina Blum (co-directed with Margarethe von Trotta, West Germany, 1975) [v], **Coup de Grace** (West Germany, 1976) [v], **The Tin Drum** (West Germany, 1980) [v], Circle of Deceit (West Germany, 1982), **Swann in Love** (West Germany/France, 1984) [v], Death of a Salesman (U.S.A., 1985) [v].

Ettore Scola (Italy, b. 1931)

While Fellini steals headlines with his uneven but always lively films, Scola has been quietly stealing international audiences from the maestro. His elegant, superbly shot films usually deal with romance, intrigue and seduction. His style often employs a hybrid of social satire, Italian neorealism and heartfelt drama.

We All Loved Each Other So Much (Italy, 1975) [v], **A Special Day** (Italy, 1977)

[v], Viva Italia! (Italy, 1978), **Passione d'Amore** (Italy/France, 1982) [v], **La Nuit de Varennes** (France/Italy, 1982) [v], **Le Bal** (France/Italy, 1983) [v], Macaroni (Italy, 1985) [v], La Famiglia (Italy/France, 1986).

Martin Scorsese (U.S.A., b. 1942)

Scorsese's career is as schizophrenic as some of the unforgettable characters he has created in his films. Since 1973, he has effortlessly moved between making intelligent but unconventional Hollywood films and highly personal artistic statements that reflect his affection for the tough urban landscape in which he grew up. He is the first American filmmaker to opt for intensely real characterizations, and his genius with the camera makes their struggles immediate and often harrowing.

Boxcar Bertha (U.S.A., 1972), **Mean Streets** (U.S.A., 1973) [v], Alice Doesn't Live Here Anymore (U.S.A., 1974) [v], **Taxi Driver** (U.S.A., 1976) [v], New York, New York (U.S.A., 1977) [v], **The Last Waltz** (U.S.A., 1978) [v], Raging Bull (U.S.A., 1978) [v], **The King of Comedy** (U.S.A., 1983) [v], **After Hours** (U.S.A., 1985) [v], The Color of Money (U.S.A., 1986) [v], The Last Temptation of Christ (U.S.A., 1988) [v].

Bertrand Tavernier (France, b. 1941)

Unmoved by his generation's embrace of the French New Wave, ex–film critic Tavernier's work encompasses the romanticism of earlier French auteurs, reflective social and political criticism, and mainstream Hollywood. His style is often deliberate, at times bordering on rambling, but he is always able to capture subtle human moments in the context of almost any genre from documentary and docudrama to film noir and science fiction.

The Clockmaker (France, 1974) [v], Let Joy Reign Supreme (France, 1975), The Judge and the Assassin (France, 1976), **Deathwatch** (France/Germany, 1980) [v],

A Week's Vacation (France, 1982), **Coup de Torchon** *(Clean Slate)* (France, 1982) [v], *Mississippi Blues* (U.S.A., 1984), **A Sunday in the Country** (France, 1984) [v], **Round Midnight** (U.S.A./France, 1986) [v].

François Truffaut (France, 1932–1983)

With fellow former film critics Godard, Chabrol and Renoir, Truffaut founded the French New Wave. Truffaut's most-remembered films are his autobiographical Antoine Doniel coming-of-age series and his films mixing romance and suspense derived from his lifelong affection for Renoir and Hitchcock. Whether successful or not, all of Truffaut's films are full of wonderful human touches, perceptive social comment and dazzling camera work.

The 400 Blows (France, 1959) [v], **Shoot the Piano Player** (France, 1960) [v], **Jules and Jim** (France, 1961) [v], *Fahrenheit 451* (France/England, 1966), **Stolen Kisses** (France, 1968) [v], *Two English Girls* (France, 1972) [v], **Day for Night** (France, 1973) [v], **The Story of Adele H.** (France, 1975) [v], **Small Change** (France, 1976) [v], **The Man Who Loved Women** (France, 1977) [v], **The Green Room** (France, 1978) [v], **The Last Métro** (France, 1980) [v], **The Woman Next Door** (France, 1981), **Confidentially Yours** (France, 1983) [v].

Margarethe von Trotta (Germany, b. 1942)

Champion of the feminist cause, von Trotta is considered by many to be one of the best women filmmakers working today. She is known for her rigorous, often melancholy approach to stories dealing with the symbiotic relationships between two women, and their struggles to overcome enormous personal and societal obstacles.

The Lost Honor of Katharina Blum (co-directed with Volker Schlondorff, West Germany, 1975) [v], *The Second Awakening of Christa Klages* (West Germany, 1977), **Sisters, or the Balance of Happi-**

ness (West Germany, 1979), *Marianne and Juliane* (Germany, 1981), *Sheer Madness* (Germany, 1983), *Rosa Luxemburg* (Germany, 1986).

Andrzej Wajda (Polish, b. 1926)

Considered one of the most talented filmmakers to emerge from Eastern Europe, Wajda's productions from the 1950s through the 1970s were often sharp indictments of the repression in Poland. In the 1980s, Wajda left Poland to direct larger multinational co-productions and establish himself with mass audiences. His films combine unorthodox visual compositions with a near-documentary style that is well-suited for his socially and politically sensitive themes.

Kanal (Poland, 1957) [v], *Ashes and Diamonds* (Poland, 1958) [v], *Everything for Sale* (Poland, 1968), *The Promised Land* (Poland, 1974), **Man of Marble** (Poland, 1977), *Without Anesthetic* (Poland, 1979), *Man of Iron* (Poland, 1981), **Danton** (France/Poland, 1983) [v], **A Love in Germany** (Germany/France, 1983) [v], *Chronicle of a Love Affair* (Poland, 1986).

Peter Weir (Australia, b. 1944)

Weir is the leader of the current growth of Australian cinema. His ability to transform low-budget, ordinary genre pictures into art eventually propelled him into big-budget Hollywood productions. Even his Hollywood films mix mesmerizing camera work with unpredictable, metaphysical story lines that articulate the specialness of a local culture.

The Cars That Ate Paris (Australia, 1974), **Picnic at Hanging Rock** (Australia, 1975), **The Plumber** (Australia, 1978) [v], **The Last Wave** (Australia, 1978) [v], **Gallipoli** (Australia, 1981) [v], *The Year of Living Dangerously* (Australia, 1983) [v], *Witness* (U.S.A., 1985) [v], *The Mosquito Coast* (U.S.A., 1986) [v].

Wim Wenders
(Germany, b. 1945)

Co-founder of the German New Wave, Wenders has emerged in the last decade as one of Germany's leading innovators. His early films were heavily influenced by American rock and roll and Japanese director Yasujiro Ozu, but Wenders has matured into a compelling stylist, often exploring themes of alienation and the search for trends amid a newly evolving international popular culture.

The Goalie's Anxiety at the Penalty Kick (West Germany, 1972), *The Scarlet Letter* (West Germany/Spain, 1973), *Alice in the Cities* (West Germany, 1974) [v], *The Wrong Move* (West Germany, 1975), *Kings of the Road* (West Germany, 1976), **The American Friend** (West Germany/France, 1977) [v], *The State of Things* (U.S.A./West Germany/Portugal, 1982), **Hammett** (U.S.A., 1982) [v], **Paris, Texas** (U.S.A./West Germany, 1984) [v], *Tokyo-Ga* (West Germany/U.S.A., 1985), **Wings of Desire** (West Germany, 1988) [v].

Lina Wertmuller
(Italy, b. 1928)

Wertmuller abandoned a career in theater to apprentice with Fellini, and by the early 1970s, she hit full stride with a series of often controversial comedies combining sex and leftist politics. Using a frenetic narrative style, her early films are known for their outrageous satire, unappealing chauvinist men and degrading female stereotypes. Her work in the late seventies has been criticized for being confusing, excessive and superficial.

The Seduction of Mimi (Italy, 1972) [v], **Love and Anarchy** (Italy, 1973) [v], **All Screwed Up** (Italy, 1974) [v], **Swept Away** (Italy, 1974) [v], **Seven Beauties** (Italy, 1976) [v], *The End of the World in Our Usual Bed in a Night Full of Rain* (Italy/U.S.A., 1978), **A Joke of Destiny, Lying in Wait Around the Corner Like a Bandit** (Italy, 1983) [v], **Sotto, Sotto** (Italy, 1984) [v], *Camorra* (Italy, 1986) [v].